DEFERENCE IN INTERNATIONAL COURTS AND TRIBUNALS

Deference in International Courts and Tribunals

Standard of Review and Margin of Appreciation

Edited by
LUKASZ GRUSZCZYNSKI
and
WOUTER WERNER

cost
EUROPEAN COOPERATION
IN SCIENCE AND TECHNOLOGY

OXFORD
UNIVERSITY PRESS

OXFORD
UNIVERSITY PRESS

Great Clarendon Street, Oxford, OX2 6DP,
United Kingdom

Oxford University Press is a department of the University of Oxford.
It furthers the University's objective of excellence in research, scholarship,
and education by publishing worldwide. Oxford is a registered trade mark of
Oxford University Press in the UK and in certain other countries

First Edition published in 2014

Impression: 1

Published in the United States of America by Oxford University Press
198 Madison Avenue, New York, NY 10016, United States of America

British Library Cataloguing in Publication Data
Data available

Library of Congress Control Number: 2014938492
ISBN 978–0–19–871694–5

Printed and bound by
CPI Group (UK) Ltd, Croydon, CR0 4YY

Acknowledgements

The editors acknowledge the financial support provided by the European Cooperation in Science and Technology (COST), an intergovernmental framework aimed at facilitating the collaboration and networking of scientists and researchers at European level. COST is supported by the European Union (EU) Seventh Framework Programme (FP7) through a dedicated Coordination and Support Action (CSA) and is funded by the European Commission. For more information on COST, see <http://www.cost.eu>. This volume has been prepared within the context of COST Action IS1003 ('International Law Between Constitutionalisation and Fragmentation: the role of law in the post-national constellation').

The editors also wish to acknowledge the financial support provided by the Polish National Science Center within the national grant DEC-2011/01/M/HS5/03846.

Last but not least, the editors would like to thank all the participants of the two conferences held in Seville and Lund, where the main directions of this book were determined. A special thanks goes to Professor Dr Daniel García San José from the Law Faculty of the University of Seville who was the great host for our kick-off meeting. Finally, we are grateful to the PAS Institute of Law Studies in Warsaw and VU University Amsterdam for their institutional support.

Table of Contents

III. EUROPEAN UNION LAW

IV. INTERNATIONAL HUMAN RIGHTS LAW

V. OTHER INTERNATIONAL COURTS

Table of Cases

EUROPEAN

Court of Justice of the European Union – Court of Justice

Court of Justice of the European Union – General Court (Court of the First Instance)

European Court/Commission of Human Rights

INTERNATIONAL

GATT Dispute Settlement Panel Report

Inter-American Court/Commission on Human Rights (IACtHR/IACHR): judgments and advisory opinions

Inter-American Commission on Human Rights (IACHR): reports

International Court of Justice (ICJ)

International Tribunal for the Law of the Sea (ITLOS)

NATIONAL

Belgium

Germany

United Kingdom

United States of America

Table of Instruments

List of Abbreviations

AC	Appeal Chamber
ACHR	American Convention on Human Rights
AJIL	American Journal of International Law
Anti-Dumping Agreement	Agreement on Implementation of Article VI of GATT 1994
BIT	bilateral investment treaty
BYIL	British Yearbook of International Law
CJEU	Court of Justice of the European Union
CLJ	Cambridge Law Journal
CMLR	Common Market Law Review
DARSIWA	Draft Articles on Responsibility of States for Internationally Wrongful Acts
DMA	doctrine of the margin of appreciation
DOJ	Department of Justice
DRC	Democratic Republic of Congo
DSU	Understanding on Rules and Procedures Governing the Settlement of Disputes
EC	European Community
ECHR	European Convention on Human Rights
ECJ	European Court of Justice
ECR	European Court Reports
ECtHR	European Court of Human Rights
EEZ	exclusive economic zone
EHRR	European Human Rights Reports
EJIL	European Journal of International Law
ELJ	European Law Journal
ELR	European Law Review
ESCR	economic, social and cultural rights
EU	European Union
FCC	Federal Constitutional Court
FET	fair and equitable treatment
FRY	Federal Republic of Yugoslavia
GATT	General Agreement on Tariffs and Trade
GATS	General Agreement on Trade in Services
GLJ	German Law Journal
GM	genetically modified
GMO	genetically modified organism
GPA	Agreement of Government Procurement
IACHR	Inter-American Commission on Human Rights
IACtHR	Inter-American Court of Human Rights
ICC	International Criminal Court
ICCPR	International Covenant on Civil and Political Rights
ICESCR	International Covenant on Economic, Social and Cultural Rights

ICJ	International Court of Justice
ICLQ	International & Comparative Law Quarterly
ICSID	International Centre for the Settlement of Investment Disputes
ICTY	International Criminal Tribunal for the former Yugoslavia
IEL	international economic law
IAHRS	Inter-American Human Rights System
ITLOS	International Tribunal for the Law of the Sea
IUU	illegal, unregulated and unreported (fishing)
JIDS	Journal of International Disputes Settlement
JIEL	Journal of International Economic Law
JWT	Journal of World Trade
LOSC	Law of the Sea Convention
LGBT	lesbian, gay, bisexual, transsexual
MEA	multilateral environmental agreement
MERCOSUR	Mercado Común del Sur (Common Market of the South)
MOA	margin of appreciation
NAFTA	North American Free Trade Agreement
NGO	non-governmental organization
OAS	Organization of American States
OJLS	Oxford Journal of Legal Studies
OSPAR	Convention for the Protection of the Marine Environment of the North-East Atlantic
OUP	Oxford University Press
PCIJ	Permanent Court of International Justice
PTC	Pre-Trial Chamber
SC	Security Council
SPS Agreement	Agreement on the Application of Sanitary and Phytosanitary Measures
TBT Agreement	Agreement on Technical Barriers to Trade
TEU	Treaty on European Union
TFCN	Treaty of Friendship, Commerce and Navigation
TFEU	Treaty on the Functioning of the European Union
TRIPS Agreement	Agreement on Trade-Related Aspects of Intellectual Property Rights
UDHR	Universal Declaration of Human Rights
UN	United Nations
UN Charter	Charter of the United Nations
UNCITRAL	United Nations Commission on International Trade Law
UNCTAD	United Nations Conference on Trade and Development
UNTS	United Nations Treaty Series
PMRA	Pest Management Regulatory Agency (Canada)
VCLT	Vienna Convention on the Law of Treaties
VMS	vessel monitoring system
WA	Warrant of Arrest
WTO	World Trade Organization
WTR	World Trade Review
YILC	Yearbook of the International Law Commission

List of Contributors

Mónika Ambrus, PhD, Lecturer in Public International Law at the Faculty of Law, University of Groningen

Uladzislau Belavusau, PhD, Assistant Professor at the Faculty of Law, VU University Amsterdam

Diane Bernard, PhD, Senior Researcher at the Belgian National Fund for Research and *professeur invitée* at the Saint-Louis University—Brussels

Veronika Bílková, PhD, Assistant Professor at the Faculty of Law, Charles University in Prague

Ilona Cheyne, Professor at the School of Law, Oxford Brookes University

Patrycja Dąbrowska-Kłosińska, PhD, Assistant Professor at the Center for Europe, University of Warsaw

Bernard Duhaime, Professor at the Faculty of Law and Political Science, University of Québec (Montreal)

Lukasz Gruszczynski, PhD, Assistant Professor at the Institute of Law Studies, Polish Academy of Sciences (Warsaw)

Caroline Henckels, PhD, Vice-Chancellor's Post-Doctoral Research Fellow at the Faculty of Law, UNSW Australia (The University of New South Wales)

Alexia Herwig, PhD, Assistant Professor at the University of Antwerp

Michael Ioannidis, PhD, Senior Research Fellow, Max Planck Institute for Comparative Public Law and International Law (Heidelberg)

Erlend M. Leonhardsen, Research Fellow at Scandinavian Institute of Maritime Law, Department of Petroleum and Energy Law, Faculty of Law, University of Oslo

Andrei Mamolea, PhD Candidate at the Graduate Institute of International and Development Studies (Geneva)

Ernst-Ulrich Petersmann, Emeritus Professor of International and European Law at the European University Institute (Florence)

Benedikt Pirker, PhD, Post-doctoral Assistant at the Institute of European Law, University of Fribourg

Chiara Ragni, PhD, Assistant Professor of International Law at the University of Milan

Rosemary Rayfuse, Professor at the Faculty of Law, UNSW Australia (The University of New South Wales) and Con-Joint Professor at the Faculty of Law, Lund University

Asja Serdarevic, PhD, Researcher at the Centre for European Law, Vrije Universiteit Brussel

Valentina Vadi, PhD, Reader at the Faculty of Law, Lancaster University

Pieter Van Cleynenbreugel, PhD, Assistant Professor at the Europa Institute, Leiden Law School

Wouter Werner, Professor at the Centre on the Politics of Transnational Law, Faculty of Law, VU University Amsterdam

Karolina Wierczynska, PhD, Assistant Professor, Institute of Law Studies, Polish Academy of Sciences (Warsaw)

1

Introduction

Lukasz Gruszczynski and Wouter Werner

Rights and obligations of States are determined by rules of international law. Indirectly, however, they may be also controlled by specific legal methodologies used by international courts and tribunals when adjudicating matters involving States' measures and actions. Both the standard of review and/or margin of appreciation are examples of such methodological devices. International courts use them, implicitly or explicitly, as tools to determine the degree of deference that is granted to States in their implementation of international legal obligations. Although the issue may appear to be of a technical nature, in practice it can have far-reaching consequences, determining the extent of international obligations and, as a consequence, the outcomes of adjudications. Surprisingly, the applicable standard of review (or margin of appreciation) is almost never articulated in the provisions of relevant treaties (with the World Trade Organization (WTO) Anti-Dumping Agreement being a notable exception), and its determination by a court is seen as an expression of the Court's prerogative to define its own procedures.[1]

The concept of standard of review has its roots in common law tradition and it is employed in two different contexts. First, it is used by the courts in their examination of actions of other branches of government, eg as to the constitutionality of legislative acts (by US Congress), or of governmental agencies as to their compliance with delegated powers. Secondly, it also describes the extent of scrutiny applied by a higher court over a decision of a lower court. In all these instances the question is how much deference is (or should be) granted by the reviewing body to the decisions or other actions of other bodies (legislative, executive or judicial). In theory, standard of review may range from very intrusive to very deferential, with many intermediate variations in between. Depending on the level of intrusiveness one may distinguish various specific standards: such as *de novo*, substantial evidence, reasonableness, abuse of discretion, clearly erroneous. The *de novo* standard of review is the most intrusive, with

[1] Jean-Pierre Cot, 'Margin of Appreciation' in Rüdiger Wolfrum (ed), *Max Planck Encyclopedia of Public International Law.* Online version available at <http://opil.ouplaw.com/home/epil> (accessed 18 March 2014), para 12.

a court able to reassess and overturn any determination made by a body whose act is reviewed, while the 'clearly erroneous' standard is usually the least intrusive with a court upholding the decision or act under review unless it is clearly erroneous. Deferential standards of review are justified by various reasons, ranging from the epistemic superiority of the initial decision-maker (which is considered to be in a better position to make a particular decision or determination) through to considerations of democratic legitimacy and to the specific allocation (and balance) of powers between different branches of government in a particular constitutional setting.[2] Sometimes, a pragmatic argument is also made for reducing the workload for a reviewing body (a lower, ie more deferential, standard of review will discourage appeals/challenges), thus allowing it to concentrate on the most important cases.[3]

In the international context, standard of review can be defined as 'the nature and intensity of review by [an international] court or tribunal of decisions [or other actions that involve some form of prior determination] taken by governmental authority'.[4] Standard of review therefore determines the extent of discretionary powers enjoyed by national authorities in making certain decisions, and affects the allocation of power between national and international levels. Similarly, as in the case of domestic practice, it may concern factual determinations (eg deciding whether a national measure is supported by sufficient scientific evidence), legal determinations (eg as to the compliance of national legislative measures with international obligations), or mixed questions of fact and law (eg the correlation between the justification of the legal norm at stake and scientific expert opinions). At the same time, the concept of standard of review is not explicitly recognized by all international courts. While some of them address the issue directly (eg WTO panels and the Appellate Body and some international investment tribunals), others do so only implicitly by simply showing various degrees of deference to domestic authorities (eg the International Court of Justice (ICJ)). Nevertheless, as discussed in the specific contributions in this volume, the rationale that stands behind the self-restraint of international judicial organs, as well as the way it is used, is strikingly similar, irrespective of whether a particular body addresses the concept of standard of review or not in its analysis. The fact is that international courts, depending on the obligation in question and their institutional setting, afford various levels of deference to governmental authorities.

[2] As discussed by several authors in this volume, similar second-order reasons are used to justify deferential standards of review at the international level (cf eg Chapter 7 by Caroline Henckels, Chapter 6 by Michael Ioannidis, and Chapter 12 by Alexia Herwig and Asja Serdarevic).

[3] For more detailed discussion in the US context, see eg Kelly Kunsch, 'Standard of Review (State and Federal): A Primer', 18 *Seattle University Law Review* 11 (1994–1995); Thomas W. Merrill, 'Judicial Deference to Executive Precedent', 101 *Yale Law Journal* 969 (1992); Jeffrey S. Lubbers, *A Guide to Federal Agency Rulemaking*, 4th edn (Chicago, IL: ABA Publishing, 2006).

[4] Jan Bohanes and Nicolas Lockhart, 'Standard of Review in WTO Law', in Daniel Bethlehem et al (eds), *The Oxford Handbook of International Trade Law* (Oxford: Oxford University Press, 2009), 379.

While the legal doctrine concerning standards of review arises from common law, the concept of margin of appreciation[5] is rooted in the European legal tradition. For example, French administrative law uses the concept *marge d'appreciation*, while German law recognizes a similar notion of administrative discretion (*Ermessensspielraum*).[6] At the international level, 'margin of appreciation' is normally associated with international human rights law,[7] but many commentators see it as a methodology (or doctrine) of general application which is used by different international courts.[8] What is generally agreed upon is that it was developed by the European Court of Human Rights (ECtHR) in the context of the European Convention on Human Rights (ECHR)[9] and later used by other international human rights judicial bodies, such as the Inter-American Court of Human Rights (IACtHR).[10] Although the concept can be traced back to the activities of the European Commission of Human Rights in the 1950s (eg *Greece v UK* (1958)), the fundamental case in this regard is *Handyside v UK* (1976), where the ECtHR held that:

> [b]y reason of their direct and continuous contact with the vital forces of their countries, State authorities are in principle in a better position than the international judge to give an opinion on the exact content of these requirements [rights provided by the Convention] as well as on the 'necessity' of a 'restriction' or 'penalty' intended to meet them.[11]

The margin of appreciation concept is based on the recognition that the international obligations contained in the ECHR can be legitimately complied with in different ways. One may therefore define it 'as the breadth of deference that the Court is willing to grant to the decisions of national legislative, executive, and judicial decision-makers'[12] or the 'room for manoeuvre the Strasburg institutions are prepared to accord national authorities in fulfilling their obligations'.[13]

[5] For more detailed discussion on margin of appreciation, see Chapter 13 by Mónika Ambrus (Section I), Chapter 8 by Erlend Leonhardsen (Section III), and Chapter 16 by Bernard Duhaime (Section IV).

[6] Yutaka Arai-Takahashi, *The Margin of Appreciation Doctrine and the Principle of Proportionality in the Jurisprudence of the ECHR* (Oxford: Intersentia, 2002) 2–3.

[7] For criticism of margin of appreciation as applied in the human right context see eg Eyal Benvenisti, 'Margin of Appreciation, Consensus and Universal Standards', 31 *International Law and Politics* 843 (1999).

[8] Arai-Takahashi, *The Margin of Appreciation Doctrine*, 4; Yuval Shany, 'Toward a General Margin of Appreciation Doctrine in International Law?', 16(5) *EJIL* 907 (2006).

[9] For details of the historic developments, see Dean Spielmann, 'Allowing the Right Margin: The European Court of Human Rights and the National Margin of Appreciation Doctrine: Waiver or Subsidiarity of European Review?', 14 *Cambridge Yearbook of European Legal Studies* 381 (2011–2012).

[10] See the discussion in Chapter 16 by Bernard Duhaime (Section IV). But note that the concept of margin of appreciation was explicitly rejected by the United Nations Human Rights Committee (Communication No. 511/1992, *Ilmari Lansman et al v Finland*, Communication No. 511/1992, UN Doc. CCPR/C/57/1 (1996).

[11] *Handyside v the United Kingdom* (app. no. 5493/72), ECtHR 1976, para 48.

[12] William W. Burke-White and Andreas von Staden, 'Private Litigation in a Public Law Sphere: The Standard of Review in Investor-State Arbitrations', 35 *Yale Journal of International Law* 283 (2010).

[13] Steven Greer, *The Margin of Appreciation: Interpretation and Discretion under the European Convention on Human Rights* (Strasbourg: Council of Europe Publishing, 2000), 5.

Of course, the above does not mean that deference granted to States under margin of appreciation is unlimited. To the contrary, the Court is consistent in holding that its role as a supervisory organ requires assessing whether a State acted within the boundaries of its authority protected by the margin of appreciation. The scope of deference granted by the Court is also very context-specific and varies according to the circumstances of a case and the specific ECHR provision(s) under consideration. In some cases, Member States are given only a narrow margin of appreciation (eg with respect to rights provided in Arts 2–3 ECHR), while in others a wide margin of appreciation is granted (eg with respect to national security justifications or the protection of public morals). Margin of appreciation, similarly to standard of review, may relate to factual determinations, legal determinations, or mixed questions of fact and law (eg whether a public emergency exists and whether the measures taken are strictly necessary as provided by Article 15 ECHR).[14]

The two concepts may therefore be regarded as referring to the same thing, although in reverse fashion (ie a wide margin of appreciation equals a low standard of review, and vice versa). The way they are applied determines the degree of deference granted by international courts to States' actions, with the margin of appreciation explicitly acknowledging the existence of such deference, while standard of review is, on its face, a procedural tool that in and of itself does not mandate any specific level of deference. Both of them however operate (or may operate) as a tool for either judicial self-restraint or judicial 'activism'. As a consequence, margin of appreciation can be understood as a methodological approach employed by a court that is simply one of the forms (albeit with its own particularities) of a standard of review.[15]

The deference that is shown by international courts and tribunals through application of a deferential standard of review or wide margin of appreciation is explained by various reasons. Some authors argue that deference reflects, or should reflect, the respect of international courts for national sovereignty and self-determination, and may be connected with the *dubio mitius* principle,[16] which requires international courts to choose, from among several admissible interpretations, the one that involves the minimum of obligations for the parties to the dispute. This also corresponds with the recognition that normative requirements in international treaties can usually be met by a range of measures that are within the legal parameters of international obligations. Others argue that

[14] Arai-Takahashi, *The Margin of Appreciation Doctrine*, 2 (note however that some second-order reasons differ between margin of appreciation and deferential standard of review, see eg the discussion by Erlend Leonhardsen in Chapter 8).

[15] Cot, 'Margin of Appreciation', paras 2 and 11. A similar stance is also taken by Shany, 'Toward a General Margin of Appreciation'; Burke-White and von Staden, 'Private Litigation', 304–11. Others however see it as a unique approach (doctrine) taken by courts in the field of international human rights law (eg Andrew Legg, *The Margin of Appreciation in International Human Rights Law: Deference and Proportionality* (Oxford: Oxford University Press, 2012) 2). See also Chapter 17 by Chiara Ragni in this volume (Section V).

[16] Steven P. Croley and John H. Jackson, 'WTO Dispute Procedures, Standard of Review and Deference to National Governments', 90 *AJIL* 193 (1996).

national governments are better placed to make complex factual determinations and political choices than international tribunals (because of the superior democratic legitimacy enjoyed by domestic decision-makers, or resulting from their greater expertise in ascertaining complex factual and political situations). In the context of margin of appreciation a respect for plurality among Member States is also frequently referred to (ie lack of common practice among Member States, which would indicate a lack of universal consensus on a specific matter).[17]

Standard of review also needs to be distinguished from the burden of proof and standard of proof. The first is a procedural rule indicating which party to a dispute bears the burden of persuasion with regard to establishing (disputed) facts and/or mixed questions of fact and law. On the other hand, the standard of proof can be defined as 'the threshold of probability that must be exceeded in the adjudicator's evaluation of the evidence in order for the adjudicator to reach judgments about the existence of historical facts and to apply legal concepts to historical facts to reach legal conclusions.'[18] The most common standard of proof in international adjudication is 'preponderance of the evidence' (ie a determination that 'the evidence adduced by one party weights heavier, on the basis of reasonable probability, than the evidence produced by the other side'), with occasional reliance on proof beyond a reasonable doubt.[19] Although the both concepts are analytically distinct, in practice they cannot be completely separated from each other. While the standard of review defines the extent to which an appellate or supervisory court can interfere in particular matters, the rules regarding the burden and particularly the standard of proof are inherently applicable in determining which matters fall within or outside the scope of the Court's sphere of review.[20]

This brings us to the core of this book. The initial idea of having a collection of articles on deference in different international settings was conceived in the course of the research undertaken within the COST Action IS1003 'International Law between Constitutionalisation and Fragmentation: The Role of Law in the Post-national Constellation'. The call for papers for a kick-off conference organized at the end of 2012 attracted many interesting proposals and eventually brought a diverse group of international law scholars to the University of Seville. Despite all the existing differences, the discussion also showed that various international courts, when it comes to the issue of deference, are confronted with the same problems and use similar methods to deal with them. This was a promising

[17] Legg, *The Margin of Appreciation*, 27–31.

[18] John J. Barcelo III, 'Burden of Proof, Prima Facie Case and Presumption in WTO Dispute Settlement', 42(1) *Cornell International Law Journal* 23 (2009) at 30; see also Katherin Del Mar, 'The International Court of Justice and Standards of Proof', in Karine Bannelier, Theodore Chistakis and Sarah Heathcote (eds), *The ICJ and the Development of International Law. The Lasting Impact of the Corfu Channel Case* (New York: Routledge, 2011).

[19] Rüdiger Wolfrum, 'International Courts and Tribunals, Evidence', in Rüdiger Wolfrum (ed), *Max Planck Encyclopedia of Public International Law*. Online version available at <http://opil.ouplaw.com/home/epil> (accessed 18 March 2014), paras 75–7.

[20] For a more extensive discussion on the relationship between standard of review and standard of proof, see Chapter 13 by Mónika Ambrus and Chapter 14 by Uladzislau Belavusau, both in this volume.

sign for a collective edition that would discuss two specific mechanisms that are used in this context—standard of review and margin of appreciation. We also noted that while the literature on standard of review used in national courts (particularly with respect to the USA and some European countries) was considerable, there were only a few books that analysed this problem in the context of international courts and tribunals.[21] At the same time, there was a growing interest in the scientific community on the topic, although most authors concentrated on the activities of a specific international court, thus providing only a fragmentary picture of current trends in international law. The follow-up meeting in 2013 at the Lund University confirmed that this initial idea could be turned into reality. Most of the participants saw the scientific potential of the topic and expressed their interest in participation in the editorial project. This group was subsequently supplemented with some additional authors that could cover the practice of other international courts and tribunals. And after more than a year of intense work, the book has been finally born.

The aim of this collection is therefore to look at two concepts that are conventionally used by international courts and tribunals in order to grant deference to national governments. The discussion is organized around two issues put forward by the editors: (i) relevance of the concept of standard of review/margin of appreciation in the jurisprudence of specific courts and the mode of its application; and (ii) extent of (ie more intrusive or less intrusive) scrutiny and reasons for deference granted by a specific international court to a respondent State. These issues are also used as guides to integrate different contributions into a study, and provide readers with a basis for making both theoretical and practical comparisons between the practices as developed and applied in different international legal regimes. In addition, all the comparative chapters also analyse existing convergences and divergences in the practice of different courts and tribunals and attempt to identify their underlying reasons.

The selection of the specific courts and tribunals discussed here, as well as the space dedicated to them, was based on two factors. First, it reflects the actual or potential prominence of applicable standards of review/margin of appreciation within a specific adjudication system. While the issue is frequently addressed by both adjudicators and scholars in the context of WTO and EU law, it has only started to be recognized by international investment tribunals, and in the case of the ICJ, ITLOS (International Tribunal for the Law of the Sea) and the International Criminal Court (ICC), it still remains underappreciated. Secondly, it reflects the specific interests of contributing authors, who in principle remained free to choose, within designated limits, both their research question and method of analysis. As editors, we also preferred contributions that transcend the

[21] In the 'older' literature this includes the monographs by Arai-Takahashi, *The Margin of Appreciation Doctrine and Matthias Oesch, Standards of Review in WTO Dispute Resolution* (Oxford: Oxford University Press, 2004); more recently, Ross Becroft, *The Standard of Review in WTO Dispute Settlement, Critique and Development* (Cheltenham: Edward Elgar Publishing, 2012), and Legg, *The Margin of Appreciation*.

traditional analysis used in the context of standards of review/margin of appreciation (especially in those fields where substantial scholarship already exists). This is the case, for example, for the chapters by Ambrus and Belavusau, both of which look at standard of review (margin of appreciation) through the lens, respectively, of standard of proof and expert participation. As a consequence, while the scope of the book is comprehensive, it does not pretend to exhaust all relevant topics. The volume should be seen as a collection of essays on the topic of deference in international law (as expressed in two mechanisms: margin of appreciation and standard of review) rather than as a companion or a handbook.

This also means that the book is characterized by a plurality of approaches taken by the contributing authors. Granting such a freedom was our deliberate decision, as we believe that some variety in approaches helps to highlight the complexities involved in any discussion on deference and gives the reader different perspectives on the topic. However, while we have supported diversity in approaches, we have also been aware that the reader must be oriented to the interconnections between the various approaches. Consequently, all authors were instructed to disclose their basic assumptions and define the concepts that are central for their arguments.

The volume is divided into five parts. Part I includes four contributions and looks at the concepts of standard of review from a more general or theoretical perspective and explores the 'external limits' of judicial review, such as principles of democracy, good faith, and public policy. All chapters in this section take a comparative approach, examining the practices of different international tribunals. Part I begins with Chapter 2 (immediately after this introduction), in which Ernst-Ulrich Petersmann analyses the inherent powers of international courts, as recognized in the customary law requirements of interpreting international treaties and settling related disputes in conformity with the principles of justice and international law. He argues that multilevel trade and investment adjudication lacks a coherent 'constitutional justification' and often neglects the 'cosmopolitan functions' of modern economic law and adjudication. In this context, he proposes a more coherent 'judicial methodology' in multilevel economic adjudication in order to protect human rights, principles of justice, 'judicial comity' and the transnational rule of law for the benefit of citizens, thus setting the limits for both the scope of judicial review and the deference that is awarded to States by international tribunals. According to him, by acknowledging the 'dual nature' of modern legal systems and protecting the 'object and purpose' of economic rules, not only in terms of rights of governments but also of citizens and other economic actors, economic adjudication can become more legitimate and more coherent.

In Chapter 3 Ilona Cheyne examines whether a State has the power to choose its own public policy, a step which logically precedes any evaluation of the measure used to implement that policy and the corresponding problem of the character and intensity of the review applied in this context. She notes that the choice of applicable standard of review is normally shaped by the substantive content of defined legal obligations, but in the case of public policy such content remains open-ended, and there are only few obvious legal markers to offer guidance. Cheyne identifies different methodological approaches taken by EU courts, WTO dispute settlement bodies and investment tribunals when dealing with public policy exceptions, each of them providing a different level of deference. Deference appears most restricted in the case of the EU and more liberal in the WTO, and there is significant variation in the practice of arbitral tribunals. Substantive and threshold controls act as filters in the EU, and to a lesser extent in the WTO. Investment treaties, on the other hand, apparently pose a much higher barrier to unilateral public policy acts by making public policy a criterion of lawful expropriation rather than a defence against compensatory liability. On the other hand, according to Cheyne, evidential and procedural controls are a common form of test, certainly at the basic level of reviewing a public policy measure on the grounds of good faith. She concludes that overall there appears to be significant convergence of practices in reviewing measures justified as public policy.

Chapter 4, authored by Benedikt Pirker, proposes Ely's procedural democracy doctrine as a possible approach to justifying and evaluating the legitimacy of different standards of review used by international courts and tribunals in cases of value conflicts. The procedural democracy doctrine inquires into whether specific values, such as constitutional rights, are under-represented in a democratic political system, and the extent to which this under-representation requires virtual representation of these values by means of judicial review. Based on this theorem, backed up by some insights into the doctrine of procedural democracy in United States constitutional law, the chapter examines the practical potential of international adjudicators such as the Court of Justice of the European Union (CJEU), the WTO Appellate Body, and international investment tribunals to apply the procedural democracy doctrine. It identifies two variables that can help determine the intensity of the review: values that are central to the system of democratic process in which adjudicating bodies participate as institutions; and the nature of the violation of such values.

Andrei Mamolea in Chapter 5 examines the relevance of good faith review in establishing a breach of international obligations. Mamolea argues that in practice international courts and tribunals frequently engage in good faith reviews, even where the applicable legal rule does not include a 'psychological' element. Open-textured standards permit the consideration of a State's intent as an aggravating factor and there are three ways that a State's intent can be found improper. In particular, an improper intent may be discriminatory, it may fall outside the permissible intents described in the 'clawback clause' of a treaty, or it may be described broadly as arbitrary and unreasonable. Mamolea also notes that, unlike with some other questions of fact, international courts and tribunals actually grant no deference to a State's *post hoc* characterizations of its own intent. Instead, a State benefits from a historic presumption against bad faith that manifests itself as a high standard of proof for the claimant. Mamolea concludes by stating that apart from this presumption, there are no brakes on the intrusiveness of an international court or tribunal regarding subjective facts.

Part II concentrates on the problem of the applicable standards of review in the practice of WTO dispute settlement bodies, North American Free Trade

Agreement panels, and international investment tribunals. It starts with the contribution of Michael Ioannidis (Chapter 6), who investigates the applicable standard of review in the WTO context. The author criticizes the current usage of standards of review by the WTO adjudicating bodies, noting in particular that notions such as 'objectiveness' or 'reasonableness' fail to give a clear answer to the question why some domestic decisions are awarded greater deference than others. The chapter proposes to abandon the current approach to applicable standard of review based on the indeterminate notion of 'objectiveness' in favour of a more qualified perspective, focusing on the concrete reasons offered by the WTO adjudicating bodies. In this context, Ioannidis identifies national sovereignty, domestic expertise, and respect for basic procedural guarantees as primary reasons. Finally, the contribution argues that decisions resulting from domestic procedures sufficiently open to the consideration of foreign interests should be given greater deference than those taken behind doors, closed to the foreigners affected by them.

In Chapter 7 Caroline Henckels takes the discussion into the area of international investment law. She recognizes that investment tribunals have not yet developed a coherent and principled approach to standard of review in relation to disputes involving the exercise of public power by host States. Henckels notes that some tribunals have employed a strict review, while others have shown a measure of deference to host States. In the latter instance, tribunals seem to rely on two key factors: (a) the desirability of regulatory autonomy and the host State authorities' proximity to their populations; and (b) the authorities' greater institutional competence and expertise. Henckels recognizes that this emerging approach to deference echoes the jurisprudence of other international and supranational courts and tribunals performing similar functions (eg WTO panels, the CJEU and the ECtHR) and argues that future investment tribunals should, cognisant of the desirability of deference in certain circumstances (ie in situations of normative or empirical uncertainty), exercise restraint in their assessment of matters that are more appropriately the province of national authorities. She concludes with the observation that such an approach would achieve a more balanced relationship between the protection of foreign investment and a host State's regulatory autonomy.

The contribution of Erlend Leonhardsen (Chapter 8) also concerns international investment law. The author analyses the recent shift in States' practice concerning international investment obligations, arguing that States increasingly seek to create or extend the existing margin of appreciation in new investment treaties. Against this background, he explores the concept of margin of appreciation in European human rights law, recognizing it as an inspiration for both governments and arbitrators. Yet, the article cautions against mechanical transplantation of the ECtHR concept to the field of investment arbitration. While the chapter applauds deference based on the epistemic superiority of national experts or procedural qualities of a domestic regulatory process, it remains rather sceptical with respect to the role that should be played by democratic-based deference in the context of international investment arbitration. The chapter concludes with the observation that the governmental push for more regulatory discretion has broadened the margin of appreciation enjoyed by States.

The last chapter of Part II (Chapter 9), written by Lukasz Gruszczynski and Valentina Vadi, compares the standards of review applied by WTO panels and investment tribunals in assessing national measures that are based on prior complex factual determinations of a scientific character. The chapter shows that the practices of dispute settlement bodies in both areas express many similarities. Although none of the systems has developed an abstract and general standard of deference, the analysis of the jurisprudence shows that a considerable degree of deference is granted to States in this specific context. This deference expresses itself in dispute settlement bodies' focus on 'reasonableness' rather than 'correctness' of specific scientific claims, showing that these bodies are well aware of their epistemic limitations. On the other hand, the chapter recognizes certain differences existing between the two systems. Investment tribunals remain more concerned with the overall quality of the regulatory process, while WTO panels are more active in testing the internal (scientific) legitimacy of measures. The authors also conclude that the adoption of the methodological-based approach does not exclude per se an intense scrutiny into the science underlying a national measure.

Part III turns to EU law and examines the practice of the CJEU in selected areas. Chapter 10, authored by Pieter Van Cleynenbreugel, analyses the standards of review relied upon by the CJEU in its assessment of national procedural choices, and in particular the role of the notion of mitigated procedural autonomy. This notion refers to the deferential scope of review maintained by the CJEU, according to which Member States remain competent to determine their own procedural rules for the application EU law in their legal systems. The court only intervenes into these determinations in cases where equivalence or effectiveness requirements have not been complied with. Consequently, EU-structured notions of equivalence and effectiveness provide mitigating conditions to unfettered national procedural competences in the area of EU law. The chapter argues in particular that four different review standards can be inferred within the seemingly coherent narrative of mitigated procedural autonomy. These four standards allow the CJEU to evaluate national procedural choices on a sliding scale of comprehensiveness. The simultaneous co-existence of such divergent standards can be explained, according to the author, by a crypto-federal understanding of European integration.

Chapter 11, by Patrycja Dąbrowska-Kłosińska, investigates the problem of the applicable standard of judicial review in risk regulation cases before the CJEU. Such disputes are particularly difficult as they frequently involve conflicting or insufficient scientific evidence, while formulating legal determinations requires the interpretation of open terms and discretionary provisions. Dąbrowska-Kłosińska describes how the CJEU moved from a deferential approach to a more restrictive one. As a result, the Court is more directly engaged in scientific questions through extensive proceduralization and review of the plausibility of evidence. She concludes that while such a standard offers more possibilities for the EU courts to construct the functioning of the internal market, influence national competences, institutional and normative structures, as well as play a role in the convergence of international standards through a strong reliance on scientific expertise, this is done at the cost of the disparity between a declared and a de facto intensity of review and the accompanying uncertainty in predicting possible outcomes in individual cases.

Chapter 12, co-authored by Alexia Herwig and Asja Serdarevic, compares the standards of review in necessity and proportionality analysis in the jurisprudence of the CJEU concerning the internal market and WTO dispute settlement bodies. The chapter argues that judicial deference by the CJEU and WTO is appropriate to questions of fact and mixed legal–factual questions whenever the facts or considered normative judgments are uncertain, as is frequently the case in necessity and proportionality analysis. In particular, the authors submit that the nature of handling uncertainties (ie through fair and inclusive decision-making procedures that provide legitimacy for subsequent decisions) requires the court to put an emphasis on the procedure rather than on substance of the decision under review. This means that deference with respect to substance should be combined with an intrusive review exercised by courts over the procedural fairness of the way the decision was taken. In this context, the chapter argues that the CJEU's vetting of procedural guarantees, coupled with deference to substantive determinations as regards EU acts, is a sound approach which should be applied more widely also in the review of Member States' acts and by WTO dispute settlement bodies.

Part IV concentrates on international human rights law and reviews various aspects of the margin of appreciation doctrine (as well as other mechanisms used to grant deference to States) in the case law of the ECtHR and the IACtHR. The discussion starts with a chapter by Mónika Ambrus (Chapter 13), which looks at the concept of margin of appreciation through the lens of standard of proof. Based on a close reading of case law, Ambrus concludes that the concepts of standard of review and standard of proof are closely connected as the degree of discretion (which is determined by the margin of appreciation doctrine) also relates to the extent to which the allegations have to be proven by the State in order to be accepted by the reviewing court (this aspect is determined by standard of proof). Against this background, Ambrus explores the standards of proof applied by the ECtHR as well as the factors influencing their determination. Taking into account Franck's theory of procedural fairness, she argues that the Court's assignment or application of the standards of proof largely fails to meet the relevant criteria, and are opaque and incoherent.

The following chapter by Uladzislau Belavusau (Chapter 14) analyses the role that is played by expertise in the recent (2008–12) hate speech cases decided by the ECtHR. Belavusau argues that the Court has worked on the basis of three, not necessarily compatible, models when dealing with hate speech cases: (a) a low standard of proof model, relying on an implicit role of experts; (b) a higher standard of proof model, leaving room for an explicit accent on expertise; and (c) an instrumental model with an over-reliance on expertise, resulting in a non-intrusive standard. As a result, the case law on hate speech fails to offer clear guidance on how the Court should review expert opinions, in part because, as

Belavusau argues, the Court has so far not been willing to clarify the criteria for expert evidence.

The next contribution by Veronika Bílková (Chapter 15) discusses the concept of 'standard of equivalent protection' as a specific standard of review used within European human rights law. Such a standard provides that no detailed review of measures adopted under the EU system is needed, provided the system ensures the material and procedural standards of human rights protection equivalent to that of the ECHR, and that there is no manifest deficiency in the protection in a concrete case. Bílková argues that, despite certain shortcomings, the standard strikes an acceptable balance between the effort to avoid engaging in the indirect scrutiny of the EU law (and decisions of the CJEU), and the need for the ECtHR to remain the final guardian with respect to the ECHR. She also concludes that the planned accession by the EU to the ECHR does not necessarily ring the death-knell to the standard, due to the specific nature of review undertaken with its help. As a consequence, the standard of equivalent protection could be preserved either as a new admissibility criterion for cases directed against the EU institutions, or as an instrument of substantive review.

The last chapter in Part IV (Chapter 16), authored by Bernard Duhaime, goes beyond the European setting and turns its attention to the Inter-American system. It investigates the extent to which the IACHR and IACtHR express deference to States in their implementation of the American Convention of Human Rights. In this context, the author identifies different mechanisms that serve this aim, such as the fourth instance formula (constraining the Inter-American institutions in their review of decisions of domestic judicial bodies regarding factual determinations and the application of local laws), the margin of appreciation doctrine, and other forms of deference. The chapter notes that the Inter-American institutions have been rather reluctant to defer to domestic legislative, administrative and judicial institutions when assessing human rights violations cases. According to Duhaime, part of the System's hesitation to defer seems to come from the limited capacity that national agencies have often shown in effectively protecting human rights in the region. Nevertheless, he also adds that as the Western Hemisphere progresses towards democracy and consolidates its institutions and practices towards States governed by the rule of law (with effective judicial authorities), one could expect a greater use of the margin of appreciation doctrine by both the Commission and Court.

The final part—Part V—covers other international courts and tribunals where the jurisprudence on the standard of review/margin of appreciation is more sparse, but nonetheless too important to be neglected. This includes in particular the ICJ, ITLOS, and the ICC. The section starts with the contribution of Chiara Ragni (Chapter 17), which examines application of the doctrine of judicial deference to other bodies' actions or to national decision-making in the practice of the ICJ. The chapter attempts to answer the question whether good faith can be regarded as a standard of review, as the jurisprudence of the Court seems to suggest, and how it has been applied (or should have been applied) in practice. The chapter next turns to another question and asks whether, in situations where the ICJ has allowed a degree of discretion to the State in the assessment of international law norms, this attitude could be regarded as amounting to judicial deference towards national decision-making, and if so, whether the margin of appreciation doctrine may be applied.

The chapter on the ITLOS (Chapter 18), authored by Rosemary Rayfuse, analyses the prompt release jurisprudence of the tribunal with a view to identifying the criteria used by ITLOS in adjudicating and reviewing State conduct in such cases. Rayfuse notes that while coastal States are given a wide discretion under the Convention on the Law of the Sea to adopt laws and regulations relating to the exercise of their sovereign rights in their exclusive economic zones, these rights are also subject to the interests of flag States. This was translated into practice by the tribunal's holding that the balance between these interests is to be found in the application, not of total deference to coastal State measures, but rather of an international standard of reasonableness as determined by the tribunal. That standard requires the rejection of excessive or disproportionate domestic penalties and the objective application of relevant criteria embodying the internationally recognized concepts of fairness, humanity and due process.

The last two chapters discuss the practice of the ICC. Karolina Wierczynska (Chapter 19) analyses the approach of the Court in admissibility proceedings initiated by States, concentrating on the same person and same conduct tests, as well as the criteria used to assess the quality of a national proceeding. In this context, Wierczynska pays special attention to two related mechanisms that control the extent of the Court's scrutiny: standard of review and standard of proof. After analysing the relevant case law, she concludes that both standards are still *in statu nascendi*, with the ICC applying a case-by-case methodology. Wierczynska calls for a more principled approach, which would provide States with a clear set of the criteria that make a particular case admissible. In doing so, she argues that although the Court needs to take into account different objectives of the Rome Statute, a special place should be occupied by the complementarity principle. The chapter by Diane Bernard (Chapter 20) also focuses on the complementarity of the ICC, interpreted in terms of 'deference' and/or demands on States regarding their reaction to mass atrocities. Through a discussion of complementarity's various aspects, Bernard shows how the concept is read through the prism of ending impunity, sometimes to the detriment of alternative responses to mass atrocities. Yet, Bernard argues, this does not result in a hierarchical structure which subdues States to the power of the ICC. Rather, complementarity spurs pluralism, with States and the ICC commonly engaged in the project of ending impunity.

Returning to the main questions that are embedded in this volume, a few observations can be made. As may be expected, the chapters clearly show the effect of the increasing specialization of international law. The position adopted by courts and tribunals is partly determined by the specific legal framework of a functional regime and the history, main concerns, expertise and vocabularies that come with it. Yet it would be a mistake to treat this volume primarily as an example of functional fragmentation, with different regimes creating incompatible world views based on their own idioms, expert language, and structural bias.[22] The contributions to this volume show that the world of international law looks more complicated, and often more paradoxical, than that. For one thing, functional imperatives do not speak for themselves; they always have to be read against the broader political and historical context in which courts operate—a context that co-determines how courts see their role and their position towards deference. As the chapter by Duhaime (Chapter 16) illustrates, for example, the position of the IACtHR resulted from an understanding of what human rights review meant in the context of the history and the political realities of the continent. Human rights courts operating in different political contexts may very well come to different conclusions within the same specialized field of human rights. Secondly, even within one and the same court or tribunal it is not uncommon to see diverging positions towards the question of judicial review. A good example is provided by Belavusau's chapter (Chapter 14) on ECtHR jurisprudence in hate speech cases, or the contribution by Herwig and Serdarevic (Chapter 12) concerning CJEU case law. Belavusau shows how the ECtHR uses different—and largely incompatible—methodologies, resulting in different attitudes towards deference in its case law. Herwig and Serdarevic demonstrate how the CJEU differentiates between measures taken by national authorities and those adopted by organs of the EU. The very same functional imperatives work out differently when applied to different agents, in light of the Court's understanding of the nature and *telos* of the EU legal order. Thirdly, the chapters show that approaches towards the intensity of review often transcend particular functional fields. Across international law, courts and tribunals use overlapping criteria to determine the intensity of judicial review. Whether it is human rights law, trade law, investment, the law of the sea, European law or general international law, courts tend to rely on more or less the same tropes to delineate the scope of their own review. Criteria that come up across virtually all functional fields include the importance of the legal provision in question, the openness of the provision concerned, proportionality, reasonableness, good faith, and the soundness of procedures to establish scientific expertise. In addition, across functional fields overlapping reasons for deference or intrusive review are offered, including epistemic limitations, democratic legitimacy, separation of powers, the integrity of the legal order, and the need to protect the values laid down in legal documents. As several chapters set out, all these criteria still leave room for many different interpretations and diverging positions of courts towards acts by other public authorities. What is shared across the board therefore is more a common vernacular, a language that adjudicators use in different contexts in order to legitimize their substantive choices. Finally, the contributions to this volume confirm the existence of a practice of inter-institutional referencing across international law. In this context, the practice of arbitration in investment law is worth mentioning. As set out by Gruszczynski and Vadi (Chapter 9), arbitrators have consistently held that investment law is not a self-contained regime, but is also

[22] Martti Koskenniemi, 'The Politics of International Law—20 Years Later', 20(1) *EJIL* 7 (2009).

open to insights and approaches developed in other fields in international law. When it comes to the judicial assessment of scientific expertise, for example, one can find overlapping approaches in WTO law and investment law. Another illustration is provided in Leonhardsen's chapter (Chapter 8), which explains how the margin of appreciation doctrine developed by the ECtHR has inspired investment arbitrations. Yet another example of inter-institutional referencing can be found in EU law, where the CJEU attaches significant weight to the expert findings of other international organizations when confronted with questions of scientific proof (see Chapter 11 by Dąbrowska-Kłosińska). Recourse to the practices of international organizations in other functional fields helps reduce the complexities and political sensitivities that come with many questions that are brought before judicial bodies across international law.

PART I

GENERAL ISSUES/ COMPARATIVE PERSPECTIVES

2

Judicial Standards of Review and Administration of Justice in Trade and Investment Law and Adjudication

Ernst-Ulrich Petersmann

I. Introduction

This contribution begins by exploring how the intensity and standards of judicial review of governmental measures in international economic law (IEL) depend on how courts comply with their task of dispute settlement 'in conformity with principles of justice and international law', including 'human rights and fundamental freedoms for all' (Section II). Section III focuses on the judicial obligation to protect the rule of law in IEL. Section IV argues that 'consistent interpretation' of the legal and 'dispute settlement *system*' of the World Trade Organization (WTO) requires that the existing diverse 'standards of review' for the Appellate Body, dispute settlement panels, arbitral decisions and domestic judicial review of trade restrictions and distortions be applied in a more coherent way so as to realize the WTO objective of 'providing security and predictability to the multilateral trading system'. In Section V the cooperation among national and transnational courts and arbitral tribunals in international commercial and investment law is examined in a comparative fashion. Section VI posits that the 'consistent interpretation principles' underlying national and international legal systems require the expansion of 'judicial comity' and the multilevel judicial protection of legal security, rule of law and non-discriminatory conditions of competition, not only in terms of rights of governments, but also of citizens and corporate actors participating in the international division of labour and in the collective supply of international public goods.

II. Access to Justice and Standards of Review in IEL

The term 'judicial standards of review' refers to the intensity and scope of judicial review of (1) the relevant facts, (2) the applicable law, and (3) the application of the law to the facts (eg compliance by administrative decision-makers with legislation or prior decisions); they must be clarified through judicial interpretation of the applicable rules, including those on access to justice and judicial deference. The outcome of adjudication often depends on the applicable standard of review and the allocation of powers among individuals and political and judicial institutions. International law, as codified in the Vienna Convention on the Law of Treaties (VCLT), requires that 'disputes concerning treaties, like other international disputes, should be settled in conformity with the principles of justice and international law', including 'human rights and fundamental freedoms for all' (Preamble and Article 31). The International Court of Justice (ICJ) refers not only to requirements of 'proper administration of justice' in clarifying procedural principles of due process of law (such as equality between the parties, specification of legal claims, effects of non-appearance in court, inherent powers, and duties to indicate provisional measures);[1] the Court also takes it for granted that '[w]hatever the legal reasoning of a court of justice, its decisions must by definition be just, and therefore in that sense equitable';[2] and that '[e]quity as a legal concept is a direct emanation of the idea of justice. The Court whose task is by definition to administer justice is bound to apply it'.[3]

IEL, compared to other fields of international law, provides more legal and judicial remedies for governments and non-governmental actors at the national, transnational and international levels of regulation. As a result, IEL evolves also in response to thousands of decisions by national and international courts and arbitral tribunals at the request of citizens. Even though IEL remains structured by treaties among States, the 'public international law' paradigm of IEL is increasingly challenged by 'constitutional law', 'global administrative law', 'economic paradigms' of IEL and 'international private law' traditions in commercial law and arbitration, so as to adjust IEL and adjudication to globalization and to the universal human rights obligations of all States.[4] The more courts acknowledge human rights as 'the foundation of freedom, justice and peace in the world' (Preamble, Universal Declaration of Human Rights (UDHR)) and as universally-recognized in numerous UN (United Nations) legal instruments, the more judges will recognize the need for reviewing the principles of 'Westphalian justice' (eg in investment disputes in the ICJ based on 'diplomatic protection') in the light of human rights principles (eg access to justice) and other 'cosmopolitan principles of justice' (eg freedom of contract and arbitration).

[1] For references to the relevant ICJ jurisprudence see eg Giuliana Ziccardi Capaldo (ed), *Repertory of Decisions of the International Court of Justice 1947–1992, Vol II* (Dordrecht: Martinus Nijhoff, 1995), at 777, 781, 825, 855, 935.

[2] ICJ, *North Sea Continental Shelf (Federal Republic of Germany v the Netherlands)*, Judgment, ICJ Rep 1969, para 88.

[3] ICJ, *Continental Shelf (Tunisia v Libyan Arab Jamahiriya)*, Judgment, ICJ Rep 1982, para 71.

[4] On the diverse conceptions of IEL, see Ernst-Ulrich Petersmann, *International Economic Law in the 21st Century: Constitutional Pluralism and Multilevel Governance of Interdependent Public Goods* (Oxford: Hart Publishing, 2012).

Such citizen-oriented standards of judicial review increasingly prompt courts to interpret legal requirements arising from 'due process of law' and to 'balance' public and private interests, or economic and non-economic principles (such as 'public morals'), in different ways compared with State-centred standards of judicial review, which are characterized by judicial deference towards State sovereignty. For instance, in contrast to the finding in the *Mavrommatis* dispute that 'once a State has taken up a case on behalf of one of its subjects before an international tribunal, in the eyes of the latter the State is sole claimant',[5] the ICJ—in its *Diallo* judgment of 2010—reviewed breaches of human rights of the foreign investor Diallo in the light of the jurisprudence of UN and regional human rights bodies rather than focusing only on the rights of Diallo's home State.[6] By justifying IEL and its judicial interpretations not only in terms of rights of governments, but also in terms of citizens entitled to transnational rule of law and fundamental rights, IEL and adjudication thereof can become more legitimate and coherent instruments of the multilevel protection of international public goods (PGs) and the individual rights of citizens. The judicial exercise of *jura novit curiae* powers, and the judicial distribution of the 'burden of proof' regarding factual claims (eg regarding 'fair and equitable treatment' by the host State), may legitimately differ depending on whether governmental measures are challenged by private actors or by other States.

In the process of clarifying incomplete treaty rules and dispute settlement procedures, courts are often confronted with diverse 'semantic uses' of legal terms (like justice, human rights, democracy), 'reasonable disagreement' on their legal interpretation, and the conflicting interests of private and public economic actors invoking 'principles of justice' underlying economic regulation (eg 'equitable market shares', 'fair price comparisons'). As IEL is embedded in broader legal systems, economic rules must be construed and justified in conformity with the 'primary rules of conduct' and 'secondary rules of recognition, change and adjudication' of the applicable legal systems.[7] Legal interpretations of IEL must also 'fit' the specific economic rationality of IEL, with due respect for the normative reality and legitimacy of 'constitutional pluralism' among States and peoples with diverse democratic preferences and constitutional traditions (eg in their definitions of 'public order'). The customary law requirement of interpreting treaties and settling disputes 'in conformity with principles of justice' and human rights confirms the view that judges should interpret IEL, in conformity with its rule-of-law objectives and underlying principles of justice, as expressing 'a coherent conception of justice and fairness': 'Law as integrity asks judges to assume, so far as this is possible, that the law is structured by a coherent set of principles about justice and fairness and procedural due process, and it asks them to enforce

[5] *Mavrommatis Palestine Concessions (Greece v United Kingdom)*, Judgment No. 2, 1924 PCIJ, Series A, No. 2, at 12.

[6] ICJ, *Ahmadou Sadio Diallo (Guinea v Democratic Republic of Congo)*, Judgment, ICJ Rep 2010.

[7] On legal systems as a union of 'primary' and 'secondary rules', see Herbert L.A. Hart, *The Concept of Law* (Oxford: Oxford University Press, 1994), Chapter V.

these in the fresh cases that come before them, so that each person's situation is fair and just according to the same standards.'[8] Hence, to the extent IEL is no longer construed only as 'international law among States' and 'global administrative law', but also as 'constitutional', 'cosmopolitan' and 'multilevel economic regulation', judicial interpretation and clarification of the rules and principles of economic law (eg on 'fair and equitable treatment', non-discrimination, legal security, property rights) require focusing not only on the texts and contexts of treaties among States; their object and purpose, such as the WTO objective of 'sustainable development', must also be clarified in conformity with the human rights obligations of all States, requiring due regard for the rights and interests of all affected persons. For example, just as investment treaty guarantees of 'legal security' are interpreted as justifying corresponding rights of investors, the WTO obligations of 'providing security and predictability to the multilateral trading system' (Article 3 Understanding on Rules and Procedures Governing the Settlement of Disputes (DSU)) may justify 'reasonable expectations' not only on the part of governments, but also of non-governmental economic actors and citizens as 'democratic principals' of legitimate governance institutions in the twenty-first century. The IEL guarantees of individual access to national and international courts and arbitral tribunals should be construed in conformity with guarantees of access to justice in human rights conventions such as the European Convention on Human Rights (ECHR) (Articles 6, 13) and the International Covenant on Civil and Political Rights (ICCPR) (Articles 2:3, 9:4, 14:1, and 14:3). The more globalization transforms *national PGs* demanded by citizens into *international PGs* that national constitutions can protect only together with international law and multilevel governance institutions, the more important become the multilevel guarantees of 'access to justice', extending legal accountability and judicial remedies beyond civil and political rights of citizens. For instance:

- Some national Constitutions have responded to systemic governance failures by providing for broad legal and judicial remedies whenever 'rights are violated by public authority' (Article 19:4 German Basic Law).
- Some regional economic agreements (like the Lisbon Treaty) are explicitly committed to facilitating 'access to justice' (Article 67(4) Treaty on the Functioning of the European Union), the 'rule of law' (Article 2 Treaty on European Union (TEU)) and the 'right to an effective remedy and to a fair trial' whenever 'rights and freedoms guaranteed by the law of the Union are violated' (Article 47 EU Charter of Fundamental Rights).
- The General Agreement on Tariffs and Trade (GATT) and the WTO Agreements include a large number of requirements to make judicial, arbitral or administrative tribunals and independent review procedures available, not only at international governance levels among WTO Members, but also in domestic legal systems in the field of GATT (cf Article X), the WTO

[8] Ronald Dworkin, *Law's Empire* (Cambridge, MA: Harvard University Press, 1986) 225, 243.

Anti-Dumping Agreement (cf Article 13), the WTO Agreement on Customs Valuation (cf Article 11), the Agreement on Pre-shipment Inspection (cf Article 4), the Agreement on Subsidies and Countervailing Measures (cf Article 23), the General Agreement on Trade in Services (GATS) (cf Article VI), the Agreement on Trade-Related Aspects of Intellectual Property Rights (TRIPS Agreement, cf Articles 41–50, 59) and the Agreement of Government Procurement (GPA) (cf Article XX).

- In international investment law, the legal guarantees of access to justice at national and international levels (eg in the ICJ) have become supplemented by more than 2,800 bilateral and regional treaty guarantees of access to transnational arbitration.
- Some environmental conventions—like the 1998 Aarhus Convention on Access to Information, Public Participation in Decision-Making and Access to Justice in Environmental Matters—protect 'access to a review procedure before a court of law or another independent and impartial body established by law' (Article 9) in transnational environmental regulation.
- UN and regional human rights covenants (eg Article 34 ECHR, the Optional Protocol to the UN Covenant on Economic, Social and Cultural Rights) increasingly extend protection of individual access to legal and (quasi-) judicial remedies in case of violation of economic and social rights beyond national courts, albeit subject to prior exhaustion of local remedies.

The terms 'effective remedy' and 'access to justice' are often used interchangeably to protect:

- individual rights to effective access to a dispute resolution body;
- rights to fair proceedings;
- rights to timely resolution of disputes;
- rights to adequate redress; and
- the principle of efficiency and effectiveness of legal remedies.[9]

In view of the global economic, environmental and poverty crises and the failures of many UN Member States to respect, protect and fulfil their human rights obligations both inside and beyond national jurisdictions, citizens and courts of justice increasingly insist on 'constitutional' and 'human rights approaches' to transnational economic regulation, for instance by claiming that—similar to multilevel human rights law, international criminal law, European economic integration law, international investment and commercial law and arbitration—international trade law should also be interpreted, developed and protected as a rights-based, participatory system of multilevel governance protecting individual access to justice and the rule of law more effectively by holding governments

[9] Cf European Union Agency for Fundamental Rights, *Access to Justice in Europe: An Overview of Challenges and Opportunities* (Luxembourg: Publication Office of the European Union, 2011).

accountable for their welfare-reducing violations of IEL in mutually beneficial cooperation among citizens across national frontiers. Just as multilevel economic regulation inside the European Economic Area (EEA) protects market freedoms and social rights as fundamental rights, subject to limited regulatory powers of the thirty-one EEA Member States and EU/EEA institutions, so too the human right to 'a social and international order in which the rights and freedoms set forth in this Declaration can be fully realized' (Article 28 UDHR) calls for linking IEL to the human rights obligations of all governments, as already proposed by US President Roosevelt in his 'Four Freedoms' speech of 1941, explaining the need for 'a world founded upon four essential human freedoms' (ie freedom of speech, freedom of belief, freedom from fear and freedom from want). The multilevel 'governance failures' in protecting global PGs (like human rights, poverty reduction, sustainable development) confirm that human rights—notwithstanding their protection also of individual, democratic and cultural diversity and 'constitutional pluralism'—must remain the common 'foundation of freedom, peace and justice in the world' in order to establish 'conditions under which justice and respect for the obligations arising from treaties and other sources of international law can be maintained' (Preamble, UN Charter).

III. Judicial Obligations to Protect the Rule of Law in IEL

Similar to Article III of the US Constitution, many constitutional, legislative and international rules create 'judicial powers' without specifying the intensity and 'standards' of judicial review of legislative and executive measures and the scope of judicial protection of the 'rule of law'. In common law countries, the power of judicial review was understood as deriving from the duty of judges to decide disputes in accordance with the law of the land, including principles of equity if the common law failed to provide adequate legal and judicial remedies.[10] In constitutional democracies and international courts of justice, judges often infer the scope of their judicial powers from the tasks assigned to them, as in the 1803 judgment in *Marbury v Madison*, where the Chief Justice of the US Supreme Court, John Marshall, declared that for '(t)hose who apply the rule to particular cases, must of necessity expound and interpret that rule', and 'if both the law and the constitution apply to a particular case...the court must determine which of these conflicting rules governs the case'; '(t)his is of the very essence of judicial duty'.[11] In a

[10] Cf Philip Hamburger, *Law and Judicial Duty* (Cambridge, MA: Harvard University Press, 2008). The historical division between common law courts and equity courts in England (where the Court of Chancery provided additional remedies in certain situations if the common law courts failed to do so) illustrates the long-standing claim by theories of justice (eg Aristotle, *Nicomachean Ethics* (Indianapolis: Hackett Publishing, 1999), at 1137b–1138a) that equitable interpretation and application of the law may require judges to address particular circumstances of the dispute through reasonable interpretations applying 'principles of justice' and other 'rules of reason' so as to do justice in the face of unforeseen, particular circumstances of disputes.

[11] *Marbury v Madison* (1803), Cranch, Reports 1, at 178–9.

similar manner judges in *international courts* have interpreted their task to 'ensure that in the interpretation and application of the Treaties the law is observed' (cf Article 19 TEU) as implying an inherent control over the scope and intensity of judicial review. The more national and international law protects the 'rule of law'—including 'strict observance of international law' (eg in Articles 2 and 3 TEU)—in order to safeguard human rights and other PGs,[12] the more legislative, administrative and judicial rule-clarification must remain restrained by legal and institutional 'checks and balances'.[13] Judicial self-restraint vis-à-vis violations of the rule of law—eg by the Court of Justice of the European Union (CJEU) in reviewing EU violations of international treaties ratified by parliaments for the benefit of citizens (such as WTO law)—remains contested by adversely affected citizens.[14] Even if judicial standards of review are specified in international rules (like Articles 1904 NAFTA, 17 WTO Anti-Dumping Agreement), their scope may depend on their constitutional context, the procedural and substantive rules being examined, as well as on the inherent powers of courts to administer justice. The mandate of impartial and independent review may prompt international courts to exercise 'strict scrutiny' of *national* interpretations of IEL rules; yet the particular nature of rules (eg human rights) may justify granting national 'margins of appreciation'; and the *administrative* procedures for fact-gathering may justify *judicial* deference to factual determinations by national authorities. The 'checks and balances principle', aimed at attaining a division of powers among political and judicial bodies inside *national* constitutional systems may be inappropriate for *international* legal systems without a common 'demos', without effective parliamentary control and without inquisitorial judicial procedures protecting individuals against abuses of powers. As illustrated by the refusal of European courts to apply international rules which violate human rights, courts may define the transnational 'rule of law' beyond just the rights of governments if they fail to provide individual access to legal and judicial remedies against abuses of power. The human rights to justification of governmental restrictions of individual freedom and of access to justice also justify judicial review of whether inter-governmental and executive acts remain consistent with the constitutional rights of citizens, democratic legislation, and with international guarantees of the rule of law ratified by national parliaments for the benefit of citizens.

[12] Since the 1948 UDHR, human rights instruments emphasize that human rights 'should be protected by rule of law' and by legal justifications of governmental restrictions of human freedom subject 'to an effective remedy by the competent national tribunals for acts violating the fundamental rights granted…by the constitution or by law' (cf the Preamble and Articles 8 and 29 UDHR). On UN protection of rule of law beyond the State see the annual reports by the UN Secretary-General on 'The rule of law at the national and international levels' (*Delivering Justice: Programme of Action to Strengthen the Rule of Law at the National and International Levels. Report by the Secretary-General*, A/66/749, 16 March 2012).

[13] Cf Petersmann, *International Economic Law*, Chapter V.

[14] Cf Ernst-Ulrich Petersmann, 'Can the EU's Disregard for "Strict Observance of International Law" (Article 3 TEU) Be Constitutionally Justified?' in Marco Bronckers et al (eds), *Trade and Competition Law in the EU and Beyond* (Cheltenham: Edward Elgar Publishing, 2011), 214–25.

In view of the lack of a unitary demos beyond nation States, and the ineffective control of inter-governmental agreements by most parliaments, international rule of law may be better evaluated in terms of 'principles of transnational justice' (eg in terms of legal and judicial protection of human rights, individual access to courts) than in terms of State sovereignty and democracy principles, which—like the equal voting powers of citizens—do not exist in international legal regimes. Broad constitutional guarantees of equal freedoms as a 'first principle of justice'—as reflected in Article 2 of the German Basic Law and in the EU Charter of Fundamental Freedoms—protect comprehensive 'rights to justification' of all governmental restrictions of human freedom. They may justify 'cosmopolitan' rather than State-centred 'Westphalian' interpretations of IEL, giving priority—eg in judicial 'proportionality balancing' of legislative or administrative restrictions—to fundamental rights of citizens over the regulatory discretion of governments. In case of indeterminate legal terms and unforeseen risks, constitutional 'principles of precaution' may prompt courts to go beyond 'conservative justice' (in the sense of rule-following) and apply principles of equity and 'reformative justice' (eg taking into account scientific uncertainty regarding health and environmental risks justifying precautionary measures). Rather than limiting their standard of judicial review to whether national risk assessments are 'supported by coherent reasoning and respectable scientific evidence and, in this sense, objectively justifiable',[15] international judicial bodies may also adopt an extensive interpretation of their inherent review powers (eg the revision powers of annulment committees established under Article 52 of the World Bank Convention establishing the International Centre for the Settlement of Investment Disputes (ICSID)) if the lack of international appellate review, as well as of national court review, of ICSID arbitration justifies 'emergency relief' in case of important errors of law delegitimizing the arbitral award.[16]

IV. Judicial Standards of Review in WTO Law

Most statutes of international courts (eg Article 38 ICJ Statute) define the 'functions', 'applicable law' and 'powers' of the court without using the term 'standard of review'. Hence judges determine the standard of review to be applied through interpretation of the rules and procedures that are applicable for the settlement of the dispute before them. Similarly, the DSU describes the 'function of panels' (Article 11), the Appellate Body (Article 17), the Dispute Settlement Body (DSB, cf Articles 16, 17, 20 ff), arbitration proceedings (cf Articles 21, 22, 25) and 'expert review groups' (DSU Appendix 4) without using the terms 'standard of

[15] Appellate Body Report, *Australia—Measures Affecting the Importation of Apples from New Zealand*, WT/DS367/AB/R, 17 December 2010, para 213.

[16] Cf the 2010 ICSID ad hoc Committee annulling the award in *Sempra v Argentina*: 'a manifest error of law may, in an exceptional situation, be of such egregious nature as to amount to a manifest excess of powers' (ICSID Case No. ARB/02/16, Decision on annulment, 29 June 2010).

review' or 'margin of appreciation'. However, the general dispute settlement procedures of the DSU are supplemented by special dispute settlement procedures in numerous WTO agreements[17] which elaborate more specific standards of review. For instance:

- Article 17.6 of the Anti-Dumping Agreement provides that:

> (i) in its assessment of the facts, the panel shall determine whether the authorities' establishment of the facts was proper and whether their evaluation of the facts was unbiased and objective. If the establishment of the facts was proper and the evaluation was unbiased and objective, even though the panel might have reached a different conclusion, the evaluation shall not be overturned; (ii) the panel shall interpret the relevant provisions of the Agreement in accordance with customary rules of interpretation of public international law. Where the panel finds that a relevant provision of the Agreement admits of more than one permissible interpretation, the panel shall find the authorities' measure to be in conformity with the Agreement if it rests upon one of those permissible interpretations.

- An additional Ministerial Decision of 15 April 1994 states that:

> [t]he standard of review in paragraph 6 of Article 17 of the Agreement on Implementation of Article VI of GATT 1994 shall be reviewed after a period of three years with a view to considering the question of whether it is capable of general application.

- The 1994 GPA—by requiring each contracting party to establish domestic 'challenge procedures' providing, *inter alia*, for '(a) rapid interim measures to correct breaches of the Agreement' and '(c) correction of the breach of the Agreement or compensation for the loss or damage suffered'—clarifies that the legal standard of domestic review includes the relevant WTO rules.
- Similarly, Article 4 of the WTO Agreement on Pre-Shipment Inspection prescribes 'independent review procedures' for the settlement of disputes among pre-shipment inspection bodies and exporters, whose 'object...shall be to establish whether, in the course of the inspection in dispute, the parties to the dispute have complied with the provisions of this Agreement' (Article 4(f)).

The WTO agreements include additional requirements for *domestic* judicial and other dispute settlement procedures and remedies that do *not* specify the domestic applicability of WTO rules, for instance in 'the prompt review and correction of administrative action relating to customs matters' (Article X:3(b) GATT), of 'administrative decisions affecting trade in services' (Article VI:2(a) GATS), or in the judicial protection of intellectual property rights (cf Articles 41–59 TRIPS Agreement). Yet each WTO Member 'shall ensure the conformity of its laws, regulations and administrative procedures with its obligations as provided in the

[17] Cf Ernst-Ulrich Petersmann, *The GATT/WTO Dispute Settlement System* (London: Kluwer Law International, 1997), at 223 ff.

annexed Agreements' (Article XVI:4 WTO Agreement) and ensure that all measures of general application affecting trade in goods and services are administered 'in a uniform, impartial and reasonable manner' (Articles X GATT, VI GATS). Furthermore good faith interpretation of WTO law requires 'consistent interpretations' and 'judicial comity' in conformity with the legal presumptions in national and international legal systems (eg in Article 31 VCLT) that governments want to act in conformity with all their international legal obligations. National judicial interpretations of trade rules which disregard the WTO obligations of the country concerned run counter to the DSU objective of 'providing security and predictability to the multilateral trading system' (Article 3 DSU) by ensuring 'the conformity of... laws, regulations and administrative procedures with... [WTO] obligations' (Article XVI:4 WTO Agreement). Inadequate 'judicial comity' between WTO, regional and national trade adjudication reduces the overall coherence of the WTO legal and dispute settlement system, often at the request of trade diplomats interested in limiting their judicial accountability. The WTO provisions for 'non-violation complaints' and 'situation complaints' (eg in terms of Articles XXIII GATT and GATS) go beyond domestic legal and judicial remedies by also protecting principles of equity, reciprocity and good faith in WTO law.

According to Article 11 DSU:

> a panel should make an objective assessment of the matter before it, including an objective assessment of the facts of the case and the applicability of and conformity with the relevant covered agreements, and make such other findings as will assist the DSB in making the recommendations or in giving the rulings provided for in the covered agreements.

In *EC—Hormones*, the Appellate Body clarified this 'objective assessment test' as follows: 'So far as fact-finding by panels is concerned... the applicable standard is neither *de novo* review as such, nor "total deference", but rather the "objective assessment of the facts"'.[18] In subsequent findings concerning the review by panels of decisions on safeguards measures, the Appellate Body repeated: 'panels must not conduct a *de novo* review of the evidence nor substitute their judgment for that of the competent authority'.[19] In *US—Softwood Lumber VI (Article 21.5—Canada)*, the Appellate Body clarified that, even though a panel 'must take care not to assume itself the role of initial trier of facts, nor to be passive by "simply accept(ing) the conclusions of the competent authority"', the panel in that case had 'failed to engage in the type of critical and searching analysis called for by Article 11 of the DSU'.[20] In *US—Continued Suspension*, the Appellate Body found that instead of determining whether the risk assessment was supported

[18] Appellate Body Report, *EC Measures Concerning Meat and Meat Products (EC—Hormones)*, WT/DS26/AB/R, 13 February 1998, para 117.

[19] Appellate Body Report, *United States—Transitional Safeguard Measure on Combed Cotton Yarn from Pakistan*, WT/DS192/AB/R, 5 November 2001, para 74.

[20] Appellate Body Report, *United States—Investigation of the International Trade Commission in Softwood Lumber from Canada (US—Softwood Lumber VI (Article 21.5—Canada))*, WT/DS277/AB/RW, 9 May 2006, paras 93, 113.

by coherent reasoning and reputable scientific evidence, the panel had wrongly sought to determine whether the risk assessment relied upon by the EU was based on correct scientific evidence.[21] Numerous Appellate Body reports have clarified that specific WTO provisions could justify specific (eg more deferential) standards of review, declaring for example that: 'an "objective assessment" under Article 11 DSU must be considered in the light of the obligations of the particular covered agreement at issue in order to derive the more specific contours of the appropriate standard of review'.[22] In reviewing the legality of prior national decisions (eg on risk assessments and technical regulations for health protection, national safeguards, anti-dumping and countervailing duty decisions), panels must act as the 'reviewer of agency action rather than as initial trier of fact'[23] and may have to respect the rationality of domestic determinations based on the evidence before the domestic authority. The standard applied by WTO dispute settlement bodies in reviewing general domestic rules implementing WTO obligations (such as the prohibitions of trade discrimination in GATT Articles I and III) does not provide for 'margins of appreciation'; it tends to be strict regarding both issues of fact and of WTO legal consistency in order to provide 'security and predictability to the multilateral trading system' and 'preserve the rights and obligations of Members under the covered agreements' (Article 3:2 DSU).[24] The Appellate Body's pragmatic focus on deriving 'specific standards of review' by interpreting the particular context of specific WTO rules, procedures and the 'measures at issue' does not exclude also taking into account general administrative, constitutional and procedural law principles,[25] provided the standard of review remains consistent with the objectives and textual limitations of WTO rules.[26]

Article 17.6 DSU limits the scope of appellate review to 'issues of law covered in the panel report and legal interpretations developed by the panel'. Yet,

[21] Appellate Body Report, *United States—Continued Suspension of Obligations in the EC—Hormones Dispute*, WT/DS320/AB/R, 14 November 2008, para 590.

[22] Appellate Body Report, *United States—Countervailing Duty Investigation on Dynamic Random Access Memory Semiconductors (DRAMS) from Korea*, WT/DS296/AB/R, 20 July 2005, para 184. On the deference criteria in WTO law and standards of review see Chapter 6 by Michael Ioannidis in this volume.

[23] Appellate Body Report, *US—DRAMS*, para 188. On WTO standards of review regarding scientific evidence see Chapter 9 by Lukasz Gruszczynski and Valentina Vadi in this volume.

[24] On the different kinds of 'measures at issue', the distinction between 'as such' claims and 'as applied' claims, and the generally strict WTO standards of review see Ross Becroft, *The Standard of Review in WTO Dispute Settlement. Critique and Development* (Cheltenham: Edward Elgar Publishing, 2012), at 28 ff.

[25] Such as access to justice, due process of law, procedural rules on burden of proof and judicial economy, transparent and inclusive democratic deliberation, effectiveness of WTO disciplines on trade-distorting national measures, and inherent judicial powers necessary for administering justice.

[26] In *EC—Hormones*, the Appellate Body emphasized: 'The standard of review applicable in proceedings under the SPS Agreement...must reflect the balance established in that Agreement between the jurisdictional competencies conceded by the Members to the WTO and the jurisdictional competencies retained by the Members for themselves. To adopt a standard of review not clearly rooted in the text of the SPS Agreement itself, may well amount to changing that finely drawn balance; and neither a panel nor the Appellate Body is authorized to do that' (Appellate Body Report, *EC—Hormones*, para 115).

appeals challenging non-compliance with the 'objective assessment' requirement of Article 11 DSU may also require the review of both *factual issues* and of *application of the law to the facts*. While the Appellate Body examines legal issues *de novo*, Article 11 limits the standard of review for *factual* and related *law application issues* to whether the panel made 'objective assessments'. Even though Article 11 'articulates with... sufficient clarity the appropriate standard of review... in respect of both the ascertainment of facts and the legal characterization of such facts under the relevant agreements',[27] it often remains difficult 'to clearly distinguish between issues that are purely legal, purely factual, or are mixed issues of law and fact',[28] as for instance when a panel examined municipal law and its consistency with WTO obligations.

The 'primary rules of conduct' and the 'secondary rules' of recognition, change, and adjudication of the legal and 'dispute settlement system of the WTO' (Article 3 DSU) are aimed not only at preserving 'the rights and obligations of Members under the covered agreements' but also at 'providing security and predictability to the multilateral trading system' (Article 3 DSU) for the benefit of private and public actors in economic markets. The WTO guarantees—of non-discriminatory market access for private goods and services; of private intellectual property rights; and of individual access to domestic courts in order to examine 'alleged breaches of the Agreement' (Article XX:2 GPA), or whether non-governmental parties 'have complied with the provisions of this Agreement' (Article 4(f) Agreement on Pre-Shipment Inspection)—acknowledge that 'raising standards of living, ensuring full employment and a large and steadily growing volume of real income and effective demand' (WTO Preamble) for the benefit of citizens are the ultimate economic values justifying the 'multilateral trading system'. Similarly, the rule of law for the benefit of citizens can be viewed as the ultimate legal value justifying the WTO dispute settlement system. The linking of WTO obligations to domestic dispute settlement and enforcement provisions—eg in Article 42 TRIPS Agreement ('Members shall make available to right holders civil judicial procedures concerning the enforcement of any intellectual property right covered by this Agreement')—reflects the 'cosmopolitan function' of WTO law for the benefit of citizens engaged in international trade, notwithstanding the sovereign freedom of WTO Members to decide on their respective (eg 'monist' or 'dualist') modalities of implementing WTO obligations in their national legal systems. Just as human rights, regional economic integration law, and international criminal and environmental law provide for the multilevel legal and judicial protection of cosmopolitan rights, so too interpreting WTO rules 'in conformity with principles of justice' and 'human rights and fundamental freedoms for all' justifies the judicial protection of precise and unconditional WTO obligations for the benefit not only of governments, but also of citizens relying on the transnational rule of law in international trade. States and governments derive their moral value from

[27] Appellate Body Report, *EC—Hormones*, para 116.

[28] Appellate Body Report, *EC and Certain Member States—Measures Affecting Trade in Large Civil Aircraft*, WT/DS316/AB/R, 1 June 2011, para 1314.

respecting the constitutional and cosmopolitan rights of citizens, rather than vice versa. The procedural and substantive 'domestic law functions' of WTO obligations depend—as in the case of judicial 'standards of review'—on the particular context of WTO rules and of their incorporation into domestic legal systems. For instance, inasmuch as *domestic justifications* of judicial deference towards national regulatory agencies controlled by national parliaments may not be persuasive in the *international context* of WTO disputes (eg over the correct interpretation of 'fair price comparison' requirements of WTO anti-dumping rules), the Appellate Body has so far adopted a restrictive application of the statutory standard of review set forth in Article 17.6 of the WTO Agreement on Implementation of Article VI GATT. Also the DSB has not endorsed proposals for extending this specific standard of review to other WTO agreements.[29]

V. Judicial Standards of Review in International Investment Law

Just as WTO adjudication (as in the 'bananas disputes' from 1991 to 2012) remains characterized by 'member-driven governance'—prioritizing the rights of governments over the rights of citizens—so too the few international investment disputes adjudicated in the ICJ remain dominated by Westphalian conceptions of the 'diplomatic protection' of investors by their home States, without offering effective and speedy remedies for private investors.[30] Yet, in contrast to the disregard of WTO rules by most domestic courts and the accompanying adjudication showing deference to governmental claims for 'freedom of manoeuver',[31] international commercial, investment, intellectual property and regional economic

[29] In *EC—Bed Linen*, for example, the Appellate Body noted that the practice of 'zeroing' was inconsistent with the Anti-Dumping Agreement, and therefore the panel 'was not faced with a choice among multiple "permissible" interpretations which would have required it, under Article 17.6(ii), to give deference to the interpretation relied upon by the European Communities' (Appellate Body Report, *European Communities—Anti-Dumping Duties on Imports of Cotton-Type Bed Linen from India*, WT/DS141/AB/R, 12 March 2001, para 65). In *US—Steel* the Appellate Body noted, however, that it did not exclude the possibility of WTO agreements admitting more than one permissible interpretation (Appellate Body Report, *United States—Anti-Dumping Measures on Certain Hot-Rolled Steel Products from Japan*, WT/DS184/AB/R, 23 August 2001, para 61). It remains to be clarified whether Article 17.6 can be legally justified (eg on grounds of the *in dubio mitius* presumption of general international law) as being consistent with the customary methods of treaty interpretation.

[30] The 2010 merits judgment in the *Diallo* case was the first investment dispute in the ICJ where a breach of an individual's rights was established; the 2012 judgment on compensation in the same *Diallo* case was the first ICJ judgment awarding damages for human rights violations—fourteen years after the proceedings were filed in 1998. In the *ELSI* case (*Case concerning Elettronica Sicula SPA (ELSI)*, Judgment, ICJ Rep 1989), the ICJ judgment was rendered more than twenty years after the investment dispute was first submitted to Italian courts.

[31] The term 'freedom of manoeuvre' continues to be used by both the political EU institutions and the EU Court (eg in Joined Cases C-120 P and C-121/06 P *Fabbrica italiana accumulatori motocarri Montecchio SpA (FIAMM) and Others v Council of the European Union* [2008] ECR I-6513, para 119) as the main justification for their disregard of legally binding WTO rules and WTO dispute settlement rulings.

integration treaties and related agreements on the recognition and enforcement of foreign arbitral awards (like the 1958 New York Convention and the 1965 ICSID Convention) provide for multilevel judicial protection of private commercial and investor rights, subject to narrowly defined legal exceptions (eg if 'recognition or enforcement of the award would be contrary to the public policy of that country', cf Article V New York Convention). This more effective judicial protection of commercial and investor rights than of transnational trading rights is related to 'protection biases' in many national legal traditions, and illustrates the interrelationships between legal interpretation and 'standards of review'. Freedom of contract, commercial and property rights, and individual rights to petition for protection from imports (eg under anti-dumping and safeguards laws) are legally and judicially more protected in national and international legal systems than individual freedoms to import and export (eg as protected under Article 2:1 German Basic Law, German trade legislation and EU common market law subject to democratic legislation).[32]

The more than 2,800 bilateral investment treaties (BITs), providing for arbitration between States as well as for investor–State arbitration, have given rise to hundreds of arbitral awards which increasingly refer to each other, despite the fact that they are legally binding only on the parties to the dispute. Because of the diversity of potential conflicts (eg among public and private, economic and non-economic interests), BITs usually refrain from defining judicial 'standards of review'. Similarly, in view of the freedom of choice among alternative dispute settlement procedures, investment tribunals also tend to refrain from defining general 'standards of judicial review'. The public law nature of BITs, multilateral investment treaties (like the ICSID Convention), and multilateral arbitration agreements (like the New York Convention) prompts arbitrators to rely less on their commercial arbitration traditions (eg of private party autonomy and confidentiality) and include more public law standards for the balancing of public and private, and economic and non-economic interests.[33] The diverse jurisdictions and 'judicial paradigms' of private and public, and national and international investment adjudication may entail different 'standards of review' (eg depending on the interpretation of the applicable law). For instance, the general jurisdiction of the ICJ enabled issuance of a merits judgment in the 2010 *Diallo* case, establishing violations of fundamental rights under applicable human rights treaties, which an ICSID tribunal—due to the limitation on its jurisdiction to 'any legal dispute arising directly out of an investment' (Article 25 ICSID Convention)—might have found to be beyond its competence. Yet ICSID tribunals have emphasized

[32] Also US courts hold 'that no one has a vested right to trade with foreign nations': 'When the people granted Congress the power "to regulate Commerce with foreign Nations"... they thereupon relinquished at least whatever right they, as individuals, may have had to insist upon the importation of any product' (*Arjay Associates Inc. v Bush*, 891 F.2d 981, 898 (Fed. Cir. 1989)).

[33] Cf Pierre-Marie Dupuy, Francesco Francioni and Ernst-Ulrich Petersmann (eds), *Human Rights in International Investment Law and Arbitration* (Oxford: Oxford University Press, 2009). On standards of review in international investment law see Chapter 8 by Erlend Leonhardsen in this volume.

that their limited jurisdiction must not imply a limitation on the scope of the applicable law. For instance, inasmuch as WTO adjudication permits only prospective judicial remedies, investors have increasingly requested financial compensation in investment arbitration on the ground that WTO dispute settlement rulings had established illegal discrimination against foreign investors violating both BIT and WTO obligations (eg due to 'umbrella clauses' transforming WTO commitments into BIT obligations).

Investor–State arbitrators based on United Nations Commission on International Trade Law (UNCITRAL) procedures, perceiving themselves to be 'private service providers' in the context of the national legal order at the seat of arbitration, may decide on their powers to adjudicate (eg for dealing with anti-suit injunctions issued by the court of another State, *lis pendens*, the arbitrator's *jura novit curiae* powers) and on the applicable 'standard of review' (eg as derived from contract law principles of 'equality of the parties') in a different way than investor–State arbitrators based on ICSID rules, perceiving themselves to be public law judges acting on behalf of a worldwide 'arbitral legal order', recognized and enforced in 148 contracting States (2013). Most ICSID tribunals interpret investment treaties and their 'standard of review' by invoking Article 31 VCLT. Their public law function justifies their perception of themselves as more than just 'private dispute resolution service providers' referring only to arguments presented by the parties to the dispute. The inevitable balancing of public and private interests also justifies independent, legal assessments *proprio motu* following the maxim of *jus novit curia*, according to which a court should—of its own motion—apply any rule of law relevant to the facts and to the dispute resolution. On the other hand, if the legal rule has not been explicitly pleaded, judges may feel bound to respect 'party autonomy', for instance if the invocation of 'exception clauses' remains within the discretion of the parties to the dispute.[34] Tribunals increasingly admit the inherent conflicts between public and private interests and 'public law' and 'private law' perspectives in investment law; hence adjudicators acknowledge the need for 'balancing' all public and private interests involved, such as private claims focusing on investor rights and government claims that tribunals should always defer to government discretion and to inter-governmental interpretations limiting the jurisdiction of tribunals, even retroactively, in pending investment disputes.[35] In *EDF Services v Romania* (2009), the arbitral tribunal emphasized that:

> The idea that legitimate expectations, and therefore FET [fair and equitable treatment], imply the stability of the legal and business framework, may not be correct if stated in an overly-broad and unqualified formulation. The FET might then mean the virtual freezing

[34] On the two types of 'dispute-oriented tribunals' and 'legislator-oriented tribunals' see Ole K. Fauchald, 'Legal Reasoning of ICSID Tribunals: An Empirical Analysis', 19(2) *EJIL* 301 (2008).

[35] See the 'Interpretive Note' issued by the NAFTA Federal Trade Commission on 31 July 2001 in order to limit the judicial articulation of stricter standards by NAFTA investment tribunals: 'The concepts of "fair and equitable treatment" and "full protection and security" do not require treatment in addition to or beyond that which is required by the customary international law minimum standard of treatment of aliens'. On the importance of deference in investor–State arbitration see Chapter 7 by Caroline Henckels in this volume.

of the legal regulation of economic activities, in contrast with the State's normal regulatory power and the evolutionary character of economic life. Except where specific promises or representations are made by the State to the investor the latter may not rely on a bilateral investment treaty as a kind of insurance policy against the risk of any changes in the host State's legal and economic framework. Such expectation would be neither legitimate nor reasonable.[36]

The judicial balancing between public and private rights and interests may legitimately differ depending on the relevant constitutional context and 'principles of justice', for instance if democracy is legally defined in terms of 'parliamentary freedom' to regulate (as in many Anglo-Saxon democracies) rather than in terms of equal constitutional rights of citizens, limiting majoritarian 'rule by law' (as in many European 'constitutional democracies'). As in international trade adjudication, judicial review of national determinations of complex facts may be limited in investment adjudication. The allocation of procedural burdens of proof may also be influenced by diverse judicial conceptions of investment law, for instance as *restraining public regulatory powers* for the benefit of cosmopolitan rights rather than as *serving primarily public interests*.[37] Table 1 illustrates how investor–State arbitration may require a more complex 'proportionality balancing' (eg of property rights with other human rights) than inter-governmental WTO disputes, even though the latter may likewise include claims to respect 'margins of appreciation' in the legislative protection of 'public morals' and other public interests.

Table 1

• Principles used by tribunals for resolving jurisdictional overlaps include, *inter alia*, '*lis pendens*', '*res judicata*', comity, '*forum non conveniens*', 'fork in the road preclusion' (*electa una via*), joinder or *de facto* consolidation of different claims, agreed settlement of disputes, voluntary waiver of the right to initiate proceedings, agreed designation of a specific *forum*, or withdrawal of consent to a certain dispute settlement mechanism.[38]
• Principles used by tribunals for deciding whether a regulatory activity (eg by a government-owned corporation) can be 'attributed' to the State (in terms of State responsibility) include, *inter alia*: formal authority to exercise public power; functional exercise of government power; private action under governmental control and instructions; agreed *lex specialis* rules (eg 'umbrella clauses' in BITs); State failure to grant 'full protection and security' and prevent 'denial of justice'.[39]

(*Continued*)

[36] *EDF (Services) Ltd v Romania*, ICSID Case No. ARB/05/13, Arbitral Award, 8 October 2009, at para 217.

[37] On these competing conceptions of 'public–private divides' see Alex Mills, 'Antinomies of Public and Private at the Foundations of International Investment Law and Arbitration', 14(2) *JIEL* 469 (2011) 500–2.

[38] For case examples see Leonila Guglya, 'The Interplay of International Dispute Resolution Mechanisms: The Softwood Lumber Controversy', 2(1) *JIDS* 175 (2011).

[39] For case examples see Mills, 'Antinomies' at 500–2.

Table 1 ***Continued***

• On the 'balancing' of competing 'development dimensions' see *Lemire v Ukraine* (2010): 'Economic development is an objective which must benefit all, primarily national citizens and companies, and secondarily foreign investors. Thus, the object and purpose of the Treaty is not to protect foreign investments *per se*, but as an aid to the development of the domestic economy. And local development requires that the preferential treatment of foreigners be balanced against the legitimate right of Ukraine to pass legislation and adopt measures for the protection of what as a sovereign it perceives to be its public interest.'[40]
• Principles for examining 'indirect expropriation' include, *inter alia*: 'non-discriminatory treatment' and 'regulation for a public purpose, which is enacted in accordance with due process' without impairing 'specific commitments' by the government to the foreign investor; 'fair and equitable treatment' (FET); 'interference with the use of property which has the effect of depriving the owner, in whole or in significant part, of the use or reasonably-to-be-expected economic benefit of property even if not necessarily to the obvious benefit of the host State'[41]; 'substantial deprivation' or permanent 'disappearance' of the economic value of the investor's property; legitimate public interests; 'fair balance' of public and private interests involved.[42]
• Even though most BITs do not refer to human rights, human rights are increasingly being raised in investment treaty lawsuits by host States, investors, third parties or judges in order to justify governmental restrictions or 'affirmative action policies', investment treaty breaches, protection of investor rights or interpretations of investment rules (eg on FET, 'protection and security' obligations, a 'state of necessity', 'public order', 'just compensation') in conformity with human rights (such as rights of access to water, essential medicines and information, rights of indigenous people). Due to their different procedures, jurisdictions and applicable laws, investment and human rights tribunals risk resolving 'overlapping disputes' (eg over property expropriations, denial of justice, due process claims, claims for moral damages arising out of government interferences into rights of investors) in different ways.[43]

The often one-sided focus of BITs on the protection of vaguely formulated investor rights has prompted some countries to withdraw from the ICSID Convention

[40] *Joseph Charles Lemire v Ukraine*, ICSID, Award on Jurisdiction, 14 January 2010, Case No. ARB/06/18, para 273.

[41] *Metalclad Corporation v The United Mexican States*, ICSID, Final Award, 30 August 2000, Case No. ARB/97/1, 40 ILM 36, para 103.

[42] Cf *LG&E Energy Corp., LG&E Capital Corp., and LG&E International, Inc. v Argentine Republic*, ICSID, Award, 3 October 2006, Case No. ARB/02/1, at para 194: 'The question remains as to whether one should only take into account the effects produced by the measure or if one should consider also the context within which a measure was adopted and the host State's purpose. It is this Tribunal's opinion that there must be a balance in the analysis both of the causes and the effects of a measure in order that one may qualify a measure as being of an expropriatory nature. It is important not to confound the State's right to adopt policies with its power to take an expropriatory measure'. On the competing 'public purpose', 'police powers' and 'effects-doctrines' in the relevant case law, see Ursula Kriebaum, 'Regulatory Takings: Balancing the Interests of the Investor and the State', 8 *Journal of World Investment and Trade* 717 (2007).

[43] For overviews of the relevant case law, see Dupuy et al, *Human Rights*. The pertinent ISCID jurisprudence is also influenced by the different roles of host States, foreign investors and third parties (eg as perpetrators or victims of human rights violations) and the diverse legal contexts; in *Biloune and Marine Drive Complex Ltd v Ghana*, UNCITRAL Award, 27 October 1989, for instance, Ghana had neither ratified the ICCPR nor the African Convention on Human Rights of 1981.

(eg Bolivia and Venezuela), or to refrain from providing for investor–State arbitration in future economic agreements (eg Australia since 2010). Other countries have responded by providing for 'general exceptions' and appellate review procedures in 'new generation BITs' (eg Canada and the USA), or by encouraging ICSID annulment committees to construe their revision powers broadly.[44] The fact that judicial decisions and scholarly opinions have become the most frequently used interpretive arguments in ICSID jurisprudence illustrates the primary role of judges and jurisprudence in the interpretation of general legal principles and standards of modern investment law. Yet, the legitimacy of investment tribunals continues to be undermined by the non-publication of arbitral awards, confidentiality and lack of transparency of many arbitral procedures. The EU Court's case law on the lack of standing of arbitral tribunals to request preliminary rulings from the Court is influenced by this inadequate transparency of investment arbitration and the fear that arbitrators may neglect or incorrectly apply EU law relevant in the context of the settlement of commercial and investment disputes.

VI. Multilevel Judicial Governance in IEL Requires 'Judicial Comity' Based on 'Cosmopolitan Constitutionalism'

The multilevel regulation of international PGs depends on 'judicial comity' between national, transnational and international tribunals in their joint task of protecting the transnational rule of law for the benefit of citizens as subjects of modern international law.[45] Notwithstanding the lack of legally binding precedents (*stare decisis*) in global trade and investment law, the compliance by national and European courts and WTO dispute settlement panels with the Appellate Body's jurisprudence on the inconsistency of 'zeroing' with the WTO legal requirements of 'fair price comparisons' in anti-dumping proceedings illustrates a welcome willingness on the part of national and international courts to modify their jurisprudence to bring it into conformity with WTO dispute settlement jurisprudence.[46] Also, Article 1904 North American Free Trade Agreement

[44] Cf the finding of the ICSID annulment Committee in the *Sempra v Argentina* arbitration. The arbitration award was deemed to amount to a manifest excess of powers owing to the erroneous interpretation of the treaty-based emergency exception in terms of the customary law defence of necessity (as codified in Article 25 of the ILC Articles on State Responsibility) rather than in terms of Article XI of the underlying BIT. Previous ICSID jurisprudence had excluded the erroneous application of the proper law as a valid reason for annulment.

[45] The ICJ judgment in *LaGrand (Germany v USA), Merits*, ICJ Rep 2001, and the jurisprudence of the CJEU, the EFTA Court and the ECtHR offer many examples of judicial recognition of individuals as subjects of rights under international treaties. The International Law Commission's codification of the rules on State responsibility is explicitly 'without prejudice to any right, arising from the international responsibility of a State, which may accrue directly to any person or entity other than a State' (Article 33:2); cf James Crawford, *The ILC's Articles on State Responsibility. Introduction, Text and Commentaries* (Cambridge: Cambridge University Press, 2002), at 209 ff.

[46] Cf Sungjoon Cho, 'Global Constitutional Lawmaking', 31 *University of Pennsylvania Journal of International Law* 621 (2010).

(NAFTA) dispute settlement panels have repeatedly followed WTO dispute settlement findings.[47] In instances where national and regional courts disregarded WTO rules (eg in MERCOSUR[48] case law on imports of re-treaded tyres into Brazil), WTO dispute settlement bodies deciding on the same subject matter (eg imports of re-treaded tyres into Brazil) rightly refrained from judicial comity and insisted on compliance with WTO obligations.[49] The human right 'to a social and international order in which the rights and freedoms set forth in this Declaration can be fully realized' (Article 28 UDHR) justifies the interpretation of WTO guarantees—of equal freedoms, non-discriminatory conditions of competition, individual access to legal and judicial remedies, and good faith implementation of WTO obligations—in domestic legal systems in conformity with the 'consistent interpretation' requirements of national and international legal systems so as to provide 'security and predictability to the multilateral trading system', not only in terms of rights of governments but also for the benefit of citizens and their human rights to transnational 'rule of law' (Preamble, UDHR).[50] Inasmuch as the multilevel legal and judicial protection of commercial, investment, human rights law and regional economic law has protected fundamental rights, rule of law and legal accountability more effectively than power-oriented Westphalian conceptions of 'international law among sovereign States', so too the multilevel WTO dispute settlement system should protect IEL guarantees of freedom, non-discrimination and rule of law for the benefit of citizens, even if the international rules were addressed to States without explicitly providing for cosmopolitan rights. From a human rights perspective aimed at empowering citizens and protecting them against abuses of power (eg in non-inclusive, governmental decision-making), modern IEL should be understood—like democratic constitutionalism—as a cosmopolitan legal system for constituting, limiting, regulating and justifying multilevel governance aimed at protecting international PGs as demanded by citizens 'in conformity with principles of justice' and 'human rights and fundamental freedoms'. This multilevel judicial protection of cosmopolitan rights must complement political governance in order to protect constitutional and human rights more effectively in international economic relations.

[47] Cf Jorge A. Huerta-Goldman, 'Trade Remedies Disputes—Reciprocal Relationships between WTO and NAFTA Tribunals', in Filippo Fontanelli et al (eds), *Shaping Rule of Law through Dialogue* (Groningen: Europa Law Publishing, 2010), 319–43.

[48] Mercado Común del Sur (Common Market of the South).

[49] Cf Ernst-Ulrich Petersmann, 'Administration of Justice in the WTO: Did the WTO Appellate Body Commit "Grave Injustice"'? 8 *The Law and Practice of International Courts and Tribunals* 329 (2009).

[50] On the 'consistent interpretation principle', see Andre Nollkaemper, *National Courts and the International Rule of Law* (Oxford: Oxford University Press, 2011) 139–65.

3

Deference and the Use of the Public Policy Exception in International Courts and Tribunals

Ilona Cheyne

I. Introduction

The concepts of standard of review and deference govern the way in which international courts and tribunals evaluate the legality of a State's actions.[1] Standard of review can be seen as a measure of intensity of a tribunal's examination.[2] Deference here is taken to mean the tribunal's acknowledgement of the primacy of the State to make decisions and the need to avoid substituting the State's judgment with its own. As Caroline Henckels points out, the need for this restraint will occur when the tribunal has a different opinion as to the correct course of action or where there is uncertainty, either in interpretation of the law or the facts, or because there is no correct objective answer.[3] The tribunal defers to the right of the State to decide in these cases and, in this sense, deference is located within the broader category of standard of review. In essence, the conflict to be resolved is between the State as domestic regulator and the State as international guarantor.

Neither deference nor standard of review is well understood in international law, and it is proposed here to use the 'public policy' justification contained in various trade and commercial legal regimes as a revealing perspective on the power relationships mediated through international courts and tribunals.[4] The use of public policy in these regimes provides clear examples of contestation between

[1] Sungjoon Cho, 'Global Constitutional Lawmaking', 31 *University of Pennsylvania Journal of International Law* 621 (2010), 643–4.

[2] Matthias Oesch, *Standards of Review in WTO Dispute Resolution* (Oxford: Oxford University Press, 2004); Steven P. Croley and John H. Jackson, 'WTO Dispute Procedures, Standard of Review, and Deference to National Governments', 90 *AJIL* 193 (1996). See also Chapter 2 by Ernst-Ulrich Petersmann (Section I) and Chapter 17 by Chiara Ragni (Section I), both in this volume.

[3] Caroline Henckels, Chapter 7 in this volume (Section II).

[4] Different terminology, such as ordre public, public interest or public purpose, exist but for ease of discussion 'public policy' will be the term used here.

legally negotiated legal obligations and the retention of unilateral policy freedom. At this stage, the enquiry is primarily concerned with identifying, ordering and classifying approaches to deference when public policy is used as a justification for State action and asking whether there is any convergence of approach.

The question here is whether a State has the power to choose its own public policy, and it logically precedes the evaluation of the measure used to implement that policy.[5] The concept of public policy is, of course, extraordinarily wide. It is found in international and transnational legal systems governing a range of subjects from child custody rules to corruption to registration of trade marks. The indeterminate category of exception defined simply as 'public policy' can be conceptually distinguished from substantively defined policy exceptions such as human health or environmental protection. However, the claim is not based on an entirely self-judging clause and it therefore invites more than a mere review of good faith on the part of the State.[6] Equally, the undefined character of public policy makes it problematic to use a standard of review equivalent to a margin of appreciation doctrine. In sum, the lack of objective criteria to employ in reviewing unilateral acts under the public policy justification gives it a particularly intriguing character. It may possess its own independent, substantive meaning or it may simply be a residual category exception. It offers a substantively open-ended balancing mechanism that operates at the pressure points between independence and cooperation, autonomy and integration. The public policy justification therefore speaks to the questions of allocation of power and relationships of power that lie at the heart of the concept of deference.

This enquiry can be placed in the wider context of constitutionalism discourse, broadly understood to engage with questions of power, coherence and normativity.[7] It

[5] For a discussion of proportionality and proportionality *stricto sensu*, see Benedict Kingsbury and Stephan W. Schill, 'Public Law Concepts to Balance Investors' Rights with State Regulatory Actions in the Public Interest—the Concept of Proportionality', in Stephan W. Schill (ed), *International Investment Law and Comparative Public Law* (Oxford: Oxford University Press, 2010) and Caroline Henckels, 'Indirect Expropriation and the Right to Regulate: Revisiting Proportionality Analysis and the Standard of Review in Investor–State Arbitration', 15(1) *JIEL* 223 (2012). See also the discussion in Chapter 12 by Alexia Herwig and Asja Serdarevic in this volume.

[6] Stephan Schill and Robyn Briese, '"If the State Considers": Self-Judging Clauses in International Dispute Settlement', 13 *Max Planck Yearbook of United Nations Law* 61 (2009); ICJ, *Case Concerning Military and Paramilitary Activities in and Against Nicaragua (Nicaragua v United States of America), Merits*, Judgment, ICJ Rep 1986, para 282 (necessity claim can only be self-judging if explicitly expressed); followed in ICJ, *Case Concerning Oil Platforms (Islamic Republic of Iran v United States of America)*, Judgment, ICJ Rep 2003, para 43. See also Chapter 17 by Chiara Ragni (Sections II and III) and Chapter 5 by Andrei Mamolea in this volume.

[7] Kumm, for example, describes the use of constitutional language by international lawyers as a way of describing examples of 'a coherent legal order'. See Mattias Kumm, 'The Cosmopolitan Turn in Constitutionalism: On the Relationship between Constitutionalism in and beyond the State', in Jeffrey L. Dunoff and Joel P. Trachtman (eds), *Ruling the World? Constitutionalism, International Law, and Global Governance* (Cambridge: Cambridge University Press, 2009) at 259. And see Jeffrey L. Dunoff, 'Constitutional Conceits: The WTO's "Constitution" and the Discipline of International Law', 17 *EJIL* 647 (2006), 651–6, identifying from the literature three perspectives of institutional, normative and judicial constitutionalization. See also Chapter 2 by Ernst-Ulrich Petersmann (Section II), noting 'The customary law requirement of interpreting treaties and settling disputes "in conformity with principles of justice" and human rights confirms the view that judges

is not possible to do justice to the full constitutionalism debate here, but a few remarks may help to set the context and explain the approach taken in this study. Broadly speaking, the concept of international constitutionalism embraces ideas of higher status norms and legislative, executive or adjudicative powers exercised by international institutions. It is an idea that is often used to promote the protection of individual human rights, interrogate the impact of powerful dispute settlement mechanisms, and reflect concerns about the fragmentation of international law.[8] It is driven partly by precepts of liberalism and their reflection in modern constitutions, particularly domestically protected fundamental rights, which may be threatened by the power and reach of international organizations.[9] It also responds to the significant loss, or delegation, of sovereign powers to make and interpret legal obligations in an expanding international legal sphere.[10] A key characteristic of constitutionalism is the creation and administration of general principles at international level, and the search for a coherent view of deference is equally a search for a functional expression of a general principle. Consequently, this study adopts a pragmatic or functionalist approach to the idea of constitutionalism as it searches for common approaches in the use of standard of review and deference.[11]

The arguments behind constitutionalism are relevant to the question of how or why deference occurs. Two principal theoretical approaches may demonstrate the connection. One approach looks for a doctrine of deference operating within the 'constitutional' context of the regime or international law as a whole; the other is based on the view that the boundary of State discretion is determined by the meaning of the relevant legal provision discovered through traditional forms of treaty interpretation.[12] The first tends towards a uniform concept of deference; the second makes deference and intensity of review contingent on the circumstances of each case. A doctrine of deference is often derived from broad factors such as democratic accountability or superior expertise.[13] In contrast, focusing on the meaning

should interpret IEL [international economic law]—in conformity with its rule-of-law objectives and underlying principles of justice—as expressing "a coherent conception of justice and fairness"'.

[8] Jeffrey L. Dunoff and Joel P. Trachtman, 'A Functional Approach to International Constitutionalization', in Dunoff and Trachtman, *Ruling the World?*, 6–9.

[9] Karolina Milewicz, 'Emerging Patterns of Global Constitutionalization: Toward a Conceptual Framework', 16 *Indiana Journal of Global Legal Studies* 413 (2009).

[10] Mattias Kumm, 'The Legitimacy of International Law: A Constitutionalist Framework of Analysis', 15 *EJIL* 907 (2004).

[11] See Dunoff and Trachtman, 'A Functional Approach', 9–18.

[12] There is considerable literature on this topic. See eg Christine E.J. Schwöbel, *Global Constitutionalism in International Legal Perspective* (Leiden: Martinus Nijhoff, 2011); Mattias Kumm, 'The Cosmopolitan Turn in Constitutionalism', 258; Oliver Diggelmann and Tilmann Altwicker, 'Is There Something Like a Constitution of International Law? A Critical Analysis of the Debate on World Constitutionalism', 68 *Zeitschrift für ausländisches öffentliches Recht und Völkerrecht* 623 (2008); Jan Klabbers, Anne Peters and Geir Ulfstein (eds), *The Constitutionalization of International Law* (Oxford: Oxford University Press, 2009); Dunoff and Trachtman, *Ruling the World?*.

[13] See eg Andrew Legg, *The Margin of Appreciation in International Human Rights Law: Deference and Proportionality* (Oxford: Oxford University Press, 2012); T.R.S. Allan, 'Human Rights and Judicial Review: A Critique of "Due Deference"', 65 *CLJ* 671 (2006); Aileen Kavanagh, 'Defending Deference in Public Law and Constitutional Theory', 126 *Law Quarterly Review* 222 (2010); T.R.S. Allan, 'Judicial Deference and Judicial Review: Legal Doctrine and Legal Theory', 127(1) *Law Quarterly Review* 96 (2011).

of a legal provision is predominantly a process anchored in legal interpretative techniques. While both approaches may lead to a finding of non-justiciability, the conceptual and theoretical reasoning behind such a conclusion is significantly different. The enquiry into whether and to what extent discretionary power has been retained by the State in public policy cases must therefore engage with this division of ideas.

Without fully embracing any constitutionalist model (though recognizing the value of the concept as a heuristic device), the analysis here will focus on trade and commercial legal regimes that are institutionalized to different levels. The European Union (EU), the World Trade Organization (WTO), and international investment agreements represent a sliding scale of international institutionalization, common standard-setting, adjudicative oversight, and application of higher norms. Nonetheless, all three regimes have been embroiled in controversy over the power of individual States to determine their own public policy goals. In the case of the EU, there has been a long-running dispute over the constitutional nature of the EU itself and increasing disquiet expressed about the encroachment by EU law on national policy discretion.[14] The WTO has attracted criticism for the power of its dispute settlement process, *inter alia*, because of the imbalance with the institutional weakness of the rest of the organization.[15] Finally, one of the most difficult questions in international investment agreements arises from an increasing number of claims of indirect expropriation against apparently normal regulatory acts of host governments.[16]

While the variation between these regimes does not necessarily allow direct comparison, they all engage with questions as to the level of deference their respective courts and tribunals show, or should show, to the explicit public policy claims of States. In particular, they offer an opportunity to identify the techniques and principles developed to determine where power lies in these different institutional and legal contexts. This chapter identifies five core approaches in the practice of the EU, the WTO, and international investment treaties: (i) an assumption that deference to the State is not unrestricted; (ii) controls over the substantive meaning of public policy; (iii) controls exercised through a required threshold of seriousness; (iv) controls exercised through evidential demands; and (v) procedural controls. The five core approaches may blur and overlap, but examining these

[14] See Joseph H.H. Weiler and Marlene Wind (eds), *European Constitutionalism Beyond the State* (Cambridge: Cambridge University Press, 2003); Neil Walker, 'Reframing EU Constitutionalism', in Dunoff and Trachtman, *Ruling the World?*, 149.

[15] Deborah Z. Cass, *The Constitutionalization of the World Trade Organization* (Oxford: Oxford University Press, 2005); Robert Howse and Kalypso Nicolaidis, 'Legitimacy and Global Governance: Why Constitutionalizing the WTO Is a Step Too Far', in Roger B. Porter et al (eds), *Efficiency, Equity, and Legitimacy: The Multilateral Trading System at the Millennium* (Washington: Brookings Institution, 2001), 227; Joel P. Trachtman, 'The Constitutions of the WTO', 17 *EJIL* 623 (2006); Dunoff, 'Constitutional Conceits'.

[16] Susan D. Franck, 'The Legitimacy Crisis in Investment Treaty Arbitration: Privatizing Public International Law Through Inconsistent Decisions', 73 *Fordham Law Review* 1521 (2005); Stephan W. Schill, 'W(h)ither Fragmentation? On the Literature and Sociology of International Investment Law', 22 *EJIL* 875 (2011).

different elements of standard of review should help to reveal whether there is a pattern of convergence or divergence in the types and levels of control operating across international and transnational systems.

II. Public Policy in Action

A. EU law

A public policy defence is a relatively common feature of primary and secondary EU law and consequently the Court of Justice of the European Union (CJEU) has developed a rich jurisprudence on the question. The discussion here will primarily focus on the example of Article 36 Treaty on the Functioning of the European Union (TFEU) which lists derogations to the principle of free movement of goods.[17] These derogations include, *inter alia*, grounds of public morality, public policy or public security and the protection of health and life of humans, animals or plants. Whereas most of the grounds for derogation are named and thereby defined, the category of public policy is left open-ended as to its substantive meaning. Notwithstanding the lack of textual guidance, the Court has consistently set boundaries around the discretion of Member States to define and act upon public policy. In particular, the use of the derogation must be subject to the supervision and control of the European Community (Union), and be strictly interpreted.[18]

In principle, the Court has excluded use of the derogation to protect policies that undermine the objectives of the Treaty or secondary legislation. The Court has reasoned that only non-economic policies that were not liable to prejudice the fundamental principles of the Treaty were intended to be protected.[19] Unilateral economic public policy measures will therefore be excluded. However, the derogation can be used for policies that regulate economic sectors, such as the collection of taxation, even if they have significant economic and social impact because they do not directly undermine the objectives of the Treaty.[20] Likewise, public policy measures may be unacceptable if they impinge on fundamental freedoms. For example, measures affecting the free movement of persons, such as residential

[17] The public policy exception can also be found in other provisions regarding the free movement of persons, services and capital, see Articles 45(3), 52(1) and 65 TFEU. It can also be found in a number of directives, for example, Council Directive 2010/24/EU of 16 March 2010 concerning mutual assistance for the recovery of claims relating to taxes, duties and other measures, OJ L 84/1; Article 5(2)(c); Council Directive 2009/50/EC of 25 May 2009 on the conditions of entry and residence of third-country nationals for the purposes of highly qualified employment, Article 5(1)(f), OJ L 155/17; Directive 2004/38/EC of 29 April 2004 on the right of citizens of the Union and their family members to move and reside freely within the territory of the Member States, OJ L 158/77, Article 27.

[18] Case 41/74 *Yvonne van Duyn v Home Office* [1974] ECR 1337, p. 1350; Case C-30/77 *Régina v Pierre Bouchereau* [1977] ECR 1999, para 33; Case 36-75, *Roland Rutili v Ministre de l'intérieur* [1975] ECR 1219, para 27.

[19] Case 7/61 *Commission v Italy (Re Quantitative Restrictions on Imports of Pork Products into Italy)* [1961] ECR 317.

[20] Case C-434/10 *Petar Aladzhov v Zamestn director na Stolichna direktsia na vatreshnite raboti kam Ministerstvo na vatreshnite raboti* [2011] ECR I-11659, para 38.

conditions for social security benefits or tax relief schemes, must be based on the individual conduct of the person involved rather than as a general policy.[21]

Under the same principle, unilateral acts that are incompatible with harmonizing legislation cannot be protected by the use of derogations.[22] Although this is relatively straightforward in the case of, say, unilateral legislation that distorts the common mechanism for setting the price of milk in the EU,[23] it does raise conceptual problems in the case of the public policy defence. For example, when attempts were made to prevent the export of calves for crating in other EU Member States, strongly held beliefs about animal cruelty were largely dismissed by the Court.[24] The crucial factor was the existence of legislation controlling the relevant animal welfare issues, and arguments as to public policy were taken to be subsumed within the animal welfare heading.[25] It therefore seems problematic to employ public policy arguments in the presence of harmonizing legislation. At the very least, a completely independent ground of public policy would have to be offered.

The use of the public policy derogation is therefore focused on measures that do not undermine the objectives of EU primary or secondary legislation. However, the level of discretion retained by Member States still remains substantively undefined. Furthermore, the Court has accepted that there will be differences in the way each Member State conceives of public policy and that, consequently, it will 'vary from one country to another and from one era to another.'[26] It might appear from this that the subject matter of the public policy derogation is left largely to the discretion of Member States. In practice, however, the Court has imposed a number of controls.

First, the Court has imposed a threshold of seriousness to justify derogation from EU legal obligations. Thus the measure must be designed to protect 'a fundamental interest of society' to which there is a 'genuine and sufficiently serious

[21] *Aladzhov*, para 42. Case C-406/04 *Gérald De Cuyper v Office national de l'emploi* [2006] ECR I-6947, para 40 (residence conditions for social security); Case C-76/05 *Herbert Schwarz and Marga Gootjes-Schwarz v Finanzamt Bergisch Gladbach* [2007] ECR I-6849, para 94 (tax relief for school fees); Case C-544/07 *Uwe Rüffler v Dyrektor Izby Skarbowej we Wrocławiu Ośrodek Zamiejscowy w Wałbrzychu* [2009] ECR I-3389, para 74 (health insurance tax relief). The same condition applies to other social benefits, such as the provision of legal aid to ensure access to a court under the European Convention of Human Rights. See C-279/09 *DEB Deutsche Energiehandels- und Beratungsgesellschaft mbH v Bundesrepublik Deutschland* [2010] ECR I-13849, paras 42, 52, 62.

[22] Case 5/77 *Carlo Tedeschi v Denkavit Commerciale s.r.l.* [1977] ECR 1555, para 35; Case C-150/88 *Kommanditgesellschaft in Firma Eau de Cologne & Parfümerie-Fabrik, Glockengasse n. 4711 v Provide Srl.* [1989] ECR 3891, para 28; Case C-37/92 *Criminal proceedings against José Vanacker and André Lesage and SA Baudoux combustibles* [1993] ECR I-4947, para 9; Case C-5/94 *The Queen v Ministry of Agriculture, Fisheries and Food, ex parte: Hedley Lomas (Ireland) Ltd.* [1996] ECR I-2553, para 18; Case C-1/96 *The Queen v Minister of Agriculture, Fisheries and Food, ex parte Compassion in World Farming Limited* [1998] ECR I-1251, para 47.

[23] Case C-283/03 *AH Kuipers v Productschap Zuivel* [2005] ECR I-04255, para 18.

[24] Case C-1/96 *Compassion in World Farming*, para 67.

[25] Case C-1/96 *Compassion in World Farming*, para 66.

[26] Case C-36/02 *Omega Spielhallen- und Automatenaufstellungs-GmbH v Oberburgermeisterin der Bundesstadt Bonn (Omega)* [2004] ECR I-9609, para 31.

threat'.[27] Fundamental interests include the protection of human rights.[28] In addition, the Court has accepted public policy measures dealing with recovery of tax, controlling drug tourism, the protection of currency and the elimination of surnames denoting noble origins.[29] However, the need to show a sufficiently serious threat can be balanced out by the relative importance of the protected interest.[30] In *Aladzhov*, for example, measures to recover tax liabilities could only be protected if they were in response to exceptional circumstances relating to the nature or the amount of the debt.[31] In contrast, the fundamental interest at stake in *Omega* was human dignity set in the context of German constitutional principles and human rights principles.[32] The prohibited version of a laser shooting game, which involved shooting directly at other players, was accepted by the Court as a sufficiently serious threat without further enquiry.

Second, the Court has insisted that there be sufficient evidence of the need for the public policy measure.[33] Where an interest cannot be presumed to be fundamental by reference to reliable sources such as constitutional principles, objective justification for its importance will be needed. It will not be sufficient to show administrative inconvenience, nor generalized fears about threats to the environment or human health.[34] There is a clear link here with the requirement that there be a 'serious threat' but the need for evidence here is not a substantive test.

Third, the case law suggests the need for a test of 'publicness'. The Court has been reluctant to accept evidence of strong public opinion on its own for the purposes of the public policy derogation.[35] However, no question has been raised about public policy implemented in the form of legislation, presumably because it is a formal act of adoption. This appears to be a form of procedural control.

There is evidence of all five of the core approaches to public policy in the case law of the Court. There is restricted deference which acknowledges some discretion on the part of the Member States, but only within the boundaries laid down by the Court as part of the EU's supervision and control. Substantively, the Court has excluded policies that run counter to the fundamental purpose of the Union

[27] Case C-208/09 *Ilonka Sayn-Wittgenstein v Landeshauptmann von Wien* [2010] ECR I-13693, para 86; Case C-36/02 *Omega*, para 30; Case C-54/99 *Association Eglise de scientologie de Paris and Scientology International Reserves Trust v The Prime Minister* [2000] ECR I-1335, para 17; Case 30-77 *Bouchereau*, para 35; Case 36-75 *Rutili*, para 28.

[28] Case C-36/02 *Omega*; Case C-112/00 *Schmidberger v Austria* [2003] ECR I-5659.

[29] Case C-434/10 *Aladzhov*; Case C-137/09 *Josemans v Burgemeester van Maastricht* [2010] ECR I-13019; Case 7/78 *R v Thompson* [1978] ECR 2247; Case C-208/09 *Sayn-Wittgenstein*.

[30] C-434/10 *Aladzhov*, para 35. See also Case 36-75 *Rutili*, paras 26–7; Case 30-77 *Bouchereau*, para 35; Joined Cases C-482/01 and C-493/01 *Georgios Orfanopoulos and Others and Raffaele Oliveri v Land Baden-Württemberg* [2004] ECR I-5257, para 66; Case C-33/07, *Ministerul Administrației și Internelor—Direcția Generală de Pașapoarte București v Gheorghe Jipa* [2008] ECR I-05157, para 23.

[31] Case C-434/10 *Aladzhov*, para 40.

[32] Case C-36/02 *Omega*, paras 33–5.

[33] Case C-165/08 *Commission v Poland* [2009] ECR I-06843, para 53; Case 124/81 *Commission v United Kingdom* [1983] ECR 203, para 35; Case C-320/03 *Commission v Austria* [2005] ECR I-9871, para 71; Case C-141/07 *Commission v Germany* [2008] ECR I-06935, para 47.

[34] Case C-165/08 *Commission v Poland*, para 54.

[35] Case C-1/96 *Compassion in World Farming*, paras 66–7; Case C-165/08 *Commission v Poland*, para 55.

or to agreed policies embedded in harmonizing legislation. The Court has also imposed a threshold of seriousness which prevents public policy measures from interfering with trade and other EU concerns unless they are deemed to be necessary in the face of serious threats against fundamental interests. Evidence is less explicitly required where public policy is implemented through formal public acts, is drawn from particularly authoritative sources such as constitutional principles or arises from commonly shared values across the EU.

In so far as the Court's persistent aim is to ensure that the EU's objectives are fulfilled, it appears to promote a doctrine of deference that excludes Member States' competence regardless of the importance, necessity, or public policy nature of a particular measure. It uses the common purpose behind the EU as a boundary marking the limits of deference. This is distinct from the idea of a doctrine of deference constituted by external factors, such as democratic accountability, because here the rule appears to be rooted in general principles of treaty interpretation such as effectiveness. The evidential and procedural controls can be seen as an exercise of normal judicial prudence over claims that would impinge on the rights of other Member States. However, the threshold of seriousness developed by the Court, requiring the interest to be fundamental and the threat to it sufficiently serious, is different in nature. It can be seen as a subset to the general principle that the common objectives of the EU should not be undermined, but the Court has effectively introduced a proportionality assessment between the rights of the Member States to follow their own public policy needs and the rights of other Member States to enjoy free movement of goods. This assessment is less objective than excluding economic public policy measures that would otherwise render the objectives of the EU ineffective, because it demands (without explanation or support from the text itself) a judgment to be made by the Court over the judgment of the Member State. This suggests an allocation of power in favour of the Court by the Court, and thus has constitutional implications beyond mere treaty interpretation.

B. WTO law

The standard of review in WTO law is, for the most part, taken to be the duty of the panel to make 'an objective assessment' under Article 11 Understanding on Rules and Procedures Governing the Settlement of Disputes (DSU).[36] An objective assessment is

[36] Understanding on Rules and Procedures Governing the Settlement of Disputes, 15 April 1994, Marrakesh Agreement Establishing the World Trade Organization, Annex 2, 1869 UNTS 401. Article 11 provides, *inter alia*, that 'a panel should make an objective assessment of the matter before it, including an objective assessment of the facts of the case and the applicability of and conformity with the relevant covered agreements'. The only exception is the very different standard of review contained in Article 17.6 of the Agreement on Implementation of Article VI GATT, 15 April 1994, Marrakesh Agreement Establishing the World Trade Organization, Annex 1A, 1868 UNTS 201 (Anti-Dumping Agreement) which grants a high degree of deference, limiting the panel's evaluation to whether the facts were properly established and the evaluation was 'unbiased and objective'. See also Ernst-Ulrich Petersmann, Chapter 2 (Section IV).

not a *de novo* review of the decision, nor is it complete deference.[37] Instead, the Appellate Body has insisted that the objective assessment test is applied in accordance with customary international law rules of treaty interpretation.[38] The implication is that deference should be determined by the interpretation of legal provisions rather than by doctrine.

This survey begins with a brief examination of one of the exceptions contained in Article XX of the General Agreement on Tariffs and Trade (GATT). The general exceptions in Article XX are, for the most part, already defined and include, for example, the protection of human health under Article XX(b) or the conservation of inexhaustible natural resources under Article XX(g).[39] Article XX(d), however, protects the right of individual States to enact measures in an undefined policy category. Specifically, it protects measures 'necessary to secure compliance with laws or regulations' that are not inconsistent with the GATT. Although some examples are given, such as the protection of consumers from deception, the provision as a whole is an open-ended category in the sense that the nature of the law or regulation for which compliance is sought is not exhaustively defined.[40] In this respect, it is similar to the explicit public policy derogation in Article 36 TFEU.

The Appellate Body has interpreted the necessity test embedded in the provision (and in Article XX(b) on the protection of human, animal or plant life or health) as requiring a weighing and balancing approach. Broadly speaking, the purpose is to ensure that measures brought under the exceptions of Article XX using the necessity test are proportionate. The weighing and balancing process involves three elements: the contribution that the measure makes towards achieving its objective, the impact of the measure on trade, and, most interestingly for this discussion, the importance of the 'common interests or values' at the heart of the measure.[41] It is particularly significant when Article XX(d) is at issue. In *Canada—Wheat Exports and Grain Imports*, for example, the panel categorized controls over grain handling that were designed to protect quality assurance and the reputation of Canadian products in export markets as 'essentially commercial in nature'.[42] While it recognized that

[37] Appellate Body Report, *EC Measures Concerning Meat and Meat Products (EC—Hormones)*, WT/DS26/AB/R, WT/DS48/AB/R, 13 February 1998, paras 116–19.

[38] Appellate Body Report, *EC—Hormones*, paras 117–8.

[39] Obviously there are questions about the exact scope of these nominate exceptions, for example, how extensively animal welfare standards can be protected under the protection of animal life or health. See Laura Nielsen, *The WTO, Animals and PPMs* (Leiden: Martinus Nijhoff Publishers, 2007); Robert Howse and Joanna Langille, 'Permitting Pluralism: The Seal Products Dispute and Why the WTO Should Accept Trade Restrictions Justified by Noninstrumental Moral Values', 37 *Yale Journal of International Law* 367 (2012).

[40] The full provision reads, 'necessary to secure compliance with laws or regulations which are not inconsistent with the provisions of this Agreement, including those relating to customs enforcement, the enforcement of monopolies operated under paragraph 4 of Article II and Article XVII, the protection of patents, trade marks and copyrights, and the prevention of deceptive practices'.

[41] Appellate Body Report, *Korea—Measures Affecting Imports of Fresh, Chilled and Frozen Beef*, WT/DS161/AB/R, WT/DS169/AB/R, 10 January 2001, para 162. 'The more vital or important those common interests or values are, the easier it would be to accept as "necessary" a measure designed as an enforcement instrument.'

[42] Panel Report, *Canada—Measures Relating to Exports of Wheat and Treatment of Imported Grain*, WT/DS276/R, 27 September 2004, upheld by Appellate Body Report WT/DS276/AB/R, para 6.224.

such an interest was important, the panel judged that this was less important than the protection of human life and health.[43] In *Dominican Republic—Import and Sale of Cigarettes*, on the other hand, efficient tax collection was recognized as a 'most important interest for any country and particularly for a developing country'.[44] There is evidently a threshold of seriousness control being used here, though it is not as pre-emptive as the equivalent in EU law which excludes any consideration of policy that falls below the threshold. In the case of Article XX(d) and the weighing and balancing process, a policy will not be excluded in principle (save for inconsistency with the GATT) but its importance will be compared to the impact of the trade measure and how much it contributes to fulfilling the policy objective.

In comparison with Article XX(d) GATT, Article XIV(a) of the General Agreement on Trade in Services (GATS), which provides an exception based on public morals or maintaining public order, is more explicit on the threshold of seriousness. Article XIV(a) notes that the exception can only be invoked where there is a 'genuine and sufficiently serious threat . . . posed to one of the fundamental interests of society.'[45] This agreement was drafted more recently than the GATT and explicitly echoes the approach of the EU's Court. However, it is important because it requires the WTO dispute settlement bodies to make an assessment of importance and offers textual guidance in doing so. Panels have therefore given deliberate consideration to the importance of relative interests. Thus in *US—Gambling*, a case that involved Article XIV(a) GATS, the panel found that concern about money-laundering, organized crime, fraud, underage gambling and pathological gambling constituted 'very important societal interests' and were 'vital and important in the highest degree'.[46] However, it is only under the explicit wording of the provision that this is a required threshold, and it would certainly be more controversial to apply a similarly high threshold to Article XX(d), which does not textually suggest any intention to restrict the scope of Members' policy discretion. To this extent, the weighing and balancing process developed in WTO law is more cautiously applied according to the specific wording of its provisions than the threshold controls developed by the EU's Court from principle.

A brief comment could also be made about Article 2.2 Agreement on Technical Barriers to Trade (TBT Agreement).[47] This provision permits measures designed to achieve legitimate objectives, including national security requirements, the prevention of deceptive practices, and protection of human health or safety, animal or plant life or health, or the environment. There has been little case law under

[43] Panel Report, *Canada—Wheat Exports and Grain Imports*, para 6.224.

[44] Panel Report, *Dominican Republic—Measures Affecting the Importation and Internal Sale of Cigarettes*, WT/DS302/R, 19 May 2005, as modified by Appellate Body Report WT/DS302/AB/R, para 7.215.

[45] General Agreement on Trade in Services, 15 April 1994, Marrakesh Agreement Establishing the World Trade Organization, Annex 1B, 1869 UNTS 183, 294, fn 5 to Article XIV.

[46] Panel Report, *United States—Measures Affecting the Cross-Border Supply of Gambling and Betting Services*, WT/DS285/R, 20 April 2005, as modified by Appellate Body Report WT/DS285/AB/R, para 6.492.

[47] Agreement on Technical Barriers to Trade, 15 April 1994, Marrakesh Agreement Establishing the World Trade Organization, Annex 1, 1868 UNTS 120.

this agreement until recently but so far the policy behind a measure has always been accepted as legitimate for the purposes of the provision. So, for example, in *EC—Sardines* the objective of protecting consumers from deception was not questioned.[48] In *US—COOL*, providing consumers with information about the country of origin of food was accepted,[49] as was a policy of reducing youth smoking in *US—Clove Cigarettes*.[50] Finally, in *US—Tuna II (Mexico)*, the protection of dolphins in the eastern tropical Pacific Ocean was found to be legitimate.[51] Although it is difficult to draw firm conclusions from such a small sample of cases, even the most hostile panel has seemed reluctant to reject the acceptability of the policy underlying a measure.[52] However, it should be noted that measures directed at providing protectionist benefits to domestic producers is precluded by the explicit provision in Article 2.1.[53] Thus the text itself precludes measures that would undermine the objective of the treaty and thereby avoids the need to rely on a more general principle such as effectiveness.

The Appellate Body's rejection of the complete deference argument and its insistence on the use of ordinary international customary law rules of treaty interpretation suggest greater emphasis on treaty interpretation and the exercise of good faith than on a constitutional, doctrinal approach. As a result, deference is applied to the discretion of Members to use Article XX(d) and Article 2.2 TBT Agreement, but is more severely curtailed by the explicit wording in Article XIV(a) GATS. Although the case law is not exhaustive, it is unlikely that a panel or the Appellate Body would feel able to exclude the substantive policy choices of a Member except in cases of obvious or deliberate interference with trade where the effectiveness of the agreement at issue was at stake. Threshold controls are evident

[48] Appellate Body Report, *European Communities—Trade Description of Sardines*, WT/DS231/AB/R, 23 October 2002.

[49] Appellate Body Report, *United States—Certain Country of Origin Labelling (COOL) Requirements*, WT/DS384/AB/R, WT/DS386/AB/R, 23 July 2012.

[50] Appellate Body Report, *United States—Measures Affecting the Production and Sale of Clove Cigarettes*, WT/DS406/AB/R, 24 April 2012.

[51] Appellate Body Report, *United States—Measures Concerning the Importation, Marketing and Sale of Tuna and Tuna Products*, WT/DS381/AB/R, 13 June 2012.

[52] Even the panels in the original *Tuna Dolphin* cases, who went to considerable lengths to deny the applicability of Article XX(b) and (g), did not question the legitimacy of a policy to save dolphins outside the territorial control of the United States although arguably it would have been possible to do so. See GATT Panel Report, *United States—Restrictions on Imports of Tuna*, DS21/R, 3 September 1991, unadopted, BISD 39S/155; GATT Panel Report, *United States—Restrictions on Imports of Tuna*, DS29/R, 16 June 1994, unadopted. Indeed, the Appellate Body in *US—Shrimp* was much more cautious about recognizing the validity of protecting endangered turtles under Article XX(g) (measures relating to the conservation of exhaustible natural resources). It declined to rule on whether the provision had jurisdictional limits, but suggested that there should be a link between the protected resource and the country in question which was satisfied in that case by a 'sufficient nexus' between turtles that migrated through American waters and the US. Appellate Body Report, *United States—Import Prohibition of Certain Shrimp and Shrimp Products*, WT/DS58/AB/R, 6 November 1998, para 133.

[53] Article 2.1 TBT Agreement reads: 'Members shall ensure that in respect of technical regulations, products imported from the territory of any Member shall be accorded treatment no less favourable than that accorded to like products of national origin and to like products originating in any other country.'

in applying the necessity test in Article XX(d) cases, when the relative importance of the interest being protected becomes part of the general weighing and balancing process. Evidential controls are in place to ensure that an objective assessment can be made, and procedural controls are based on the explicit reference to laws and regulations in the Article XX(d), measures adopted or enforced in Article XIV(a) GATS, and technical regulations with which compliance is mandatory in Article 2.2 TBT Agreement.[54] Again, the predominant approach is based on textual interpretation of treaty provisions.

C. Investment agreements

The focus in this section is on the controversial area of indirect expropriation claims under international investment agreements. Expropriation in its direct form occurs when there is transfer of legal title and benefit or, in the words of one tribunal, 'forcible appropriation by the State of the tangible or intangible property of individuals by means of administrative or legislative action'.[55] The usual conditions laid down in international investment agreements for lawful expropriation of foreign investment are non-discrimination, due process of law, payment of compensation and a public purpose.[56] If the measure is found not to satisfy the public purpose criterion, therefore, the expropriation is illegal.[57] Compensation is payable for both lawful and unlawful expropriation, although the basis on which it is calculated may be different.[58]

Indirect expropriation occurs when title stays with the investor but control and use of the investment is impaired to a degree equivalent to outright taking. It has been described in this way:

> covert or incidental interference with the use of property which has the effect of depriving the owner, in whole, or in significant part, of the use of reasonably-to-be-expected economic benefit of property even if not necessarily to the obvious benefit of the host State.[59]

[54] Defined in Annex I of the TBT Agreement.

[55] *LG&E Energy Corp., LG&E Capital Corp., and LG&E International, Inc. v Argentine Republic*, ICSID Case No. ARB/02/2, Decision on Liability, 3 October 2006, para 187.

[56] See Rudelf Dolzer and Christoph Schreuer, *Principles of International Investment Law* (Oxford: Oxford University Press, 2008) 90–1. The terminology used may vary but the general sentiment is the same. See, for example, Article 1110(1) of NAFTA; Article 6(1) of the Hong Kong–Australia Agreement for the Promotion and Protection of Investments. Variations include the requirement that 'the measures are taken in the public interest', see eg Article 6 of the Netherlands–Malawi Agreement on Encouragement and Reciprocal Protection of Investments 2003; Article 13(1) of the Energy Charter Treaty 1994, 34 ILM 373 (1995).

[57] *ADC Affiliate Limited and ADC & ADMC Management Limited v The Republic of Hungary*, Award, ICSID Case No. ARB/03/16, 2 October 2006, paras 429–33 (failure to substantiate claims of public interest); *Ioannis Kardassopoulos and Ron Fuchs v The Republic of Georgia*, ICSID Case No. ARB/05/18 and ARB/07/15, Award, 3 March 2010, para 391 (arguable on the evidence that expropriation in public interest).

[58] Compensation for lawful expropriation is usually assessed by reference to market value at the date of taking, but unlawful expropriation gives rise to compensation under normal international customary law rules governing the whole loss. See *ADC v Hungary*, Award, paras 481–3; *LG&E v Argentina*, Award, 25 July 2007, para 58.

[59] *Methanex Corporation v United States of America*, Final Award (3 August 2005), Part IV—Chapter D, para 4, quoting from *Metalclad Corp. v United Mexican States*, ICSID Case No.

Indirect expropriation claims are therefore problematic because they argue that property has been expropriated by acts apparently aimed at a legitimate regulatory purpose such as environmental or health protection. In these cases, the host State is likely to resist paying compensation by claiming that no expropriation has taken place and the tribunal will be faced with issues that speak directly to questions of the State's freedom of action to enact public policy.[60]

Extending public policy beyond a criterion of lawful expropriation to larger questions of State power highlights the importance and difficulty of determining the appropriate standard of review and deference. In one sense, the answer is straightforward. Public purpose is a criterion of legal expropriation and a State signing the investment agreement has accepted that such acts will give rise to compensation if foreign investments are sufficiently seriously affected.[61] In practice, however, tribunals have not always found it easy to deal with public policy measures in such clear-cut terms. The question remains whether a State's power to conduct its own public policy should be safeguarded even in cases where there is an expropriatory effect. The existence of sufficient interference is a question of fact, but the scope of public policy discretion is a question of law that needs to be framed and resolved as a matter of deference by the tribunal to the State's judgment.

With regard to standard of review, the case law suggests that arbitral tribunals do not give complete deference to the host State and any claim of public policy will have to be justified. However, they have often acknowledged that deference is due.[62] To find the proper level of deference, two principal tests have emerged. The first is whether sufficient interference has occurred to constitute expropriation and in some cases this is the only test employed. However, reluctance to penalize public policy measures by a finding of expropriation has resulted in other tribunals introducing a second test. This test focuses on the purpose and intent behind the challenged measure when determining whether there is liability to compensate.

There are three lines of thought on how these two tests might be applied.[63] One is that the degree of destruction of the property right is the most relevant factor. A genuinely environmental measure that completely or substantially removed a

ARB(AF)/97/1, Reply, para 216. The type of property that may be expropriated is extensive, including intellectual property, goodwill, and market share. See *Pope & Talbot, Inc. v The Government of Canada*, Interim Award, para 96; *S.D. Myers v Government of Canada*, UNCITRAL, Partial Award, 13 November 2000, para 281.

[60] Public policy issues are also involved in complaints about fair and equitable treatment, but unfortunately space does not allow discussion here.

[61] Rosalyn Higgins, 'The Taking of Property by the State: Recent Developments in International Law', 176 *Recueil des Cours* 259 (1982-III) at 331; W. Michael Reisman and Robert D. Sloane, 'Indirect Expropriation and its Valuation in the BIT Generation', 74 *BYIL* 115 (2003), 121.

[62] *S.D. Myers*, Partial Award, para 261; *Chemtura Corporation v Government of Canada*, Award, 2 August 2010, para 134; *Glamis Gold, Ltd v United States of America*, ICSID, Award, 8 June 2009, para 779. See also discussion in Chapter 7 by Caroline Henckels (Section IV.C.3).

[63] These echo, but do not entirely map on to, the categorization by Henckels of the three approaches taken by tribunals to the exercise of police powers. She identifies 'sole effects', an exception to expropriation and a purpose and effect approach. See Henckels, 'Indirect Expropriation', 223.

property right in practice would, in this view, constitute expropriation regardless of its underlying purpose.[64] This 'sole effect doctrine' focuses on the consequences of the State's act rather than the intention behind it, in response to the problem of expropriatory acts that 'cloak expropriatory conduct with a veneer of legitimacy'.[65] Thus the State's right to regulate will not necessarily preclude a successful action for compensation for the ensuing expropriation.[66]

The second line of thought is that the normal exercise of regulatory powers should be safe from a claim of expropriation. It has been said that '[E]xpropriations tend to involve the deprivation of ownership rights; regulations are a lesser interference. The distinction between expropriation and regulation screens out most potential cases of complaints concerning economic intervention by a State and reduces the risk that governments will be subject to claims as they go about their business of managing public affairs.'[67] In other words, normal regulation will not usually result in sufficient interference to constitute expropriation. In *Saluka v Czech Republic*, however, the tribunal stated a more sweeping principle that would exclude certain regulatory acts from the scope of expropriation altogether:

> It is now established in international law that States are not liable to pay compensation to a foreign investor when, in the normal exercise of their regulatory powers, they adopt in a non-discriminatory manner bona fide regulations that are aimed at the general welfare.[68]

A useful example of this type of thinking can be seen in *Methanex*, a case that turned directly on whether the nature rather than the impact of the environmental legislation constituted expropriation. The complaint arose from a ban on a petrol additive believed to contaminate drinking water. Methanex argued, *inter alia*, that the ban had deprived it of a substantial portion of its investments, including

[64] The degree of interference required is not consistently described, ranging from 'significant' (*Metalclad*, para 103) to 'such a degree of interference as to sterilise its business' (*Corn Products International, Inc v United Mexican States*, ICSID Case No. ARB(AF)/04/01, 15 January 2008, para 92). In *Chemtura*, the tribunal abandoned any attempt to find a general principle, taking the view that determining whether there has been a 'substantial deprivation' is a 'fact-sensitive exercise' which could not be 'conducted on the basis of rigid binary rules' (para 249).

[65] Reisman and Sloane, 'Indirect Expropriation and its Valuation, 121. See *Compañía del Desarrollo de Santa Elena, SA v The Republic of Costa Rica*, ICSID Case No. ARB/96/1, Award, 17 February 2000; *Técnicas Medioambientales Tecmed, S.A. v The United Mexican States*, ICSID Case No. ARB(AF)/00/2, Award, 29 May 2003; *Fireman's Fund Insurance Company v The United Mexican States*, ICSID Case No. ARB(AF)/02/01, Award, 17 July 2006; *Too v Greater Modesto Insurance Associates and the United States of America*, Award, 29 December 1989, 23 Iran-USCTR (1989), 378.

[66] See Kathryn Gordon and Joachim Pohl, 'Environmental Concerns in International Investment Agreements: A Survey', *OECD Working Papers on International Investment, No. 2011/1*, 22; Laura Henry, 'Investment Agreement Claims Under the 2004 Model US BIT: A Challenge for State Police Powers?', 31 *University of Pennsylvania Journal of International Law* 935 (2010), 1004–5; Justin R. Marlles, 'Public Purpose, Private Losses: Regulatory Expropriation and Environmental Regulation in International Investment Law', 16 *Journal of Transnational Law and Policy* 275 (2007).

[67] *S.D. Myers*, para 282; *Marvin Roy Feldman Karpa v United Mexican States*, ICSID Case No. ARB(AF)/99/1, 16 December 2002, para 103.

[68] *Saluka Investments BV v Czech Republic*, Ad hoc-UNCITRAL Arbitration Rules, Partial Award, 17 March 2006, para 255.

its share of the relevant Californian and US markets. In particular, it argued that the US measures were not intended to serve a public purpose as required under the conditions of Article 1110 North American Free Trade Agreement (NAFTA).[69] The tribunal rejected the idea that the ban on methanol was a political sham.[70] It found that a proper risk assessment had been carried out, which displayed 'a serious, objective and scientific approach to a complex problem'. Although there was not complete scientific agreement, the assessment should not be rejected on that basis. The important point was that it had been subjected to 'public hearings, testimony and peer-review' and the fact that it was derived from 'open and informed debate' reaffirmed that it was genuine environmental legislation.[71] Here the tribunal seemed to be interested both in the weight of objective evidence for the existence and seriousness of the risk addressed by the legislation and in the public process by which that risk was assessed. Together they were sufficient to outweigh the actual expropriatory interference caused by the measure.[72]

A third approach seeks to combine both of these approaches by balancing the effect of a measure against its purpose. In *Tecmed v Mexico*, the tribunal accepted that regulatory acts were in principle capable of giving rise to expropriation. The measures should be tested to see if they were 'proportional to the public interest…and to the protection legally granted to investments.'[73] This approach has been expanded elsewhere with a test of unreasonableness, covering arbitrariness, discrimination, disproportion and unfairness.[74]

In the last two approaches, it may be significant that tribunals have often referred to the right of States to exercise their 'police powers'. This concept, drawn from the US law of takings, is traditionally considered to include the protection of public health, safety or morals.[75] It suggests a value category that is narrower than the public policy criterion for lawful expropriation and can justify avoiding compensation liability altogether. Whereas ordinary regulation is unlikely in practice to create sufficient interference to constitute expropriation, the nature of police powers may be enough to protect them from penalty when expropriation would otherwise have occurred.

[69] *Methanex*, Final Award, Part IV—Chapter D, para 2.

[70] *Methanex*, Part III—Chapter A, para 101; Part IV—Chapter E, para 20.

[71] *Methanex*, Final Award, Part IV—Chapter D, para 14. See also *Chemtura v Canada*, para 254 (finding that the challenged decision was not arbitrary because, *inter alia*, it was based on valid science and made in good faith).

[72] See also *Chemtura v Canada* (ban on lindane), para 266; Todd Weiler, 'Methanex Corp. v. USA Turning the Page on NAFTA Chapter Eleven?', 6 *Journal of World Investment & Trade* 903 (2005), 918–19; Ursula Kriebaum, 'Regulatory Takings: Balancing the Interests of the Investor and the State', 8 *Journal of World Investment & Trade* 726 (2007).

[73] *Tecmed*, Award, 29 May 2003, paras 121–2.

[74] *El Paso Energy International Company v The Argentine Republic*, ICSID Case No. ARB/03/15, Award, 31 October 2011, paras 237–43. See also *Azurix Corp. v The Argentine Republic*, ICSID Case No. ARB/01/12, Award, 14 July 2006, para 311 (drawing on the approach of the European Court of Human Rights); *LG&E v Argentina*, Decision on Liability, paras 189–95; *Continental Casualty Company v The Argentine Republic*, ICSID Case No. ARB/03/9, Award, 5 September 2008, paras 276–7.

[75] J. Brandeis, Dissenting Opinion in *Pennsylvania Coal Co. v Mahon*, 260 US 393 (1922): 'restriction imposed to protect the public health, safety or morals from dangers threatened is not a taking.'

There is no need here to examine the case law in detail to try to determine what is the correct test, even if that were possible given the variety of reasoning displayed by arbitral tribunals. The point is that tribunals are required to determine what standard of review they think is appropriate. If the test is whether a measure has a public purpose in order to determine whether it is a lawful act of expropriation, the level of review can be quite light because the tribunal need only determine that the act falls within the broad sphere of public policy. There is no need to delve any further. However, if the tribunal accepts that a public policy measure is capable of falling outside the definition of expropriation, a more complex review needs to be carried out and a much more detailed analysis of the purpose and nature of the measure will be required.

The practical implications of choosing the appropriate level of review may be serious, since using the impact test as the sole or decisive criterion may effectively deny States the right to regulate.[76] The obligation they have undertaken in the investment agreement must be fulfilled either by refraining from regulation or paying compensation, which may amount to the same thing for many countries.[77] Indeed, because of the costs of indirect expropriation claims, some States have redrafted expropriation provisions to make the standard of review by tribunals less onerous.[78] So, for example, a deliberate expansion of deference can be found in Annex B(4)(b) of the US 2012 Model Bilateral Investment Treaty (BIT) which excludes (except in rare circumstances) non-discriminatory measures designed to protect legitimate public welfare objectives from the definition of indirect expropriation.[79] As well as defining environmental protection more specifically, BITs

[76] Andrew T. Guzman, 'Why LDCs Sign Treaties That Hurt Them: Explaining the Popularity of Bilateral Investment Treaties', 38 *Virginia Journal of International Law* 639 (1998), 657–8; Gus Van Harten, 'Reforming the NAFTA Investment Regime' unpublished paper available at SSRN: <http://ssrn.com/abstract=1687263> (accessed 28 March 2014), noting that Canada has withdrawn regulatory proposals in the light of threatened expropriation claims under NAFTA, at 3.

[77] The recent complaint by the tobacco manufacturer Philip Morris against the Australian mandatory plain packaging of cigarettes under the Hong Kong–Australia BIT demonstrates the point. The claim is for 'significant financial loss, potentially amounting to billions of dollars'. See *Philip Morris Asia Limited v The Commonwealth of Australia*, Notice of Claim, 21 November 2011, at 12. Complaints against plain packaging laws have also been brought under the WTO dispute settlement procedure by the Dominican Republic, Honduras, Ukraine, Cuba, and Indonesia.

[78] Some countries have expressed a desire to withdraw from investment arbitration altogether. Bolivia, Ecuador and Venezuela withdrew from the ICSID Convention in 2007, 2009 and 2012 respectively. See Christoph Schreuer, 'Denunciation of the ICSID Convention and Consent to Arbitration' in Michael Waibel et al (eds), *The Backlash against Investment Arbitration: Perceptions and Reality* (Alphen aan den Rijn: Kluwer Law International, 2010), 353; UNCTAD, 'Denunciation of the ICSID Convention and BITS: impact on Investor–State Claims', *IIA*, December 2010: No. 2. Also see the Australian government's statement of its intention to avoid investment arbitration, April 12, 2011 discussed in Jürgen Kurtz, 'The Australian Trade Policy Statement on Investor–State Dispute Settlement', 15(22) *ASIL Insights* (2011); Jürgen Kurtz, 'Australia's Rejection of Investor–State Arbitration: Causation, Omission and Implication', 27(1) *ICSID Review* 65 (2012); Muthucumaraswamy Sornarajah, 'Evolution or Revolution in International Investment Arbitration? The Descent into Normlessness' in Chester Brown and Kate Miles (eds), *Evolution in Investment Treaty Law and Arbitration* (Cambridge: Cambridge University Press, 2011) at 638. See also Chapter 8 by Erlend Leonhardsen (Section II) in this volume.

[79] US Model BIT, Annex B(4)(b): 'Except in rare circumstances, non-discriminatory regulatory actions by a Party that are designed and applied to protect legitimate public welfare objectives, such

recently entered into by Belgium provide for the right of each party to establish its own levels of domestic environmental protection, policies and priorities with the correlative power to legislate.[80] In addition, the US Model BIT 2004 and NAFTA provide that nothing in the agreements is to 'be construed to prevent a Contracting Party from adopting, maintaining or enforcing any measure otherwise consistent with this Agreement that it considers appropriate to ensure that investment activity in its territory is undertaken in a manner sensitive to environmental concerns'.[81] This type of self-judging clause is intended to increase the degree of deference owed by the tribunal, to the point where its role is limited to ensuring good faith.[82]

To summarize, the area of investment arbitration over expropriation claims is not easy to navigate, largely because of the difference of analysis and emphasis displayed by different tribunals. The standard of review required by an investment arbitration tribunal will depend very largely on how it interprets the scope of expropriation and the specific wording of the investment agreement. In particular, deference appears to depend on how crucial it is to classify the measure as a relevant act of public policy. Where compensation for expropriation may be payable regardless, the scrutiny appears to be less searching. If the remedy of compensation is potentially excluded, the scrutiny will be correspondingly more intense.

The three lines of thought—sole effect, context and purpose, and proportional balancing—seem to exhibit different modes of review. The first relies on simple textual interpretation of the obligations undertaken by host States. The second line of thought indicates a degree of discomfort with classifying normal State regulation as expropriation with its accompanying penalty of compensation. The tribunals that have accepted the possibility of excluding expropriation altogether seem to have found another, more narrow, concept of public policy that transcends the criterion used for lawful expropriation. When applied, it resembles a principle of full deference to the right of the State to choose and implement its own public policy in good faith. The emphasis then shifts to the evidential and procedural aspects of the measure that lay at the heart of the tribunal's reasoning in *Methanex*.

The third line of thought has moved tribunals' analysis from strict textual interpretation or full deference to a more nuanced evaluation of the relative harm caused by a measure and its importance to the achievement of the public purpose. The review of the proportionality of the actual measure in the light of the objective to be achieved and its impact on investment means that the State's right to choose and implement its public policy is still untouched in principle, although evaluated against the interests of third parties. The third approach therefore suggests a more constitutional approach to balancing the rights and duties of all

as public health, safety, and the environment, do not constitute indirect expropriations'; and see Canada Model BIT, Annex B.13(1).

[80] Belgium and Luxembourg–Guatemala BIT (2005), Article 13(1).

[81] US Model BIT 2012, Article 12(5); NAFTA, Article 1114(1).

[82] Schill and Briese, 'If the State Considers'.

the actors involved, while leaving the right to choose public policy objectives in the hands of the individual State. In so far as this can be identified as a form of doctrine of deference, it may also be explained by a pragmatic functionalism that attempts to curb excess on both sides.

III. Conclusions

The concept of public policy is particularly interesting because its underdetermined character and scope offer a paradigm example of the difficulties in ascertaining the appropriate standard of review by international courts and tribunals. The need to wrestle with a mixture of law and policy in a situation where there is little textual assistance helps to throw the meaning of deference into sharp relief. To be sure, each legal regime provides its own twist on the meaning and scope of the role of public policy and hence on the power of an international court or tribunal to review its use. However, the fundamental questions are broadly similar across the international spectrum and permit a level of heuristic reasoning and tentative conclusions.

States rely on their national decision-making powers when they invoke the public policy justification. However, its open-ended character means that international courts and tribunals are likely to fall back on general principles drawn from common objectives and values when searching for the boundaries of unilateral discretion. Thus the concept of constitutionalism in the sense of a coherent legal order, common aims and normative framework and, where it exists, a sophisticated institutional structure allocating legislative and adjudicative powers seems to possess significant explanatory power. However, even in the highly institutionalized context of the EU, finding a coherent level of deference is difficult when faced with the wide range of trade and social values that can be pleaded. Indeed, a similar mix of values exists in the less institutionalized environment of investment treaty arbitration, such as the desire to promote and protect foreign investment, the need to respect the national sovereignty of the host State over its internal affairs, and the accepted importance of social values such as human health or taxation. Whereas these value conflicts have traditionally been mediated through the mechanism of compensation, the trend towards treating some forms of indirect expropriation as non-compensable goes beyond the textual meaning to privilege commonly held values, particularly those contained within the scope of 'police powers'. A similar approach can be seen in the WTO. The weighing and balancing process appears to rest on a presumption that any value being protected under the open-ended scope of Article XX(d) will be a common interest or value, even though the only textual limitation is that the law being implemented must not be contrary to the GATT.

Although the underlying reasoning may be different, at least in tone, in no case is there a doctrine of complete deference. The concept of public policy retains an independent meaning despite its lack of textual definition. Deference appears most restricted in the case of the EU and more liberal in the WTO, and there is significant variation in the practice of arbitral tribunals. Substantive and threshold controls act as filters in the EU and to a lesser extent in the WTO concerning Article XX(d) GATT, excluding certain types of measures and interests that conflict with the common aims and objectives written into the treaties. Investment treaties, on the other hand, pose a higher barrier to unilateral public policy acts by making public policy a criterion of lawful expropriation rather than a defence against compensatory liability. Despite this, tribunals have begun to feel the need to recognize common and shared values that States should be able to protect without the threat of financial penalty. This recognition may not always be explicitly drawn from textual provisions in a treaty but rather from a shared concept of value.

As a separate though related form of review, each regime requires the public policy interest to be both important and under serious threat. This is most expressly seen in the case law of the EU. In WTO law, a threshold of high seriousness is a condition of Article XIV(a) GATS but it is unlikely that this would be applied in practice in the absence of explicit wording in Article XX(d). Indeed, the disparity of membership and limited objectives of the WTO compared to the EU would suggest that a greater level of deference would be more appropriate. In the case of investment arbitration, it is arguable that the focus on 'police powers' is intended to carve out a particularly important category of public policy which lies beyond the reach of investment treaties and their expropriation provisions.

On a different note, evidential and procedural controls can be seen primarily as a method of reviewing the good faith behind a public policy measure. There is little to suggest that more objective justification is required for public policy exceptions than for any other. Procedural controls are relevant but not often explicitly raised. Most measures that are reviewed are legislative in nature and their status as public policy is not seriously questioned. However, the process by which the regulation in *Methanex* came about was crucial for determining its public policy status and may offer a useful precedent where the good faith of a measure is questioned.

In sum, there appears to be significant convergence of practice in reviewing measures justified as public policy. The acknowledgement of a wide but not unlimited discretion is accompanied by the use of all five control techniques. However, the undefined character of the public policy justification highlights another strand—the concept of common or shared interests—as a method of setting boundaries on unilateral State discretion. The case law demonstrates that tribunals will employ the concept of shared interests as part of determining the appropriate standard of review and due deference even when those interests have not been expressed and refined through negotiated processes such as legislation. This idea of commonality finds its roots in a functional need, rather than an overriding normative source such as human rights. It acts as a benchmark when assessing the legitimacy of public policy, including the extent and nature of its impact on other members of the group.

Interests are ranked in relative importance but according to a common scale of shared interests. Beyond the substantive, procedural and evidential controls, therefore, there appears to be a more constitutional form of control operating besides mere textual interpretation. This may have wider implications, notably when interpreting other, more explicitly defined, areas of State policy discretion.

4

Democracy and Distrust in International Law

The Procedural Democracy Doctrine and the Standard of Review Used by International Courts and Tribunals

*Benedikt Pirker**

I. Introduction

The standard of review employed by international courts and tribunals varies both in substance and in the terminology used. Concerns over fragmentation in international law are arguably involved, and they not only concern the separation and potential incoherence between substantive legal norms, but also between methodologies used by international courts and tribunals.[1] The standard of review is one prominent example: to what extent is the difference in the degree of deference granted by various international courts and tribunals justified? Such differences are of course only a problematic development if there are no sound reasons for the diverging positions. What we are looking for is not a unified solution, but a unified way of thinking about substantially similar problems, which may then result in legitimately different outcomes. This is what this chapter suggests: there is nothing intrinsically wrong with courts and tribunals in various regimes of international law using different standards of review, however there should be some sort of common justificatory framework within which the decision on a standard of review is taken. This chapter suggests that the procedural democracy doctrine developed by John Ely[2] in United States constitutional law can provide, at least in part, such a framework.

There are a number of ways to define what 'standard of review' means. For some, it is very closely linked to the standard of proof, ie the degree to which a

* The author is grateful to Markus Kern, Robert Mosters, Wouter Werner and Lukasz Gruszczynski for insightful comments on earlier versions of this chapter and to the participants at the 2012 workshop at the Universidad de Sevilla for fruitful discussions.

[1] Andreas Paulus, 'International Adjudication' in Samantha Besson and John Tasioulas (eds), *The Philosophy of International Law* (New York: Oxford University Press, 2010) 208.

[2] John H. Ely, *Democracy and Distrust—A Theory of Judicial Review* (Cambridge, MA: Harvard University Press, 1980).

party must prove its claim for it to be accepted prima facie by an adjudicative body.[3] For the purpose of this chapter, we treat the *standard of review* as the question of how intrusively a court or tribunal should assess a measure (or a decision) that establishes a certain balance between competing interests. Should they generally exercise deference to those who adopted the measure? Or can certain characteristics appearing in the case at issue require that a measure be struck down if the adjudicator is convinced they point towards bias in the decision? The standard of review is thus a question of allocation of power. It implicitly involves the issue of subsidiarity, ie whether the decision was or is to be taken at the appropriate level.[4] A number of criteria can play a role in this decision. We focus here on the legitimacy of courts and tribunals reviewing questions of value-conflict and the resulting trade-offs. Typically, a first-level decision-maker's choices must be assessed by a judiciary body. If these first-level decision-makers are legislators, they are often concerned with broad policy choices. Administrative agencies as first-level decision-makers are typically more engaged with technical decisions. Legislators are, therefore, more relevant here. The choice of a standard of review is, for an adjudicator, part[5] of the question of the degree to which they perceive themselves as able to monitor and review the reconciliation of values found by a first-level decision-maker. Their power of review requires, in our view, justification.

Our present suggestion is thus also to be understood as limited. It suggests one criterion that ought to be added to the elements considered and balanced by courts and tribunals when deciding upon the standard of review used in judging cases. It should be underlined that it is not the only way of looking at the topic of legitimacy in choosing a particular standard of review. In her chapter, Ambrus uses the notion of fairness as set out by Franck to discuss the legitimacy of choosing a standard of review, focusing for this purpose on criteria such as transparency and coherence.[6] By contrast, Ely's thesis combines elements of process and of substantive values, in the context of the United States' system of constitutional law, to provide an explanation and justification for judicial review and the choice of a particular standard of review.

In Section II, we set out Ely's 'procedural democracy doctrine'. Section III contrasts the background of United States constitutional law with the background of international adjudication and explains the grounds upon which we can transpose

[3] See eg Mónika Ambrus, Chapter 13 in this volume (Section I), who discusses the connection between the concept of margin of appreciation (being a variation of standard of review) and standard of proof. Another approach is to extrapolate common threads in the jurisprudence of different legal regimes; see Ilona Cheyne, Chapter 3 in this volume, Section I (using the example of public policy exceptions).

[4] Matthias Oesch, *Standards of Review in WTO Dispute Resolution* (Oxford: Oxford University Press, 2003) 23.

[5] The term 'part' of the question is used here deliberately, as the use or non-use of the proportionality analysis as a technique to apply norms is also of crucial importance here, as witnessed by the current vivid debate in the literature; see generally Benedikt Pirker, *Proportionality Analysis and Models of Judicial Review—A Theoretical and Comparative Study* (Groeningen: Europa Law Publishing, 2013).

[6] See Mónika Ambrus, Chapter 13 in this volume (Section III).

Ely's procedural democracy doctrine to this different context. Section IV warns of some possible pitfalls that must be taken into account. We then sketch out, in Section V, some suggestions on how adjudicators such as the World Trade Organization's (WTO's) Appellate Body, the Court of Justice of the European Union (CJEU) or tribunals active in international investment arbitration could approach the question of the appropriate standard of review in their particular settings.

II. The Procedural Democracy Doctrine: Ely's 'Democracy and Distrust'

Ely centrally posits the need to understand judicial review through the lens of representation reinforcement; where democratic majority decision-making fails as a process, a court is legitimized to intervene. A central problem of constitutional interpretation in the United States has always been the absence of a comprehensive catalogue of fundamental rights. During the drafting process, no full agreement could be found between those in favour of an explicit listing of fundamental rights and others afraid that such a list might unduly exclude other rights not included.[7] As a result, in 1791 the Bill of Rights (in the form of ten amendments) was adopted, with the Ninth Amendment specifically providing that the 'enumeration . . . of certain rights [,] shall not be construed to deny or disparage others retained by the people'. The Bill of Rights explicitly protects only a limited number of rights such as the freedom of speech and of the press or the free exercise of religion. Since a number of fundamental interests are not explicitly enshrined in the Constitution, the interpreter of the Constitution must find a solution regarding how to ensure their protection. The Supreme Court has 'studiously avoided' use of the Ninth Amendment to accomplish this purpose,[8] but instead turned to the due process clauses contained in the Fifth and Fourteenth Amendments, developing the doctrine known as 'substantive due process'.

By means of this doctrine, the Court has filled in what it determined to be lacunae in rights protection, and thus brought important values within the scope of its review powers. Put simply, it has based its review on a finding that the violation of a fundamental right not explicitly laid down in the Constitution constitutes a violation of due process and an arbitrary exercise of power.[9] It is against this

[7] See for more context Michael J. Faber, *Our Federalist Constitution—The Founder's Expectations and Contemporary American Government* (El Paso: LFB Scholarly Publishing, 2011) 250–1.

[8] Kurt T. Lash, 'Three Myths of the Ninth Amendment', 56 *Drake Law Review* 875 (2007–2008), 875.

[9] The Supreme Court thus protected predominantly individual economic rights (see eg on the liberty of contract: *Allgeyer v Louisiana*, 165 US 578 (1897) at 589, or the famous decision of *Lochner v State of New York*, 198 US 45 (1905)). But other rights were also protected by means of this doctrine; see eg *Meyer v Nebraska*, 262 US 390 (1923) at 399, where the Due Process Clause is held to protect a freedom which includes 'the right of the individual to contract, to engage in any of the common occupations of life, to acquire useful knowledge, to marry, establish a home and bring up children, to worship God according to the dictates of his own conscience, and generally to enjoy

background that Ely tried to introduce a solution apart from value-imposition by a court.

Taking a historical perspective on the development of the United States Constitution, Ely suggested that '[n]o finite list of entitlements can possibly cover all the ways majorities can tyrannize minorities'.[10] In his view, the best way to make sense of a Constitution with an incomplete list of fundamental values to be protected, and provisions too broad to be interpreted by themselves, is to employ a procedural, participation-based interpretation. In particular in the light of clauses like the Equal Protection Clause of the Fourteenth Amendment, the central idea ought to be that the denial of the representation of minorities had to be prevented.[11] There is, in his view, no prohibition on treating a minority less favourably as a result of a democratic, majority-based decision-making process; but no majority may ever systematically deprive a minority of its rights of representation. In Ely's view, three central arguments underpin the representation-reinforcing reading he gives to the Constitution.

First, by its very nature, the Constitution is not so much about defending one particular governing ideology; it rather enshrines a particular process of government that is concerned with the way in which liberty can be defended rather than with the definition of what liberty encompasses in substance.[12] The central reason why there is judicial review in the system of the Constitution is not that judges are better equipped than legislators to define substantive values, but rather because as lawyers they are particularly qualified in questions relating to process, ie to determine whether participation and representation rights in the democratic process have been respected for all groups.[13]

Second, the fact that the Constitution is all about representative government puts great emphasis on the values that facilitate 'clearing the channels of political change'.[14] The First Amendment, with its emphasis on freedom of speech and the later amendments securing the right to vote, are prime examples for Ely.[15]

Third, a representation-based view of the Constitution must also take into account that 'a voice and a vote' may not be enough, so that judicial review must ask more profound questions.[16] In theory, given a system where minorities can always strike deals and create coalitions on the political market to improve their lot through the channels of political change, no illegitimate interference with a minority's rights should be possible. In practice, the 'political market' can fail to function properly due to prejudice, which blinds some groups to the overlapping interests of others, prevents cooperation, and results in systematic neglect of some

those privileges long recognized at common law as essential to the orderly pursuit of happiness by free men.'

[10] Ely, *Democracy and Distrust*, 81. [11] Ely, *Democracy and Distrust*, 82.

[12] Ely, *Democracy and Distrust*, 100–1.

[13] Ely, *Democracy and Distrust*, 102–3, suggesting an 'antitrust' rather than a 'regulatory' approach to judicial review.

[14] Ely, *Democracy and Distrust*, 105.

[15] Ely, *Democracy and Distrust*, 106 ff and 116 ff, respectively.

[16] Ely, *Democracy and Distrust*, 135.

groups' interests.[17] By means of judicial review, a court should examine whether prejudice exists in a particular situation where a minority seems to be less favourably treated.[18] Generalizations and stereotypes used by the legislator are of course a necessity for law-making, inasmuch as law is based on drawing distinctions. Prejudice, however, results in drawing unfavourable distinctions for the wrong reasons, and it can be shown to be at work when a review of legislation reveals a significantly high number of counter-examples to legislative generalizations.[19]

Ely's way of thinking can arguably be transposed, with some minor modifications, to the work of international courts and tribunals and the standard of review they ought to choose. Judicial 'second-guessing' should take a back seat as long as there seems to be appropriate representation of the relevant interests in the domestic political process. In our view, Ely's thesis is thus not so much about procedural review replacing a court's need to base its review and standard of review on particular values; rather, it complements the need for adjudicators to choose such values with a process-based justification. In terms of the standard of review, intrusive review is thus required where the basic values inherent in the functioning of the political process are impaired, or where particular values or interests are systematically disadvantaged in the outcomes of said process.[20] In order to transpose this idea, however, it is necessary to first examine what these values are in international legal regimes.

III. Transposing Ely's Procedural Democracy Doctrine to the Level of International Courts and Tribunals

As a starting point, we must be mindful of the caveat already alluded to in the introduction. Namely, as has been noted in the literature, 'constitutional' solutions proposed for specialized international judiciaries run the risk of becoming overambitious in trying to bring order into an apparently chaotic, fragmented situation of international law, without taking into account that a certain functional diversification is a natural characteristic for today's international law. The response to fragmentation cannot be a desperate attempt to find unifying solutions at all costs, ignoring the specialization of international tribunals.[21] Furthermore, there is also the danger of using an apparently neutral technical vocabulary to hide a particular structural bias or ideology adhered to. This problem has gained in importance with the diversification and specialization of international law, coupled with the emergence of separate, highly technical vocabularies for each separate 'regime' of international law.[22] As a consequence, in approaching this issue we must

[17] Ely, *Democracy and Distrust*, 153.
[18] Ely, *Democracy and Distrust*, 154.
[19] Ely, *Democracy and Distrust*, 157.
[20] Ely, *Democracy and Distrust*, 103.
[21] In 'Constitutionalism Lite', 31 *International Organizations Law Review* 31 (2004), 49, Jan Klabbers speaks colourfully of the danger of a 'knee-jerk response' of constitutionalism to the fear of fragmentation.
[22] See Martti Koskenniemi, 'The Politics of International Law—20 Years Later', 20 *EJIL* 12 (2009).

carefully consider and justify what ideas can be transposed from Ely's contribution to the international legal level, and how such ideas must be adapted, pointing out both the benefits international adjudicators can draw from such an approach as well as the pitfalls they will inevitably face. As to the ideas themselves, we must keep a sceptical eye on them, as is subsequently set out using the example of process-based review which, despite its designation, requires a choice of substantive values.

With this caveat in mind, we can turn now to a detailed assessment of how the procedural democracy doctrine could be fruitful for the determination of an appropriate standard of review for international courts and tribunals. The central idea is that the United States Constitution, which establishes a system predominantly concerned with the protection of due process, representation and participation of all groups, can arguably help us to answer this difficult question. One of the central points of criticism addressed to international courts and tribunals is that they are not well-equipped to make substantive value choices. Typically, judges on the bench are high-profile international lawyers, not necessarily familiar with a particular domestic legal system or the socio-economic and political context of the country whose actions are to be reviewed against the benchmark of an international treaty. One could thus argue that the case against having such judges fill in gaps in international treaties with—at worst—personal value choices is even stronger than in the case of the US Supreme Court. Thus, while the proposal to focus on process and on judges as guardians of due process is in principle promising, some conceptual details remain and need to be fleshed out.

In the first instance, one might ask why international courts or tribunals should feel influenced in any way by the operation of a domestic legal process? From a purely formal perspective, international law is not necessarily interested in questions of domestic governance. In principle, domestic law cannot be an excuse for a violation of international law; dictatorships can join international organizations.

This point is of course easier to answer for courts like the European Court of Human Rights (ECtHR). Being called upon to interpret the European Convention on Human Rights, it operates in quite a similar setting to that of a domestic constitutional court. The constitutionalization of this international legal regime has been much commented upon in the doctrine.[23] If we take a closer look at the Court's function in relation to domestic political processes, we can observe that its role is mostly to defend minimum standards of protection for Convention rights against the potential majoritarian bias of domestic democratic decision-making in those situations where all domestic safeguard mechanisms have failed.[24] As the ECtHR stated itself, 'democracy does not simply mean that

[23] See eg Alec Stone Sweet, 'Sur la constitutionalisation de la Convention européenne des droits de l'homme', 80 *Revue trimestrielle des droits de l'homme* 923 (2009). Sceptical on this development Stephanie Hennette-Vauchez, 'Constitutional v International? When Unified Reformatory Rationales Mismatch the Plural Paths of Legitimacy of ECHR Law', in Jonas Christoffersen and Mikael R. Madsen (eds), *The European Court of Human Rights between Law and Politics* (Oxford: Oxford University Press, 2011) 152–3.

[24] See for a historic overview of the development of the system of the European Convention from a limited safeguard against totalitarianism towards a 'European Bill of Rights' Ed Bates, *The*

the views of a majority must always prevail: a balance must be achieved which ensures the fair and proper treatment of minorities and avoids any abuse of a dominant position'.[25]

It is, however, much more difficult to establish the link between a domestic legal process and appropriate representation of minorities in the less clear cases of 'quasi-constitutional' international courts and tribunals. Take the WTO dispute settlement system as an example.[26] Why should the Appellate Body be concerned in any way with thinking about the representation of minorities? The disputes before it typically concern traders (both domestic and foreign) and their interests, and at first glance, the whole treaty system is about fairly arcane matters such as custom duties or import restrictions. A closer look, however, reveals that even in international treaties which do not contain human rights provisions, we can observe traces of representation reinforcement through the dispute settlement mechanism contained in a treaty. Some suggest using different sources than Ely, in order to avoid reading international treaties, which typically do not enshrine any clearly defined values akin to fundamental or constitutional rights of individuals, as though they were domestic constitutions.[27] Procedural views such as Habermas' procedural theory of justice argue that legitimacy ought to be primarily based on fair procedures rather than on questions of substantive values.[28] The advantage of this approach would be that the focus is not so much on the introduction of values by the adjudicator. It should be kept in mind, however, that the problem of substantive value choices cannot fully be avoided thereby. Accessibility, transparency and requirements of justification through reasons are also values that courts use to examine whether a procedure can be accepted as sufficiently fair and inclusive. The added value of Ely's approach is his concrete suggestion as to how procedural review and representation reinforcement can be justified.

The best conceptual basis for such representation reinforcement was set out by Ely in his discussion of 'virtual representation'. Historically, this concept originates from the context of the independence movement in the American colonies. Originally, when the inhabitants of the colonies claimed that there could be 'no taxation without representation', the British reply was that beyond the mere sending of representatives to parliament (the colonies were not represented), representation could also take a virtual form: the electors of representatives were inextricably linked to the non-electors and would certainly ensure that the latter's interests would be appropriately represented. While this theory proved most certainly not to be applicable to the concrete case of the American colonies, nonetheless, the general idea of such 'virtual representation' has continued to find

Evolution of the European Convention on Human Rights—From Its Inception to the Creation of a Permanent Court of Human Rights (Oxford: Oxford University Press, 2010) 6 ff.

[25] *Sørensen and Rasmussen v Denmark* (app. nos. 52562/99 and 52620/99), ECtHR 2006, para 58.

[26] For the mere case of simplicity, we focus here on the Appellate Body.

[27] See in this regard Michael Ioannidis, Chapter 6 in this volume (Section IV).

[28] Jurgen Habermas, *Between Facts and Norms: Contributions to a Discourse Theory of Law and Democracy. Translated by William Rehg* (Cambridge: Polity Press, 1996).

acceptance in a variety of situations. The so-called 'Commerce Clause' of the United States Constitution can be taken as an example: in this case, the prohibition of discrimination against out-of-staters was aimed to ensure that the fate of this group, typically non-resident and powerless, would be linked to the fate of local groups similarly situated, who possessed representation and power. The local group thereby would ensure the 'virtual representation'.[29] In-state traders would use their representation power to lobby against any unreasonable tax or regulatory burdens; simultaneously, their efforts would benefit both them and out-of-state traders.[30]

The concept is not only limited to the domestic constitutional level. International legal provisions—in particular in international economic law—can follow a strikingly similar rationale. Returning to our example of WTO law, the national treatment obligation contained in eg, the General Agreement on Tariffs and Trade (GATT) prescribes the same linking of outsiders' fate with that of local economic actors. With this in mind, it can be suggested that the interpretation of GATT by the Appellate Body is an exercise of judicial review following a logic comparable to that of representation reinforcement in United States constitutional law. The WTO Appellate Body would thus focus not so much on substantive values, but rather on the question whether the interests of outside traders have been appropriately represented in the domestic political process.

There are, of course, counter-arguments to this virtual representation approach. Regan examined the argument of virtual representation both in United States constitutional law and WTO law.[31] In his view, there is a central flaw in the argument that foreign traders may not be represented. He argues that in order to achieve overall efficiency, from an economic standpoint, there is actually no need to represent their interest. Protectionism, which disadvantages these traders, will not only harm them, but harm in-state consumers as well. Thus the latter represent the interests of out-of-state traders and ensure an efficient allocation of resources.[32] This would weaken the claim for representation reinforcement through judicial review, and support a deferential approach with respect to the standard of review. However, it is arguable whether this 'replacement representation' necessarily works in practice. If a court or tribunal has doubts about whether consumers are effectively represented in the political process, there may continue to be a need to reinforce representation through judicial review. Arguably, it may quite often be the case that consumers are a fragmented group with much less influence on the decision-making process than the concentrated interest group of

[29] Ely, *Democracy and Distrust*, 83. [30] Ely, *Democracy and Distrust*, 82 and 84.

[31] Donald H. Regan, 'The Supreme Court and State Protectionism: Making Sense of the Dormant Commerce Clause', 84 *Michigan Law Review* 1091 (1986); Donald H. Regan, 'The Meaning of "Necessary" in GATT Article XX and GATS Article XIV: The Myth of Cost-Benefit Balancing', 6 *WTR* 347 (2007).

[32] Donald H. Regan, 'Judicial Review of Member-State Regulation of Trade within a Federal or Quasi-Federal System: Protectionism and Balancing, "Da Capo"', 99 *Michigan Law Review* 1853 (2001), 1860.

producers.[33] Thus, while valuable in certain cases Regan's criticism cannot refute Ely's concept of 'virtual representation' as a whole.

There is thus no convincing reason to suggest that Ely's approach could not be followed in principle by international courts and tribunals. As part of choosing a standard of review, international courts and tribunals can therefore look at violations of values that are particularly important to the functioning of the domestic democratic process, or at the systematic disadvantageous treatment of particular groups in a State. In case of such findings, they would then use a more intrusive standard of review.

IV. Some Caveats

Before sketching some preliminary suggestions as to how Ely's ideas have been or could be used in the future by specific international courts and tribunals, a number of points should be addressed.

One difficulty is that it is clear that even such representation reinforcement or procedure-based approaches rely, at least to a minimum extent, on substantive values. The very judgment as to whether a certain party has been appropriately represented requires defining whether this very party has a legitimate participation interest. Procedural review remains based on substantive choices. Ely's contribution can thus also be understood as making us aware of the need to appropriately justify the choices of values on which procedural review is to be based, and as warning us not to perceive approaches of procedural review as an easy panacea.

If courts and tribunals thus remain central to some extent to identification of the benchmarks of their review, some further potential problems need to be addressed. First, review of domestic democratic processes requires a definition of what such a process is. Based on Ely, we could suggest that not only regimes of international law protecting fundamental rights qualify for securing representation reinforcement. Also under other treaties States have signed up to obligations which may require appropriate respect for foreign interests in their domestic political process. But the evaluation of domestic democratic processes could prove difficult, and could be viewed as necessarily prone to bias in favour of certain preconceived forms of democracy.[34] Adjudicators must thus be aware that there is no unique form in which such a process is established, even at the level of different democratically governed States. Absurd rulings could result from an overtly formalist approach in this case: an adjudicator could—at least in theory—condemn

[33] For an economist's point of view on the problem of 'rent-seeking' groups, see Anne Krueger, 'The Political Economy of the Rent-Seeking Society', 64 *The American Economic Review* 291 (1974).

[34] See also Caroline Henckels, 'Balancing Investment Protection and the Public Interest: The Role of the Standard of Review and the Importance of Deference in Investor–State Arbitration', 4 *JIDS* 197 (2013). On the limited case law on democratic deference in investment arbitration see Erlend Leonhardsen, Chapter 8 in this volume (Section IV.C).

the same measure in one case and not in another, merely based on the fact of the 'erroneous procedure' by which it was adopted in the 'offending' State.

A different problem may arise from the fact that courts and tribunals at the international level are often much more specialized in comparison to domestic supreme or constitutional courts. This means that they are focused on a specific interest. This focus is of course not problematical as such.[35] But it could lead them to overemphasize the value central to their legal regime, and accordingly to evaluate cases in a biased manner.[36] There is no easy remedy to this danger, except for awareness by adjudicators of the need to explicitly justify their choice of a standard of review.

Summing up, if courts and tribunals take into account Ely's proposals they can justify their chosen standard of judicial review based on their assessment of the underlying process and principles of adequate representation. If they have justifiable doubt that such representation has been achieved, courts and tribunals can assume that they are entitled to replace such representation through the 'virtual' form of their review, and intervene even if it means overturning to some extent substantive value choices made by a lower-level decision-maker. Viewed in this light, one can posit that the inevitable problem of second-guessing substantive value choices is somewhat alleviated by the theoretical grounds provided in Ely's thesis. Nonetheless, there remains a need for substantive value choices by adjudicators for the purpose of establishing which group has a legitimate interest in the first place, and can thus potentially be considered to have been systematically disadvantaged.

In the following brief case studies, we sketch out reflections as to how adjudicators could, in some selected international legal regimes, assess the values represented and how the choice of a standard of review could ensure that pertinent groups are effectively represented.

V. The Procedural Democracy Doctrine and International Adjudication

A. The WTO dispute settlement system

Ely's thesis would require that in WTO law, as noted before, adjudicators would look at violations of values that are particularly important to the functioning of the domestic democratic process, ie at systematic disadvantageous treatment of particular groups within a State. Their review would become more intrusive if

[35] See for a theoretical exploration of the issue Pirker, *Proportionality Analysis*, 68 ff.

[36] With respect to such overemphasis on values intrinsic to a legal regime to the detriment of external values, see eg Ralf Michaels and Joost Pauwelyn, 'Conflict of Norms or Conflict of Laws? Different Techniques in the Fragmentation of International Law' in Tomer Broude and Yuval Shany (eds), *Multi-Sourced Equivalent Norms in International Law* (Oxford: Hart Publishing, 2011) 36–7. See also on the difficult role of adjudicators in science-based disputes Lukasz Gruszczynski and Valentina Vadi, Chapter 9 in this volume (Section IV).

such elements appear. Using the example of an older debate on GATT, it can be shown that there remains a need to first define, to some extent, the substantive values at stake before the concerned group's need for representation through judicial review can be identified.

At first view, the group that would potentially require representation is easily identified as foreign traders. But what rights do they actually possess which require protection by the WTO adjudicative bodies? In order to assess the appropriate standard of review more thoroughly, we need to reflect in more depth about what the value of 'trade' enshrined in GATT really means. The debate over what GATT is all about can give us some useful insights. Typically, using national treatment as the central norm of the agreement some have suggested in the past that GATT enshrines market access for foreign traders. But opposing views see the agreement more as a limited set of obligations. Foreign traders would be represented differently under each of these constellations. Based on the market access view,[37] a broader number of measures would be subject to review. A large number of measures may prevent market access, making an examination necessary as to whether there are indications in the process of measures which neglect to take into account the interests of foreign traders. The net would be cast wider.

A limited, and today more accepted, reading interprets GATT as an incomplete contract, including most centrally a pledge of non-discriminatory treatment of imported products.[38] This would leave domestic policies largely unbound, apart from fixed levels of tariffs and the pledge not to discriminate.[39] Based on this first step, a panel would thus start to look for discrimination. Then, having cast the net, a panel would require some indication that there is a need for representation reinforcement to set its standard of review. Clear-cut cases of discrimination will be very likely to fall foul of GATT's disciplines. But sudden and sharp changes of policy causing, eg substantial de facto discrimination could also be an indication of discrimination, as could accompanying measures which soothe the impact of measures for domestic groups, such as domestic consumers or economic operators, which would otherwise lobby in favour of the interests of traders generally.[40]

[37] The term 'right of access' is used by Rob Howse and Donald H. Regan, 'The Product/Process Distinction—An Illusory Basis for Disciplining "Unilateralism" in Trade Policy', 11 *EJIL* 249 (2000), 257. See eg Erich Vranes, *Trade and the Environment—Fundamental Issues in International Law, WTO Law, and Legal Theory* (Oxford: Oxford University Press, 2009) 191–3, who explains the corresponding rather broad interpretation of national treatment that ensues.

[38] For an exploration of the idea of GATT as an incomplete contract see Henrik Horn and Petros Mavroidis, 'Still Hazy after All These Years: The Interpretation of National Treatment in the GATT/WTO Case-law on Tax Discrimination', 15 *EJIL* 39 (2004), 53–4.

[39] Petros Mavroidis, *Trade in Goods—The GATT and the Other Agreements Regulating Trade in Goods* (Oxford: Oxford University Press, 2007) 215. A more extensive discussion of these ideas in other WTO covered agreements can be found in Pirker, *Proportionality Analysis*, 286 ff.

[40] See eg the famous Supreme Court decision in the case of *West Lynn Creamery, Inc. v Healy* at 200, where a non-discriminatory tax was offset to in-State economic operators by means of an accompanying subsidy which 'mollified' the representation of the local interest.

B. The Court of Justice of the European Union

As regards the first step, similarly in EU law much depends on the reading one takes of the internal market freedoms[41] enshrined in the Treaty on the Functioning of the European Union (TFEU). They could be understood as rights of individuals to access another Member State's market, or more limited as the idea that no discrimination should occur. In the latter case the representation of the powerless foreigners is again tied to the fate of the locals.

The CJEU has constantly opted for an extensive reading of the central prohibition of quantitative restrictions on imports and measures having an equivalent effect enshrined in Article 34 TFEU. However, opposing views can be found in the doctrine which would favour a less extensive scope given to Article 34 TFEU and a focus instead on discrimination.[42] In contrast, by embracing a reading of Article 34 as essentially a traders' right the Court held boldly in *Procureur du Roi v Dassonville* that '[a]ll trading rules enacted by Member States which are capable of hindering, directly or indirectly, actually or potentially, intra-Community trade are to be considered as measures having an effect equivalent to quantitative restrictions'.[43] A very wide range of Member State regulations would thus come under intensive scrutiny by the CJEU.[44]

To some extent, because of the wide range of measures falling under the Court's review as established in this first step, in the second step the Court has struggled to find a coherent approach to defining a standard of review. Review of Member State measures against the benchmark of internal market freedoms is, generally speaking, quite intrusive. Under its version of the 'principle of proportionality' the Court has understood all derogations from market freedoms by Member States in order to pursue public interests at the national level as 'exceptions' which must be read narrowly, and thus imposed the burden of proof on the Member State.[45] The standard of review embraced by the Court thus puts great emphasis on market integration, to the detriment of domestic regulatory autonomy.[46] At the same

[41] For the sake of conciseness, our focus is here limited to the internal market freedoms in EU law, with a focus on the free movement of goods as perhaps the most well-known. Of course, the other market freedoms as well as EU citizenship or the elaborate system of fundamental rights protection in EU law would merit consideration in their own right, but for reasons of space cannot be provided here.

[42] Nicolas Bernard, 'On the Art of Not Mixing One's Drinks: *Dassonville* and *Cassis de Dijon* Revisited' in Miguel P. Maduro and Loic Azoulai (eds), *The Past and Future of EU Law—The Classics of EU Law Revisited on the 50th Anniversary of the Rome Treaty* (Oxford: Hart Publishing, 2010), 462–3. See also the well-known critique by Miguel P. Maduro, *We, the Court: The European Court of Justice & the European Economic Constitution* (Oxford: Hart Publishing, 1998).

[43] Case 8/74 *Procureur du Roi v Benoît and Gustave Dassonville* [1974] ECR 837, para 5.

[44] It should, of course, be mentioned that the Court later narrowed down to some extent the scope of its review in cases such as Joined Cases C-267/91 and C-268/91 *Criminal Proceedings against Bernard Keck and Daniel Mithouard* [1993] ECR I-6097.

[45] Case 36/75 *Roland Rutili v Minister for the Interior* [1975] ECR 1219, paras 26–7.

[46] Takis Tridimas, *The General Principles of EU Law* (Oxford: Oxford University Press, 2006) 193–4. This is not just a past tendency. A rather recent study remarks that the number of national measures failing the Court's review is increasingly compared to the situation ten or twenty years ago; see Catherine Barnard, 'Derogations, Justifications and the Four Freedoms: Is State Interest Really

time, the reasons for this approach are difficult to discern from the case law. Arguably, Ely's thesis could help in making the chosen approach more clear and transparent.

Some developments pointing in this direction can be found in recent CJEU jurisprudence. The Court seems to enquire more frequently into unusual, inconsistent features in Member State measures, an approach which is closer to looking at a potential, systematic and less favourable treatment of a disenfranchised group, as Ely would suggest. Recently, review has thus focused increasingly on the 'consistent and coherent' operation of Member State measures.[47] Furthermore, there are some proposals which would limit the broad market access reading given to the internal market freedoms, and focus on measures which create a burden for new market entrants, thereby favouring competitors already established on the market[48]—which can be read as a need for the CJEU to base its review on a finding of systematic disadvantageous treatment of newcomers, who are typically foreign traders.

C. Tribunals active in international investment arbitration

In international investment arbitration, problems can be identified in a similar manner at the two levels of, firstly, defining the pertinent group and identifying its interests to be protected through representation reinforcement; and, secondly, of choosing the correct standard of review based on the circumstances of the case at issue.

First of all, if a tribunal active in international investment law wants to develop a standard of review based on the ideas of representation reinforcement, it faces the somewhat complex question of what or whose interest exactly is being protected. The group concerned is rather straightforward to identify: foreign investors are to be protected from neglect in the political process of the host State. But the breadth of the value at issue, ie whose representation can investors ask to be reinforced through the mechanism of investment arbitration, proves to be difficult to determine.

One view would suggest a parallel to the right to property. Investors would thus enjoy a right to property, and a wide-ranging number of intrusions into this right ought to be closely examined by a tribunal. There are, however, some points that cast doubt on the 'right to property' perspective. What is laid down in investment treaties is not so much a right to have one's property respected, but rather the conditions under which expropriation may be lawful.[49] The other standards of protection

Protected?' in Catherine Barnard and Okeoghene Odudu (eds), *The Outer Limits of European Union Law* (Oxford: Hart Publishing, 2009) 295.

[47] Gjermund Mathisen, 'Consistency and Coherence as Conditions for Justification of Member State Measures Restricting Free Movement', 47 *CMLR* 1021 (2010).

[48] Gareth Davies, 'Understanding Market Access: Exploring the Economic Rationality of Different Conceptions of Free Movement Law', 11 *GLJ* 671 (2010), 678 ff.

[49] See for insightful observations on this point Joost Pauwelyn, *Optimal Protection of International Law: Navigating between European Absolutism and American Voluntarism* (Cambridge: Cambridge University Press, 2008) 145.

laid down for foreign investors in investment treaties are quite general and it would appear to be a stretch to simply equate them with the right to property as enshrined in various domestic constitutions and international human rights treaties.[50] Also, the circle of beneficiaries is quite specific: only possession of an 'investment' entitles a party to protection through arbitration.[51] Furthermore, the way in which investment arbitration procedure operates as a remedy is additional, rather than subsidiary. Human rights mechanisms typically can only be appealed to once domestic mechanisms of protection have failed. Investment arbitration often excludes the need to exhaust domestic legal remedies,[52] and thus offers the investor a way to simply avoid the judiciary of the host State altogether.[53] With respect to a case involving the right to property, the rationale of investment arbitration seems thus to follow the paradigm of an insurance policy rather than that of defending human rights.[54] From an insurance policy perspective, claims would much more go in the direction of how to calculate actual loss of property in order to establish the appropriate compensation. With rights protection, one could argue in favour of more comprehensive claims of restitution or positive obligations to protect property, even *ex ante* for future cases. This distinction can play a significant role both for the scope of review and for the consequences of breaches of investment treaties.

An alternative view would posit the value to be centrally protected in investment law as encompassing foreign investment as a public interest, based on its beneficial economic effect, although much definitional work remains to be done in this regard.[55] The very notion of investment is disputed in the case law, as the controversy over the *Salini* decision demonstrates.[56] Both the case law and doctrine continue to quarrel over the admissibility of adding a 'public interest' dimension to the notion of investment.[57]

[50] Similarly sceptical on this point Markus Perkams, 'The Concept of Indirect Expropriation in Comparative Public Law—Searching for Light in the Dark' in Stephan Schill (ed), *International Investment Law and Comparative Public Law* (Oxford: Oxford University Press, 2010) 148.

[51] Jorge D. Taillant and Jonathan Bonnitcha, 'International Investment Law and Human Rights' in Marie-Claire Cordonier Segger et al (eds), *Sustainable Development in World Investment Law* (Alphen aan den Rijn: Wolters Kluwer, 2011) 76–7.

[52] Jan Wouters and Nicolas Hachez, 'The Institutionalization of Investment Arbitration and Sustainable Development' in Marie-Claire Cordonier Segger et al (eds), *Sustainable Development in World Investment Law* (Alphen aan den Rijn: Wolters Kluwer, 2011) 636.

[53] On this potentially troubling aspect of investment arbitration, see in more detail Tom Ginsburg, 'International Substitutes for Domestic Institutions: Bilateral Investment Treaties and Governance', 25 *International Review of Law and Economics* 107 (2005), 119.

[54] See also Benedikt Pirker, 'Seeing the Forest without the Trees—The Doubtful Case for Proportionality Analysis in International Investment Arbitration', *Highly Commended Essay, Society of International Economic Law/Cambridge University Press Essay Prize 2011*, 1–19 (available at <http://www.sielnet.org> (accessed 7 May 2014)).

[55] Andreas Kulick, 'Book review, Stephan W. Schill (ed.), International Investment Law and Comparative Public Law. Oxford: Oxford University Press, 2010', 22 *EJIL* 917 (2011), 920.

[56] *Salini Costruttori SpA and Italstrade SpA v Kingdom of Morocco*, ICSID Case No. ARB/00/4, Decision on Jurisdiction, 23 July 2001, para 52.

[57] In the *Salini* case, the criterion of a contribution to the economy of the host State was added as necessary for some activity to qualify as an investment. See, with references to further case law, Diane A. Desierto, 'Development as an International Right: Investment in the New Trade-Based IIAs', 3 *Trade, Law and Development* 296 (2011), 302 ff. For a sceptical view, based

Nonetheless, the rationale of investment as a public interest appears somewhat more convincing. This does not fully invalidate the idea of representation reinforcement through judicial review by investment tribunals, but arguably influences the way in which they ought to perceive the scope of their review. Not every intrusion into property rights would fall within the scope of review. Rather, some at least cursory indications of purposeful neglect of foreign investors in the political process of a host State should be required to justify intervention through the judicial review of an arbitral tribunal.

Secondly, as regards the intrusiveness of the review it appears that the case law has paid insufficient attention to the issue of choosing a standard of review. Only in few decisions can some remarks be taken as indicating some reflections akin to representation reinforcement. In *TECMED* the tribunal held, based on references to ECtHR case law, that it had to be taken into account that foreign investors had a reduced or even no participation in the taking of decisions which affect them, since they had no political rights as nationals of the host State.[58] In *Lemire v Ukraine* the tribunal suggested that foreigners were 'more exposed than domestic investors to arbitrary actions of the host State' because they lacked political rights. As a consequence, they ought to be given a 'wider scope of protection'.[59]

However, it is not clear from the above-mentioned cases exactly how these declarations influenced the standard of review. Generally, tribunals do not discuss in much detail their standard of review. The tribunal in *Lemire v Ukraine* seemed, at least in part, to be heading in the right direction, examining, beyond mere formal participation rights, whether a foreign investor was less privileged in the framework of a domestic public procurement procedure because it did not have the political clout of local competitors, and suggesting that investment arbitration ought to achieve a 'level playing field'.[60] By contrast, it is also very possible to imagine situations where political rights play no role at all, such as when a foreign investor is actually a powerful local player through its subsidiary in the host State and as an economic factor and important employer.[61]

VI. Conclusions

The aim of this chapter has been to present how Ely's thesis concerning the procedural democracy doctrine could be fruitful in the context of international courts and tribunals. While the doctrine is rooted in the United States constitutional system and its democratic political process, we have shown that its concepts can be transposed to international legal regimes and can help, for example,

on the *travaux préparatoires* of the ICSID Convention, see Julian D. Mortenson, 'The Meaning of 'Investment': ICSID's Travaux and the Domain of International Investment Law', 51 *Harvard International Law Journal* 257 (2010).

[58] *Tecnicas Medioambientales TECMED, SA v United Mexican States*, ICSID Case No. ARB/AF/00/2, Award, 29 May 2003, para 122.

[59] *Joseph Charles Lemire v Ukraine*, ICSID Case No. ARB/06/18, Award, 28 March 2011, para 57.

[60] *Lemire v Ukraine*, paras 64–5.

[61] See also Perkams, 'The Concept', 111 fn 16.

adjudicators in international economic law to ensure that they are looking for the 'right' problems. Standards of review are rarely laid out in the broad provisions of international treaties. Textbook approaches using literal interpretations are thus unlikely to be of much help in asking and answering the right questions in order to define an appropriate standard of review.

As has been shown via some reflections on WTO law, EU law and international investment law, concrete proposals can be drawn from Ely's views. Adjudicators first need to clearly define the particular group whose representation they are called on to ensure and exactly which interest(s) or right(s) such a group possesses. This can help to cast the net in the right way. Secondly, in order to know when to use an intrusive standard of review (making it more likely to strike down a measure under review), adjudicators should strive to define the values central to the system of democratic process in which they participate as representation-reinforcing institutions. They should then review more strictly which acts constitute violations of these values. Furthermore, they should review more intrusively where a suspicion of prejudice, in Ely's terms, arises, ie when particular interests seem to have been systematically disadvantaged as indicated by the outcome of a democratic process.

The procedural democracy doctrine is thus not to be equated with a purely procedural review, ie an exclusive focus on procedure to the neglect of substantive values. On the contrary, it is necessary to define such values and review measures in light of them. But the objective of judicial review is arguably better met if international courts and adjudicators act as guardians of representation reinforcement where it is necessary, rather than as guarantors of what they personally perceive as the optimal outcome in every situation of value conflict.

While certainly not revolutionary, this proposal could convince judges and arbitrators to invest more time in the elaboration of the standard of review in cases where the reconciliation of competing values found by a first-level decision-maker, such as a legislator, is at stake. The procedural democracy doctrine is arguably a useful tool to structure the adjudicator's thinking and to make the reasoning of international courts and tribunals more transparent and consistent.

5

Good Faith Review

Andrei Mamolea

I. Introduction

Good faith is a basic principle of international law. But to what extent is good faith review relevant to establishing breach? The question has received insufficient attention in the literature, and international courts and tribunals often vocally deny the importance of a State's subjective intent[1] even as they have relied on subjective evidence to establish breach.[2] This has nurtured the widely held assumption that subjective intent is both too difficult to prove and too slippery to interpret for it to play any meaningful role in international law. Statements that 'proving a State's bad faith can be an extremely difficult task' or 'almost impossible' are now ubiquitous in both international law scholarship and jurisprudence.[3] Many contend that good faith is simply not justiciable and international courts and tribunals must instead defer to the State's own characterization of subjective facts.

And yet, even a cursory survey of the case law reveals that international courts and tribunals frequently engage in good faith review to establish breach of an international obligation, even where the applicable legal rule does not include a 'psychological' element.[4] Evidence of a State's subjective intent

[1] 'Subjective intent' is 'the intention or knowledge of relevant State organs or agents' (Draft Articles on Responsibility of States for Internationally Wrongful Acts (DARSIWA), UN GAOR, 53d Sess., Supp. No. 10 at 70, UN Doc. A/56/10 (2001)). For reasons that will soon be apparent, this chapter will examine only one type of subjective intent: good faith.

[2] Donald Regan, 'Judicial Review of Member-State Regulation of Trade within a Federal or Quasi-Federal System: Protectionism and Balancing, Da Capo', 99 *Michigan Law Review* 1853 (2001), 1886, fn 51 ('courts that claim not to be interested in legislative motive or in subjective evidence cannot be taken at their word'). Unfortunately, Regan never elaborates on this important side comment.

[3] See eg Jeswald W. Salacuse, *The Law of Investment Treaties* (Oxford: Oxford University Press, 2010) 243 ('proving a state's bad faith can be an extremely difficult task'); Pierre-Hugues Verdier, 'Cooperative States: International Relations, State Responsibility and the Problem of Custom,' 42 *Virginia Journal of International Law* 839 (2002), 854 ('proving a state's negligence would be almost impossible'). For a fuller discussion of the literature and history see my work-in-progress, 'A History of the Struggle to Define Subjective Intent in International Law' (forthcoming).

[4] See eg *Methanex Corporation v United States of America*, First Partial Award, NAFTA Arbitration Tribunal 7 August 2002, para 158; Panel Report, *Mexico—Tax Measures on Soft Drinks and Other Beverages*, WT/DS308/R, 24 March 2006, paras 8.91–8.95; ICJ, *Armed Activities on the Territory of the Congo (Democratic Republic of Congo v Uganda)*, Judgment ICJ Rep 2005, para 109.

is neither impossible to retrieve nor judicially unmanageable. Open-textured standards permit the consideration of a State's intent as an aggravating factor and there are three ways that a State's intent can be found improper. An improper intent may be discriminatory, it may fall outside the permissible intents described in the 'clawback clause' of a treaty, or it may be described quite broadly as arbitrary and unreasonable. A State's intent is proven in much the same way that an individual's intent is proven in domestic law, by circumstantial evidence relating to the words and deeds of the State's agents. Though a few unique issues arise from the 'complex and multifaceted' nature of a State's decision-making process,[5] case law confirms that these same methods of proof are no less available in international law. There is ultimately nothing exotic about the methods of proof and interpretation employed in this type of review.

Good faith is treated as a question of fact.[6] But unlike with some other questions of fact, international courts and tribunals grant no deference to a State's *post hoc* characterizations of its own intent. Good faith is not for the State to self-judge. International courts and tribunals apply *de novo* review and once a court decides to examine evidence of bad faith, the State is afforded no deference. Instead, it benefits from a historic presumption against bad faith that manifests itself as a high standard of proof for the claimant.[7] The absence of different standards of intrusiveness in good faith review is responsible for the central problem that this chapter seeks to address.

The chapter briefly looks at good faith review across different bodies of international law to document the remarkable convergence regarding what this type of review should entail. This is particularly noteworthy as some scholars have recently claimed that 'the paucity of case law on [good faith review] means that arbitral tribunals will have to develop their own approaches to whether the good faith requirement has been met.'[8] This process is already in motion. The chapter argues that good faith review is more common than previously suggested and that it has developed in the direction of uniformity. Specifically, different international

[5] *S.D. Myers Inc. v Canada*, First Partial Award and Separate Opinion, Ad hoc—UNCITRAL Arbitration Rules, 8 ICSID Reps 18, 13 November 2000, para 161 ('The intent of government is a complex and multifaceted matter. Government decisions are shaped by different politicians and officials with differing philosophies and perspectives'); see also Gaetano Arangio-Ruiz, 'State Fault and the Forms and Degrees of International Responsibility: Questions of Attribution and Relevance', in Michael Virally (ed), *Le Droit International au Service de la Paix, de la Justice et du Développement* (Paris: A. Pedone, 1991) 35 ('The consequence of complexity…is that an act of a State as an international person is composed mostly, if not always, of a plurality of acts and attitudes emanating from different organs situated frequently at different levels in the hierarchy of the State's mastodontic structure').

[6] Arangio-Ruiz, 'State Fault', 34 ('the question whether wilful intent or any degree of culpa is present in a given instance is a question of fact, just as the very existence of the act of a State is a question of fact').

[7] See F.V. García-Amador, *Second Report*, 2 *YILC* 104 (1957) 122 ('the basic principle apparent in previous codifications, in the decisions of international tribunals, and in the works of the learned authorities is that there is a presumption against responsibility').

[8] William W. Burke-White and Andreas von Staden, 'Investment Protection in Extraordinary Times: The Interpretation and Application of Non-Precluded Measures Provisions in Bilateral Investment Treaties', 48 *Virginia Journal of International Law* 307 (2008), 378.

tribunals operating in different functional regimes generally apply the same standard of review when analysing subjective evidence of a State's intent.

Unfortunately, they diverge markedly on the question of proof. In particular, there is no consensus regarding the type of subjective facts that are unsuitable for good faith review. Such inconsistency is damaging to the legitimacy of these courts and should be overcome. But because of the widely held assumption that good faith review simply does not occur, there has been no scholarly discussion of this problem. International courts and tribunals increasingly rely on subjective evidence when it is available, and will continue to do so as States become more porous. As a consequence, scholars must address the phenomenon in order to ensure that subjective facts are used properly. This chapter takes an important first step in that direction by examining good faith review and suggesting potential limits.

II. Standard of Review for Good Faith Review

The first place one would look for guidance on the role of subjective intent would be the Draft Articles on the Responsibility of States for Internationally Wrongful Acts. Surprisingly, considering the inattention given to the subject by scholars, the commentary to the Draft Articles acknowledges that a State's blameworthy psychological attitudes may indeed play a role in international law.[9] The commentary lists a variety of mental elements with potential legal consequence, including 'intention', 'knowledge', 'fault', 'culpability', 'negligence' and 'want of due diligence', and does not purport to exclude any others.[10] However, there is no framework in place to determine how international courts and tribunals should approach subjective facts for each cause of action. Unhelpfully, the commentary twice professes not to give any guidance on this question.[11] Then only a few paragraphs later the commentary contradicts itself. Despite refusing to 'lay down any presumption', the commentary then promptly does so: 'In the absence of any specific requirement of a mental element in terms of the primary obligation, it is only the act of a State that matters, independently of any intention.'[12] This passage is wrong to suggest that, 'in the absence' of an essential mental element, 'it is only the act of a State that matters'. This is a false dichotomy. The case law reveals that there is also a third category—a broad middle zone in which intent is neither essential nor irrelevant, but instead may be an optional aggravating factor.

[9] The text of DARSIWA itself refers to a State's 'knowledge' in the context of shared State responsibility. See DARSIWA Articles 16, 17, 18. It also refers to 'wilful or negligent action or omission' in the context of the claimant's contributory fault in causing the injury (Article 39 DARSIWA). But it does not make any reference to any mental elements in the context of breach: see Article 2 DARSIWA. According to Article 2, the only two elements necessary for an act to be found in violation of international law are that the act is 'attributable to the State' and, creating a conspicuous tautology, 'a breach of an international obligation of the State.'

[10] See Article 2, cmt 3 DARSIWA.

[11] Article 2, cmt 3 DARSIWA.

[12] Article 2, cmt 10 DARSIWA.

Open-textured standards allow the consideration of a State's intent as an aggravating factor. Of these standards, one of the most widely litigated is the 'vague and elastic' international minimum standard for the treatment of aliens, famously set out in the *Neer v United Mexican States* case[13] by the US–Mexico Claims Commission.[14] The *Neer* case is cited in nearly every modern investment law dispute for the proposition that aliens are owed protection only from injuries amounting to 'an outrage'. The rest of this familiar passage hides important methodological truths in plain sight. First, *Neer* explicitly names a pair of subjective facts that point to a breach, 'bad faith' and 'wilful neglect of duty', as well as an objective one, 'an insufficiency of governmental action...that every reasonable and impartial man would readily recognize'. Second, *Neer* does not display any preference for either sort of factual evidence. Under *Neer*, subjective facts and objective facts are equally valid alternative means of demonstrating a violation of the international minimum standard.[15]

International case law demonstrates that for a wide range of causes of action the methodological situation is the same as that expressed in *Neer*. A claimant may succeed either by showing objective facts that demonstrate that a State acted improperly, or by showing subjective facts that demonstrate an improper intent. Considering the scholarly consensus that subjective intent is both too difficult to define or to prove, one would expect an analysis of objective facts to be the preferred route for identification of breach. In fact, the subjective route persists because the application of a legal standard is always awkwardly elastic, even when applied to objective facts. An international tribunal will inevitably have considerable discretion to determine whether 'every reasonable and impartial man' would recognize a State's conduct to constitute 'insufficiency of government action,' or, as the Restatement of Foreign Relations expresses this concept, action that is not 'commonly accepted as within the police power of states'.[16] This discretion is not always a blessing.[17] Inquiries can become highly theoretical or even political

[13] *Neer v United Mexican States* (*US v Mexico*) 4 RIAA 60 (1926). Neer, a US citizen and mine superintendent in Mexico, was murdered by a group of armed men. The Commission announced the *Neer* formula in adjudicating his wife's claim that Mexico's failure to prevent or punish the crime was a violation of the international minimum standard for the treatment of aliens.

[14] Yoshiro Matsui, 'Transformation of the Law of State Responsibility', 20 *Thesaurus Acroasium* 5 (1993), 9. For a recent iteration of the subjective approach of the *Neer* standard see *Alex Genin, Eastern Credit Limited, Inc. and A.S. Baltoil v The Republic of Estonia,* ICSID Case No. ARB/99/2, Award, 25 June 2001, para 367 (including as acts that would violate the fair and equitable treatment standard, 'acts showing a wilful neglect of duty, an insufficiency of action falling far below international standards, or even subjective bad faith').

[15] *Neer.* Only six months prior to the *Neer* case, the PCIJ made an almost identical statement that evidence of subjective and objective intent was of equivalent value for demonstrating a breach of an anti-expropriation provision in a treaty. 'In the Court's opinion, such [expropriation] has not taken place in the present case. The act in question does not *overstep the limits of the normal administration* of public property and was *not designed* to procure for one of the interested Parties an illicit advantage.' *Certain German Interests in Polish Upper Silesia (Germany v Poland), Merits,* 1926 PCIJ, Series A, No. 7, 37–38 (emphasis added).

[16] Restatement (Third) of Foreign Relations Law of the United States, para 712, cmt g. (1987).

[17] For example, the ECtHR's version of this inquiry, the doctrine of the margin of appreciation, has been widely criticized for being 'slippery and elusive as an eel': George Letsas, *Theory of Interpretation of the European Convention* (Oxford: Oxford University Press, 2007) 3–4 (adding

debates about the role of a 'reasonable' government.[18] Often, evidence of a State's 'bad faith' or 'wilful neglect of duty' may provide a firmer basis for decision—or at least the comforting appearance of one—when either the objective facts or the relationship between the objective facts and the 'commonly accepted' boundaries of the police power are unclear. Even where a State's improper intent is not an essential element of breach, its presence will greatly increase the practical likelihood that an international tribunal will rule against the State. The way in which international courts divide proper from improper intent thus becomes a central problem in the open-textured standards that allow good faith review.

In general, there are three ways that the intentions of States are found to be improper during good faith review. An improper intent may be described as discriminatory, it may fall outside the permissible intents described in the 'claw-back clause' of a treaty, or it may be described quite broadly as arbitrary and unreasonable.

A. Discrimination

Rules against discrimination can be found in every corner of international law and, as in the *Neer* case, they incorporate no preference for subjective or objective evidence. When they are available, subjective facts can play a role in establishing discrimination or lack of fair and equitable treatment in an investment arbitration.[19] In *S.D. Myers*, the claimant showed that various Canadian ministers made statements before parliament explaining that various Canadian policies, including a tax on certain periodicals and a ban on the shipment of toxic waste into the US for environmentally safe disposal, were intended to protect Canadian industries. The Canadian Minister of the Environment, for example, had declared that 'the handling of PCBs should be done in Canada by Canadians'.[20]

Convinced by this evidence of 'protectionist intent', the tribunal found that Canada had discriminated against foreign owners of a waste disposal company in violation of North American Free Trade Agreement (NAFTA) Article 1105.[21] The tribunal stated in clear language that 'a statement by the lead Minister in the House of Commons with respect to government policy on an issue is ordinarily to be accepted at face value as stating official government policy and the rationale

that it has also been criticized for 'inconsistency or lack of clarity,' and for 'mask[ing] the real basis for the decision').

[18] See also chapters by Ilona Cheyne (Chapter 3), Lukasz Gruszczynski and Valentina Vadi (Chapter 9) and Caroline Henckels (Chapter 7) in this volume.

[19] *Waste Management, Inc. v United Mexican States*, Award, ICSID Case No. ARB(AF)/00/3, 20 April 2004, para 123 ('Evidence of collusion between CANACO and the City with respect to the conduct of the arbitration or of discrimination against Acaverde on account of its foreign ownership would have been very material, but there is no such evidence before the Tribunal').

[20] *S.D. Myers, Inc. v Government of Canada*, First Partial Award, 13 November 2000, para 116.

[21] *S.D. Myers* at paras 162, 195. While the tribunal acknowledged that Canada's underlying goal was 'legitimate' and 'consistent with the policy objectives of the Basel Convention', the 'protectionist intent' of the measures contravened the non-discrimination NAFTA Article 1105 (para 263).

behind it.'[22] In subsequent decisions the NAFTA tribunal gamely accepted invitations to locate improper intent.[23] The jurisprudence of the UN Human Rights Committee and the European Court of Human Rights (ECtHR) confirms this openness to both subjective and objective facts.[24] For example, in two recent cases the ECtHR relied heavily on newspaper interviews given by the mayors of Warsaw and Moscow in order to establish that the respondent States had violated Article 14 of the European Convention on Human Rights.[25]

The World Trade Organization (WTO) Appellate Body has also relied on both subjective and objective facts to find taxes and regulations discriminatory. Typically, the Appellate Body employs the 'asymmetric impact test' which is based entirely on objective evidence to determine that, in the aggregate, conditions of competition favour domestic over foreign producers.[26] But the WTO dispute settlement system also permits an alternative means of proving breach based on subjective facts alone.[27] In *Canada—Periodicals* the Appellate Body declined to apply the asymmetric impact test and instead focused its attention on protectionist statements made by Canadian ministers before the parliament.[28] This approach was affirmed in *Mexico—Tax Measures on Soft Drinks and Other Beverages*, where the panel examined comments made at a meeting of the Mexican Chamber of Deputies during which deputies noted that the measure had failed to achieve its non-fiscal protectionist objective of safeguarding the domestic sugar cane industry. The panel concluded that the measure's 'protective effect' on Mexican domestic production of sugar did not appear 'to be an unintended effect, but rather an intentional objective'.[29]

[22] *S.D. Myers* at para 161. Just as public statements of government policy may be used to demonstrate a State's intent, so may the conspicuous absence. See eg *ADC Affiliate Ltd and ADC & ADMC Management Ltd v The Republic of Hungary*, Final Award, ICSID Case No. ARB/03/16, IIC 1, 2 October 2006.

[23] *Methanex Corporation v United States of America*, Final Award, pt IV, ch. E, 3 August 2005, para 20 and *Glamis Gold, Ltd v United States of America*, Award, 8 June 2009, paras 794, 797. See also Chapter 3 by Ilona Cheyne (Section II.C) in this volume.

[24] *Simunek v Czech Republic*, UNHRC Commission, Communication No. 516/1992 UN Doc. CCPR/C/54/D/516/1992 at para 11.7 ('A politically motivated differentiation is unlikely to be compatible with article 26'); *Timishev v Russia* (app. nos. 55762/00 and 55974/00), ECtHR 2006, para 43 (relying on conflicting internal investigations).

[25] *Alekseyev v Russia* (app. nos. 4916/07, 25924/08 and 14599/09) ECtHR 2010; *Case of Bączkowski and others v Poland* (app no. 1543/06), ECtHR 2007, para 27.

[26] See Lother Ehring, 'De Facto Discrimination in WTO Law: National and Most-Favored-Nation Treatment—Or Equal Treatment?', *Jean Monnet Working Paper No. 12/2001.*

[27] See eg Appellate Body Report, *Japan—Taxes on Alcoholic Beverages*, WT/DS8/AB/R, WT/DS10/AB/R, WT/DS11/AB/R, 1 November 1996, paras 27–8. See also Nicolas Diebold, *Non-Discrimination in International Trade in Services* (Cambridge: Cambridge University Press, 2010) 84 ('in reality, the Appellate Body did nothing else under this test than covertly looking at the intent and purpose of the regulation.') This alternative approach should not be confused with the 'aims and effects' test, a method used to determine whether products are 'like'. I am addressing a different set of cases where regulatory purpose is relevant to the 'less favourable treatment' determination under GATT Article III. See Amelia Porges and Joel P. Trachtman, 'Robert Hudec and Domestic Regulation: The Resurrection of Aim and Effects', 37 *JWT* 783 (2003), 791, 793, 796.

[28] Appellate Body Report, *Canada—Certain Measures Concerning Periodicals*, WT/DS31/AB/R, 30 July 1997, para 30.

[29] Panel Report, *Mexico—Tax Measures on Soft Drinks and Other Beverages*, WT/DS308/R, 24 March 2006, paras 8.91–8.95. The Appellate Body now embraces a cautious approach to subjective

Finally, the opportunity to address subjective intent is often available to the respondent in cases where the claimant has presented objective facts demonstrating differential treatment. Instead of responding in kind with objective facts, the State may present evidence that it possessed a 'reasonable justification' for the differential treatment that was unrelated to the prohibited bases of discrimination.[30] If the respondent is successful, the international tribunal will find that no discrimination occurred entirely on the basis of subjective facts. Although tribunals, rather than treaty-drafters, are responsible for the existence of this avenue of rebuttal, there exists a treaty-based parallel: the 'clawback clause'.[31]

B. Absence of a designated legitimate aim

The application of the treaty-based clawback clauses is practically quite similar to the judicial construction of the term 'discrimination'. After a claimant demonstrates that the State has committed the actions or omissions that are prohibited by the primary rule, the claimant may then present either objective or subjective evidence to show the State's violation is not covered by the clawback clause.[32] By presenting objective evidence, the claimant may demonstrate that the State's conduct was not necessary and proportionate to any of the purposes sanctioned by the clawback clause. Alternatively, but not under WTO law, the claimant may demonstrate that the State's actual intent did not reflect any of those sanctioned purposes by presenting subjective evidence. Unlike in discrimination cases, however, the respondent must respond in kind. To persuade a tribunal that its actions were in fact covered by the clawback clause, the State can only rebut subjective evidence with subjective evidence and objective evidence with objective evidence.

Most of the relevant case law arises under human rights conventions. In the case of *Open Door and Dublin Well Woman v Ireland*, the ECtHR found that an Irish law prohibiting the distribution of literature advocating abortion was in violation of the Convention.[33] The subjective evidence of Ireland's actual intent was unhelpful to the claimant, because the ECtHR found the law to be sincerely

facts (see Appellate Body Report *United States—Certain Country of Origin Labeling (COOL) Requirements*, WT/DS384/AB/R, 23 July 2012, para 420).

[30] *Belgian Linguistics* (app. nos. 474/62, 1677/62, 1691/62, 1769/63, 1994/63 and 2126/64), ECtHR 1968; *Parkerings-Compagniet AS v Republic of Lithuania*, ICSID Case No. ARB/05/8, 11 September 2007, para 368 ('to violate international law, discrimination must be unreasonable or lacking proportionality, for instance, it must be inapposite or excessive to achieve an otherwise legitimate objective of the State. An objective justification may justify differentiated treatments of similar cases').

[31] Treaties often impose sweeping obligations in bright line rules that are not susceptible to intent analysis and then create more open-textured exceptions that require evidence of a State's proper intent. These exceptions, known as clawback clauses, usually incorporate a 'specified number of published reasons' that are contemplated as proper, justifying intents. Rosalyn Higgins, 'Derogations under Human Rights Treaties', 48 *BYIL* 281 (1978).

[32] Although the respondent normally bears the burden of proof in this context, in practice the claimant may present evidence that the violation is not covered by the clawback clause.

[33] *Open Door and Dublin Well Woman v Ireland* (app. nos. 14234/88 and 14235/88), ECtHR 1992.

motivated to protect the 'profound moral values... reflected in the stance of the majority of the Irish people.'[34] The claimant succeeded instead by presenting objective facts to show that the restriction on expression was not necessary and proportionate to the aim.[35] By contrast, in *Vereinigung ender Künstler v Austria*, the ECtHR saw no need to assess whether the Austrian restriction on freedom of expression was necessary and proportionate to the protection of public morals, because the 'wording of the... legislation' and 'the relevant court decisions' demonstrated that protection of morals was not in fact the actual intention of the State.[36]

The International Court of Justice (ICJ) has applied the same bifurcated approach to clawback clauses in a number of recent cases. In its advisory opinion addressing the *Construction of a Wall in the Occupied Palestinian Territory*, the ICJ considered the clawback clauses under both the International Covenant on Civil and Political Rights (ICCPR) and the International Covenant on Economic, Social and Cultural Rights (ICESCR), and held that Israel's actions violated the ICCPR based on the objective facts of its disproportionate conduct, while Israel's actions violated the ICESCR based on the subjective fact of Israel's intent.[37] More recently, in *Mutual Assistance in Criminal Matters*, the ICJ examined the clawback clause in a mutual legal assistance treaty stipulating that a request could be refused only for a few narrowly defined purposes, including the protection of national security. The ICJ analysed the reasoning of a French investigating judge's opinion to confirm that it was based on 'the essential interests of France'.[38] It found that the judge's decision to refuse assistance did indeed 'fall within the scope' of the bilateral treaty's national security exception.[39] The subjective intent of the French judge had been proper.

Though it is not generally thought of in this way, the relationship between Articles 2(4) and 51 of the UN Charter is also structured like a clawback clause. While Article 2(4) creates a bright-line rule that broadly prohibits the use of force, Article 51 makes an exception for measures that are necessary and proportionate to the legitimate aim of self-defence. This structure, as with other clawback clauses, permits claimants to succeed based on either objective or subjective evidence. In the *Oil Platforms* case, the ICJ explicitly described

[34] *Open Door and Dublin Well Woman* at para 63. Since the Irish people had 'expressed in [a] 1983 referendum' their belief that life begins at conception, the ECtHR was persuaded that the State's actual intent fell within the scope of the clawback clause.

[35] The ECtHR was 'struck' in particular by the 'perpetual restraint on the provision of information,' the 'sweeping nature of this restriction', and the basic fact that the restricted information 'may be crucial to a woman's health and well-being' (*Open Door and Dublin Well Woman* at paras 69–77).

[36] *Vereinigung Bildender Künstler v Austria* (app. no. 68354/01), ECtHR 2007, para 31.

[37] ICJ, *Legal Consequences of the Construction of a Wall in the Occupied Palestinian Territory*, Advisory Opinion, ICJ Rep 2004, para 136.

[38] ICJ, *Mutual Assistance in Criminal Matters (Djibouti v France)*, ICJ Rep 2008, paras 140, 150–2.

[39] *Djibouti v France*. Yet although the judge had acted with the proper motivates, the court also found that the failure to follow the proper objective procedures rendered the refusal unlawful. *Mutual Assistance in Criminal Matters*, paras 150–2. For an extended analysis of this case see Chapter 17 by Chiara Ragni (Section III).

the first factor in this inquiry, 'the criteria of necessity and proportionality,' as a 'strict and objective' component of this cause of action.[40] In the *Nicaragua* case, decades prior, the ICJ connected the second factor to an inquiry into 'whether the State in question was itself convinced that it was acting in self-defence'.[41] The subjective component of this justification inquiry was again confirmed in *Armed Activities*, when the ICJ looked to the statements of Ugandan leaders, declarations issued by the Ugandan High Command, and the decision of Uganda not to report its actions to the UN as evidence that Uganda's intentions 'were not consonant with the concept of self-defence as understood in international law'.[42] In both cases, the respondent States were held responsible for violations of the UN Charter's prohibition against the use of force on the basis of subjective facts.

Finally, in the realm of trade law, GATT Article XX incorporates a series of clawback clauses, although the case law has so far only addressed the objective component of these provisions. The prominence of the word 'necessary' in each of these permissible exceptions seems to permit an analysis of necessity and proportionality based on objective facts, whereas the chapeau's stipulation that these clawback clauses not be subverted for use as 'disguised restriction on international trade' implies an inquiry based on subjective evidence.[43]

C. Unreasonableness or arbitrariness

'Unreasonableness' or 'arbitrariness,' the third means by which international tribunals incorporate a State's intent into an analysis of breach, is also the hardest to pin down. Discriminatory intent can be traced to a prohibited act usually set out in a treaty. Clawback clauses, similarly, list the discrete purposes that may justify an otherwise prohibited form of conduct. Notions of 'arbitrary' or 'unreasonable' State intent, by contrast, are left open for interpretation. They are therefore the most likely to lead to thorny political questions about the limits on government conduct. Nonetheless, as in the case law addressing discrimination and clawback clauses, arbitrariness and unreasonableness may be proven either by objective or subjective proof. For example, objective evidence that a State's legislation leaves 'an unfettered discretion to the executive,' or fails to be published in an 'adequately accessible' form, has led the ECtHR to conclude that the State's conduct had been arbitrary.[44] In other cases, subjective evidence of arbitrariness or unreasonableness has also been found to violate these prohibitions. The investment tribunal

[40] *Oil Platforms (Islamic Republic of Iran v United States of America)*, ICJ Rep 2003, para 73.

[41] *Military and Paramilitary Activities in and against Nicaragua (Nicaragua v United States of America) (Merits)*, ICJ Rep 1986, at paras 200, 234–6.

[42] *Armed Activities*, paras 119, 143.

[43] Mads Andenas and Stefan Zleptnig, 'Proportionality: WTO Law in Comparative Perspective', 42 *Texas International Law Journal* 370 (2007).

[44] *Hasan and Chaush v Bulgaria* (app. no. 30985/96), ECtHR 2000, paras 84–9. This led the ECtHR to the conclusion that Bulgaria, acting through a semi-governmental figure, the Grand Mufti of Bulgarian Muslims, had violated the requirement that all restrictions on human rights be 'prescribed by law'.

in *LG&E v Argentina* held that prohibitions of arbitrariness permitted claimants to succeed against a respondent State by demonstrating the absence of 'a rational decision-making process' and 'reasoned judgment'.[45] In the case of *Khamidov v Russia*, the ECtHR also held that a State's administrative or judicial decisions were unlawful where 'the decisions' themselves 'appear arbitrary or manifestly unreasonable'.[46]

The most difficult issue for litigants and tribunals in determining the existence or absence of this form of intent, undoubtedly, is simply its indeterminacy. In general, international tribunals have found that a State's intent to enrich itself at the expense of the claimant is particularly easy to determine as improper. In *Gusinskiy v Russia*, the ECtHR found that the State had violated the European Convention because it had used the public law mechanisms of prosecution and imprisonment merely 'to intimidate' the claimant 'as part of [a] commercial bargaining strateg[y]'.[47] Similarly, in *Siemens v Argentina*, the investment tribunal found that the State had acted 'for the sole purpose of reducing its costs, unsupported by any declaration of public interest.'[48] Naturally, since States have an obligation to preserve the public treasury for the provision of public services, it is not easy to see the division in this area between proper and improper intent. Even more troubling, tribunals seem to disfavour State action that is 'motivated by political considerations', as the *Biwater Gauff v Tanzania* tribunal suggested.[49] Likewise, in *Eureko v Poland*, a second investment tribunal found that the respondent State had acted in a 'purely arbitrary' manner because Polish government officials had been driven by 'Polish politics' to take control of the claimant's insurance company.[50] Since States' governments are political entities by definition, the division between proper and improper State intent in this area seems particularly amorphous.[51]

In each and every one of these cases, including those involving self-judging national security exceptions, the international court or tribunal was well within its remit to consider subjective evidence.[52] An international tribunal may always

[45] *LG&E Energy Corp., LG&E Capital Corp., and LG&E International, Inc. v Argentine Republic*, ICSID Case No. ARB/02/1, Decision on Liability, 3 October 2006, para 158.

[46] *Khamidov v Russia* (app. no. 72118/01), ECtHR 2007.

[47] *Gusinskiy v Russia* (app. no. 70276/01), ECtHR 2004, paras 75–6.

[48] *Siemens A.G. v Argentine Republic*, ICSID Case No. ARB/02/08, Award, 6 February 2007, para 308.

[49] *Biwater Gauff (Tanzania) Ltd v United Republic of Tanzania*, ICSID Case No. ARB/05/22, 24 July 2008, para 500. See also *Técnicas Medioambientales Tecmed SA v United Mexican States*, ICSID Case No. ARB(AF)/00/2, Award, 29 May 2003 at para 132. But see *Methanex v United States*, Final Award, pt IV, ch D, para 9.

[50] *Eureko BV v Republic of Poland*, Judgment on Setting Aside of Award, RG 2005/1542/A, IIC 99 paras 231–4 (2006).

[51] The analysis is more straightforward when it focuses purely on procedural rights. See eg *Bayindir Insaat Turizm Ticaret Ve Sanayi AS v Islamic Republic of Pakistan*, ICSID Case No. ARB/03/29, Decision on Jurisdiction, 14 November 2005, para 252 ('the Tribunal finds that Bayindir cannot infer a breach of due process simply from NHA's [National Highway Authority's] Chairman writing to the Minister of Communication that "[o]ur legal counsel will defend the case and get [a favourable outcome] after appearing in Court"').

[52] Good faith review is the most basic and universal form of judicial review, as Ilona Cheyne has noted in her contribution to this volume (see Chapter 3, Section I).

seek out the real intent that lies beneath the pretexts offered during adjudication. At first blush all this would suggest that good faith is simple, straightforward, and presents no interpretive or evidentiary complications. Yet a few problems persist because of the 'complex and multifaceted' nature of a State's decision-making process. The claimant must satisfy a high standard of proof in order to prove that the State acted in bad faith. But what precisely does that involve? The absence of different standards of intrusiveness in good faith review means that there is no guidance regarding the types of subjective facts that are unsuitable for review. The following section suggests that there are at least two such types of facts.

III. Propensity Evidence and Adverse Inferences

A State's intent is the intent of its agents, whether they serve administrative, judicial, or legislative roles. Though international law once viewed the State as separate and distinct from its agents, the current understanding is that the 'organs and servants of the state *are* "the state"'.[53] Ascertaining whether a State's agent possessed a particular intent at a legally relevant moment is treated as 'a question of fact, just as the very existence of an act of a State is a question of fact.'[54] In seeking to discharge its burden of proof with respect to a State's intent, the claimant must resort to circumstantial evidence. In this regard, international law is no different from domestic law. Because no third party observer can directly view a human being's thoughts, inferences based on circumstantial evidence are the only 'practically available' means of reconstructing an individual's decision-making process.[55] There are, however, several unique issues where international law is different from domestic law. The most important of these for our purposes is the prohibition on propensity evidence.

Propensity evidence is proof that a respondent State has exhibited certain behaviours in the past and is thus most likely to have exhibited the same behaviours during the specific events at issue in a trial. International tribunals have repeatedly rejected this method of proving a State's intent. This is surprising for several reasons. First, international law actually permits propensity evidence to establish a State's objective conduct in some circumstances. Second, international legal procedure owes more to civil law, which lacks a rule against this type of

[53] Rosalyn Higgins, 'Accountability and Liability: The Law of State Responsibility', in Rosalyn Higgins, *Problems and Process: International Law and How We Use It* (Oxford: Oxford University Press, 1995) 146, 151.

[54] Arangio-Ruiz, 'State Fault', 35.

[55] According to Wigmore, author of the best-known treatise on Anglo-American evidence law, an individual defendant's blameworthy psychological attitudes may only be established through the defendant's 'conduct, as indicating the inward existence of a design' or his 'words', whether these words are '[o]bscure intimation and allusions' or '[e]xplicit threats to do injury'. John Henry Wigmore, *The Principles of Judicial Proof as Given by Logic, Psychology, and General Experience* (Boston: Little, Brown and Company, 1913) 120–1 (referring to the 'conduct' and 'words of a person' as the only 'practically available' evidence of a design or plan).

evidence.[56] Third, even common law, which bars evidence to prove conduct in conformity with a propensity, allows it for subjective facts: 'motive, opportunity, intent, preparation, plan, knowledge…or absence of mistake.'[57] Finally, human rights tribunals permit the use of propensity evidence to prove objective conduct in conformity with a propensity in certain cases—even though this is precisely the use for propensity evidence that the common law most vehemently opposes. This last practice helps shed some light on the reason international courts are so allergic to propensity evidence and require a high standard of proof.

In the 'forced disappearance' cases decided by the Inter-American Court of Human Rights (IACtHR) and ECtHR, a claimant may shift her burden of proof to the respondent State simply by showing that the State has previously engaged in a general practice of forced disappearances.[58] The justification for permitting this sort of propensity evidence is a simple 'relative cost of proof' argument.[59] A State with a track record of abducting its own citizens is much more likely to possess information about the whereabouts of a disappeared victim than the victim's family members. Such States are assigned the burden of proving that they did not abduct the victim because 'otherwise, it would be impossible to prove that an individual has been disappeared; in the majority of cases'.[60] This prohibitive 'cost of proof' rationale applies equally to the internal decision-making process of a State.[61] Yet international tribunals have been resistant to using propensity evidence to prove a State's intent.

In *Rumeli v Kazakhstan*, the claimant presented the investment tribunal with a number of reports by the press, UN bodies, and non-governmental organizations (NGOs),[62] which 'tended to establish that the whole country,

[56] Mirjan R. Damaska, *Evidence Law Adrift* (New Haven: Yale University Press, 1997). See also Mirjan Damaska, 'Propensity Evidence in Continental Legal Systems', 70 *Chicago-Kent Law Review* 55 (1994), 61.

[57] See Federal Rules of Evidence para 404(b). See also Durward V. Sandifer, *Evidence Before International Tribunals* (Chicago: Foundation Press, 1975) 176 ('Whether or not by conscious purpose, the practice of international tribunals in the admission of evidence has developed a pattern comparable to that of the liberal system of procedure of the civil law countries.'); Mojtaba Kazazi, *Burden of Proof and Related Issues: A Study on Evidence Before International Tribunals* (The Hague: Kluwer Law International, 1996) 185 (linking this influence to 'the absence of a jury in the judicial system of civil law countries').

[58] *Valasquez-Rodriguez (Honduras)* (1988), IACtHR, Series C, No. 4; *Neira Alegria et al (Peru)* (1995), IACtHR, Series C, No. 21.

[59] On the 'relative-cost-of-proof theory' see Michelle Grando, *Evidence, Proof, and Fact-Finding in WTO Dispute Settlement* (Oxford: Oxford University Press, 2010) 201; Bruce Hay, 'Allocating the Burden of Proof', 72 *Indiana Law Journal* 651 (1997), 677.

[60] See eg *Velasquez-Rodriguez* at para 124.

[61] Indeed many scholars have cited cost of proof as the reason for their opposition to the examination of States' intent in international law. See Verdier, 'Cooperative States', 854 ('Under contemporary conditions, proving a state's negligence would be almost impossible, since it would require the production of the relevant evidence, most of which is likely to be in possession of the indicted state.')

[62] *Rumeli Telekom A.S. and Telsim Mobil Telekomunikasyon Hizmetleri A.S. v Republic of Kazakhstan*, ICSID Case No. ARB/05/16, Award, 29 July 2008, para 710 (citing to reports from the UN Economic and Social Council, the International Eurasian Institute for Economic and Political Research, and the Bureau of Democracy).

the whole political system and the whole economy of Kazakhstan are controlled by President Nazarbayev'.[63] Nonetheless, 'the Tribunal [wa]s unable on this material to conclude with the necessary degree of conviction that there was a wider conspiracy involving the President' with the goal of intentionally depriving the claimant of his investment.[64] Similarly, in two cases brought by claimants of Roma heritage,[65] the claimants failed to show that Bulgaria possessed discriminatory intent, despite producing numerous reports by UN bodies and NGOs suggesting that Bulgaria had a general practice of discriminating against its Roma citizens.[66] Finally, in *Chile—Taxes on Alcoholic Beverages*, the Appellate Body overruled the panel that had partially based its ruling regarding a Chilean tax on previous instances of discriminatory taxation and regulation by the Chilean government. It concluded that States 'should not be assumed, in any way, to have *continued* previous protection or discrimination through the adoption of a new measure. This would come close to a presumption of bad faith'.[67]

This last statement holds the key to international law's distaste for using propensity evidence to prove intent. As the Permanent Court of International Justice (PCIJ) held in 1932, the bad faith of a State 'cannot be presumed'.[68] Since that time, Bin Cheng and other scholars have concluded that this statement constitutes a general principle of law.[69] This principle that bad faith cannot be presumed is not just a legal politesse, a way of avoiding dignitary harm,[70] but stands in for a host of normative and practical considerations. From the allocation of burden of proof to the need to ensure State compliance with international law, there are many reasons against assuming bad faith. The problem is also tightly bound with

[63] *Rumeli v Kazakhstan* at para 710.

[64] *Rumeli v Kazakhstan* at para 715. See also *Methanex v United States*, Final Award, para 70. In *Methanex v United States*, the investment tribunal rejected the claimant's resort to a 'treasure trove of...evidence' uncovered by the US Congress regarding the general tendency of US politicians to trade political favours for campaign contributions, because this 'treasure trove' did not prove that the politician whose activities were the subject of the case, California Governor Gray Davis, himself had an intent to favour local ethanol producers over foreign ones (para 30).

[65] *Nachova and others v Bulgaria* (app nos. 43577/98 and 43579/98), ECtHR 2005; *Velikova v Bulgaria* (app no. 41488/98), ECtHR 2000, para 94.

[66] *Nachova v Bulgaria* at para 53 (citing to the Human Rights Project and Amnesty International and Council of Europe's European Commission against Racism and Intolerance); *Velikova v Bulgaria* at para 87, citing to the Report of the Special Rapporteur on Torture to the United Nations Commission on Human Rights UN Doc. E/CN.4/1997/7 and the United Nations' Special Rapporteur on Contemporary Forms of Racism, Racial Discrimination, Xenophobia and Related Intolerance (UN Doc. E/CN.4/1999/15). The ECtHR's position against propensity evidence is also evident in *Cobzaru v Romania* (app no. 48254/99), ECtHR 2007 para 95.

[67] Appellate Body Report, *Chile—Taxes on Alcoholic Beverages*, WT/DS87/AB/R, WT/DS110/AB/R, 12 January 2000, para 74.

[68] *Free Zones of Upper Savoy and District of Gex (France v Switzerland)*, 1932 PCIJ, Series A/B, No. 46.

[69] Gerald Fitzmaurice, 'The Law and Procedure of the International Court of Justice, 1951–54: General Principles and Sources of International Law', 35 *BYIL* 183 (1959), 209 ('There is always a natural reluctance to ascribe bad faith to States, in the sense of a deliberate intention knowingly to circumvent an international obligation').

[70] Hersch Lauterpacht, *Oppenheim's International Law*, 8th edn (1955) 282 (noting the 'fundamental right of reputation').

adverse inference method of discerning intent, which has been widely suggested as a method for deriving proof of subjective intent.

International courts generally enjoy the discretion to draw adverse inferences from the refusal to produce evidence.[71] But they have avoided such measures.[72] Periodically, scholars will call on courts to be more aggressive in using this method to shift the evidentiary burden onto the respondent. Even judges have occasionally argued that an overweening concern about impartiality has undermined their ability to provide access to information.[73] The most recent episode of this phenomenon was the *Genocide Convention* case,[74] where evidence that may have linked the Serbian government to the Republic of Srpska was excluded because of Serbian national security concerns.[75]

The problem with drawing adverse inferences from the failure to provide evidence of subjective intent is not merely that it will invite annulment but that it will erode important normative and institutional limits on the ability of the courts to inquire into certain types of evidence.[76] That in turn will threaten their legitimacy.

Open-textured standards allow courts the discretion to weigh evidence for fact-patters that drafters cannot anticipate. Yet this discretion is not boundless. The problem can be reframed as such: how can judges maintain their legitimacy even as they tread into an area that has long been considered forbidden by theorists and State delegates? How should international courts tailor, in a common law fashion, the doctrines and presumptions necessary to ensure that outcomes are just, efficacious, and in line with the desire of the drafters? The general silence that has marked the subject of intent has also deprived judges of rules of judicial prudence. Fortunately, as international courts and tribunals begin to rely on subjective intent they are also reaching some common conclusions about the kind of subjective facts that are not suitable for good faith review. This has been the case with propensity evidence and facts derived from adverse inferences. But on many other important questions they have taken multiple contradictory positions. Unfortunately, these other problems cannot be examined within the confines of this short chapter.[77]

[71] 'The powers of the Court in matters concerning evidence are wide.' Dissenting Opinion of Judge Schwebel, ICJ, *Military and Paramilitary Activities in and against Nicaragua*, para 132. See also Statute of the ICJ Articles 49 and 62(1); Ruth Teitelbaum, 'Recent Fact-Finding Developments at the International Court of Justice', 6 *Law & Practice of International Courts & Tribunals* 119 (2007), 130–1.

[72] For example, the ICJ has never drawn an adverse inference from a State's failure to produce evidence. See Teitelbaum, 'Recent Fact-Finding Developments at the International Court of Justice', 119, 129.

[73] ICJ, *Oil Platforms*, para 321 (dissenting opinion of Judge Owada).

[74] ICJ, *Application of the Convention on the Prevention and Punishment of the Crime of Genocide (Bosnia and Herzegovina v Serbia and Montenegro) (Merits)*, ICJ Rep 2007.

[75] Marko Milanović, 'State Responsibility for Genocide: A Follow Up', 18 *EJIL* 669 (2007), 677.

[76] Stephan W. Schill, *International Investment Law and Comparative Public Law* (Oxford: Oxford University Press, 2010) 683–4.

[77] Above all, international courts and tribunals have approached in very different ways two perennial yet largely unaddressed problems that beleaguer good faith review, determining whether low-ranking officers can express a State's intent (a nexus/threshold problem) and ascertaining the

IV. Conclusions

Case law confirms that international courts and tribunals frequently engage in good faith review to establish breach of an international obligation, even where the applicable legal rule does not include a 'psychological' element. Open-textured standards permit the consideration of a State's improper intent as an aggravating factor. The presence of such intent is a question of fact and is proven in much the same way that an individual's intent is proven in domestic law, by circumstantial evidence relating to the words and deeds of the State's agents. But unlike with some other questions of fact, international courts and tribunals grant no deference to a State's *post hoc* characterizations of its own intent. Instead, it benefits from a historic presumption against bad faith that manifests itself as a high standard of proof for the claimant. Apart from this presumption, there is no brake on the intrusiveness of an international court or tribunal regarding subjective facts. The absence of different standards of intrusiveness in good faith review is a serious problem.

In particular, there is only a partial consensus regarding the type of subjective evidence that is unsuitable for review. What is clear is that the standard of intrusiveness should differ based on the type of the evidence.[78] This chapter has highlighted two types of subjective evidence where the State should continue to benefit from greater deference. Future work will have to locate other forms of subjective evidence whose review undermines the traditional presumption of good faith. In an age when evidence is easier to store and transmit, evidence of subjective intent and the practice of good faith review will become more common. This chapter has suggested ways to avoid potential pitfalls.

reliability of internal investigations. These problems and the phenomenon of good faith review will be more comprehensively addressed in a future article entitled 'Minds of State: Subjective Intent in International Law'.

[78] Chiara Ragni has argued in Chapter 17 of this volume that inquiries into good faith involve a reasonableness test. I contend that reasonableness is not a standard of review, but a necessary element of any inquiry into good faith. As Michael Ioannidis has argued in Chapter 6 of this volume, 'the lines between allegedly different degrees of deference are notoriously blurred.' It therefore makes more sense to analyse the adjudicative process, which for good faith review is inextricably intertwined with the nature of the evidence at hand (cf Chiara Ragni, Chapter 17, Section IV; Michael Ioannidis, Chapter 6, Section II.C).

PART II

INTERNATIONAL INVESTMENT LAW AND WTO LAW

6

Beyond the Standard of Review

Deference Criteria in WTO Law and the Case for a Procedural Approach

Michael Ioannidis

I. Introduction

In the final days of the eight-year-long Uruguay Round of negotiations, very few deal-breaker issues were still left open. Perhaps surprisingly, one of them was the standard of review.[1] The fact that debates on that issue continued until the very end of the negotiations illustrates how important it was deemed to be by the contracting parties. Indeed, the final text of the Uruguay Round Agreements is among the few international instruments that makes an explicit reference to the standard of review.[2] But it was not only the Uruguay Round negotiators who saw the standard of review as a decisive concept for the future development of the multilateral trading system—the adjudicating bodies also shared this view.[3] In *EC—Hormones*, the Appellate Body addressed the standard of review as an issue directly affecting 'the balance established... between the jurisdictional competences conceded by the Members to the World Trade Organization (WTO) and the jurisdictional competences retained by the Members for themselves.'[4] For both WTO negotiators and adjudicators, thus,

[1] John H. Jackson, 'Remarks, Panel on Trading in a Post-Uruguay World: The New Law of the GATT/World Trade Organization', 88 *Proceedings of the Annual Meeting (American Society of International Law)* 136 (1994), 139; Steven P. Croley and John H. Jackson, 'WTO Dispute Procedures, Standard of Review, and Deference to National Governments', 90 *AJIL* 193 (1996), 194; Matthias Oesch, *Standards of Review in WTO Dispute Resolution* (Oxford: Oxford University Press, 2003) 76 et seq.

[2] Article 17.6 of the Agreement on Implementation of Article VI of the General Agreement on Tariffs and Trade 1994, 15 April 1994, Marrakesh Agreement Establishing the World Trade Organization, Annex 1A, 1868 UNTS 201 (Anti-Dumping Agreement).

[3] See Claus-Dieter Ehlermann, 'Six Years on the Bench of the "World Trade Court": Some Personal Experiences as Member of the Appellate Body of the World Trade Organization', 36 *JWT* 605 (2002), 621.

[4] Appellate Body Report, *European Communities—Measures Concerning Meat and Meat Products (EC—Hormones)*, WT/DS26/AB/R, WT/DS48/AB/R, 13 February 1998, paras 115–17.

the standard of review has been a cardinal issue. Considering the language used by the Appellate Body in *EC—Hormones*, one could even say it is a *constitutional* issue.[5]

II. Importance and Approaches

A. Standard of review and allocation of authority

The fact that the standard of review is a basic concept for arranging the relationship between various decision-makers is well known from domestic settings. In most legal orders based on the principle of the separation of powers, the standard of review emerged as a basic tool for understanding the power arrangements between the different branches of government. How much authority is allocated to reviewing courts compared to the legislature (in constitutional review) or the administrative authorities (in administrative review) is a question that courts and academic commentators often approach by using the concept of standard of review.[6]

With the growth of international regulation and adjudication, this question has come to exceed national boundaries. Actually, the issues surrounding the standard of review are even more challenging at the international level,[7] because international courts and the reviewed authorities belong to different legal orders. Whereas in domestic settings the standard of review is associated with the allocation of power between *different branches of a single polity*, at the international level, it *also* refers to the relationship between *two different levels*—the domestic and the international. In other words, while an intrusive standard of review employed by a domestic court means more power for the judiciary vis-à-vis the legislature or the administration, an intrusive standard of review employed by an international court means more power for the judiciary *and at the same time* more power for the

[5] See Croley and Jackson, 'WTO Dispute Procedures', 195; Deborah Z. Cass, 'The "Constitutionalization" of International Trade Law: Judicial Norm-Generation as the Engine of Constitutional Development in International Trade', 12 *EJIL* 39 (2001), 57 et seq.

[6] As in domestic and other international institutions, the question of the standard of review in WTO might be relevant in various contexts. This chapter will focus only on one of them, namely the standard used by the adjudicating bodies when reviewing decisions made by national authorities: parliaments, administrative agencies, or courts. This demarcation leaves out of the scope of this contribution the standard applied by the Appellate Body, WTO's higher judicial body, when reviewing decisions of the ad hoc established panels. On that, see Appellate Body Report, *European Communities—Measures Affecting Asbestos and Asbestos-Containing Products*, WT/DS135/AB/R, 5 April 2001, para 161; Simon Lester, 'The Development of Standards of Appellate Review for Factual, Legal and Law Application Questions in WTO Dispute Settlement', 4 *Trade, Law and Development* 125 (2012); Jan Bohanes and Nicolas Lockhart, 'Standard of Review in WTO Law' in Daniel Bethlehem et al (eds), *The Oxford Handbook of International Trade Law* (Oxford: Oxford University Press, 2009) 421 et seq.

[7] See Armin von Bogdandy and Ingo Venzke, 'Beyond Dispute: International Judicial Institutions as Lawmakers', 12 *GLJ* 979 (2011).

international level of governance.[8] Thus, at issue here is not only the allocation of power between different organs of the same legal order, but also between State and international institutions.[9]

B. (Im)balance of powers and the WTO

The above general remarks are also valid for the WTO. As with other international regimes using the same or similar concepts, the standard of review is seen as reflecting a 'finely drawn balance'[10] about where power is located: with the WTO or its Members.[11] This would already be enough to explain why the standard of review was so important during the Uruguay Round negotiations. There could be, however, an additional concern that made the standard of review such an important concept for WTO law. This concerns the particular institutional architecture of the WTO.

As has been explained by several authors, the Marrakesh Agreement established an international organization with a very strong judicial branch but with anaemic law-making capacities.[12] According to the Understanding on Rules and Procedures Governing the Settlement of Disputes (DSU), the decisions of the adjudicating bodies are binding even without the consensus of all WTO Members.[13] That means that the WTO Members have delegated to the adjudicating bodies autonomous decision-making power. At the same time, the dispute settlement mechanism is currently the *only* branch of the WTO with real power to flesh out the open-textured provisions of WTO law.[14] The WTO does not have specialized rule-making organs able to regulate international trade on a day-to-day basis,[15] and the moribund Doha Round clearly shows the limits of legislating by means

[8] See Lukasz Gruszczynski, 'Standard of Review of Health and Environmental Regulations by WTO Panels' in Geert Van Calster and Denise Prévost (eds), *Research Handbook on Environment, Health and the WTO* (Cheltenham: Edward Elgar Publishing, 2013) 733–4.

[9] See Croley and Jackson, 'WTO Dispute Procedures', 194–5.

[10] Appellate Body Report, *EC—Hormones*, para 115.

[11] Andrew T. Guzman, 'Determining the Appropriate Standard of Review in WTO Disputes', 42 *Cornell International Law Journal* 45 (2009), 49.

[12] Armin von Bogdandy, 'Law and Politics in the WTO—Strategies to Cope with a Deficient Relationship', 5 *Max Planck Yearbook of United Nations Law* 609 (2001); Thomas Cottier and Satoko Takenoshita, 'The Balance of Power in WTO Decision-Making: Towards Weighted Voting in Legislative Response', 58 *Aussenwirtschaft* 171 (2003).

[13] Articles 16.4 and 17.14 of the Understanding on Rules and Procedures Governing the Settlement of Disputes, 15 April 1994, Marrakesh Agreement Establishing the World Trade Organization, Annex 2, 1869 UNTS 401. See also Articles 6.1 and 22.6 DSU.

[14] See Cass, 'The "Constitutionalization" of International Trade Law', 55–6.

[15] Some of the WTO subsidiary bodies have undertaken the task of interpreting and further developing WTO law, and the adjudicating bodies have occasionally attached weight to such decisions; see, for example, Appellate Body, *United States—Measures Concerning the Importation, Marketing and Sale of Tuna and Tuna Products*, WT/DS381/AB/R, 13 June 2012, para 361. This activity could be perceived as a form of secondary soft-law-making. Such decisions, together with rules promulgated in the form of waivers (Article IX:3 of the Marrakesh Agreement Establishing the World Trade Organization (WTO Agreement), 15 April 1994, 1867 UNTS 154) or authoritative interpretations (Article IX:2 WTO Agreement) can be seen as a form of law-making activity of WTO organs. Nevertheless, their importance and function cannot be compared with the

of single-package treaty-making. Most authors recognize that empowerment of the adjudicating bodies, without an effective legislative check, might give them a disproportionately powerful role in defining the rules of international trade. This institutional asymmetry leads to an obvious question of legitimacy. Given the wide scope of WTO law, the adjudicating bodies often have the last word on issues of fundamental importance, such as environmental and health standards.

This imbalance between legislative and judicial organs makes the discussion concerning the intrusiveness of the standard of review even more important. In contrast to the domestic context, where the application of an overly intrusive standard of review by the courts might trigger the corrective reaction of other decision-makers, such as the legislature, there is, practically speaking, no such mechanism in the WTO. If the adjudicating bodies opt for a less deferential standard of review, rejecting, for example, a national consumer protection rule as incompatible with WTO law, there is no legislator at the international level to introduce a corrective norm.[16] Using an intrusive standard of review in this institutional context means, in effect, that the intrusion cannot be fought back.

C. How to study the standard of review

Despite the central role of the standard of review in the debate on power allocation, it remains a notoriously elusive concept.[17] Sometimes it is approached in terms of courts' willingness to show deference or respect towards the reviewed decision,[18] while on other occasions it is defined in terms of aggressiveness.[19] For our present purposes, the standard of review is approached as a concept indicating the willingness (or unwillingness) of a court to substitute the assessments of other bodies exercising authority, such as the legislature or the administration, with its own assessments.[20] Viewed from this perspective, the concept of standard of review is one of the instruments used by courts and commentators to make visible the allocation of power between adjudicating bodies and other decision-makers.[21]

sophisticated law-making procedures characterizing domestic legal orders or even those of regimes such as the EU.

[16] Compare here with EU, where an effective supranational regulator exists. On this point, see Joseph Weiler, 'Epilogue: Towards a Common Law of International Trade' in Joseph Weiler (ed), *The EU, the WTO, and the NAFTA: Towards a Common Law of International Trade* (Oxford: Oxford University Press 2000) 214–15.

[17] For recent analysis, see Ross Becroft, *The Standard of Review in WTO Dispute Settlement: Critique and Development* (Cheltenham: Edward Elgar Publishing, 2012); Daniel Lovric, *Deference to the Legislature in WTO: Challenges to Legislation* (Alphen aan den Rijn: Wolters Kluwer, 2010); Oesch, *Standards of Review.*

[18] Croley and Jackson, 'WTO Dispute Procedures', 194.

[19] Guzman, 'Determining the Appropriate Standard of Review', 45.

[20] Avery H. Kolers, 'Dynamics of Solidarity' 20 *Journal of Political Philosophy* 365 (2012), 375. See also Bohanes and Lockhart, 'Standard of Review in WTO Law', 379; Appellate Body Report, *United States–Definitive Safeguard Measures on Imports of Certain Steel Products*, WT/DS248/AB/R, WT/DS249/AB/R, WT/DS251/AB/R, WT/DS252/AB/R, WT/DS253/AB/R, WT/DS254/AB/R, WT/DS258/AB/R, WT/DS259/AB/R, 10 December 2003, para 300.

[21] Other such instruments are proportionality and the margin of appreciation.

That being said, there appear to be many ways in which the standard of review can be studied. One approach is to enumerate cases and try to group them together with a view to identifying patterns followed by courts over a specific period of time.[22] This exercise can be meaningful for making informed predictions about how courts may proceed in similar cases in the future. It might also help create categories based on different degrees of deference, such as *de novo* review, review for reasonableness, or review for arbitrariness.[23] Nevertheless, this often proves to be a difficult and elusive task. The lines between allegedly different degrees of deference are notoriously blurred, and the courts' practice changes rapidly and is highly case-specific. The danger exists that one becomes trapped in a futile casuistry and reaches conclusions simply stating the obvious: 'that the applicable standard of review depends on the case at issue'.[24]

Another risk when studying the standard of review is to overcharge the analytical capacity of concepts as broad and vague as 'reasonableness' or 'objectiveness'. Courts often use such concepts to describe the standard of review they apply, and so do many authors. However, we can seldom discern a court's attitude towards other instances of authority simply by saying that it engages in '*de novo*' or 'reasonableness' review. As will be discussed—and this is the central point of this chapter—to approach the standard of review using such undefined terms offers little to clarify the real underlying issue: the criteria used by courts when they award deference. This requires asking what motivates an international court to give greater weight to the decision of a domestic instance in one case, and less in another. Are there considerations related to expertise, democracy, or procedure that play a decisive role? Moreover, this approach can also assume a critical dimension, investigating the question of when a court should offer greater deference to the reviewed instance.

This chapter investigates these questions by focusing on three points. The first point is the limited analytical capacity of the notion of standard of review as it is currently used by most WTO commentators and panels. Although WTO negotiators discussed the issue extensively during the Uruguay Round, the final wording offers little to direct the adjudicating bodies when deciding questions of deference. This is not to say that the WTO adjudicating bodies have been less deferential than they should; the Appellate Body in particular has been especially sensitive to domestic decisions. This chapter thus firstly examines whether the concept of standard of review offers legal discourse an instrument useful for understanding, assessing, and criticizing the ways international courts allocate

[22] For an impressive example of this kind of research in US law, see William N. Eskridge Jr and Lauren E. Baer, 'The Continuum of Deference: Supreme Court Treatment of Agency Statutory Interpretations from Chevron to Hamdan', 96 *The Georgetown Law Journal* 1083 (2007–2008).

[23] See eg, Martha S. Davis, 'Basic Guide to Standards of Judicial Review', 33 *South Dakota Law Review* 469 (1988).

[24] See Appellate Body Report, *United States—Investigation of the International Trade Commission in Softwood Lumber from Canada—Recourse to Article 21.5 of the DSU by Canada*, WT/DS277/AB/RW, 9 May 2006, para 93.

power between themselves and domestic authorities. The second point on which this chapter focuses concerns the adoption of a more qualified perspective to the question of deference by focusing on the reasons offered by the WTO adjudicating bodies when deciding to respect some domestic decisions more than others. The third point centres around my suggestion that the most convincing of these reasons are those that focus on the inclusiveness of the procedure that culminated in the reviewed decision. In short, decisions resulting from procedures sufficiently open to consideration of foreign interests should merit greater deference than those taken behind closed doors.

III. Positive Regulation of the Standard of Review and Its Limits

A. Sector-specific and general clauses

As discussed in Section II.C above, the drafting of the WTO provisions regarding the standard of review was the object of long discussions. Not surprisingly, the final decision reflects a difficult compromise. WTO law does not contain a general standard of review, uniformly applicable to all international trade disputes. Despite efforts aimed at a general formulation that would require the adjudicating bodies to show deference to national measures,[25] the only such explicit reference is in the Anti-Dumping Agreement. According to Article 17.6 of the Anti-Dumping Agreement:

> (i)... If the establishment of the facts [by the competent domestic authorities] was proper and the evaluation was unbiased and objective, even though the panel might have reached a different conclusion, the evaluation shall not be overturned;
> (ii)... Where the panel finds that a relevant provision of the Agreement admits of more than one permissible interpretation, the panel shall find the authorities' measure to be in conformity with the Agreement if it rests upon one of those permissible interpretations.

This clause is applicable only to disputes concerning anti-dumping measures. The Decision of the Ministerial Conference on Review of Article 17.6 of the Agreement of the Implementation of Article VI of the General Agreement on Tariffs and Trade 1994 calls for the Contracting Parties to re-examine the anti-dumping-specific standard of review after three years 'with a view to considering the question of whether it is capable of general application'.[26] However,

[25] Holger Spamann, 'Standard of Review for World Trade Organization Panels in Trade Remedy Cases: A Critical Analysis', 38 *JWT* 509 (2004), 510.

[26] Decision of the Ministerial Conference on Review of Article 17.6 of the Agreement of the Implementation of Article VI of GATT 1994, Marrakesh Agreement Establishing the World Trade Organization, Ministerial Decisions, Declarations and Understanding, 15 April 1994, 1867 UNTS 75. Relevant here is also the Declaration on Dispute Settlement Pursuant to the Agreement on Implementation of Article VI of GATT 1994 or Part V of the Agreement on Subsidies and Countervailing Measures, Marrakesh Agreement Establishing the World Trade Organization,

the WTO Members have not as of yet taken up this task, and no Ministerial Conference has pronounced itself on the relevance of the principles declared in Article 17.6 of the Anti-Dumping Agreement for disputes outside the field of anti-dumping. Thus, with regard to disputes arising under the other Covered Agreements, directions about the appropriate degree of scrutiny can be derived only indirectly, from general clauses.

Article 11 DSU, requiring panels to make 'an objective assessment' of the matter before them, eventually became the most important textual basis for the WTO standard of review outside of anti-dumping.[27] In *EC—Hormones*, the leading WTO case in this context, the Appellate Body stated that this provision 'articulates with great succinctness but with sufficient clarity the appropriate standard of review for panels in respect of both the ascertainment of facts and the legal characterization of such facts under the relevant agreements'.[28] Subsequent rulings have almost religiously followed this path, claiming that the 'objective assessment' requirement, contained in Article 11 DSU, is the starting point whenever the standard of review becomes an issue in any field of WTO law outside of anti-dumping.[29]

B. The limits of regulating the standard of review by means of treaty law

One would certainly expect an adjudicator to approach every case 'objectively'. However, the 'objectiveness' requirement offers little guidance to the WTO adjudicating bodies as to how much they should respect domestic decisions.[30] What makes a determination 'objective' needs further clarification. Even Article 17.6 of the Anti-Dumping Agreement, despite its more detailed drafting, leaves basic questions unanswered. This clause instructs panels to award deference to domestic authorities any time they find that a relevant provision of

Ministerial Decisions, Declarations and Understanding, 15 April 1994, 1867 UNTS 78. In this declaration, the Ministerial Conference recognized, 'with respect to dispute settlement pursuant to the Agreement on Implementation of Article VI of GATT 1994 or Part V of the Agreement on Subsidies and Countervailing Measures, the need for the consistent resolution of disputes arising from anti-dumping and countervailing duty measures'.

[27] Although not intended as a provision setting a specific standard of review, see Debra P. Steger, 'Comment in the Panel "Dispute Settlement: Jurisprudential and Procedural Features"' in Mads Andenas and Federico Ortino (eds), *WTO Law and Process* (London: BIICL, 2005) 408.

[28] Appellate Body Report, *EC—Hormones*, para 116.

[29] For the latest decision, see Appellate Body Report, *United States—Measures Affecting Imports of Certain Passenger Vehicle and Light Truck Tyres from China*, WT/DS399/AB/R, 5 October 2011, paras 122 et seq. Consider also Appellate Body Report, *Argentina—Safeguard Measures on Imports of Footwear*, WT/DS121/AB/R, 12 January 2000, paras 117–18.

[30] Jacques H.J. Bourgeois, 'GATT/WTO Dispute Settlement Practice in the Field of Anti-Dumping Law' in Ernst-Ulrich Petersmann (ed), *International Trade Law and the GATT/WTO Dispute Settlement System* (London: Kluwer Law International, 1997) 300; G. Axel Desmedt, 'Hormones: "Objective Assessment" and (or as) Standard of Review', 1 *JIEL* 695 (1998), 698; Bohanes and Lockhart, 'Standard of Review in WTO Law', 383; Catherine Button, *The Power to Protect: Trade, Health and Uncertainty in the WTO* (Oxford: Hart Publishing, 2004) 171 et seq.

the Anti-Dumping Agreement 'admits of more than one permissible interpretation'. Some authors read this formulation as requiring panel restraint 'with sufficient clarity'.[31] It seems, however, that the word 'permissible' does little to reduce the spectrum of interpretative options that WTO adjudicators enjoy. The Appellate Body in *US—Steel* gave a good indication of this problem, signalling that the difference between the general standard of review, as derived by Article 11 DSU, and the particular one, applied to anti-dumping disputes, is much more blurred.[32] In fact, there has not yet been a single case where the adjudicating bodies explicitly found that a provision of the Anti-Dumping Agreement would allow more than one permissible interpretation.[33]

In short, the wording of the Covered Agreements leaves much open with regard to the appropriate standard of review in WTO law. The Delphic dictum of the Appellate Body in *EC—Hormones* is illustrative of how broadly a panel can read the relevant provisions. In a much-cited passage of this decision, the Appellate Body ruled that 'the applicable standard is neither de novo review as such, nor "total deference", but rather the "objective assessment of the facts."'[34] However, the spectrum between '*de novo* review' and 'total deference' is too broad for a notion as indeterminate as 'objective assessment' to bridge it, and many authors have expressed their scepticism as to whether this phrase provides any concrete guidance at all regarding the applicable standard of review.[35] Yet this specific formula has been repeated in a long series of panel and Appellate Body decisions.[36] Similarly, recourse by the Appellate Body to a dictionary-based definition of 'proper establishment' in *Thailand—H-Beams* rendered the not-particularly-helpful results of 'accurate' and 'correct'.[37] Again, these references offer a notoriously weak touchstone for contesting the evaluations of the adjudicating bodies.

Similar analytical problems burden the distinction between the standard of review applied to questions of law and the one relevant for questions of facts—a distinction often drawn by authors,[38] and also reflected in Article 17.6 of the

[31] Oesch, *Standards of Review*, 95.

[32] Appellate Body Report, *United States—Anti-Dumping Measures on Certain Hot-Rolled Steel Products from Japan*, WT/DS184/AB/R, 23 August 2001, para 55. See also Panel Report, *European Communities—Definitive Anti-Dumping Measures on Certain Iron or Steel Fasteners from China*, WT/DS397/R, 28 July 2011, as modified by the Appellate Body Report, WT/DS397/AB/R, para 7.3; Oesch, *Standards of Review*, 145. For the insistence of the US to a 'less intrusive' standard of review in the field of anti-dumping, see Statement of Administrative Action for the Uruguay Round Agreements Act, Pub. L. 103-465 Statute 4809 (1994), 19 USC 3501, para 12.

[33] Oesch, *Standards of Review*, 181.

[34] Appellate Body Report, *EC—Hormones*, para 117.

[35] See Spamann, 'Standard of Review in Trade Remedy Cases', 528–9; Bohanes and Lockhart, 'Standard of Review in WTO Law', 383.

[36] See Oesch, *Standards of Review*, 106.

[37] Appellate Body Report, *Thailand—Anti-Dumping Duties on Angles, Shapes and Sections of Iron or Non-Alloy Steel and H-Beams from Poland*, WT/DS122/AB/R, 5 April 2001, para 11, with reference to The New Shorter Oxford English Dictionary. See also Panel Report, *United States—Transitional Safeguard Measure on Combed Cotton Yarn from Pakistan*, WT/DS192, 5 November 2001, as modified by Appellate Body Report, WT/DS192/AB/R, fn 193 to para 7.35.

[38] See Claus-Dieter Ehlermann and Nicolas Lockhart, 'Standard of Review in WTO Law', 7 *JIEL* 491 (2004), 496 et seq; Bohanes and Lockhart, 'Standard of Review in WTO Law', 385 et seq; Oesch, *Standards of Review*, 16 et seq; Becroft, *The Standard of Review*, 8–10.

Anti-Dumping Agreement.[39] However, beyond the question of whether or not a certain event did occur in time and in space, which the Appellate Body has clearly categorized as a question of fact,[40] the line between the two notions is unclear. As it has been noted in the context of domestic judicial review, this distinction is often affected by pragmatic considerations, based on the courts' willingness to intervene or not intervene.[41] The problem with drawing an analytically clear line between two allegedly different standards of review is obvious with regard to the legal qualification of 'established facts' from the perspective of WTO law, such as whether the import of a certain quantity of products amounts to an 'increased quantity' for the purposes of Article 2.1 of the Safeguard Agreement, or whether the evaluation of a certain industrial practice as harmful for human health offers 'sufficient scientific evidence' within the meaning of Article 2 of the Agreement on the Application of Sanitary and Phytosanitary Measures (SPS Agreement).[42] This is treated as a question of fact by some[43] and as a legal question by others.[44] The problem with such a dichotomy is connected with the difficulty of drawing a clear-cut distinction between the successive steps of legal argumentation, and cannot be further analysed here. For present purposes, suffice it to say that deference in each of these steps cannot be defined beforehand, but, as it will be argued in more detail, with reference to the specific considerations that make it more suitable for the adjudicating bodies or domestic authorities to decide each step.

In sum, the Uruguay Round Agreements give little textual guidance as to the applicable standard of review. Both the anti-dumping-specific and the general standard of review, based on Article 11 DSU, allow the adjudicating bodies to retain almost uncontested power over the issue of deference.[45] This means that, ultimately, the panels and the Appellate Body have 'little choice but to do what judicial organs throughout the world do in such situations: base [their] decisions on relevant policy considerations'.[46] For example, the adjudicating bodies might be more willing to award deference to domestic decisions when they recognize that it is based on superior domestic expertise or when they believe that the decision-maker has followed a transparent and deliberative procedure. As Andrew Guzman notes, however, it is crucial that these criteria are identified and adequately scrutinized.[47] Actually, it is the reference to these criteria that allows for a meaningful assessment of judicial decisions, rather than generalizations about 'more' or 'less' intrusive courts or obscure notions such as 'permissible' or 'adequate'.

[39] See Appellate Body Report, *US—Steel*, para 54.
[40] Appellate Body Report, *EC—Hormones*, para 132.
[41] Paul Craig, *Administrative Law*, 7th edn (London: Sweet & Maxwell, 2008) 243.
[42] See Button, *The Power to Protect*, 166–7; Spamann, 'Standard of Review in Trade Remedy Cases', 525–7; Bohanes and Lockhart, 'Standard of Review in WTO Law', 384.
[43] See Spamann, 'Standard of Review in Trade Remedy Cases', 526.
[44] Appellate Body Report, *EC—Hormones*, para 132.
[45] Croley and Jackson, 'WTO Dispute Procedures', 204.
[46] Guzman, 'Determining the Appropriate Standard of Review', 53.
[47] Guzman, 'Determining the Appropriate Standard of Review', 53.

C. Judicial criteria for awarding deference

A significant problem in the standard-of-review debate is that adjudicators do not always make explicit the criteria upon which they base their decisions on deference. Often, courts stop short of giving persuasive (or indeed any) explanations why some domestic measures fall, for example, within the category of 'permissible interpretation' and others do not. Sometimes, they simply resort to self-referential explanations, such as 'the Panel's job was not to conduct a *de novo* investigation.'[48] Other times, adjudicators offer cumulatively more than one reason supporting their view.

In the following section, a general categorization will be attempted, systematizing some of the reasons that seem to be the most important to the WTO adjudicating bodies when called upon to decide whether or not to grant deference. To some extent, this transforms the discussion on the standard of review from a quantitative one to a more qualitative one. Instead of examining the standard of review as a general choice of a point along the 'more intrusive—less intrusive' continuum, the focus is put on the patterns of justification followed by the adjudicating bodies. Of course, this cannot be an exclusive catalogue. It rather seeks to serve a mapping function, allowing for reasoned criticism of the choices of the adjudicating bodies, and paving the way for arguing for the merits of a procedural standard of review.

1. *Sovereignty*

Respect for national sovereignty is one of the first criteria that have been suggested for directing the WTO adjudicating bodies to show more deference to domestic determinations. In their influential article published immediately after the establishment of the WTO, Steven Croley and John Jackson focused on the role that sovereignty could play in determining the WTO standard of review.[49] Here, the basic argument is that WTO Members have committed themselves to certain limitations regarding the exercise of their sovereign powers in the field of international trade. States, however, have only committed themselves to the specific limitations contained in the WTO Agreements, and no additional constraints can be imposed on them without their consent. An intrusive standard of review could empower the adjudicating bodies to interfere with the Members' sovereign choices even when there is no adequate consensual and textual basis for this. Eventually, an intrusive standard could add to the international obligations agreed to by the WTO Members in Marrakesh, contrary to what Article 3.2 DSU prescribes.

The Appellate Body, albeit arguing in a different context, has hinted that this argument might be indeed of some relevance for WTO law. In *EC—Hormones*, the Appellate Body found that the adjudicating bodies cannot 'lightly assume that

[48] GATT Dispute Settlement Panel Report, *Korea—Anti-Dumping Duties on Imports of Polyacetal Resins from the United States*, ADP/92 and Corr. 1, 27 April 1993, para 57.

[49] Croley and Jackson, 'WTO Dispute Procedures', 211.

sovereign States intended to impose upon themselves the more onerous, rather than the less burdensome, obligation',[50] supporting this finding with a reference to the principle of *in dubio mitius*. This principle, as understood by the Appellate Body, requires an international adjudicator to interpret treaties 'in deference to the sovereignty of States'.[51]

As such, however, the sovereignty criterion begs the question of *why* domestic sovereignty deserves respect by an international adjudicator in the case at issue. Moreover, the fact that an international provision is drafted broadly enough to trigger a discussion over the proper standard of review does not necessarily mean that the contracting parties intended to exclude the relevant domestic decisions from international scrutiny. On many occasions, issues are left open in international negotiations because States are unwilling or unable to reach agreement, preferring to defer their solution to a later time and/or a third party. Most of the time, thus, the *in dubio mitius* principle will not be conclusive for deciding how much deference the WTO adjudicating bodies need to show to domestic assessments. Indeed, the WTO adjudicating bodies have refrained from giving further weight to the sovereignty argument when discussing the applicable standard of review.

2. *Democratic accountability*

One of the powerful reasons suggested in favour of deference is that domestic decision-makers enjoy superior democratic legitimacy vis-à-vis international courts.[52] Assuming that the domestic authority at issue is embedded in an effective democratic system, the argument is that the reviewing international court should respect its democratic credentials and better responsiveness to the considerations of domestic constituencies. In the early *Hatter's Fur* case, the respective working party argued that 'it is natural that governments should on occasion be greatly influenced by social factors, such as local employment problems'.[53] The 'responsibility and representativeness' of governments has also appeared as a consideration, albeit only en passant, in the review of Sanitary and Phytosanitary (SPS) measures, which touch upon sensitive issues in the field of public health.[54] In *EC—Hormones*, the panel

[50] Appellate Body Report, *EC—Hormones*, para 165.

[51] Appellate Body Report, *EC—Hormones*, fn 154.

[52] For the connection between democratic legitimacy and the standard of review in international courts, see Andreas von Staden, 'The Democratic Legitimacy of Judicial Review Beyond the State: Normative Subsidiarity and Judicial Standards of Review', 19 *International Journal of Constitutional Law* 1023 (2012). For the general issues regarding international courts and democratic legitimacy, see von Bogdandy and Venzke, 'Beyond Dispute'.

[53] GATT Panel Report, *United States—Withdrawal of a Tariff Concession under Article XIX (Fur Felt Hat Bodies)*, GATT/CP/106, 22 October 1951, para 48. The working party went on to qualify this assertion by saying that a country's power to consider domestic social factors finds its limits when 'the weight attached by the government concerned to such factors [is] clearly unreasonably great'.

[54] See Appellate Body Report, *EC—Hormones*, paras 124 and 198; Appellate Body Report, *United States—Continued Suspension of Obligations in the EC—Hormones Dispute*, WT/DS320/AB/R, 14 November 2008 and *Canada—Continued Suspension of Obligations in the EC—Hormones Dispute*, WT/DS321/AB/R, 14 November 2008, paras 529 and 680; Appellate Body Report, *EC—Asbestos*, para 178.

indicated that, whereas risk assessment can be more intensively reviewed, the choice of risks that a community is willing to undertake is an issue for 'political bodies'.[55]

Popular as the argument of domestic accountability might be, it is not sufficient to justify deference. The main reason behind the establishment of the multilateral trading system is the recognition that the decisions adopted by domestic authorities in the field of international trade have repercussions beyond their respective jurisdictions.[56] A domestic decision that affects the condition of foreign actors cannot be deemed legitimate only on the basis that it responds to the considerations of *domestic* constituencies.[57] International trade interdependencies make the regulation of trade a concern for international constituencies as well. This means that the fact that domestic authorities, legislatures, agencies, or courts, are more accountable to a country's citizens[58] does not give them full democratic credentials, and cannot be conclusive when it comes to the assessment of their decisions from a WTO perspective. Additionally, the openness of the procedure to foreign interests and arguments would be necessary for a proper democratic justification of deference. I return to this point in Section IV of the chapter.

3. *Expertise*

In the domestic context, one important criterion for deciding on the applicable standard of review is expertise. For example, domestic courts often justify their decision to show deference to the executive on the basis that the latter is better positioned to ascertain complex facts and make difficult policy evaluations. Greater information, knowledge, and time resources are supposed to give other authorities an advantage over courts; an advantage that deserves to be respected by adjudicators.[59]

Similar arguments are also relevant on the international plane, especially in a context as information-intensive as international trade. State authorities, having much greater capabilities with regard to information gathering and assessment, might reasonably claim that they are in a better position than a WTO panel to evaluate issues such as whether the import of certain product can cause 'serious injury' to the domestic industry.[60] One could actually distinguish two different

[55] Panel Report, *EC Measures Concerning Meat and Meat Products (EC–Hormones), Complaint by the United States*, WT/DS26/R/USA, 13 February 1998, as modified by Appellate Body Report, WT/DS26/AB/R, WT/DS48/AB/R para 8.94 ('an assessment of risks is, at least for risks to human life or health, a *scientific* examination of data and factual studies; it is not a policy exercise involving social value judgments made by political bodies').

[56] See Croley and Jackson, 'WTO Dispute Procedures', 209.

[57] Yuval Shany, 'Toward a General Margin of Appreciation Doctrine in International Law?', 16 *EJIL* 907 (2006), 920. On the question of how to square transborder externalities with democratic accountability, see Robert Keohane, 'Global Governance and Democratic Accountability' in David Held and Mathias Koenig-Archibugi, *Taming Globalization: Frontiers of Governance* (Cambridge: Polity Press, 2003); Eyal Benvenisti, 'Sovereigns as Trustees of Humanity: On the Accountability of States to Foreign Stakeholders', 107 *AJIL* 295 (2013).

[58] If they are. This argument apparently does not hold for autocratic domestic polities.

[59] See Shany, 'Toward a General Margin of Appreciation', 918–19.

[60] See Guzman, 'Determining the Appropriate Standard of Review', 54–6; Oesch, *Standards of Review*, 56.

issues here. The first is how panels address the expertise of domestic authorities with regard to the application of their own, domestic laws, and the second is how they treat their capacity in making determinations requiring scientific expertise.

Regarding the first question, the Appellate Body confirmed in *Thailand—Cigarettes (Philippines)* that 'a Member is normally well-placed to explain the meaning of its own law',[61] noting, however, 'that this does not relieve a party of its burden to adduce arguments and evidence necessary to sustain its proposed interpretation'.[62] Of course, this statement is far from clear regarding the weight that the adjudicating bodies are willing to give to the fact that a domestic authority might be more knowledgeable of the (domestic) rules it is called upon to apply.[63] The criterion of expertise here seems to tilt the balance towards greater deference to a Member's interpretation of its own laws, but this interpretation must be substantiated by additional evidence.[64]

With respect to scientific expertise, the Appellate Body ruled in *US/Canada—Continued Suspension* that a panel should not substitute its own scientific judgement for that of the domestic authority.[65] The Appellate Body suggested that, in the context of scientific assessments, greater deference to domestic decisions is justified by the better capacities of national authorities, compared to panels, in conducting scientific research.[66] This means that the adjudicator's task is not to determine whether the risk assessment is correct, but rather to review 'whether that risk assessment is supported by coherent reasoning and respectable scientific evidence and is, in this sense, objectively justifiable'.[67]

The Appellate Body further qualified this requirement by distinguishing between two tasks that domestic authorities need to accomplish in order for their conclusions to be respected when it comes to scientific expertise. Firstly, domestic decision-makers need to ensure that the scientific basis on which their decisions are based constitutes 'legitimate science according to the standards of the relevant scientific community'.[68] Although the domestic decision need not represent the

[61] Panel Report, *China—Measures Affecting the Protection and Enforcement of Intellectual Property Rights*, WT/DS362, 20 March 2009, para 7.28.

[62] Appellate Body Report, *Thailand—Customs and Fiscal Measures on Cigarettes from the Philippines*, WT/DS371/AB/R, 15 July 2011, fn 253 to para 159.

[63] See Oesch, *Standards of Review*, 196.

[64] See Appellate Body Report, *United States—Countervailing Duties on Certain Corrosion-Resistant Carbon Steel Flat Products from Germany*, WT/DS213/AB/R and Corr.1, 19 December 2002, para 157; Bohanes and Lockhart, 'Standard of Review in WTO Law', 416 et seq.

[65] Appellate Body Reports, *US/Canada—Continued Suspension*, paras 590 and 612; Appellate Body Report, *Australia—Measures Affecting the Importation of Apples from New Zealand*, WT/DS367/AB/R, 17 December 2010, para 225. On the applicable standard of review in WTO cases dealing with issues of scientific expertise, see Chapter 9 by Lukasz Gruszczynski and Valentina Vadi in this volume.

[66] Appellate Body Report, *Australia—Apples*, para 225. See also Appellate Body Report, *EC—Hormones*, para 117 ('Many panels have in the past refused to undertake *de novo* review, wisely, since under current practice and systems, they are in any case poorly suited to engage in such review'); Panel Report, *US—Combed Cotton Yarn*, para 7.32 ('Panels are less equipped and might have less expertise in fact-finding than national authorities').

[67] Appellate Body Reports, *US/Canada—Continued Suspension*, para 590.

[68] Appellate Body Report, *Australia—Apples*, para 220.

majority of scientific views,[69] it must come 'from a respected and qualified source' and have 'the necessary scientific and methodological rigour to be considered reputable science'.[70]

Secondly, the reasoning articulated by the domestic authority on the basis of this scientific evidence must be 'objective and coherent'.[71] In other words, a panel should review whether the particular conclusions drawn by the Member in assessing the risk 'find sufficient support in the scientific evidence relied upon'.[72] This second requirement, referring to the sufficiency of the connection between the scientific evidence and the ultimate conclusion reached by the domestic regulator, is the most critical.[73] In some of its latest decisions, the Appellate Body seems to request that the panels reconstruct in detail the logic and reasoning followed by the domestic authority in order to accept its superior access to scientific expertise.[74] That brings this criterion very close to the one focusing on the 'quality of the reasoning' supporting domestic authorities' decisions. This is discussed below.

4. *Quality of reasoning: the 'all relevant factors' and 'reasoned explanation' tests*

Beyond scientific assessments, complex factual determinations pose a significant challenge for determining the criteria for deference. According to the Appellate Body in *US—Lamb*, the objective-assessment requirement anchored in Article 11 DSU requires the adjudicating bodies to satisfy themselves that two criteria are fulfilled, a formal and a substantive. The formal criterion requires domestic authorities to 'evaluate all relevant factors', while the substantive one is that they provide 'a reasoned and adequate explanation' of how the facts support their determination.[75] Further elaborating on the content of these two requirements, the Appellate Body ruled that:

> [a] panel must find, in particular, that an explanation is not reasoned, or is not adequate, if some *alternative explanation* of the facts is plausible, and if the competent authorities' explanation does not seem adequate in the light of that alternative explanation.[76]

69 Appellate Body Report, *EC—Hormones*, para 194.

70 Appellate Body Reports, *US/Canada—Continued Suspension*, para 591.

71 Appellate Body Reports, *US/Canada—Continued Suspension*, para 591.

72 Appellate Body Reports, *US/Canada—Continued Suspension*, para 591; Appellate Body Report, *Australia—Apples*, para 220.

73 Appellate Body Reports, *US/Canada—Continued Suspension*, para 590; Appellate Body Report, *Australia—Apples*, para 253.

74 Appellate Body Report, *Australia—Apples*, paras 224–6.

75 Appellate Body Report, *United States—Safeguard Measures on Imports of Fresh, Chilled or Frozen Lamb Meat from New Zealand and Australia*, WT/DS177/AB/R, WT/DS178/AB/R, 16 May 2001, para 103. See also Appellate Body Report, *Argentina—Footwear*, para 121; Appellate Body Report, *United States—Definitive Safeguard Measures on Import of Circular Welded Carbon Quality Line Pipe from Korea*, WT/DS202/AB/R, 8 March 2002, para 217; Appellate Body Report, *US—Softwood Lumber VI* (*Article 21.5—Canada*), para 93.

76 Appellate Body Report, *US—Lamb*, para 106 (emphasis in the original); restated in Appellate Body Report, *US—Tyres (China)*, para 123.

In *US—Cotton Yarn*, the Appellate Body restated the 'all relevant factors' and 'reasoned and adequate explanation' tests,[77] and in *US—Steel* indicated that these criteria are not relevant only for the interpretation of some WTO provisions, but might be of general application.[78] Indeed, the requirement that all relevant facts are examined and a reasoned explanation is offered has gradually become a standard phrase for trade-remedy cases.[79] Of course, the main issue left open by this requirement is which explanation would count as 'adequately reasoned' in the eyes of the adjudicating bodies.

As expected, the Appellate Body stated that this 'will inevitably depend on the facts and circumstances of the case and the particular claims'.[80] Nevertheless it also stated that some general lines of inquiry could be relevant for most cases.[81] In *US—Softwood Lumber VI (Article 21.5—Canada)*, the Appellate Body ruled that the adjudicator need to review:

> whether the reasoning of the authority is coherent and internally consistent. The panel must undertake an in-depth examination of whether the explanations given disclose how the investigating authority treated the facts and evidence in the record and whether there was positive evidence before it to support the inferences made and conclusions reached by it. The panel must examine whether the explanations provided demonstrate that the investigating authority took proper account of the complexities of the data before it, and that it explained why it rejected or discounted alternative explanations and interpretations of the record evidence.

As is known from domestic constitutional and administrative law, the reason-giving criterion is popular among courts that deeply scrutinize legislative or administrative decisions, but are also concerned with critics raising the separation-of-powers argument. From the perspective of courts, the advantage of the adequate reasoning requirement is that it lies on the borderline between procedural and substantive review. On the one hand, reason-giving can be understood as a simply formal requirement, requiring that the administrative body states the reasons for its decision—regardless of how convincing these reasons are.[82] On the other hand, the requirement to give reasons might extend to their substantive quality by demanding that the reasons submitted are also *good* reasons. The importance of this distinction cannot be overestimated. By reassessing the merits of the explanation offered by the original decision-maker, courts essentially substitute their own assessment for that of the original decision-maker. This means the transformation of 'a mild, essentially procedural requirement into a draconian, substantive one'.[83]

[77] Appellate Body Report, *US—Combed Cotton Yarn*, para 74, adding that a domestic explanation cannot be deemed inadequate in the light of evidence that became available *after* the domestic decision was made, see paras 77–79.

[78] See Appellate Body Report, *US—Steel*, para 276; Guzman, 'Determining the Appropriate Standard of Review', 61.

[79] Oesch, *Standards of Review*, 118.

[80] Appellate Body Report, *US—Softwood Lumber VI (Article 21.5—Canada)*, para 93.

[81] Appellate Body Report, *US—Softwood Lumber VI (Article 21.5—Canada)*, para 93.

[82] Martin Shapiro, 'The Institutionalization of European Administrative Space' in Alec Stone Sweet, Wayne Sandholtz and Neil Fligstein (eds), *The Institutionalization of Europe* (Oxford: Oxford University Press, 2001) 99.

[83] Martin Shapiro and Alec Stone Sweet, *On Law, Politics, and Judicialization* (Oxford: Oxford University Press, 2002) 235. As noted in the context of US law, 'the most crucial aspect of the

Although the Appellate Body has been eager to stress that the 'all relevant facts' and 'reasoned explanation' tests do not substitute the views of the adjudicating bodies for those of the competent domestic authorities,[84] the rejection of certain domestic explanations as inadequate is little less than that.[85] This, however, does not mean that by using this criterion the Appellate Body goes beyond its mandate or acts contrary to Article 3.2 DSU. The purpose of showing the limits of the 'adequate explanation' test is to point out that, on many occasions, it does not offer a decisive criterion for awarding deference. An additional basis is needed for deciding what makes one explanation better than others. It is here suggested that this criterion could be the procedure followed for the adoption of the contested decision.

5. *Participation and procedural due process*

On many occasions, the WTO adjudicating bodies have tied their assessments on the 'objectiveness' or 'appropriateness' of the reviewed decision to the procedure followed by domestic authorities in order to arrive at the contested decision. According to this criterion, domestic authorities that respect international due process standards and reach their conclusions after having sufficiently considered foreign arguments deserve more deference than authorities reaching their decisions behind closed doors.

In *US—Lamb* and *US—Steel*, the Appellate Body linked the sufficiency of the explanation offered by the domestic authorities with the procedure they followed before adopting the trade-restrictive measure at issue in each case.[86] It is characteristic that in *US—Steel* the Appellate Body, answering to the US objections that the Safeguard Agreement does not explicitly establish an 'adequate explanation' requirement, read this condition as:

> 'a shorthand' for the obligations that '*are* in the Agreement', that is, that the published report of the competent authorities must, pursuant to Article 3.1, contain 'reasoned conclusions' on 'all pertinent issues of fact and law' and, under Article 4.2(c), it must also contain 'a detailed analysis of the case', including 'a demonstration of the relevance of the factors examined.'[87]

Indeed, on many occasions, WTO law regulates in minute detail how domestic authorities should conduct the investigations upon which they base their decisions.[88] For example, the Anti-Dumping Agreement requires national decision-makers to arrive at their conclusions only after having respected basic

giving-reasons requirement may be that it serves as a way of softening and somewhat disguising substantive judicial review. Thus, the requirement softens and disguises the ultimate dilemma of judicial review' (247).

[84] See Appellate Body Report, *US—Steel*, para 299.

[85] Spamann, 'Standard of Review in Trade Remedy Cases', 541.

[86] Appellate Body Report, *US—Lamb*, para 105; Appellate Body Report, *US—Steel*, para 299.

[87] Appellate Body Report, *US—Steel*, para 300.

[88] See in detail Michael Ioannidis, *Due Process and Participation Rights in WTO Law* (Cambridge: Cambridge University Press, forthcoming 2014).

due process guarantees, including the publication and notification of relevant documents, the granting of sufficient rights to participation, and the support of the final decision with adequate reasons.[89] Although in *Thailand—H-Beams* the Appellate Body was sceptical in using the observance of such procedural safeties as a criterion for awarding deference to domestic decision-makers,[90] many authors have suggested that the requirement for 'proper establishment of facts' should be read as requiring domestic authorities to employ fair procedures, including adequate opportunity to interested parties to respond to the record and bring forward their own view on the facts.[91]

Even in contexts where there is no equivalent to Article 17.6 of the Anti-Dumping Agreement, adherence to procedural standards appears to be an important criterion for adopting a deferential approach.[92] As Claus-Dieter Ehlermann and Nicolas Lockhart aptly observe, where WTO law regulates domestic procedures with sufficient detail, aimed at securing due process standards, there is a strong argument for a more deferential stance towards the findings of domestic authorities that respect those WTO-imposed procedural rules.[93] In a similar vein, Joanne Scott notes the connection between 'a higher level of scrutiny of procedural requirements in the course of adoption of decisions . . . and a lower level of scrutiny of the substantive compatibility of those decisions with the agreements'.[94]

Openness to the consideration of foreign arguments has also been used by the adjudicating bodies beyond trade-remedy cases as a criterion for deciding the issue of deference. In *US—Cotton Yarn*, the Appellate Body connected the level of scrutiny of the domestic decision with the participation of interested parties in the relevant procedure, noting that:

> Article 6 [ATC Agreement] does not require the participation of all interested parties in the process leading to the determination. We consider, therefore, that the exercise of due diligence by a Member is all the more important in reaching a determination under Article 6 of the *ATC*.[95]

Finally, the *US—Shrimp*[96] decision offers an example of how procedure and participation might play a role in deference considerations even in cases where no such requirement can be directly derived by positive WTO law. In that case, the Appellate Body was called upon to examine whether a US import prohibition

[89] See Articles 6.1, 6.9, 6.12, 12.1 and 12.2 Anti-Dumping Agreement.

[90] Appellate Body Report, *Thailand—H-Beams*, para 117.

[91] Garry N. Horlick and Peggy A. Clarke, 'Standards for Panels Reviewing Anti-dumping Determinations under the GATT and WTO' in Ernst-Ulrich Petersmann, *International Trade Law and the GATT/WTO Dispute Settlement System* (London: Kluwer Law International, 1997) 319. See, however, Oesch, *Standards of Review*, 91.

[92] Bohanes and Lockhart, 'Standard of Review in WTO Law', 395.

[93] Ehlermann and Lockhart, 'Standard of Review in WTO Law', 507–8.

[94] Joanne Scott, 'Comment in the Panel "Dispute Settlement: Jurisprudential and Procedural Features"' in Mads Andenas and Federico Ortino (eds), *WTO Law and Process* (London: BIICL, 2005) 410.

[95] Appellate Body Report, *US—Cotton Yarn*, para 76.

[96] Appellate Body Report, *United States—Import Prohibition of Certain Shrimp and Shrimp Products*, WT/DS58/AB/R, 6 November 1998.

was 'not applied in a manner which would constitute a means of arbitrary or unjustifiable discrimination between countries where the same conditions prevail, or a disguised restriction on international trade'.[97] Among the reasons why the Appellate Body ultimately found the US measure inconsistent with GATT was that US authorities did not respect the due process rights of foreign interests.[98] In particular, US agencies failed to afford the complainants with a 'formal opportunity... to be heard, or to respond to any arguments that may be made against it' as well as to provide for a formal written, reasoned decision, prior notification, and opportunity for review.[99]

To better understand the potential of this approach one might consider the alternative way in which the Appellate Body could have proceeded here.[100] That would have been to assess whether the decision of US agencies was *substantively* correct. In order to make this assessment, the Appellate Body would have had to second-guess the US decision, balancing competing interests and making a substantive decision on the similarity of environmental conditions between the disputing parties.[101] Instead of this, the Appellate Body took a 'proceduralist turn',[102] connecting the discriminatory nature of the US measure to the failure of US authorities to hear the arguments of foreign interested parties.[103] In so doing, the Appellate Body effectively disciplined its own law-making potential and relocated the decision-making power back to the domestic level,[104] under the condition that it is exercised after the meaningful consideration of affected foreign interests.

IV. The Case for a Procedural Standard of Review in WTO Law

There are strong arguments why the procedure-oriented and participation-reinforcing criterion should receive more attention by the adjudicating bodies when deciding questions of deference. This idea has been a recurring topic in domestic settings, both at the level of constitutional and administrative review.

[97] Article XX General Agreement on Tariffs and Trade 1994, 15 April 1994, Marrakesh Agreement Establishing the World Trade Organization, Annex 1A (GATT), 1867 UNTS 187.

[98] See Richard B. Stewart and Michelle Ratton Sanchez Badin, 'The World Trade Organization: Multiple Dimensions of Global Administrative Law', 9 *International Journal of Constitutional Law* 556 (2011), 571.

[99] Stewart and Ratton Sanchez Badin, 'Multiple Dimensions', 571.

[100] Shaffer distinguishes between five alternatives open to the Appellate Body, see Gregory Shaffer, 'Power, Governance, and the WTO: a Comparative Institutional Approach' in Michael Barnett and Raymond Duvall (eds), *Power in Global Governance* (Cambridge: Cambridge University Press, 2005) 141–2.

[101] Shaffer, 'Power, Governance, and the WTO', 153.

[102] Shaffer, 'Power, Governance, and the WTO', 153.

[103] Appellate Body Report, *US—Shrimp*, para 177. See Patricia I. Hansen, 'Transparency, Standards of Review, and the Use of Trade Measures to Protect the Global Environment', 39 *Virginia Journal of International Law* 1017 (1999), 1053; Joanne Scott, 'European Regulation of GMOs: Thinking about "Judicial Review" in the WTO', in Ellen Vos and Michelle Everson (eds), *Uncertain Risks Regulated* (New York: Routledge, 2009) 308.

[104] See Shaffer, 'Power, Governance, and the WTO', 153.

In administrative law, domestic courts often focus on transparency and participation as criteria for giving leeway to administrative determinations.[105] In constitutional adjudication, the orientation of courts to a process-perfecting role instead of second-guessing parliamentary decisions has been suggested as a way out of the notorious 'counter-majoritarian difficulty'. According to this view, courts are better placed to secure the procedural conditions of legitimate decision-making, ensuring that diverse arguments have been exposed and considered during the making of the contested decision.[106] Transparency, broad opportunities for access, and the giving of reasons have been identified as basic criteria on which courts should focus to accomplish this task of procedural oversight. According to Christopher Zurn, for example, the proper task of a constitutional adjudicator is not to overturn the substantive choices of elected legislatures, but to ensure that the latter have formed their decisions after an open and deliberative exchange of arguments.[107] But also in the supranational context of the EU, the procedural criterion has been suggested as a potential response to the critics of the Court of Justice of the European Union. Miguel Poiares Maduro, the Court's former Advocate General, has prominently suggested that, instead of second-guessing domestic regulatory choices, the Court should rather focus on ensuring 'that there is no under-representation of the interests of nationals of other Member States' in the national decision-making process.[108]

In the case of the WTO, opting for a procedural and participation-reinforcing criterion may offer an institutionalized mechanism of external accountability and a corrective to the 'in-built parochialism' of nation States.[109] Thomas Cottier refers to the application of this criterion as 'compensation by process',[110] arguing that when WTO substantive provisions leave broad discretion to the adjudicating bodies, the observance of procedural guarantees shall be given a predominant role. By requiring domestic decision-makers to consider diverse scientific and societal considerations it becomes less likely that the final decision expresses protectionist aims.[111] Stefan Zlepting, in suggesting a 'deliberation test' for WTO law, has also

[105] For more details for the lessons that can be learnt from domestic administrative law for WTO adjudication, see Michael Ioannidis, 'A Procedural Approach to the Legitimacy of International Adjudication: Developing Standards of Participation in WTO Law', 12 *GLJ* 1175 (2011), 1177 et seq.

[106] For one of the most elaborate theories in this context, see John Hart Ely, *Democracy and Distrust: a Theory of Judicial Review* (Cambridge, MA: Harvard University Press, 1980). For the relevance of Ely's theory at the international level, see Chapter 4 by Benedikt Pirker in this volume.

[107] Christopher F. Zurn, *Deliberative Democracy and the Institutions of Judicial Review* (New York: Cambridge University Press, 2007). For a procedural theory of justice that has proven very influential in this context, see Jürgen Habermas, *Between Facts and Norms: Contributions to a Discourse Theory of Law and Democracy*, trans. William Rehg (Cambridge: Polity Press, 1997).

[108] Miguel P. Maduro, *We, the Court: The European Court of Justice and the European Economic Constitution* (Oxford: Hart Publishing, 1998) 173.

[109] Christian Joerges and Jürgen Neyer, 'Politics, Risk Management, World Trade Organisation Governance and the Limits of Legalisation', 30 *Science and Public Policy* 219 (2003), 221. For the merits of this approach see also Ioannidis, 'A Procedural Approach'.

[110] Thomas Cottier, 'Risk Management Experience in WTO Dispute Settlement' in Thomas Cottier (ed), *The Challenge of WTO Law: Collected Essays* (London: Cameron May, 2007) 163.

[111] Cottier, 'Risk Management Experience', 163.

powerfully advocated for a procedural criterion for deference, which would make respect to domestic decisions contingent upon the quality and openness of the procedure which produced them.[112]

The basic premise of all these approaches is that international trade is a field of common interest for a variety of international actors. In this field of unavoidable economic and social interaction, decisions made by one or some actors often have a significant impact on foreigners.[113] This creates a need for coordination and the establishment of mechanisms through which the 'external' effects of their activity can be internalized.[114] Viewed from this perspective, the respect of basic due process and participation standards by domestic decision-makers is a genuinely democratic postulate, requiring that those having an interest in a decision should also be given notice thereof and some form of voice.[115] As Robert Howse notes, the obligation of domestic authorities to justify their decisions to outsiders is a central element of the legitimacy of the international trade regime.[116] Opting for a procedural criterion for awarding deference might thus promote the idea of 'structuring a democratic regulatory process that is fair to outsiders as well as insiders, and as countering the possibility of hidden or embedded discrimination'.[117]

In practical terms, a participation-enhancing concept of deference could be based on a number of techniques. The scrutiny of domestic measures in the light of open-textured provisions should take into account to what extent foreign interests were effectively considered by the domestic regulator.[118] The WTO adjudicating bodies should thus afford broader deference to domestic authorities when assessing their compliance with the requirements of 'necessity' or 'less restrictive means', making, however, such deference contingent upon the fulfilment of minimum due process requirements.[119] Similar considerations should underlie the application of the requirement of 'reasonableness' in Article X:3(a) GATT or that

[112] Stefan Zlepting, 'The Standard of Review in WTO Law: An Analysis of Law, Legitimacy and the Distribution of Legal and Political Authority', 6 *European Integration Online Papers* (2002) (<http://eioporat/eiop/pdf/2002-017pdf> (accessed 28 March 2014)).

[113] For this argument in the EU context, see Christian Joerges, '"Deliberative Political Processes" Revisited: What Have we Learnt About the Legitimacy of Supranational Decision-Making', 44 *Journal of Common Market Studies* 779 (2006), 790. For a connection of the standard of review with the aim of protecting individual citizens as subjects of modern international law, see Chapter 2 by Ernst-Ulrich Petersmann in this volume.

[114] For the model of 'coordinated interdependence' as the most persuasive approach to the WTO, see von Bogdandy, 'Law and Politics in the WTO', 651 et seq.

[115] See Joerges, '"Deliberative Political Processes" Revisited'.

[116] Robert Howse, 'Democracy, Science, and Free Trade: Risk Regulation on Trial at the World Trade Organization', 98 *Michigan Law Review* 2329 (2000), 2356–7.

[117] Robert Howse, 'The Legitimacy of the World Trade Organization' in Jean-Marc Coicaud and Veijo Heiskanen (eds), *The Legitimacy of International Organizations* (Tokyo: United Nations University Press, 2001) 370 (footnote omitted).

[118] Armin von Bogdandy, 'Rechtsnatur und Finalität der WTO—eine Analyse der Präambel' in Hartmut Bauer et al, *Wirtschaft im offenen Verfassungstaat: Festschrift für Reiner Schmidt zum 70 Geburtstag* (Munchen: Beck, 2006) 37.

[119] Ioannidis, 'A Procedural Approach', 1200. See also the conclusions reached by Alexia Herwig and Asja Serdarevic in Chapter 10 in this volume.

of 'the objective assessment' in Article 11 DSU.[120] It must be acknowledged that defining which interests should be granted participation rights is not an easy task. Courts, however, are better placed to address this kind of question than to make complicated assessments about sensitive political issues, such as public health. Moreover, rules of thumb can be developed. For example, foreign parties that are singled out by a specific domestic decision should enjoy a presumption that their interests have not been adequately represented in the relevant domestic discourse, and thus require special access rights.

Moreover, this approach can be relevant not only where WTO law regulates domestic procedures in detail, such as in anti-dumping and safeguard cases, but also in those fields where positive WTO procedural rules are sparser, such as in the context of the SPS Agreement and Article XX GATT.[121] The adjudicating bodies can utilize the existing procedural requirements[122] and follow a proceduralist reading of broadly drafted provisions, as indicated in *US—Shrimp*. This approach cannot, of course, substitute international substantive regulation and does not affect the interpretation of provisions as clear as tariff concessions. For the cases, however, where the wording of WTO law leaves substantial discretion to the adjudicating institutions,[123] a procedural approach may be a convincing alternative.

V. Conclusions

Despite the continuing scholarly and judicial interest in the standard of review, many things remain unclear, both about the content of the concept itself and its usefulness in legal discourse. This contribution has raised three points. Firstly, that the current debate on the standard of review continues to be dominated by obscure and indeterminate notions such as 'objectiveness' and 'reasonableness'. These concepts essentially hide the important normative choices on which courts base their decisions, do not allow for reasoned criticism of the adjudicating bodies' practice, and ultimately go against the declared intention of the WTO to reinforce predictability in the multilateral trading system. Secondly, it is suggested that the focus of both panels and commentators shifts to the reasons that the adjudicating bodies give (or fail to give) when deciding to grant deference to

[120] Article 11 DSU. See Zlepting, 'The Standard of Review in WTO Law'.

[121] For a different view on this point, see Button, *The Power to Protect*, 215–16.

[122] Both the SPS Agreement and the TBT Agreement require Member States intending to enact a technical regulation to provide adequate notice, to allow other States to make comments on it, to discuss these comments upon request, and to take the comments and the resulting discussion into account when eventually deciding on the measure at hand; see Article 2.9.4 Agreement on Technical Barriers to Trade, 15 April 1994, Marrakesh Agreement Establishing the World Trade Organization, Annex 1A (TBT Agreement), 1868 UNTS 120, and 5(d) Annex B Agreement on the Application of Sanitary and Phytosanitary Measures, 15 April 1994, Marrakesh Agreement Establishing the World Trade Organization, Annex 1A (SPS Agreement), 1867 UNTS 493. Consider also Article 2.10.3 TBT Agreement and 6(c) Annex B SPS Agreement. In more detail, see Ioannidis, 'A Procedural Approach', 1193 et seq.

[123] Shany, 'Toward a General Margin of Appreciation', 913.

domestic authorities. Of course, this does not mean that courts' ultimate power in giving their own version of the meaning of broadly drafted provisions ceases to exist.[124] Legal rules will always be indeterminate, and courts will always have the privilege to give the last word on their meaning. Nevertheless, reasoned criticism of their stance will be greatly enhanced if we focus on the reasons they suggest as relevant for deference and even require them to make those reasons explicit. Moreover, as this chapter suggested in the third point raised herein, a procedural, participation-reinforcing criterion for awarding deference would better meet the institutional specificities of the WTO, offering a mechanism to respond to a structural question for international law, namely the exclusion of foreigners from domestic decision-making. Such a criterion would allow the WTO adjudicating bodies to function as guardians of procedural legitimacy, focusing on the control of the inclusiveness of domestic procedures without 'supplanting the substance of national regulatory policies'.[125] As Bohanes and Lockhart observe, there is no 'correct' standard of review.[126] There can be, however, criteria for awarding deference that better meet the requirements of a one international legal regime than another.

[124] See Ioannidis, 'A Procedural Approach', 1181.

[125] John O. McGinnis and Mark L. Movsesian, 'The World Trade Constitution', 114 *Harvard Law Review* 511 (2000), 580.

[126] Bohanes and Lockhart, 'Standard of Review in WTO Law', 380.

7

The Role of the Standard of Review and the Importance of Deference in Investor–State Arbitration

*Caroline Henckels**

I. Introduction

Standards of review employed by tribunals in investor–State arbitration are a critical factor in determining whether States may permissibly regulate or take other actions to promote public welfare without being liable to compensate foreign investors. Strict approaches taken by investment tribunals to standards of review have attracted criticism, and although a number of recent cases embrace the concept of deference, tribunals have not yet developed a coherent approach to the concept. This chapter argues that investment tribunals should afford a measure of deference to States in situations of normative or empirical uncertainty, where the characteristics of primary decision-makers make them better placed to have primary responsibility for deciding an issue.

Section II of this chapter discusses the concepts of the standard of review and deference in the context of international adjudication. Section III provides a brief overview of the approaches taken by investment tribunals to the concept of deference. Arguing that the two principal rationales for deference in international adjudication are (a) regulatory autonomy and proximity and (b) relative institutional competence and expertise, Section IV explores the treatment of these forms of deference by investment tribunals in comparative perspective. Section V reflects on the emerging discourse of deference in investor–State arbitration, noting the lack of analytical transparency in the decided cases. The chapter concludes that the adoption by tribunals of a principled and appropriately deferential approach to the standard of review would achieve a more balanced relationship between the protection of foreign investment and state autonomy to act in the public interest. However, it is desirable that tribunals be more explicit in their reasoning, setting out the rationale for their approach.

* This is a revised version of an article published in 4 *JIDS* 197 (2013).

II. The Standard of Review in Context

Standards of review—defined for the purpose of this chapter as the degree of scrutiny of the decision of a primary decision-maker employed by an adjudicator—reflect the horizontal allocation of authority between a legal system's primary decision-makers and its adjudicators.[1] In international and supranational legal systems, standards of review also influence the vertical relationship between adjudicators and States.[2] Standards of review in this context aim to strike an appropriate balance between the need for compliance with international obligations and national autonomy.[3] Overly lenient review may undermine the negotiated balance of rights and obligations in international treaties.[4] Yet, international regimes also depend on a degree of deference in structuring relationships between States and international courts and tribunals.[5] The application of strict standards of review may give rise to compliance issues, reform of relevant legal instruments to curtail adjudicative discretion, withdrawal of States from the jurisdiction of the court or tribunal, and failure to comply with court or tribunal decisions—all of which are situations that have arisen in international investment law.

In domestic legal systems, perceived judicial overreach or 'wrong' decisions may be remedied on appeal or by the passage of legislation to mandate how future cases should be dealt with.[6] However, there is no appellate mechanism in international investment law to discipline first-instance decisions and there are extremely limited opportunities for the review of awards. Nor do most investment treaties provide a procedure that can be triggered in response to tribunal decisions, such as the North American Free Trade Agreement (NAFTA) Commission through which the NAFTA parties can issue authoritative interpretations of relevant investment rules.[7] These institutional features all mean that the manner in which tribunals approach the question of State liability is crucial, and in particular, how

[1] Eg Matthias Oesch, *Standards of Review in WTO Dispute Resolution* (Oxford: Oxford University Press, 2004) 23; Jan Bohanes and Nicholas Lockhart, 'Standard of Review in WTO Law' in Daniel Bethlehem et al (eds), *The Oxford Handbook of International Trade Law* (Oxford: Oxford University Press, 2009) 378, 379.

[2] Eg Steven P. Croley and John H. Jackson, 'WTO Dispute Procedures, Standard of Review, and Deference to National Governments', 90 *AJIL* 193 (1996), 194–5, 197; Oesch, *Standards of Review*, 23, 28; Bohanes and Lockhart, 'Standard of Review', 381; Daniel Lovric, *Deference to the Legislature in WTO Challenges to Legislation* (Alphen aan den Rijn: Kluwer, 2010) 60; Anthea Roberts, 'The Next Battleground: Standards of Review in Investor–State Arbitration' in Albert J. Van Den Berg (ed), *Arbitration—The Next Fifty Years* (Alphen aan den Rijn: Kluwer, 2012) 170, 175–6, 178.

[3] Eg Bohanes and Lockhart, 'Standard of Review', 381.

[4] Tsai-fang Chen, 'The Standard of Review and the Roles of ICSID Arbitral Tribunals in Investor–State Dispute Settlement', 5 *Contemporary Asia Arbitration Journal* 23 (2012), 30; Roberts, 'The Next Battleground', 180.

[5] Stephan W. Schill, 'Deference in Investor–State Arbitration: Re-Conceptualizing the Standard of Review', 3 *JIDS* 577 (2012), 577, 589.

[6] See Benedict Kingsbury and Stephan W. Schill, 'Public Law Concepts to Balance Investors' Rights with State Regulatory Actions in the Public Interest—The Concept of Proportionality' in Stephan W. Schill (ed), *International Investment Law and Comparative Public Law* (Oxford: Oxford University Press, 2010) 75, 102.

[7] Kingsbury and Schill, 'Public Law Concepts', 75, 102

tribunals approach the applicable standard of review. In light of concerns that investment tribunal decisions have had an overly intrusive effect on the regulatory autonomy of States, employing standards of review that reflect an appropriate allocation of power between tribunals and States may be one way, within the current system of investor–State arbitration, for the law to achieve an appropriate balance between public and private interests.[8]

Standards of review are dependent on a number of factors, including stipulation[9] or guidance[10] in the treaty text, the extent of interference with the legal regime's primary norm,[11] the nature of the primary norm[12] and degree of specificity with which it is expressed,[13] the degree of international harmonization or consensus with respect to the subject matter of the measure,[14] the level of dependence the court or tribunal has on other organs in the legal system and whether it desires to manifest respect for the primary decision-maker for strategic reasons,[15] and the characteristics of and ambit of discretion enjoyed by primary decision-makers. This latter category is the concept of deference.

Deference involves an adjudicator exercising restraint in adjudication where there is uncertainty as to what the 'right' conclusion to an issue should be (whether empirically or normatively).[16] The concept of deference can, therefore, be divided into the categories of normative deference and empirical deference.[17] Normative deference relates to the uncertainties that arise where decision-making is based on value judgements, whereas empirical deference relates to situations of uncertainty

[8] See William Burke-White and Andreas von Staden, 'Private Litigation in a Public Law Sphere: The Standard of Review in Investor–State Arbitrations', 35 *Yale Journal of International Law* 283 (2010), 285–6; Schill, 'Deference', 579.

[9] See eg Article 17(6)(i) Anti-Dumping Agreement.

[10] See eg Article 22(2)(b) Australia–United States Free Trade Agreement; Article 144 TFEU.

[11] See eg Case C-131/93 *Commission v Germany (Crayfish)* [1994] ECR I-3303, paras 21–5; *Dickson v the United Kingdom* [GC], (app. no. 44362/04), ECtHR 2007, para 78; Appellate Body Report, *Korea—Measures Affecting Imports of Fresh, Chilled and Frozen Beef*, WT/DS161/AB/R, WT/DS169/AB/R, 10 January 2001, para 163; Julian Rivers, 'Proportionality and Variable Intensity of Review', 65 *CLJ* 174 (2006), 205–6; Janneke Gerards, 'Pluralism, Deference and the Margin of Appreciation Doctrine', 17 *ELJ* 80 (2011), 112.

[12] For example, the ECtHR applies a less strict standard of review to interferences with property rights than the right to privacy. The CJEU also takes a more stringent approach to review of Member State measures impeding free movement than in relation to EU measures ostensibly taken in furtherance of the aims of the TFEU.

[13] Yuval Shany, 'Toward a General Margin of Appreciation Doctrine in International Law?', 16 *EJIL* 907 (2005), 910, 914. See also Federico Ortino, 'The Investment Treaty System as Judicial Review', 24 *American Review of International Arbitration* 437 (2013), 463–4, comparing the (broad) obligation to afford fair and equitable treatment with the (specific) prohibition on coercion and harassment in international investment law.

[14] See eg Shany, 'Margin of Appreciation'; Benn McGrady, *Trade and Public Health: The WTO, Tobacco, Alcohol and Diet* (Cambridge: Cambridge University Press, 2010) 147, 182.

[15] Andrew T. Guzman, 'International Tribunals: A Rational Choice Analysis', 157 *University of Pennsylvania Law Review* 171 (2008), 184; Aileen Kavanagh, *Constitutional Review under the UK Human Rights Act* (Cambridge: Cambridge University Press, 2009) 197.

[16] Rivers, 'Variable Intensity', 199, 203; Kavanagh, *Constitutional Review*, 169–70; Alan D.P. Brady, *Proportionality and Deference under the UK Human Rights Act: An Institutionally Sensitive Approach* (Cambridge: Cambridge University Press, 2012) 68, 107.

[17] Robert Alexy, *A Theory of Constitutional Rights* (Oxford: Oxford University Press, 2002) 388–425.

in relation to knowledge and factual findings.[18] Adjudicators will determine whether deference is appropriate in the circumstances by evaluating the extent of their role and capabilities vis-à-vis the primary decision-maker and the desirability of interfering with a particular decision without regard to the merits of possible substantive outcomes.[19]

If a court or tribunal determines that a measure of deference is appropriate, it will attach weight to the reasons given by a primary decision-maker for its decision and will refrain from making or from acting on the adjudicator's own assessment of the matter.[20] The degree of deference employed by a court or tribunal will fall on a continuum bounded by total deference to the primary decision-maker at one end, and substitutionary (*de novo*) review at the other.[21] The degree of deference an adjudicator affords will range from treating the views of the primary decision-maker in relation to a matter as persuasive (meaning that an adjudicator assesses the issue but takes account of the decision-maker's views) to treating those views as conclusive (where an adjudicator declines to assess the issue, relying solely on the assessment of the decision-maker).[22] For example, a court or tribunal might require only that certain procedures be followed, place a low evidential burden on the government in relation to an issue for determination, assess whether the authorities' conclusions were reasonable, accord substantial weight to the views of authorities, or require rigorous justification of certain matters.[23]

III. Approaches to Deference in Investor–State Arbitration: A Mixed Bag

Investment treaties typically do not address the relationship between the standards of investment protection (such as indirect expropriation, fair and equitable treatment and national treatment) and the continuing powers of States to regulate

[18] See Brady, *Proportionality and Deference*, 68; Lukasz Gruszczynski and Valentina Vadi, Chapter 9 of this volume, Section IV.

[19] See Croley and Jackson, 'WTO Dispute Procedures', 194–5; Oesch, *Standards of Review*, 24; Shany, 'Margin of Appreciation', 913; Rivers, 'Variable Intensity', 204; Aileen Kavanagh, 'Deference or Defiance? The Limits of the Judicial Role in Constitutional Adjudication' in Grant Huscroft (ed), *Expounding the Constitution: Essays in Constitutional Theory* (Cambridge: Cambridge University Press, 2008) 184, 190; William W. Burke-White and Andreas von Staden, 'Investment Protection in Extraordinary Times: The Interpretation and Application of Non-Precluded Measures Provisions in Bilateral Investment Treaties', 48 *Virginia Journal of International Law* 307 (2008), 370–1; Kavanagh, *Constitutional Review*, 240.

[20] Mark Elliott, 'Proportionality and Deference: The Importance of a Structured Approach' in Christopher Forsyth et al (eds), *Effective Judicial Review: A Cornerstone of Good Governance* (Oxford: Oxford University Press, 2010) 264, 268.

[21] Oesch, *Standards of Review*, 14–15; Kavanagh, 'Deference or Defiance?', 184–6, 190. Total deference differs from non-justiciability: non-justiciability is a substantive bar on adjudication: see Andrew Legg, *The Margin of Appreciation in International Human Rights Law: Deference and Proportionality* (Oxford: Oxford University Press, 2012) 26–7.

[22] Kavanagh, *Constitutional Review*, 172–3; Bohanes and Lockhart, 'Standard of Review', 383.

[23] See Rivers, 'Variable Intensity', 177–82, 203; Mads Andenas and Stefan Zleptnig, 'Proportionality: WTO Law in Comparative Perspective', 42 *Texas International Law Journal* 371 (2006), 392–3; Elliott, 'Proportionality and Deference', 269, 282–4.

and take other actions in the interest of their populations. Nor, like most other treaties, do they generally stipulate the applicable standard of review,[24] meaning that tribunals must rely on their inherent powers in the determination of the appropriate standard of review to the extent that the treaty text does not shed light on the matter.[25] Investment tribunals have affirmed the existence of inherent powers, although not specifically in relation to standards of review.[26] To date, no investment tribunal has set out a coherent framework for determining the appropriate standard of review to apply with respect to disputes involving the exercise of public power by States,[27] although a number of tribunals have referred to the desirability of deference in their decision-making and/or have adopted a deferential approach.

A. NAFTA tribunal decisions

The clearest examples of a deferential approach have occurred in the NAFTA context, where many tribunals have approached the standard of review with the perspective of a need for institutional balance between investment protection and regulatory autonomy. NAFTA tribunals and tribunal members issuing separate opinions have referred on many occasions to the desirability of deference, policy space and regulatory autonomy, and have stated that their role was not to second-guess the policy decisions of governments.[28] For example, the *S.D. Myers* tribunal referred to 'the high measure of deference that international law generally extends to the right of domestic authorities to regulate matters within their own borders', a perspective that influenced its approach to determining the legitimacy of the government's objective and the methodology it adopted in reviewing the necessity of the measure.[29] The *Glamis* tribunal noted the expertise of authorities

[24] But see eg Article 18(2) US Model BIT 2012, which provides a self-judging non-precluded measures clause.

[25] See Chester Brown, 'The Inherent Powers of International Courts and Tribunals', 76 *BYIL* 195 (2005), 225–7; Shany, 'Margin of Appreciation', 911; Article 44 ICSID Convention: '[if] any question of procedure arises which is not covered by this Section or the Arbitration Rules or any rules agreed by the parties, the Tribunal shall decide the question'; Appellate Body Report, *EC Measures Concerning Meat and Meat Products (EC–Hormones)*, WT/DS26/AB/R, WT/DS48/AB/R, 13 February 1998, paras 114–17.

[26] See eg *Libananco Holdings Co. Limited v Republic of Turkey*, ICSID Case No. ARB/06/8, Award, 2 September 2011, para 78.

[27] See Schill, 'Deference', 579–80: investment tribunals invoke the concept of deference 'as a mantra rather than…as part of a theoretical framework structuring the power relations between states and tribunals.'

[28] *S.D. Myers v Government of Canada*, UNCITRAL, Partial Award, 13 November 2000, para 263 and Separate Opinion of Arbitrator Schwartz, para 233; *Pope & Talbot Inc. v The Government of Canada*, UNCITRAL (NAFTA), Interim Award, 26 June, 2000; Award on Merits, 10 April 2001, paras 123, 128, 155; *International Thunderbird Gaming Corporation v The United Mexican States*, UNCITRAL (NAFTA), Award, 26 January 2006, para 127; *United Parcel Service of America Inc. v Government of Canada*, UNCITRAL (NAFTA), Award, 24 May 2007, Separate Statement of Arbitrator Cass, paras 119–21, 125 (although not supporting a wholly deferential approach); *Glamis Gold, Ltd v United States of America*, UNCITRAL (NAFTA), Award, 8 June 2009, paras 625, 779, 803–5.

[29] *S.D. Myers v Canada*, para 263.

in determining the appropriateness of the challenged measure, and referred to the desirability of democratically legitimate decision-makers having primary responsibility for balancing the interests of the investor, the environment and communities affected by mining projects.[30]

There are few NAFTA cases in which it could be argued that a tribunal adopted an excessively strict approach to the standard of review. One explanation for these explicit acknowledgements of the desirability of deference by NAFTA tribunals relates to the actions taken by the NAFTA parties in response to the unanticipated wave of claims against the US in the first few years following NAFTA's inception.[31] Decisions such as *Metalclad*, which took an expansive approach to the obligation of fair and equitable treatment, influenced the parties to take steps to clarify the extent of the obligation by issuing a binding Note of Interpretation, stating that fair and equitable treatment in the context of NAFTA did not require treatment over and above that required by the customary international law minimum standard of treatment of aliens.[32] The customary international law standard proscribes only treatment that is egregious or in bad faith, thereby providing greater scope for States to act without risking liability. Although this clarification concerns the normative content of fair and equitable treatment rather than deference based on the characteristics of decision-makers, there is some overlap between these matters: the narrower the interpretation of fair and equitable treatment, the greater the potential for more deferential review of governmental conduct that falls short of the customary international law threshold for breach.[33]

NAFTA tribunals also appear to be motivated by strategic concerns in relation to their approach to the applicable standard of review, in terms of maintaining the institution of NAFTA as an instrument of economic integration. This echoes the approaches of other international and domestic courts and tribunals.[34] In *Glamis*, the tribunal stressed that maintaining the integrity of NAFTA's investment chapter required it to decide the case with an awareness of the systemic implications of its decision, noting the NAFTA parties' 'indefinite commitment to the deepening of their economic relations' and remarking that 'the long-term maintenance of this commitment requires both governmental and public faith in the integrity of the process of arbitration.'[35] There

[30] *Glamis Gold v US*, paras 181, 625, 779, 803–5.

[31] See Gus Van Harten, *Investor–State Arbitration and Public Law* (Oxford: Oxford University Press, 2007) 88, 145–6; Roland Kläger, *'Fair and Equitable Treatment' in International Investment Law* (Cambridge: Cambridge University Press, 2011) 62–70.

[32] *Metalclad Corporation v United Mexican States*, ICSID Case No. ARB(AF)/97/1, Award, 30 August 2000, paras 75–6; NAFTA Commission, *Note of Interpretation of Certain Chapter 11 Provisions*, 31 July 2001.

[33] See Schill, 'Deference', 582: standards of review differ from the content given by adjudicators to substantive treaty obligations that permit greater or lesser autonomy for States, although the two may be closely connected.

[34] See eg George Letsas, *A Theory of Interpretation of the European Convention on Human Rights* (Oxford: Oxford University Press, 2007) 3–4; Kavanagh, 'Deference or Defiance?', 203–4.

[35] *Glamis Gold v US*, para 8.

is also evidence of strategic concerns influencing deference in cases where tribunals have held that it was permissible for governments to pursue initiatives designed to assist the State's economy.[36] In the earlier case of *Loewen,* however, the tribunal referred to the viability of NAFTA in order to justify a decision that is regarded as taking an intrusive approach to review, taking the view that it would be undesirable for a foreign investor to not receive a remedy for injustice.[37]

Although it might be argued that the imperative of maintaining continued support for an institution such as the NAFTA regime is not generally present in investment law given the dominance of bilateral treaties between capital-importing and capital-exporting States, it remains to be seen whether tribunals adjudicating disputes under other regional or plurilateral agreements will adopt a similarly strategic approach to the standard of review. It might, however, be argued that this factor may be a relevant consideration more broadly. Although investment tribunals do not depend on the support of States for their continued existence (governments having given general consent to the arbitration of disputes on signing investment treaties), individual arbitrators are dependent the continued use of their services and are thus subject to their own constraints in terms of not alienating their stakeholders. It is arguable that investment tribunals might increasingly respond to concerns expressed by States in relation to regulatory autonomy—in particular the threat of exit—by adopting a less strict approach to the standard of review.[38]

B. Non-NAFTA tribunal decisions

Outside of the context of NAFTA, the situation is more complex. A number of tribunals have taken strict approaches to the standard of review. Most notably, these decisions include the first tranche of claims against Argentina in relation to emergency measures adopted in response to its 1999–2001 economic crisis,[39] but also in other cases relating to the Argentine crisis[40] and in cases where

[36] *S.D. Myers v Canada*, para 255; *GAMI v Mexico*, paras 46, 52–6, 114; *UPS v Canada*, paras 146, 149; *Archer Daniels Midland Company and Tate & Lyle Ingredients Americas, Inc. v. The United Mexican States*, ICSID Case No. ARB (AF)/04/5, 21 November 2007, paras 44–7, 55.

[37] *Loewen Group, Inc. and Raymond L. Loewen v United States of America*, ICSID Case No. ARB(AF)/98/3, Award, 26 June 2003, para 242. See Van Harten, *Investor–State Arbitration*, 146–7; Jürgen Kurtz, 'Access to Justice, Denial and Justice and International Investment Law: A Reply to Francesco Francioni', 20 *EJIL* 1077 (2009), 1081.

[38] See Anthea Roberts, 'Clash of Paradigms: Actors and Analogies Shaping the Investment Treaty System', 107 *AJIL* 45 (2013), 89.

[39] See *CMS Gas Transmission Company v The Republic of Argentina*, ICSID Case No. ARB/01/08, Decision on Jurisdiction, 17 July 2003; *Enron Corporation and Ponderosa Assets LP v Argentine Republic*, ICSID Case No. ARB/01/3, Award, 22 May 2007; *Sempra Energy International v The Argentine Republic*, ICSID Case No. ARB/02/16, Award, 18 September 2007; *National Grid Plc. v The Argentine Republic*, UNCITRAL, Award, 3 November 2008, para 247.

[40] *Suez, Sociedad General de Aguas de Barcelona SA and InterAgua Servicios Integrales del Agua SA v The Argentine Republic*, ICSID Case No. ARB/03/17, Decision on Liability, 30 July 2010, paras 215–28; *Suez, Sociedad General de Aguas de Barcelona SA and Vivendi Universal SA Argentina and AWG v The Argentine Republic*, ICSID Case No. ARB/03/19, Decision on Liability, 30 July 2010, paras 235–48.

tribunals disagreed with authorities as to the legitimacy for the State's reasons for acting.[41] However, several other tribunals have explicitly affirmed the right to regulate and the need to avoid second-guessing government policies (but such expressions of the need for deference are less prevalent outside of the context of NAFTA). For example, the *Total* tribunal stressed the importance of recognizing the right to regulate in determining whether the State had breached fair and equitable treatment in the context of the economic crisis.[42] Other tribunals, such as the *Lemire* and *Continental* tribunals, have referred to the undesirability of substituting their judgment for that of regulators with respect to the question of the suitability or likely effectiveness of the challenged measures vis-à-vis their objectives.[43]

IV. Rationales for Deference in Investor–State Arbitration

A. A multi-factorial approach

Deference is not a concept that is amenable to concretization in terms of a doctrine readily applicable to a given case.[44] The concept is flexible in the sense that adjudicators assess their own capacity to decide an issue and display restraint to the extent that their capacity is limited. Determining whether to afford deference and on what basis requires consideration of whether the qualities of and discretion enjoyed by government actors will make them better qualified to have primary responsibility for deciding or determining an issue.[45] This determination entails the consideration of a number of contextual factors including the nature, processes and institutions of the primary decision-maker.[46] The totality of these factors—which may pull in different directions—are taken into account in determining the appropriate degree of deference.[47]

[41] *Metalclad v Mexico*, paras 48, 90–8; *Technicas Medioambientales Tecmed SA v The United Mexican States*, ICSID Case No. ARB(AF)/00/2, Award, 29 May 2003, paras 154, 157–8, 164, 166, 172–3.

[42] *Total v Argentina*, paras 122–3. However, in relation to its review of other measures, the tribunal arguably took an overly strict approach that did not pay sufficient regard to the situation of empirical uncertainty existing during Argentina's economic crisis (at paras 325–35).

[43] *Joseph Charles Lemire v Ukraine*, ICSID Case No. ARB/06/18, Decision on Jurisdiction and Liability, 14 January 2010, para 283; *Continental v Argentina*, paras 198–9, 233.

[44] See Michael Beloff, 'The Concept of Deference in Public Law', 11 *Judicial Review* 213 (2006), 223; Michael Taggart, 'Proportionality, Deference, *Wednesbury*', 1 *New Zealand Law Review* 423 (2008), 458.

[45] See Croley and Jackson, 'WTO Dispute Procedures', 194–5; Oesch, *Standards of Review*, 24; Shany, 'Margin of Appreciation', 913; Rivers, 'Variable Intensity', 203–4; Kavanagh, 'Deference or Defiance?' 190; Kavanagh, *Constitutional Review*, 240; Burke-White and von Staden, 'Non-Precluded Measures', 370–1.

[46] Gerards, 'Pluralism, Deference', 99.

[47] Oesch, *Standards of Review*, 23; Taggart, 'Proportionality, Deference', 458.

B. The comparative inquiry

Attempting to theorize standards of review in relation to investor–State arbitration must take into account the de facto function of investment tribunals as part of the system of public law governance of the State whose measures are at issue, given that disputes involve aggrieved individuals bringing claims against government agencies in relation to the exercise of public power.[48] Such claims often involve legal issues that would ordinarily be considered to be constitutional or administrative in nature, and raise the issue of the horizontal dimension of the standard of review in terms of the balance of power between different branches of government. Consideration of standards of review must also take account of investment tribunals' role as international adjudicators of treaty-based disputes. It is crucial to recognize this dual function in theorizing methods and standards of review, because tribunals are constrained by the rules of treaty interpretation and are not bound by and are arguably less likely to take into account principles of public law developed in domestic legal systems. Standards of review in the international and supranational context are of particular relevance, as the international dimension adds increased sensitivity to the question of the appropriate standard of review due to adjudicators' lack of embeddedness in the State polity, their competence, legitimacy and accountability.[49]

Viewing investor–State arbitration in this light opens the door for consideration of how other legal systems performing similar functions have dealt with standards of review. Given that the body of decided investment cases does not reveal a clear approach to dealing with these issues, comparative perspectives can assist in formulating an understanding of how investment tribunals could approach the standard of review in their determination of claims involving the exercise of public power by demonstrating what has been done in relation to similar issues in other jurisdictions.[50] The comparative case law discussed in this chapter focuses on the review of national measures by the Court of Justice of the European Union (CJEU), the approach taken by the European Court of Human Rights (ECtHR) in property cases, and the approach adopted by World Trade Organization (WTO) tribunals to measures interfering with liberalized trade. These courts and tribunals all rule on the lawfulness of legislation and other measures affecting private rights and interests (whether held by individuals or more generally, such as

[48] See *International Thunderbird v Mexico*, Separate Opinion of Arbitrator Wälde, para 13; Gus Van Harten and Martin Loughlin, 'Investment Treaty Arbitration as a Species of Global Administrative Law', 17 *EJIL* 121 (2006); Van Harten, *Investor–State Arbitration*; Santiago Montt, *State Liability in Investment Treaty Arbitration: Global Constitutional and Administrative Law and the BIT Generation* (Oxford: Hart, 2009); Stephen W. Schill, 'International Investment Law and Comparative Public Law—An Introduction' in Schill (ed), *International Investment Law*, 3.

[49] Eg Croley and Jackson, 'WTO Dispute Procedures', 194; Oesch, *Standards of Review*, 23, 28, Bohanes and Lockhart, 'Standard of Review', 381; Lovric, *Deference*, 60; Rahim Moloo and Justin Jacinto, 'Standards of Review and Reviewing Standards: Public Interest Regulation in International Investment Law', in *Yearbook of International Investment Law and Policy 2011–2012* (New York: Oxford University Press, 2013) 539, 540.

[50] Montt, *State Liability*, 166; Kingsbury and Schill, 'Public Law', 78–9.

market access) in terms of compliance with the treaty-based obligations of States. In this respect, they perform broadly common functions compared to investment tribunals in relation to the standard of review.

This is not, however, to gloss over institutional and other differences between these regimes as they affect the standard of review. For example, the political context and values that are protected in EU law and under the European Convention on Human Rights (ECHR) may produce a stricter standard of review that may be not appropriate for investor–State arbitration. The EU's institutional goals of positive integration and market building are imperatives that have provided a basis for European judicial activism in relation to national measures, while the CJEU affords greater deference to measures adopted by European institutions.[51] The ECtHR can draw on a relatively closer degree of consensus among ECHR parties with respect to the circumstances in which it is legitimate to limit rights, which might make it more appropriate to engage in strict scrutiny but equally, the ECHR requires applicants for review to exhaust local remedies, indicating that a deference is appropriate because the challenged measure has already been reviewed by another independent body.[52] Some further caveats apply in a more practical sense. Both the CJEU and the ECtHR may be criticized for lacking a coherent framework setting out the factors affecting the intensity of review.[53] In the WTO context, apart from certain areas under the Sanitary and Phytosanitary (SPS) Agreement[54] and in the context of trade remedies,[55] tribunals have not explicitly considered questions of institutional structure in terms of the circumstances in which reliance on the characteristics of primary decision-makers might affect the intensity of review. Nor has the Appellate Body provided substantive guidance to panels with respect to the standard of review they should apply, apart from stating that the standard of review generally applicable in WTO disputes is neither *de novo* review nor 'total deference', in part because panels are poorly suited to engage in substitutionary review.[56]

Despite these caveats, analysis of the case law and associated literature suggests that there are two key reasons why the views of governments may be considered

[51] Eg Paul Craig, 'Judicial Review, Intensity and Deference in EU Law' in David Dyzenhaus (ed), *The Unity of Public Law* (Oxford: Hart Publishing, 2004) 335, 344–5; Catherine Button, *The Power to Protect: Trade, Health and Uncertainty in the WTO* (Oxford: Hart Publishing, 2004), 211–12; Kurtz, 'Adjudging the Exceptional', 367–8.

[52] Schill, 'Deference', 597.

[53] See eg Steven Greer, *The Margin of Appreciation: Interpretation and Discretion under the European Convention on Human Rights* (Strasbourg: Council of Europe, 2000), pp. 5, 8, 32; Gerards, 'Pluralism, Deference', 90–1.

[54] See Appellate Body Report, *US/Canada—Continued Suspension of Obligations in the EC—Hormones Dispute*, WT/DS320/AB/R, WT/DS321/AB/R, 16 October 2008, paras 587–98. See Lukasz Gruszczynski and Valentina Vadi, Chapter 9, Section II of this volume.

[55] See Appellate Body Report, *United States—Measures Affecting Imports of Certain Passenger Vehicle and Light Truck Tyres from China*, WT/DS399/AB/R, 5 October 2011, paras 123–5 (safeguard measures); Article 17.6 Anti-Dumping Agreement (stipulating the applicable standard of review for dumping investigations).

[56] Article 11 DSU. See Appellate Body Report, *EC—Hormones*, para 117. See Claus-Dieter Ehlermann and Nicholas Lockhart, 'Standard of Review in WTO Law', 7 *JIEL* 491 (2004), 495.

to be more reliable than those of adjudicators in situations of normative or empirical uncertainty. These are: the desirability of regulatory autonomy and decision-making by actors that are proximate to or embedded in the national polity, and the practical advantages that inhere in reliance upon decision-makers with institutional competence and expertise. The regulatory autonomy and proximity rationale is relevant in situations of normative uncertainty, whereas the institutional competence and expertise rationale is relevant in situations of empirical uncertainty. Both bases for deference relate, at a broad level, to the legitimacy of an international tribunal having primary decision-making responsibility. However, each rationale relates to different characteristics of primary decision-makers and to different aspects of the decision-making processes of adjudicators. These are discussed in turn.

C. Regulatory autonomy and proximity

1. Overview

States have broad discretion to enact laws and take other actions in furtherance of the public interest. Courts and tribunals exhibiting deference on the basis of regulatory autonomy do so with the understanding that national authorities should be the main determinant of the public interest in situations of normative uncertainty.[57] The concern is that the adversarial process may not in all cases be able to effectively substitute governmental decision-making where that decision-making entails value judgement or political judgement.[58] A related issue is the proximity of the court or tribunal to the national polity: governments may be more competent to discern and evaluate local conditions, as they are usually more closely acquainted with local issues, sensitivities and traditions.[59] The CJEU, the ECtHR and WTO tribunals exhibit deference on this basis, where the circumstances of the case highlight their non-representative nature or give rise to concerns of proximity. Such cases typically involve polycentric issues (involving the consideration and balancing of a number of divergent interests), value judgements, or matters of sensitivity or controversy such as social policy or the acceptable level of risk to health or the environment.[60]

One criticism that might be made of this rationale for deference is that governments can always make a claim to the desirability of regulatory autonomy

See also Michael Ioannidis, Chapter 6, Section III.B in this volume (noting the difficulties inherent in applying Article 11 DSU).

[57] See eg Ali Riza Çoban, *Protection of Property Rights within the European Convention on Human Rights* (London: Ashgate, 2004) 200; Elliott, 'Proportionality and Deference', 276, 281; Brady, *Proportionality and Deference*, 71–2. However, this area might also attract deference on the basis of empirical uncertainty in circumstances where the treaty provision stipulates permissible objectives but there is uncertainty as to whether the pleaded objective comes within the relevant rubric: see Brady, *Proportionality and Deference*, 70, 153–4.

[58] Gerards, 'Pluralism, Deference', 86.

[59] Eg Oesch, *Standards of Review*, 57; Shany, 'Margin of Appreciation', 919; Letsas, *Theory of Interpretation*, 90–1; Gerards, 'Pluralism, Deference', 85, 98, 110; Burke-White and von Staden, 'Private Litigation', 331–3.

[60] Eg Case C-491/06 *Danske Svineproducenter v Justitsministeriet* [2008] ECR I-3339, paras 31, 38, 40; Case C-275/92 *Her Majesty's Customs and Excise v Schindler* [1994] ECR I-1039, paras

or to greater proximity to communities affected by the relevant decision.[61] The non-embedded nature of adjudicators may also be important in assuring the neutrality of the court or tribunal—indeed, this was the impetus for the establishment of investor–State arbitration rather than the use of domestic courts to resolve disputes between foreign investors and States.[62] In this respect, while it might be argued that decisions of governments are always worthy of a certain degree of deference on the basis of the desirability of regulatory autonomy and decision-making by embedded actors (a presumption in favour of a degree of deference for its own sake), only in situations of normative uncertainty will the circumstances attract a greater degree of deference.[63]

In some situations, however, it is desirable that adjudicators apply more stringent scrutiny to the justification for a measure, such as where authorities have been subject to capture by domestic industries.[64] Deference would not seem to be appropriate with respect to State conduct taken with a discriminatory or other impermissible motive. Arguably, there is no situation of normative uncertainty giving rise to the need for deference on the basis of regulatory autonomy and proximity in such situations, because whether government action was taken with (for example) a protectionist motive is generally an issue that can be objectively determined.[65]

2. *The relevance of deference on this basis*

Deference on the basis of regulatory autonomy and proximity is especially relevant to the determination of whether the State's asserted objective serves the public interest. This inquiry in many cases operates as a prerequisite for a finding that the State has acted lawfully. While treaty provisions may set out the legitimate objectives towards which a measure may permissibly be directed, such as in the Treaty on the Functioning of the European Union (TFEU), the ECHR and WTO agreements,[66] few investment treaties stipulate permissible bases for regulation.[67] In the absence of such stipulation in the treaty text, the direct evaluation

60–1; Case C-83/94 *Criminal proceedings against Peter Leifer* [1995] ECR I-3231, para 35; *James and others v the United Kingdom* (app. no. 8793/79), ECtHR 1986, para 46; *Lithgow v the United Kingdom* (app. nos. 9006/80, 9262/81, 9263/81, 9265/81, 9266/81, 9313/81, 9405/81), ECtHR 1986, para 122; *Jahn v Germany* [GC] (app. nos. 46720/99, 72203/01 and 72552/01), ECtHR 2005, para 91; *Handyside v UK* (app. no. 5493/72), ECtHR 1976, para 48; *Wingrove v the United Kingdom* (app. no. 17419/90), ECtHR 1996, para 58; Appellate Body Reports, *EC—Hormones*, paras 124, 187; *Korea—Beef*, para 176; *European Communities—Measures Affecting Asbestos and Asbestos-Containing Products*, WT/DS135/AB/R, 5 April 2001, paras 168, 178; Panel Report, *United States—Measures Affecting the Cross Border Supply of Gambling and Betting Services*, WT/DS285/R, 25 April 2005, para 6.461.

[61] See Schill, 'Deference', 24.

[62] Roberts, 'The Next Battleground', 179.

[63] Kavanagh, 'Deference or Defiance?', 192–193; Kavanagh, *Constitutional Review*, 190–6.

[64] See Gerards, 'Pluralism, Deference', 87–8.

[65] Andreas von Staden, 'Deference or No Deference, That Is the Question: Legitimacy and Standards of Review in Investor–State Arbitration', 2 *Investment Treaty News* 3 (2012), 4.

[66] See eg TFEU, Article 36; ECHR, Article 8; General Agreement on Tariffs and Trade (GATT), Article XX.

[67] But see eg defining measures deemed not to be indirectly expropriatory by reference to permissible regulatory objectives: Australia–US FTA (2004) Annex 11-B, Article 4; Common Market

of the legitimacy and/or importance of a particular regulatory objective may be regarded as transgressing the role of national decision-makers.[68] Provided that a measure does not pursue a discriminatory, protectionist or otherwise impermissible objective, this rationale for deference suggests that investment tribunals should display restraint and refrain from second-guessing the importance of the objective or the desired level of protection or achievement of it.[69] Tribunals may hold different opinions to States as to the desirability of enacting regulations or taking other actions in a particular policy area or as to the role of the State, but making findings as to the legitimacy of the State's regulatory objective on the basis of such normative disagreement risks significant incursions into State autonomy.

The regulatory autonomy and proximity rationale for deference is also relevant to the question of whether a measure reflects a fair balance (proportionality) between the interests of foreign investors and States, or whether a measure is 'reasonable'.[70] Tribunals have increasingly referred to considerations of proportionality[71] and reasonableness[72] in determining State liability. Regulatory autonomy-based considerations (including the issue of proximity to affected communities) are relevant to this assessment, as the question of proportionality or reasonableness will, as a value judgement, legitimately be the source of disagreement, risking highly subjective decision-making that is influenced by adjudicators' own political, ideological and economic beliefs and assumptions.[73] This may be of particular concern where the determination of proportionality or reasonableness is made by international or supranational adjudicators that are not embedded within the local community—a factor that national judges can rely on to bolster their adjudicative legitimacy.[74] An argument can be made that

for Eastern and Southern Africa, *Investment Agreement for the COMESA Common Investment Area* (2007) Article 20(8). Non-precluded measures clauses also stipulate relevant objectives that a measure may permissibly be directed to: see eg Canada–Peru BIT, Article 10(c) (2007); China–New Zealand FTA, Article 200 (2008).

[68] See eg Miguel Poiares Maduro, *We, the Court: The European Court of Justice and the European Economic Constitution* (Oxford: Hart Publishing, 1998) 59; Çoban, *Property Rights*, 199.

[69] See Van Harten, *Investor–State Arbitration*, 144–5.

[70] See Caroline Henckels, 'Indirect Expropriation and the Right to Regulate: Revisiting Proportionality Analysis and the Standard of Review in Investor–State Arbitration', 15 *JIEL* 223 (2012), 250–4.

[71] See eg *Tecmed v Mexico*, para 122; *Saluka v Czech Republic*, paras 304–7; *Glamis Gold v US*, paras 625, 803–4; *Total v US*, paras 123, 162, 164, 197, 301–2, 309, 332, 429.

[72] See eg *Parkerings-Compagniet AS v Republic of Lithuania*, ICSID Case No. ARB/05/8, Award, 11 September 2007, para 332; *Continental v Argentina*, para 254; *Merrill & Ring Forestry LP v The Government of Canada*, UNCITRAL (NAFTA), Award, 31 March 2010, para 213; *Impregilo SpA v Argentine Republic*, ICSID Case No. ARB/07/17, Award, 21 June 2011, para 291.

[73] Eg Neumann and Türk, 'Necessity Revisited', 231–3; Arwel Davies, 'Interpreting the Chapeau of GATT Article XX in Light of the "New" Approach in *Brazil—Tyres*', 3 *JWT* 507 (2009), 525; Brady, *Proportionality and Deference*, 21; Henckels, 'Indirect Expropriation', 250 (with further references).

[74] Eg Greer, *Margin of Appreciation*, 414; Gabrielle Marceau and Joel P. Trachtman, 'A Map of the World Trade Organization Law of Domestic Regulation of Goods' in George A. Bermann and Petros C. Mavroidis (eds), *Trade and Human Health and Safety* (New York: Cambridge University Press, 2006) 9, 49.

in the context of international adjudication, governments should bear primary responsibility for balancing the interests of stakeholders in the course of governance, particularly where a measure has been adopted following wide public participation or in response to public concerns.[75] In many cases, it will be more appropriate for national decision-makers to make this assessment, or for tribunals to attach significant weight to their views.[76]

3. *International investment cases*

Several tribunals have referred to this rationale in affording a measure of deference to a State.[77] For example, the *Lemire* tribunal referred to Ukraine's 'inherent right to regulate its affairs and adopt laws in order to protect the common good of its people, as defined by its Parliament and Government'.[78] The tribunal affirmed that a high degree of deference was due 'in cases when the purpose of [the challenged measure] affects deeply felt cultural or linguistic traits of the community.'[79] The *Continental* tribunal stated that it was 'not its mandate to . . . censure Argentina's sovereign choices as an independent state' or to 'make any political or economic judgment on Argentina's policies and of the measures adopted to pursue them'.[80] The tribunal also referred to ECtHR jurisprudence in relation to the idea that proximate decision-makers were better placed to determine what was in the State's interest, 'because of their direct knowledge of their society and of its needs.'[81] The *Glamis* tribunal indicated that it would not substitute its own view for the question of whether the challenged measures (which included tightened regulatory controls on mining sites to protect the landscape and cultural heritage) were adopted in the public interest, stating that the relevant test was whether there was a 'manifest lack of reasons for the legislation'.[82] The tribunal held that it would respect the legislature's attempt to achieve an appropriate balance of interests, noting that 'governments must compromise between the interests of competing parties and, if they were bound to please every constituent . . . with each piece of legislation, they would be bound and useless.'[83] Further, the *Paushok* tribunal stated that 'the fact that a democratically elected legislature has passed legislation that may be considered

[75] See eg Gerards, 'Pluralism, Deference', 86; Legg, *Margin of Appreciation*, 69.

[76] See eg Donald H. Regan, 'The Meaning of "Necessary" in GATT Article XX and GATS Article XIV: The Myth of Cost–Benefit Balancing' 6 *WTR* 347 (2007), 349; Elliott, 'Proportionality and Deference', 264, 271, 284; Tor-Inge Harbo, 'The Function of the Proportionality Principle in EU Law', 16 *ELJ* 158 (2010) 165; Jud Matthews and Alec Stone Sweet, 'All Things in Proportion? American Rights Review and the Problem of Balancing', 60 *Emory Law Journal* 101 (2011), 114.

[77] See also, discussing deference in this area, Erlend Leonhardsen, Chapter 8, Section IV.C in this volume.

[78] *Lemire v Ukraine*, para 505.

[79] *Lemire v Ukraine*, para 505.

[80] *Continental v Argentina*, paras 198–9, 233.

[81] *Continental v Argentina*, para 181, citing *Jahn v Germany*.

[82] *Glamis Gold v US*, paras 803, 805.

[83] See *Glamis Gold v US*, paras 625, 803–5.

as ill-conceived, counter-productive and excessively burdensome' would not necessarily entail a breach of the treaty.[84]

However, this approach is not uniform. For example, in both the *Tecmed* and *Metalclad* cases, authorities had relied from previous representations that they would grant permits for the construction or operation of hazardous waste facilities. Both tribunals held that the authorities had acted for impermissible political purposes in responding to civil society concerns, which included community opposition to the locations of the facilities and to their environmental impacts.[85] The *Tecmed* decision is notable for the tribunal's statement that it would afford 'due deference' to the State in defining and implementing its public policies and that it was 'undisputable' that States could exercise their 'sovereign powers' without liability.[86] However, the tribunal did not appear to actually consider why it would have been appropriate to afford deference in the circumstances. This strict approach affected its conclusion as to the proportionality of Mexico's actions: the tribunal found that the authorities' objective was insufficiently important to outweigh the impact on the investor's interests.[87] In the context of the Argentine economic crisis, the *CMS, Enron* and *Sempra* tribunals took a strict approach to the question of whether the situation was of sufficient severity to affect Argentina's 'essential security interests' (a prerequisite for successful invocation of the treaty's emergency measures clause).[88] Although more recent tribunals reviewing these measures have distanced themselves from this position and have adopted a more institutionally sensitive approach that echoes the approaches of other courts and tribunals in this respect,[89] these early decisions demonstrate the crucial connection between the applicable standard of review and State liability for measures adopted in the public interest. The approaches of these tribunals, in substituting their views for the importance of the challenged measures' objective, the existence of a crisis situation or appropriate balance between public and private interests, is unsatisfactory from the perspective of the need for international investment law to provide sufficient policy space for States.

Nevertheless, as noted above, in some circumstances the question of whether the State was pursuing the public interest is not a question that attracts deference because no situation of normative uncertainty arises. In this respect, it is arguable that at least some tribunals have been overly deferential. The *GAMI* tribunal held that Mexico's actions in nationalizing loss-producing sugar mills was plausibly connected with its avowed objective of ensuring the solvency of the industry,

[84] *Sergei Paushok, CJSC Golden East Company and CJSC Vostokneftegaz Company v The Government of Mongolia*, Award on Jurisdiction and Liability, UNCITRAL, 28 April 2011, para 299.

[85] *Metalclad v Mexico*, paras 86, 92, 109; *Tecmed v Mexico*, paras 126–7; cf *Parkerings v Lithuania*, paras 392, 396.

[86] *Tecmed v Mexico*, para 122; Henckels, 'Indirect Expropriation', 232–3.

[87] *Tecmed v Mexico*, paras 133–49.

[88] *CMS v Argentina*, paras 322, 355; *Enron v Argentina*, paras 306–7; *Sempra v Argentina*, paras 348–9.

[89] See *LG&E v Argentina*, para 195; *Continental v Argentina*, paras 180–1, 187; *Total v Argentina*, para 197. See also *El Paso v Argentina*, para 402; *Asian Agricultural Products Ltd. v Republic of Sri Lanka*, ICSID Case No. ARB/87/3, Dissenting Opinion of Arbitrator Asante, 15 June 1990, para 74.

but did not probe the relationship between the measure and its objective any further.[90] More searching scrutiny may have uncovered protectionist intentions, given that the nationalizations took place in the context of a longstanding dispute between the US and Mexico regarding market access for Mexican sugar and US imports of high-fructose corn syrup into the Mexican market.[91] Similarly, it is arguable that the *UPS* tribunal did not sufficiently scrutinize the connection between a measure requiring Canadian periodicals to be delivered by the public postal service rather than by courier companies. The tribunal accepted Canada's argument that the measure was necessary to ensure nationwide delivery of Canadian periodicals in order to strengthen cultural identity, but did not appear to fully examine whether there were real impediments to the investor providing the service.[92]

D. Relative institutional competence and expertise

1. *Overview*

The other key rationale for deference is the institutional competence and expertise of the primary decision-maker relative to the adjudicator.[93] Deference, in this respect, is a practical response to situations of empirical uncertainty.[94] Institutional features or greater expertise may render national authorities better placed to have primary responsibility for making certain decisions and determinations. For example, governments will be better placed to perform tasks such as gathering and evaluating complex information (including in relation to risk or harm), monitoring evolving situations, engaging in consultation and investigating alternative courses of action, and may have greater expertise in relation to the subject matter of the measure.[95] Courts and tribunals (both domestic and international) are often constrained by time, resource, procedural and evidentiary limitations, which may inhibit a thorough examination of all relevant material.[96] Further, courts and tribunals take decisions only in relation to the narrow matter at issue, and through the lens of legal

[90] *Gami Investments, Inc. v The Government of the United Mexican States*, UNCITRAL (NAFTA), Final Award, 15 November 2004, para 114.

[91] Jürgen Kurtz, 'The Merits and Limits of Comparativism: National Treatment in International Investment Law and the WTO' in Schill (ed), *International Investment Law*, 275–6. See WTO Panel Report, *Mexico–Anti-Dumping Investigation of High-Fructose Corn Syrup from the US*, WT/DS132/R, 24 February 2000, as modified by the Appellate Body Report, WT/DS397/AB/R; NAFTA Panel Report, *Imports of High-Fructose Corn Syrup Originating in the US (Dumping)*, MEX-USA-98-1904-01, 15 April 2002; Appellate Body Report, *Mexico—Tax Measures on Soft Drinks and Other Beverages*, WT/DS308/AB/R, 24 March 2006.

[92] See *UPS v Canada*, paras 173–81. See the criticism levelled at the majority decision in the Separate Statement of Arbitrator Cass, paras 131–3; Kurtz, 'National Treatment', 276.

[93] See eg Kavanagh, *Constitutional Review*, 182–90; Lovric, *Deference*, 129–30.

[94] Brady, *Proportionality and Deference*, 114.

[95] Eg Shany, 'Margin of Appreciation', 918–19; Rivers, 'Variable Intensity', 204; Guzman, 'International Tribunals', 63–4; Lovric, *Deference*, 69; Gerards, 'Pluralism, Deference', 98; Gregory Shaffer and Joel Trachtman, 'Interpretation and Institutional Choice in the WTO', 52 *Virginia Journal of International Law* 103 (2011), 148–9.

[96] See, generally, Zleptnig, 'Standard of Review', 12; Shany, 'Margin of Appreciation', 918–19; Gerards, 'Pluralism, Deference', 90, 111.

norms.[97] If a government has greater expertise in relation to the type of issue or more resources at its disposal to decide the issue, there will be reason to believe that the authorities are more likely to reach the 'correct' answer (for example, in relation to economic or scientific matters) than the court or tribunal.[98] The CJEU and ECtHR generally exhibit deference on this basis,[99] and in some cases WTO tribunals have referred to their inferior expertise in fact-finding compared to governments[100] or have been deferential in this respect.[101]

Arguably, the related rationales for deference of expertise and institutional competence are engaged in adjudication in slightly different circumstances. Where a court or tribunal affords deference to a primary decision-maker on the basis of expertise, it does so due to the reliability of the assessment made by the primary decision-maker.[102] This suggests that an adjudicator should only be deferential where the authorities can demonstrate that they have the requisite expertise and that this expertise has been relied upon in making the decision, rather affording deference on the basis that a government agency has responsibility for a particular area of government policy.[103] It is arguable, however, that the institutional competence of governments can be presumed and need not be established before a court or tribunal, on the basis that in situations of uncertainty, an adjudicator should afford a measure of deference if the institutional characteristics of the primary decision-maker suggest that it will be more likely to be correct in relation to the issue.[104]

2. *The relevance of deference on this basis*

Deference on the basis of relative competence and expertise may be relevant to the question of whether a measure is likely to be effective at achieving its objective.[105] Deference reflects that this assessment will turn on a case's specific facts

[97] Shany, 'Margin of Appreciation', 918–19.

[98] However, courts and tribunals may instead take steps to inform themselves by relying on expert evidence, appointing or consulting experts, or through *amici curiae*: eg Jorge E. Viñuales, 'Foreign Investment and the Environment in International Law: An Ambiguous Relationship', 80 *BYIL* 244 (2009), 278–9; Elliott, 'Proportionality and Deference', 274. Investment tribunals have relied on *amicus* briefs in their decision-making: see eg *Methanex Corporation v United States of America*, UNCITRAL (NAFTA), Award, 3 August 2005, Part IV, Chapter B, para 13; *Biwater Gauff v Tanzania*, para 392.

[99] Eg *Broniowski v Poland* [GC] (app. no. 31443/96), ECtHR 2004, paras 149, 162, 182; *Fredin v Sweden (No. 1)* (app. no. 12033/86), ECtHR 1991, para 48; Gráinne de Búrca, 'The Principle of Proportionality and its Application in EC Law', 13 *Yearbook of European Law* 105 (1993), 147; Gerards, 'Pluralism, Deference', 85. See also (discussing the CJEU's approach) Patrycja Dąbrowska-Kłosińska, Chapter 11 in this volume.

[100] Eg Appellate Body Report, *EC—Hormones*, para 177.

[101] Eg Appellate Body Report, *Brazil—Measures Affecting Imports of Retreaded Tyres*, WT/DS332/AB/R, 17 December 2007 paras 150–1. See Lukasz Gruszczynski and Valentina Vadi, Chapter 9, Section II in this volume.

[102] Brady, *Proportionality and Deference*, 114.

[103] Kavanagh, 'Deference or Defiance?', 201–3.

[104] Jeff King, 'Institutional Approaches to Judicial Restraint', 28 *OJLS* 409 (2008), 411–14, 425–6; cf Brady, *Proportionality and Deference*, 114–15.

[105] See eg Aharon Barak, *Proportionality: Constitutional Rights and Their Limitations* (Cambridge: Cambridge University Press, 2012), 308–9; Brady, *Proportionality and Deference*, 20–1.

and local context, and acknowledges the uncertainties inherent in regulation.[106] Competence and expertise may also be relevant to the question of whether a State's actions are necessary in the sense of whether alternative measures impacting less on the protected right or interest would equally achieve the government's objective.[107] Determining whether a State could have acted differently involves a comparison of the measure and its alternatives to determine which option impacts the least on the right or interest at issue.[108] National authorities will frequently have more complete information as to the various trade-offs made in arriving at a measure and the true costs of alternative measures, and may have special expertise in the relevant policy area or greater capacity to apprehend the social implications of regulatory options. In situations of uncertainty, such as where there is legitimate disagreement among experts or whether relevant information is difficult to obtain or interpret, it is appropriate that adjudicators exercise restraint.[109]

3. *International investment cases*

Several tribunals have granted a measure of deference to States on the basis of relative institutional competence and expertise, particularly in relation to the question of the appropriateness of measures to achieve their objectives.[110] The *Methanex* and *Chemtura* tribunals explicitly relied on the expertise of primary decision-makers in relation to their review of science-based measures. The *Chemtura* tribunal noted, in relation to authorities' assessment of the harmful nature of a pesticide on which a product ban was based, that it was not appropriate for a tribunal 'to judge the correctness or adequacy of the scientific results' or 'second-guess the correctness of the science-based decision-making of highly specialized national regulatory agencies'.[111] The *Methanex* tribunal, reviewing the scientific evidence that formed the basis for a ban on a gasoline additive, held that the scientific report relied on by authorities reflected a 'serious, objective and scientific approach to a complex problem' and noted that the report was subjected 'to public hearings, testimony and peer-review'.[112] The *Glamis* tribunal cautioned that it was not its role to 'supplant its own judgment of underlying factual material…for that of a qualified domestic agency' nor 'become archaeologists or ethnographers' in determining the appropriateness of administrative decisions.[113] The tribunal

[106] See eg Barak, *Constitutional Rights*, 308–9.

[107] See Andrew D. Mitchell and Caroline Henckels, 'Variations on a Theme: Comparing the Concept of "Necessity" in International Investment Law and WTO Law', 14 *Chicago Journal of International Law* 287 (2013).

[108] See eg de Búrca, 'Proportionality', 108, 111; Elliott, 'Proportionality and Deference', 270–1, 274, 282.

[109] See Burke-White and von Staden, 'Private Litigation', 30.

[110] See also Erlend Leonhardsen, Chapter 8, Section IV.A in this volume.

[111] *Chemtura Corporation v Government of Canada*, UNCITRAL (NAFTA), Award, 2 August 2010, paras 134, 153.

[112] *Methanex v US*, Part III, Chapter A, paras 101–2.

[113] *Glamis Gold v US*, para 779.

referred to the authorities' 'sufficient good faith belief that there was a reasonable connection between the harm and the proposed remedy', finding the measure to be 'reasonably drafted to address its objectives' and 'rationally related to its stated purpose.'[114] This approach reflected the relative strengths of authorities and gave weight to their assessment of relevant matters. Further, the *Lemire* tribunal remarked that a State would not violate its obligations towards an investor merely because authorities made 'a decision which is different from the one the arbitrators would have made if they were the regulators', noting that 'arbitrators are not superior regulators' and that 'they do not substitute their judgment for that of national bodies applying national laws'.[115]

In the specific context of Argentina's economic crisis, some tribunals and tribunal members (*LG&E, Continental* and *Total* decisions and the Separate Opinions of Arbitrator Nikken in *AWG* and *InterAgua*) indicated that they would refrain from second-guessing the actions of the authorities, demonstrating awareness of tribunals' competence to evaluate the feasibility and effectiveness of policy options and the desirability of a less strict approach to the standard of review in the context of governmental decision-making in a time of significant empirical uncertainty.[116] In particular, the *Continental* tribunal stated, in its review of the necessity of Argentina's emergency measures, that it would not 'go into the merits in detail and to substitute its own judgment to that of the national authorities' in relation to appropriateness of the currency conversion rate adopted by authorities during the crisis, noting that 'a certain deference' and 'a margin of discretion and appreciation' was appropriate.[117] But in contrast, the earlier *CMS, Enron* and *Sempra* tribunals all approached this question with a strict standard of review, holding that a range of other measures impacting less on foreign investors were theoretically available to Argentina to deal with the crisis.[118] It is difficult to imagine how Argentina could have escaped liability according to this approach, given the panoply of potential measures available to a State to deal with an economic crisis and the disagreement among experts as to the best way to address it.[119] The *InterAgua* and *AWG* tribunals took a similarly strict approach to review in the context of the Argentine crisis. The relevant measures froze tariffs for drinking water and sewerage services with the aim of ensuring the population's access to services. These tribunals held that other actions would have impacted less on the

[114] *Glamis Gold v US*, paras 803, 805.

[115] *Lemire v Ukraine*, para 283.

[116] *LG&E v Argentina*, paras 239–42; *Continental v Argentina*, paras 174–81; *Total v Argentina*, paras 162–5, 309; Separate Opinions of Arbitrator Nikken in *InterAgua v Argentina*, paras 37, 42; *AWG v Argentina*, paras 37, 42. See also Erlend Leonhardsen, Chapter 8, Section IV.B in this volume.

[117] *Continental v Argentina*, paras 181, 198–9, 223.

[118] *CMS v Argentina*, para 323; *Sempra v Argentina*, para 339; *Enron v Argentina*, para 300.

[119] See Button, *Power to Protect*, 211–12; Jürgen Kurtz, 'Adjudging the Exceptional at International Investment Law: Security, Public Order and Financial Crisis', 59 *ICLQ* 325 (2010), 342; Burke-White and von Staden, 'Private Litigation', 298. However, these tribunals conflated the strict requirements of the customary plea of necessity with the necessity test in the emergency measures clause: see *CMS v Argentina*, paras 320, 323, 324, 329, 355, 356, 374; *Sempra v Argentina*, para 376; *Enron v Argentina*, para 334; Kurtz, 'Adjudging the Exceptional', 341–7.

investors' interests such as 'applying a social tariff or a subsidy to the poor'.[120] These decisions are open to the criticism that tribunals did not give due consideration to whether, in the circumstances of the crisis, authorities possessed the capacity to devise and implement such measures and in this respect, these tribunals did not recognize their own institutional weaknesses in evaluating regulatory policy. The approaches taken by these tribunals risk significant incursions into regulatory autonomy.

V. An Emerging Discourse of Deference?

Strict approaches to standards of review in investor–State arbitration have resulted in tribunals finding that Argentina's general regulatory measures taken in response to its economic crisis violated the State's obligations towards foreign investors. Strict approaches are also apparent in cases in which tribunals did not appear to agree with States as to the importance of their objectives or the gravity of the situation, or where tribunals did not take account of governments' comparatively greater expertise in designing regulatory policy. Yet, an increasing number of tribunals have acknowledged the desirability of deference or have approached their review of measures with an understanding of the need for deference in situations of uncertainty for reasons of regulatory autonomy and proximity, and relative institutional competence and expertise.

While a discourse of deference may be emerging in investor–State arbitration, tribunals' approaches remain under-theorized. The reception of the concept of deference into the decision-making of investment tribunals has been a positive step, but tribunals could be more explicit in their determination of the applicable standard of review, including setting out why they have (or have not) been deferential in the circumstances.[121] As well as providing greater clarity for States and investors, articulation of the approach taken to the standard of review by investment tribunals might also improve States' decision-making processes to the extent that authorities will be able to anticipate areas of higher scrutiny and ensure that their decisions are particularly robust.[122]

It should be noted that investment tribunals have not always adopted the approach to deference that they have described. The references to deference by the *Tecmed* tribunal and its portrayal of its approach as reflecting that taken by the ECtHR is problematic, because the decision has been cited by subsequent tribunals as taking an appropriate approach to deference, whereas the tribunal reviewed the conduct of the authorities with an arguably overly strict standard of review. In the same vein, where tribunal decisions do not explicitly refer to deference or appear to disavow the concept, a closer reading of the decision may nevertheless be needed. The approach taken by the *Glamis* and *Chemtura*

[120] See *InterAgua v Argentina*, paras 215–28; *AWG v Argentina*, paras 235–48.
[121] See Kläger, *Fair and Equitable Treatment*, 248; von Staden, 'Deference', 4.
[122] See Gerards, 'Pluralism, Deference', 89.

tribunals—which both appeared to reject the concept of deference afforded on the basis of the characteristics of primary decision-makers whilst simultaneously adopting a deferential approach—is unhelpful from the perspective of clarity in legal reasoning. The *Glamis* tribunal stated that the concept of deference was implicit in the applicable standard of treatment required by fair and equitable treatment 'rather than being additive to that standard'.[123] In doing so, the tribunal appeared to conflate the normative content of fair and equitable treatment with the concept of deference based on the characteristics of primary decision-makers. The *Chemtura* tribunal stated that it would not apply a margin of appreciation in its decision-making, but then held that it would take into account the expertise of decision-makers in its review of science-based measures, which is one of the bases upon which a court or tribunal may afford a margin of appreciation.[124]

Some commentators argue that a deferential approach by investment tribunals will only be appropriate in certain predefined situations. Burke-White and von Staden argue that a deferential approach should be restricted to situations where the text of the relevant treaty provision indicates that States intend to preserve regulatory autonomy, such as non-precluded measures clauses.[125] The applicable degree of deference would be further discerned from the treaty language, with tribunals granting greater deference in relation to more open-textured treaty terms (such as non-precluded measures clauses referring to the objectives of public order or morality) than those amenable to objective determination (such as public health).[126] To be sure, States will have a range of perspectives on the concept of public morals and when it is appropriate to take action to protect them, whereas the question of whether a measure is directed at public health is more likely to be an issue that is clear-cut. However, while standards of review may be guided by and should never be inconsistent with the treaty text, restricting deference to situations where treaty text indicates an intention to preserve regulatory autonomy would not permit tribunals to take a deferential approach to the vast majority of provisions of investment treaties that do not detail or even suggest the existence of the State's continued regulatory powers.

VI. Conclusions

Investment tribunal decisions adopt a range of approaches to the standard of review when determining the legality of the exercise of public power by States. While no tribunal to date has clearly set out the rationale for the approach that it employs, the decided cases evidence a number of occasions where tribunals have

[123] *Glamis Gold v US*, para 617. [124] *Chemtura v Canada*, para 123.

[125] Burke-White and von Staden, 'Non-Precluded Measures', 370–6; Burke-White and von Staden, 'Private Litigation', 293–6; von Staden, 'Deference', 4.

[126] Burke-White and von Staden, 'Non-Precluded Measures', 372, 375.

shown a measure of deference on the basis of States' right to regulate, authorities' proximity to their communities and governments' greater institutional competence and expertise. An approach to the standard of review taking into account these rationales for deference echoes the case law of other international courts and tribunals performing similar functions.

Employing an institutionally sensitive approach to the standard of review that takes into account the desirability of regulatory autonomy, decision-making by proximate decision-makers and issues of relative institutional competence and expertise does not amount to an abdication of the adjudicatory function of tribunals[127] and will not invariably result in a high level of deference or preclude State liability.[128] Nor does such an approach politicize the adjudicatory function of investment tribunals.[129] Taking into account the relative characteristics and strengths of different actors in decision-making is, on the contrary, an essential aspect of governance, including adjudication.[130]

It is appropriate that investment tribunals continue to adopt standards of review reflecting their role as international adjudicators of disputes concerning the exercise of public power by domestic governments and, cognizant of the desirability of deference in certain circumstances, exercise restraint in situations of normative or empirical uncertainty. Such an approach would go some way towards achieving a more balanced relationship between the protection of foreign investment and States' right to regulate and take other actions in the public interest.

[127] Cf T.R.S. Allan, 'Human Rights and Judicial Review: a Critique of Due Deference', 65 *CLJ* 671 (2006), 675.

[128] Cf *Sporrong and Lönnroth v Sweden* (app. nos. 7151/75 and 7152/75), ECtHR 1982, paras 69, 73; Appellate Body Report, *Brazil—Tyres*, paras 150–1, 232–3. See Roberts, 'The Next Battleground', 177; Chen, 'Standard of Review', 28.

[129] Cf Moloo and Jacinto, 'Standards of Review', 566.

[130] See Van Harten, *Investor–State Arbitration*, 144.

8

Treaty Change, Arbitral Practice and the Search for a Balance

Standards of Review and the Margin of Appreciation in International Investment Law

Erlend M. Leonhardsen[*]

I. Introduction

Along with the rapid rise of investment treaty arbitration over the last decade, the regime has faced considerable and increasing criticism from States, scholars, and civil society.[1] This criticism has taken many forms, but in essence it has been directed towards arbitral decision-making as placing too much emphasis on investor rights and too little on State regulatory legitimacy, as well as what has been regarded as judicial activism. This arbitrator-driven regime, fuelled by narrowly drafted, imprecise treaties, yet with a high degree of delegation and strongly binding language,[2] is now experiencing a recurrence of State activity and involvement, in the form of States' utilization of the main control powers available to them under public international law: treaty exit, amendment, or renewal.[3] The response by arbitral tribunals to these State acts will, in my view, likely seek to create a new equilibrium, aimed at minimizing States' perceived need to amend or exit their investment agreements.

[*] Thanks to the participants on the 'Standard of Review in International Courts and Tribunals Rethinking the Fragmentation and Constitutionalization of International Law' Workshop, Universidad de Sevilla, Faculty of Law 26–7 October 2012, Clemens Wackernagel and the editors for helpful comments and suggestions.

[1] For examples, see eg Michael Waibel et al, *The Backlash against the Investment Arbitration* (Alphen aan den Rijn: Kluwer Law International, 2010); Erlend M. Leonhardsen, 'Looking for Legitimacy: Exploring Proportionality Analysis in Investment Treaty Arbitration', 3 *JIDS* 95 (2012).

[2] Kenneth W. Abbott et al, 'The Concept of Legalization', 54 *International Organization* 401 (2000), 401–2.

[3] As well as opting not to include State-investor dispute resolution provisions in new bilateral investment treaties (BITs) and free trade agreements (FTAs). I address many of these changes in Leonhardsen, 'Looking for Legitimacy', 107 et seq.

This chapter argues, first, that States have responded to what has been perceived as too strict standard of review of their conduct by treaty tribunals with treaty amendments, exits, and other responses at their disposal. The aim of these responses, discussed in Section II, has been to make courts grant States a larger area of discretion. Section III explores the structure of this kind of discretion in European human rights law, which in my view has largely inspired both governments and arbitrators. It is argued here that while this human rights law jurisprudence might be a useful comparison in investment treaty arbitration, the essential legal differences must be kept in mind. Section IV of this chapter explores the way in which investment treaty tribunals have, in recent decisions, reasoned with respect to deference. I conclude that while there is no clear and unified doctrine of deference in investment treaty arbitration, adjudicators are well aware of the governmental push for more regulatory discretion. Nonetheless, there appears to be a discrepancy between the approach taken by most tribunals and the States' perception of the vanishing regulatory freedom left to governments under international investment law.

II. State Voice and Treaty Amendments

According to the United Nations Conference on Trade and Development (UNCTAD), treaty preambles increasingly indicate that international investment agreements 'do not purport to promote and protect investment at the expense of other key values such as health, safety, labour protection and the environment'.[4] For instance, the 2002 BIT between the Republic of Korea and Trinidad and Tobago, the 2005 BIT between the US and Uruguay, and the 2007 Norwegian Draft Model BIT all emphasize health, safety, and the environment as important values that the BIT should not override.[5]

A similar trend is occurring in the substantive provisions that provide protection to foreign investors. For instance, it has become common for new investment treaties to specify that, except in certain grave circumstances, non-discriminatory regulatory measures that are 'designed and applied to protect legitimate public welfare objectives, such as public health, safety, and the environment',[6] do not constitute indirect expropriations. In the US 2012 Model BIT this is emphasized, *inter alia*, by specific treaty provisions that aim to do the same thing (in a negative fashion) in specific areas such as environmental rights and labour protection by clarifying what does *not* count as expropriation.

Such clauses entail a shift in *ex post* interpretative control over treaty provisions from adjudicators to States,[7] and will probably lead to a more lenient standard of

4 UNCTAD, *Bilateral Investment Treaties 1995–2006: Trends in Investment Rulemaking* (2007) 3–5.

5 Paras 6 and 4 respectively.

6 Anthea Roberts, 'Clash of Paradigms: Actors and Analogies Shaping the Investment Treaty System', 107 *AJIL* 45 (2013).

7 See generally Anthea Roberts, 'Power and Persuasion in Investment Treaty Arbitration', 104 *AJIL* 176 (2010).

review by the tribunal as far as conduct governed by these provisions is concerned. When this is combined with increasingly specific treaty provisions *ex ante*,[8] it can be seen as a visible assertion of power by States. Even though these signals through treaty amendments largely occur within bilateral treaties, they still in my view send a clear message because the investment treaty regime has proven susceptible to intra-regime spillover effects. This has taken place from a treaty design perspective, and States also display strong degrees of learning. It has also occurred in the adjudicative phase through the decision-making of arbitral tribunals.[9] Furthermore, the regime's borders vis-à-vis other regimes appear to become more and more porous in both respects.[10]

As a furthering of this trend, States have in recent investment treaties and free trade agreements (FTAs) often included broad exceptions clauses, similar to Article XX of the General Agreement on Tariffs and Trade (GATT),[11] a practice not common until the current wave of changes.[12] A somewhat far-reaching example in this regard is the Norwegian 2007 Model BIT,[13] which includes a whole section on exceptions, and which not only contains a general exception clause but also a Prudential Regulation exception clause, a cultural exceptions clause, a security exceptions clause, and a taxation exceptions clause. All of these are in addition to a very narrow expropriation protection clause, which is almost identical to the property protection clause in Article 1 of the first Additional Protocol to the European Convention on Human Rights (ECHR).

Textually, the combination of such changes invites adjudicators to employ a lax standard of review, by which I mean the 'degree of scrutiny' tribunals display vis-à-vis governments in assessing factual and legal matters.[14] As a result, tribunals afford considerable discretion to a State.

There are several possible approaches to interpreting these exceptions. More specifically, these considerations often take the form of a necessity analysis, in which a variety of approaches has been taken by tribunals so far,[15] but where even the stricter approaches seem to allow for the acceptance of regulatory discretion of a State.[16] In my view the most likely approach is to consider these exceptions

[8] Roberts, 'Clash of Paradigms', 47.

[9] See Leonhardsen, 'Looking for Legitimacy', 104 et seq for my take.

[10] See Ole Kristian Fauchald, 'The Legal Reasoning of ICSID Tribunals—an Empirical Analysis', 19 *EJIL* 301 (2008).

[11] Roberts, 'Clash of Paradigms', 47. See eg the broad exceptions clause in Article 10 of the 2004 Canadian Model BIT, incorporated verbatim eg in the 2006 Canada–Peru BIT.

[12] Andrew Newcombe and Lluís Paradell, *Law and Practice of Investment Treaties: Standards of Treatment* (Alphen aan den Rijn: Kluwer Law International, 2009) 499.

[13] Draft Model Norwegian Bilateral Investment Treaty (19 December 2007), available at <www.regjeringen.no/upload/NHD/Vedlegg/hoeringer/Utkast%20til%20modellavtale2.doc> (accessed 28 March 2014).

[14] Caroline Henckels, 'Indirect Expropriation and the Right to Regulate: Revisiting Proportionality Analysis and the Standard of Review in Investor-State Arbitration', 15 *JIEL* 223 (2012), 238.

[15] See eg Andrew D. Mitchell and Caroline Henckels, 'Variations on a Theme: Comparing the Concept of "Necessity" in International Investment Law and WTO Law', 14 *Chicago Journal of International Law* 93 (2013).

[16] Eg *Suez, Sociedad General de Aguas de Barcelona SA, and InterAgua Servicios Integrales del Agua SA v The Argentine Republic*, ICSID, Decision on Liability, 30 July 2010, para 217.

as 'intended to provide greater regulatory flexibility to host States in pursuing the specific legitimate objectives established in the exceptions'.[17] From this starting point, I go on to consider more thoroughly the function of this 'regulatory flexibility' as the result of a lenient adjudicatory standard of review, a result which can also be described using the increasingly common label of 'margin of appreciation' (MOA).

My argument here is essentially that the MOA is a tool of judicial strategy to affect a judicial body's standard of review, functioning mainly (but not only) as a way to protect its legitimacy by limiting the impact of its decision-making responsibility.[18] I postulate that the notion of a MOA was developed in the European Court of Human Rights (ECtHR),[19] in a similar context as that currently seen in investment treaty arbitration. Moreover, States can, and do, amend treaties to facilitate the adjudicative application of the doctrine, such as when the Norway Model BIT incorporated the text of ECHR protocol 1 rather than the common expropriation clause (as in its older BITs). Indeed, as Fawcett, a leading early ECHR lawyer, put it, 'The notion of a margin of appreciation is to be found expressed in only one provision of the Convention, Article 1(2) of the [first Additional] Protocol.'[20] It was precisely this language the Norwegian government put in its Model BIT, presumably because the government wanted tribunals to grant it a margin of appreciation.

As European lawyers noted in the 1960s when the doctrine was being developed, the MOA might have been necessary simply to avoid withdrawals from the ECHR. As with investment treaty arbitration tribunals today,[21] these were 'the facts of political life' with which the European human rights bodies of that day and age had to live, and had they 'adopted the role of a European "busybody" it is likely that a good number of States would withdraw from the Convention.'[22] Something similar reportedly occurred during the *Loewen* case,[23] where one of the arbitrators, appointed by the US Department of Justice (DOJ), was allegedly told by a DOJ representative: 'You know... if we lose this case we could lose NAFTA.' This seems to have influenced the arbitrator's decision-making.[24]

[17] Newcombe and Paradell, *Law and Practice*, 502.

[18] In a domestic setting, see eg Aileen Kavanagh, 'Deference or Defiance? The Limits of the Judicial Role in Constitutional Adjudication' in Grant Huscroft (ed), *Expounding the Constitution: Essays in Constitutional Theory* (Cambridge: Cambridge University Press, 2008) 184, 203–7.

[19] Clovis Morrisson Jr, 'The Margin of Appreciation in European Human Rights Law', 6 *Revue des Droit de l'Homme* 263 (1973).

[20] James E.S. Fawcett, *The Application of the European Convention on Human Rights* (Oxford: Oxford University Press, 1968) 248.

[21] See further Leonhardsen, 'Looking for Legitimacy'.

[22] D.R. Gilmour, 'The Sovereignty of Parliament and the European Commission of Human Rights', *Public Law* 62 (1968) at 70.

[23] *Loewen Group, Inc. and Raymond L. Loewen v United States of America*, ICSID (NAFTA), Award on Merits, 26 June 2003, Case No. ARB (AF)/98/3.

[24] David Schneiderman, 'Judicial Politics and International Investment Arbitration: Seeking an Explanation for Conflicting Outcomes', 30 *Northwestern Journal of International Law & Business* 383 (2010). See also Caroline Henckels, Chapter 7 in this volume (Section III.A).

Not only, then, is deference 'a rational response to uncertainty' of a legal and factual nature.[25] It is also a rational response to the problem of institutional weakness that characterizes international courts and tribunals in times when, such as in international investment law today, States and those who influence States voice strong criticism. A high degree of deference in such instances essentially works as a way to delegate the 'decisional burdens' to the State, thereby minimizing the costs for international courts and tribunals of making controversial and difficult decisions.[26] For these reasons, it is worthwhile examining the development of this doctrine somewhat more closely.

III. State Voice and Adjudicative Response: The Margin of Appreciation

The international law origin of MOA is commonly traced to the ECtHR, and sometimes to domestic administrative law, though Bjørge has in a recent work argued that its proper origin can be found in general international law.[27] MOA can be defined broadly as the freedom of States to act within international regulatory regimes; 'the latitude of deference or error which the judicial organs will allow to national legislative, executive, administrative and judicial bodies before it is prepared' to regard an act or omission attributable to the State as breach of the treaty.[28] A recent development, which I believe largely corresponds to the amendments in investment treaties described above, was the writing of the MOA doctrine into the preamble of the ECHR as per Article 1 of additional protocol no. 15 of 16 May 2013.[29] This development, which comes at a critical time for the Court, in my view underlines the crucial international political context of the doctrine.

Until the additional protocol enters into force, the basis of the Court's application of the doctrine can be seen in, for instance, the famous *Handyside* judgment,[30] which concerned freedom of expression under Article 10 of the ECHR. In that case the Court held that the second paragraph of Article 10 leaves to the parties 'a margin of appreciation'.[31] It then went on to limit the margin left to the State. Because the Court is responsible for 'ensuring the observance of the [State Parties'] engagements' it is also 'empowered to give the final ruling on whether a "restriction" or "penalty" is reconcilable with the freedom or right protected by the ECHR'.[32]

[25] Kavanagh, 'Deference or Defiance?', 186.

[26] Cass Sunstein and Edna Ullmann-Margalit, 'Second-Order Decisions', 110 *Ethics* 5 (1999), 10–12.

[27] Eirik Bjørge, 'The Margin of Appreciation: Where Does it Come from and Where Is It Headed?' (unpublished manuscript on file with the author).

[28] Ronald St. J. Macdonald, 'The Margin of Appreciation' in Ronald St. J. Macdonald et al (eds), *The European System for the Protection of Human Rights* (Dondrecht: Martinus Nijhoff, 1993) 83, 84.

[29] The protocol will enter into force when all the parties have consented to it.

[30] *Handyside v United Kingdom* (app. no. 5493/72), ECtHR 1976.

[31] *Handyside v United Kingdom*, para 48.

[32] *Handyside v United Kingdom*, para 49.

The broad definition I gave above represents the different legal solutions underlying the doctrine as a label. On one hand, adjudicators can refrain from substituting their judgment for the judgment of the State on a particular matter under this label.[33] On the other hand they can also employ the label as a way of saying that they find the judgment of the State justifiable.[34] In the former instance, the court or tribunal does not exercise judicial review at all, while in the latter judicial review is exercised, but no breach found. It is not always apparent which of the described uses of the label is exercised in a particular application of the doctrine.[35]

A. The margin of appreciation as a second-order reason

These various functions can point us towards another, less opaque, understanding of MOA, suggested by Legg, as the 'judicial practice of assigning weight to the respondent State's reasoning in a case on the basis of one or more of three external factors: democratic legitimacy; the common practice of States; and expertise'.[36] Legg regards these as 'second-order reasons' to uphold the State's original decision, by which he refers to Joseph Raz's distinction between first and second-order reasons.[37] First-order reasons can be regarded as intrinsic to the choice between two conflicting values, because one is valued over the other by the decision-maker in that particular instance.[38] Second-order reasons, on the other hand, are reasons 'to act for a reason or refrain from acting for a reason'.[39] While it is not always necessarily clear exactly which reason a decision is actually based on—neither to the outside observer nor perhaps even to the decision-maker—this perspective is helpful because it allows us to emphasize the values being deferred to. A weakness is that we do not know what role, if any, is played by elements such as the desire to pass the costs and burdens of making controversial decisions on to others.[40]

Viewed in this perspective, then, adjudicators act on the basis of second-order reasons each time they show deference. As the tribunal put it in *Electrabel,* its task was not:

> to sit retrospectively in judgment upon Hungary's discretionary exercise of a sovereign power, not made irrationally and not exercised in bad faith... [Electricity price regulation]...is...a difficult discretionary exercise involving many complex factors. In short, Hungary would enjoy a reasonable margin of appreciation in taking such measures before being held to account.[41]

[33] Macdonald, 'The Margin of Appreciation', 85.

[34] Macdonald, 'The Margin of Appreciation', 85.

[35] Macdonald, 'The Margin of Appreciation', 85.

[36] Andrew Legg, *The Margin of Appreciation in International Human Rights Law: Deference and Proportionality* (Oxford: Oxford University Press, 2012) 17.

[37] Joseph Raz, *Practical Reasons and Norms* (Oxford: Oxford University Press, 1999) 36.

[38] For instance, freedom of expression is valued above the right to privacy.

[39] Raz, *Practical Reasons*, 39.

[40] See Kavanagh, 'Deference or Defiance?'; Sunstein and Ullmann-Margalit, 'Second-Order Decisions'.

[41] *Electrabel SA v Republic of Hungary*, ICSID Case No. ARB/07/19, Decision on Jurisdiction, Applicable Law and Liability, 30 November 2012, para 8.35.

In other words, deference in this sense means that the second-order reason, such as the regulatory expertise of the decision-maker the tribunal defers to, is given greater weight than the first-order reason, the values that must be balanced in the case.

The degree of deference will vary according to the specific context in which the decision is made, based on factors such as 'the nature of the... right at issue, its importance for the individual and the nature of the activities concerned'.[42] The degree of deference varies between legal regimes as well. It can sometimes be less in investment treaty arbitration than in European human rights law because the second-order reasons have different weight in the two regimes. A good example is what Legg refers to as 'the common practice of States', which is crucial in the ECHR but plays a limited role in investment treaty arbitration. However, there are also legal reasons for this difference. Let us look at this from yet another angle.

B. Two concepts of the margin of appreciation

It is possible to identify two different uses of the MOA doctrine in the jurisprudence of the ECtHR.[43] These are useful to distinguish its different impact in human rights cases and investment treaty arbitration. The first of these ('the substantive concept') is used to address the relationship between the freedom of the individual and collective goals.

1. *The substantive MOA concept*

In all cases where an interference by the State with the freedom of an individual is established by the ECtHR but not deemed to amount to a violation of a right, the role of the MOA is to identify the point when an interference amounts to a violation. The most important criterion for identifying the distinction between a permissible and non-permissible interference is the principle of proportionality. In the words of one observer, this 'non-absoluteness of the Convention freedoms [is] the main idea behind the substantive [MOA] concept'.[44] This substantive concept is what States are trying to create in the new investment agreements with broad exceptions clauses described above.

The principle of proportionality often serves as an important tool for investment arbitration tribunals in similar situations, although not necessarily under the MOA label. This is so because in these instances the ECtHR can be said to utilize the concept 'to express a final conclusion as to whether a particular interference with an individual right amounts to a violation all things considered'.[45]

[42] *Buckley v the United Kingdom* (app. no. 20348/92), ECtHR 1996, para 74.

[43] George Letsas, 'Two Concepts of the Margin of Appreciation', 26 *Oxford Journal of Legal Studies* 705 (2006).

[44] Letsas, 'Two Concepts', 718.

[45] Letsas, 'Two Concepts', 712 (italics omitted); *Lindheim and others v Norway* (app. nos. 13221/08 and 2139/10), ECtHR 2012, para 134. From an investment arbitration perspective,

In his concurring opinion in *Odievre v France*, Judge Rozakis remarked that the proportionality test (expressed as a necessity test) was for him:

the crucial test to be applied in the circumstances of the case. Indeed, when... the Court has in its hands an abundance of elements leading to the conclusion that the test of necessity is satisfied by itself and embarks on a painstaking analysis of them, reference to the margin of appreciation should be duly confined to a subsidiary role.[46]

Notably, however, the ECtHR's necessity tests differ from those employed so far in investment treaty arbitration in that they are qualified by the additional phrase 'in a democratic society'. This phrase serves as a limit upon the MOA. All else equal, this would seem to imply that without this phrase the margin is wider. This seems to be the case with ECtHR property protection jurisprudence (where the provision does not include the 'democratic society' qualification), although it hardly seems to be true for investment treaty arbitration so far—presumably because the treaty texts so far have been very different.

In general the idea of democracy in the Court's case law can be understood as respect for democracy as a process, which is what we might consider as the inner core of the second-order value the MOA ought to protect. This can be thought of more broadly as institutional quality requirements. Marks has suggested that the *Mellacher* decision, a case about rent control legislation under the property protection clause, can be interpreted in this manner.[47] There it was observed that the proportionality of the measures in question had been disputed both in parliament and in public debate.[48]

The Court seemed to agree with this procedural aspect of democracy, by noting that it would 'respect the legislature's judgment as to what is in the general interest unless that judgment be manifestly without reasonable foundation'.[49] This form of deference can play a role in investment treaty arbitration as well, in the sense that, as noted above, the value of democratic process or deliberation can be considered as a second-order value which leads to arbitral tribunals giving due deference to States.[50] However, very different types of governments and democracies appear before investment treaty tribunals. Normatively, one could imagine judicial scrutiny over the type and content of democratic process behind a particular

see eg *Técnicas Medioambientales Tecmed, SA v The United Mexican States*, ICSID, Award, 29 May 2003, para 122. On the relationship between the MOA and the proportionality principle in investment treaty arbitration, see Henckels, 'Indirect Expropriation' and Leonhardsen, 'Looking for Legitimacy'.

[46] *Odievre v France* (app. no. 42326/98), ECtHR 2002, Concurring opinion of Judge Rozakis.

[47] Susan Marks, 'The European Convention on Human Rights and its "Democratic Society"', 66 *BYIL* 209 (1995), 218.

[48] *Mellacher and others v Austria* (app. nos. 10522/83, 11011/84 and 11070/84), Report of the Commission 1988, para 211.

[49] *Mellacher and others v Austria* (app. nos. 10522/83, 11011/84 and 11070/84), ECtHR 1989, para 45. But see the property control case *Lindheim and others v Norway*, where the government makes a similar argument (para 118), which the Court does not appear to have addressed.

[50] There are powerful reasons for such deference. Besides the normative argument in defence of democracy per se, contemporary political theory also emphasizes the superior epistemic power of group decision-making, such as that made in parliaments. See eg Hélène Landemore, *Democratic*

governmental decision that a respondent government claims should be treated with deference by a tribunal.

To sum up, if tribunals determine that a particular measure was enacted pursuant to thorough deliberation by lawmakers, or enacted/adopted by de facto and de jure independent domestic courts, regulators and prosecutors in the course of due process, this ought to mean that they allow for an MOA. In other words, arbitrators ought to respect evidence of good governance as a second order value. Conversely, the standard of review may legitimately be stricter if these formal aspects are not in place. This is not to say that States will react well to such scrutiny by tribunals, which means that it carries potential costs. For instance, strict scrutiny may lead to requests for amendments or even withdrawal from the treaty in question.[51]

2. *The structural MOA concept*

This brings us to the second of the two concepts of the MOA ('the structural concept').[52] It is used to address the intensity of the scrutiny of the international adjudicator. For the ECtHR, as for arbitral tribunals, this implies deferral to the judgment made by the national authorities, because it is not their role to be a 'fourth' national court.[53] For instance, in the case of *Deutsche Bank v Sri Lanka*, the dissenting arbitrator pointed to the high measure of deference the domestic judiciary was entitled to.[54]

The structural MOA concept, however, highlights one of the more important differences between international investment law and the ECHR. This is related to the key function of the ECtHR as harbinger and protector of democracy,[55] a role ill-fated if the review of legitimate governmental acts is too strict. The approach taken by the ECtHR in striking the right balance between the

Reason: Politics, Collective Intelligence and the Rule of the Many (Princeton: Princeton University Press, 2013).

[51] Venezuela noticed its denunciation of the American Convention of Human Rights on 12 September 2012. Reportedly, this was partly due to several judgments finding a breach of the independent judiciary requirement. International Justice Reform Center, 'Venezuela Denounces American Convention on Human Rights as IACHR Faces Reform', 19 September 2012. Available at <http://www.ijrcenter.org/2012/09/19/venezuela-denounces-american-convention-on-human-rights-as-iachr-faces-reform> (accessed 28 March 2014).

[52] See also Mónika Ambrus, Chapter 13 in this volume, who explores this structural concept from the perspective of standards of proof.

[53] Letsas, 'Two Concepts', 706. See however the interesting explanation by the NAFTA tribunal in *Loewen* (para 242): ('[W]e find nothing in NAFTA to justify the exercise by this Tribunal of an appellate function parallel to that which belongs to the courts of the host nation').

[54] *Deutsche Bank v Democratic Socialist Republic of Sri Lanka*, ICSID Case No. ARB/09/2, Dissenting Opinion of Makhdoom Ali Khan, 31 October 2012, para 106, referring to *S.D. Myers, Inc v Government of Canada*, Partial Award, 13 November 2000, para 236 (though the reference should probably have been to para 263, and in *S.D. Myers* the statement was made in the context of general regulatory authority, not courts).

[55] See eg *United Communist Party of Turkey and others v Turkey* (app. no. 19382/92), ECtHR 1998, para 45. For a look at this role from the perspective of procedural democracy, see Benedikt Pirker, Chapter 4 in this volume (Section III).

sovereignty of States and the Court's role as protector of the rights enshrined in the ECHR sometimes takes the form of a 'consensus inquiry'.[56] Legg regards this as a second-order reason,[57] but it is nonetheless a form of reasoning that has broad support in the text of the ECHR itself.

This entails that the Court examines the 'degree of consensus or harmony among the national laws of signatory States' with respect to the measure under scrutiny in order to afford the respondent State a degree of discretion in case there is no harmony of which it is not part.[58] For instance, in *X, Y and Z v United Kingdom*, it observed that there was 'no common European standard with regard to the granting of parental rights to transsexuals. Since the issues in the case, therefore, touch on areas where there is little common ground amongst [States]', they must be afforded wide discretion.[59] The MOA in these cases has less to do with the relationship between individual rights and collective goals than with that between the ECtHR and the State parties.[60]

For this reason, the latter concept is rarely employed by arbitral tribunals, nor ought it be. This is a consequence of the fact that it is not the primary role of such tribunals to function as guardians of a multilateral international convention like the ECHR.[61] That said, many good governance concepts, like institutional independence, which (as we shall see below) tribunals seem ready to provide some deference to, are certainly key ingredients in any democracy. Nonetheless this does not mean that it is either the role of investment treaty tribunals or the aim of their constitutive instruments to promote and protect democracy as a form of government.

Rather, arbitral tribunals should be seen as fulfilling the role of proper and efficient courts of first instance, albeit ones mainly charged with the task of adjudging public policy affecting foreign investors.[62] This role of tribunals should not be understood as exercising the function of an administrative review body with the aim of ensuring that 'municipal agencies perform their tasks diligently, conscientiously or efficiently. That function is within the proper domain of domestic courts and tribunals that are cognizant of the minutiae of the applicable regulatory regime'.[63] For actions and omissions of a host State towards a foreign investor that do not reach the threshold of specific substantive provisions of the applicable investment treaty—for example regulations that limit the right of the investor to utilize its investment but that do not amount to an expropriation—there is a MOA for the host government to undertake such non-discriminatory regulatory measures as it sees fit.

[56] Laurence R. Helfer and Anne-Marie Slaughter, 'Toward a Theory of Effective Supranational Adjudication', 107 *Yale International Law Journal* 273 (1997), 317.
[57] Legg, *The Margin of Appreciation*, 18.
[58] Helfer and Slaughter, 'Toward a Theory', 316–17.
[59] *X, Y and Z v the United Kingdom* (app. no. 21830/93), ECtHR 1997, at 13.
[60] Letsas, 'Two Concepts', 721.
[61] See also Caroline Henckels, Chapter 7 in this volume, at Section IV.B.
[62] See *S.D. Myers Inc v Canada*, Partial Award, para 261. See further Benedikt Pirker, Chapter 4 in this volume, at Section V.C.
[63] *Generation Ukraine, Inc. v Ukraine*, ICSID Case No. ARB/00/9, 16 September 2003, ICSID, para 20.33.

At this point, it may be useful to highlight some of the criticism against the MOA in the form of the consensus inquiry, which I have cautioned against here. This is where the MOA is used to indicate the measure of discretion given to the State parties 'in the manner in which they implement the legal standards of the treaty, taking into account their own particular national circumstances and conditions',[64] legal, cultural, social and other. It seems plausible that widespread usage of the MOA in this sense challenges the aim of achieving a high level of unity in any international legal order. Certainly, this is an argument which can be made more generally against deference in general, but removing at least one level of pluralism, or not accepting one particular second-order reason, decreases the challenge. Taking such criticism seriously, Judge de Meyer stated his belief in a partly-dissenting opinion that it was 'high time for the Court to banish [the MOA] from its reasoning. It has already delayed too long in abandoning this hackneyed phrase and recanting the relativism it implies.'[65] Similarly, following the Court's judgment in *Müller*,[66] where allegedly obscene paintings were confiscated from an exhibition by the Swiss government, Lord Lester argued that it was hard to consider human rights protection as real and effective with respect to issues thought 'injurious to public morals' when 'an interference as extreme as the confiscation of an artist's works is regarded as within the wide MOA.'[67] This concept of morals as the underlying rationale for a measure restricting the rights of applicable persons has not been as important so far in investment arbitration as it is in the ECHR, though this is not necessarily improbable, for instance in cases concerning investments in gambling facilities.

Summing up the comparison I have undertaken here, from a more narrow perspective of the underlying values and the social and political contexts in which European human rights protection and the system of investment treaty protection respectively operate, there are many differences which affect the MOA. The ECHR signatories have, at least historically, more or less shared 'the Judeo-Christian tradition, democracy, and mixed-market economies',[68] and it has been the role of the Court to promote these values and protect their legitimate differences. Investment treaty arbitration, on the other hand, has functioned in a much more diverse legal and cultural environment, in which no degree of consensus among State participants in an investment treaty regime ought to, in and of itself, justify deference.

For instance, the rather extensive fragmentation in the jurisprudence of arbitral tribunals with respect to indirect expropriation may both stem from and exacerbate differences related to 'cultural, economic and legal concepts of property,

[64] Yutaka Arai-Takahashi, *The Margin of Appreciation Doctrine and the Principle of Proportionality in the Jurisprudence of the ECHR* (Oxford: Intersentia, 2002) 1–2.

[65] *Z v Finland* (app. no. 22009/93), ECtHR 1997, Partly Dissenting Opinion of Judge de Meyer, part III.

[66] *Müller and others v Switzerland* (app. no. 10737/84), ECtHR 1988, para 16.

[67] Lord Lester, 'Freedom of Expression', 19 *Commonwealth Law Bulletin* 1722 (1993), 1725.

[68] Howard C. Yourow, *The Margin of Appreciation Doctrine in the Dynamics of European Human Rights Jurisprudence* (Dordrecht: Martinus Nijhoff, 1996) 3.

different understandings of State role, and general heterogeneity in State practice.'[69] If a tribunal were to rely on this heterogeneity as a second-order reason in order to defer judgment to government, however, it would in my view cross an unfortunate line. With this in mind, let us take a closer look at some functions of the MOA in investment treaty arbitration.

IV. The Margin of Appreciation in Investment Treaty Arbitration: Some Conclusions

The first section of this chapter demonstrated that States, through treaty amendments and new treaties, have sought recently to create larger regulatory flexibility in their domestic spheres insofar as they are governed by international investment agreements. The second section of the chapter looked at the most famous form such regulatory flexibility has taken from the adjudicative perspective, namely the MOA of the ECtHR, and drew comparisons with arbitral tribunals. It is in my view likely that these treaty changes are meant by States as signals to treaty tribunals to provide greater regulatory flexibility, and that both States and adjudicators have looked to the Strasbourg Court for inspiration and will continue to do so in order to sustain the legitimacy of the investment treaty regime. As I noted in the second section, not all the Strasbourg jurisprudence is, in this sense, apt inspiration for investment treaty arbitration. In particular, what was referred to above as 'the common practice of States' seems to play little role. With that in mind let us now attempt, from the perspective of the framework set out, to make some conclusions about how the MOA has played out so far in investment treaty awards.

A. Epistemic deference

There seems to be little place for the structural role of the MOA in investment treaty arbitration, at least in the regime's present, bilateral-centred stage. On the other hand, the epistemic-related form of deference seems to be the most widespread.[70] In these cases, relying on the distinctions I made in the previous part, expertise serves as a second-order reason for arbitration tribunals. As the tribunal in *Saluka Investments* observed:

> In the absence of clear and compelling evidence that the [Czech National Bank] erred or acted otherwise improperly in reaching its decision, which evidence has not been presented to the Tribunal, the Tribunal must in the circumstances accept the justification given by the Czech banking regulator for its decision.[71]

[69] L. Yves Fortier, 'Indirect Expropriation in the Law of International Investment: I Know It When I See It, or Caveat Investor', 19 *ICSID Review* 293 (2005).

[70] See also Chapter 7 in this volume by Caroline Henckels at Section IV.D and Chapter 9 by Lukasz Gruszczynski and Valentina Vadi at Section III.

[71] *Saluka Investments BV v The Czech Republic*, Partial Award, 17 March 2006, para 273.

In the same vein the tribunal in *Chemtura* noted that it was not its role 'to second-guess the correctness of the science-based decision-making of highly specialized national regulatory agencies'.[72] The same was the case in *Methanex*, where scientific studies differed.[73] A vivid statement in this regard can be found in *Glamis*, in which the tribunal agreed with the respondent that it was not the 'tribunal's task to become archaeologists and ethnographers and to draw a definitive conclusion as to the location of the Trail of Dreams',[74] a sacred site for Native Americans which was located near land where the claimant had mining rights. As observed in that case, it was beyond the role of the international adjudicator 'to supplant its own judgment of underlying factual material and support for that of a qualified domestic agency'.[75] A similar position was taken in *Micula*, concerning a factual decision by Swedish immigration authorities relating to the requirements of naturalization.[76]

Thus, epistemic deference can encompass a broad range of determinations, including decision-making in the sense of complex choices among competing alternatives being entrusted to experts on the matter, acceptable risk level assessment, and to expertise in establishing facts.

As mentioned above, there is in my view a powerful argument in favour of considering deference to parliaments as not only normatively sound (this is addressed in Section IV.C later in this chapter), but also epistemically. The idea behind this kind of reasoning is that group decision-making is on average better than the kind of assessment arbitrators undertake. There is so far little evidence that tribunals have followed this particular line of thinking however.

B. Deference to the responsible decision-maker in times of crisis

Like in instances of purely epistemic deference, a special category of cases is related to different alternatives available to a State in order to reach a regulatory goal. This was a very controversial topic in many of the awards related to measures enacted by Argentina during and after its 2001–02 financial crisis.[77] This is surely an issue that will only grow in importance as measures taken during the current financial crisis reach tribunals, but it is also conceivable in cases concerned more clearly with national security. In terms of second-order reasons, deference in these cases encompass elements of both epistemic and democratic deference,

[72] *Chemtura Corporation v Government of Canada*, Ad Hoc NAFTA Arbitration under UNCITRAL Rules, Award, 2 August 2010, para 134.

[73] *Methanex Corporation v United States of America*, UNCITRAL (NAFTA), Final Award, 3 August 2005, Part III, Chapter A, para 101.

[74] *Glamis Gold, Ltd. v United States of America*, Award (UNCITRAL), 8 June 2009, para 779.

[75] *Glamis Gold v US*, para 779.

[76] *Ioan Micula and others v Romania*, ICSID Case No. ARB/05/20, Decision on Jurisdiction and Admissibility, 24 September 2008, paras 94–5. The deference here, however, was not shown to the respondent but to Sweden for the purpose of determining whether the foreign investor qualified under the Sweden/Romania BIT.

[77] See generally on these cases Henckels, 'Indirect Expropriation', 223 and Leonhardsen, 'Looking for Legitimacy'.

but they are sufficiently different to be treated independently, especially because the difficult question usually revolves around the appropriate degree of scrutiny of decision-making in crisis-like situations. This was a prominent problem in the early days of the ECHR as well, which illustrates well the function of the MOA in times when an adjudicative body's political and social support is fragile. As an early writer commented with respect to the ECHR, the MOA 'emerged from situations in which governments were faced with civil disturbances, riots, possibly large-scale acts of violence from sizable segments of the population, perhaps even intervention from outside'.[78]

If MOA is indeed a useful juridical tool in these situations, it is interesting to observe that there seem to be two main approaches taken so far, one of which appears to support this proposition, and one of which does not. On the one hand, some tribunals have recognized that there may be several legitimate regulatory responses in a crisis.[79] The tribunal in *Continental Casualty* emphasized this point, noting that its:

> objective assessment must contain a significant [MOA] for the State applying the particular measure: a time of grave crisis is not the time for nice judgments, particularly when examined by others with the disadvantage of hindsight.[80]

On the other hand some other tribunals, deciding on the same facts, have taken a stricter approach,[81] basically denying that there existed an MOA at all under the applicable treaty provision.[82] Consequently, the task of the Tribunal, as it was argued in *Sempra* and *Enron*, was 'to determine whether the choice made was the only way available'.[83]

Still, even this stricter approach seems to acknowledge deference to States in general with respect to economic policy choices, something which perhaps relates more to the epistemic deference mentioned above: 'While one or the other party would like the Tribunal to point out which alternative was recommendable, it is not the task of the Tribunal to substitute its view for the Government's choice

[78] Morrisson, 'The Margin of Appreciation', 267.

[79] *LG&E Energy Corp., LG&E Capital Corp., and LG&E International, Inc. v Argentine Republic*, ICSID, Decision on Liability, 3 October 2006, para 239; *Continental Casualty Company v The Argentine Republic*, ICSID, Award, 5 September 2008; *Total SA v The Argentine Republic*, ICSID Case No. ARB/04/01, Award 27 December 2010 paras 164–5; and the two similar Separate Opinions of Professor Nikken in *Suez, Sociedad General de Aguas de Barcelona SA, and InterAgua Servicios Integrales del Agua SA v The Argentine Republic* and *AWG Group et al v Argentine Republic*, both Decision on Liability, July 30 2010, paras 34, 37. Generally this approach is subject mainly to minimum review. As Nikken put it, 'what should be subject to scrutiny is whether these measures conform to the canons of good governance in a modern and well-organized State', para 34. See also *Pope & Talbot Inc. v The Government of Canada*, UNCITRAL (NAFTA), Award on Damages, 31 May 2002, para 155.

[80] *Continental Casualty v Argentina*, para 181.

[81] *CMS Gas Transmission Company v The Republic of Argentina*, ICSID Case No. ARB/01/8, Award, 12 May 2005; *Enron Corporation and Ponderosa Assets, LP v Argentine Republic*, ICSID, Award, 22 May 2007; *Sempra Energy International v The Argentine Republic*, ICSID, Award, 28 September 2007.

[82] Article XI of the US–Argentina BIT.

[83] *Sempra Energy International v Argentina*, para 351; *Enron Corporation and Ponderosa Assets v Argentina*, para 309.

between economic options.'[84] It seems clear that there is no uniform approach to the margin of appreciation in these cases, but earlier treaty approaches carried a clear risk that crucial decision-making powers have been ceded to arbitrators.

C. Democratic deference and institutional quality control

I noted above that the Strasbourg approach could be interpreted so as to give greater deference to measures when they have been thoroughly debated by the legislature. I have found little evidence that this approach has been followed by arbitrators so far. Nonetheless, it is reiterated that it could be a useful starting point.

The best example is perhaps *Glamis*, where the tribunal seemed to put weight on the procedural democratic aspects of the measures in question. It agreed with the respondent's starting point 'that governments must compromise between the interests of competing parties and, if they were bound to please every constituent and address every harm with each piece of legislation, they would be bound and useless.'[85] This had consequences for the issue whether the legislation in question was 'arbitrary' and thus could entail a breach of the fair and equitable treatment (FET) standard. A similar analysis follows from *Lemire*, where the tribunal noted that 'arbitrators are not superior regulators; they do not substitute their judgment for that of national bodies applying national laws'.[86] As the tribunal held in *Frontier Petroleum*, as long as such conclusions are reached by plausible interpretations, the State enjoys 'a certain margin of appreciation in determining what [its] own conception of international public policy is'.[87]

A more convoluted approach was taken in *Tecmed*. In that case the measures in question had been taken by, *inter alia*, the National Ecology Institute, ie they had not been subject to deliberative reasoning. The tribunal appeared to respect internal divisions of power, however, by acknowledging that due deference must be shown to the State 'when defining the issues that affect its public policy or the interests of society as a whole, as well as the actions that will be implemented to protect such values.'[88] That being said, it is somewhat unclear what, if anything, this deference meant in practice.

In light of recent case law, similar arguments can be made with respect to institutional quality requirements under the label of good governance, exemplified by prosecution, domestic court and central bank decision-making. For instance, in

[84] *Sempra Energy International v Argentina*, para 351; *Enron Corporation and Ponderosa Assets v Argentina*, para 309.

[85] *Glamis Gold v US*, para 804.

[86] *Joseph Charles Lemire v Ukraine*, ICSID, Decision on Jurisdiction and Liability, 24 October 2010, para 283.

[87] *Frontier Petroleum Services Ltd. v The Czech Republic*, UNCITRAL, Final Award, 12 November 2010, para 527.

[88] *Tecmed v Mexico*, para 122. Similarly, *Electrabel v Hungary*, para 8.35.

Vanessa Ventures Ltd. v Venezuela, the investor argued that it had been mistreated by the domestic courts in Venezuela, which 'were less than independent and impartial', and that this amounted to breach of the FET standard.[89] The Tribunal did not exclude that such a determination could be possible,[90] though it rejected the claim on the basis of lack of evidence, a bar it indicated was high, and noted that something like this had to be proved in each case.[91] These are considerations which arguably may be extended to inquiry into the structure of the judicial system. Article 6 ECHR is, for instance, interpreted in this manner (requiring 'an appearance of independence'),[92] and the American Convention on Human Rights and the International Covenant on Civil and Political Rights contain similar provisions.[93]

Here we can also point to more due process-related aspects of domestic adjudicative actions. This can also be discussed under FET standards and can be used to distinguish legitimate regulatory activity from indirect expropriation. For instance, in *Deutsche Bank v Sri Lanka*, the majority held that the Supreme Court acted in breach of due process requirements in this manner, and that the actions taken by the Central Bank amounted to 'financially motivated and illegitimate regulatory expropriation by a regulator lacking in independence.'[94] These justifications were used by the tribunal to deny discretion to the government decisions. Similarly, in *Rompetrol v Romania*, prosecutorial authority that involved 'procedural irregularities' towards the investor amounted to a breach of the FET requirement, again inspired by ECHR Article 6.[95] Somewhat similarly, in the *Occidental* case the tribunal noted that it could accept 'that some punishment or other step [against Claimant] may well have been justified, or at the very least defensible',[96] but such punishment could not be disproportional to the acts it addressed. In other words, the government had discretionary powers to enact measures against the investor, but its discretion did not go beyond what was considered proportional.

These examples provide two perspectives on deference in defence of what I would term 'democracy as a value in the broad sense'. On the one hand, this includes deference to thoroughly-debated parliamentary decisions. On the other, it entails non-deference to decisions made by governmental bodies where either the decision or even the structure of the decision-making body as such failed to reach minimum quality requirements concerning the appearance of impartiality and abuse of powers.

[89] *Vanessa Ventures Ltd. v Bolivarian Republic of Venezuela*, ICSID Case No. ARB/05/8, Award, 16 January 2013, para 217.

[90] See also eg *Parkerings-Compagniet v Lithuania*, ICSID, Award, 11 September 2007, para 318.

[91] *Vanessa Ventures v Venezuela*, para 228.

[92] *Langborger v Sweden* (app. no. 11179/84) ECtHR 1989, para 32.

[93] Articles 8(1) and 14(1) respectively.

[94] *Deutsche Bank v Sri Lanka*, para 524.

[95] *The Rompetrol Group NV v Romania*, ICSID Case No. ARB/06/03, Award, 6 May 2013, para 279.

[96] *Occidental Petroleum Corporation and Occidental Exploration and Production Company v The Republic of Ecuador*, ICSID Case No. ARB/06/11, Award, 5 October 2012, para 450.

It is not entirely unproblematic that these awards are based on vague treaty standards and both explicit and implicit analogies from human rights law, where the treaty texts are much more clear and detailed.[97] Nonetheless, neither is it clear that such scrutiny by investment tribunals ought to be seen as judicial overreach. The treaty changes discussed in Section I would hardly have affected these findings, and the jurisprudence is not too much out of sync with international trends. Hopefully, this might signal a future for investment treaty arbitration towards a kind of inquiry that is less open to critique than earlier trends.

V. Conclusions

In this chapter I have argued that States increasingly seek to create a margin of appreciation for themselves in new investment treaties, something which probably arises from dissatisfaction with current tribunal practice. Still, there is ample evidence that tribunals do provide a margin of appreciation in a variety of instances, in particular giving deference to national experts and non-discriminatory regulatory decisions.

Compared with European human rights law, the role of democratic deference is thus far underplayed in investment treaty arbitration, but I do not believe that tribunals are primarily to blame. This non-occurrence could be due to the fact that well-reasoned legislative acts are not that likely to give rise to credible investment treaty claims worth the costs of pursuing in international tribunals, and to the extent that they are, the bar for winning a claim in such circumstances seems high. On the other hand, tribunals increasingly seem to look at institutional and procedural aspects of decision-making, where evidence of abuse of powers or conflict of interests leads to striking down regulations, with little discretion left to the government.

This does not mean that ceding sovereignty through investment treaties is something States should do except for good reasons and with due consideration, a kind of diligence many of the earlier treaties were not always subject to. I think this has changed today, as evidenced by the new and amended treaties mentioned in the first part of this chapter. That being said, while I believe that tribunals will take this signal, thousands of old-school investment treaties continue to operate. To the extent that they do, and to the extent that they are to be taken seriously, the States that have negotiated, signed and ratified them will perhaps have to live with the risks that are entailed in being part of international legal regimes, both in terms of loss of domestic policy control and/or monetary costs.

[97] See more of this critique in Leonhardsen, 'Looking for Legitimacy'.

9

Standard of Review and Scientific Evidence in WTO Law and International Investment Arbitration

Converging Parallels?

Lukasz Gruszczynski and Valentina Vadi[*]

I. Introduction

World Trade Organization (WTO) dispute settlement bodies and investment treaty tribunals are increasingly confronted with national regulatory measures based on prior complex factual determinations made at the national level, frequently of a scientific character. This may relate to regulations in various fields such as environmental protection or the promotion of public health. In this context, the question as to which standards of review apply becomes crucial. Are WTO panels and arbitral tribunals expected to go into details of scientific determinations made at the municipal level and assess their merits, or rather should they express some degree of deference when reviewing such determinations?[1]

The answer is not an easy one, especially considering that the concept of standard of review is far less developed and consistent in international investment law and arbitration compared with other areas of international law. The boom in investment arbitrations is relatively recent, and arbitral tribunals tend to address the problems posed by applicable standard of review implicitly or *en passant* (if at all).[2] As far as the standard of review applicable to

[*] Lukasz Gruszczynski acknowledges that his research was financed by the Polish National Science Center pursuant to grant number DEC-2011/01/M/HS5/03846. This chapter reflects the authors' views only and the usual disclaimer applies. Lukasz Gruszczynski authored the introduction, Sections II and IV.A, while Valentina Vadi authored Sections III, IV.B, and the conclusions. The authors gratefully acknowledge the reciprocal inputs.

[1] For analysis of similar questions in the EU context, see Patrycja Dąbrowska-Kłosińska, Chapter 11 in this volume.

[2] But cf Ross Becroft, *The Standard of Review in WTO Dispute Settlement. Critique and Development* (Cheltenham: Edward Elgar Publishing, 2012), 24 (arguing that in many cases the

scientific determination is concerned, one should also add that until recently, such questions were rather rare in arbitral proceedings. This situation contrasts with the practice developed within the WTO, where the problem of applicable standard of review, including the issue of what degree of scrutiny should be applied to municipal scientific determinations, has been extensively addressed, both by adjudicating bodies and scholars. However, this does not necessarily mean that such jurisprudence is of better quality than that of arbitral tribunals.

This brings us to the core problem addressed in this chapter. Our aim is to compare the standards developed in both fields (in particular as applied to national scientific determinations) and enquire whether the two systems are converging or diverging and whether useful insights can be drawn for both fields from such analysis. In a previous article, 'Standards of Review in International Investment Law and Arbitration', we examined how, given its hybrid features, investment treaty law and arbitration can be analogized to different national and regional systems as well as subsystems of international law (eg domestic administrative review, review undertaken by international courts and tribunals as well as commercial arbitration) and demonstrated how these different analogies have an impact on the selected standards of review.[3] This chapter moves the discussion forward, comparing and critically assessing the approaches adopted by investment arbitration and WTO adjudication respectively with regard to scientific evidence. The reasons for juxtaposing the two systems with regard to the issue are as follows. First, international investment law and international trade law belong to the same branch of international law, namely international economic law. Second, beyond a mere taxonomic justification and, more substantively, the nature of problems that both systems encounter, is similar—ie investment arbitration tribunals and WTO adjudicative bodies are frequently required to assess national regulatory measures protecting certain non-economic values against a set of obligations of a purely economic character (unlike, for example, other international courts and tribunals). Third, a few WTO agreements touch upon various aspects of international investment law.[4] Consequently, portions of WTO law can be regarded as a part of the international investment regime. Finally, the WTO jurisprudence on the issue of standards of review is well developed as compared to other sections of international law, thus providing rich practical material for investigation.

problem of applicable standard of review is irrelevant as the investment tribunals are 'merely deciding on whether an international obligation has been observed').

[3] For details see Valentina Vadi and Lukasz Gruszczynski, 'Standards of Review in International Investment Law and Arbitration: Multilevel Governance and the Commonweal', 16(3) *JIEL* 613 (2013), 618–22.

[4] Eg Agreement on Trade-Related Aspects of Intellectual Property Rights, 15 April 1994, Marrakesh Agreement Establishing the World Trade Organization, Annex 1C, 1869 UNTS 299, Agreement on Trade Related Investment Measures, 15 April 1994, Marrakesh Agreement Establishing the World Trade Organization, Annex 1A, 1868 UNTS 186, General Agreement on Trade in Services, 15 April 1994, Marrakesh Agreement Establishing the World Trade Organization, Annex 1B, 1869 UNTS 183. New investment rules were initially agreed as a part of the WTO Doha Development Round agenda but afterwards withdrawn at the Cancun meeting in 2003.

There are, however, reasons that may also speak against comparing the two fields. As already mentioned, the existing investment arbitration jurisprudence on the treatment of scientific evidence is still very limited. This obviously makes any generalization (and subsequent comparison) more difficult or even premature. In addition, while the problem of applicable standard of review over scientific determinations is mostly relevant in the context of the WTO Agreement on the Application of Sanitary and Phytosanitary Measures (SPS Agreement),[5] which provides for specific science-based criteria, none of the international investment treaties contains comparable language. As a consequence, the two regimes require a scrutiny and critical assessment being cognizant of their inherent differences. Bearing in mind these observations, we nevertheless hold that there is analytical merit in considering the current developments in these two fields to verify whether they are converging and/or diverging.

This chapter proceeds as follows. The first part (Section II) briefly explains the concept of standard of review and examines its application in the WTO context, concentrating on particularities connected with the assessment of scientific evidence. The second part (Section III) turns to international investment arbitration, discussing standards used by investment tribunals when confronted with national scientific determinations. In the third part (Section IV), we connect the previous discussion by identifying similarities and differences between the two systems as well as the reasons behind possible convergences and/or divergences. In this context, we also indicate some arguments that support rather deferential approach of both WTO panels and investment arbitration tribunals towards domestic scientific determination. Section V concludes.

This chapter specifically addresses the problem of standard of review as applied when the WTO panels and investment arbitration tribunals are asked to assess the scientific aspects of a decision/action taken by a State.[6] Consequently, our observations and subsequent conclusions do not necessarily extend to other instances of review.[7] This also means that our argument should not be understood as a general call for deference in WTO law or international investment arbitration. At the same time, such a narrow approach seems to be justified as the review of scientific facts generates its own unique problems.[8]

[5] Agreement on the Application of Sanitary and Phytosanitary Measures, 15 April 1994, Marrakesh Agreement Establishing the World Trade Organization, Annex 1, 1867 UNTS 493.

[6] For more general discussion on the standard of review in the WTO context, see Chapter 6 by Michael Ioannidis in this volume.

[7] WTO panels apply different levels of scrutiny depending on the agreement. See eg Claus-Dieter Ehlermann and Nicolas Lockhart, 'Standard of Review in WTO Law', 7(3) *JIEL* 491 (2004), 496.

[8] Note however that both Henckels and Leonhardsen identify a deferential approach as an appropriate response in all cases that concern the question of epistemic superiority of national authorities (see Caroline Henckels, Chapter 7, and Erlend Leonhardsen, Chapter 8, both in this volume).

II. WTO, Standard of Review, and Scientific Evidence

Standard of review can be defined as 'nature and intensity of a court's scrutiny of the legal validity of a legislative or administrative decision'.[9] To put it differently, standard of review can be understood either as 'the degree of deference or discretion that the court accords to legislator or regulator' or 'the degree of intrusiveness or invasiveness into the legislator's or regulator's decision-making process'.[10] These quotes aptly indicate the two extremes of the applicable standard of review. On the one hand, such a standard can be fully deferential with a court/tribunal only entitled to check the procedural compliance of a body that adopted a measure or took an action. On the other hand, it can be intrusive (so-called '*de novo* review'), with a reviewing organ able to test the substantive merits of an examined decision and substitute prior determinations (including scientific ones) with its own. Of course between these two extremes there are a number of less or more deferential types of review.

In the WTO context, the Appellate Body characterized the *de novo* and deferential standards as follows:

> [*de novo* review] would allow a panel complete freedom to come to a different view than the competent authority of the Member whose act or determination is being reviewed. A panel would have to 'verify whether the determination by the national authority was correct—both factually and procedurally'... Under a 'deference' standard, a panel... should not seek to redo the investigation conducted by the national authority but instead examine whether the 'procedure' required by the relevant WTO rules had been followed.[11]

WTO law, except for the Anti-Dumping Agreement,[12] does not explicitly mandate any specific standard of review to be followed by panels. It was the Appellate Body that interpreted Article 11 of the Understanding on Rules and Procedures Governing the Settlement of Disputes (DSU)[13] as determining such a standard. In a widely quoted passage, the Appellate Body explained that the applicable standard of review with respect to factual determinations 'is neither *de novo* review as such, nor "total deference", but rather the "objective assessment of the facts"', adding that 'many panels have in the past refused to undertake *de novo* review, wisely, since under current practice and systems, they are in any case poorly suited to

[9] Ehlermann and Lockhart, 'Standard of Review', 493.

[10] Jan Bohanes and Nicolas Lockhart, 'Standard of Review in WTO Law' in Daniel Bethlehem et al (eds), *The Oxford Handbook of International Trade Law* (Oxford: Oxford University Press, 2009) 379.

[11] Appellate Body Report, *EC Measures Concerning Meat and Meat Products (EC—Hormones)*, WT/DS26/AB/R, WT/DS48/AB/R, 13 February 1998, para 111.

[12] Article 17.6 of the Agreement on Implementation of Article VI GATT, 15 April 1994, Marrakesh Agreement Establishing the World Trade Organization, Annex 1A, 1868 UNTS 201.

[13] Understanding on Rules and Procedures Governing the Settlement of Disputes, 15 April 1994, Marrakesh Agreement Establishing the World Trade Organization, Annex 2, 1869 UNTS

engage in such a review'.[14] Although the standard indicated by the Appellate Body falls short of providing a meaningful guidance for panels (ie both deferential and intrusive review can be objective),[15] it has nevertheless become a point of reference in subsequent disputes.[16]

Since the objective standard does not explain the required level of scrutiny, it is necessary to look more closely at the approach(es) taken by WTO panels in specific disputes under particular agreements. When it comes to the review of scientific facts, the most important is the case law under the SPS Agreement. The treaty introduces certain disciplines in the area of sanitary and phytosanitary protection, requiring, among other things, that SPS measures be based on scientific principles and not be maintained without sufficient scientific evidence.[17] This general obligation is explained in Article 5.1, which obliges WTO Members to base their SPS measures on a formal assessment that would evaluate the possibility or probability of risks to human, animal or plant life or health.

The early SPS case law, probably except for the Appellate Body report in *EC—Hormones*,[18] adopted rather intrusive review that came very close to *de novo* enquiry.[19] WTO panels investigated into the quality, persuasive force and correctness of scientific findings made on the domestic level and substituted them with their own determinations. For example, in *Japan—Apples*, the Appellate Body made clear that objective review does not require a panel to give any 'precedence to the importing Member's evaluation of scientific evidence' or to accord a degree of discretion to such Member in the manner in which it chooses, weighs, and evaluates scientific evidence.[20] Another panel, although admitting that its task was not to undertake a new risk assessment, also added that in fact its position was similar to that of a national body producing such an assessment.[21] This suggests (and is subsequently reflected in the reasoning of the report) that the panel saw its role as an ultimate arbiter of correctness (and not reasonableness) of

401, Article 11 (providing in the relevant part that 'a panel should make an objective assessment of the matter before it, including an objective assessment of the facts of the case').

[14] Appellate Body Report, *EC—Hormones*, para 117.

[15] Ehlermann and Lockhart, 'Standard of Review', 495; Michael Ming Du, 'Standard of Review under the SPS Agreement after EC–Hormones II', 59 *ICLQ* 441 (2010) at 443; see also Michael Ioannidis, Chapter 6 in this volume.

[16] For more general discussion on external limits of WTO review see Ernst-Ulrich Petersmann, Chapter 2 in this volume.

[17] SPS Agreement, Article 2.2.

[18] Although the Appellate Body explicitly refused in that case to adopt deferential reasonableness standard that was postulated by the European Communities (and which would be based on the standard provided by the Anti-Dumping Agreement), in fact it took a rather deferential approach when assessing scientific backup of the EC measure.

[19] Similarly Ming Du, 'Standard of Review', 448; Bohanes and Lockhart, 'Standard of Review', 412.

[20] Appellate Body Report, *Japan—Measures Affecting the Importation of Apples*, WT/DS245/AB/R, 10 December 2003.

[21] Panel Report, *United States—Continued Suspension of Obligations in the EC—Hormones Dispute*, WT/DS320/R, 14 November 2008, as modified by Appellate Body Report WT/DS320/AB/R.

scientific determinations that formed a basis for the domestic measure.[22] As the panel observed in its report:

> [w]hile, on some occasions, we followed the majority of experts expressing concurrent views, in some others the divergence of views were such that we could not follow that approach and decided to accept the position(s) which appeared, in our view, to be the most specific in relation to the question at issue and to be best supported by arguments and evidence.[23]

As correctly summarized by Fukunaga, panels in the earlier SPS case law 'made their own factual determinations as to whether a risk existed, comparing their conclusions with those reached by the respondents'.[24] In a similar vein, Ming Du observed that:

> the panel's role seems to have shifted to finding out what the 'correct science' is, as opposed to whether [a Member's] interpretation of scientific evidence is an honest, reasonable, and coherent account, even if it differs from the opinions given by the panel's scientific experts.[25]

This initial approach was modified in the more recent case law. The Appellate Body in *US—Continued Suspension* opted for a more deferential standard. In particular, it confirmed that the task of a WTO panel under the SPS Agreement consists in reviewing, and not redoing, risk assessment. As a consequence, a panel cannot substitute its own scientific judgments for that of the national risk assessor. Equally, 'the review power of a panel is not to determine whether the risk assessment undertaken by a WTO Member is correct, but rather to determine whether that risk assessment is supported by coherent reasoning and respectable scientific evidence'.[26] To this end, the Appellate Body set out a fairly detailed methodology to be followed by panels when confronted with a domestic risk assessment. First, a panel must identify the scientific evidence that forms a basis of a specific SPS measure. As a second step, a panel has to verify the epistemic quality of such evidence (whether it 'comes from a respected and qualified source'). In this context, there is no need for a panel to check the correctness of scientific data and a mere assessment of its defensibility (as a scientific claim according to the methodological parameters of a specific discipline) is sufficient. Subsequently, the panel should assess whether the reasoning articulated on the basis of the scientific evidence is objective and coherent (ie rational relationship between evidence and conclusions). Fourth, a panel must determine whether

[22] For more detailed discussion of specific examples of intrusive review, see Lukasz Gruszczynski, 'Standard of Review of Health/Environmental Regulation by WTO Panels', in Gert Van Calster and Denise Prévost (eds), *Research Handbook on Environment, Health and the WTO* (Cheltenham: Edward Elgar Publishing, 2013), 740–3.

[23] Panel Report, *US—Continued Suspension*, para 7.420.

[24] Yuka Fukunaga, 'Standard of Review and "Scientific Truths" in the WTO Dispute Settlement System and Investment Arbitration', 3(3) *JIDS* 559 (2012) at 564.

[25] Ming Du, 'Standard of Review', 449.

[26] Appellate Body Report, *US—Continued Suspension of Obligations in the EC—Hormones Dispute*, WT/DS320/AB/R, 14 November 2008, para 590.

there is a sufficient connection between the results of the risk assessment and the SPS measure at issue.[27] The Appellate Body, while confirming the right of a panel to seek the assistance of experts, also warned that 'the purpose of a panel consulting with experts is not to perform its own risk assessment'.[28] Overall this standard appears to be relatively deferential as it puts the emphasis on methodological rather than substantive aspects (eg defendable scientific claim versus the best available science).[29]

The subsequent SPS case law (ie *Australia—Apples*)[30] only partially confirmed the deferential nature of the required review. Although, the Appellate Body repeated that a panel is only expected to determine whether a specific claim can be regarded as 'legitimate' science (and not the best science),[31] it also accepted a rather intrusive examination into the reasoning included in a risk assessment (the third step of the analysis described above). Consequently, it is not enough for a panel to inquire whether such reasoning falls within a range that could be considered legitimate by the scientific community.[32] In this context, the Appellate Body also rejected the Australian claim that the task of the panel was limited to determining whether alleged flaws in the reasoning of risk assessment were sufficiently serious to undermine reasonable confidence in the assessment as a whole.[33] The approach proposed by the Appellate Body obviously opens the possibility of a quite intrusive investigation into the reasoning of risk assessment (including its assumptions, intermediate and final conclusions), with a panel able to substitute its own judgments for those of the national risk assessor. As a consequence, it may be argued that the approach merely replaces the previous *de novo* review with respect to the underlying science with an intrusive enquiry into the methodological dimension of risk assessment.

What remains uncontroversial is that the existence of risk can be shown either qualitatively or quantitatively, while domestic SPS measures can be based on both majority and minority scientific opinions (the latter if they come from qualified and respected sources). This obviously affects the level of scrutiny that may be applied by WTO panels (eg by barring a panel from condemning a measure simply because it is based on divergent rather than mainstream science). There is also a considerable level of deference with respect to policy choices made by WTO Members as to the maximum level of risk they are ready to tolerate.[34] Panels are in principle prohibited from inquiring into the appropriateness of the

[27] Appellate Body Report, *US—Continued Suspension*, para 591.
[28] Appellate Body Report, *US—Continued Suspension*, para 592.
[29] Similarly Jacqueline Peel, *Science and Risk Regulation in International Law* (Cambridge: Cambridge University Press, 2010), 218.
[30] Appellate Body Report, *Australia—Measures Affecting the Importation of Apples from New Zealand*, WT/DS367/AB/R, 17 December 2010.
[31] Appellate Body Report, *Australia—Apples*, para 225.
[32] Appellate Body Report, *Australia—Apples*, para 231.
[33] Appellate Body Report, *Australia—Apples*, para 258.
[34] Cf Ehlermann and Lockhart, 'Standard of Review', 517.

acceptable level of protection and need to accept the level chosen by a particular Member.

Outside the SPS Agreement, the applicable standard of review with respect to scientific facts remains relatively deferential.[35] As noted by the panel in *EC—Asbestos*, a case decided under the General Agreement on Tariffs and Trade (GATT) 1994,[36] 'it is not its function to settle a scientific debate, not being composed of experts in the field of the possible human health risks posed by asbestos. Consequently, the Panel does not intend to set itself up as an arbiter of the opinions expressed by the scientific community'.[37] In this specific case the limited role of the panel only required assessing whether evidence was sufficient to conclude that there was a human health risk and whether the measure was necessary to achieve the regulatory goal of France (and not to determine whether risk 'objectively' exists, eg according to the best available science). In line with the SPS Agreement, minority scientific opinions may form an equally valid basis for a measure as mainstream science. WTO Members are also free to set any level of protection they deem appropriate and panels are not allowed to question the rationality of such choices.[38] A similarly deferential approach was taken by the panel in the *Brazil—Tyres*.[39] In particular, the panel did not require any specific evaluation, according to the best available science, of the risk posed by the improper management of used tyres in Brazil and accepted evidence of a general nature (eg the Basel Convention Technical Guidelines on the Identification and Management of Used Tyres, reflecting the global consensus on the matter) and of indirect character relating to practices in other countries (eg the European Union, United Kingdom).[40] Under the Technical Barriers to Trade (TBT) Agreement,[41] the panel only touched upon the issue of standard of review applicable to scientific evidence in *US—Tuna II (Mexico)*.[42] Similarly to the approach taken under GATT 1994, it was interested in determining whether specific claims were sufficiently substantiated by the respondent, rather than whether they represented the best available science.[43]

[35] Although one also has to admit that the case law is rather limited, while the panels rarely explicitly speak about standard of review applicable to scientific determinations. One reason that could explain this situation is the fact that scientific controversies in trade disputes, except for SPS cases, are still occasional.

[36] GATT, 15 April 1994, Marrakesh Agreement Establishing the World Trade Organization, Annex 1, 1867 UNTS 187.

[37] Panel Report, *European Communities—Measures Affecting Asbestos and Asbestos-Containing Products*, WT/DS135/R, 5 April 2001, as modified by Appellate Body Report, WT/DS135/AB/R, para 8.181.

[38] Eg Appellate Body Report, *European Communities—Measures Affecting Asbestos and Asbestos-Containing Products*, WT/DS135/AB/R, 5 April 2001, para 168.

[39] Panel Report, *Brazil—Measures Affecting Imports of Retreaded Tyres*, WT/DS332/R, 17 December 2007, as modified by Appellate Body Report WT/DS332/AB/R, para 7.77.

[40] Panel Report, *Brazil—Tyres*, paras 7.61, 7.68 and fn 1118.

[41] Agreement on Technical Barriers to Trade, 15 April 1994, Marrakesh Agreement Establishing the World Trade Organization, Annex 1, 1868 UNTS 120.

[42] Panel Report, *United States—Measures Concerning the Importation, Marketing and Sale of Tuna and Tuna Products*, WT/DS381/R, 13 June 2012, as modified by Appellate Body Report WT/DS381/AB/R.

[43] Panel Report, *US—Tuna II (Mexico)*, para 7.504.

III. Standard of Review over Scientific Facts in Investment Arbitration

While earlier investment tribunals showed little deference to the scientific assessment by the relevant national regulatory bodies,[44] more recent tribunals have expressed a certain degree of deference to national authorities in disputes that require complex factual determinations of a scientific character. This 'return of the State'[45] is clearly visible under the North American Free Trade Agreement (NAFTA). Since the NAFTA was successfully negotiated, investor–State arbitration under its Chapter 11 has put the regulatory spaces of the parties under pressure. A growing stream of arbitrations has focused on the interplay between public health regulations by the host State and the NAFTA Chapter 11 substantive provisions. Among the arbitration claims filed by investors against host States as a result of the latter's regulation are those relating to: the adoption of discrimination policies; the expropriation of a given investment; and the violation of the fair and equitable treatment (FET) standard. In a nutshell, the question is how to reconcile the need to promote public health with the promotion of foreign direct investment. Can the host State adopt precautionary policies? To what extent can and should policy influence risk regulation? Should the investor be compensated if its toxic products are banned from the market? Which standard of review should arbitral tribunals adopt to assess scientific evidence?

In *S.D. Myers v Canada*, the tribunal rejected the claim that the ban on the export of polychlorinated biphenyl (PCB) constituted an expropriation, because the ban was temporary and there was no appropriation or transfer of benefits to the host State. The tribunal affirmed that 'regulatory conduct by public authorities is unlikely to be the subject of legitimate complaint under Article 1110 NAFTA, although the tribunal does not rule out that possibility'.[46] Somehow, this case theoretically distinguished between legitimate regulation and indirect expropriation and put emphasis on the fact that there was no appropriation and the property was not taken from the owner. Furthermore, the *S.D. Myers* tribunal considered that a breach of Article 1105 occurs:

> only when it is shown that an investor has been treated in such an unjust or arbitrary manner that the treatment rises to the level that is unacceptable from the international perspective. That determination must be made in the light of the high measure of deference that international law generally extends to the right of domestic authorities to regulate matters within their own borders. The determination must also take into account any specific rules of international law that are applicable to the case.[47]

[44] See eg *Metalclad Corporation v The United Mexican States*, ICSID, Award, 30 August 2000, Case No. ARB(AF)/97/1.

[45] José E. Alvarez, 'The Return of the State', 20(2) *Minnesota Journal of International Law* 223 (2009). See also Erlend Leonhardsen, Chapter 8 in this volume.

[46] *S.D. Myers, Inc. v Government of Canada*, Partial Award, 13 November 2000, para 281.

[47] *S.D. Myers v Canada*, para 263.

In *Waste Management II v Mexico*,[48] the arbitral tribunal acknowledged that:

the minimum standard of treatment of fair and equitable treatment is infringed by conduct attributable to the State and harmful to the claimant if the conduct is arbitrary, grossly unfair, unjust or idiosyncratic, is discriminatory and exposes the claimant to sectional or racial prejudice, or involves a lack of due process leading to an outcome which offends judicial propriety—as might be the case with a manifest failure of natural justice in judicial proceedings or a complete lack of transparency and candour in an administrative process. In applying this standard it is relevant that the treatment is in breach of representations made by the host State which were reasonably relied on by the claimant.[49]

At the same time, the tribunal stated that such standard of review is 'a flexible one which must be adapted to the circumstances of each case.'[50] This holding was restated in a subsequent arbitration, *Gami Investments v Mexico*.[51]

Correctly, arbitral tribunals have declared that it is not their task to second-guess the regulatory autonomy of the host State. As the *S.D. Myers* tribunal put it:

When interpreting and applying the 'minimum standard', a Chapter 11 tribunal does not have an open-ended mandate to second-guess government decision-making. Governments have to make many potentially controversial choices. In doing so, they may appear to have made mistakes, to have misjudged the facts, *proceeded on the basis of a misguided economic or sociological theory*, placed too much emphasis on some social values over others and adopted solutions that are ultimately ineffective or counterproductive. The ordinary remedy, if there were one, for errors in modern governments is through internal political and legal processes, including elections.[52]

In *Glamis Gold v US*, which related to the alleged expropriation of a mine to protect indigenous heritage and presented analogous issues of reviewing national determinations based on specific knowledge—namely archaeology—the respondent argued that: 'in reviewing State agency or departmental decisions and actions, international tribunals as well as domestic judiciaries favour deference to the agency so as not to second guess the primary decision-makers or become "science courts"'.[53] The tribunal disagreed 'that domestic deference in national court systems is necessarily applicable to international tribunals'. Instead, it found that the standard of deference was already 'present in the standard as stated, rather than being additive to that standard'.[54]

In *Methanex*, as scientific evidence showed that MTBE (methyl tertiary-butyl ether) contaminated groundwater and was difficult and expensive to clean up, the State of California enacted legislation to prevent the commercialization and

[48] *Waste Management, Inc. v United Mexican States*, ICSID, Award, 30 April 2004, Case No. ARB(AF)/00/3, paras 94 and 98.

[49] *Waste Management II*, para 98. [50] *Waste Management II*, para 99.

[51] *Gami Investments, Inc. v The Government of the United Mexican States*, UNCITRAL Award, 15 November 2004, para 96.

[52] *S.D. Myers*, para 261; *Gami v Mexico*, para 93 (emphasis added).

[53] *Glamis Gold, Ltd v United States of America*, ICSID, Award, 8 June 2009, para 617.

[54] *Glamis Gold v US* (emphasizing that 'The idea of deference is found in the modifiers "manifest" and "gross" that make this standard a stringent one; it is found in the idea that a breach requires

use of MTBE. Methanex, a Canadian investor, initiated arbitration against the United States of America, claiming compensation resulting from losses caused by the ban on the use of a gasoline additive. Methanex submitted that the Californian regulation was tantamount to expropriation within NAFTA Article 1110, as the US measures were not meant to serve a public purpose, but rather to seize the company's market share and to favour the domestic ethanol industry. Since no compensation was paid, Methanex argued that this violated due process of law and the minimum standard of treatment. However, the tribunal decided that there was no expropriation because it was 'a non-discriminatory regulation for a public purpose, which is enacted in accordance with due process and, which affects, *inter alios*, a foreign investor or investment'.[55]

The *Methanex* tribunal ascertained the non-discriminatory character of the measure and its public purpose by looking at the procedure through which the national measure had been adopted. By examining the scientific study carried out by the University of California (the UC Report), the tribunal held that the UC Report reflected a serious, objective and scientific approach, and that it was also subjected to open and informed debate such as public hearings, testimony and peer-review: 'its emergence as a serious scientific work from such an open and informed debate is the best evidence that it was not the product of a political sham'.[56] The award did not suggest that the Report was scientifically correct, nor did it take a position on its scientific truths. Nonetheless, the reasoning highlights that governments may regulate risks where there are competing scientific views: in this context, emphasis will be put on *due process*.

More recently, in *Chemtura v Canada* the tribunal endorsed a deferential review, concentrating on the reasonableness rather than the correctness of the scientific determination made by domestic regulatory bodies.[57] The *Chemtura* case concerned the question of whether the Government of Canada should pay compensation to a United States agricultural pesticide manufacturer for its ban of lindane, a pesticide used on canola. As Canada's Pest Management Regulatory Agency (PMRA)[58] banned lindane on the basis of the risk assessment findings,[59] Chemtura initiated arbitral proceedings at the Permanent Court of Arbitration, requesting the reinstatement of all registrations relating to its lindane products and/or the damages resulting from Canada's alleged breaches.[60] According

something greater than mere arbitrariness, something that is surprising, shocking, or exhibits a manifest lack of reasoning').

[55] *Methanex Corporation v United States of America*, UNCITRAL (NAFTA), Final Award, 3 August 2005, Part IV, Chapter D, 4.

[56] *Methanex v US*, Part II, Ch. D, paras 7–22, and Part. III, Ch. A, paras 1–36.

[57] *Chemtura Corporation (formerly Crompton Corporation) v Government of Canada*, Award, 2 August 2010.

[58] The Pest Management Regulatory Agency is the federal agency 'responsible for the regulation of pest control products in Canada. Its primary objective is to prevent unacceptable risks to people and the environment from the use of pest control products.' *Chemtura v Canada*, para 10.

[59] *Chemtura v Canada*, para 29.

[60] *Crompton Corporation v Government of Canada*, Notice of Intent to Submit a Claim to Arbitration, 6 November 2001; Second Notice of Intent, 4 April 2002; Third Notice of Intent, 19

to Chemtura, the regulation was not based on a rigorous scientific risk assessment,[61] discriminated against foreign investors by requiring the use of substitute Canadian products in lieu of lindane, and amounted to an indirect expropriation. Therefore, according to the firm, Canada was in violation of NAFTA Article 1103 (Most Favoured Nation Treatment), Article 1105 (minimum standard of treatment) and Article 1110 (expropriation).[62]

The tribunal held that Canada did not violate its obligations under NAFTA. With regard to the standard of review, the tribunal stated that such an assessment is not 'an abstract assessment circumscribed by a legal doctrine about the margin of appreciation of specialized regulatory agencies', rather it 'must be conducted *in concreto*'.[63] The tribunal held that 'the assessment of fact [was] an integral part of its review under Article 1105 NAFTA' and that 'in assessing whether the treatment afforded to the claimant's investment was in accordance with the international minimum standard, the Tribunal must take into account all the circumstances, including the fact that certain agencies manage highly specialized domains involving scientific and public policy determinations'.[64]

First, the tribunal found that the respondent had not breached Article 1105 NAFTA. As Article 1105 NAFTA seeks to ensure that investors from NAFTA States benefit from regulatory fairness, the tribunal investigated whether the review of lindane was conducted in good faith and whether it breached the due process rights of the claimant.[65] In the tribunal's view, 'the evidence of the record [did] not show bad faith or disingenuous conduct on the part of Canada' but 'it show[ed] that the Special review was undertaken by the PMRA in pursuance of its mandate and as a result of Canada's *international obligations*'.[66] Although the tribunal noted at the outset that 'it [was] not its task to determine whether certain uses of lindane are dangerous' and that 'the rule of a Chapter 11 Tribunal is not to second-guess the correctness of the science-based decision-making of highly specialized national regulatory agencies',[67] the tribunal '[could] not ignore the fact that lindane has raised increasingly serious concerns both in other countries and at the international level since the 1970s'.[68] On one hand, the tribunal noted that 'the position of the claimant as to whether lindane itself present[ed] unacceptable health and environmental risks [was] somewhat ambiguous'.[69] On the other hand, the tribunal deemed that the respondent had 'amply established the existence of such concerns' by referring to a number of countries banning or restricting the use of lindane and international legal instruments further signalling international concern about the human health and environmental

September 2002. Notice of Arbitration (Related to the First and Second Notice of Intent) 17 October 2002; and Notice of Arbitration (Related to the Third Notice) 10 February 2005. These documents are available at <http://www.international.gc.ca/trade-agreements-accords-commerciaux/disp-diff/crompton_archive.aspx?lang=en&view=d> (accessed 28 March 2014).

[61] *Chemtura v Canada*, para 52.
[62] *Chemtura v Canada*, para 92. [63] *Chemtura v Canada*, para 92.
[64] *Chemtura v Canada*, para 123. [65] *Chemtura v Canada*, para 145.
[66] *Chemtura v Canada*, para 138 [emphasis added].
[67] *Chemtura v Canada*, para 134. [68] *Chemtura v Canada*, para 135.
[69] *Chemtura v Canada*, para 133.

effects of the chemical.[70] For instance, the 1998 Aarhus Protocol on Persistent Organic Pollutants to the 1979 Convention on Long-Range Transboundary Air Pollution[71] restricted the use of lindane and required the reassessment of this chemical product.[72] Moreover, in 2009 lindane was included in the list of chemicals designated for elimination under the Stockholm Convention on Persistent Organic Pollutants.[73]

The tribunal found that the review of lindane was not conducted in such a manner that reached the threshold necessary to constitute a violation of the minimum standard of treatment: '[as] a sophisticated registrant experienced in a highly regulated industry, the Claimant could not reasonably ignore the PMRA's practices and the importance of the evaluation of exposure risks within such practices'.[74] More importantly, with regard to the risk assessment, the tribunal affirmed that 'scientific divergence... cannot in and of itself serve as a basis for a finding of breach of Article 1105 of NAFTA.'[75]

Second, the tribunal held that the respondent did not breach Article 1103 NAFTA.[76] With regard to the allegation that the claimant's investment was discriminated in any form, the tribunal found that this allegation had no factual basis.[77]

Third, the tribunal found that no expropriation had occurred,[78] holding that 'since the sales from lindane products were a relatively small part of the overall sales of Chemtura,... the interference of the Respondent with the Claimant's investment [could] not be deemed "substantial"'[79] and that:

> [I]n any event... the measures challenged by the Claimant constituted a valid exercise of the Respondent's police powers. The PMRA took measures within its mandate, in a non-discriminatory manner, motivated by the increasing awareness of the dangers presented by lindane for human health and the environment. A measure adopted under such circumstances is a valid exercise of the State's police powers and, as a result, does not constitute an expropriation.[80]

Other interesting investment disputes concerning scientific evidence relate to plain packaging and pharmaceutical products, respectively. As both disputes are still pending, it is not possible at this stage to foresee which standards of review the relevant tribunals will adopt.[81]

[70] *Chemtura v Canada*, para 133.

[71] Aarhus Protocol on Persistent Organic Pollutants to the 1979 Convention on Long-Range Transboundary Air Pollution of 24 June 1998, in force 23 October 2003, 2230 UNTS 79.

[72] *Chemtura v Canada*, para 135.

[73] *Chemtura v Canada*, para 136. Stockholm Convention on Persistent Organic Pollutants of 22 May 2001, in force 17 May 2004, 40 ILM (2001) 532 (note that the Appellate Body adopted an analogous approach in *EC—Asbestos*).

[74] *Chemtura v Canada*, para 149.

[75] *Chemtura v Canada*, para 154.

[76] *Chemtura v Canada*, para 237.

[77] *Chemtura v Canada*, para 234.

[78] *Chemtura v Canada*, para 267.

[79] *Chemtura v Canada*, para 263.

[80] *Chemtura v Canada*, para 266.

[81] For more details on these disputes, see Valentina Vadi, 'Global Health Governance at a Crossroads: Trademark Protection v. Tobacco Control in International Investment Law', 48 *Stanford Journal of International Law* 93 (2012); Valentina Vadi, 'The Beauty of Unity? Intellectual

IV. Critical Assessment: Converging Parallels?

A. The WTO acquis

WTO dispute settlement bodies certainly express a certain degree of deference to national authorities in disputes that require complex factual determinations of a scientific character. This is clearly visible under the GATT 1994 and TBT Agreement. Even under the SPS Agreement one may observe a recent shift (ie *US—Continued Suspension*) in the direction of deferential review that concentrates on reasonableness rather than correctness of the scientific determination made by a domestic regulator. The case law is also consistent in holding that the national levels of protection are not subject to any review by the WTO, while a regulatory measure can be based on either majority or minority scientific views. At the same time, admittedly the dispute settlement bodies are not willing to entirely abdicate from the position of final arbitrator over scientific controversies. In *Australia—Apples* the Appellate Body admitted that the investigation into the national reasoning articulated on the basis of scientific evidence is relatively intrusive. Due to the reasons discussed below, this is a regrettable development.

In this context, it is worth noting that while there are some merits of strict review,[82] multiple reasons speak in favour of the deferential approach (albeit not a total deference as this would turn some WTO obligations into a mere formality and could weaken the whole system) of WTO panels, and more generally of any international court or tribunal, with respect to evaluation of scientific facts.[83] Probably the most important one is the limited epistemic competence of such bodies to assess the correctness of scientific evidence, which in turn considerably increases the risk of rendering wrong decisions. This was actually explicitly recognized by the Appellate Body when it observed that 'a panel is not well suited to conduct scientific research and assessment itself'.[84] Panellists are experts in international trade law and perhaps in international economics, but not in scientific matters. Although they can be assisted by scientific experts (in fact this was the case in all SPS disputes), this can only partially address the problem of limited epistemic competence.[85] In particular, panels still need to decide how to interpret

Property Rights v. Public Health in International Investment Arbitration' in Christian J. Tams and Rainer Hoffmann (eds), *Investment Law and Its Others* (Berlin: Nomos, 2012) 167–90.

[82] Arguably the main advantage of *de novo* review is the possibility of having a neutral third party (eg a WTO panel or an investment arbitral tribunal) review all the aspects of a given dispute without any default deference for the determinations made by the defendant. *De novo* review may also strengthen international obligations and improve the consistency of the particular legal system (as the discretion of States will be limited). Nevertheless, and as discussed in this section, we believe that overall the reasons for deference are much stronger. See also Andrew T. Guzman, 'Determining the Appropriate Standard of Review in WTO Dispute Resolution', 42 *Cornell Journal of International Law* 45 (2009).

[83] As to other reasons that may justify a deferential approach of WTO panels outside assessment of scientific facts, see Michael Ioannidis, Chapter 6 in this volume.

[84] Appellate Body, *Australia—Apples*, para 225.

[85] For more detailed discussion see Lukasz Gruszczynski, 'The Role of Experts in Environmental and Health Related Trade Disputes in the WTO: Deconstructing Decision-Making Processes'

opinions of experts, how to choose between conflicting views, or what kind of inferences to make therefrom. This is rarely an easy task, especially if answers are formulated in conditional language that reflects the uncertainties inherent in scientific research. An additional layer of difficulty is also added by the lack of a proper scientific institutional infrastructure that the panels could rely on, and the time constraints built into the WTO dispute settlement system.[86] At the same time, it should be noted that this observation is true not only with regard to scientific evidence as such but also applies to the reasoning articulated on the basis of scientific evidence. Panels are in no way better equipped to decide on the correctness of intermediate conclusions on risk assessments or expert judgments used to compensate for uncertainties. Both aspects are highly complex and go beyond the limited epistemic competence of panels. On the other hand, scientific determinations, which form a basis for a contested measure, are usually made by highly specialized domestic regulatory agencies. Arguably in most cases those agencies will be better placed than panels to assess risks or to undertake other scientific enquiry.

Secondly, regulatory science—ie science applied in the policy (regulatory)-making process, including risk or environmental impact assessment—is not a purely scientific task; rather it has both scientific and non-scientific components depending on the specific socio-cultural conditions of a particular country.[87] Such assessments inevitably involve the subjective judgments of the assessors and reflects their attitudes towards particular risks, values of the relevant community in which the experts are acting (which may affect how the problem is framed), and other normative elements such as the required level of protection or the selected approach to deal with uncertainties. Consequently, the same set of scientific data may produce entirely different estimates in various jurisdictions. A panel seems to be worse placed to make such judgments than the WTO Member that conducted research and evaluated scientific evidence in the context of its specific risk frames and concerns.[88] If a panel ends up imposing on the WTO Members its own vision of science (as would be the case in a *de novo* review), these normative and context-dependent elements will be lost, and the ultimate determination may fail to produce a correct result. As summarized by Peel in the context of the SPS Agreement:

> an intrusive panel review of a WTO Member's risk assessment, drawing heavily on expert views (especially if these views are accepted uncritically), thus risks supplanting the risk framings considered important by advising experts for those deemed important by the WTO Member in carrying out the risk assessment.[89]

in Mónika Ambrus et al (eds), *Irrelevant, Advisors or Decision-Makers? The Role of 'Experts' in International Decision-Making* (Cambridge: Cambridge University Press, 2014, forthcoming).

[86] Andrew Guzman, 'Dispute Resolution in SPS Cases', in Dan Horowitz et al (eds), *Ten Years of WTO Dispute Settlement* (London: International Bar Association, 2007), 229.

[87] See generally David Winickoff et al, 'Adjudicating the GM Food Wars: Science, Risk, and Democracy in World Trade Law', 30 *Yale Journal of International Law* 81 (2005).

[88] Cf Catherine Button, *Power to Protect. Trade, Health and the World Trade Organization* (Portland: Hart Publishing, 2004) at 181.

[89] Jacqueline Peel, 'Of Apples and Oranges (and Hormones in Beef): Science and the Standard of Review in WTO Disputes under the SPS Agreement', 61 *ICLQ* 427 (2012), 443.

Thirdly, as noted in the literature, the potential costs of a mistake on the side of the WTO dispute settlement bodies appear to be considerably higher in health-related disputes, as compared to other trade disagreements. Some additional costs may also be generated by problems in compliance. Domestic health measures regulate very sensitive areas which were always considered within the core of national sovereignty. Due to the high values at stake, it may be simply politically unviable to comply with a WTO ruling. Potential costs here relate not only to additional distortions of international trade resulting from the suspension of a concession in response to non-compliance, but also to the harm that is caused to the credibility (and perceived legitimacy) of the WTO as such. If Members do not comply with rulings, the whole dispute settlement system is called into question.[90]

B. Investment jurisprudence

Arbitral tribunals have increasingly shown a rather deferential standard of review—albeit not a total deference—when reviewing regulatory measures with a scientific aspect.[91] This development is a positive one for a number of reasons. First, like the WTO adjudicative bodies, arbitral tribunals have little if any epistemic competence to assess the correctness of the relevant scientific evidence. Arbitrators are international law experts but may not have expertise in scientific matters.[92] As Koskenniemi explains, international law 'does not operate on the basis of demonstrable, even less empirical truths...',[93] but rather the correctness of the legal decision is 'a product of legal practice, argument, persuasion, not its precondition'.[94] On the other hand, the scientific determinations which form the basis for a contested measure are usually made by specialized domestic regulatory agencies. Arguably, in most cases, specialized agencies will be better placed than international adjudicators to assess risk or to undertake other scientific enquiry.

Second, regulation concerning public health lies at the very heart of State sovereignty. Due to their impact on public welfare, health/environment-related disputes differ from other investment or trade-related disputes. A perceived lack of consideration for paramount health concerns might fuel the so-called 'legitimacy crisis' of investment arbitration.

Third, as already mentioned, risk regulation has a hybrid nature in that it involves both scientific and non-scientific—namely legal and political—aspects.[95] Policy

[90] Guzman, 'Dispute Resolution', 230.

[91] See generally Valentina Vadi, *Public Health in International Investment Law and Arbitration* (London: Routledge, 2012). See also Caroline Henckels, Chapter 7 in this volume.

[92] See generally Stephan Schill, 'W(h)ither Fragmentation? On the Literature and Sociology of International Investment Law', 22(3) *EJIL* 875 (2011).

[93] Martti Koskenniemi, 'Law, Teleology and International Relations: An Essay in Counterdisciplinarity', 26 *International Relations* 1 (2012), 19.

[94] Koskenniemi, 'Law, Teleology and International Relations', 19.

[95] Lukasz Gruszczynski, *Regulating Health and Environmental Risks under WTO Law: Critical Analysis of the SPS Agreement* (Oxford: Oxford University Press, 2010) 147–55.

makers 'rely on the epistemic capital of science in articulating new policies'.[96] Yet, regulation remains a social science; the governance of risk 'cannot be left to scientists alone–for both epistemic and political reasons'.[97] When regulating scientific matters, regulators will have to take into account the specific preferences of their constituency, depending on the specific socio-cultural conditions of their country.

Arguably, a case for deferential review would be weaker if one analogized investment arbitration to international commercial arbitration. In such cases, as correctly noted by Fukunaga, 'factual findings by tribunals [would] exclusively depend on the persuasiveness of each party's case; deference to any of the parties [would] ha[ve] little place'.[98] Commercial disputes involve private entities, with a tribunal acting as 'impartial referee'.[99] Yet, despite some similarities between investment arbitration and commercial arbitration—eg the selection of arbitrators by parties, the confidential nature of the proceeding, and some procedural matters—international commercial arbitration generally involves private parties and concerns disputes of a commercial nature while investment arbitration involves States and private actors. As we argued elsewhere,[100] international investment arbitration should be regarded as a dispute settlement mechanism among those available under international law—such as the WTO dispute settlement mechanism—thus calling for public international law standards.

The examined investment arbitrations address the concerns of an alleged 'legitimacy crisis' of investor–State arbitration, indicating that this mechanism is responsive to societal concerns. The *Chemtura* case is a paradigmatic example of this new trend.[101] First, the *Chemtura* award shows that in case of scientific uncertainty and a plurality of scientific opinions, adjudicators may put emphasis on the scientific method and on due process, particularly with regard to transparency and public participation.[102] While 'the rule of a Chapter 11 Tribunal is not to second-guess the correctness of the science-based decision-making of highly specialized national regulatory agencies',[103] the tribunal's enquiry focused on the question of whether policy makers adopted reasonable scientific methods and due process in the risk assessment. In this sense, as Wälde and Kolo put it, investor–State arbitration 'can be seen as a desirable constraint over the domestic political process' and 'a step towards good governance in international economic relations'.[104] Second, with regard to the standard

[96] Oren Perez and Reut Snir, 'Global Environmental Risk Governance under Conditions of Scientific Uncertainty: Legal, Political and Social Transformations', 2(1) *Transnational Environmental Law* 7 (2013), 7–8.

[97] Perez and Snir, 'Global Environmental Risk Governance', 13.

[98] Fukunaga, 'Standard of Review', 570.

[99] Fukunaga, 'Standard of Review', 570.

[100] See generally Vadi and Gruszczynski, 'Standards of Review'.

[101] For in depth analysis and critical assessment, see Valentina Vadi, 'Overlapping Regulatory Spaces: The Architecture of NAFTA Chapter 11 and the Regulation of Toxic Chemicals', 4 *European Journal of Risk Regulation* 586 (2011).

[102] Marcos Orellana, 'The Role of Science in Investment Arbitrations Concerning Public Health and the Environment' 17(1) *Yearbook of International Environmental Law* 48 (2006) at 54 (arguing in favour of the adoption of the margin of appreciation doctrine in investment arbitration).

[103] *Chemtura v Canada*, para 134.

[104] Thomas Wälde and Abba Kolo, 'Environmental Regulation, Investment Protection and "Regulatory Taking" in International Law', 50 *ICLQ* 811 (2001), 846. Similar observation in the

of review,[105] the *Chemtura* tribunal noted that it would not apply an abstract level of deference when scrutinizing the conduct of States, but that it would weigh all the circumstances, including 'the fact that certain agencies manage highly specialized domains involving scientific and public policy determinations'.[106] Third, by placing some weight on the fact that many countries had taken steps to ban and restrict the use of lindane and by referring to multilateral environmental agreements (MEAs), the tribunal implicitly confirmed the view that international investment law does not constitute a self-contained regime; rather it must be interpreted in the light of public international law. Comparative assessments were used as a tool to assess the reasonableness of a given regulatory measure. While the existence of MEAs did not shield the regulatory action of the host State from review, it constituted evidence of the government's good faith vis-à-vis Chemtura and its products.[107] Finally, the adoption by the arbitral tribunal of the police powers doctrine has to be welcomed too. While the importance of protecting aliens in international law is incontestable, it is important to keep in mind that investment guarantees do not provide absolute protection, but may be limited for legitimate reasons. Having said this, one also needs to admit that in all of the mentioned awards, judicial economy was exercised, and certain theoretical elements were only mentioned in passing—one would have appreciated a more extensive reasoning on the type of review conducted by the arbitral tribunals.

The practice of international investment tribunals and WTO panels present some notable convergences. Although both systems refuse to explicitly recognize an abstract and general standard of deference (eg in the form of a margin of appreciation doctrine) applicable to national scientific determinations, they also reject the idea of an intrusive *de novo* review, arguably acknowledging their limited epistemic competence in scientific matters. In this context, they both concentrate on reasonableness rather than correctness of specific scientific claims.[108] This includes an acknowledgement that minority scientific views may serve as a possible justification equally as mainstream science.[109] Overall, the relevant practice seems to indicate a preference for a deferential stance of review in scientific disputes.

On the other hand, the practice of international investment tribunals and WTO panels also present some notable divergences, in particular with regard to the issue of optimal design of judicial scrutiny over national risk regulation measures. Investment tribunals are concerned with the quality of regulatory process—eg reviewing the transparency and inclusiveness of the regulatory

context of WTO law was made by Robert Howse, 'Democracy, Science and Free Trade—Risk Regulation on Trial at the WTO', 98 *Michigan Law Review* 2329 (1999–2000), 2330.

[105] See generally Orellana, 'The Role of Science'.

[106] *Chemtura v Canada*, para 123.

[107] On the need for comparative surveys of best regulatory practices, see generally Piet Eeckhout, 'The Scales of Trade—Reflections on the Growth and Functions of the WTO Adjudicative Branch', 13(1) *JIEL* 3 (2010).

[108] The European Union has also adopted a similar approach (cf Patrycja Dąbrowska-Kłosińska, Chapter 11 in this volume).

[109] As discussed in Section III this was expressly acknowledged by the Appellate Body in *EC—Asbestos* (at para 155) and indirectly admitted by the *Chemtura* tribunal when it observed that scientific divergence could not have in and of itself served as a basis for a finding violation of international investment obligations.

processes.[110] WTO panels, on the other hand, tend to show a distinct interest in the internal (scientific) legitimacy of measures. This dissimilarity may be explained by the textual difference of the applicable law in the relevant disputes. While international investment agreements tend to be vague on scientific matters, the SPS Agreement explicitly includes scientific criteria for assessing the legality of regulatory measures, thus compelling WTO panels to engage in some form of scientific enquiry—irrespective of whether such enquiry would be deferential or intrusive. SPS provisions also affect the way that WTO panels approach scientific questions outside the realm of the agreement, to ensure cross-sectoral dialogue among the covered agreements as well as increase the consistency and predictability of the relevant reports. In turn, this may lead to paradoxical results, with WTO panels admitting their limited epistemic competences and at the same time sometimes engaging in the details of science (at least under the SPS Agreement). This is a trap that arguably has been (and should be) avoided by arbitral tribunals.

Moreover, until recently, the issue of the standard of review that should be applied to prior national scientific determinations used to be more pressing in the context of WTO law than in international investment arbitration. This explains the quantity of cases relating to scientific matters adjudicated before WTO bodies. Yet, the recent boom of investment arbitrations shows that this issue has become crucial in investment arbitration too; and there is also scope for increasing dialogue among the two fora when taking into account the emergence of analogous disputes arising from the same regulatory measures.[111]

V. Conclusions

The question of standard of review plays a key role in regulatory disputes as it concerns 'the allocation of power between national governments and international institutions on matters of vital concern'.[112] Among these, public health and environmental protection lie at the heart of State sovereignty. At the same time, there is a risk that governments use domestic regulation to deflect their

[110] See eg *Grand River Enterprises Six Nations Ltd, et al v United States of America*, UNCITRAL (NAFTA), Award, 12 January 2011, para 212 (stating that 'a good case could be made that consultations should have occurred with governments of the Indian tribes or nations in the United States whose members and sovereign interests could, and apparently are, being affected by the MSA and related measures to regulate commerce in tobacco. Retail tobacco businesses are in many Indian reservations across the country, constituting important sources of income and catalysing other economic activity among indigenous communities').

[111] Cf *Australia—Certain Measures Concerning Trademarks, Geographical Indications and Other Plain Packaging Requirements Applicable to Tobacco Products and Packaging*, dispute DS435 (Panel established on 25 September 2013) with *FTR Holding SA (Switzerland), Philip Morris Products SA (Switzerland) and Abal Hermanos SA (Uruguay) v Oriental Republic of Uruguay*, ICSID, Request for Arbitration, 19 February 2010, Case No. ARB/10/7).

[112] Steven P. Croley and John H. Jackson, 'WTO Dispute Procedures, Standard of Review, and Deference to National Governments', 90 *AJIL* 193 (1996), 194.

international commitments. As a consequence, regulatory measures in both areas have increasingly been challenged before investment treaty tribunals and the WTO adjudicative bodies under the relevant trade and investment treaty provisions. Like other international courts and tribunals, international economic fora may have a *Missionsbewusstsein* or 'in-built bias' in that they have a limited mandate.[113] WTO panels and arbitral tribunals have no mandate to adjudicate the correctness of State measures under public health law. Rather, their mandate is to adjudicate on the eventual violation of relevant trade and investment treaty standards respectively. While their review of public health regulations can strengthen the rule of law and good governance in this area, an overly intrusive review may undermine State regulatory autonomy and the pursuit of legitimate public policy goals. In turn this may fuel the alleged 'legitimacy crisis' of the two international economic law regimes. Against this background, this chapter argues that there are good reasons for international adjudicators to adopt a deferential standard of review—albeit not a total deference—and to respect State regulatory autonomy as well as allow States to select a given level of health protection and adopt reasonable measures in the pursuit of public health objectives.

This chapter compares the approaches adopted by arbitral tribunals and WTO adjudicative bodies in order to offer a roadmap to adjudicators, scholars and practitioners. This scrutiny aims at providing a fresh synopsis of the current tensions between a strict scrutiny and a more deferential approach in international economic law adjudication. We are not arguing that WTO adjudication and investment arbitration should necessarily borrow from each other. Rather, our analysis focuses on a more analytical level, in that it shows that there are both convergences and divergences between the two fields as regards the ways in which their dispute settlement bodies deal with scientific evidence.

The practice of international investment tribunals and WTO panels present some notable convergences. The reasons for a deferential standard of review over national scientific determinations are generally the same for both WTO panels and international investment arbitration tribunals. WTO adjudicative bodies as well as investment treaty arbitral tribunals are willing to adopt a deferential stance when reviewing State regulation in public health matters, in particular when confronted with scientific determinations made at the municipal level. At the same time, they both accept that an intrusive *de novo* review should not be conducted. On the other hand, the practice of international investment tribunals and WTO panels also present some notable divergences, which may be explained by the textual differences in the applicable treaties.

Finally, this chapter also shows that recent arbitral tribunals have shown a relatively sophisticated approach to reviewing State conduct in public health matters. Whether this sophisticated approach will be maintained in subsequent awards

[113] Yuval Shany, 'No Longer a Weak Department of Power? Reflections on the Emergence of a New International Judiciary', 20(1) *EJIL* 73 (2009), 81.

remains to be seen—there is no binding precedent in investment arbitration, and there is no Appellate Court to eventually promote a de facto precedent. On the other hand, while the Appellate Body has stated that 'WTO Members have a large measure of autonomy to determine their own policies on the environment',[114] the question as to whether this theoretical acknowledgement has been fully put into practice remains open to debate.

[114] Appellate Body Report, *Standards for Reformulated and Conventional Gasoline*, WT/DS2/AB/R, 20 May 1996, para 634.

PART III

EUROPEAN UNION LAW

10

National Procedural Choices before the Court of Justice of the European Union

Pieter Van Cleynenbreugel

I. Introduction

Rules governing civil, criminal and administrative procedures have long remained bulwarks of Member State sovereignty in an increasingly integrated European Union (EU).[1] The Court of Justice of the European Union (CJEU or the Court)[2] has confirmed the importance of such sovereignty through an extensive body of case law devoted to a judicially-created *principle of national procedural autonomy*.[3] According to that principle, Member States remain at liberty to designate the courts responsible for enforcing EU law at the national level and to determine the procedural rules governing such application. National choices are nevertheless subject to judicial scrutiny by the CJEU.[4] Such scrutiny allows the Court to directly review national procedural choices from the vantage point of EU law.

Despite being consistently relied on in the Court's case law, the conceptual language of procedural autonomy does not in itself provide insight into the *intensity* with which the Court reviews national procedural choices. The Court's

[1] Rachael Craufurd Smith, 'Remedies for Breaches of EU Law in National Courts: Legal Variation and Selection' in Paul Craig and Gráinne de Búrca (eds), *The Evolution of EU Law* (Oxford: Oxford University Press, 1999) 298.

[2] According to Article 19(1) of the Treaty on the European Union, [2008] OJ C115/13, the Court of Justice of the European Union is comprised of the Court of Justice, the General Court, and specialized tribunals (presently only the Civil Service Tribunal). When referring to the CJEU, this chapter refers to all three judicial bodies. When referring to the Court or the Court of Justice, it refers to the Court as one judicial body, excluding the General Court and the Civil Service Tribunal.

[3] On the principle of national procedural autonomy, see among many others Constantinos Kakouris, 'Do the Member States Possess Judicial Procedural Autonomy?', 34 *CMLR* 1389 (1997); Walter Van Gerven, 'Of Rights, Remedies and Procedures', 37 *CMLR* 500 (2000); Michael Dougan, 'The Vicissitudes of Life at the Coalface: Remedies and Procedures for Enforcing Union Law before the National Courts' in Craig and de Búrca (eds), *The Evolution of EU Law*, 407 (for general overviews).

[4] Sacha Prechal and Rob Widdershoven, 'Redefining the Relationship between "Rewe-effectiveness" and Effective Judicial Protection', 4 *Review of European Administrative Law* 31 (2011).

constitutional inability to rule directly on the validity of national procedural choices contributes to the lack of clear review standards in this regard.[5] Within the seemingly uniform language of 'procedural autonomy', different review standards can nevertheless be detected. This chapter identifies those standards and explains their simultaneous co-existence.

The chapter proceeds in five sections, the first being this introduction. Section II sketches the conceptual framework of national procedural autonomy guiding the Court's review of national procedural choices. Section III outlines how this conceptual framework fails to grasp the *intensity* of CJEU review. It additionally offers an alternative setting in which such intensity can be captured by identifying four concurrently applicable standards of review of national procedural choices. Section IV explains the continuous co-existence of those different standards of review, despite the lack of clear dividing benchmarks governing their application. In doing so, it relies on a *crypto-federal* account of EU integration through law. According to that account, the Court adheres to different standards of review with a view towards protecting the *process and project* of European integration as an end in itself. To that end, it encapsulates the different review standards within a process-based *integration-reinforcement* narrative. Section V offers conclusions.

II. The Classical National Procedural Autonomy Narrative

The establishment of a more integrated European legal space did not automatically invalidate national rules. According to the narrative adopted, those rules would continue to operate within the umbrella framework provided by EU law. National regulatory autonomy would only be diminished to the extent that EU law directly harmonized national legal provisions, or to the extent that these provisions constituted an unjustifiable limitation on the effective realization of EU law.[6] In its important 1963 *van Gend & Loos* judgment, the Court of Justice acknowledged that EU Treaty provisions—and instruments adopted on the basis of them[7]—were directly applicable within and across all participating legal orders. In addition, sufficiently precise rules of EU law were to be interpreted as granting rights to individuals under EU law.[8] Those rights were deemed invocable before a

[5] Article 267 of the Treaty on the Functioning of the European Union [2008] OJ C115/47 only allows the Court to rule on the interpretation of the Treaties or the validity of Union acts, see for example Case C-130/93 *Lamaire tegen Nationale Dienst voor Afzet van Land- en Tuinbouwprodukten* [1994] ECR I-3215, para 10; Case C-506/04 *Graham J. Wilson v Ordre des avocats du barreau de Luxembourg* [2006] ECR I-8613, paras 34–5; and Case C-296/06 *Telecom Italia SpA v Ministero dell'Economia e delle Finanze, Ministero delle Comunicazioni* [2008] ECR I-801, para 17.

[6] See for that approach in the realm of the EU's internal market law, most notably Case 120/78 *Rewe-Zentral AG v Bundesmonopolverwaltung für Branntwein* [1979] ECR 649.

[7] See Case 41/74 *Yvonne van Duyn v Home Office* [1974] ECR 1337. EU Directives comprise a notable exception, see Article 288 TFEU.

[8] Case 26/62 *NV Algemene Transport- en Expeditie Onderneming van Gend & Loos v Netherlands Inland Revenue Administration* [1963] ECR 3 (English Special Edition, at 1). On the existence and invocability of rights, see Van Gerven, 'Of Rights', 502.

national judge in accordance with national procedural law. *In the absence of harmonized EU law on the matter*, national provisions continued to govern the designation and division of jurisdictional competences, access to court and judicial remedies, and the procedural rules that allowed for the application of those remedies (procedural rules *stricto sensu*).

With a view towards guaranteeing the effective application of EU law in national procedural systems, the Court of Justice structured and sanctioned an EU-wide principle of national procedural autonomy.[9] This principle maintains that 'it is for the domestic legal system of each Member State to designate the courts having jurisdiction and to determine the procedural conditions governing actions at law intended to ensure the protection of rights citizens derive…from [EU] law'.[10] EU law nevertheless restrains unfettered national procedural autonomy. The Court consistently holds that national remedies or procedural rules applicable to EU rights-based claims 'must be no less favourable than those governing similar domestic actions (principle of equivalence) and must not render practically impossible or excessively difficult the exercise of rights conferred by [Union] law (principle of effectiveness)'.[11] National rules that breached either condition had to be disapplied, as a matter of the primacy of EU law over conflicting national provisions.[12] The possibility or obligation for national judges to refer matters to the Court for a 'preliminary ruling' on the interpretation of EU law allowed the Court to indirectly assess the compatibility of national rules with those conditions.[13]

[9] The Court for the first time referred to a self-standing principle of procedural autonomy in C-201/02 *The Queen on the application of Delena Wells v Secretary of State for Transport, Local Government and the Regions* [2004] ECR I-723, para 65.

[10] Among others, Case 33/76 *Rewe-Zentralfinanz eG et Rewe-Zentral AG v Landwirtschaftskammer für das Saarland* [1976] ECR 1989, para 5; Case 45/76 *Comet BV v Produktschap voor Siergewassen* [1976] ECR 2043, para 13; Case C-312/93 *Peterbroeck, Van Campenhout & Cie SCS v Belgian State* [1995] ECR I-4599, para 12; Case C-432/05 *Unibet (London) Ltd and Unibet (International) Ltd v Justitiekanslern* [2007] ECR I-2271, para 39; Joined Cases C-222/05 to C-225/05 *J. van der Weerd and others* (C-222/05), *H. de Rooy sr. and H. de Rooy Jr.* (C-223/05), *Maatschap H. en J. van 't Oever and others* (C-224/05) *and B.J. van Middendorp* (C-225/05) *v Minister van Landbouw, Natuur en Voedselkwaliteit* [2007] ECR I-4233, para 28; Case C-268/06 *Impact v Minister for Agriculture and Food and others* [2008] ECR I-2483, para 44. See also John McKendrick, 'Modifying Procedural Autonomy: Better Protection for Community Rights', 8 *European Review of Private Law* 565 (2000).

[11] Case C-432/05 *Unibet (London) Ltd and Unibet (International) Ltd v Justitiekanslern*, para 43; more recently see Case C-452/09 *Tonina Enza Iaia and others v Ministero dell'Istruzione, dell'Università e della Ricerca and others* [2011] ECR I-4043, para 16; Case C-262/09 *Wienand Meilicke and others v Finanzamt Bonn-Innenstadt* [2011] ECR I-5659, para 55. For applications of the principle of equivalence, see Case C-326/96 *B.S. Levez v T.H. Jennings (Harlow Pools) Ltd.* [1998] ECR I-7835, paras 43–4; C-63/08 *Virginie Pontin v T-Comalux SA* [2009] ECR I-10467, para 45; Case C-591/10 *Littlewoods Retail and others v Her Majesty's Commissioners of Revenue and Customs* [2012] OJ C295/5, para 31; Case C-93/12 *ET Agrokonsulting-04-Velko Stoyanov v Izpalnitelen direktor na Darzhaven fond "Zemedelie" - Razplashtatelna agentsia* [2013] OJ C225/28, para 38; on the principle of effectiveness in general, see Matej Accetto and Stefan Zleptnig, 'The Principle of Effectiveness: Rethinking its Role in Community Law', 11 *European Public Law* 375 (2003).

[12] See on the requirement of disapplication, Pieter Van Cleynenbreugel, 'Judge-Made Standards of National Procedure in the Post-Lisbon Constitutional Framework', 37 *European Law Review* 92 (2012).

[13] At the same time, the preliminary reference mechanism directly allowed national courts to question the compatibility of national legislation with EU law. In doing so, EU law provides

In addition, the Court recognized more extensive individual entitlements to effective judicial protection.[14] Relying on such entitlements, it imposed specific access to justice requirements and EU-wide remedies. National procedural systems had to incorporate those requirements and remedies into national law.[15]

The relationship between effective judicial protection and national procedural autonomy is far from clear. Both concepts have been argued to constitute flip sides of the same coin.[16] Depending on the concrete circumstances of the case at hand, the Court would flip this coin and opt for a particular approach. Both the negative obligations of equivalence and effectiveness and the positive obligation to ensure effective judicial protection have served to shape a framework within which EU law mitigates and structures *national procedural autonomy*.

More recently, the national procedural autonomy narrative has extended beyond national procedural choices in the absence of EU legislative harmonization. Recent case law demonstrates that the Court also relies on the 'procedural autonomy' language to justify interventions into national legal orders in instances where de facto supranational procedural harmonization effectively took place.[17] The Court additionally seems willing to more directly interpret and rely on the binding EU Charter of Fundamental Rights and the obligation it incorporates to guarantee effective judicial protection.[18] The Charter, in this understanding,

national judges with an incentive to rely on EU law in order to remove undesirable national provisions from the national legal order. Article 267 of the Treaty on the Functioning of the European Union (TFEU) states that where a preliminary issue is raised in a case pending before a court or tribunal of a Member State against whose decisions there is no judicial remedy under national law, that court or tribunal shall bring the matter before the Court. See, on that requirement, Koen Lenaerts et al, *Procedural Law of the European Union* (London: Sweet & Maxwell, 2006) 69.

[14] Case 222/84 *Marguerite Johnston v Chief Constable of the Royal Ulster Constabulary* [1986] ECR 1651, para 17; see in detail Anthony Arnull, 'The Principle of Effective Judicial Protection: An Unruly Horse?', 36 *European Law Review* 51 (2011).

[15] See in general Michael Dougan, *National Remedies before the Court of Justice. Issues of Harmonisation and Differentation* (Portland: Hart Publishing, 2004) 229–93.

[16] Prechal and Widdershoven, 'Redefining the Relationship', at 46, for a perspective on that interrelationship.

[17] In the realm of EU competition law, Case C-439/08 *Vlaamse federatie van verenigingen van Brood- en Banketbakkers, Ijsbereiders en Chocoladebewerkers (VEBIC) VZW* [2010] ECR I-12471, para 63; EU environmental law, Case C-240/09 *Lesoochranárske zoskupenie v Ministerstvo životného prostredia Slovenskej republiky* [2011] ECR I-1255, para 52 and Joined Cases C-128/09, C-129/09, C-130/09, C-131/09, C-134/09 and C-135/09, *Antoine Boxus, Willy Roua* (C-128/09), *Guido Durlet and others* (C-129/09), *Paul Fastrez, Henriette Fastrez* (C-130/09), *Philippe Daras* (C-131/09), *Association des riverains et habitants des communes proches de l'aéroport BSCA (Brussels South Charleroi Airport) (ARACh)* (C-134/09 and C-135/09), *Bernard Page* (C-134/09), *Léon L'Hoir, Nadine Dartois* (C-135/09) *v Région wallonne* [2011] ECR I-9711, paras 55–7 and Case C-182/10, *Marie-Noëlle Solvay and others v Région wallonne* [2012] OJ C98/5, para 41; EU asylum law, Case C-69/10, *Brahim Samba Diouf v Ministre du Travail, de l'Emploi et de l'Immigration* [2011] ECR I-7151, para 41.

[18] Article 6 TEU and Charter of Fundamental Rights of the European Union, 30 March 2010, [2010] OJ C 83/02, 389. See also Case C-279/09 *DEB-Deutsche Energiehandels- und Beratungsgesellschaft mbH v Bundesrepublik Deutschland* [2010] ECR I-13849, paras 29–30; Johanna Engström, 'The Principle of Effective Judicial Protection after the Lisbon Treaty. Reflection in the Light of Case C-279/09 DEB Deutsche Energiehandels- und Beratungsgesellschaft mbH', 4 *Review of European Administrative Law* 53 (2011).

provides an additional supranational starting point for the review of national procedural choices.

III. Supranational Review Standards: United in Diversity?

Despite its apparent conceptual clarity, the judicially-crafted language of national procedural autonomy does not provide insight into the *standards of review* the CJEU employs to scrutinize national procedural rules. Such standards reflect the *intensity* with which the Court assesses the autonomy of Member States to design their own procedural systems. Although the Court does not explicitly refer to the standard of review concept in its case law, four implicit standards of review can be concurrently identified in the sphere of national procedural rules. Those standards can be subdivided into categories of *marginal, intermediate, negative comprehensive* and *positive comprehensive* review.

A. Marginal review

The first—and 'lightest'—standard provides for only a marginal review of national procedural choices. It enables the Court to assess whether or not an institutional, procedural or remedial provision reasonably fits within the EU framework. This standard seeks to consider the function a particular—and potentially restrictive—rule plays in the *national procedural framework*. The Court will, in that regard, specifically consider:

> the role of that provision in the procedure, its progress and its special features, viewed as a whole, before the various national instances. In the light of that analysis the basic principles of the domestic judicial system, such as protection of the rights of the defence, the principle of legal certainty and the proper conduct of procedure must, where appropriate, be taken into consideration.[19]

In doing so, the Court only scrutinizes national procedural choices on a very abstract level. It classically defers a concrete judgment on the compatibility of the national rule to the national judge that referred the matter as a preliminary ruling. It will be the responsibility of that judge to establish to what extent the abovementioned principles justify the application of a particular national rule. An important precedent can be found in the 1995 *van Schijndel and van Veen* judgment. In that case, the Court stated that a national rule impeding a judge from invoking a provision of EU law on his or her own motion was:

> justified by the principle that, in a civil suit, it is for the parties to take the initiative, the court being able to act of its own motion only in exceptional cases where the

[19] Joined Cases C-430/93 and C-431/93 *Jeroen van Schijndel and Johannes Nicolaas Cornelis van Veen v Stichting Pensioenfonds voor Fysiotherapeuten* [1995] ECR I-4705, para 19.

public interest requires its intervention. That principle reflects conceptions prevailing in most of the Member States as to the relations between the State and the individual; it safeguards the rights of the defence; and it ensures proper conduct of proceedings by, in particular, protecting them from the delays inherent in examination of new pleas.[20]

In this ruling, the Court summarily maintained that those justifications suffice to rely on the applicability of the national rule.[21] Although it did assess those justifications, the Court did not specify the circumstances in which such a rule could effectively be considered to impede the effective application of EU law. The national court mainly had to maintain and apply its rule in the case at hand. In a similar vein, the 2007 *Unibet* judgment held that:

it is for the national courts to interpret the procedural rules governing actions brought before them…in such a way as to enable those rules, wherever possible, to be implemented in such a manner as to contribute to the attainment of the objective…of ensuring effective judicial protection of an individual's rights under Community law.[22]

The Court found that the presence of a remedial claim for damages in accordance with Swedish law sufficed for Unibet to obtain effective protection of its rights under EU law. Once again, the Court did not consider whether the national remedial action for damages would be sufficient to ensure the effective protection of EU rights.[23] Its mere availability sufficed to not warrant EU judicial interest. That concrete assessment was left to the national court to make.[24]

The marginal review standard reflects a particular allocation of procedural competences between the Union courts and the national legal orders. According to that allocation, the Court is responsible for identifying the nature and extent of Union rights. At the same time, the Court presumes that national procedural systems are able to accommodate EU rights.[25] Marginal review thus starts from an assumption that national procedural law complies with the EU's equivalence and effectiveness standards. From that vantage point, the Court engages in an abstract investigation of the procedural system at hand. It specifically refrains from engaging in a concrete investigation of national remedial and procedural standards and their effects on a particular EU right. Without clear guidance from the Court, the referring national court is obliged to apply the contested national rule in an EU rights-friendly way.

[20] Joined Cases C-430/93 and C-431/93 *Jeroen van Schijndel and Johannes Nicolaas Cornelis van Veen*, para 21. Qualifying this approach as a procedural rule of reason, Sacha Prechal, 'Community Law in National Courts: The Lessons from Van Schijndel', 35 *CMLR* 690 (1998).

[21] Joined Cases C-430/93 and C-431/93 *Jeroen van Schijndel and Johannes Nicolaas Cornelis van Veen*, para 22.

[22] Case C-432/05 *Unibet (London) Ltd and Unibet (International) Ltd*, para 44.

[23] Case C-432/05 *Unibet (London) Ltd and Unibet (International) Ltd*, para 49.

[24] Case C-432/05 *Unibet (London) Ltd and Unibet (International) Ltd*, para 54.

[25] Van Gerven refers to such approach as an effectiveness approach, as opposed to a more stringent adequateness approach; see Van Gerven, 'Of Rights', 503.

B. Intermediate review

The *intermediate review* standard builds upon the marginal review standard, but proposes a more direct review of national procedural choices. Intermediate review enables the Court to directly assess a specific national procedural rule in the light of EU law principle of equivalence or effectiveness directly circumscribing Member States' procedural choices. That assessment allows the Court to specifically instruct national judges to *disapply* the offending national rule as a matter of EU law. A national judge will then have to continue proceedings on the basis of the remaining national rules in force.

The Court's judgment in *Peterbroeck* exemplifies this approach. In that judgment, the Court evaluated a national rule impeding judges from invoking particular EU law pleas on their own motion. Contrary to its approach in *van Schijndel*, the Court held that since the litigant could invoke a particular plea only within a limited time period, the Court should be able to intervene in order to maintain the coherent application of EU law in cases where the litigant refrained from invoking the EU law argument within that prescribed limitation period.[26] In particular, it held that:

> [EU] law precludes application of a domestic procedural rule whose effect, in procedural circumstances such as those in question in the main proceedings, is to prevent the national court, seized of a matter falling within its jurisdiction, from considering of its own motion whether a measure of domestic law is compatible with a provision of [EU] law when the latter provision has not been invoked by the litigant within a certain period.[27]

The Court identified a direct conflict between the national rule and the supranational standard and mandated the national court to preclude the application of that rule. The *Impact* case offers a more recent example. In that case, the Court held that the principle of effectiveness:

> requires that a specialized court which is called upon, under the, albeit optional, jurisdiction conferred on it by the legislation transposing [a Union Directive], to hear and determine a claim based on an infringement of that legislation, must also have jurisdiction to hear and determine an applicant's claims arising directly from the directive itself in respect of the period between the deadline for transposing the directive and the date on which the transposing legislation entered into force if it is established that the obligation on that applicant to bring, at the same time, a separate claim based directly on the directive before an ordinary court would involve procedural disadvantages liable to render excessively difficult the exercise of the rights conferred on him by [EU] law. It is for the national court to undertake the necessary checks in that regard.[28]

While this judgment was rendered in the shadow of a transposed EU Directive, it particularly focused on national procedural rules on access to justice that had not

[26] Case C-312/93 *Peterbroeck, Van Campenhout & Cie SCS*, para 6.
[27] Case C-312/93 *Peterbroeck, Van Campenhout & Cie SCS*, para 21.
[28] Case C-268/06 *Impact*, para 55.

been the subject of harmonization.[29] In this case, the Court precluded the application of a particular national rule to the extent that it imposed procedural disadvantages on the parties involved. It first identified a conflict between a requirement of EU law and a disadvantageous national procedural rule, and subsequently suggested the latter's disapplication to the national judge.[30]

Intermediate review differs from marginal review in two respects. First, the Court explicitly *establishes* a conflict between a supranational standard and a national rule. In a marginal review case, the Court operates from a reasonable presumption that the national procedural system *in abstracto* complies with EU law. Second, the Court more explicitly guides the national court in disapplying a particular conflicting national rule. In doing so, it indirectly promotes changes to national procedural systems. Relying on the language that EU law *precludes the application of* a particular national procedural rule,[31] it indirectly mandates the national judge to disapply a particular national procedural rule and to decide the case in accordance with the remainder of national procedural standards.

C. Negative comprehensive review

A *comprehensive review* standard projects a more intensive review of national procedural rules or standards. Contrary to a marginal or intermediate standard of review, the Court investigates the specific conditions governing the operation of the national procedural system, identifies a *potential* future conflict that may arise in the realm of enforcing EU rights, and proposes an effective *remedy* to avoid this conflict from occurring. This remedy is either directed at generally *removing* the contested standard from the national legal order and/or at *replacing* it with a new EU-wide standard.

Negative comprehensive review only aims at removing a contested standard from a national legal order. It focuses on the identification of a *potentially systemic* and *indirect* conflict between an EU standard and a national rule of procedure. Whilst the application of a national procedural rule might present a problem in the specific case referred, the Court especially frames the conflict as having a potentially broader and more general scope. To the extent that the national rule would remain in force, future conflicts of a different nature and scope cannot be excluded. As a result, the Court relies on stronger language to project or mandate the disapplication of the national rule at hand. It particularly relies on an explicit reference to the principle of primacy of EU law over national law to impose the disapplication of the national procedural rule(s).[32] In doing so, it

[29] Case C-268/06 *Impact*, para 50.

[30] Case C-268/06 *Impact*, para 54: the Court did not refer to disapplication directly. Rather, it claimed that it would be for the national court to interpret the domestic jurisdictional rules in such a way that, wherever possible, they contribute to the attainment of the objective of ensuring effective judicial protection of an individual's rights under EU law.

[31] Intermediate review can also result in the position that EU law does not preclude a particular rule. For a recent example, see Case C-292/10 *G v Cornelius De Visser* [2012] OJ C133/5, para 42.

[32] See on the primacy principle, Case 6/64 *Flaminio Costa v ENEL* [1964] ECR 585; Case 11/70 *Internationale Handelgesellschaft v Einfuhr- und Vorratstelle für Getreide und Futtermittel* [1970] ECR 1125; Case 106/77 *Amministrazione delle Finanze dello Stato v Simmenthal SpA* [1978] ECR

effectively neutralizes the application of a national procedural rule as a matter of EU law in both the present and potential future disputes. National judges *and national legislators or executives* are required to *remove* the conflicting national rule entirely from the national legal order, thus extending beyond the concrete dispute at hand. If they fail to do so, it could result in a successful Member State liability action equally grounded in EU law and supervised by the Court.[33]

The Court's *Simmenthal* judgment clearly reflects this approach. In that judgment, the Court explicitly stated that:

> any recognition that national legislative measures which encroach upon the field within which the [European Union] exercises its legislative power or which are otherwise incompatible with the provisions of [EU] law had any legal effect would amount to a corresponding denial of the effectiveness of obligations undertaken unconditionally and irrevocably by Member States pursuant to the Treaty and would thus imperil the very foundations of the [Union].[34]

As a result, a national procedural rule stating that national courts should 'request or await the actual setting aside by the national authorities empowered so to act of any national measures which might impede the direct and immediate application of community rules' was to be removed.[35] More recently, the *Lucchini* judgment mandated the removal of a national rule on *res iudicata* which would have impeded the effective application of EU state aid law.[36] Once again, the language of EU law primacy was used to justify the national rule's removal.

D. Positive comprehensive review

The most intense review standard presently relied upon by the Court proposes a *positive comprehensive review* of national procedural provisions. In addition to providing a comprehensive review of national procedural provisions that result in their disapplication, the Court in these cases effectively determines the terms of the actual or potential conflict between supranational and national law. In determining these terms, it seeks to *avoid* future conflicts by directly superimposing a

629; Case 102/79 *Commission v Belgium* [1980] ECR 1487, para 15; Case 149/79 *Commission v Belgium* [1980] ECR 3903, para 19; Case C-473/93, *Commission v Luxemburg* [1996] ECR I-3255, para 26; Case C-285/98 *Tanja Kreil v Bundesrepublik Deutschland* [2000] ECR I-105, para 23. See also Matej Avbelj, 'Supremacy or Primacy of EU law—(Why) Does it Matter?', 17 *ELJ* 744 (2011).

[33] On Member State liability, see Joined Cases C-6/90 and C-9/90 *Andrea Francovich and Danila Bonifaci and others v Italian Republic* [1991] ECR I-5357; Joined Cases C-46/93 and C-48/93 *Brasserie du Pêcheur SA v Bundesrepublik Deutschland and The Queen v Secretary of State for Transport, ex parte: Factortame Ltd and others* [1996] ECR I-1029. See also Nicolo Zingales, 'Member State liability vs. National Procedural Autonomy: What Rules for Judicial Breach of EU Law?', 11 *GLJ* 419 (2010).

[34] Case 106/77 *Simmenthal SpA*, paras 17–18.

[35] Case 106/77 *Simmenthal SpA* at para 24.

[36] Case C-119/05 *Ministero dell'Industria, del Commercio e dell'Artigianato v Lucchini SpA*, [2007] ECR I-6199, para 61. See also Paolise Nebbia, 'Do the Rules on State Aids Have a Life of Their Own? National Procedural Autonomy and Effectiveness in the Lucchini Case', 33 *European Law Review* 427 (2008).

supranational alternative to the conflicting national rule. That supranational alternative is meant to serve as an EU-wide standard of adequate national procedure(s) throughout all the Member States.[37] The *positive* dimension attached to this comprehensive review lies in the Court taking on the role of establishing procedural standards. In addition to mandating the national rules' disapplication, the Court itself crafts a standard of adequate procedure that will subsequently have to be implemented at all national levels. In this way, the Court aims to directly ensure the effective application (*effet utile*) of EU rights in national procedural systems.[38]

The most remarkable positive comprehensive intervention can be found in the realm of EU-wide remedies. Unsatisfied with the scope and availability of remedies within national legal orders, the Court of Justice directly mandated the establishment of EU-wide remedies. These remedies have included an action for damages on the basis of Member State liability[39] and the provision of interim injunctive relief,[40] to name but a few. In all these instances, the Court identified a gap in the national procedural structures. It subsequently interpreted EU law to accommodate that gap and avoid potential future conflicts with national law. In doing so, it imposed a particular remedy on national legal orders. That remedy had to be fitted into the existing framework of national procedural rules. To the extent that such a fit could not be provided for, the national framework had to be adapted.[41]

A similar approach has guided the case law on specific national procedural rules. The Court's approach in cases involving particular national time limits is illustrative in that regard.[42] In *Emmott*, the Court directly maintained that national time limits could not begin to run until the transposition period of an EU Directive had ended. Although EU law did not govern time limits, the Court argued that the effectiveness of EU law would be imperilled in cases where the commencement of time limits were placed prior to the transposition deadline.[43] More recently, the case of *Francisco Javier Rosado Santana* confirmed this position. In that case, the Court referred to national procedural autonomy with respect to time limits governing proceedings against the outcome of competitions in the Andalusian civil service. Since the EU law provisions at stake in that case did not directly govern time limits, the Court relegated the matter to national procedural

[37] See for a conceptualization of that perspective in the language of procedural autonomy, Pieter Van Cleynenbreugel, 'Transforming Shields into Swords. The Vebic Judgment, Adequate Judicial Protection Standards and the Emergence of Procedural Heteronomy in EU Law', 18 *Maastricht Journal of European and Comparative Law* 511 (2011).

[38] See for that position, Van Gerven, 'Of Rights', 504.

[39] See the case law references in note 33.

[40] Case C-213/89 *The Queen v Secretary of State for Transport, ex parte: Factortame Ltd and others* [1990] ECR I-2433.

[41] Van Cleynenbreugel, 'Transforming Shields', 532.

[42] On national time limits, see Mariolina Eliantonio, *Europeanisation of Administrative Justice? The Influence of the ECJ's Case Law in Italy, Germany and England* (Groningen: Europa Law Publishing, 2008) 71–83.

[43] Case C-208/90 *Theresa Emmott v Minister for Social Welfare and Attorney General* [1991] ECR I-4269, para 23.

autonomy. It nevertheless concluded that should the application of the time limits result in the impossibility for a claimant to assert rights under EU law, the starting point of the time limit should be placed at a later stage.[44] In so doing, the Court imposed a direct obligation on national legal orders to set the starting point at a later moment in time.[45]

E. Four distinctive review standards

While the language of national procedural autonomy emphasizes national diversity, mitigated by the need for a coherent application of EU law in national legal orders, the four review standards adopt a more dynamic perspective. They directly focus on the assessment assumption, the object of review, and the practical consequences of a review of national procedural rules. The four standards illustrated above are summarized in Table 2.

The identified review standards provide an analytical device to grasp the diverging intensities in the review of national procedural choices. At the same time however, the abovementioned standards allow us to more accurately project and predict the possible *outcomes* of different 'procedural autonomy' analyses.

Recent case law indicates that the Court might be willing to extend the comprehensiveness of its review to situations where the fundamental right to effective judicial protection, incorporated in Article 47 of the Charter, applies, in the absence of any other concrete harmonizing EU law provisions.[46] In doing so, the Court directly grounded a positive comprehensive review approach into the EU constitutional framework. It also employs the language of EU fundamental rights

Table 2. Overview of supranational standards of review of national procedural rules.

Supranational review standard	*Assessment assumption*	*Object of review*	*Practical consequences*
marginal review	no perceived conflict	national legal system: abstract	national judge's discretion
intermediate review	resolution of actual conflict	specific national rule: concrete	EU-imposed disapplication
negative comprehensive review	indirect resolution of potential conflict	concrete	EU-imposed removal; 'primacy'
positive comprehensive review	direct avoidance of actual or potential conflict	concrete	EU-adequateness standard; 'effet utile'

[44] Case C-177/10 *Francisco Javier Rosado Santana v Consejería de Justicia y Administración Pública de la Junta de Andalucía* [2011] ECR I-7907, paras 97–9.

[45] See also Pieter Van Cleynenbreugel, 'The Confusing Constitutional Status of Positive Procedural Obligations in EU Law', 5 *Review of European Administrative Law* 98 (2012).

[46] See most directly, Case C-279/09 *DEB*, para 33; see also *Samba Diouf* and *Boxus* referred to in note 17.

and national procedural autonomy to design a new framework in which comprehensive EU intrusion into national procedural spheres is considered legitimate. If and to the extent that a provision of national procedural law goes against the requirements directly read into Article 47 of the Charter, the Court would be able to adopt a negative or positive comprehensive review approach, ie to remove the contested national provision from the legal order and even to impose a new EU-wide standard of adequate national procedure instead. Since the right to effective judicial protection applies in all instances where the Charter applies,[47] Article 47 therefore potentially provides an instrument to establish a new equilibrium between EU review and national autonomy. No national procedural provision would, under this approach, escape the potential comprehensive scrutiny projected by EU law. The Court's case law, however, does not, to date, go as far as to impose more intensified review in any national procedural autonomy case. It continues to simultaneously rely on more deferential review standards.[48]

IV. Diversified in Unity: Integration-Reinforcement as an Explanatory Framework

Section III demonstrated that, despite the seemingly uniform language focused on 'national procedural autonomy', four standards of review can be distinguished based on intensity and outcome assessment in the Court's case law. The overview and assessment of cases in the previous sections shows that the four review standards have not operated in distinctive and clearly demarcated timeframes. All the standards of review have rather operated simultaneously and somewhat unpredictably throughout the case law. This section seeks to conceptualize the simultaneous and unpredictable co-existence of these standards of review through the lens of judicially-sanctioned EU *crypto-federalism*.

The explanation proceeds in two parts. The first subsection argues that the simultaneous appearance of four standards of review could be conceptually captured by the notion of crypto-federalism. Building upon such a crypto-federal conception, this subsection outlines the Court's role within it, as a crypto-federal standard-setter. The second subsection additionally identifies an *integration-reinforcement* approach underlying crypto-federalism. That approach

[47] On the scope of application of the Charter, see Piet Eeckhout, 'The EU Charter of Fundamental Rights and the Federal Question', 39 *CMLR* 945 (2002). Advocating a broad interpretation of the Charter's scope, see Joined Cases C-411/10 and C-493/10 *N. S.* (C-411/10) *v Secretary of State for the Home Department* and *M. E. and others* (C-493/10) *v Refugee Applications Commissioner and Minister for Justice, Equality and Law Reform* [2012] OJ C49/8, para 68.

[48] Case C-177/10 *Francisco Javier Rosado Santana*, para 56 and Case C-41/11 *Inter-Environnement Wallonie ASBL and Terre wallonne ASBL v Région wallonne* [2012] OJ C118/6, para 42, stating that 'in the absence of provisions in that directive on the consequences of infringing the procedural provisions which it lays down, it is for the Member States to take, within the sphere of their competence, all the general or particular measures necessary to ensure [that EU procedural law requirements are complied with]'. Those judgments were rendered following the *DEB, Samba Diouf* and *Boxus* judgments mentioned in note 17.

justifies the Court's continued reliance on different standards of review as a *means* to protect the project of European integration as a dynamic and ongoing project. It also justifies the continuous co-existence of different standards of review as a necessary precondition of the EU's political 'integration through law'.

A. Diverging standards as a necessary precondition to judicially-sanctioned crypto-federalism

The reliance on a vague principle of procedural autonomy to structure the scope of review over national procedural choices reflects a well-known technique of EU integration. The Court explicitly relies on a non-identified EU integration target to justify and promote an increasingly federalized legal order in which it situates itself at that order's apex.[49] This approach is commonly referred to as *crypto-federalism*. Crypto-federalism maintains that focus on the end goals of EU integration would detract attention from the *process and project* of such integration, so it focuses particularly on that *process and project* to justify ever more integration. This focus on process effectively impedes substantive discussions on the limits of EU intervention and allows the Court to continuously refine the process of review in order to achieve more—or better—integration.[50] An additional feature of this framework is that it will be left to the Court to outline what more—and better—integration amounts to. As such, the Court is effectively able to determine the boundaries of legitimate EU integration.

Different standards of review also impact upon the allocation of powers within the EU system.[51] In determining and applying diversified standards of review, the Court of Justice also enables national courts to act as supranationally mandated procedural standard setters. To the extent that the Court engages in marginal or intermediate review, national courts effectively function as residual autonomous bodies. They can continue to rely on national law, albeit within the confines of a supranationally-determined procedural framework. In cases where the Court proceeds in accordance with comprehensive review, it directly entrusts national courts with the obligation to disapply a contested national rule and/or to replace it with an EU-wide standard of adequate national procedure. That EU-wide standard serves as a benchmark, which grants an important implementing role to national judges. They will first of all be responsible for the application and incorporation of that standard in the national legal order. Second, they will have the opportunity to bring problematic issues before the Court by way of reference for a preliminary ruling. The framing of these questions sets the stage for the scope of review engaged in by the Court. To the extent that the national court frames a matter as requiring more comprehensive EU review, the Court will indeed be enticed to

[49] For a similar understanding of the Court's role in the design of its proportionality test, see the contribution by Alexia Herwig and Asja Serdarevic in Chapter 12 of this volume.

[50] See Giandomenico Majone, *Europe as the Would-be World Power. The EU at Fifty* (Cambridge: Cambridge University Press, 2008) 77–8.

[51] See also Benedikt Pirker, Chapter 4 of this volume.

engage in such and involve the national court in implementing the requirements it elaborates. In such manner, the national courts will interact directly with the supranational judiciary. They become effective agents of the Court of Justice in the national legal orders.

The simultaneous availability of four different standards of review allows the Court of Justice to shift the allocation of procedural competences between national and supranational governance levels, depending on the felt necessities of each case. As a result, different standards justify a flexible and court-centred federalist image of procedural intervention. The singular language of national procedural autonomy, mitigated by EU law, effectively captures this narrative: national systems remain at liberty to develop a procedural framework, but at the same time that framework needs to be subject to judicial modification at either the supranational or the national level. The differing standards of review serve to accommodate these different needs.

On a more general level, the Court's involvement in national procedural choices and its resulting cooperation with national courts are legitimized by a particular image of national *democratic* decision-making in a *supranational* legal context. According to this image, Member States have deliberately surrendered a part of their national sovereignty to enable the integration of national legal systems in a supranational setting.[52] While Member States are considered to embody the necessary political and legal *expertise* to design appropriate procedural frameworks, the Court serves to steer such expertise to include attention to the interests of peoples and States beyond the classic nation-state boundaries. In this way, the Court serves as a supranational constitutional gatekeeper ensuring that the *majoritarian* idea of sustained legal integration is not frustrated by particular national procedural choices.[53] Supranational *standards of review*, in this image, establish the boundaries within which national (legislative and judicial) experts can structure national procedural law.[54] Building on that argument, it can be submitted that the Court generally defers substantive judgments on national procedural choices to *experts*—in this case national legislators and judges—whilst determining the 'procedural' conditions within which national experts can effectively render decisions.[55] In determining such 'procedural' conditions however, the Court directly or indirectly influences the shape and format that the nationally structured expert decisions may take. In this way, the Court firmly positions itself as the guardian of the European integration project that Member States have voluntarily and willingly signed on to. Even if participating Member States would not have directly agreed to particular intrusions into national procedural law frameworks, the Court structures these as necessary complements of national

[52] See for that philosophy in particular, Case 26/62 *Van Gend & Loos*.

[53] On the CJEU as a majoritarian actor, see Miguel Poiares Maduro, *We, the Court: The European Court of Justice and the European Economic Constitution* (Portland: Hart Publishing, 1998).

[54] See Michael Ionnaides, Chapter 6 of this volume, for a similar perspective on trade law.

[55] For more on that perspective see Patrycja Dąbrowska-Kłosińska, Chapter 11 of this volume, reflecting a similar position in instances where 'experts' comprise independent scientific advisors rather than national legislatures or judges.

democratic law-making procedures under a supranational 'integration through law' framework.

B. Crypto-federalism as process-oriented constitutional review

This crypto-federal conceptualization of the differently-structured standards of review does not, however, explain when to rely on a particular standard of review. It justifies the emergence of different standards of review as organizing a level playing field among national and supranational judges, but cannot provide clear guidelines on when to apply marginal, intermediate or comprehensive standards of review.

The crypto-federal emphasis on the process and project of integration nevertheless provides an insight into the reasons why different procedural review standards should be relied on. To the extent that a crypto-federal account seeks to justify the process of European integration, different standards of review serve to consolidate and structure that process.[56] In this image, the intervention of a European Court into the operations of national procedural systems serves to maintain the effectiveness of the European integration process. To the extent that Member States' procedural systems frustrate that process, more intense scrutiny of national procedural choices should take place. In the same vein, to the extent that the supranational legislator decides directly to harmonize national procedural standards, the Court should be able to structure the side-effects of such harmonization in accordance with a supranational logic. Both instances allow the Court to protect the ongoing *process* of European integration as an end in itself.

This results in an *integration-reinforcement* framework,[57] where the Court intervenes to the extent warranted by the process of European integration. Rather than maintaining a concrete substantive goal, the Court structures its review operations to maintain the *operational integrity* of the European project. Accordingly, the different standards of review serve to maintain, protect or promote the process of European integration as an end in itself. To the extent that the *continuous process* of integration is imperilled, a comprehensive review is warranted to avoid future and potential conflicts from emerging.[58] In cases where the envisaged conflicts are only minor or even virtually non-existent, marginal review also serves to maintain the *process* of European integration. Where a conflict is tailored to a particular case and does not appear to extend beyond the realm of that case, intermediate review is sufficient to protect the integration process. In this understanding, all

[56] For a similar normative account, see Benedikt Pirker, Chapter 4 of this volume.

[57] Integration-reinforcement mirrors the theory of *representation-reinforcement* advocated in US constitutional law. According to that theory, legislation impeding on the rights of discrete and insular minorities warrants more intense judicial scrutiny; see John Hart Ely, *Democracy and Distrust. A Theory of Judicial Review* (Cambridge, MA: Harvard University Press, 1980) 135–79. See also Alexander Bickel, *The Least Dangerous Branch: The Supreme Court at the Bar of Politics*, 2nd edn (New Haven: Yale University Press, 1986).

[58] For a comparable account, see the contribution of Alexia Herwig and Asja Serdarevic, Chapter 12 of this volume.

review standards serve to protect the process of European integration as an ongoing and substantively indeterminate *perpetuum mobile* that needs to move in order to be meaningful.[59]

This *integration-reinforcement* framework confirms the crypto-federal narrative underlying the national procedural autonomy discourse. It seeks to justify the emergence of divergent standards of review as an instrument to protect the *process* of European integration and to structure national democratic decision-making processes within a supranational mind-set. National procedural rules should serve the end of making the process of European integration work. The Court only intervenes to the extent that these rules do not function in such a way. National legislators and national courts are considered as nationally embedded *experts* responsible for establishing well-functioning procedural frameworks under the direct supervision of the Court. The potentiality to extend comprehensive review contained in Article 47 of the Charter serves as an effective safeguard to incline national courts to act as exponents of the CJEU's effective judicial protection logic. To the extent that these national courts can be trusted as cooperative actors, the CJEU will not be called upon to rely on its comprehensive review trump card.

The existence of diversified standards of review thus provides the Court with different instruments with which to respond to any frustration of the integration process. The Court itself has so far nevertheless refrained from making clear where, when and how the integration process would be frustrated to such an extent that more comprehensive CJEU intervention would be warranted. As a result, the scope of the *integration-reinforcement* approach remains rather unpredictable and highly dependent on the contextual particularities of the specific cases brought before the Court.

V. Conclusions

This contribution analyzed the CJEU's approach to national procedural autonomy from a more dynamic point of view. It has sought to distinguish four standards, reflecting a different intensity in the review of national procedural choices. The four standards are concurrently applicable, both in earlier as well as recent cases. Each standard of review relies on different *assessment assumptions*, structures the *object* of review differently, and seeks to impose different *practical consequences* on national legal orders.

Whilst the standards of review structure national law in the absence of harmonized procedural standards, recent case law has also applied the 'national procedural autonomy' framework to fields of procedural harmonization. The CJEU in those instances has effectively preferred to rely on a comprehensive review standard. Those 'procedural harmonization' examples more generally demonstrate that the Court relies on a procedural autonomy framework—supported

[59] Majone, *Europe*, 75.

by four different review standards—to justify and extend its competences over national procedural frameworks. A crypto-federal approach justifies and legitimizes such an extension of competences, as it seeks to establish a level playing field between national judges and the Court of Justice. At the same time however, this approach does not in itself explain what standard of review will be relied upon in a particular case. This contribution therefore additionally identified an *integration-reinforcement* image. In accordance with that image, the Court would apply more rigorous review standards to the extent that national legislative and judicial frameworks can no longer be trusted to continue the *process* of European integration. If national procedural actions are deemed to frustrate that process, more intense judicial intervention would be warranted.

11

Risk, Precaution and Scientific Complexity before the Court of Justice of the European Union

*Patrycja Dąbrowska-Kłosińska**

I. Introduction

In adjudicating cases underpinned by uncertainty of risk and potential dangers to human and animal health and the environment, a particularly demanding task for the Court of Justice of the European Union (the CJEU or the Court) has been the application of the precautionary principle and the powers of Member States to derogate from the European Union (EU) internal market rules.[1] These judgments have been extensively analysed.[2] The authors of these analyses have been increasingly exploring the roles and methodologies of courts under the conditions of risk and uncertainty.[3]

The main challenges result from a necessity to assess the often enormous factual density of regulatory solutions, the application of complex normative conditions relating to the competing interests and values (internal market vs human,

* I acknowledge the support of the Jean Monnet Fellowship 2012/2013 in the Global Governance Programme at the Robert Schuman Center for Advanced Studies, European University Institute in Florence. An extended version of this chapter was published in RSCAS EUI Working Papers series 63 (2013), as 'EU Courts, Global Risks, and the Health and Environmental Safety Revisited: On Nuances of a Less Deferential Standard of Review'.

[1] See Joanne Scott and Ellen Vos, 'The Juridification of Uncertainty: Observations on the Ambivalence of the Precautionary Principle Within the EU and the WTO' in Christian Joerges and Renaud Dehousse (eds), *Good Governance in Europe's Integrated Market* (Oxford: Oxford University Press, 2002) 253–86.

[2] See eg Ellen Vos, 'The European Court of Justice in the Face of Scientific Uncertainty and Complexity' in Mark Dawson, Bruno de Witte and Elise Muir (eds), *Judicial Activism at the European Court of Justice* (Cheltenham: Edward Elgar Publishing, 2013) 142–65; Caroline E. Foster, *Science and the Precautionary Principle in International Courts and Tribunals: Expert Evidence, Burden of Proof and Finality* (Cambridge: Cambridge University Press, 2011); Alberto Alemanno, 'The Shaping of European Risk Regulation by Community Courts', *Jean Monnet Working Papers* 18 (2008); Joseph Corkin, 'Science, Legitimacy and the Law: Regulating Risk Regulation Judiciously in the European Community', 33(2) *European Law Review* 359 (2008).

[3] See Joanne Scott and Susan Sturm, 'Courts as Catalysts: Rethinking the Judicial Role in New Governance', 13(3) *Columbia Journal of European Law* 565 (2007).

consumer, animal and environmental safety), and the scope of discretion of national and EU authorities.[4] The difficulty is linked to the fact that in these cases, when deciding on factual determinations, the courts are often faced with conflicting or insufficient scientific evidence while having to formulate legal determinations involving the interpretation of open terms and discretionary provisions.[5] Moreover, judicial review needs to address the relationship between risk, science and uncertainty, as well as the so-called 'paradox of expertise'.[6] The latter relates to the de facto scientific uncertainty caused either by an insufficiency of specific knowledge or an abundance of diverging interpretations of scientific data, which makes it difficult to issue a final judgment (for example, when national and EU scientific opinions are in conflict).[7] Altogether, deciding on risk often implies political determinations.[8]

Taking into account the existing scholarship, this chapter examines judicial reasoning in risk regulation cases from the perspective of the standard of review. It takes a doctrinal-positivist approach and uses as case studies the decisions rendered by the CJEU in the face of some of the risks to health and environmental safety. The standard of review applied by EU Courts in these complex cases not only has important effects on the Member States' powers, the functioning of the internal market and the construction of the EU policies in the area of human and animal health and the protection of the environment, but also globally, because some protective measures within the EU can be claimed as incompatible with the World Trade Organization (WTO) framework.[9] Moreover, identifying the relevant standard of review can assist in determining the role which should be played by the CJEU, both internally and at the international level, in the context

[4] See generally Miguel Poiares Maduro, *We, the Court: The European Court of Justice and the European Economic Constitution* (Oxford: Hart Publishing, 1998); Nicolas de Sadeleer, 'The Precautionary Principle in European Community Health and Environmental Law: Sword or Shield for the Nordic Countries?' in Nicolas de Sadeleer (ed), *Implementing the Precautionary Principle: Approaches from the Nordic Countries, EU and USA* (London: Earthscan, 2007) 10–58.

[5] See eg the recent judgments in cases T-257/07 *France v Commission* [2011] ECR II-05827, its appeal, Case C-601/11P, judgment of the Court of 11 July 2013, nyr, and C-36/11 *Pioneer Hi Bred Italia Srl v Ministry of Food, Agriculture and Forestry Policy*, nyr.

[6] Ulrich Beck, *Risk Society: Towards a New Modernity* (London: Sage Publications, 1986).

[7] Cf a controversial study by Gilles-Eric Séralini et al, 'Long Term Toxicity of a Roundup Herbicide and a Roundup-tolerant Genetically Modified Maize', 50(11) *Food and Chemical Technology* 4221 (2012) and the response by the European Food Safety Authority, 'Review of the Séralini et al (2012), 'Publication on a 2-year Rodent Feeding Study with Glyphosate Formulations and GM Maize NK603 as Published Online on 19 September 2012 in Food and Chemical Toxicology', 10(10) *EFSA Journal* 2910 (2012).

[8] See generally Cass R. Sunstein, *Risk and Reason: Safety, Law, and the Environment* (Cambridge: Cambridge University Press, 2002) and Jenny Steele, *Risks and Legal Theory* (Oxford: Hart Publishing, 2004).

[9] See Lukasz Gruszczynski, 'SPS Measures Adopted in Case of Insufficiency of Scientific Evidence: Where Do We Stand after EC-Biotech Products Case' in Julien Chaisse and Tiziano Balmelli (eds), *Essays on the Future of the World Trade Organization* (Geneva: Edis, 2008) 91–140 and also Chapter 9 by Lukasz Gruszczynski and Valentina Vadi and Chapter 12 by Alexia Herwig and Asja Serdarevic in this volume. Cf further cases C-504/04 *Agrarproduktion Staebelow GmbH v Landrat des Landkreises Bad Doberan* [2006] ECR I-00679; Joined Cases C-58/10-68/10 *Monsanto SAS and others v Ministry of Agriculture and Fisheries* [2011] ECR I-07763; and Case T-475/07 *Dow AgroSciences Ltd and Others v Commission* [2011] ECR II-05937.

of the complex regime of transnational risk regulation and the fragmentation of international law.[10]

From the standpoint of standard of review, there have been several trends which can be identified in the case law of the CJEU in this field.[11] That is, there was an established tradition of EU Courts applying a deferential standard of review in risk cases involving scientific complexity (although somewhat less deferential towards the Member States than to the EU bodies).[12] This approach has been changing gradually over time, and especially after 2002, when the famous judgments in the *Pfizer* and *Alpharma* cases were issued.[13] It is argued that since those decisions, EU Courts have shown increasing willingness to involve themselves in the process of weighing the merits of scientific opinions and assessing their quality and validity.[14]

One sign of this change, in comparison to the earlier judgments, has been the Court increasingly extending the scope of judicial review to embrace questions relating to the factual basis of scientific evidence, risks and methodologies for their assessment. This transformation has been equally visible in cases involving both national measures and EU decisions. The expanded scope of review has necessarily modified the CJEU's intensity of scrutiny, which means that the applicable standard of review has become less deferential generally.[15] At the same time, it can be observed that the EU Courts still appear to be less willing to grant a broad discretion to national authorities when they invoke protective measures based on risk and precaution, than they do to EU institutions when they perform risk management duties.[16]

In order to present the new tendency in the applicable standard of review, this chapter extracts the principles, terms and conditions that EU Courts apply without strictly differentiating between judgments reviewing Member States and EU measures. It also treats the Court of Justice (CJEU) and the General Court as one functional institution. This is justified by the fact that the broadened scope of judicial review, the applicable judicial reasoning and the resulting structural implications are fairly similar in cases involving both the EU and the

[10] Cf Robert O. Keohane and David G. Victor, 'The Regime Complex for Climate Change', 9(1) *Perspectives on Politics* 7 (2011).

[11] See also Chapter 7 by Caroline Henckels, Chapter 9 by Lukasz Gruszczynski and Valentina Vadi and Chapter 12 by Alexia Herwig and Asja Serdarevic, all in this volume, for the analysis of the similar issues in different jurisprudential contexts.

[12] See Ellen Vos, 'The European Court of Justice', 143 and 145 ff; Alberto Alemanno, *Trade in Food—Regulatory and Judicial Approaches in the EC and the WTO* (Colwick: Cameron May, 2007), 325 ff.

[13] Case T-13/99 *Pfizer Animal Health v Council* [2002] ECR II-3305 and Case T-70/99 *Alpharma v Council* [2002] ECR II-3495.

[14] Alberto Alemanno, 'EU Risk Regulation and Science: The Role of Experts in Decision-making and Judicial Review' in Ellen Vos (ed), *European Risk Governance—Its Science, its Inclusiveness and its Effectiveness* (Mannheim: Connex Report Series No. 6, 2008), 59–63.

[15] See also Ellen Vos, 'The European Court of Justice', 144.

[16] Cf Patrycja Dąbrowska and Patricia Quillacq, 'Science Goes to Court. Some Considerations on the Precautionary Principle in the Community Jurisprudence' in Francesco Francioni (ed), *The Future of Environmental Law: International and European Perspective*, EUI Law Working Paper 5 (2006) 59–70.

Member States' risk regulation measures, and it is the actual outcome of judgments that varies, depending on whether it is a national regulatory measure or EU-level decision, towards a relatively more frequent approval of the Member States' regulations.[17]

In view of the above, this chapter analyses the standard of judicial review applied by the CJEU in risk regulation case law. The chapter proceeds by first briefly describing the relevant, normative context (Section II), then exploring the scope of judicial review, including the review of powers and procedural guarantees (Section III). Finally, in Section IV it presents the implications of the examined standard of judicial review.

II. The Scope and Normative Context of the Analysis

The scope *ratione materiae* of the analysis includes the case law of the CJEU regarding product safety and environmental regulations adopted to avoid transnational risks on the EU internal market (eg the use of food and feed, pharmaceuticals, pesticides, genetically modified organisms, effects of radioactive substances, etc). The study is based on a non-exhaustive list of the case law wherein EU Courts have been faced with complex political, scientific and factual questions. The scope, *ratione personae*, of the analysis in this chapter will focus on judgments assessing national derogations from the internal market, but will also include judgments on EU-level measures relevant for the allocation of national regulatory powers in risk regulation cases. That is, the specificity of the EU constitutional structure and procedural provisions often imply that judicial review of EU administrative decisions involves deciding, either directly or indirectly, on national powers.[18]

Accordingly, on the basis of Article 36 of the Treaty on the Functioning of the European Union (TFEU) and in the absence of EU harmonization, Member States can invoke the protection of health and life of humans, animals or plants to justify the rules which constitute a restriction of trade within the internal market. The CJEU accepts that Member States can legitimately determine the level of protection which they accord to public health and furthermore has declared that their discretion 'relating to the protection of public health is particularly wide where it is shown that there is still uncertainty in the current state of scientific research'.[19] At the same time, however, Member States' measures are subject to

[17] But see eg Case T-182/06 *Netherlands v Commission* [2007] ECR II-01983 and reversing judgment of the Court annulling the contested Commission's decision to the derogating advantage of the Member State: Case C-405/07P *Netherlands v Commission* [2008] ECR I-08301.

[18] Eg under the Article 114 TFEU procedure (see Case T-69/08 *Poland v Commission* [2010] ECR II-05629) or when a Member State is outvoted in the qualified majority voting on risk regulatory measure and files a complaint against an EU institution (T-257/07 *France v Commission* [2011] ECR II-05827).

[19] Case C-333/08 *Commission v France*, para 86. Cf also cases C-319/05 *Commission v Germany* [2007] ECR I-9811 and C-270/02 *Commission v Italy* [2004] ECR I-01559.

the principle of proportionality, which is carefully applied by the CJEU against the factual basis of the national defence.[20]

Second, on the basis of Article 114 TFEU, Member States can derogate from an EU measure on approximation of national laws (regulation, directive).[21] In particular, according to Article 114(4), Member States may *maintain* divergent national legislation *after* the adoption of a harmonization measure when they deem it necessary on grounds of major needs referred to in Article 36 TFEU, or relating to the protection of the environment or the working environment. Pursuant to Article 114(5), Member States are empowered to *introduce* divergent national provisions, but the conditions are detailed. The justification for national legislation must be based on *new scientific evidence* relating to the protection of the environment or the working environment on the grounds of a problem specific to that Member State and arising after the adoption of a harmonization measure.[22] Both provisions provide the Commission with the authority to approve or reject such national provisions, and the decision is later subject to judicial review by the CJEU.[23]

Third, Member States can adopt protective measures on the basis of safeguard clauses contained in EU regulations or directives approximating national laws, which traditionally contain provisions allowing a product which poses risk to human health or the environment to be withdrawn from the market.[24] National measures are usually subject to the Commission's and/or comitology's acceptance and a possible review by the CJEU.[25]

The majority of the cases where Member States adopt measures restricting the functioning of the internal market on the grounds of human health and safety or the environment concern the application of the precautionary principle. Although interpretations of its content differ,[26] it nevertheless constitutes one of the guiding principles in the EU's legal reasoning with respect to risk regulation.[27] According

[20] See Paul Craig and Gráinne de Búrca, *EU Law Text Cases Materials*, 5th edn (Oxford: Oxford University Press, 2011), 672–4 and Case C-333/08 *Commission v France* [2010] ECR I-00757, para 90. Cf also Chapter 12 by Alexia Herwig and Asja Serdarevic in this volume.

[21] See Case C-512/99 *Germany v Commission* [2003] ECR I-845; Joined Cases T-366/03 and T-235/04 *Land Oberösterreich and Austria v Commission* [2005] ECR II-4005; T-234/04 *Netherlands v Commission* [2007] ECR II-04589; Case T-69/08 *Poland v Commission* [2010] ECR II-05629; Case T-182/06 *Netherlands v Commission* [2007] ECR II- 01983, and Case C-405/07P *Netherlands v Commission* [2008] ECR I-08301.

[22] See Case C-3/00 *Denmark v Commission* [2003] ECR I-2643, para 58.

[23] See generally Isidora Maletic, *The Law and Policy of Harmonisation In Europe's Internal Market* (Cheltenham: Edward Elgar Publishing, 2013); Nicolas de Sadeleer, 'Procedures for Derogations from the Principle of Approximation of Laws under Article 95 EC', 40 *CMLR* 911 (2003).

[24] See cases: C-58/10-68/10 *Monsanto SAS and Others v Ministry of Agriculture and Fisheries*; C-165/08 *Commission v Poland* [2009] ECR I-06843; C-236/01 *Monsanto Agricoltura Italia SpA and Others v Presidenza del Consiglio dei Ministri and Others* [2003] ECR II-8105 and C-6/99 *Association Greenpeace France and Others v Ministere de l'Agriculture et de la Pêche and Others* [2000] ECR I-1651.

[25] See Patrycja Dąbrowska, 'GM Foods, Risk, Precaution and the Internal Market: Did Both Sides Win the Day in the Recent Judgment of the European Court of Justice?', 5(2) *GLJ* 151 (2004).

[26] See Verlee Heyvaert, 'Facing the Consequences of the Precautionary Principle in European Community Law', 31 *ELR* 185 (2006).

[27] Article 191 TFEU. See Koen Lenaerts, '"In the Union We Trust": Trust-enhancing Principles of Community Law', 41 *CMLR* 317 (2004); Elizabeth Fisher, *Risk Regulation and Administrative Constitutionalism* (Oxford: Hart Publishing, 2007).

to the General Court, it is a general principle of EU law which requires public authorities:

> to take appropriate measures to prevent specific potential risks to public health, safety and the environment, by giving precedence to the requirements related to the protection of those interests over economic interests.[28] [In addition] where there is scientific uncertainty as to the existence or extent of risks to human health, the precautionary principle allows the institutions to take protective measures without having to wait until the reality and seriousness of those risks become fully apparent... or until the adverse health effects materialise.[29]

Hence, the scientific uncertainty regarding risk needs to be viewed as influencing the scope of Member States' discretion to take protective measures.[30]

The discretion to exercise political risk management (eg a decision to withdraw a product) can be called 'substantive precaution'[31] because public authorities enjoy power to determine the level of acceptable risk for society and the possibility to adopt protective measures. The procedural constraints imposed on this discretion can be referred to as 'formal precaution' or the proceduralizing role of the precautionary principle, inasmuch as the powers and duties of public administrations to take protective measures under conditions of scientific uncertainty are constrained by procedural guarantees.[32] These issues will be further examined in the analysis in Section III below.

III. The Scope of Judicial Review

Let us now turn to analysis of the scope of EU Courts' review in risk regulation cases, bearing in mind that while the applicable judicial reasoning is fairly similar for both the EU and the Member States' measures, but the actual outcomes of judgments are more often affirmative with respect to EU-level decisions. Still, it appears from the reading of the case law that it is possible and justified to frame common conditions regarding the scope and intensity of applicable judicial review in these types of cases. Their common feature is the need to protect human health or the environment often in the light of inconclusive scientific evidence and on the basis of the precautionary principle.

[28] See eg Joined Cases T-74/00, T-76/00, T-83/00 to T-85/00, T-132/00, T-137/00 and T-141/00 *Artegodan and Others v Commission* [2002] ECR II-4945, paras 183 and 184; and Case T-392/02 *Solvay Pharmaceuticals v Council* [2003] ECR II-4555, para 121.

[29] Case T-257/07 *France v Commission*, paras 66–8; C-236/01 *Monsanto*, para 111. See also Case C-504/04 *Agrarproduktion Staebelow*, para 39 and T-13/99 *Pfizer*, paras 139 and 141.

[30] Case C-41/02 *Commission v Netherlands* [2004] ECR I-11375, para 51.

[31] Oliver Segnana, 'The Precautionary Principle: New Developments in the Case Law of the Court of First Instance', 3(10) *GLJ* 5 (2002).

[32] Joanne Scott, 'The Precautionary Principle before the European Courts' in Richard Macrory (ed), *Principles of European Environmental Law* (Groningen: Europe Law Publishing, 2004), 63–5. See also Case C-41/02 *Commission v Netherlands*, paras 48–56.

A. Review of powers exercised by national (and EU) authorities

It follows from the construction of the EU legal framework and its interpretation by the CJEU, that in the implementation of risk regulation underpinned by scientific uncertainty it is the public institutions (national administrative authorities, the EU Commission) who 'must carry out complex assessments' and 'complex technical evaluations' of knotty scientific and factual problems. Consequently, they enjoy 'a broad discretion' in defining policy objectives and making political choices about the required level of protection and the 'appropriate means of action' necessary to fulfil these objectives (ie to make a decision with respect to the level of risk and the level of protection that is deemed appropriate).[33] If the EU Courts later review this 'broad' discretion, a certain logic of reasoning can be extracted from their judgments, described below.

First, according to the CJEU, complexity of technical and scientific determinations and of the acceptable level of risk imply that the judicial review is limited.[34] It is often observed by the EU Courts in this context:

> That broad discretion and those complex assessments imply a limited power of review on the part of the Courts of the European Union. That discretion and those assessments have the effect that review by the Courts as to the substance is limited to verifying whether the exercise by the institutions of their powers is vitiated by a manifest error of appraisal, whether there has been a misuse of powers, or whether the institutions have manifestly exceeded the limits of their discretion.[35]

In other words, the CJEU does not substitute the public authorities in the assessment of complex facts. It is explained that:

> in order to establish that that institution committed a manifest error in assessing complex facts…, the evidence adduced by the applicant must be sufficient to make the factual assessments used in the act implausible… Subject to that review of plausibility, it is not the Court's role to substitute its assessment of complex facts for that made by the institution which adopted the decision.[36]

Secondly, when exercising its review of the plausibility of evidence, the CJEU emphasizes that the above limits do not affect its duty to:

> establish whether the evidence relied on is factually accurate, reliable and consistent but also whether that evidence contains all the information which must be taken into account in order to assess a complex situation and whether it is capable of substantiating the conclusions drawn from it.[37]

[33] Case C-333/08 *Commission v France*, paras 85–6; Case C-192/01 *Commission v Denmark* [2003] ECR I-09693, paras 42–3. See also Case T-257/07 *France v Commission*, para 84 and C-405/07 P *Netherlands v Commission*, para 54.

[34] Cf Case C-333/08 *Commission v France*, para 87; Case C-192/01 *Commission v Denmark*, para 46 for the national context. See also Joined Cases C-211/03, C-299/03 and C-316-318/03 *HLH Warenvertriebs GmbH and Orthica BV v Germany* [2005] ECR I-05141, paras 74–9 for analogies between the EU and national judicial review.

[35] Case T-257/07 *France v Commission*, para 85. See also eg Case C-236/01 *Monsanto*, para 135.

[36] Case T-257/07 *France v Commission*, para 86. Cf also Case C-333/08 *Commission v France*, paras 94–8.

[37] Case C-405/07 P *Netherlands v Commission*, para 55. Cf Case T-257/07 *France v Commission*, for the judicial discussion on national versus EU-level scientific evidence.

It follows from the above passage that the examination of plausibility of evidence creates a duty for the Court to verify the submitted evidence in the light of rather far-reaching criteria, that is factual accuracy, reliability and consistency. In the case of scientific evidence, which is often a key element in such complex disputes, the Court's examination presupposes an assessment of the quality and validity of scientific opinions. In addition, the EU Courts must also check the completeness of the information and its capability of supporting the deductions made. Altogether, this implies that the review of plausibility of evidence opens the possibility for the CJEU to extend its formally limited scope of review to a wide range of issues in the process of evaluation of scientific merits and facts.

Finally, the EU Courts often emphasize that their role is to examine carefully the authorities' observance of EU law guarantees in administrative procedures. The CJEU explains that in the EU legal order 'those guarantees include, in particular for the competent institution, the obligations to examine carefully and impartially all the relevant elements of the individual case and to give an adequate statement of the reasons for its decision'.[38] What's more, the risk assessment process belongs to these guarantees, as it has been specified in judgments that 'a scientific risk assessment carried out as thoroughly as possible... is an important procedural guarantee whose purpose is to ensure the scientific objectivity of the measures adopted and preclude any arbitrary measures'.[39]

The above-cited passages reveal an interesting story about the steps and content of the CJEU's reasoning. Formally speaking, the authorities enjoy broad discretion (powers) with regard to the realization of a given policy and must make complex assessments, and the EU Courts pursue a limited review of the exercise of these powers. Their review is limited to the verification that the exercise of powers was not affected by a manifest error of assessment (appraisal), and that there was no misuse of powers and/or that the institutional discretion was not manifestly exceeded.[40] The establishment of manifest error in assessment of complex facts in a given case means that the Court does not substitute its own assessment for the institution's assessment of complex facts, either technical or scientific facts. But it does review the plausibility of factual evidence submitted regarding the factual assessments. This 'plausibility review' of evidence is pursued with a view towards assessing whether it substantiates the conclusions drawn from it, whether it 'contains all the information which must be taken into account in order to assess a complex situation', and whether it is 'factually accurate, reliable and consistent'.[41] In consequence therefore, the formally limited scope of judicial review does not preclude, and moreover, it requires a de facto substantive, and detailed evaluation of the plausibility of submitted evidence ('duty to establish'). Next, the EU Courts review the observance of

[38] Case C-405/07 P *Netherlands v Commission*, paras 56–7; see also Case C-192/01 *Commission v Denmark*, para 56.

[39] Case C-236/01 *Monsanto*, para 107; and Case T-257/07 *France v Commission*, para 89. Cf also Case C-333/08 *Commission v France*, paras 88–90 for the national context.

[40] See eg Case T-257/07 *France v Commission*, para 265.

[41] Case C-405/07 P *Netherlands v Commission*, para 55; Case T-257/07 *France v Commission*, para 87. See also Case C-41/02 *Commission v the Netherlands*, para 59.

procedural guarantees by public authorities in view of their claimed wide discretion when they exercise risk management and apply the precautionary principle in risk regulation cases.[42] These guarantees include the obligation to examine 'carefully and impartially' each individual case, to perform *ex ante* scientific risk assessment, give reasons for the action (burden of proof), perform cost–benefit analysis, and apply the principle of proportionality.[43] Finally, the review of the exercise of national discretion inevitably includes an evaluation whether the measures constitute a means of arbitrary discrimination.

To sum up, the EU Courts apply a logic of reasoning which aims, formally, to combine a broad scope of the institutional discretion with a limited scope of judicial review of administrative powers. Interestingly, however, it appears that this same logic leads to the extension of the applicable scope of review and results in a less deferential review than originally intended.[44] The de facto more restrictive approach to the standard of review is based on two tools: review of procedural guarantees and review of the plausibility of evidence submitted. Moreover, the EU Courts combine these two tools by declaring that scientific risk assessment, which is usually the main content of evidence, is a crucial procedural guarantee, and acknowledging the proceduralizing role of the precautionary principle.[45]

B. Review of procedural guarantees

It is now necessary to turn to the content of the procedural guarantees and their requirements as formulated by the CJEU because they constitute a yardstick against which the judicial review is carried out. Within this framework, the conditions for scientific risk assessment, scientific evidence, and the application of the precautionary principle—which is directly linked to scientific uncertainty—are of paramount significance.[46]

1. Conditions for scientific risk assessment and the approach to risk

The CJEU declares that:

> [A] scientific risk assessment is a scientific process which is commonly accepted as consisting, in so far as possible, in the identification and characterisation of a hazard, the assessment of exposure to the hazard and the characterisation of the risk. In such a situation, 'risk' thus constitutes the degree of probability that the acceptance of certain measures or

[42] Cf Case T-257/07 *France v Commission*, para 89.

[43] Eg Case C-333/08 *Commission v France*, paras 90–1; Case C-41/02 *Commission v Netherlands*, paras 48–56. See also Chapter 12 by Alexia Herwig and Asja Serdarevic in this volume.

[44] Cf in this context the interesting analysis of deference in the investor–State arbitration in Chapter 7 by Caroline Henckels in this volume.

[45] See Scott, 'The Precautionary Principle'; Scott and Sturm, 'Courts as Catalysts'.

[46] Cf Chapter 9 by Lukasz Gruszczynski and Valentina Vadi in this volume.

practices will adversely affect the interests safeguarded by the legal order. 'Hazard' is commonly used in a broader sense and describes any product or procedure capable of having an adverse effect on human health.[47]

This definition implies that the Court differentiates between the process of risk assessment and the notion of risk, which is characterized in descriptive terms. Further analysis reveals the approach of EU Courts to risk assessment, the risk assessment process, and scientific uncertainty in cases where measures to protect public health or the environment are taken.

a) The EU Courts' approach:

    1) there is a demonstration of the existence of 'real' or 'specific' risk for public health or the environment or a 'genuine threat' to public health, and consequently, the identification of the potentially adverse effects arising from a phenomenon;[48]
    2) risk assessment and preventive measures 'cannot properly be based on a purely hypothetical approach to the risk' nor 'founded on mere conjecture which has not been scientifically verified';[49]
    3) the reality and the extent of risk do not need to be '*fully demonstrated*' or '*fully apparent*', but its existence must be backed up by the scientific data available when the measure is taken '*since zero risk does not exist in practice*'.[50]

b) The risk assessment process. According to the CJEU, the risk assessment process should fulfil several conditions:

    1) the object of risk assessment 'is to appraise the degree of probability of harmful effects on human health . . . and the seriousness of those potential effects';[51]
    2) a risk assessment process should be carried out 'as thoroughly as possible' and 'as complete as possible in the particular circumstances of an individual case' on the basis of scientific evidence.[52]

[47] Case C-41/02 *Commission v the Netherlands*, para 47; also Cases: T-475/07 *Dow AgroSciences Ltd*, paras 146–147; T-13/99 *Pfizer*, paras 147 and 156.

[48] Case C-41/02 *Commission v the Netherlands*; Case C-236/01 *Monsanto*, para 109; and Case C-333/08 *Commission v France*, para 87.

[49] See Case C-236/01 *Monsanto*, para 105–6; Case C-192/01 *Commission v Denmark*, para 49; Case C-41/02 *Commission v the Netherlands*, para 52; and Case C-333/08 *Commission v France*, para 91–6. See also Case T-229/04 *Sweden v Commission* [2007] ECR II-2437, para 161.

[50] See Case T-257/07 *France v Commission*, para 76. See also Scott and Vos, 'The Juridification of Uncertainty', 264–5.

[51] Case C-41/02 *Commission v the Netherlands*, paras 48–9; Case C-192/01 *Commission v Denmark*, paras 47–8; C-24/00 *Commission v France* [2004] ECR I-01277, paras 54–5. See also Case C-77/09 *Gowan Comércio Internacional e Serviços Lda v Ministero della Salute* [2010] ECR I-13533, paras 75–6.

[52] Cases T-257/07 *France v Commission*, para 89 and C-236/01 *Monsanto*, para 107.

c) Risk, scientific uncertainty and the precautionary principle. The Court explains that:

Where it proves to be impossible to determine with certainty the existence or extent of the alleged risk because of the insufficiency, inconclusiveness or imprecision of the results of studies conducted, but the likelihood of real harm to public health persists should the risk materialise, the precautionary principle justifies the adoption of restrictive measures.[53]

These citations demonstrate that the Court differentiates between two 'extremes' on a risk continuum: 'real risk', the likelihood of which justifies protection (subject to the proportionality test); and 'hypothetical' or 'zero' risk, that in fact does not exist in practice. The scientific uncertainty lies somewhere in between the two extremes, especially when the risk assessment process is not able to provide a definitive conclusion because the evidence is insufficient, inconclusive or incomplete. The result, or rather difficulty, is that in such a situation the precautionary principle can or even must be applied, but the application of precaution nevertheless requires that the 'likelihood of real harm persists'.[54]

The requirements for both the scientifically backed real risk and for the risk assessment process mean a high standard with respect to the burden of proof and scientific evidence for the relevant EU authorities/Member States. The Court explains that 'risk' corresponds to the degree of probability which seems to refer to quantifiable numbers (statistical probability; while the term 'plausibility' is reserved to the evaluation of evidence). This implies a rather restrictive judicial review, with a great reliance on science as a source of omniscient knowledge in risk regulation.[55]

2. *Scientific evidence*

The assessment of scientific issues and risk assessment should be 'entrusted by the institution to scientific experts' who are able to give their opinion in an 'independent, objective and transparent manner', and scientific advice must be 'founded on the principles of excellence, transparency and independence'.[56] If a scientific opinion is procedurally vitiated (eg not provided in an independent manner), its (un)lawfulness will also affect the subsequent decision of the authorities.[57]

Moreover, the scientific evidence that supports protective measures needs to reflect the current state-of-the-art and be of the highest available quality at the time of taking a preventive measure. This means that the scientific evidence must contain the most recently available information and 'the results of international scientific research'.[58] To this end, and to establish the state of scientific knowledge,

[53] Eg Case C-192/01 *Commission v Denmark*, paras 52–3.

[54] See Case T-257/07 *France v Commission*, para 75.

[55] See also Anne-Marie Janssen and Marjolein B.A. van Asselt, 'The Precautionary Principle in Court: An Analysis of Post-Pfizer Case Law' in Marjolein B.A. van Asselt, Esther Versluis and Ellen Vos (eds), *Balancing between Trade and Risk Integrating Legal and Social Science Perspectives* (New York: Routledge, 2013) 216.

[56] Eg Case T-257/07 *France v Commission*, paras 73 and 89.

[57] See Alemanno, 'EU Risk Regulation and Science', 55.

[58] Case C-41/02 *Commission v the Netherlands*, para 47.

the CJEU not only often refers extensively to the opinions of EU agencies, eg the European Food Safety Authority, but also to standards external to the EU legal system, which include manuals, guidelines or opinions of international standards bodies and international organizations, for example, UN bodies such as the Food and Agriculture Organization, the World Health Organization or the Codex Alimentarius Commission, and even US agencies.[59]

However, the scientific evidence need not be conclusive regarding 'the reality of the risk and the seriousness of the potential adverse effects were that risk to become a reality' and the results of conducted studies can be imprecise, incomplete or insufficient.[60] The CJEU agrees that it is impossible to carry out a full scientific risk assessment when available scientific data are of an 'inadequate nature'.[61] Further, the evidence can outline the scientific inconclusiveness (and uncertainty) regarding 'the reality of risk and the seriousness of the potential adverse effects were that risk to become a reality', but it is nevertheless necessary that scientific risk assessments provide 'sufficiently reliable and cogent information' on the scientific questions raised and on the facts.[62] The soundness of scientific evidence will also determine the necessity of protection for the proportionality test.[63]

Finally, it needs to be highlighted that the EU Courts rely mainly on the so-called 'partisan' expert evidence brought in by the parties or other sources of secondary scientific evidence. By doing so, it refers to the quality of expertise that has already been employed by other bodies, including the expertise of the EU agencies, and the self-commissioning of the experts' reports remains truly exceptional[64] (although there are clear provisions regulating experts' testimony in the rules of procedures).[65] This allows the EU Courts and judges to rely on their own experience while assessing the evidence and the legitimation of the EU institutionalized scientific experts (eg agencies).[66] In addition, it is a safe exercise because references to the already published and known scientific opinions do not pose the 'danger' of vesting judicial powers in an external, commissioned expert, whose evidence could bring an unexpected outcome that would have to be dealt with in the judgment.[67]

[59] Alemanno, 'EU Risk Regulation and Science', 39 and 52. See also C-236/01 *Monsanto*, para 79.

[60] Case C-192/01 *Commission v Denmark*, para 52; and C-41/02 *Commission v the Netherlands*, para 54.

[61] Eg Case C-77/09 *Gowan Comércio Internacional*, paras 75–6.

[62] Case C-236/01 *Monsanto*, paras 112–13; see also Dąbrowska-Kłosińska, 'EU Courts', 13.

[63] Cf also Chapter 12 by Alexia Herwig and Asja Serdarevic in this volume.

[64] See Eric Barbier de la Serre and Anne-Lise Sibony, 'Expert Evidence before the EC Courts', 45 *CMLR* 45 941 (2008), 948–9 ff for the further explanation of the various reasons lying behind this reluctance.

[65] Article 25 of the Statute, Protocol (No. 3) on the Statute of the Court of Justice of the European Union, annexed to the Treaties, as amended by Regulation No. 741/2012 of 11 August 2012 amending the Protocol on the Statute of the Court of Justice of the European Union and Annex I thereto OJ L 228/1 and Articles 63–75, in particular Article 70 of the Expert's report of the Procedural Rules of the Court of Justice, OJ 2012 L 265/1.

[66] Alemanno, 'EU Risk Regulation and Science', 64.

[67] Barbier de la Serre and Sibony, 'Expert Evidence before the EC Courts', 958–64.

3. Scientific uncertainty and the scope of authorities' discretion in the application of the precautionary principle

It follows from the above (Section III.A.2) that scientific uncertainty regarding the existence and extent of alleged risk affects the precise scope of the Member States' (and EU institutions') discretion to take protective measures on the basis of the precautionary principle. Hence, while formulating the requirements and conditions for scientific risk assessment, the CJEU seems to be aware of the problem of uncertainty in the complex assessments of facts, and for this reason it stipulates that:

> [i]n a number of cases, the assessment of those factors will demonstrate that there is much uncertainty, in science and in practice, in that regard. Such uncertainty, which is inseparable from the precautionary principle, affects the scope of the Member State's discretion and thus also the manner in which the precautionary principle is applied.[68]

At the same time, the reasoning of the CJEU on the relationship between scientific evidence, its uncertainty, and the reality or likelihood of risk can cause confusion in determining precisely the discretion of public authorities to apply the precautionary principle. As a consequence, this gives the CJEU not only the possibility to conduct a more restrictive review of administrative powers, but also to decide in a rather flexible manner whether or not to uphold a given measure. Several remarks outlining the difficulties should be added here.

First, the discretion in application of protective measures in accordance with the precautionary principle as defined by the CJEU, seems broadened if it is impossible to carry out a full scientific risk assessment because of inadequacy or incompleteness of available scientific data.[69]

Second, the evaluation of scientific evidence and the drawing of conclusions therefrom by public authorities requires a de facto earlier pre-definition: of the level of protection which is deemed necessary for public health and the level of risk (critical probability threshold) which is acceptable for society in the given circumstances of an individual case. Political institutions are to:

> determine the critical probability threshold for adverse effects on public health, safety and the environment and for the seriousness of those possible effects which, in their judgement, is no longer acceptable for society and above which it is necessary, in the interests of protecting public health, safety and the environment, to take preventive measures in spite of any existing scientific uncertainty.[70]

In essence, this means making a decision whether or not to apply the precautionary principle, because 'where there is uncertainty as to the existence or extent of risks to the health of consumers, the institutions may take protective measures without having to wait until the reality and the seriousness of those risks become fully apparent'.[71]

[68] Case C-41/02 *Commission v the Netherlands*, para 51.
[69] Eg Case C-77/09 *Gowan Comércio Internacional*, paras 75–6.
[70] Case T-257/07 *France v Commission*, para 78.
[71] See eg Cases C-236/01 *Monsanto*, paras 111–12, and T-13/99 *Pfizer*, para 139.

Third, when national authorities are faced with a level of risk which they find to be unacceptable for the society, as it exceeds their pre-defined critical probability threshold, they are 'bound, by reason of the precautionary principle, to adopt provisional risk management measures necessary to ensure a high level of protection'.[72] The CJEU has also held that a safeguard clause gives specific expression to the principle which must, where relevant, constitute an 'integral part of the decision-making processes leading to the adoption of any measure for the protection of human health'.[73] As Scott rightly observes, the Court by this statement declared, albeit implicitly, that this principle can impose on Member States' positive obligations to act in accordance with the precautionary principle in decision-making processes.[74] What's more, Member States and EU institutions are also obliged to review the measures taken in a reasonable period in order to see if new elements change the perception of risk, or new scientific evidence justifies the application of less restrictive measures.[75]

Finally, the CJEU points out that 'a level of risk deemed unacceptable for society will depend on the assessment made by the competent public authority of the particular circumstances of each individual case'.[76] Under the obligation to examine 'carefully and impartially' each individual case, this statement brings back the requirements of the scientific risk assessment process and other procedural guarantees which the CJEU envisages for making the decisions in risk regulation cases. All these conditions will be subject to review by the EU Courts.

IV. Standard of Review Applied by the CJEU and Its Implications

A very literal reading of the scope of judicial review as explained in the judgments of the CJEU can prompt the conclusion that EU Courts enjoy a limited power in this respect and that the applicable standard of review is narrowed down to a strict interpretation of normative conditions (legal determinations).

However, a more functional and in-depth reading of the case law reveals that this interpretation does not hold entirely true. Paradoxically, as signalled above, through proceduralization (declaring that scientific risk assessment is a procedural guarantee, proceduralizing the role of the precautionary principle, and elaborating procedural conditions for decision-making in face of scientific uncertainty) and review of the plausibility of evidence, the CJEU reviews indirectly (or sometimes even directly) factual determinations (scientific evidence) and political choices (level of risk) of public authorities. Thus, a formally limited standard of judicial review often becomes de facto a much more

[72] Case T-257/07 *France v Commission*, para 81 (referring to EU institutions).
[73] Case C-236/01 *Monsanto*, paras 110 and 133 (referring to national authorities).
[74] Joanne Scott, 'The Precautionary Principle', 51.
[75] Case C-504/04 *Agrarproduktion Staebelow*, para 40.
[76] Case T-257/07 *France v Commission*, para 80.

intensive one. At the same time, engaging in questions of risk, risk assessment and scientific evidence seems to have led the CJEU to an intolerance of uncertainty (imposing a strict scientific discipline on the decision-making processes) and an extensive reliance on partisan expert opinion and external standards. This can have positive effects in terms of upholding the EU Courts' authority internally as well as on the convergence with international standards (eg in the WTO context), but it can bring about unreliability regarding the actual outcomes of the CJEU judgments. In other words, it is difficult to predict with any certainty when it will uphold and when it will reject the risk management choices of public authorities at the EU and national levels, which can have undesirable consequences for individual parties.[77] The more intensive standard of review in risk regulation cases has further implications. Through the exercise of its judicial review, the CJEU engages in several reasoning processes and interpretative interventions, which produce the consequences described below (1–6).

1. *Construing procedural guarantees*

In view of the above analysis, regulatory authorities have several procedural obligations when making decisions under conditions of scientific uncertainty (and pursuant to the precautionary principle). These include the duty to examine carefully and impartially all the relevant aspects of the individual case, to provide reasons in case scientific opinion is disregarded in the final decision on risk, to perform scientific risk assessment and cost–benefit analysis, and to apply the principle of proportionality.[78]

2. *Structuring decision-making processes on risk through a proceduralized version of the precautionary principle*

In view of the EU Court's case law, precaution should be seen as a principle rather than a rule.[79] This explains why precaution draws attention to the 'process' by which a decision is made, and requires decision-makers to take into account the problems created by scientific uncertainty in the setting of standards, the purpose of which is to protect human health or the environment. This 'process' includes questions of who participates in decision-making, what should be taken into account, or how regulatory decision-making is structured. Accordingly, the necessity of consultation with scientific bodies and the integration of scientific risk assessment into decision-making processes is recognized as an important procedural guarantee in sectors where the precautionary principle applies.

[77] See a critical comment by Alberto Alemanno, 'Case C-77/09, Gowan Comercio Internacional e Servicos Lda v Ministero della Salute, Judgment of the Court of Justice (Second Chamber) of 22 December 2010, nyr', 48(4) *CMLR* 1329 (2011).

[78] Eg Cases C-6/99 *Greenpeace*, para 33 and C-236/01 *Monsanto*, paras 111–12.

[79] Cf Fisher, *Risk Regulation*.

3. *Determining institutional make-up*

The procedural duty to undertake scientific risk assessment as defined by the EU Courts additionally influences the make-up of public authorities. The assessment of risk must be delegated to experts,[80] while the determination of the level of risk which is deemed unacceptable for society must be entrusted to 'institutions responsible for the political choice of determining an appropriate level of protection for society'.[81] As a consequence, the CJEU also indirectly defines the roles of the different actors involved in risk analysis.

4. *Reinforcing the role of science*

The designation of scientific risk assessment as a procedural guarantee reinforces the role of scientific expertise in the decision-making processes. It also allows the Court to review indirectly the issues of risk and uncertainty in relation to the scientific evidence.

5. *Ensuring the revisability and reflexivity of EU law*

Through its review of risk regulation measures, especially those based on Article 114 or safeguard clauses, the CJEU also contributes to the facilitation of reflexivity and revisability of EU law. The results of judicial review (eg invalidity of an act) often oblige policy-makers either to modify the relevant provisions or enact new regulations. Moreover, the CJEU insists that competent authorities timely review both their perception of risk and risk assessment, as well as the need for the measures in question.[82]

6. *Converging with international standards and expertise*

Finally, it can be claimed that CJEU promotes external standards and attempts to ensure convergence with the results of research conducted at the international level and within international organizations.[83] For example, in the *KYDEP* case regarding maximum radioactive tolerances in foodstuffs, the Court referred to opinions of national experts, the recommendations of the International Commission on Radiological Protection, and to the instructions of the US Food and Drug Administration.[84] The methodology of the Court in the *Monsanto* case on genetically modified food can also be cited here. In that ruling, the CJEU appeared to shift emphasis from a formal reading of the legalized scientific notions towards their teleological interpretation in order to uphold, in the EU regime, the

[80] See Scott, 'The Precautionary Principle', 51.
[81] Case T-257/07 *France v Commission*, para 78.
[82] Eg Case C-504/04 *Agrarproduktion Staebelow*, para 40.
[83] See Alemanno, 'EU Risk Regulation and Science', 39, 45 and the case law quoted therein.
[84] See Case C-146/91 *KYDEP v Council and Commission* [1994] I-04199, paras 40–3.

controversial concept of substantial equivalence, a concept which was recognized at the international level.[85]

V. Concluding Remarks

The analysis of the relevant CJEU case law in the area of risk regulation confirms that there has been a certain evolution of its standard of review, moving from a deferential to a more restrictive one. While the EU Courts still formally declare that they exercise a 'limited' judicial review, they have de facto developed a less deferential standard of review of regulatory measures through, paradoxically, the extensive proceduralization and review of the plausibility of evidence. It seems that, in reality, the standard of review described herein offers more possibilities for the EU Courts to construct the functioning of the internal market, influence national competences and institutional and normative structures, as well as play a role in the convergence of international standards through a strong reliance on scientific expertise. At the same time, this is done at the cost of a disparity between the declared and de facto intensity of review, and instability in the foreseeability of the possible outcomes of individual cases.

Further, it should be noted that through its frequent reference to the results of international research, scientific evidence and findings of other international organizations, the CJEU amplifies the significance of international regulation for the EU system and points towards the possibility of convergence of the applicable standards. The reasoning of the EU Courts is science-based and highly resonates with the wording of the WTO panel reports, which would indicate not only an appreciation of international developments, but also a will to maintain consistency between the EU rules and transnational standards of review.[86]

Finally, the more open engagement of the EU Courts in the elaboration of the role of different institutions (assessing and managing risks) in decision-making processes, together with the recognition of structures/bodies which could exercise legitimate peer review in such complex cases, can improve the quality of decisions.[87] The CJEU will also need to frankly engage in methodological questions and take a stance on the value of differing scientific opinions and the 'newness' of scientific evidence, which is a pre-condition of many regulatory decisions. The establishment of some kind of institutionalized cooperation (network?) with other national and international courts and bodies faced with similar disputes could perhaps additionally assist European judges in making complex determinations in the area of risk regulation.

[85] See Dąbrowska, 'GM Foods'.

[86] See Joanne Scott, 'European Regulation of GMOs: Thinking About "Judicial Review" in the WTO' in Ellen Vos and Michelle Everson (eds), *Uncertain Risks Regulated* (London: Routledge Cavendish, 2009) 295–321.

[87] Alemanno, 'EU Risk Regulation and Science', 65–6.

12

Standard of Review for Necessity and Proportionality Analysis in EU and WTO Law

Why Differences in Standards of Review Are Legitimate

*Alexia Herwig and Asja Serdarevic**

I. Introduction

The intrusion into the regulatory autonomy of Member States of the European Union (EU) and World Trade Organization (WTO) Members, and the sensitivity of adjudicatory bodies to non-trade values in disputes concerning regulatory trade barriers are key points in the evaluation of the legitimacy of EU and WTO law. The extent of regulatory autonomy and sensitivity to non-trade values are dependent on judicial approaches to the standard of review and to balancing through the proportionality analysis. This chapter analyses whether the approaches to standard of review for proportionality and necessity in the EU and WTO are legitimate. As the legal and constitutional issues at stake in the proportionality and necessity analysis are similar in both EU and WTO law, they serve as a good testing ground for the plausibility of various prescriptive proposals for calibrating the standard of review.

Before going further it is worth defining the central concept of this chapter. We understand the standard of review as the level of scrutiny applied by a court in its review. The standard of review is of great importance with respect to the role of the adjudicative body in relation to the other actors of the legal system, both vertically and horizontally. In unitary liberal democratic States, it concerns the horizontal relationship between constitutional courts, representative parliamentary bodies and the executive authorities. Thereby, the standard of review implicates the balancing of individual rights against the democratic will of the majority, of substance against procedure, and of the coherence of the law under scrutiny with other legal norms (notably constitutional norms, but also, eg norms of procedure concerning law-making). From the point of view of

* We are thankful to the editors of this volume and to Gert Straetmans for helpful comments on this chapter. All errors remain our own.

multilevel legal systems themselves, the standard of review concerns the vertical relationship between adjudicatory bodies and lower-level institutions, and raises questions about the balance of unity against diversity. In other words, the standard of review adopted by adjudicatory bodies is intricately linked to constitutional-type legal questions.

In the context of proportionality analysis in the EU and the WTO, the standard of review is directly relevant to the *vertical* relationship between the international organization and its Members. In the EU, it is also relevant to the *horizontal* relationship between the European courts and the law-making and executive bodies of the EU, that is, between institutions at the same level of governance.

The principle of proportionality is an important tool for adjudicatory bodies to reconcile the regulatory freedom of legislatures and executives with the objective of ensuring market access across national borders. The principle is applied in some form in both EU and WTO law. In the EU,[1] it places limitations on Union actions as well as Member States' measures that restrict trade within the EU. When it comes to acts of the Union, the principle is applied to confer the necessary discretion required by EU institutions, while in the case of Member States' measures, the aim is rather to limit their regulatory freedom (through a more intrusive standard of review). The role of the proportionality test in WTO law is not clear and has been a subject of discussion among both academics and practitioners.[2] WTO agreements do not explicitly provide for a proportionality test, but they contain several necessity tests.[3] The most prominent is Article XX of the General Agreement on Tariffs and Trade (GATT),[4] which calls for the analysis of the contribution that a measure makes towards achieving the regulatory objective, weighed against its trade-restrictiveness in light of the importance of the regulatory objective.[5] In practice, the standard of review employed in the WTO has varied for the different parts of the necessity and proportionality analysis, depending on the issues at stake.

[1] Case C-180/96 *United Kingdom v Commission* [1998] ECR 2265, para 96.

[2] See Axel Desmedt, 'Proportionality in WTO law', 4(3) *JIEL* 441 (2001); Meinhard Hilf, 'The Power, Rules and Principles—Which Orientation for WTO/GATT Law?', 4(1) *JIEL* 111 (2001); Mads Andenas and Stefan Zlepting, 'Proportionality: WTO Law in Comparative Perspective', 42 *Texas International Law Journal* 371 (2007); Andrew D. Mitchell, *Legal Principles in WTO Disputes* (Cambridge: Cambridge University Press, 2008).

[3] See Article XI(2)(b), (c); Article XX GATT 1994; Article XIV(a), (b), (c) and Article VI(4) GATS; Articles 3.2, 8.1, 27.2 TRIPS.

[4] See GATT Panel Report, *US—Section 337 of the Tariff Act of 1930*, L/6439, 7 November 1989, para 5.26; GATT Panel Report, *Thailand—Restrictions on Importation of and Internal Taxes on Cigarettes*, DS10/R, 7 November 1990, para 75; Panel Report, *United States—Standards for Reformulated and Conventional Gasoline*, WT/DS2/R, 29 January 1996, as modified by Appellate Body Report WT/DS2/AB/R, paras 6.25–6.28; Appellate Body Report, *Korea—Measures Affecting Imports of Fresh, Chilled and Frozen Beef*, WT/DS/161/AB/R, 10 January 2001, paras 161–2.

[5] See Appellate Body Report, *Korea—Beef*; Appellate Body Report, *United States—Measures Affecting the Cross-Border Supply of Gambling and Betting Services*, WT/DS285/AB/R, 20 April 2005, which confirmed applicability of this test to the General Agreement on Trade in Services (GATS).

II. Principle of Proportionality

A. Principle of proportionality in EU law

The principle of proportionality in the Treaty on European Union (TEU) stipulates that the content and form of Union actions must not exceed what is necessary to achieve the objectives of the TEU and the Treaty on the Functioning of the European Union (TFEU).[6]

The Treaty of Rome (which is an earlier version of the TFEU) mentioned the principle only in limited terms,[7] and it was only the European Court of Justice (ECJ, or the Court) that developed it. The principle has been primarily used in two situations: to review the validity of Union measures and of Member States' actions.[8] It was first addressed by the Court in the context of the European Coal and Steel Community Treaty.[9] The Court held that 'in accordance with a generally-accepted rule of law such an indirect reaction by the High Authority to illegal action on the part of the undertakings must be in proportion to the scale of that action.'[10] In 1971, the Court relied explicitly on the principle of proportionality and laid down its distinctive characteristics in *Internationale Handelsgeschellschaft*.[11] It derived the principle from the rule of law and held that 'the individual should not have his freedom of action limited beyond the degree necessary in the public interest.'[12] The Court considered the proportionality principle so fundamental and apparent that its presence in the Community (Union) legal order was deemed to be self-evident and it did not need further clarification.[13]

In order to examine whether a particular measure (Union's or Member State's) complies with the principle of proportionality, three sequential, cumulative tests are applied: suitability, necessity and proportionality *stricto sensu*. The suitability test requires that the measure in question is suitable or appropriate to achieve the objectives it pursues;[14] in other words it asks for a causal connection between the

[6] Article 5(4) TFEU.

[7] Article 3(b) of the Treaty Establishing the European Economic Community, 25 March 1957, 298 UNTS 3.

[8] Federico Ortino, *Basic Legal Instruments for the Liberalisation of Trade: A Comparative Analysis of EC and WTO Law* (Oxford and Portland: Hart Publishing, 2004) 403; see also Nicholas Emilio, *The Principles of Proportionality in European Law: A Comparative Study* (London: Kluwer Law International, 1996) 24; Takis Tridimas, 'Proportionality in Community Law: Searching for the Appropriate Standard of Scrutiny' in Evelyn Ellis (ed), *Principle of Proportionality in the Laws of Europe* (Oxford: Hart Publishing, 1999) 65.

[9] Tridimas, 'Proportionality in Community Law', 69; see also Case 8/55 *Federation Charbonniere Belgique v High Authority* [1954-56] ECR 292.

[10] Case 8/55 *Federation Charbonniere Belgique*, para 299.

[11] Case 11/70 *Internationale Handelsgesellschaft mbH v Einfuhr - und Vorratsstelle fur Getreide und Futtermittel* [1970] ECR 1125.

[12] Case 11/70 *Internationale Handelsgesellschaft*, para 1147.

[13] Emiliou, *The Principles of Proportionality*, 135.

[14] Andenas and Zlepting, 'Proportionality: WTO Law', 387; see also Juka Snell, *Goods and Services in EC Law: A Study of the Relationship Between the Freedoms* (Oxford: Oxford University Press, 2002) 196; Tor-Inge Harbo, 'The Function of the Proportionality Principle in EU Law', 16(2) *ELJ* 165 (2010).

measure adopted and the aim pursued.[15] However, it is not entirely clear how suitable a measure must be. 'Suitable' seems to imply a less strict causal relationship than 'indispensable', while at the same time being less flexible than merely 'useful'. This step of the proportionality analysis aims mainly at establishing a minimum level of 'reasonableness' in the relationship between the regulatory instrument and its public policy objective, without the Court of Justice of the European Union (CJEU) having to consider whether the Member State's measure is the best alternative in relation to the specific objective pursued, or the negative effects on other interests.[16]

The necessity test requires that the objective of the measure cannot be achieved by other means that are less restrictive and produce the same result.[17] This test has an underlying purpose: that the adopted measure should be the least trade-restrictive in pursuing non-trade related domestic policy objectives. The Court takes into account the level of trade-restrictiveness of a measure in comparison to all other regulatory instruments. However, the necessity test entails a degree of difficulty, because the Court must compare the regulatory and trade-restrictive effects of actual and hypothetical measures.[18]

For example, the CJEU in *Adrien de Peijper* held that the measure was not necessary because the national authorities could have pursued the same objective with the same effect by adopting other means which were less restrictive to trade within the Community.[19] In this case, the Court clearly set the 'least restrictive means' test. In *Familiapress*, the Court held that it was for the national courts to assess whether the national prohibition was 'proportionate to the aim of maintaining press diversity and whether that objective might be attained by measures less restrictive of both intra-Community trade and freedom of expression.'[20] In *Schindler*, the Court gave considerable latitude to the Member State explaining that the latter must have sufficient room to manoeuvre to determine what is necessary to protect those taking part in lotteries, and justified the measure in question because of the high risk of crime or fraud.[21]

The third element of the principle of proportionality is the proportionality *stricto sensu*. The disputed measure is analysed as to whether its effects are disproportionate or excessive compared to the interests affected.[22] The Court will assess whether the measure reviewed imposes an excessive burden on the individual,

[15] Desmedt, 'Proportionality in WTO Law', 444.

[16] Ortino, *Basic Legal Instruments*, 405–6.

[17] Andenas and Zlepting, 'Proportionality: WTO Law', 388; Tridimas, 'Proportionality in Community Law', 68; Emiliou, *The Principles of Proportionality*, 29.

[18] Ortino, *Basic Legal Instruments*, 406.

[19] Case 104/75 *Officier Van Justitie v Adriaan de Peijper* [1976] ECR 613, 636; see also Case C-348/93 *Alpine Investments* [1995] ECR I-1141.

[20] Case C-368/95 *Vereinigte Familiapress Zeitungsverlags- und vertriebs GmbH v Heinrich Bauer Verlage* [1997] ECR I-3689, I-3717.

[21] Case C-275/92 *Her Majesty's Customs and Excise v Gerhart Schindler and Jörg* [1994] ECR I-1039.

[22] Robert Alexy, *A Theory of Constitutional Rights* (Oxford: Oxford University Press, 2002) 66–7: refers to the proportionality *stricto sensu* as the 'balancing requirement'.

even though it may be suitable and necessary. While the suitability and necessity tests are primarily about balancing trade against non-trade interests with respect to factual possibilities, proportionality analysis *stricto sensu* is about balancing and weighing competing objectives.[23]

In EU law, the necessity test dominates most cases where the CJEU applies the proportionality test. In fact, the Court tries to disguise proportionality *stricto sensu* as the necessity test and it almost never addresses the third element.[24] Consequently, even though the three-tier test has received some support from the European judiciary,[25] in practice the Court does not distinguish between the second and the third elements of the test.[26] In the cases when the CJEU explicitly applied proportionality *stricto sensu*, it has usually balanced and weighed the objectives submitted by the Member States to justify their domestic measures against the Union interests.

B. Standard of review in applying the principle of proportionality in the EU

The three steps of the principle of proportionality were set out clearly in *Fedesa*.[27] However, subsequent CJEU case law has developed in two different directions depending whether the subject of review concerns EU secondary legislation or a Member States' measure.[28]

EU measures are usually subjected to a test of manifest disproportionality, while the Member States' measures are subject to a least-restrictive means test.[29] The CJEU will only nullify an EU measure if it finds it manifestly inappropriate to achieve the objective it is aiming to realize. When the Court applies the manifestly inappropriate test, it examines the reasons proffered by the Union's institution,[30] but its inquiry searches for gross misjudgement rather than improving the ratio of regulatory benefits to economic costs. In contrast, the CJEU overturns Member

[23] Andenas and Zlepting, 'Proportionality: WTO Law', 388.

[24] Ortino, *Basic Legal Instruments*, 471; see also Andenas and Zlepting, 'Proportionality: WTO Law', 389; Takis Tridimas, *The General Principles of EU Law* (Oxford: Oxford University Press, 2006), 139–40.

[25] See Opinion of Advocate General van Gerven in Case C-159/90 *Society for the Protection of Unborn Children Ireland Ltd v Grogan* [1991] ECR I-4685 and the Opinion of Advocate General in Case 331/88 *Fedesa* [1990] ECR I-4023 at 4051; Case C-169/91 *Stoke-on-Trent v B&Q* [1992] ECR I-6635; see also Tridimas, *General Principles*, 139.

[26] Tridimas, *General Principles*, 139–40.

[27] Case C-331/88 *R v Minister of Agriculture, Fisheries and Food and Secretary of State for Health, ex parte: Fedesa and others* [1990] ECR I-4023, para 13; Joined Cases C-300/93 and C-362/93 *Antonio Crispoltoni v Fattoria Autonoma Tabacchi* and *Giuseppe Natale and Antonio Pontillo v Donatab Srl* [1994] ECR I-4863, para 40; Case C-180/96 *United Kingdom v Commission* [1998] ECR I-2265, para 96; Case C-189/01 *H. Jippes and others v Minister van Landbouw, Natuurbeheer en Visserij* [2001] ECR I-5689, para 80.

[28] Wolf Sauter, 'Proportionality in EU Law: A Balancing Act?', *TILEC Discussion Paper No. 2013-003*, 6–7, available at <http://ssrn.com/abstract=2208467> (accessed 28 March 2014).

[29] Sauter, 'Proportionality in EU Law', 5–6. See Tridimas, *General Principles*, 138; Gráinne de Búrca, 'The Principle of Proportionality and Its Application in EC Law', 13 *Yearbook of European Law* 105 (1993), 146.

[30] Paul Craig, *EU Administrative Law*, 2nd edn (Oxford: Oxford University Press, 2012) 601.

States' measures if there is a less restrictive, effective alternative (least-restrictive means test).[31] When the principle is invoked in order to challenge the compatibility with EU law of national measures affecting one of the fundamental freedoms, the Court balances Union interests against national ones.[32]

It has been suggested that the nature of the interest to be protected is relevant to the manner in which the Court applies the principle of proportionality,[33] as well as the degree of harmonization achieved with respect to certain policies at the EU level.[34] The level of harmonization indicates the degree to which a common policy exists and/or the degree to which the Member States have acceded to a common regime. The Court gives more leeway to the Member States if the subject of the measure in question falls more within the jurisdiction of the Member States, such as combating crime and fraud, as opposed to economic activities, which fall primarily within the jurisdiction of the EU. Hence, in the absence of harmonization, the least-restrictive means test is unlikely to be applied with intense scrutiny to the actions of the Member States. But it should be noted that if a measure constitutes an infringement of one of the four fundamental freedoms, the Court will scrutinize it more strictly even if it was adopted by the EU institutions.[35]

When a national measure creates an obstacle or restricts the free movement of goods in the Union, the CJEU is strict even if a Member State claims the protection of human health as its reason for restricting trade.[36] A good example is *Commission v Germany*, in which Germany imposed a total ban on the use of additives in beer, arguing that it was necessary to protect the health of the many German beer drinkers.[37] Nevertheless, the Court held that the German ban was illegal and disproportionate to the aim it was trying to pursue for several reasons: the use of additives was permitted in other Member States and Germany allowed it in other drinks; the exclusion of all additives by Germany highlighted the ban's disproportionate nature; and the lack of proportionality was obvious since there was no specific procedure laid down in such a way that traders could obtain authorization to use certain additives.[38] In *Danish Bottles*, while the Court recognized a recycling system as an essential means of protection of the environment that may justify the necessary and proportional restriction of the free movement of goods, nevertheless it held that since the Danish system could only

[31] Harbo, 'The Function of the Proportionality Principle', 172.

[32] Tridimas, 'Proportionality in Community Law', 66.

[33] Jan H. Jans, 'Proportionality Revisited', 27(3) *Legal Issues of Economic Integration* 239 (2000), 246.

[34] Wolf Sauter and Harm Schepel, *State and Market in European Union Law: The Private and Public Spheres of the Internal Market before the EU Courts* (Cambridge: Cambridge University Press, 2009); Damian Chalmers, Gareth Davies and Giorgio Monti, *European Union Law*, 2nd edn (Cambridge: Cambridge University Press, 2010) 206–7.

[35] See Case C-331/88 *R v Minister of Agriculture, Fisheries and Food ex parte Fedesa*; Case 104/75 *Adriaan de Peijper* and Case C-348/93 *Alpine Investments,* which concerned a national measure infringing fundamental freedoms.

[36] Tridimas, *General Principles*, 225.

[37] Case C-178/84 *Commission v Germany* [1987] ECR 1227.

[38] *Commission v Germany*; see also Natalie McNelis, 'The Role of the Judge in the EU and WTO. Lessons from the BSE and Hormones Cases', 4(1) *JIEL* 698 (2001), 204.

accommodate a limited number of bottle types, it was not necessary and therefore disproportionate.[39] In *Criminal Proceedings against Harry Franzén*, which involved a licensing system for the import of alcoholic beverages, the Court held that the Swedish government did not establish that such regime was proportionate to the public health aim pursued, nor that such a regime could not be pursued by a less restrictive means.[40] Thus it can be seen that while in matters of public health the Court has mostly followed a cautious approach, it still applies a strict approach to the principle of proportionality.

Even though the Court has been driven by an integration paradigm in the least-restrictive means test, it has conferred a margin of discretion on Member States in cases such as consumer protection, notwithstanding considerable harmonization. The fact that one Member State imposes less restrictive measures than others does not mean that the others' measures are disproportionate and hence incompatible with EU law.[41]

In setting the standard of review of Union acts in the area of the common commercial policy and the common agriculture policy, the CJEU has considered the role of the Commission as guardian of the Treaty and its enormous technical expertise. Hence, while the Court held in *Fedesa* that the legality of a measure adopted can be affected if the measure is manifestly inappropriate having regard to the objective which the competent institution is seeking to pursue,[42] it did not examine whether there were less restrictive measures able to achieve the same aim, but held that since the Council of Ministers enjoyed discretion and made no obvious error in considering the measure appropriate, the Council was entitled to take the position that the objectives pursued could not be achieved by any other measure.[43] The expression 'manifestly inappropriate' delineates what the Court perceives to be the limits of its judicial function when reviewing measures which involve different choices of economic policy by EU institutions.

However, it must be noted that the Court will look not only at whether the case concerns EU measures or national measures, but will also take into consideration whether the contested measure affects fundamental rights.[44] For example, *Internationale Handelsgeschellschaft* [45] and *Hauer*[46] concerned property rights and EU measures, while the cases *Adrien de Peijper* and

[39] Case 302/86 *Commission of the European Communities v Kingdom of Denmark (Danish Bottles)* [1988] ECR-4607, para 6.

[40] Case C-189/95 *Criminal Proceedings against Harry Franzén* [1997] ECR I-5909, para 76.

[41] Case C-348/93 *Alpine Investments*; Case C-110/05 *Commission v Italy* [2009] ECR I-519, para 65; Case C-124/97 *Markku Jahani Läärä, Cotswold Motorcycle Ltd and Oy Translatlantic Software Ltd v Kihlakunnansyyttäja (Jyväskylä) and Suomen Valtio* [1999] ECR I-6067, para 37.

[42] Case C-331/88 *Fedesa*, para 14. For an analysis with respect to tightening review by looking at the quality of evidence in complex factual cases, see the contribution of Dąbrowska-Kłosińska at Chapter 11 in this volume.

[43] Case C-331/88 *Fedesa*, para 16.

[44] Harbo, 'The Function of the Proportionality Principle', 173.

[45] Case 11/70 *Internationale Handelsgesellschaft v Einfuhr-und Vorratsstelle Getreide.*

[46] Case 44/79 *Hauer v Land Rheinland-Phalz* [1979] ECR 3727.

Alpine Investments concerned the four fundamental freedoms and national measures. In *Internationale Handelgesellschaft* and *Hauer*, the Court found the Community measures to be proportionate, while in the latter cases national measures were found to be not proportionate. There are reasons to assume that the Court was stricter in the latter cases not because they involved national measures while the former involved Community acts, but rather because the latter constituted infringements of one of the four freedoms, whereas the former did not.[47]

It is clear that the proportionality principle is a flexible one which the CJEU applies with varying degrees of judicial scrutiny, from being considerably deferential to a rigorous and searching examination of the justification for a measure in question.[48] When the Court applies the proportionality test, both in the case of Member State and EU measures, it uses differing degrees of strictness depending on several factors, as follows:

1. The nature of the measure in question and the degree of discretion given to the institution adopting it are of crucial importance. If the power of appraisal given to an institution is broader, then the Court will exercise a less comprehensive review.
2. If the measure severely affects private interests, then it is more difficult to establish its necessity. A penalty charge is more restrictive to commercial freedom than the refusal of a subsidy, and the Court imposes a higher standard on the authorities to justify it.
3. The objective of the measure and the type of interest are also very important: public health considerations,[49] as well as nuclear safety[50] and public security,[51] might be given priority over economic interests.
4. In sensitive areas, such as an abortion,[52] Sunday closing hours,[53] human dignity,[54] and gambling and lottery cases,[55] the Court has been reluctant to substitute its own views for those of the Member States and has engaged in more lenient tests.

[47] Harbo, 'The Function of the Proportionality Principle', 172–3; Craig, *EU Administrative Law*, 629–30.

[48] De Búrca, 'The Principle of Proportionality', 105; see also Paul Craig, 'Proportionality, Rationality and Review', *New Zealand Law Review* 265 (2010), 268.

[49] Case C-331/88 *Fedesa*, para 13.

[50] Case C-308/90 *Advanced Nuclear Fuels v Commission* [1993] ECR I-309.

[51] Case C-120/94 *Commission v Greece* [1996] ECR 1513, per Advocate General Jacobs.

[52] Case C-159/90 *Society for the Protection of Unborn Children Ireland Ltd v Stephen Grogan and others*.

[53] Case C-169/91 *Stoke-on-Trent v B&Q*.

[54] C-36/02 *Omega Spielhallen,-und Automatenaufstellungs GmbH v Bundesstad Bonn* [2004] ECR I-9609.

[55] Case C-275/92 *Schindler* [1994] ECR I-1039; see also Gert Straetmans, 'Case C-124/97, Läärä, Judgment of the Court of 21 September 1999 and Case C-67/98, Zenatti, Judgment of the Court of 21 October, 1999', 37(4) *CMLR* 991 (2000), 991–2.

5. If the measures restricting economic freedom are of a temporary nature, then the measure could be justified more easily.[56]

In its review of Union measures, the CJEU has aimed at achieving a balance between the objective of the measures and their adverse effect on individual freedoms and created a path to more unity within the Union. The Court has, from the beginning of the Union, promoted European integration, which explains its bias and 'favouritism' towards the measures adopted by the institutions of the EU.[57] However, at the same time the Court has tried to preserve diversity, for instance in consumer law cases.

C. Standard of review and application of the principle of proportionality in the WTO

In the WTO, the standard of review concerns the question whether the Appellate Body or WTO panels should defer to or 'second-guess' the legal interpretations, application of law, and findings of fact of the WTO Members.[58] There is nothing in the WTO agreements that specifically provides for the standard of review, except for Article 17.6 of the Anti-Dumping Agreement, nor is there an express provision for the principle of proportionality, even though it has been suggested that it is one of the basic principles of the multilateral trading system.[59]

In the *EC—Hormones* case, the Appellate Body defined the standard of review for all WTO agreements (unless provided otherwise in a specific agreement) and held that standard of review must respect the balance established between the jurisdictional competences given to the WTO by its Members and the competences that the Members kept for themselves.[60] According to the Appellate Body, the proper standard of review is an 'objective assessment of the matter'.[61] As per Article 11 DSU, 'a panel should make an objective assessment of the matter before it, including an objective assessment of the facts of the case and the applicability of and conformity with the relevant covered agreements.' According to the Appellate Body, this standard of review is articulated with great succinctness but sufficient precision.[62]

The Appellate Body has read the principle of proportionality into WTO law in its interpretation and application of Article XX GATT.[63] It held that the task of interpreting and applying Article XX (chapeau) is to find a balance between the

[56] Tridimas, 'Proportionality in Community law', 76–7; Tridimas, *The General Principles*, 173–4.

[57] Tridimas, *The General Principles*, 193; Harbo, 'The Function of the Proportionality Principle', 172.

[58] Andenas and Zlepting, 'Proportionality: WTO Law', 393.

[59] Hilf, 'The Power, Rules and Principles', 120.

[60] Appellate Body Report, *European Communities—Measures Concerning Meat and Meat Products (EC—Hormones),* WT/DS26/AB/R, WT/DS48/AB/R, 13 February 1998, para 117.

[61] Appellate Body Report, *EC—Hormones*, para 116.

[62] Appellate Body Report, *EC—Hormones*, para 116.

[63] Appellate Body Report, *United States—Import Prohibition of Certain Shrimp and Shrimp Products*, WT/DS58/AB/R, 6 November 1998.

right of a Member to invoke an exception under Article XX and the rights of other WTO Members under various substantive provisions of the GATT, so that the rights do not cancel each other out and distort and impair the balance of rights and obligations given to the Members by the agreement.[64]

In the *US—Gasoline* case, the Appellate Body set a three-tiered test for applying Article XX GATT: 1) whether a measure falls within the scope of one of the public policy exceptions proclaimed in the above-mentioned GATT article; 2) if so, whether it is necessary or related to the aim it purports to achieve; and 3) whether the application of the measure in question complies with the criteria provided in the chapeau of Article XX.[65]

With respect to the necessity test, the Appellate Body in the *EC—Asbestos* case held that the WTO Members have the right to determine the level of health protection they consider appropriate in a given situation.[66] A Member cannot be required to substitute a measure with an alternative which is less protective simply because it is less trade-restrictive.[67] In *EC—Asbestos*, doubts about the comparability of protection levels from the controlled use of asbestos with the levels resulting from a ban sufficed for the Appellate Body to reject 'controlled use' as a reasonably available, less restrictive alternative.[68]

The necessity test in Articles XX(b) and (d) has been extensively addressed in the case law. In the *US—Gasoline* case, the panel set the standard for the necessity test by inquiring whether measures consistent, or less inconsistent, with the GATT were reasonably available.[69] The subsequent *Korea—Beef* case seems to add an analysis of proportionality *stricto sensu* to the examination of necessity. In particular, the Appellate Body held that in order to evaluate the necessity of measures which are not indispensable, three factors had an impact on whether such measures could be accepted as necessary (two for and one against): a high importance of the objective the measure pursues and a high degree of contribution to realizing the end result weighed in favour of the necessity of the measure; while significant trade-restrictive effects weighed against its necessity.[70] According to the Appellate Body, this weighing and balancing is part of the determination of whether or not a reasonably available alternative exists.[71] In *US—Gambling*, the Appellate Body explained that it envisages a two-step test: the necessity test using the *Korea—Beef* factors, combined with an inquiry into reasonably available alternative measures, in the light of the importance of the interest at stake.[72]

[64] Appellate Body Report, *US—Shrimp*, para 159.

[65] Appellate Body Report *United States—Standards for Reformulated and Conventional Gasoline*, WT/DS2/AB/R, 20 May 1996, paras 22–4.

[66] Appellate Body Report, *European Communities—Measures Affecting Asbestos and Asbestos-Containing Products*, WT/DS135/AB/R, 5 April 2001, para 168.

[67] Appellate Body Report, *EC—Asbestos*, para 171.

[68] Appellate Body Report, *EC—Asbestos*, para 174.

[69] Panel Report, *US—Gasoline*, para 6.20.

[70] Appellate Body Report, *Korea—Beef*, paras 161–3.

[71] Appellate Body Report, *Korea—Beef*, para 166.

[72] Appellate Body Report, *US—Gambling*, para 307.

In *Brazil—Tyres*,[73] both the panel and the Appellate Body effectively relaxed their scrutiny of the availability of alternative measures in two ways: firstly by holding that the analysis does not require quantification of the risk, nor of the contribution of a measure or alternative to the achievement of the objective;[74] and secondly by requiring a genuine means-end relationship between the measure and the objective.[75] This has been labelled as a suitability test.[76] The Appellate Body was willing to assess the importance of the regulatory objectives at stake according to proportionality *stricto sensu* because it considered environmental protection to be merely an important interest and not a vital interest as in previous cases.[77]

The issue that arises is whether the approaches taken in *EC—Asbestos* and *Korea—Beef* on the one hand, and in *Brazil—Tyres* on the other, are reconcilable. The Appellate Body stated in *EC—Asbestos* that WTO Members can determine the level of protection they want to achieve; yet it also showed willingness in *Brazil—Tyres* to assess the importance of the regulatory objectives at stake according to proportionality *stricto sensu*. One can argue that the two tests are inconsistent unless the assessment of the importance of the regulatory objective can only be used to give more deference to WTO Members in cases of doubt about the comparative effectiveness of measures proposed as alternatives in achieving the sought-after levels of protection. In other words, when there is scientific and technical certainty that only the disputed measure achieves the desired level of protection, the importance of the regulatory objective at stake will not be used to question the measure.[78] *Mutatis mutandis*, when it is clearly established that the disputed measure is not necessarily the only effective measure to achieve the desired level of protection, the importance of the regulatory objective at stake should not be used to grant more deference to WTO Members.

III. Theoretical Framework—Proposals on the Standard of Review

A threshold problem is what type of issue under judicial review is appropriate for deference or strict scrutiny. According to Shany, deference should apply to fact-finding and fact-assessing exercises (mixed questions of law and fact), but not to legal interpretation.[79] We share his opinion inasmuch as *de novo* review of

[73] Appellate Body Report, *Brazil—Measures Affecting Imports of Retreaded Tyres*, WT/DS332/AB/R, 17 December 2007.

[74] Chad P. Bown and Joel P. Trachtman, 'Brazil—Measures Affecting Imports of Retreaded Tyres: A Balancing Act', 8(1) *WTR* 85 (2009), 85–135.

[75] Appellate Body Report, *Brazil—Tyres*, para 210.

[76] Bown and Trachtman, 'Brazil—Tyres', 133.

[77] Appellate Body Report, *Brazil—Tyres*, para 210.

[78] In *Korea—Beef*, the Appellate Body confirmed that it excluded indispensable measures from balancing.

[79] Yuval Shany, 'Toward a General Margin of Appreciation Doctrine in International Law?', 16(5) *EJIL* 907 (2006), 909–11, 913.

legal interpretations promotes legal uniformity and ensures that the same legal obligations apply to all legal subjects. Shany further submits that deference should be limited to inherently uncertain norms *inter alia* standards such as proportionality assessment, because they can only give limited normative guidance which deference would not erode.[80] Inasmuch as standards connect law to more or less complex facts and indicate a preference for diversity and decentralization, they are a good case for deference.[81] Our comparative analysis of the CJEU and WTO dispute settlement bodies has shown that they apply different standards of review even within proportionality analysis. In the following subsections, we examine whether the key justifications used by the CJEU and WTO dispute settlement bodies for adjusting standards of review are normatively convincing.

A. Adjusting the standard of review depending on the issues at stake in the norm under review

Both the CJEU and Appellate Body scrutinize important public policy interests more lightly, but tighten their review the heavier the policy's impact on private interests is. This suggests that both adjudicatory bodies see stricter review as more justified to the extent they are exercising the function of protecting the interests of individuals affected by trans-boundary externalities. In their approach, deference to majoritarian will-formation is contingent on the type of public policy pursued, ie the importance of the public policy. This raises the question of whether it is normatively convincing to adjust the standard of review depending on the issues at stake. Do courts become guardians of substantive principles and rights primarily when individual interests are at stake? And is protection of the democratic procedures of will-formation particularly important when important public policies are at stake? It should be noted that prescriptive analyses of the standard of review carried out by several scholars have provided support for the way the CJEU and Appellate Body adjust their standards depending on whether important trade interests or important public policies are at stake.

Craig argues that strict scrutiny of core economic freedoms is generally justified. He suggests that a harder look at proportionality in such cases is justified, because proportionality becomes the key way to distinguish lawful from unlawful regulation of commerce, since discrimination is not essential to finding a violation of Article 34 TFEU (as it equally applies to non-discriminatory measures having equivalent effect to a quantitative restriction).[82] Craig also considers that the centrality of equality underlying the four freedoms and an allegation of their prima facie breach justifies a strict standard for reviewing proportionality of the exceptions contained in Article 36 TFEU.[83]

[80] Shany, 'Toward a General Margin', at 913–4.

[81] Shany, 'Toward a General Margin', 915. For a similar argument in relation to CJEU review of EU acts, see Craig, *EU Administrative Law*, 601 and for the International Court of Justice's (ICJ's) approach to standard-type norms, see Chiara Ragni's contribution to this volume at Chapter 17.

[82] Craig, *EU Administrative Law*, 630.

[83] Craig, *EU Administrative Law*, 630–1.

However, if indeed it is the importance of equality (in other words, non-discrimination) that justifies strict scrutiny, then it would seem to follow that, inasmuch as discrimination is not at issue with indistinctly applicable and merely restrictive regulations of commerce, *less strict* scrutiny is called for. Secondly, the fact that proportionality becomes central to sorting out lawful from unlawful regulations, where restrictive effects of regulatory measures suffice for a possible violation of Article 34, does not explain why the CJEU should take a hard look at the situation, unless one is committed to the normative position that State intervention in the economy is prima facie suspect. We doubt this commitment is normatively sensible and analytically sustainable, because with some restrictive regulations of commerce the link to product-specific regulation becomes ever more tenuous, so that establishing the necessary inconsistency with Article 34 TFEU is already a close call. The EU Sunday trading cases exemplify this, because shop closing hours are more directly concerned with the protection of workers and family life than regulating any product. Should not the CJEU give *more* deference because it is no longer reviewing a regulation that is blameworthy because it is protectionist, but rather a genuine mandate of the State to regulate for the common well-being of its citizens?[84]

Other commentators in European and international law adopt a more nuanced position. Gerards, in her comparison of the European Court of Human Rights and the CJEU, argues that courts should take a hard look when potential infringements of procedural rights relevant for democracy, fundamental individual rights or key treaty objectives (fundamental economic freedoms) are at issue.[85] However, a relationship to national constitutional values (eg the importance of human dignity in the German constitution given the country's dark past) calls for adjusting to an intermediate review even if the 'hard look' factors are present.[86] Shany's position on the standard of review to be adopted by international courts is similar. He argues that because of the limited democratic accountability of international courts with non-elected judges, deference is called for where the international law norm regulates primarily internal matters (human rights) as opposed to outward-looking norms designed to protect foreigners from extra-territorial effects in other States where deference is not appropriate.[87] Similarly, von Staden argues that on the grounds of democracy inward-looking norms (eg human rights)

[84] Note that this argument also applies to the Appellate Body when considering necessity in the Sanitary and Phytosanitary Measures (SPS) and Technical Barriers to Trade (TBT) Agreements, which can be violated without discrimination.

[85] Janneke Gerards, 'Pluralism, Deference and the Margin of Appreciation Doctrine', 17 *ELJ* 80 (2011), 118–19.

[86] Gerards, 'Pluralism, Deference', 17. Delmas-Marty and Izroche agree that significant differences in policies call for a wider margin of appreciation. See Mirellie Delmas-Marty and Marie-Laure Izroche, 'Marge Nationale d'Appréciation et Internationalisation du Droit: Réflexions sur la Validité Formelle d'un Droit Commun Pluraliste', 52 *Revue internationale de droit comparé* 753 (2000), 778–9.

[87] Shany, 'Toward a General Margin', 919–21.

should be reviewed with a deferential standard of review, but not outward-looking norms dealing with cross-border externalities.[88]

GATT Articles XX and XXI and Article 36 TFEU look like good testing ground for this type of argument, since they invoke inward-looking norms, appropriate for deference, together with a standard type norm in the form of the necessity test as a justification for inconsistencies with core economic freedoms.[89]

A first difficulty with the common position of Shany and von Staden is that GATT Articles XX and XXI as well as Article 36 TFEU invoke inward-looking norms but do so within outward-looking legal systems, which seek to make their Member States accountable for the extra-territorial effects they produce on trade.[90] The categories of inward- and outward-looking norms do not provide useful guidance on how to calibrate the standard of review, and Shany admits as much.[91] An argument might be raised that once the adjudicatory body gets to the exception clause, the outward-looking norm protecting core economic freedoms has already been provisionally found to be infringed, so that 'hard look' factors no longer apply. But this argument is unduly formalistic because of course the exception clause is intimately tied to the question of whether there has in fact been a violation.

Finally, we would question that using human rights-based exceptions to restrict trade or deny national treatment is a purely inward-looking matter. Firstly, inadequate human rights protection in nation-States affects the fairness of the EU and international treaty-making and is therefore important for the democratic character of EU and international law. Secondly, a failure to protect human rights in another State matters to autonomous, *moral* agents abroad insofar as it implicates their moral judgement and raises the question of whether or not to intervene. This may explain why human rights protection within nation-States is of common international concern as an *erga omnes* norm, and not just an inward-looking matter.

Recall that Gerards argues that intermediate review is called for when national constitutional values or legitimate pluralism are at stake, together with the core free movement guarantees in EU law. But why must such review be intermediate? Is it simply because of the evening-out effect of the factors supporting strict scrutiny and deference, which are individually justified on other grounds? Such a

[88] Andreas von Staden, 'The Democratic Legitimacy of Judicial Review Beyond the State', 10(4) *International Journal of Constitutional Law* 1023 (2012).

[89] Shany himself characterizes GATT Article XXI as a deference norm, since this Article refers to action a WTO Member considers necessary to protect its essential security interests.

[90] Eg Petros C. Mavroidis, *Trade in Goods* (New York: Oxford University Press, 2007), 12–20; Christian Joerges, 'Free Trade in Hazardous Products. The Emergence of Transnational Governance with Eroding State Government', 10(4) *European Public Affairs Review* 553 (2005); Robert Howse and Nicolaidis Kalypso, 'Democracy without Sovereignty: The Global Vocation of Political Ethics' in Tomer Broude and Yuval Shany (eds), *The Shifting Allocation of Authority in International Law. Considering Sovereignty, Supremacy and Subsidiarity* (Oxford: Hart Publishing, 2008) 167.

[91] Shany concedes that the outward-/inward-looking distinction is of limited guidance only, but this admission raises the question of what else should guide courts in granting deference for reasons of democracy. He fails to answer this, instead only pointing to a few instances where courts should not grant deference. Shany, 'Toward a General Margin', 920–1.

simple offsetting would not accord with the importance of the public policy issues that can be at stake. We submit that constitutional rights are usually more important than economic interests. As a result, adjudicatory bodies should err on the side of constitutional rights through lenient review if the potential impact on the constitutional right is severe, and tighten the review only gradually as the impact on such right gets lighter. Only in WTO cases concerning developing countries can trade interests be very important for human well-being and justify a stricter review if the impact is prima facie severe.

A preliminary conclusion therefore is that the categorization of objectives into important ones does not work in the abstract. It is normatively unconvincing and of limited analytical usefulness. Given that the importance of the issues at stake requires a context-dependent and case-specific assessment, adjudicatory bodies have to provide more detailed normative reasons for the importance of interests than a simple declaratory statement. They need to explain the extent to which objectives are related to core human interests (which lie at the heart of the legitimacy of law and constitutions) in the context of the specific facts of each case.

At this juncture, we should examine Shany's and von Staden's argument on the limited democratic accountability of judges. There is reason to be cautious in transposing the arguments in the nation-State context about counter-majoritarian courts interfering with democratic decision-making to the supra- or international level. When the CJEU, WTO panels and the Appellate Body assess the proportionality of market regulation by States, they do not adjudicate matters which have already gone through a fully inclusive, democratic decision-making procedure, because foreign interests are not represented in national decision-making procedures. Adjudication serves as a corrective measure to the democratic problem of non-inclusion of all affected interests.[92]

To us, the fact that a measure has been enacted following democratic decision-making procedures weighs in favour of deference if we have a normative reason for disposing of the matter through democratic procedures which do not always coincide with the importance of the policy. For instance, we have no normative reason for applying simple majority parliamentary procedures to constitutional rights, intelligence services or the trial of criminals, all of which concern very important human interests. We have particularly strong normative reasons for parliamentary procedures where (i) our considered normative judgements are uncertain and the vote is the only way to come to a decision, or (ii) when perfect procedural fairness can be completely or nearly attained.[93] However, if we rely on procedure, it is all the more crucial that the decision-making procedure is actually fair, both procedurally and substantively; in other words that it ensures the

[92] See also the contribution of Michael Ioannidis at Chapter 6 in this volume.

[93] Consider Rawls' example of the cake-cutting procedure, where formal fairness probably suffices to make the distribution fair. In the example, the one who cuts the cake has to choose his or her slice last and thus probably end up with the smallest piece, ensuring that the cake-cutter cannot tailor the distribution to his or her advantage. John Rawls, *A Theory of Justice* (Oxford: Oxford University Press, 1999) 74.

equality of the affected interests, both as regards the actual ability for input and control as well as the decision rule.

If one accepts the above, courts have an important role to play in ensuring the fairness of procedures by examining whether or not standards of transparency, inclusion of affected interests (formal and substantive) and reason-giving have been met. In other words, while there is a democratic reason for courts to grant deference in substantive questions, there is a corresponding democratic reason for courts to review the fairness of the decision-making procedure.[94]

In this sense, the CJEU is adopting a sensible approach when it couples a wide margin for substantive determinations in Union acts with an inquiry into the appropriateness of the decision-making procedure, and when it tightens its review of national measures and looks at the procedural quality of decision-making when Member States impose inconsistent levels of protection vis-à-vis foreign and domestic operators, or across the country.[95] The Appellate Body has on occasion fashioned procedural tests as well, notably in relation to the chapeau of GATT Article XX, where in *US—Shrimp* it examined whether or not the administrative decision-making process provided due process rights.[96] It has also done so in trade remedies cases, where it reviewed whether the authorities examined all the relevant facts, evaluated them in an unbiased manner and explained how the facts supported the determinations made.[97] A similar test could be used for the necessity analysis, but probably needs to be supplemented with even more guarantees of procedural fairness, depending on the extent to which important moral interests of persons are affected by the national measure.

In this respect, it is necessary to consider the position of Ehlermann and Lockhart. They argue that *de novo* review is excluded where a WTO agreement explicitly mandates an investigative procedure, since it provides procedural guarantees.[98] Where none is mandated as in GATT Article XX, but a WTO Member elects to perform such a process, they doubt whether this fact makes deference appropriate, since the obligation of supporting national measures with evidence is open-ended and contemporary, not historical as in trade remedy cases.[99] Chen

[94] For a similar argument, see Stefan Zlepting, 'The Standard of Review in WTO Law: An Analysis of the Law, Legitimacy and the Distribution of Legal and Political Authority', *European Integration Online Papers*, Vol. 6, No. 17 (2002). Zlepting argues that a well-functioning public discourse must be transparent and grant due process rights for all stakeholders. He suggests a lighter standard of review should apply if the national measure has passed a deliberation test fashioned after the jurisprudence in WTO trade remedies cases. Ioannidis, in Chapter 6 of this volume, argues that WTO panels or the Appellate Body should generally grant deference as long as due process and participatory rights were granted in the national decision-making procedure. In our view, this argument ignores the fact that for some issues, the procedural quality of decision-making is less relevant than substantive considerations of justice or rationality.

[95] Craig, *EU Administrative Law*, 632, Koen Lenaerts, 'Consumer Protection, Free Movement and Harmonisation' in Evelyne Terryn, Gert Straetmans and Veerle Colaert (eds), *Landmark Cases of EU Consumer Law* (Antwerp: Intersentia, 2013), at 116–17.

[96] Zleptnig, 'Standard of Review in WTO Law', 17.

[97] Zleptnig, 'Standard of Review in WTO Law', 17.

[98] Claus-Dieter Ehlermann and Nicolas Lockhart, 'Standard of Review in WTO Law', 7(3) *JIEL* 491 (2004), 513.

[99] Ehlermann and Lockhart, 'Standard of Review', 514–17.

however takes the opposite view. According to him, even if such procedural obligations are missing, it can still be appropriate for WTO dispute settlement bodies to reject *de novo* review so long as the legal provision implies the need for a policy determination or national investigation.[100] Since the concept of standard of review refers to the deference granted to national determinations, it follows that deference should be granted whenever the legal provision implies one.[101] Conversely, legal provisions that only require the existence of certain 'raw' facts, but not their establishment through a national determination, should be subject to *de novo* review.[102] 'Raw facts' are distinct from provisions that require drawing legal conclusions on the basis of facts pursuant to standards such as necessity.[103] Here, what the panel is called on to review is actually a legal matter (conformity with the necessity test).[104] Moreover, Chen argues that a provision implying a national determination with less precision should result in deference because of the *in dubio mitius* principle, according to which States should be presumed to have taken on rather less, than more, onerous obligations.[105]

We submit that both of the positions have shortcomings because they are too formalistic. Whether or not deference on grounds of democracy or procedural safeguards is appropriate depends in the first place on whether democratic procedures are appropriate for regulating a matter. The legitimacy of policies in GATT Article XX or Article 36 TFEU does not hinge equally on the democratic quality of the procedure through which they were made. For instance, public health protection policies cannot be legitimized by a simple vote; they also require substantive justification, while non-anthropocentric environmental protection can be legitimized on the basis of preference aggregation.

B. Adjustments to the standard of review because of the limited capacity of courts relative to public institutions at the lower level of governance

The CJEU uses the complexity of facts and fact-based judgements as a justification for lighter review, suggesting that it sees its capacity as more limited, relative to Member States' legislative, executive and judicial authorities. This raises the question of when the capacity of the CJEU and WTO dispute settlement bodies is smaller, and why. Several commentators agree that courts adjust the standard of review depending on their strengths and weakness in terms of access to facts and their ability for discretionary judgement.

[100] Tsai-fang Chen, 'What Exactly is the Panel Reviewing: the First Step in the Standard of Review Analysis in the WTO Dispute Resolutions', 4 *Asian Journal of WTO Health Law and Policy* 467 (2009), 471, 481–3, 489.

[101] Chen, 'What Exactly is the Panel Reviewing', 481.

[102] Chen, 'What Exactly is the Panel Reviewing', 482, 489, 497. Chen gives the example of GATT, Article III:2, first sentence (likeness and taxation in excess).

[103] Chen, 'What Exactly is the Panel Reviewing', 486.

[104] Chen, 'What Exactly is the Panel Reviewing', 486.

[105] Chen, 'What Exactly is the Panel Reviewing', 507.

Craig submits that institutional reasons concerning the legal effect of treaty provisions and the remedies available to individuals should affect the standard of review of proportionality, in particular the fact that proportionality cases can come to the CJEU through preliminary references by national courts under Article 267 TFEU. The task for the CJEU then is to balance, through a more deferential standard of review, the need for uniformity against the need to respect the role of national courts to apply EU law and in particular their better access to the facts in the underlying legal procedure.[106] However, where particularly complex matters are at stake, as for instance in *Familiapress*, which involved balancing of the interests in free movement, press diversity, and freedom of expression, Craig sees the CJEU as better placed for this complex task, and thus stricter scrutiny as justified.[107] Although WTO law has no preliminary reference procedure, the question about the respective expertise of WTO dispute settlement bodies and that of national legislatures or executives also arises here.

Guzman contends that the standard of review should take account of the respective institutional capacities of WTO dispute settlement bodies and national authorities.[108] WTO dispute settlement bodies enjoy the advantage of neutrality, while national authorities have better access to local knowledge and political preferences.[109] The WTO dispute settlement bodies' advantages are comparatively more important for matters of legal interpretation, the formal requirements imposed on investigative procedures, and the analysis of objective, accepted evidence, since they are not context-dependent nor do they involve subjective judgement.[110]

The advantages of national authorities become more important if the establishment of evidence requires judgement and discretion, and in particular if evidence is disputed and facts are uncertain.[111] Panels and the Appellate Body are ill-equipped for discretionary judgement which is necessarily connected to political priorities and cultural values, while the risk of protectionism and bias remains constant relative to other WTO provisions.[112] Shany justifies judicial deference with the argument that the limited possibilities for participation and the constraints of legal reasoning make courts less suitable to resolve complex factual issues, as compared to State bureaucracies.[113]

A common theme amongst the three commentators is access and (in)ability of supra- and transnational adjudicatory bodies to handle local facts and complex or

[106] Craig, *EU Administrative Law*, 636–9.

[107] Craig, *EU Administrative Law*, 637–9.

[108] Andrew T. Guzman, 'Determining the Appropriate Standard of Review in WTO Disputes', 42 *Cornell International Law Journal* 45 (2009), 46, 57.

[109] Guzman, 'Determining the Appropriate Standard of Review', 52–6.

[110] Guzman, 'Determining the Appropriate Standard of Review', 57–64.

[111] Guzman, 'Determining the Appropriate Standard of Review', 64–9. On the influence of scientific uncertainty and normative judgement on standard of review in the international economic law and EU context, see also the contributions of Lukasz Gruszczynski and Valentina Vadi (Chapter 9) and of Patrycja Dąbrowska-Kłosińska (Chapter 11) to this volume.

[112] Guzman, 'Determining the Appropriate Standard of Review', 69, 71, 72. Similarly, Damian Chalmers, Christos Hadjiemmanuil and Giorgio Monti, *European Union Law: Texts and Materials* (Cambridge: Cambridge University Press, 2006) 846.

[113] Shany, 'Toward a General Margin', 918.

uncertain facts. A theme of discord is the ability of adjudicatory bodies to handle the balancing of complex interest, with Guzman seeing the WTO's dispute settlement bodies as too removed from political preferences to exercise discretionary judgement, while Craig considers the CJEU as better equipped than national courts to perform complex interests balancing.

In our view, the point about the capacity of the adjudicatory bodies to deal with local or complex facts requires nuancing. Some local or complex facts may be perfectly accessible and intelligible, with the help of the experts that the CJEU and the WTO dispute settlement bodies can call on, and may not raise difficult issues of interest balancing so that there is no difference in their capacity to handle these issues. Where adjudicatory bodies may be performing less well than bureaucracies or parliaments is in cases involving uncertainty, ie when current knowledge yields limited predictive abilities.[114] Here, the wisdom of the many, united in bureaucracies or specialized parliamentary committees, may be greater because where no one can credibly claim to be a true expert, the many may simply err less often than courts, composed of only a few individuals. What's more, when there is uncertainty, empirical facts can only provide limited guidance concerning the appropriate course of action. A reaction to uncertainty therefore necessarily involves a greater degree of discretionary, normative judgement.

If complexity arises because multiple important human interests have to be balanced against each other, greater judicial deference is called for because the uncertainty of normative judgement with respect to the comparative importance of the interests and factual uncertainty about their effects and interferences will tend to increase, and resolving the matter through fair decision-making procedures with public deliberation becomes more important. Relative to national bureaucracies and parliaments, the CJEU and WTO dispute settlement bodies are also at a disadvantage when a multiplicity of public policy factors have to be balanced for legal-institutional reasons because the proportionality analysis of the general exceptions of the GATT and Article 36 TFEU involve the balancing of two factors: the principal, relevant public policy and the objective of restricting obstacles to trade.[115] However, a comprehensive policy might contain elements which also serve other purposes. For instance, a public policy might have as its principal purpose the protection of health of consumers but it might also serve further purposes, such as the promotion of fair trade practices. Promotion of fair trade practices may not contribute to the principal purpose and, if not fitting under the public policy exceptions, is not easily justifiable.[116] The CJEU could examine the proportionality of the elements relevant for the fair trade

[114] Similarly Guzman, 'Determining the Appropriate Standard of Review', 68–71.

[115] Chalmers points out that this presumption of coherence and unitary public policy objectives in proportionality analysis is problematic. See Chalmers, *European Union Law*, 846.

[116] Note also that under the TBT Agreement with its open-ended list of objectives, the same concern does not arise. Note also that this chapter was written prior to the WTO Panel Report in *EC—Seals*, which raises concerns about how the panel, and later the Appellate Body, handle multi-purpose policies. See Alexia Herwig, 'Lost in Complexity? The WTO's Panel Report in the EU Seals Case', 5 *European Journal of Risk Regulation* 97 (2014), 101.

objectives by inquiring whether they constitute a means of arbitrary discrimination or a disguised restriction under Article 36 TFEU. Panels or the Appellate Body might assess the proportionality of the fair trade objective under the chapeau of Article XX. They could ask whether the measure is applied in a manner so as to cause arbitrary or unjustifiable discrimination or a disguised restriction on trade. Textually, however, such a move is doubtful because the chapeau concerns the way a policy is applied, whereas the fair trade purpose really concerns the substance of the policy.

When matters concern complex balancing of several important human interests with high levels of uncertainty, we posit that judicial deference is appropriate. We thus disagree with Craig that the CJEU necessarily is in a better position to conduct complex interests balancing. In the example of *Familiapress*, the Austrian court in our view enjoyed two advantages. Firstly, it knew how large a threat a crossword prize competition in print media was to Austrian press diversity, because it had a sense of the factors affecting readership. Secondly, it could evaluate the importance of the constitutional rights to be balanced because it was familiar with how other Austrian constitutional cases involving a variety of parties evaluated their importance, whereas the CJEU had to make its judgement in an isolated instance of the case referred to it by the national court. This reason for deference applies even more forcefully to WTO panels and the Appellate Body, which enter into contact with national legal systems and constitutional values on an even more ad hoc basis.

Having made the case that the CJEU and WTO dispute settlement bodies should defer when well-considered normative judgements are uncertain and decision-making procedures gain in importance for making an authoritative and legitimate normative judgement, at this juncture we should also evaluate the argument that the supra- and international adjudicatory bodies are too far removed from political preferences to take a hard look at cases involving policy judgement. Guzman's argument implies that governments should generally follow political preferences and cultural values in matters requiring discretionary judgement. We would question this assumption. Indeed, the whole idea of legitimate political authority is based on the notion that the State should not endorse the visions of any particular culture, tradition or religion and should not simply aggregate and follow public preferences, but rather should make decisions in a manner that is fair and does not lead to unjust outcomes.[117] Put differently, proximity to local preferences is valuable only if they are compatible with the fundamental right(s) involved. And as we have argued, this is principally the case where considered normative judgements remain uncertain. Where considered normative judgements are certain (that is, where the just resolution of an issue can be arrived at through reflection) but public preferences diverge, it is for the preferences to change. Consequently, in these cases, proximity to local preferences is irrelevant for the legitimacy of a decision and deference would not be justified.

[117] Rawls, *A Theory of Justice*, 3–4, 16–17, 394–5.

The effect of national regulations on foreign trade interests raises precisely the potential problem of the fairness of taking account of people's preferences and, with them, the State's distance to foreign cultures, traditions and other relevant matters. Until we can determine that the national regulation is non-protectionist, we do not know whether proximity to political preference is valuable or negative. Thus to argue, as Guzman does, that the danger of protectionism is relevant for assessing the importance of neutrality versus expertise is putting the cart before the horse. Whether or not there is a specific (rather than a general, abstract) danger of protectionism depends on the analysis of the facts in the light of the legal requirements, which in turn depends on the standard of review employed.

In concluding our evaluation of CJEU and WTO practice in relation to situations involving complex facts or interest-balancing, we submit that the complexity or the existence of local facts is insufficient to justify deference in every case. However, deference is justified where facts are uncertain or multiple, important human interests have to be balanced against each other, and the considered normative judgements are uncertain. Against this backdrop, the justification the CJEU uses for deference needs refining, and the WTO dispute settlement bodies should start calibrating their standard of review more to the extent of factual or normative uncertainty. However, the greater deference the CJEU exhibits in the proportionality assessment of Union acts compared to Member State actions, and the relevance it accords to the extent of harmonization in a particular field, is justified because Union action does not suffer from the problem of non-representation of affected interests in the Union, making it harder to impose protectionist preferences.

C. Pluralism as an argument for deference

In the EU, the CJEU has generally refrained from intensive scrutiny if public policy approaches in Member States are not homogenous, suggesting that it is concerned about giving greater protection to diversity relative to the need for uniformity. The CJEU's approach raises the question of whether pluralism can work as a sufficient normative reason for according deference. In the WTO, diversity amongst its Members is bound to be even greater than in the EU, which raises the question of whether WTO dispute settlement bodies should also accord more deference in such situations.

Some commentators consider pluralism to be an independent argument for deference. According to Gerards, legitimate pluralism of moral or ethical opinions is a good reason for the CJEU to grant deference, even if core free movement guarantees are at stake.[118]

[118] Gerards, 'Pluralism, Deference', 118–19. Delmas-Marty and Izroche agree that significant differences in policies call for a wider margin of appreciation. See Delmas-Marty and Izroche, 'Marge Nationale d'Appréciation', 753–80: 778–9.

Is pluralism really an independent normative reason for deference? We may think of pluralism as legitimate because reasonable people can reasonably disagree about a matter. In other words, a disputed arrangement can have a basis in an overlapping consensus on shared normative principles, even if the precise details remain contested.[119] But then one wonders what difference the margin of appreciation makes to the substantive outcome of a case? If there is a legitimate reason for diversity, there is also a strong reason for the adjudicatory bodies to consider the disputed measure to be a proportionate response *anyway*. Moreover, in order to determine whether or not differences are legitimate, courts already have to look to the facts of the case and in particular the proportionality of interest balancing; that is, the necessity for infringing on core economic freedoms and the intensity with which the various interests are affected, and their importance. In other words, courts should provide the same kind of reasoning on the importance of objectives we recommended earlier.

We therefore conclude that pluralism is not an independent normative reason for deference. Deference is not warranted if a matter is highly independent of the context. This context-independency will typically apply to the core of constitutional rights guarantees. Video games which involve shooting, which were at issue in the *Omega* case, are as much an assault on human dignity in Germany as they are in the UK, and access to abortion and related information, at issue in *Grogan and others*, raises the same issues of the right to life, human dignity and freedom of expression in Ireland as everywhere else. For context-dependent matters (eg how to realize equal education opportunities, how to organize social security), it all depends on whether the CJEU or WTO dispute settlement bodies can obtain access to the facts through the help of experts, and whether or not the facts and required normative judgements are certain.

As a consequence of these reflections, we consider that the CJEU should adjust its practice of using pluralism as such as a justification for deference, and that greater diversity amongst Members is not per se a reason for granting more deference.

IV. Conclusions

Delmas-Marty and Izroche stress the need for pluralism to be legally ordered or bounded in order to avoid arbitrariness and anarchy.[120] In this contribution, we have subjected CJEU and WTO practice on standard of review to a comparative evaluation. We have argued that judicial deference by the CJEU and WTO dispute settlement bodies is appropriate on questions of fact and mixed legal–factual questions when the facts or considered normative judgements are uncertain, because bureaucracies or legislatures can rely on more sources of information and

[119] Charles F. Sabel and Oliver Gerstenberg, 'Constitutionalising an Overlapping Consensus: The ECJ and the Emergence of a Coordinate Constitutional Order', 16 *ELJ* 511 (2010).

[120] Delmas-Marty and Izroche, 'Marge Nationale d'Appréciation', 769.

because uncertainty (whether factual or normative) puts more emphasis on procedure as a form of legitimization. We have also argued that deference on substance should coincide with the courts actively vetting the procedural fairness of the way the decision was reached.

We submit that in this manner the possible conflicts between substance and procedure, rights and democratic will, and unity versus diversity can be minimized. If the considered normative judgements are relatively certain and context-independent (eg what constitutes an interference with the right to life or human dignity), the issue can be decided on the substance and deference to pluralism is not warranted. If the considered normative judgements are uncertain, authoritative dispositions require more procedural legitimization and consequently courts have less of a role to play in fine-tuning the complex interest-balancing and more of a reason for allowing diversity.

Against this backdrop, the CJEU's vetting of procedural guarantees, coupled with deference to substantive determinations as regards EU acts, is a sound approach which should also be used more widely in the review of Member States' acts as well as by WTO panels and the Appellate Body. WTO panels and the Appellate Body should also move towards a more explicit endorsement of deference in cases involving factual or normative uncertainty. In the WTO, comparatively greater deference to a Member's factual determinations and the legal conclusions drawn therefrom is often appropriate because a strict scrutiny standard of the correctness of determinations and policy conclusions increases the risk of false negatives on the side of the non-trade public policy interest.[121] In the WTO, such types of errors cannot be corrected easily because of the need to obtain a consensus to prevent the adoption of dispute settlement reports or amend WTO law, whereas in the EU a legislative procedure exists to correct erroneous judicial decisions.[122]

[121] A false negative would arise where the CJEU or WTO dispute settlement bodies mistakenly determine that there is no risk to the public policy, when in fact there is one.

[122] On the anaemic legislative capacity of the WTO, see also Chapter 6 by Michael Ioannidis in this volume.

PART IV

INTERNATIONAL HUMAN RIGHTS LAW

13

The European Court of Human Rights and Standards of Proof

An Evidentiary Approach towards the Margin of Appreciation

*Mónika Ambrus**

I. Introduction

The margin of appreciation doctrine, as devised in the case law of the European Court of Human Rights (ECtHR, also referred to as the Court), has different applications. George Letsas distinguished two main forms of the doctrine: the so-called *substantive* and *structural* uses of the concept. While the former focuses on 'the relationship between individual freedoms and collective goals', the latter addresses 'the limits or intensity of the review of the European Court of Human Rights in view of its status as an international tribunal'.[1] Given that the first form focuses on how two interests are balanced with each other, it can also be described as the *proportionality* principle, whereas the structural form can be identified as the 'original' concept of *margin of appreciation*.[2]

* The author is grateful for the useful comments of Lukasz Gruszczynski and Wouter Werner. In addition, special thanks go to Sascha Grievink for her research assistance.

[1] George Letsas, 'Two Concepts of the Margin of Appreciation', 26 *OJLS* 705 (2006), 706.

[2] For further nuances see, *inter alia*, Howard C. Yourow, *The Margin of Appreciation Doctrine in the Dynamics of European Human Rights Jurisprudence* (Dordrecht: Martinus Nijhoff Publishers, 1996); Yutaka Arai-Takahashi, *The Margin of Appreciation Doctrine and the Principle of Proportionality in the Jurisprudence of the ECHR* (Oxford: Intersentia, 2002); Letsas, 'Two Concepts'; Jan Kratochvíl, 'The Inflation of the Margin of Appreciation by the European Court of Human Rights', 29 *Netherlands Quarterly of Human Rights* 324 (2011), 324; Eva Brems, 'The Margin of Appreciation Doctrine in the Case-Law of the European Court of Human Rights', 56 *Zeitschrift für Auslandisches Öffentliches Recht und Volkrecht* 240 (1996); Jeffrey A. Brauch, 'The Margin of Appreciation and the Jurisprudence of the European Court of Human Rights: Threat to the Rule of Law', 11 *Columbia Journal of European Law* 113 (2004–2005); Steven Greer, *The Margin of Appreciation: Interpretation and Discretion under the European Convention on Human Rights* (Strasbourg: Council of Europe Publishing, 2000). On the elaboration of the application of the doctrine of margin of appreciation within the Inter-American system, see Bernard Duhaime, Chapter 16 in this volume.

The focus in this chapter will be placed on this latter, 'original' meaning of the doctrine, which will simply be referred to as the *margin of appreciation*. In this meaning, the margin of appreciation essentially delineates the relationship between the State and the Court, which is also referred to as the principle of subsidiarity.[3] This principle aims to find a balance between the sovereignty of States on the one hand, and the Court's supervisory role on the other.[4] As has been often pointed out, this balance is based on the idea of the Convention being the lowest common denominator, thus giving ample space for national diversity in the protection of human rights.[5] In this original meaning, the margin of appreciation focuses on the extent to which a State has discretion in a particular case, and at the same time it also delineates the *level of scrutiny* applied by the Court. Conceptually, the 'level of scrutiny' refers to the intensity with which the *fact-finding body* examines the facts and arguments submitted by the parties, so it is the flip side of the margin of appreciation. In terms of evidentiary law, it can be argued that the degree of discretion also determines the extent to which the allegations have to be proven by the State in order to be accepted by the Court, which is called the *standard of proof*.[6]

The standard of proof is defined for the party who bears the burden of persuasion with regard to a certain factual or mixed factual and legal questions. Pursuant to the general rules of evidence the party alleging something is obliged to prove it. Within the framework of the European Convention on Human Rights (ECHR, also referred to as the Convention)[7] this rule means that the individual (applicant) has to prove that there was an interference with one of his or her rights enshrined in the Convention, and if such is proven, it is for the respondent State to prove that the interference can be justified, provided such a justification is permitted by the applicable provision. Accordingly, if justification is possible, one can also talk about the standard of proof of the respondent.

The rules on the allocation of the burden of proof also imply that in cases where justification is not possible, the State's standard of proof and thus the margin of appreciation doctrine do not play a role. However there are exceptions to this

[3] Although its origin, as explained by Carozza, lies in the acknowledgement of pluralism, diversity and human dignity, the emphasis here will be placed on its institutional consequences at the international level. Paolo G. Carozza, 'Subsidiarity as a Structural Principle of International Human Rights Law', 97 *AJIL* 38 (2003), 40–9.

[4] For more on the meaning of the doctrine of margin of appreciation/standard of review, see also Benedikt Pirker (Chapter 4) and Bernard Duhaime (Chapter 16), both in this volume. Duhaime makes an interesting distinction between the 'fourth instance doctrine' and the 'doctrine of margin of appreciation'.

[5] See also Council of Europe, 'The Margin of Appreciation', available at <http://www.coe.int/t/dghl/cooperation/lisbonnetwork/themis/echr/paper2_en.asp> (accessed 30 September 2013).

[6] Justice Harlan defined the 'standard of proof' in his concurring opinion in the *In Re Winship* case as follows: 'a standard of proof represents an attempt to instruct the fact/finder concerning the degree of confidence our society thinks he should have in the correctness of factual conclusions for a particular type of adjudication.' *In Re Winship*, 397 US 358 (SC 1970), J. Harlan, Concurring Opinion.

[7] Convention for the Protection of Human Rights and Fundamental Freedoms (European Convention on Human Rights, as amended), 213 UNTS 222.

general conclusion. Articles 2 and 3 ECHR,[8] which are the examples *par excellence* of articles with no general exceptions clauses,[9] concern cases of alleged physical harm/suffering. These cases usually turn on proving factual questions, ie whether or not something happened or how it happened. While in principle the applicant bears the burden of proving that there has been a violation of these articles, in certain instances the burden of proving that there was no violation is placed on the respondent State. This different allocation of the burden of proof implies that, in certain Article 2 and/or 3 ECHR cases, an exceptional standard of proof, and in turn a margin of appreciation, is defined for the State.

The classical articles of the ECHR where justifications are possible are Articles 8–11 ECHR[10] and Article 14 ECHR.[11] Complaints relating to Articles 8–11 ECHR usually do not pertain to proving factual questions. Rather they involve decisions on moral or value-driven issues. In these cases the respondent has the onus to prove to a certain extent that it had good reasons to interfere with the particular right, so the respondent's standard of proof has an important role to play in each case.

The linguistic structure of Article 14 ECHR is similar to Articles 2 and 3 ECHR in that it does not contain a per se limitation clause. Nevertheless, since the very first equal treatment case of *Belgian Linguistics v Belgium*,[12] it has been accepted that a justification is embedded in this article as well. Although this inherent justification seems to make this article and the Court's examination of the case based on this article similar to cases concerning Articles 8–11 ECHR, still proving factual matters in order to establish an interference with the right is an important element in some of these cases too. Accordingly, the analysis of Article 14 ECHR cases in combination with Articles 2/3 ECHR on the one hand, and in combination with Articles 8–11 ECHR on the other, can provide interesting insights into the designation of the State's standard of proof.

With respect to Articles 8–11 and Article 14 ECHR cases, the use of the margin of appreciation doctrine, and thus the standard of proof imposed on the State, has often been criticized by both scholars and dissenting judges.[13] The most frequently-heard charges are that the Court is inconsistent and obscure in the way it delineates the applicable margin and that this discretion is used as justification instead of a proper proportionality analysis, and also that the margin of appreciation is invoked in a random fashion. These charges also indicate that as a result the Court suffers from a certain legitimacy deficit.

[8] Admittedly, there are more articles where no justification is included or embedded.

[9] The second paragraph of Article 2 ECHR cannot be regarded as a general exception clause.

[10] Although within the Convention system more articles embed the possibility of justification, Articles 8–11 ECHR are the original articles for which a clear division of interference/justification was designed.

[11] Even though it lacks a second paragraph, in essence Article 14 ECHR can also be regarded as having a two-paragraph structure.

[12] *Belgian Linguistics v Belgium* (app. nos. 1474/62, 1677/62, 1691/62, 1769/63, 1994/63, 2126/64), ECtHR 1968.

[13] Eg Kratochvíl, 'The Inflation of the Margin of Appreciation', 343; Brems, 'The Margin of Appreciation Doctrine', 256.

Against this backdrop, this chapter looks at the margin of appreciation doctrine through the lens of the standard of proof and (1) explores the standards of proof applied by the ECtHR in these three sets of cases as well as identifies the main factors that seem to influence the designation of these standards (Section II); and (2) analyses to what extent this procedural issue, as devised and applied by the Court, can be regarded as legitimate based on Thomas Franck's theory on procedural legitimacy (Section III). In the conclusion some general observations will be made on the margin of appreciation based on the standard of proof analysis (Section IV).

II. Standards of Proof in Three Sets of Cases

The following analysis looks into the standards that can be identified in the case law of the Court. The distinction between the three sets of cases is relevant because of the different procedural positions of the parties, which, as indicated above, impacts on the standard of proof. The terminology the Court uses to define the standard of proof in these cases also varies: generally, in cases where factual questions need to be proven, the Court identifies the 'standard of proof'; in cases concerning justification of the respondent State the term 'margin of appreciation' is referred to; and in equality cases (Article 14 ECHR) the term 'level of scrutiny' is most often used.[14]

A. Standard of proof in cases without a justification clause: Articles 2 and 3 ECHR

In cases referring to the violation of Articles 2 and 3 ECHR, the main issue very often is to prove whether or not certain facts are true or an event occurred. The applicant's standard of proof originally was set very high ('proof beyond reasonable doubt'),[15] meaning the application of the 'most careful scrutiny'.[16] The Court might have realized the difficulties the applicants faced in these cases, and in certain instances placed the burden of proof on the respondent State. The factors leading to this different allocation of the burden of proof, and thus to the establishment of the standard of proof for the respondent, are discussed below.

1. *Special allocation of the burden of proof*

A clear development in these cases is the identification of procedural obligations in addition to the substantive violation of these articles. In a certain set of cases the distinction between the 'substantive' and 'procedural' limbs of Articles 2 and

[14] Mónika Ambrus, *Enforcement Mechanisms of the Racial Equality Directive and Minority Protection* (Den Hague: Eleven International Publishing, 2011) 34–5.
[15] *Velikova v Bulgaria* (app. no. 41488/98), ECtHR 2000, para 70.
[16] *Velikova v Bulgaria*, para 68.

3 ECHR has led to finding a *procedural violation* of these articles where the Court was unable to find a substantive violation.[17] In another set of cases the Court also realized that the applicant could not prove beyond a reasonable doubt that there was a violation of this procedural limb of Article 2 or 3 ECHR, e.g. when the State did not carry out effective investigations into the circumstances of the case. Accordingly, in these cases the procedural violation changed the allocation of the burden of proof with regard to the violation. This happened, for instance, in *Stoica v Romania*,[18] where the lack of proper investigation created the presumption (prima facie case) that there had also been a substantive violation.[19] This prima facie case then placed the burden of proof on the respondent State, which had to convince the Court that there was no substantive violation. In these cases where the burden of proof is placed on the respondent the standard of proof with regard to the substantive violation is also proof beyond reasonable doubt. Finally, the Court also applied the special rules on the allocation of the burden of proof in some cases where the State's procedural obligation was at stake. For instance, in *Opuz v Turkey* the applicant alleged that 'the authorities had failed to safeguard the right to life of her mother, who had been killed by her husband'.[20] In the Court's view, based on the facts of the case 'the local authorities could have foreseen a lethal attack by [the attacker] H.O.'[21] Although the Court stated that the applicant needed to prove both the foreseeability of the attack and the lack of due diligence on the side of the authorities, based on the Court's deliberation it seems that the first element was indeed proven by the applicant, while the existence of due diligence needed to be proven by the respondent. The arguments of the State were strictly scrutinized, meaning that the margin of appreciation was rather narrow.

In cases where the respondent State was in possession of the evidence, even though no distinction was made between a procedural and substantive violation the Court also placed the burden of proof on the State. This special allocation of the burden of proof can mainly be observed in cases where the victim was taken into custody by State authorities. For instance, in *Velikova v Bulgaria* the Court explained, and since then has repeated several times, that:

> [w]here the events in issue *lie wholly, or in large part, within the exclusive knowledge of the authorities*, as in the case of persons within their control while in custody, strong presumptions of fact will arise in respect of injuries and death occurring during that detention. Indeed, the burden of proof may be regarded as resting on the authorities to provide a satisfactory and convincing explanation.[22]

Similarly, in the *Stoica* case the Court explained that 'where an individual raises an *arguable claim* that he has been seriously ill-treated by the police or other

[17] Eg *Tahsin Acar v Turkey* (app. no. 26307/95), ECtHR 2004, para 217.
[18] *Stoica v Romania* (app. no. 42722/02), ECtHR 2008.
[19] *Stoica v Romania*, para 80.
[20] *Opuz v Turkey* (app. no. 33401/02), ECtHR 2009, para 118.
[21] *Opuz v Turkey*, para 136, see also para 130.
[22] *Velikova v Bulgaria*, para 70 (emphasis added). See also paras 72–4.

such agents of the State unlawfully', the burden of proof should be placed on the respondent State to prove (beyond reasonable doubt) that there was no violation.[23] In these cases the Court accepted that the lack of access to evidence would place the burden of proof on the respondent, who had a high standard of proof and thus a narrow margin of appreciation.

2. *Justification elements in Article 2 ECHR*

The second paragraph of Article 2 ECHR includes a quasi-justification clause, allowing for the State to prove that the use of force did not go beyond what was 'absolutely necessary' to achieve certain purposes. This is one of the few provisions of the Convention where an almost explicit reference can be found to the applicable standard of proof. The Court's case law is rather consistent in this regard: the Court applies strict scrutiny in reviewing the governments' arguments. In the recent case of *Guiliani and Gaggio v Italy*,[24] the Court compared the 'absolutely necessary' test with the 'necessity' test under Articles 8–11 ECHR, and concluded that the former 'indicates that a stricter and more compelling test of necessity must be employed'[25] than in the case of the latter. Arguably however, both tests can be interpreted as involving a high standard of proof, the only difference being what should be proven to a high degree (a factual versus a moral question).

B. Standard of proof in cases with a justification clause: Articles 8–11 ECHR

In cases brought under Articles 8–11 ECHR, the focus is on the degree of the margin of appreciation granted to the respondent with respect to its justification. The question posed by the Court in these cases is the following: to what extent should the Court be convinced that the State was entitled to interfere with the right at stake? The degree of such conviction varies, usually described in terms of the different margins of appreciation, which can be translated as different standards of proof placed on the respondent. The Court sets out two main degrees of deference afforded to the State: wide and narrow margin of appreciation. However, it can be argued that the Court de facto also applies a third, an intermediate, margin of discretion. The analysis below will be based on these three degrees of margin of appreciation.

1. *Broad margin of appreciation—low standard of proof*

Certain factors seem to influence the Court in applying a low standard of proof (lenient scrutiny/broad margin of appreciation). Firstly, it is generally accepted by the Court that the existence of, or absence of, a consensus among the (European)

[23] See also *Anguelova v Bulgaria* (app. no. 38361/97), ECtHR 2002, para 121.
[24] *Guiliani and Gaggio v Italy* (app. no. 23458/02), ECtHR 2011.
[25] *Guiliani and Gaggio v Italy*, para 176.

States as to how to deal with a particular legal issue influences the margin of appreciation. The search for consensus is usually linked to 'sensitive moral or ethical issues',[26] where it is often difficult to stake out a consensus position.[27] For instance, in *SH v Austria* the Court explained that:

> [s]ince the use of IVF treatment gave rise then and continues to give rise today to sensitive moral and ethical issues..., and since the questions raised by the case touch on areas where there is not yet clear common ground amongst the member States, the Court considers that the margin of appreciation to be afforded to the respondent State must be a wide one.[28]

Similarly, the lack of consensus with regard to the legal position of transsexuals was the main factor influencing the broad margin of appreciation granted to the State in one of the early transsexual cases, *Sheffield and Horsham v UK*.[29]

Secondly, in some cases the nature of the right has seemed to be the decisive factor for the Court in applying a broad margin of appreciation. This was the case, for instance, in *Mouvement Raëlien Suisse v Switzerland*, where the Court established that 'States have a broad margin of appreciation in regulation of speech in commercial matters or advertising'.[30] In each of the above-mentioned cases, the Court scrutinized the respondent's arguments in a rather lenient manner, which might be described as a reasonability test, or a low standard of proof.

The lenient scrutiny applied by the Court, which in the above-mentioned cases resulted in finding no violation by the State, has been criticized both by dissenting judges of the Court as well as scholars focusing on the margin of appreciation.[31] The main point of critique is that this broad margin of appreciation in fact replaced the proportionality test in many of these cases.[32]

2. *Narrow margin of appreciation—high standard of proof*

The other end of the scrutiny continuum is the so-called 'strict scrutiny'. The Court sometimes uses different terminology to indicate that it applies this level of review: the State needs to provide 'convincing and compelling reasons'; 'the most careful scrutiny' needs to be applied; or the State has 'only a limited margin of appreciation'.

[26] *SH and others v Austria* (app. no. 57813), ECtHR 2011, para 94.

[27] On the comparative law method used in the Court's case law, see Mónika Ambrus, 'Comparative Law Method in the Jurisprudence of the European Court of Human Rights in the Light of the Rule of Law', 3 *Erasmus Law Review* 353 (2009).

[28] *SH and others v Austria*, para 97. See also *Christine Goodwin v the United Kingdom* (app. no. 28957/95), ECtHR 2002, para 85.

[29] *Sheffield and Horsham v the United Kingdom* (app. nos. 22985/93 and 23390/94), ECtHR 1998, para 57.

[30] *Mouvement Raëlien Suisse v Switzerland* (app. no. 16354/06), ECtHR 2012, para 61.

[31] See, *inter alia*, Brauch, 'The Margin of Appreciation', 133; Kratochvíl, 'The Inflation of the Margin of Appreciation', 345–7.

[32] See eg *Mouvement Raëlien Suisse v Switzerland*, Joint Dissenting Opinion of Judges Sajó, Lazarova Trajkovska and Vucinic. See also *SH and others v Austria*, Joint Dissenting Opinion of Judges Tulkens, Hirvelä, Lazarova Trajkovska and Tsotsoria, para 11.

Here too, the Court sometimes tries to explain which factors influence the extent of the margin of appreciation. The nature of the violation and the importance of the right seem to be among the most important factors. Concerning the former, for instance, in *Obukhava v Russia* the Court explained, with regard to an interference with the applicant's right to freedom of expression, that 'the dangers which restrictions of this kind pose for a democratic society are such that they call for the most careful scrutiny'.[33] As to the latter, the Court, for instance, found in *Czarnowski v Poland* that 'taking into account the seriousness of what was at stake, namely refusing an individual the right to attend the funeral of his parent, the Court is of the view that the respondent State could have refused attendance only if there had been compelling reasons and if no alternative solution... could have been found.'[34]

However, sometimes the Court does not indicate the extent of review, or applies a test different from that indicated. In these cases the following elements suggest the level of scrutiny actually applied: testing whether or not other (less stringent) means were available,[35] or looking at each and every point made by the respondent and assessing to what extent the respondent's action was proportionate. In *Guja v Moldova*, for instance, the Court did not clarify the extent of scrutiny,[36] and it carried out an extensive review.[37] In a similar vein, the Court, although it hinted at the fact that the review would not be marginal, did not explicitly make clear what the actual extent of review was in the groundbreaking *Christine Goodwin v UK* case.[38] While in the *Guja* and *Christine Goodwin* cases the Court did not indicate the extent of review to be carried out, in *Egeland and Hanseid v Norway* it applied a standard that was different from that indicated. In this case the Court explained that there was no European consensus, thus 'the respondent State should be accorded a wide margin of appreciation in [its] balancing of the conflicting interests'.[39] Notwithstanding this assessment however, the Court actually carried out a very thorough review, thus granting a narrow margin of appreciation, ie assigning a high standard of proof to the State. In reaction to this inconsistency Judge Rozakis, in his concurring opinion, criticized the 'degree of automaticity' with which the majority established the extent and applied the concept of margin of appreciation.[40] Last but not least, there are some cases where the Court indicated that it did not accept the State's claim to a wide margin of appreciation, yet the State's arguments were so weak that there was no need to actually apply strict scrutiny.[41]

[33] *Obukhova v Russia* (app. no. 34736/03), ECtHR 2009, para 22.
[34] *Czarnowski v Poland* (app. no. 2858/03), ECtHR 2009, para 32.
[35] See also *Czarnowski v Poland*.
[36] *Guja v Moldova* (app. no. 14277/04), ECtHR 2008, para 69.
[37] See *Guja v Moldova*, paras 74–97.
[38] *Goodwin v the United Kingdom*, para 91.
[39] *Egeland and Hanseid v Norway* (app. no. 34438/04), ECtHR 2009, para 55.
[40] *Egeland and Hanseid v Norway*, Concurring Opinion of Judge Rozakis, para c.
[41] See, for instance, *Alekseyev v Russia* (app. nos. 4916/07, 25924/08 and 14599/09), ECtHR 2010, para 85.

3. *'A certain margin of appreciation'—intermediate standard of proof*

Although the Court does not explicitly define and identify it, in some cases the application of an intermediate degree of scrutiny can be observed by assessing the extent to which the Court analyses States' arguments; ie its review consists neither of a detailed, thorough analysis, nor a brief superficial assessment. Another aspect might be that it does not look at the availability of alternative (and less intrusive) means, which is an indication of the application of a strict proportionality test.

When intermediate scrutiny is applied, the Court often indicates that the State enjoys a 'certain margin of appreciation'—without being precise about its extent or sometimes even about the factors that influence the extent of deference, and thus the standard of proof. For instance, in the *Dogru v France* case the Court simply stated that a 'margin of appreciation... must be left to the member States with regard to the establishment of the delicate relations between the Churches and the State'.[42] Even though the Court was silent on the applicable test, it can be argued that its review of the State's arguments was neither lenient, nor very thorough, thus it can be characterized as a 'relevancy and sufficiency' test.[43] This test is somewhat higher than one of reasonability, but it does not reach the 'compelling reasons' test.

A particular set of these cases involving the application of intermediate scrutiny concern those where the ECtHR does not elaborate on how the relationship between those factors which pull in different directions should be assessed. This approach can be observed, for instance, in *Odièvre v France*[44] and *Evans v UK*.[45] In the *Evans* case, the Court established that:

> [w]here a particularly important facet of an individual's existence or identity is at stake, the margin allowed to the State will be restricted... Where, however, there is no consensus within the member States of the Council of Europe,... particularly where the case raises sensitive moral or ethical issues, the margin will be wider.... there will also usually be a wide margin if the State is required to strike a balance between competing private and public interests.[46]

While based on the language above, the Court seems to have concluded that the margin should be wide, but it arguably applied an intermediate scrutiny, conforming to a medium level of review, or intermediate margin of appreciation. In the *Odièvre* case the Court only established that 'the State enjoys a certain margin of appreciation',[47] and did not further elaborate on the actual extent of such appreciation. It should be noted however that the majority's approach towards determining the margin of appreciation was much criticized by seven dissenting judges: in their view the Court did not consider each factor it generally takes into account.[48] In the opinion of the dissenting judges the fact that the case touched

[42] *Dogru v France* (app. no. 27058/05), ECtHR 2008, para 72.

[43] *Dogru v France*, para 73.

[44] *Odièvre v France* (app. no. 42326/98), ECtHR 2003.

[45] *Evans v the United Kingdom* (app. no. 6339/05), ECtHR 2007.

[46] *Evans v the United Kingdom*, para 77.

[47] *Odièvre v France*, para 40.

[48] *Odièvre v France*, Joint Dissenting Opinion of Judges Wildhaber, Bratza, Bonello, Loucaides, Cabral, Barreto, Tulkens and Pellonpää.

upon the right to identity, being 'an essential condition of the right to autonomy', should have required the 'fairest scrutiny'.

In *A, B and C v Ireland* the Court also enumerated the different factors and their effects, which then again seemed to pull to different directions as far as the applicable standard was concerned: an important facet of an individual's existence (narrow margin of appreciation), moral and ethical issues (broad margin of appreciation),[49] and consensus (narrow margin of appreciation). However, as opposed to its general jurisprudence concerning the importance of consensus, the Court concluded that it 'does not consider that this consensus decisively narrows the broad margin of appreciation of the State.'[50] Nevertheless, given the extent of its actual review, the applied standard can arguably be identified as intermediate. Although one of the concurring opinions observed that the consensus the Court found was not relevant to the determination of the margin of appreciation,[51] six judges in their partly-dissenting opinion criticized the Court's disregard of the impact of a consensus.[52] Interestingly, these observations of the dissenting/concurring judges indicate that the Court itself might think only in terms of two levels of scrutiny: low and high.

C. Standard of proof in Article 14 ECHR cases in combination with Articles 2/3 ECHR and Articles 8–11 ECHR

The most elaborate analysis of the standards of proof applied by the ECtHR has been provided with regard to equal treatment cases based on Article 14 ECHR.[53] Article 14 ECHR does not have an independent existence, which means that it can be invoked only in combination with another right. However, in order to be able to deal with an alleged violation of the right to equal treatment, it is not necessary for the Court to find a separate violation of this other right—as Article 14 ECHR has an autonomous meaning.

Given the difference between the State's standards of proof in Articles 2/3 ECHR and Articles 8–11 ECHR cases, and the non-independent nature of Article 14 ECHR, it is worthwhile exploring whether and to what extent the difference in the Court's approach to these two sets of cases is also present when they are invoked in combination with Article 14 ECHR.

1. Cases of Article 14 ECHR in combination with Articles 2/3 ECHR

Unsurprisingly, a development similar to that in cases of Articles 2 and 3 ECHR can be observed also in cases where Article 14 ECHR was invoked in combination

[49] *A, B and C v Ireland* (app. no. 25579/05), ECtHR 2010, para 233.

[50] *A, B and C v Ireland*, para 236.

[51] *A, B and C v Ireland*, Concurring Opinion of Judge Finlay Geoghegan, para 4.

[52] *A, B and C v Ireland*, Joint Partly Dissenting Opinion of Judges Rozakis, Tulkens, Fura, Hirvelä, Malinverni and Poalelungi, para 9.

[53] See, *inter alia*, Janneke H. Gerards, *Judicial Review in Equal Treatment Cases* (Dordrecht: Martinus Nijhoff Publishers, 2005) 103–222.

with Articles 2 and/or 3 ECHR. Even though a justification clause is embedded in Article 14 ECHR, the very first cases have not reached this phase due to the applicant's high standard of proof. In the *Velikova* case, the Court concluded that '[t]he material before it does not enable the Court to conclude beyond reasonable doubt that Mr Tsonchev's death and the lack of a meaningful investigation into it were motivated by racial prejudice'.[54] The same approach was followed in *Anguelova v Bulgaria*, in which Judge Bonello gave voice to his criticism of this high standard—also as compared to the Court's changing approach to Articles 2 and 3 ECHR.[55]

Although no reference was made to this dissenting opinion, in effect Judge Bonello's suggestions were followed in the next Article 14 ECHR combined with Articles 2/3 ECHR cases. The groundbreaking cases were *Nachova and others v Bulgaria* (*I* and *II*).[56] In the *Nachova I* case, where the Court finally found a violation of Article 14 ECHR in combination with Article 2 ECHR, the Court placed the burden of proof on the respondent State because 'the authorities have not pursued lines of inquiry that were clearly warranted in their investigation into acts of violence by State agents and have disregarded evidence of possible discrimination'.[57] Although here no explicit distinction was made between the procedural and the substantive aspects of the case, this argumentation is still similar to the reasons for 'shifting' the burden of proof in Articles 2/3 ECHR cases.[58] The effect of this different allocation of the burden of proof was that the respondent State had a high standard of proof and narrow margin of appreciation. On the suggestion of Judge Bonello in his concurring opinion in *Nachova I*,[59] the Court in *Nachova II*[60] made an explicit distinction between procedural and substantive violations. However, in the Grand Chamber's view, the procedural violation could not result in 'shifting' the burden of proof to the State in terms of the substantive limb of the case.[61] Nevertheless, the State's standard of proof with regard to its justification of the procedural violation was set high.

The Court has most likely come to realize the difficulties applicants have in these and similar cases, since in the *Stoica* case,[62] it adopted a different approach. Although again without making an explicit distinction between the procedural and substantive limbs of the alleged violation, the Court accepted that 'the burden of proof lies on the Government'.[63] Given its reasoning, it may be concluded that the Court applied strict scrutiny.

[54] *Velikova v Bulgaria*, para 94.

[55] *Anguelova v Bulgaria*, Partly Dissenting Opinion of Judge Bonello, paras 9 and 19 in particular.

[56] *Nachova and others v Bulgaria* (app. nos. 43577/98, 43579/98), ECtHR (Chamber) 2004; *Nachova and others v Bulgaria* (app. nos. 43577/98, 43579/98), ECtHR (Grand Chamber) 2005.

[57] *Nachova and others v Bulgaria* (2004), para 169; see also para 171.

[58] See eg *Velikova v Bulgaria*, para 70.

[59] *Nachova and others v Bulgaria* (2004), Concurring Opinion of Judge Bonello, para 3.

[60] For a similar approach see *Cobzaru v Romania* (app. no. 48254/99), ECtHR 2007.

[61] *Nachova and others v Bulgaria* (2005), para 157. See also *Nachova and others v Bulgaria* (2005), Concurring Opinion of Judge Sir Nicolas Bratza.

[62] *Stoica v Romania*. See also *Opuz v Turkey*, in particular para 200.

[63] *Stoica v Romania*, paras 130–1.

2. Cases of Article 14 ECHR in combination with Articles 8–11 ECHR

In cases in which Article 14 ECHR has been invoked in combination with Articles 8–11 ECHR, the Court has followed the approach adopted in relation to these latter articles. Accordingly, the emphasis is on the respondent's justification and the extent of its margin of appreciation. This is somewhat surprising in terms of discrimination law, in that showing the existence of an interference in discrimination cases is generally considered difficult.

Not only does the Court follow the same structure in these cases as in Articles 8–11 ECHR cases, it also takes similar factors into account when deciding on the actual extent of the margin of appreciation. The Court has, however, added one additional specific factor: the protected ground at stake can also have an impact on the degree of scrutiny applied. It is generally accepted in the case law that discrimination based on so-called 'suspect grounds',[64] such as racial or ethnic origin or sexual orientation, calls for a restricted margin of appreciation. This was, for instance, visible in the *Kurić* case, where the Court emphasized that '[w]here a difference in treatment is based on race, colour or ethnic origin, the notion of objective and reasonable justification must be interpreted as strictly as possible'.[65]

In addition, the Court applies all the three levels of scrutiny (low, intermediate and high standard of proof) in these cases too. The Court adopts strict scrutiny in many of the cases where there is a 'suspect ground', although it is not always clear about the level of scrutiny it applies. For instance, in the well-known *Thlimmenos v Greece* case,[66] the Court arguably applied strict scrutiny, albeit without so indicating, and in particular without explaining the reasons for applying this test. Also, as has been observed previously, the Court does not always apply the level of scrutiny it asserts is applicable.[67]

Contrary to these cases, lenient scrutiny was applied by the Court, for instance, in *Schalk and Kopf v Austria*.[68] In the Court's view, given that there was little common ground concerning the legal 'recognition of stable de facto partnerships between homosexuals' and that the issue fell within the scope of general measures of economic and social strategy, the State enjoyed a wide margin of appreciation,[69] even though 'differences based on sexual orientation require particularly serious reasons by way of justification',[70] ie sexual orientation being a suspect ground which would ordinarily have called for a high standard of proof (narrow margin of appreciation). This failure to attribute appropriate weight to the 'suspect ground' was criticized in the dissenting opinion of three judges.[71]

[64] See, *inter alia*, Gerards, *Judicial Review*, 84–5.

[65] *Kurić and others v Slovenia* (app. no. 26828/06), ECtHR 2012, para 386. See also *Alekseyev v Russia*, para 108.

[66] *Thlimmenos v Greece* (app. no. 34369/97), ECtHR 2009.

[67] *SH and others v Austria*, paras 68–9 and 76.

[68] *Schalk and Kopf v Austria* (app. no. 30141/04), ECtHR 2010.

[69] *Schalk and Kopf v Austria*, paras 92, 97 and 105.

[70] *Schalk and Kopf v Austria*, para 97.

[71] *Schalk and Kopf v Austria*, Joint Dissenting Opinion of Judges Rozakis, Spielmann and Jebens, para 8.

Last but not least, in some cases the Court's scrutiny can be characterized as intermediate.[72] In one group of these cases, a suspect ground (eg gender, sexual orientation) is combined with the (alleged) absence of a common standard. It seems that in these cases the lack of a common approach caused the Court to apply a less strict scrutiny. This can be seen, for instance, in the *Fretté v France*[73] or *Petrovic v Austria*[74] cases.[75] In the other group of these cases, the explanation given by the respondent State was so weak that there was no need for a strict scrutiny. This was the case, for instance, in *Danilenkov and others v Russia*.[76]

III. Standard of Proof and the Court's Legitimacy

As the above analysis has shown, the Court's approach towards the standard of proof, and thus the margin of appreciation, can and has been criticized from different perspectives. This criticism arguably has implications for the Court's legitimacy.[77] While the literature on the legitimacy of international law and of international organizations is abundant, Thomas Franck's theory[78] stands out among these discussions,[79] which essentially rely on or can be traced back or linked to his approach.

[72] In relation to the Court's Article 14 ECHR case law, it has been argued that this test cannot, as yet, be disclosed, but that its introduction would be desirable. Gerards, *Judicial Review*, 79–98.

[73] *Fretté v France* (app. no. 36515/97), ECtHR 2002, para 41 in particular.

[74] *Petrovic v Austria* (app. no. 20458/92), ECtHR 1998, para 40 in particular.

[75] In both cases the dissenters criticized the level of scrutiny: *Petrovic v Austria*, Dissenting Opinion of Judges Bernhardt and Spielmann; *Fretté v France*, Joint Partly Dissenting Opinion of Judge Sir Nikolas Bratza and Judges Fuhrmann and Tulkens.

[76] *Danilenkov and others v Russian Federation* (app. no. 67336/01), ECtHR 2009. See also *Savez Crkava 'Riječ Života' and others v Croatia* (app. no. 7798/08), ECtHR 2010.

[77] Benedict Pirker argues in Chapter 4 of this volume for the need for 'a common justificatory framework within which the decision on a standard of review is taken'. Placing the discussion within the context of the Court's legitimacy can also be regarded as such a framework.

[78] Thomas M. Franck, *Fairness in International Law and Institutions* (Oxford: Clarendon Press, 1995).

[79] Two main schools have also addressed the question of legitimacy in international law: Global Constitutionalism and Global Administrative Law. The idea behind both of these schools can, arguably, be traced back to the idea of Franck on substantive and procedural legitimacy. For Global Constitutionalism, see, *inter alia*, Anne Peters and Klaus Armingeon, 'Introduction—Global Constitutionalism from an Interdisciplinary Perspective', 16 *Indiana Journal of Global Legal Studies* 385, (2009); Klaudia Milewicz, 'Emerging Patterns of Global Constitutionalization: Toward a Conceptual Framework', 16 *Indiana Journal of Global Legal Studies* 413, (2009); Jan Klabbers, Anne Peters and Geir Ulfstein, *The Constitutionalization of International Law* (Oxford: Oxford University Press, 2009); Jeffrey L. Dunoff and Joel P. Trachtman (eds), *Ruling the World?: Constitutionalism, International Law, and Global Governance* (Cambridge: Cambridge University Press, 2009). For Global Administrative Law, see, *inter alia*, Benedict Kingsbury, Nico Krisch and Richard B. Stewart, 'The Emergence of Global Administrative Law', 68 *Law and Contemporary Problems* 15 (2005); Nico Krisch and Benedict Kingsbury, 'Introduction: Global Governance and Global Administrative Law in the International Legal Order', 17(1) *EJIL* 1 (2006); Daniel C. Esty, 'Good Governance at the Supranational Scale: Globalizing Administrative Law', 115 *Yale Law Journal* 1490 (2006).

In Franck's view, fairness encompasses both normative/substantive and procedural fairness. While the former refers to distributive justice, that is the proper allocation of burdens and benefits, the latter can be translated as legitimacy, namely, whether and to what extent a procedure can be accepted by the participants as fair process. Although not particularly devised for judicial decision-making, Franck's concept of legitimacy can well be applied to it. Given that standard of proof rules, and thus the assignment of the margin of appreciation, concern procedural norms, Franck's ideas on procedural fairness provide a proper framework for assessing whether and to what extent the Court's approach towards the identification of the standard of proof can be regarded as legitimate.[80] In order to assess the legitimacy of procedural rules, Franck identified a number of legitimacy indicators: determinacy, coherence, adherence and symbolic validation. These indicators will be used to assess the extent to which the methods used by the Court to adopt particular standards of proof can be regarded as legitimate. No particular attention will be paid to the indicator of symbolic validation, as that would require a different type of analysis. Leaving it aside, it may be said that these indicators essentially aim to ensure legal certainty in different ways.[81]

The case law exploration carried out in the previous Sections creates a basis for assessing the legitimacy of the Court's approach towards the margin of appreciation across the spectrum of cases, within the framework of legitimacy described by Franck's indicators. Accordingly, the subsequent analysis will focus on whether and, in particular, to what extent, the Court's choice or application of the various standards of proof can be regarded as being in compliance with the requirements of determinacy, coherence and adherence.

A. Determinacy

Franck's concept of determinacy can be equated to transparency.[82] In terms of judicial deliberation this means that courts should be able to explain the applicable rules, all the more so when they are judge-made. Concerning the standards of proof the question is whether the manner in which the different standards are assigned and applied is clear enough.

[80] Franck's idea of procedural justice, as briefly indicated above, relies on the idea of fairness, ie how to ensure a fair procedure for those participating in it. This idea can be closely linked to Ely's idea as elaborated in Benedict Pirker in Chapter 4 of this volume. Similarly to Ely's idea, Franck also combines some substantive elements with procedural requirements, and although not explained in so many words, the indicators devised by Franck can also be linked to ensuring proper participation of those whose rights have been affected. John H. Ely, *Democracy and Distrust—A Theory of Judicial Review* (New Haven, Harvard University Press, 1980). In a similar manner, Bernard Duhaime in Chapter 16 of this volume also relies on certain democratic/substantive values that influence and/or should influence the standard of review in particular instances. He pleads for a greater degree of deference when there is an independent and impartial judiciary.

[81] See also Patrick Kinsch, 'On the Uncertainties Surrounding the Standard of Proof in Proceedings before International Courts and Tribunals' in Gabriella Venturini and Stefania Bariatti (eds), *Diritti Individuali E Giustizia Internationazionale. Liber Fausto Pocar* (Milan: Giuffre, 2009), 427–8 (emphasis added).

[82] Franck, *Fairness*, 30–4.

The above analysis indicates that there is a clear distinction in this regard between two main sets of cases. In Articles 2/3 ECHR cases the factors that influenced the allocation of the burden of proof, which imposed on the States a high standard of proof, were applied in a clear, transparent manner. However, in general, the answer to the above question is in the negative in relation to Articles 8–11 ECHR cases. While in certain cases the Court gave its reasons for adopting a particular standard of proof, in other cases there were either no clear explanations (or no explanations at all) in this regard. Also, the Court has not provided a convincing explanation for the application of the factors it identified as relevant to the determination of the level of scrutiny. Some of the dissenting opinions and criticism by scholars might be explained by the difficulty the dissenting judges expressed with respect to the lack of transparency in determining the standard of proof.[83] As Judge Malinverni observed in one of his concurring opinions, it is 'essential that the case law establish clear, objective and specific criteria that make it possible to identify in which cases it is appropriate to accord States a wide margin of appreciation or, on the contrary, to limit it.'[84]

B. Coherence

The second factor in Franck's concept of legitimacy is coherence. This means that rules are applied in the same manner in similar cases, in order to exclude arbitrariness.[85] With regard to the standard of proof, this indicator can be summarized by the following question: to what extent does the Court apply the rules it has devised for determining the applicable standard of proof, and thus the margin of appreciation, in a coherent manner?[86]

There are some recurring factors, as hinted at above, that are mentioned in the case law as influencing, either directly or indirectly, the margin of appreciation. In Articles 2/3 ECHR cases these factors primarily influence the allocation of the burden of proof, and thus relate only indirectly to the margin of appreciation of the State. These factors include the following: whether the State was in possession of evidence (such as an applicant being held in custody), and substantive versus procedural obligations. In Articles 8–11 ECHR cases the following factors directly influenced the State's margin of appreciation: existence/lack of a common European standard, and the nature of the right and the policy field involved. While the application of the respective factors seems coherent in Articles

[83] See also Ignacio de la Rasilla del Moral, 'The Increasingly Marginal Appreciation of the Margin-of-Appreciation Doctrine', 7 *GLJ* 611 (2006); Oren Gross and Fionnuala Ní Aoláin, 'From Discretion to Scrutiny: Revisiting the Application of the Margin of Appreciation Doctrine in the Context of Article 15 of the European Convention on Human Rights', 23 *Human Rights Quarterly* 625 (2001).

[84] *Egeland and Hanseid v Norway*, Concurring Opinion of Judge Malinverni, para 4.

[85] Franck, *Fairness*, 38 and 41.

[86] On the question of consistency in the jurisprudence of the ECtHR, see, *inter alia*, Nick Huls, Maurice Adams and Jacco Bomhoff (eds), *The Legitimacy of Highest Courts' Rulings. Judicial Deliberations and Beyond* (Cambridge: Cambridge University Press, 2009), 424–5 and 443–4.

2/3 ECHR cases, the factors identified in Articles 8–11 ECHR cases seem to have been relied on in a somewhat random and inconsistent manner. Firstly, these factors are not mentioned and assessed systematically in each and every case.[87] With regard to Articles 8–11 ECHR cases, not all the factors are mentioned each and every time when the Court assesses the applicable standard.[88] Secondly, in Articles 8–11 ECHR cases, the effect of these factors is not always assessed consistently.[89] Thirdly, not only are the factors applied in an incoherent manner, but the exercise of defining the applicable standard of proof is not carried out in each and every case in Articles 8–11 ECHR cases.[90] Lastly, the Court has sometimes applied a standard different from what it actually defined in some cases relating to Articles 8–11 ECHR.[91] Based on this assessment one cannot help but conclude that the standard of proof is not applied in an entirely coherent manner in Articles 8–11 ECHR cases, as in fact pointed out in some of the dissenting opinions.[92]

C. Adherence

Adherence is defined by Franck as 'the vertical nexus between a single primary rule of obligation...and a pyramid of secondary rules governing the creation, interpretation, and application of such rules by the community.'[93] He argues that '[p]rimary rules unconnected to secondary rules tend to be mere ad hoc reciprocal arrangements.'[94] In the present context, this indicator can be interpreted as adherence of the designation of the standards of proof (secondary rules) to the doctrine of the margin of appreciation, interpreted as subsidiarity/deference (primary rule).[95] The question then is: to what extent does the principle of subsidiarity require and/or allow the application of different standards of proof, and thus different margins of appreciation, in the Court's deliberation?

In general, it could be argued that the mere fact that the Convention system is subsidiary to domestic legal systems would not require the application of different standards, as it is subsidiary with regard to each and every right, and not more or less subsidiary. Nevertheless, conceptually the principle of subsidiarity does not necessarily exclude the possibility of applying different standards of proof either.

Concerning Articles 8–11 ECHR, the question is: can the factors identified and applied by the Court (common European standard vis-à-vis the legal issue at stake and the nature of the right) be regarded as part of the subsidiarity discourse;[96] ie do they justify the application of different levels of scrutiny in

[87] See eg *Evans v the United Kingdom*. [88] See eg *Odièvre v France*.
[89] See eg *Schalk and Kopf v Austria*. [90] See eg *Dogru v France*.
[91] See eg *Egeland and Hanseid v Norway*.
[92] See, *inter alia, A, B and C v Ireland*, Joint Partly Dissenting Opinion of Judges Rozakis, Tulkens, Fura, Hirvelä, Malinverni and Poalelungi, paras 5, 6 and 9. See also Kratochvíl, 'The Inflation of the Margin of Appreciation', 343.
[93] Franck, *Fairness*, 41–6. [94] Franck, *Fairness*, 41.
[95] Carozza, 'Subsidiarity as a Structural Principle', 40. See also Gross and Ní Aoláin, 'From Discretion to Scrutiny', 626.
[96] See also Marjolein Busstra and Kristin Henrard, 'Conflicting Fundamental Rights: Broad Parameters for a Model of Review' (unpublished manuscript, on file with the author).

the light of the concept of subsidiarity (rather than proportionality or balancing)? The institutional relationship between the contracting parties to the ECHR and the Convention system, captured by the subsidiarity principle, is arguably not dependent on factors which are part of the balancing exercise. Accordingly, to the extent that it is used in order to give weight to one of the protected interests (ie balancing) the nature of the right should not be relied on to assign the margin of appreciation. However, it could be argued that the search for common European standards, which is carried out when there is a high 'degree of normative uncertainty',[97] might be accepted as a second-order reason or external factor[98] that also fits within the institutional relationship embedded in the subsidiarity principle.[99] In other words, this factor is not part of the balancing exercise and appears to be linked to the position of the State towards the ECtHR.

Contrary to the designation of the margin of appreciation or standard of proof in Articles 8–11 ECHR cases, in Articles 2/3 ECHR cases the allocation of the burden of proof creates the State's standard of proof, which subsequently determines the margin of appreciation. In Articles 2/3 ECHR cases the applicable standard of proof has always been high with regard to the applicant's claim, and accordingly the Court's scrutiny has always been strict. In cases where the burden of proof has 'shifted' to the State, this strict scrutiny has not been influenced by the fact that the Court had to review the State's arguments rather than the applicant's—even though some hesitation on the Court's side might be observed in this regard.[100] In these cases only the availability of evidence influences the allocation of the burden of proof, and indirectly the State's standard of proof. Originally, the standard of proof in these cases was determined by the importance or nature of the right. In other words, while the State's standard of proof was created by the procedural position of the parties, its extent was defined on the basis of the right at stake. However, in this instance the right at stake is not and cannot be part of the justificatory discourse, so it could be argued that it is an acceptable second-order reason in the light of the principle of subsidiarity—similarly as with the procedural position of the parties. As Carozza argued in relation to the subsidiarity principle, 'the nature of the right... might make it necessary to remove the interested actors of local politics further from the problem to avoid bias or distortion.'[101] Put differently, as long as the nature of the right does not influence the proportionality analysis, the principle of subsidiarity is not affected in a negative manner

[97] See Yuval Shany, 'Toward a General Margin of Appreciation Doctrine in International Law', 16 *EJIL* 907 (2005), 912–17.

[98] In Legg's view 'judges are influenced by factors outside of the immediate pros and cons of a particular decision related to their own institutional competence.' Andrew Legg, *The Margin of Appreciation in International Human Rights Law: Deference and Proportionality* (Oxford: Oxford University Press, 2012) 1.

[99] See also Legg, *The Margin of Appreciation*, 7 and in particular 103–44.

[100] See, for instance, *Nachova and others v Bulgaria* (2005), para 157.

[101] Carozza, 'Subsidiarity as a Structural Principle', 79.

by its inclusion in the designation of the margin of appreciation, and thus the standard of proof.

IV. Final Remarks on Standards of Proof

This procedural approach towards the margin of appreciation has allowed us to include in the analysis Articles 2/3 ECHR cases which are generally not part of the margin of appreciation discussion—probably because in these cases it is generally not the State which bears the burden of proof. The incorporation of certain cases of Articles 2/3 ECHR not only makes it possible to illuminate the link between the burden of proof and the standard of proof, but also enables the creation of a sharp contrast between cases relating to moral issues and factual assessments.

The analysis reveals that the standard of proof assigned by the Court is different in the two sets of cases. When the State bears the burden of proof in Articles 2/3 ECHR cases, the Court (also) applies strict scrutiny—resulting in a narrow margin of appreciation and a high standard of proof for the State. In Articles 8–11 ECHR cases one can find three levels of scrutiny: lenient, intermediate and strict, which in turn defines the particular margin of discretion of the State (and thus the standard of review adopted by the Court). The designation of the applicable standard of proof in Article 14 ECHR cases follows to a great extent that of those articles which are invoked in combination with the equality provision. The legitimacy assessment, based on the analysis of two sets of cases, signals some legitimacy gaps in the process of designating the standard of proof, in particular with regard to Articles 8–11 ECHR cases.

All in all, the original hypothesis that different standards are applied when factual and moral questions are involved has been confirmed by the analysis. It should also be noted that, based on the classical division of legal fields, facts-driven cases are mainly of a criminal law nature, while the moral-based cases are of a civil and administrative law nature. At the domestic level these legal fields are determinative of the applicable standard of proof, and this principle penetrates the international level as well. More generally, this distinction seems to relate, as Shany points out, to the determinacy/vagueness of the norms.[102] Norms of a criminal law nature are rather precise, leaving less room for interpretation, and thus requiring strict scrutiny/narrow margin of appreciation, while norms of an administrative or civil law nature are often formulated in broader terms (standard-type norms, discretionary norms, result-oriented norms),[103] allowing in general for

[102] Shany, 'Toward a General Margin of Appreciation', 913.
[103] Shany, 'Toward a General Margin of Appreciation', 912–17.

more discretion of States when they apply them, thus leading to a somewhat more lenient scrutiny/broader margin of appreciation. Naturally, certain circumstances can lead to a higher standard of proof/narrower margin of appreciation in these cases too. Depending on whether and to what extent such a distinction can be observed across international courts and tribunals and their case law, the influence of the determinacy of the norm on the standard of review might, indeed, lead to the establishment of a general margin of appreciation. Such a general margin of appreciation does not mean, however, as the analysis of Articles 8–11 and Article 14 ECHR illustrated, that its particular degree cannot be influenced by second-order reasons stemming from the institutional relationship between the State and the international (quasi-) judicial body.

14

Experts in Hate Speech Cases

Towards a Higher Standard of Proof in Strasbourg?

*Uladzislau Belavusau**

> The admission of testimony by experts (Rule 702) also exemplifies a dedication to truth, since experts are people presumed to know relevant truths.
>
> Alvin I. Goldman[1]

> As soon as the philosopher submitted his truth, the reflection of the eternal, to the polis, it became immediately an opinion among opinions. It lost its distinguishing quality, for there is no visible hallmark which marks off truth from opinion. It is as though the moment the eternal is brought into the midst of men it becomes temporal, so that the very discussion of it with others already threatens the existence of the realm in which the lovers of wisdom move.
>
> Hannah Arendt[2]

I. Introduction: Epistemic Paternalism and Standard of Proof/Review

The only neutral method to distil the 'performative' (discriminating, inciting xenophobia or provoking hostility) potential of speech is essentially rooted in epistemic paternalism.[3] It stems from the idyllic belief in some expert ability to find the truth. The imagined expert is expected to catalogue various expressions, taking into account the historical, political, socio-linguistic, forensic, and

* The author is grateful to participants and organizers (in particular to Lukasz Gruszczynski and Wouter Werner) of the workshop at the Universidad de Sevilla (October 2012), for valuable feedback: u.belavusau@vu.nl.

[1] Alvin Goldman, 'Epistemic Paternalism: Communication Control in Law and Society', 88(3) *Journal of Philosophy* 113 (1991) at 115.

[2] Hannah Arendt, *The Promise of Politics*, Jerome Kohn (ed) (New York: Schocken Books, 2005) at 12.

[3] American philosopher Alvin I. Goldman developed a classical account of epistemic paternalism. His rationale is based on the idea that epistemic paternalism allows people to avoid error

numerous other contextualizations of speech.[4] Roughly equivalent to speech act theory, this assumption signifies that certain types of speech do not just sound or appear in the semiotic space, but carry with them an action.[5] In the present chapter, this *active* potential of speech will be designated as *performative* although the classical account of philosophy of language combines three types of speech acts: locutionary, illocutionary, and perlocutionary.[6] A *locutionary act* is the act of purely uttering something. An *illocutionary act* is an act performing some function (asking, ordering, apologizing, etc). A *perlocutionary act* is an act bringing about some consequence in the actions, thoughts or feelings of the listeners or the speaker (such as persuading, convincing, frightening, enlightening, inspiring, etc). Both illocutionary and perlocutionary acts are performative. By referring to certain utterances as *performative* in the context of hate speech expertise, I address foremost the perlocutionary dimensions (ie the degree to which they *cause* subordination via concrete social effects) of speech acts beyond their illocutionary (that *constitute* subordination) and locutionary (pure uttering) dimensions.

As was recently exemplified by English judges in a case dealing with a hate speech allegation against John Terry, a Chelsea football player:

> It is axiomatic that expert evidence is not called unless a particular expertise is needed to give an opinion to the court which the court cannot readily form itself... the duty of an expert witness is to furnish the court with the necessary scientific criteria for testing the accuracy of conclusions, so as to enable the court to form its own independent judgment by the application of those criteria to the facts proved in evidence. In deciding what weight to attach to the evidence of an expert, the court should take into account the extent to which that evidence is based on other established facts.[7]

and get to truth. He examines several social practices that use epistemic paternalism: (1) based on rules of evidence, the courts refuse to admit certain types of evidence for trial, hence judges are denied from hearing that evidence, for example, hearsay evidence; (2) the US Federal Trade Commission has rules that prevent false advertising; (3) school systems may have a curriculum that does not allow for teaching some viewpoints, for example, creationism; (4) scientific journals select some papers and not others, and hence deny publication to some people's submissions (Goldman, 'Epistemic Paternalism').

[4] For a concise introduction into linguistic expertise in hate speech cases, see Gary D. Prideaux, 'Linguistic Contributions to the Analysis of Hate Language', 1(1) *International Journal of Law & Discourse* 27 (2011). For a broader study, see Kent Greenawalt, *Speech, Crime & the Uses of Language* (Oxford: Oxford University Press, 1992).

[5] *Speech act theory* was introduced by John L. Austin (in *How to Do Things with Words*) who elaborated the theory of *performatives*. The concept was further developed by John R. Searle (*Speech Acts*). The seminal units of the analysis, *performatives*, cover such utterances that when spoken—'*do* what they say at the moment of the saying by the one who is saying'. For a widely cited rhetorical reconstruction of hate speech through the methodology of speech acts, see Judith Butler, *Excitable Speech: A Politics of the Performative* (London: Routledge, 1997).

[6] For a broader outlook on philosophy of language, see Gillian Russell and Delia Graff Fara (eds), *The Routledge Companion to Philosophy of Language* (London: Routledge, 2012) at 754–69.

[7] Howard Riddle, Senior District Judge (Chief Magistrate) in the Westminster Magistrate's Court, *R v John Terry*, 13 July 2012 (Judgment), 3. The case dealt with the allegedly racist utterances by John Terry against Anton Ferdinand, a player from Queens Park Rangers. Mr Terry used the words '*fuck off, fuck off, yeah, yeah and you fucking black cunt, fucking nobhead*' and possibly other words, which were left to expert witnesses (lip readers) to establish.

At the international level, multiple questions are involved in the cognitive process of supposed truth-finding in hate speech cases:

(1) who are the relevant 'persuasive' agents or what are the relevant persuasive factors to establish the performative ('inciting') potential of the alleged hate speech utterance in procedural terms? (*burden of proof*);
(2) what constitutes the acceptable evidence of hate speech and the threshold of probability that must be exercised in evaluating this evidence to reach judgments establishing hate speech? (*standard of proof*);
(3) who is in a better position to properly assess the evidence of hate speech, considering the variety of national 'contextualizing' factors (historical background of discrimination, socio-political climate, vulnerability of particular minorities): is it the international tribunal (implying its higher impartiality) or rather the national court (better informed of the context and facts of the alleged hate speech)?

In the context of Strasbourg adjudication, this last aspect is generally encompassed by the discussion on the *margin of appreciation* (the discretional power left to the Member States of the Council of Europe).[8] In free speech cases, a lower standard of proof (for example, uncritical acceptance of the evidence brought before national courts with a low threshold of probability) usually correlates with a broad margin of appreciation left to a State (ie a low standard of review).[9]

In this respect, the standard of proof developed by the European Court of Human Rights (ECtHR) in hate speech cases[10] has been largely driven by the (explicitly or implicitly cited) expert conclusions. The absolute majority of hate speech cases before the ECtHR are those where the Court is able to reach a judgment on the basis of the information gathered in the course of

[8] In other organizations, a similar debate on the intensity of review of national measures by international tribunals is often encompassed by the terminology of the *standard of review*, see eg Chapter 9 by Lukasz Gruszczynski and Valentina Vadi in the present volume. It should be noted that beyond the Council of Europe, the notion of margin of appreciation is applied unsystematically and cautiously (see eg an account of the Inter-American Human Rights System by Bernard Duhaime in Chapter 16 of this volume).

[9] In a similar way, Mónika Ambrus in Chapter 13 in this volume associates one of the principal aspects of the *margin of appreciation* in Strasbourg jurisprudence (the extent to which the allegations have to be proven by the State in order to be accepted by the ECtHR) with the standard of proof. She draws her account on the typology of George Letsas who distinguished two forms of the margin of appreciation: *substantive* (which focuses on the relationship between individual freedoms and collective goals), and *structural* (which addresses the limits or intensity of the review of the ECtHR in view of its status as an international tribunal). See George Letsas, 'Two Concepts of the Margin of Appreciation', 26 *OJLS* 705 (2006), 706. The latter (structural) mode of the margin of appreciation thus becomes tantamount to standard of proof. For the sake of coherence in this volume, I employ a similar account of the standard of proof as being either low (broad margin of appreciation), intermediate (a certain margin of appreciation), or high (narrow margin of appreciation). Yet my major focus is the specific issue of the role (explicit, implicit, etc) of expert opinions (usually collected by national authorities) in Strasbourg hate speech judgments, which traditionally allocate an impressively broad margin of appreciation to Member States.

[10] Either leaving the issue to the *margin of appreciation* of a State or finding violation of Article 10 ECHR.

prior domestic proceedings. Therefore, this chapter does not imply the specific situation where the Court intervenes into a fact-finding procedure and assumes that a State was incapable of providing neutral factual data (which would reflect the highest standard of proof).[11] Although such a situation is not excluded and some fact-finding techniques developed by the Court imply a broader normative outlook for the role of experts in Strasbourg, this chapter focuses mainly on the use of the expert opinions and facts collected in domestic proceedings.

In order to evaluate this role of experts within the standard of proof employed by the Strasbourg Court, I revisit recent (2008–2012) hate speech cases from the ECtHR and distinguish them into three streams:

1. *Soulas et autres v France* (2008),[12] *Leroy v France* (2008),[13] *Féret v Belgium* (2009)[14] and *Vejdeland v Sweden* (2012);[15]
2. *Balsytė-Lideikienė v Lithuania* (2008);[16]
3. *Aksu v Turkey* (2012).[17]

What unites all three streams is the epistemic convenience of the Court in granting a wide margin of appreciation to the respective States. Yet on a closer reading, it appears that Strasbourg judges have been mixing largely incompatible methodologies in order to achieve that low (non-intrusive) standard.

The structure of this chapter builds on the discussion of the aforementioned streams in the recent Strasbourg jurisprudence on hate speech. Following this introduction, the second section (II.A.1) scrutinizes the margin of appreciation and the locus of expertise in *Soulas, Leroy, Féret* and *Vejdeland*, dealing with, respectively, anti-migrant, terrorism-glorifying, political and homophobic hate speech. Section II.B will zoom into a two-fold decision concerning a xenophobic interpretation of historical facts, a case that involved both Article 10 and Article 6 of the European Convention on Human Rights (ECHR) (Case *Balsytė-Lideikienė*). Section III.C turns the research focus away from Article 10 ECHR into the terrain of the right to privacy and family rights (Article 8 ECHR). It discusses the standard of proof and margin of appreciation in a most recent 'hate speech' case in Strasbourg, concerning anti-Gypsyism (*Aksu*). Finally, the conclusions deliberate on the normative role of experts in hate speech cases and address the inconsistencies in the Strasbourg standards.

[11] See Philip Leach, Costas Paraskeva and Gordana Uzelac, *An Analysis of the Fact-Finding Missions Conducted by the European Commission & the Court of Human Rights*, Report by the Human Rights & Social Justice Research Institute at London Metropolitan University (February 2009). As the authors of the report observe, the excessive backlog of cases may mean increasing pressure on Court judges and officials to not sanction fact-finding process, because they are time-consuming and expensive.

[12] *Soulas et autres v France* (app. no. 15948/03), ECtHR 2008.

[13] *Leroy v France* (app. no. 36109/03), ECtHR 2008.

[14] *Féret v Belgium* (app. no. 15615/07), ECtHR 2009.

[15] *Vejdeland v Sweden* (app. no. 1813/07), ECtHR 2012.

[16] *Balsytė-Lideikienė v Lithuania* (app. no. 72596/01), ECtHR 2008.

[17] *Aksu v Turkey* (app. nos. 4149/04 and 41029/04), ECtHR 2012.

II. Streams of Recent Hate Speech Cases in Strasbourg

I begin by distinguishing three models of the Court's engagement with expertise in its recent hate speech cases: (1) 'implicit'—so far the dominant stream of cases involving a low standard of proof; (2) 'explicit'—represented just by one recent case, where the focus on expert evidence leads to a much higher standard of proof; and finally (3) the 'extrinsic' or 'instrumental' model—reflected in a recent case where the Court over-relied on expertise in national domestic proceedings and constructed a non-intrusive standard.

A. First model: implicit role of expertise—low standard of proof

1. Soulas et autres v France (2008)

After a certain pause in the hate speech jurisprudence in Strasbourg,[18] a case appeared at the ECtHR arising out of the civil conviction of Gilles Soulas and Guillaume Faye in France, authors of a book entitled *La colonisation de l'Europe. Discours vrai sur l'immigration et l'islam*. The main goal of the book, as the authors proclaimed, was to demonstrate the alleged incompatibilities between European and Muslim civilizations. They specified that they did not intend to caricature, insult, or slur anybody, and that their motivation was to defend the inalienable right of Europeans to preserve their identity.

The case was brought to the national court by the Prosecutor, who based his claim on Articles 23 and 24 of the Press Law, which are pertinent in the context of the French prohibition of hate speech. The civil applicants were represented by *La ligue contre le racisme et l'intolérance (LICRA)* and *Le Mouvement contre le racisme pour l'amitié entre les peoples (MRAP)*. The national court (*la cour d'appel de Paris*) found the authors guilty of inciting hate propaganda. Both of them were ordered to pay a fine of €7,500.

Supposedly the French court used witness testimony (the submissions of the civil applicants) to establish socio-linguistic expertise with respect to the 'hateful' speech acts later cited in the Strasbourg decision. The French judges put an emphasis on the peculiar wording of the book, in particular the *performative* character of the phrases like 'ethnic war', 'the anti-French racism of the young generations of the immigrants' and 'ritual rapes of European women'.

The ECtHR essentially administered a standard proportionality test on the interplay of the two parts of Article 10 ECHR, without an attempt to analyse the issue under Article 17 ECHR (ie finding an outright non-acceptance of the case) or Article 14 ECHR (exploring the effect of speech against the yardstick of non-discrimination). That traditional proportionality test investigates three

[18] See Uladzislau Belavusau, 'A Dernier Cri From Strasbourg: An Ever Formidable Challenge of Hate Speech', 16(3) *European Public Law* 373 (2010).

elements in a restrictive (with respect to freedom of expression) measure (triggering hate speech): suitability of the measure, its necessity and, finally, its appropriateness. However, the Court was extremely brief in its assessment of the two elements of the proportionality test, namely (1) the suitability of the law at stake, and (2) its appropriatness. Therefore, the Court's analysis goes straight to the evaluation of 'social needs' (*besoins socials impérieux*) in order to determine the third element, (3) namely the necessity of the respective limitation.[19] Referring to its previous case law,[20] the Court mentioned the specific French problem regarding the social integration of immigrants and underlined the public necessity for a wide margin of appreciation in such delicate questions.[21] The pertinence of a broad margin of appreciation was further reinforced with reference to international instruments.[22] In terms of the proof standard, the ECtHR followed the conclusions of the domestic proceedings about the performative character of the wordings in the book, revealing the potential for the incitement of aggression in the passage 'it is only if an ethnic civil war breaks out, the solution could be found'.[23]

The case has also brought before the Strasbourg forum the ambiguous issue of comparative narratives. In their defence, the authors referred to examples of works by Taslima Nasreen, Samuel P. Huntington and Vidiadhar S. Naipul. Yet the Court did not accept this comparison as a relevant argument (*manifestement mal fondé*),[24] emphasizing the gravity of the authors' call for ethnic war through allegations that the Muslims have been consciously establishing the control over some suburbs of Paris.

The ECtHR construed the margin of appreciation in such a way that the harmful effect of speech depends on the historical, demographic, and cultural contexts. Therefore it concluded that the French courts remained within permissible limits. The Court did not engage itself in the discussion over whether it would have made a difference if the expressed views were robed in the mantle of a newspaper article, since the press is usually given higher protection in its role as watchdog. *Soulas et autres*, thus, leaves an element of uncertainty over whether one can distinguish between the narrative of a book (presuming its sociological character) and strong wording in the press. The latter traditionally plays a particular role in inspiring public debate, whereas books form a part of the academic discourse. The authors of the French book allegedly remained in the terrain of knowledge production (albeit pathologically). Thus, epistemologically the Court overlooked the discussion on reliable sources of knowledge and built its judgment on the expert account offered by the national courts. This reliance on domestic conclusions reveals a rather low standard of proof with a broad margin of appreciation left to the State.

[19] *Soulas et autres v France*, para 31. For a broader discussion on proportionality, see Chapter 12 by Alexia Herwig and Asja Serdarevic in this volume.

[20] *Soulas et autres v France*, paras 32–5.

[21] *Soulas et autres v France*, paras 36–7.

[22] *Soulas et autres v France*, para 42.

[23] *Soulas et autres v France*, para 43.

[24] *Soulas et autres v France*, paras 50–1.

2. *Leroy v France (2008)*

The second case appeared in Strasbourg as a consequence of a caricature publication in the Basque left-wing nationalist weekly *Ekaitza*. On 11 September 2001, immediately after the attacks on the World Trade Center in New York, the caricaturist Denis Leroy submitted his drawing, depicting the attack on the Twin Towers, for publication with the caption: '*Nous en avions tous rêvé... le Hamas l'a fait*' (We have all dreamt of it... Hamas did it). The caption parodied a trendy advertisement slogan: '*Vous en avez rêvé, Sony l'a fait*' (You have dreamt of it... Sony did it). Consequently, *Ekaitza* published the caricature and caption on 13 September 2001.

In the next issue *Ekaitza* published the electronic messages received by the editorial board in reaction to the drawing, as well as the feedback from the caricaturist himself, who justified his picture with a reference to anti-Americanism, underlining that he was not motivated by hatred or approval of the terroristic acts.

The local *tribunal correctionnel* (Bayonne) found that the caricature was 'unequivocally laudatory' and, therefore, fell within the classification of an act of incitement of terrorism (*apologie du terrorisme*). Consequently, it imposed a fine of €1,500 on both the publisher and the caricaturist, followed by the traditional remedy of covering the costs of the decision's publication in their weekly edition as well as in two other newspapers. In their motivation, the judges again followed the pattern of a vague socio-linguistic expertise, underlining that the usage of the pronoun 'we' (*nous*) carried with it connotations of approval.

The case made its way up to the ECtHR, where the Court went beyond the pure conventional right to freedom of expression and focused on the instruments of the Council of Europe,[25] in particular on Article 5 of the Convention of the Council of Europe for the Prevention of Terrorism (2005), which addresses the issue of public provocation to commit a terrorist act. The Court also brought to the forum the Explanation Report of the Convention (with the characterization of an *apologie du terrorisme*) as well as the Declaration about Freedom of Expression and Information in the Media in the Context of the Fight with Terrorism, also adopted in 2005. Most importantly for the purpose of this chapter, the Explanation Report on which the Court relied so heavily is essentially an extensive expert opinion. Consequently, four expert-driven factors were taken into consideration in upholding the decision of the French court: (i) the context of the publication; (ii) the date of the publication; (iii) the place of the publication; and (iv) the small size of the fine.

In *Leroy*, the ECtHR seems to be somewhat less detailed in its assessment of proportionality. Instead, the Court is more inclined to discuss the idealization of terrorist attacks and the harmful effect of the phrase 'we have all dreamt of it'. Following its approach in *Soulas*, the Court concerned itself with the psychological effect of the hateful utterances for certain communities, echoing the simplified linguistic expertise of speech acts. From such a perspective, it is not

[25] *Soulas et autres v France*, paras 19–21.

the speaker who enjoys a higher protection due to the right to free speech, but rather the (victimized) audience that needs protection in light of the principle of non-discrimination and non-admissibility of glorification of acts of massive annihilation. The Court's rhetoric transcends pure positive law and embraces certain emotional implications. Without an explicit expert reference to scholars of the effects of linguistic utterances, such as Austin and Searle, the Court nevertheless comes close to adopting the *speech act theory* in its assessment of the caption as performative, thus revealing the *perlocutionary* effect of the caricature.[26] According to this approach, certain utterances do not just 'sound' in the semiotic space of oral expressions, written texts, pictures, and songs, but *perform* as acts, bringing evident consequences with legal implications.

Likewise, the Court took into consideration the modest size of the fine and the absence of a criminal conviction, which corresponded to the established case law regarding the responsibility of journalists. Therefore, it concluded that:

> by making a direct allusion to the massive attacks on Manhattan, by attributing these attacks to a well-known terrorist organisation and by idealising this lethal project through the use of the verb 'to dream', [thus] unequivocally praising an act of death, the cartoonist justifies the use of terrorism, identifies himself through his use of the first person plural ('We') with this method of destruction, which is presented as the culmination of a dream and, finally, indirectly encourages the potential reader to evaluate positively the successful commission of a criminal act.[27]

It is perhaps indicative that the Court found the second part of Article 10 ECHR to be perfectly relevant in the case of utterances approving terrorism, setting a low standard of proof as necessary for the prevention of crime and disorder at the national level.

3. *Féret v Belgium (2009)*

In July 2009, the Small Chamber of the ECtHR rendered the judgment in *Féret v Belgium*, whereby the decision was approved by four votes to three, with a strong dissenting opinion attached based on certain specificities of the case, which distinguish it from the 2008 cases. The case emerged after a Belgian party (*Front National*) leader, Dr Daniel Féret, was convicted by a national court for incitement to racism in his leaflets advocating the deportation of immigrants, conversion of asylum seekers' centres into shelters for the homeless, and the advocacy of ethnic ghettos for the protection of the Belgian people. He was sentenced to 250 hours of community service, commutable to a ten-month prison sentence. In addition, Dr Féret was prohibited from standing for parliamentary elections for ten years. Similarly to the 2008 'French' cases, one can observe here the active role of anti-racist organizations in bringing the claim before the court. Similarly to *Soulas*, the case concerns a vigorous anti-immigration narrative; and like in *Leroy*,

[26] For more on speech act theory, see the literature cited in note 5.
[27] *Soulas et autres v France*, para 14.

it is substantially based on hate speech through images, inasmuch as one of the posters is accompanied by the inscription 'Attacks on the USA: that's couscous clan', and another displays a woman raped by a man in a turban with the caption 'The Koran says: Kill all the infidels until the point of making a great slaughter'. Once again, the Court granted the State a wide margin of appreciation in establishing the proof of hate speech, maintaining that the incitement to hatred does not necessarily require an appeal to a particular act of violence or other criminal acts. The Court also noted with approval that the Belgian authorities had imposed a ten-year period of ineligibility to stand for parliament rather than a penal sanction, in accordance with the case practice in Strasbourg to avoid a criminal conviction in hate speech cases.

The following year, the Court confirmed its approach to hate speech by politicians in the French context, in the *Le Pen v France* case (2010).[28] Through 2005–2008, the president of the radical right-wing *Front National* party, Mr Jean-Marie Le Pen, was fined by national courts for the incitement of hatred towards Muslims in interviews. The ECtHR administered a proportionality test similar to *Soulas, Leroy* and *Féret*. Yet unlike in other cases, it found Le Pen's claim that the French courts had violated Article 10 ECHR manifestly ill-founded and inadmissible.

Thus both the *Féret* and *Le Pen* cases demonstrate a similar non-intrusive standard of proof with the evidence obtained essentially from national submissions. Considering the role of politicians and the criminal measure at stake, one would have expected a much higher standard of proof required by the Court, but such was not triggered.

4. Vejdeland and others v Sweden (2012)

Perhaps one of the most significant hate speech judgments in Strasbourg appeared in 2012, in *Vejdeland v Sweden*.[29] This is the first case where the Court shed light on hate speech in terms broader than just xenophobic utterances, and embraced homophobic speech within the same proportionality test administered in its previous hate speech judgments. A radical-right Swedish organization distributed homophobic leaflets on school premises (in or nearby the pupils' lockers), alleging a conspiracy of 'gay propagandists' in the Swedish educational system, categorizing homosexual relations as perverted, vicious, and threatening to children. The members of the organization were prosecuted before Swedish courts for incitement of homophobic hatred.[30] The ECtHR acknowledged that homophobic speech should be treated in the same way as xenophobic speech, leaving a broad margin of appreciation to the State. The Court took into particular consideration the fact that the leaflets were distributed to 'impressionable and sensitive' young school

[28] *Le Pen v France* (app. no. 187788/09), ECtHR 2010.

[29] Four Swedish nationals lodged the case: Tor Fredrik Vejdeland (born 1978), Mattias Harlin (1981), Björn Täng (1987) and Niklas Lundström (1986).

[30] In July 2006, The Supreme Court of Sweden convicted the applicants under Article 8 of the Penal Code for agitation against a national or ethnic group. Hence, technically the applied provision address 'agitation against a national or ethnic group' (*hets mot folkgrupp*).

pupils, who did not have the possibility to refuse to accept them.[31] Moreover, the applicants neither attended nor had free access to the school.[32] None of the applicants was imprisoned, although the maximum sentence for this offence under Swedish law could have amounted to two years in prison.[33]

This case is important not only in terms of embedding homophobia into the frame of hate speech, but also as a clear indication of the position of the Council of Europe, where homophobia remains State-sponsored in many of its members, especially those from Eastern Europe. The recent laws prohibiting 'gay propaganda' in Russia are particularly troublesome in this respect,[34] and together with the mass violations of lesbian, gay, bisexual, transsexual (LGBT) rights as well as the prohibition of Gay Pride marches (despite the decisions of the ECtHR)[35] should be assessed against the benchmarks of statutory obligations of the Russian Federation vis-à-vis the Council of Europe. They require a highest scrutiny from Strasbourg due to the manifest reluctance of Russian authorities and courts to address the issue.[36] Moreover, considering the most recent hate speech case, *Snyder v Phelps* (2011),[37] which came before the US Supreme Court, and which also dealt with homophobic speech (albeit in the context of religious obscurantism), *Vejdeland v Sweden* reveals a further radical split between freedom of speech in the United States and in the Council of Europe.[38]

Implicit expertise for the case was provided via the third-party comments from the International Centre for the Legal Protection of Human Rights and the International Commission of Jurists, whom the President of the ECtHR had authorized to intervene in the written procedure (in accordance with Article 36(2) ECHR).[39] Once again a wide margin of appreciation was granted to the national

[31] *Vejdeland v Sweden*, para 56.
[32] *Vejdeland v Sweden*, para 56.
[33] *Vejdeland v Sweden*, para 58.
[34] The ban on 'gay propaganda amongst minors' (understood as the 'dissemination of the information amongst minors, portraying hetero- and homo-relations as equally valuable') was recently prescribed in the local laws of nine regions in Russia. A similar federal bill was adopted almost unanimously in the second reading in Russian Duma and signed into law by Vladimir Putin in June 2013.
[35] See *Bączkowski et al v Poland* (app. no. 1543/06), ECtHR 2007; *Alekseyev v Russia* (app. nos. 4916/07, 25924/08 and 14599/09), ECtHR 2010.
[36] A decision on the consolidated cases of *Bayev, Kiselev & Alekseyev v Russia* (app. nos. 31955/11, 44092/12 and 56717/12), is currently pending at the ECtHR. The plaintiffs challenge prohibition of 'gay propaganda amongst minors' in Russia.
[37] *Snyder v Phelps et al* (No. 09-751) 580 F. 3d 206, affirmed (2011). The Westboro Baptist Church picketed the funeral of a US marine who died in Iraq. During the manifestation behind the cemetery, their placards displayed inscriptions such as 'America is doomed', 'You're going to hell', 'God hates you', 'Fag troops', and 'Thank God for dead soldiers'. The US Supreme Court rejected the victimhood arguments and praised the value of the First Amendment in safeguarding prohibition of speech on content-based restrictions.
[38] For an account, see Ian Cram, 'Coercing Communities or Promoting Civilised Discourse? Funeral Protests and Comparative Hate Speech Jurisprudence', 12(3) *Human Rights Law Review* 455 (2012). Interestingly enough, in her concurring opinion in *Vejdeland v Sweden* (although agreeing with the outcome of the decision), Slovenian judge Boštjan M. Zupančic raises the *Snyder* example from the US Supreme Court, which indicates that the Court is aware of the divergent transatlantic perspective.
[39] *Vejdeland v Sweden*, paras 41–6.

authorities and a very low standard of proof approved, with the evidence brought under the national proceedings being implicitly embedded via the expert submissions from a non-governmental organization (NGO).

Thus, this most numerous stream of recent hate speech cases in Strasbourg indicates a low standard of proof/review, essentially achieved through treating the submissions before national courts as implicit expert opinions and granting a wide margin of appreciation to the State, taking the position considering that the *performative* potential of speech utterances can be better evaluated in concrete socio-historic contexts.

B. Second model: explicit accent on expertise—a higher standard of proof

In its 2008 case of *Balsytė-Lideikienė v Lithuania*, the Court for the first time extensively discussed expert opinions. Moreover, it partially satisfied the claims of the applicant, targeting the way the expert testimony is treated in domestic proceedings.

The Baltic republic of Lithuania is a vivid example of specifically Eastern European (transitional and in many respects still 'post-colonial') sensibilities towards ethnic problems. Having been under Polish and Russian dominance for almost four centuries, the Lithuanians managed to preserve their ethnic identity and even succeeded in creating their national State in the inter-war period of 1918–1940. In the 1940s, the country was once again occupied by the Soviet Army, and until 1990 was part of the Soviet Union. Due to the multinational composition of the State entities in the territory of the present-day Republic of Lithuania (formerly Grand Duchy of Lithuania, Polish-Lithuanian Commonwealth, Northern-Western Region of the Russian Empire, Lithuanian-Belarusian Soviet Socialist Republic, Soviet Socialist Republic of Lithuania, and so on), it is hard to distinguish the 'ethnic' territory of a pure Lithuanian nation. For example, in the early twentieth century, the Lithuanian-speaking population of Vilnius (nowadays the country's capital) constituted only a small minority, with Yiddish, Polish, and Belarusian speakers comprising the majority of the city's inhabitants. Before the Holocaust, Vilnius had often been called 'the Northern Jerusalem', and both Belarusian and Polish historiographies point to the particular importance of the city for their respective cultures. Meanwhile, the national question in Lithuania itself is far from being resolved. Many national historians raise territorial claims to neighbouring countries and produce manifestly xenophobic narratives.[40]

Mrs Danutė Balsytė-Lideikienė was a publisher of the annual '*Lietuvio kalendorius*' (Lithuanian calendar). The 2000 version of the calendar became particularly scandalous. The dates of the calendar were accompanied with unpleasant

[40] For a historical account (in English) of the complicated national building in the region, see Timothy Snyder, *The Reconstruction of Nations: Poland, Ukraine, Lithuania, Belarus, 1569–1999* (New Haven: Yale University Press, 2004). As an example of the legal account of the complexity of national identities in the region, see Kiryl Kascian, 'Die Litauische Verfassung und die Auslegung des Begriffes "Volk" in historischer Perspektive', 5 *Osteuropa-Recht* 290 (2008).

remarks about national minorities. In particular, it portrayed Poles as the executioners of Lithuanians (especially during the Second World War) and the Jews as the main accomplices of the Russian occupants. All three groups were blamed for the genocide-like atrocities towards the Lithuanians. Above all, the back cover of the calendar contained a map whereby the neighbouring territories of Belarus, Poland, and Russia were marked as 'ethnic Lithuanian lands under temporary occupation'. Consequently, the Lithuanian Foreign Ministry received diplomatic notes of dissatisfaction from the embassies of Belarus and Russia.

At the end of January 2000, the security intelligence authorities seized a number of copies of the calendar and stopped its distribution. The State Security Department requested that Vilnius University submit an experts' opinion as to whether the calendar promoted ethnic, racial, or religious hostility. The experts were requested to examine whether the calendar contained hateful expressions towards minorities, and/or assertions of the superiority of Lithuanians vis-à-vis other ethnic groups. Two experts, respectively history and political science professors at Vilnius University, found that the calendar could be characterized as promoting a radical ideology of nationalism, which rejected an idea of the integration of civil society, incited ethnocentrism, contained xenophobic and offensive statements (in particular with regard to the Jewish and Polish populations), and promoted territorial claims and national superiority vis-à-vis other ethnic groups. The experts nonetheless noted that the calendar did not explicitly incite violence against the Jewish population, nor did it advocate the implementation of a discriminatory policy against this ethnic group.

The national court found the administrative penalty and the seizure of the publication to be an adequate measure against the one-sided portrayal of relations among nations, which obstructed the consolidation of civil society and promoted ethnic hatred. Since the bibliographic expert revealed that the calendar contained no indication of the sources and literature that had been used, and the name of the author of each statement in the calendar was not provided, the Lithuanian court concluded that the applicant herself had prepared, published, and distributed the calendar and that she was therefore responsible for its content. The Lithuanian constitution itself prohibits hate speech in the article concerned with free speech (Article 25). Besides, the country ratified the International Covenant on Civil and Political Rights, which explicitly prohibits the advocacy of racial hatred (Article 20). The dissatisfied applicant submitted a claim to Strasbourg.

In its deliberation, the ECtHR referred to Recommendation No. R (97) 20 of the Committee of Ministers to Member States on 'Hate Speech', drafted within the framework of the Council of Europe. Interestingly enough, the Recommendation (essentially drafted as an expert opinion itself) for the first time gives a legal definition of *hate speech*, which for a long time was only a conventional academic term:

> for the purposes of the application of these principles, the term 'hate speech' shall be understood as covering all forms of expression which spread, incite, promote or justify

racial hatred, xenophobia, anti-Semitism or other forms of hatred based on intolerance, including: intolerance expressed by aggressive nationalism and ethnocentrism, discrimination and hostility against minorities, migrants and people of immigrant origin.

The Recommendation encourages the States to establish a framework for the fight against hate speech, based on the principle of proportionality.

Technically, the Court was to assess the (non-) violation of two articles of the Convention, ie Article 6 ECHR (fair trial) and Article 10 ECHR (freedom of expression). Having analysed all the materials submitted, the Court considered that neither at the pre-trial stage nor during the trial was the applicant given the opportunity to question the experts, whose opinions contained certain discrepancies, in order to subject their credibility to scrutiny or cast any doubt on their conclusions. Relying on its case law, the Court concluded that in the case in question the refusal to entertain the applicant's request to have the experts examined in open court failed to meet the requirement of Article 6(1) ECHR. The Court drew particular attention to the fact that when finding the applicant guilty, the national courts (in both instances) extensively quoted the experts' conclusions.

Similarly to the 'French' cases of several months earlier (*Soulas* and *Leroy*), the Court was mainly concerned with the third stage of the proportionality assessment, ie with the necessity linked to a 'pressing social need'.[41] Therefore, the Court underlined the sensitivity of the questions of territorial integrity and national minorities in Lithuania following the country's regaining of its independence in 1990, giving a *renvoi* to the margin of appreciation. It also linked the negative feedback from the diplomatic missions of the neighbouring countries to the obligations of Lithuania under international law, and found the 'specific language' of the applicant to be aggressive towards national minorities. Thus, the Court agreed with the conclusions of the experts that a biased and one-sided portrayal of relations among nations hindered the consolidation of civil society and promoted national hatred.[42] In this respect, this 'Lithuanian' case remains the most explicit pronouncement of Strasbourg to date about the role of expert opinions in hate speech cases. Moreover, considering the careful engagement of the Court into the procedural aspects of expert evidence, this case demonstrates a much higher standard of proof/review applied by the Court vis-à-vis the State.

C. Third model: instrumental expertise—a low standard of proof/review

The approach of Strasbourg towards widening the scope of hate speech grounds is not limitless, as was illustrated in a 2012 case, *Aksu v Turkey*. The case appeared

[41] *Balsytė-Lideikienė v Lithuania*, para 76.

[42] *Balsytė-Lideikienė v Lithuania*, para 80.

via joined petitions against academic publications in Turkey.[43] One of them challenged a book whose authors (scholars with a claimed expertise) had stated that Gypsies were engaged in illegal activities, characterized as 'thieves, pickpockets, swindlers, robbers, usurers, beggars, drug dealers, prostitutes and brothel keepers' and reproduced popular stereotypes of the Roma people as polygamist and aggressive. The domestic proceedings were largely based upon expertise from the Ministry of Culture. The publications advisory board to the Ministry (composed of seven professors) had decided the book constituted part of scientific research and did not contain any insults with malicious intent. In 1991 and 1998 respectively, the Language Association (another 'expert non-governmental organization') published two dictionaries, exposing anti-Roma stereotypes and reproducing the burlesquing of Roma in Turkish idioms.[44] In response to a petition within the national proceedings, the Language Association maintained, *inter alia*, that the definitions and expressions were based on historical and sociological reality.

Unlike in the previous streams of judgments, the Court addressed this case not under Article 10 ECHR (freedom of expression) but under Article 8 ECHR (privacy and family life), in combination with Article 14 ECHR (non-discrimination). Procedurally, this case illustrates the paradox that hate speech cases typically reach Strasbourg exclusively as claims against States by 'haters', alleging violation of their right to free speech. *Aksu* was the reverse; an attempt of an applicant to proceed with a case, seeking to impose a militant democratic vision about the non-admissibility of (anti-Roma) hate speech on a State by Strasbourg. The Court appeared to implicitly accept the expertise in the national domestic proceedings and found no violation of the Convention. Hence, the Court again established a low standard of proof /review (like in the first 'implicit' model), yet this time using explicit expertise before national tribunals (similarly to the second 'explicit' model), in a most extrinsic manner. The expertise of national linguistic organizations became instrumental in proving the scholarly, rather than hateful, purpose of Roma burlesquing, shadowing the victim narrative of the plaintiff (in a mode similar to organizations who brought claims vis-à-vis *Soulas* and *Féret*). In their dissenting opinion, three judges (including the President of the Chamber) disagreed with the majority decision, pointing out that the victimization of Roma via stereotyping had been summarized in several expert reports (in particular, the data collected by the EU's Fundamental Rights Agency).[45] They specifically indicated that those expert reports constitute 'valuable sources of information which should urge us to be more vigilant'.[46]

[43] The cases originated in two applications lodged by a Turkish national, Mr Mustafa Aksu (born in 1931). He previously filed several petitions to governmental bodies in Turkey against ethnic stereotyping of Roma in academic publications.

[44] Similar idioms could be found in other languages, eg [from the aforementioned dictionary] 'Gypsy's debt' (an unimportant debt), 'Gypsy tent' (a dirty and poor place), 'Gypsy wedding' (a crowded and noisy wedding), 'Gypsy fight' (verbal fight in which vulgar language is used), etc.

[45] Joint dissenting opinion of Judges Tulkens, Tsotsoria, and Pardalos.

[46] Joint dissenting opinion of Judges Tulkens, Tsotsoria, and Pardalos, pt 5.

III. Conclusions

In line with international human rights jurisprudence, the Strasbourg mechanism of review avoids establishing strict rules as to the quantity and quality of evidentiary material required for a judgment. In its recurrent standard of proof 'beyond reasonable doubt' (which is ironically the opposite of the low standard of proof), the Court is not constrained by any strict framework of what constitutes admissible evidence. It seems to follow a flexible approach, allowing a vast discretion on the interplay of evidence implicitly, explicitly or via privileging certain experts. The only formal constraint is Article 38(1)(a) ECHR, which establishes a duty of the Member States concerned to cooperate in the proceedings before the Court, which has been interpreted, *inter alia*, as an obligation to provide the Court with documentary evidence relating to the case: to identify, locate and ensure the attendance of witness, to comment on documents submitted to the Court; and to reply to questions posed by the Court. Neither the Convention nor the Rules contain express provisions about the standard of proof contained in the Strasbourg mechanism. This allows for a somewhat ad hoc instrumentalization of expert testimony, as becomes clear from an analysis of the recent hate speech cases. In all three streams the Court is epistemologically confident in upholding a margin of appreciation for the respective States, while mixing largely different standards of proof.

The first stream of judgments only implicitly hints at expert opinions in justifying hate speech prosecution in France, Belgium and Sweden (in issues as diverse as anti-immigration narratives, homophobic leaflets, and a cartoon with the alleged glorification of terrorism) under Article 10(2) ECHR. In the *Aksu* case, the Court uses a margin of appreciation under Article 8 ECHR as an escape from framing anti-Roma stereotyping into the same methodological assumptions as in the dominant line of hate speech cases. The Court explicitly relies on the expert opinions collected in national proceedings and justifying anti-Roma forms of speech as a part of academic freedom. Finally, the 'Lithuanian' case in Strasbourg reveals that the Court is methodologically confused with respect to its standard of proof based on the role of expert evidence and testimonies of national authorities. This fragile balancing between epistemic superiority and normative flexibility led to a decision whereby a xenophobic claimant partially satisfied her petition under Article 6 ECHR. This judgment sets a higher standard of proof offering a serious outlook on the procedural role of experts.

In none of the cases was the standard of proof/review adopted by the ECtHR set extremely high (as would be the case if the Court, eg completely neglected the national position and re-constructed the case *de novo*).[47] All examined streams identify a somewhat low-to-intermediary standard of proof, in practice resulting in full deterrence (with the acknowledgement of the experts and margin of appreciation

[47] So far the only exception—where the Court has been systematically adopting *de novo* standard of review—is the stream of hate speech cases addressing the 'Kurdish' problem in Turkey. Just to give a few examples of the large caseload which descends almost annually upon Strasbourg since the 1990s in this area:

left to the Member States). Despite the initial intuition that the engagement of experts in hate speech cases will lead to a higher standard of proof/review in Strasbourg, the present chapter reveals that overall this standard remains quite low, with the decisions left to the margin of appreciation of Member States. The Court has based its conclusions on the national expertise unpacking the context and *performativity* of particular speech utterances in the given societies.

Nonetheless, it would not be correct to assert that the Court has chosen the most non-intrusive (lowest) standard of review (ie granting a maximum deference), which would have meant simply invoking Article 17 ECHR (as requested by States in their submissions). This provision provides grounds for disregarding the contested limitation of rights with no further engagement into proportionality, if the exercise of that limited right contradicts the general values and principles of the Convention. Instead of choosing this 'easy' judicial track, the Court imposed a traditional proportionality test on the interplay between the two parts of Article 10 ECHR. This stance on the troubled relationship between Articles 10 and 17 ECHR confirms a theory that the role of Article 17 ECHR in free speech cases is reserved to disputes concerning the Holocaust denial.[48] Thus, David Keane has suggested that there is a two-tiered approach to free speech evident in the case law of the ECtHR, where this right enjoys a lesser standard of protection against Holocaust denial and related questioning of historical facts of the Second World War, which fall directly under Article 17 ECHR, than in the case of other forms of racist or hate speech, which are examined under Article 10 ECHR.[49]

- conviction for disseminating propaganda against the integrity of the State in *Arslan v Turkey* (app. no. 23462/94), ECtHR 1999; *Başkaya & Okçuoğlu v Turkey* (app. nos. 23536/94 and 24408/94), ECtHR 1999; *Gerger v Turkey* (app. no. 24919/94), ECtHR 1999;
- conviction of a member of a trade union for incitement to hatred following the publication of criticisms of State policy in south-east Turkey in *Ceylan v Turkey* (app. no. 23556/94), ECtHR 1999;
- conviction of the editor of a periodical for disseminating propaganda against the indivisibility of the State in *Erdoğdu and Ince v Turkey* (app. no. 25723/94), ECtHR 1999;
- conviction of a writer for inciting the people to hatred and hostility by writing articles strongly criticizing the Turkish authorities' policy in *Gökçeli v Turkey* (app. nos. 27215/95 and 36194/97), ECtHR 2003;
- conviction of members of several associations for incitement to hatred, via the press, on the basis of distinguishing between regions, in *Gümüs and others v Turkey* (app. no. 40303/98), ECtHR 2005.

For a detailed legal overview of free speech issues in Turkey, see a monograph by Umit Kilinç, *La liberté d'expression en Turquie à l'épreuve de la Convention Européenne des Droits de l'Homme* (Paris: L'Harmattan, 2010).

[48] Most recently the ECtHR has refused to apply recourse to Article 17 to a case concerning Armenian genocide denial, in *Perinçek v Switzerland* (app. no. 17510/08), ECtHR 2013. For a broader analysis of 'memory laws', see Uladzislau Belavusau, 'Historical Revisionism in Comparative Perspective: Law, Politics, and Surrogate Mourning', *EUI Law Research Paper* 12 (2013). For a critique of the approach in *Perinçek*, see Uladzislau Belavusau, 'Armenian Genocide v. Holocaust in Strasbourg: Trivialisation in Comparison', *Verfassungsblog: On Matters Constitutional*, available at <http://www.verfassungsblog.de/en/armenian-genocide-v-holocaust-in-strasbourg-trivialisation-in-comparison/#.U1KTwtz9PKg> (accessed 19 April 2014).

[49] David Keane, 'Attacking Hate Speech under Article 17 of the European Convention of Human Rights', 25(4) *Netherlands Quarterly of Human Rights* 641 (2007) at 642. This theory of Keane still faces, at least, one exception, namely *Norwood v the United Kingdom* (2004), where in a context somewhat similar to *Leroy*, the Court decided that a 'drawing' constituted an act

In none of those streams has the Court chosen to clarify the criteria for expert evidence, despite the fact the whole epistemological rationale for the margin of appreciation choice is based on the harm identified by expert testimony (submissions of NGOs before national courts) or by specialists (historians, sociologists, political scientists, anthropologists, psychologists, forensic experts, etc). Moreover, the Court's inconsistent attitude to evidence may potentially disrupt the whole idea of protection against hate speech, on which the jurisprudence of the Court has been based. A consistent discourse analysis based on expert evidence might have led to identification of similar rhetorical toolkits in hate speech acts, ie pertaining to all such cases.[50]

Another intriguing issue is that of NGOs submitting cases before national courts (like for example, *La ligue contre le racisme et l'intolérance* in *Soulas*), and in turn acting as expert witnesses in testifying as to the *performative* character of hate speech utterances (via collective victim stories and histories of oppression). Furthermore, in such cases the 'invisible' expertise is often reinforced by the third-party submissions. For example, in *Vejdeland* case, INTERIGHTS provided a substantial '*amicus curiae*' report with a comparative assessment of legal developments on homophobic speech: the report was authorized by the Court.[51]

A similar pattern about the role of NGOs has recently become crystallized in two hate speech cases in Luxembourg, at the Court of Justice of the European Union (CJEU). In the first case, *Centrum voor gelijkheid van kansen* (2008),[52] a Belgian firm was sanctioned under the 'Race Directive'[53] after an employer's interview announcing that he would not hire Moroccans. In the second case, *Asociaţia ACCEPT* (2013),[54] a Romanian football club faced charges under the 'Framework Directive'[55] because its patron stated that he would not keep a gay player in that team. In both cases, national anti-discrimination bodies (Belgian *Centrum voor*

incompatible with Article 17 ECHR, thus, not engaging with the proportionality test of Article 10 ECHR. The applicant displayed a window poster depicting the Twin Towers on fire, accompanied by the caption 'Islam out of Britain—Protect the British People'. The ECtHR held that the poster was incompatible with 'the values proclaimed and guaranteed by the Convention, notably tolerance, social peace, and non-discrimination' (para 43). On the inconsistent use of Article 17 ECHR, see Antoine Buyse, 'Dangerous Expressions: The ECHR, Violence and Free Speech', 63(2) *ICLQ* 491 (2014).

[50] See Prideaux, 'Linguistic Contribution', at 38–9. The author offers the toolkits as follows: targeting—inversion—code—generalization—alibi.

[51] Third-party Intervention by the International Commission of Jurists and Interights (2012), available at <http://www.ilga-europe.org/home/how_we_work/litigation/ecthr_litigation/interventions> (accessed 28 March 2014). INTERIGHTS is an international human rights law centre providing case litigation in human rights and non-discrimination.

[52] Case 54/07 *Centrum voor gelijkheid van kansen en voor racisme bestrijding v Firma Feryn NV* [2008] ECR 5187.

[53] Council Directive 2000/43/EC of 29 June 2000 implementing the principle of equal treatment between persons irrespective of racial or ethnic origin OJ L 180/22 (often referred to as 'Race Directive').

[54] Case 81/12 *Asociaţia ACCEPT v Consiliul Naţional pentru Combaterea Discriminării*, 25 April 2013, nyr. For a detailed case analysis, see Uladzislau Belavusau, 'A Penalty Card for Homophobia from EU Non-Discrimination Law: Comment on Asociaţia ACCEPT', *Columbia Journal of European Law* (2014) (forthcoming).

[55] Council Directive 2000/78/EC of 27 November 2000 establishing a general framework for equal treatment in employment and occupation, OJ L 303/16. Both the 'Framework' and 'Race' Directives were adopted under Article 19 of the Treaty on the Functioning of the European Union and share a very similar structure.

gelijkheid van kansen and Romanian *Asociaţia ACCEPT*) mobilized a cluster of (secondary) EU labour law to combat discriminatory speech. Those organizations substantially acted as experts, illustrating the *performative* character of hate speech before the courts and insisting on the relevance of the EU law, triggering the preliminary ruling procedure in Luxembourg. Likewise, it is remarkable that in *Feryn*, the Advocate General Maduro explicitly invoked speech act theory to support his conclusions on the direct discrimination stemming from the utterances of the Belgian employer,[56] in the absence of a single Moroccan employee who actually could prove he was not hired for the job on ethnic grounds.[57]

As recently whimsically noted by Robert C. Post in the US context, 'expert knowledge requires exactly what normal First Amendment [free speech] doctrine prohibits'.[58] If the First Amendment recognizes no such thing as a 'false idea', then it cannot sustain, or even tolerate, the disciplinary practices necessary to produce expert knowledge. He concludes therefore that reliance on expert testimony should be based exclusively on an established fact and not on an emotional opinion. The line between these two is often blurred of course.

Yet for the same reason (belief in the elusive nature of truth), the US Supreme Court has been permitting hate speech under the First Amendment.[59] The European approach to hate speech is based on a different assumption, ie on an intrinsic epistemological belief in the possibility of 'relevant truth' and 'false ideas'. This epistemological optimism requires a strong evidentiary pattern, which could be based on idealized experts. The review of the recent hate speech cases in Strasbourg reveals the lack of a consistent approach to speech act analysis, with no explicitly identified epistemic authorities to rely upon in that analysis. Putting this paradox into the words of Michael Walzer, 'truth is indeed another opinion'[60] and the Court does not seem willing to explain its rules for privileging certain opinions to the pedestal of truth.

[56] Opinion of Maduro AG in Case 54/07, Centrum voor gelijkheid van kansen en voor racisme bestrijding v Firma Feryn NV, para 16: 'By publically stating his intention not to hire persons of a certain racial or ethnic origin, the employer is, in fact, excluding those persons from the application process and from his workflow. He is not merely talking about discriminating, he is discriminating. He is not simply uttering words; he is performing a "speech act". The announcement that persons of a certain racial or ethnic origin are unwelcome as applicants for a job is thus itself a form of discrimination.'

[57] For a detailed review of *Feryn*, see in Uladzislau Belavusau, 'Fighting Hate Speech through EU Law', 4(1) *Amsterdam Law Forum* 20 (2012).

[58] Robert C. Post, *Democracy, Expertise, Academic Freedom. A First Amendment Jurisprudence for the Modern State* (New Haven: Yale University Press, 2012) 9.

[59] For a broader account of the epistemological difference in the rhetorical construction of free speech in the case law of the US Supreme Court and the ECtHR, see Uladzislau Belavusau, 'Judicial Epistemology of Free Speech through Ancient Lenses', 23 *International Journal for the Semiotics of Law* 165 (2010). For the general differences in the approach to hate speech in the USA and Europe, see also Frederic Schauer, *Freedom of Expression Adjudication in Europe and America: A Case Study in Comparative Constitutional Architecture, Faculty Research Working Paper Series, Harvard University, RWP05-019* (2005).

[60] Michael Walzer, 'Philosophy and Democracy', 9(3) *Political Theory* 379 (1981), 397.

15

The Standard of Equivalent Protection as a Standard of Review

Veronika Bílková

The standard of equivalent protection is one of the standards of review, albeit a specific one, known under current international law. Used in European human rights law since the 1990s, the standard of equivalent protection assumes that no detailed review of measures adopted under the EU system is needed, provided that this system ensures the material and procedural standard of human rights protection is equivalent to that of the European Convention on Human Rights (ECHR, also referred to as the Convention), and that there is no manifest deficiency in the protection in a concrete case. This chapter argues that despite certain shortcomings, the standard of equivalent protection strikes an acceptable balance between the effort by the European Court of Human Rights (ECtHR) to avoid engaging in a scrutiny of European Union (EU) law and the need for it to remain the final guardian of the Convention. It also shows that the accession by the EU to the Convention need not necessarily ring the death-knell to the standard; in fact, it could give new impulse to its further development.

I. Standard of Equivalent Protection as Standard of Review

This section introduces the standard of equivalent protection as one of the standards of review under international law. It first looks into the nature and typology of reviews and standards of review under international law (Section I.A). In the next step, it sketches the historical evolution of the standard of equivalent protection and gives an overview of the Strasbourg case law related to it (Section I.B).

A. Reviews and standards of reviews under international law

The standard of review is a concept stemming from the common law, especially its North American tradition. It can be generally defined as 'the lens through which a tribunal will evaluate the determination of a prior authority'.[1] At the domestic level,

[1] *Concrete Pipe and Prod. of Cal., Inc., v Constr. Laborers Pension Trust for S. Cal.*, 508 US 602, 623 (1993).

it has two different meanings. In the broader meaning, the prior authority could be either a political (legislative, executive) organ or a lower judicial instance. In the narrow meaning, the term is reserved to an intra-judicial review. The identity of the prior authority is crucial, as it also predetermines the standard under which the review is carried out. Judicial review of legislative and executive acts calls into play the principles of the separation of powers and of checks and balances. Although its concrete scope and procedures differ from one country to another, the review is normally organized around the principles of constitutionality/legality and of deference/margin of appreciation.[2]

The intra-judicial review takes place within one branch of government—the judiciary. The reviewing authority (higher judicial instance) tends to be in a hierarchically superior position with respect to the prior authority (lower judicial instance), both forming part of a vertical judicial structure. In this narrower context, the standard of review could be defined as the amount of deference given by one court in reviewing a decision of a lower court or tribunal. The standard again varies among countries. Thus, for instance, while the US courts traditionally resort to the 'arbitrary and capricious', 'clearly erroneous', 'plain error', and '*de novo*' standards, their Canadian counterparts invoke the standards of 'correctness' and 'reasonableness'. The standards may also differ depending on the branch of domestic law in which they are used (criminal law, administrative law, civil law, etc).

International law was able for most of its history to do without a standard of review—and, in fact, without a review itself—due to the lack of permanent judiciary. Yet, the proliferation of international courts and tribunals over the past two or three decades has made the issue relevant at the international level as well.[3] Again, a distinction needs to be made between several types of review. The first is the review carried out by international courts or tribunals with respect to measures adopted at the domestic level. That is how the term 'review' is usually understood in the law of the World Trade Organization (WTO),[4] although some authors make the effort to distinguish between this *external* review and the *internal* review undertaken within the WTO structures as such.[5] This review is not very different from the judicial review carried out at the domestic level with regard to the decisions of the legislative and executive powers; similar standards of review (legality, deference/margin of

[2] See T.R.S. Allan, 'Judicial Deference and Judicial Review; Legal Doctrine and Legal Theory', 127(1) *Law Quarterly Review* 96 (2011).

[3] See Benedict Kingsbury, 'International Courts: Uneven Judicialisation in Global Order' in James Crawford and Martti Koskenniemi (eds), *The Cambridge Companion to International Law* (Cambridge: Cambridge University Press, 2012), 205–9.

[4] See Claus-Dieter Ehlermann and Nicolas Lockhart, 'Standard of Review in WTO Law', 7(3) *JIEL* 491 (2004). See also Chapter 9 by Lukasz Gruszczynski and Valentina Vadi (Section II), and Chapter 6 by Michael Ioannidis (Section III.A–B) in this volume.

[5] Stefan Zleptnig, 'The Standard of Review in WTO Law: An Analysis of Law, Legitimacy and the Distribution of Legal and Political Authority', *European Integration Online Papers*, Vol. 6, No. 17 (2002).

appreciation, etc) are therefore used here.[6] The same holds for the second type of review that international courts and tribunals carry out with respect to decisions by international political bodies (EU organs, United Nations (UN) organs etc).[7] A relatively recent phenomenon on the international scene, this review occurs more and more frequently, especially within highly integrated international organizations such as the European Union.[8]

In addition to the two types of what could be called *external* review, two types of *internal* or *intra-judicial* review can also be distinguished. One, that of *direct intra-judicial review*, relates to the review procedures carried out within one hierarchically organized and vertically oriented system of international judiciary. This is the case in international criminal tribunals (International Criminal Tribunal for the former Yugoslavia (ICTY), International Criminal Tribunal for Rwanda, and the International Criminal Court) where appellate chambers review decisions of trial chambers, in the WTO system (panels and the Appellate Body), and in the European Court of Human Rights (Chambers and the Grand Chamber). The review undertaken in this context is similar to intra-judicial review carried out at the domestic level and its standard therefore can take inspiration from the domestic practice. For instance, the ICTY in its appeals procedure uses the 'clearly erroneous' standard when assessing errors of law and the standard of 'reasonableness' when assessing errors of fact.[9]

The last type, and the most controversial, is that of *indirect intra-judicial review*. Due to the decentralized nature of international law and overlapping jurisdiction of international judicial and quasi-judicial bodies, it may happen that two or more international courts or tribunals belonging to different functional or regional sub-systems of international law are called upon to adjudicate the same case or some aspects thereof. Although no formal hierarchy exists among these bodies, the one giving its verdict later does in fact undertake a review, albeit an indirect one, of the decision reached previously by another judicial body. Since this horizontal model differs significantly from that known within States, the domestic practice is of limited use. Rules applied to inter-State cooperation in judicial matters are not of much help either, as they mostly aim at harmonizing national laws or developing mechanisms for the mutual recognition of judgments, rather than at setting an adequate standard of review. Moreover, national courts apply their respective domestic legislation, whereas international bodies have to apply the rules of international law.

[6] See eg Yuval Shany, 'Toward a General Margin of Appreciation Doctrine in International Law?', 16(5) *EJIL* 907 (2005).

[7] Cf Chapter 17 by Chiara Ragni (Section I) in this volume.

[8] See Aindrias Ó. Caoimh, 'Standard of Proof, Burden of Proof, Standards of Review and Evaluation of Evidence in Antitrust and Merger Cases: Perspective of Court of Justice of the European Union' in Mel Marquis and Claus-Dieter Ehlermann (eds), *European Competition Law Annual 2009* (Portland: Hart Publishing, 2011), 271–85; see also Chapter 11 by Patrycja Dąbrowska-Kłosińska and Chapter 12 by Alexia Herwig and Asja Serdarevic in this volume.

[9] See Article 25 of Statute of the International Criminal Tribunal for the former Yugoslavia, Security Council resolution 827 (1993), 25 May 1993; ICTY, *Prosecutor v Ante Gotovina, Mladen Markač*, IT-06-90-A, 16 November 2012, Part 2 (Standard of Review), paras 10–15.

This indirect intra-judicial review therefore places high demands upon the international community, forcing it to look for innovative solutions which would take into account the specificities of this type of the review. The judicial body adjudicating a case later is not superior to the one which decided it previously; and is thus not in any way able to reverse or alter the original decision. Moreover the two courts or tribunals, belonging to distinct regional and/or functional subsystems of international law, do not necessarily apply the same set of norms. For instance, a case can first be considered by the ECtHR, under the ECHR, and subsequently by the UN Human Rights Committee, under the International Covenant on Civil and Political Rights. The two organs, looking into the same set of facts and applying similar norms, can hardly allow themselves to ignore the position of each other. Hence they need to undertake an indirect review and decide what standard of review they will use when doing so.

In the academic literature, this topic is mainly addressed in the framework of the debates about the fragmentation of international law and the judicialization of international relations.[10] Emphasis is placed upon the effort to avoid jurisdictional competition among courts and tribunals, thus eliminating situations in which indirect intra-judicial review could take place.[11] The question of how to proceed if such strategies fail, and under what standard, is addressed very rarely. Shany, for instance, mentions the principle of comity, under which 'courts in one jurisdiction should show respect and demonstrate a degree of deference to the… decisions in other jurisdictions'.[12] Yet, what this respect should look like and what degree of deference is to be granted remains unclear. Even scholars who do not avoid analysing cases of jurisdictional competition in detail usually focus on the relationship between norms applied by judicial bodies rather than on the relationship between these bodies themselves.[13]

Yet, despite the lack of any established theory in the matter, jurisdictional competition does take place on the international scene and courts and tribunals confronted with it need to look for an appropriate standard of review under which they could assess decisions of their judicial counterparts, while respecting the indirect nature of the review. Most of them, in line with the views held by the doctrine, seek to avoid the review, by either declining to consider the case[14] or looking at it from a different perspective than the other body.[15] Holding this position is

[10] See Yuval Shany, *Regulating Jurisdictional Relations between National and International Courts* (Oxford: Oxford University Press, 2007).

[11] Yuval Shany, *Competing Jurisdictions of International Courts and Tribunals* (Oxford: Oxford University Press, 2004). Shany identifies several strategies which help achieve this goal, such as exclusive jurisdiction provisions (Article 292 of the Treaty Establishing the European Community) and the principle of finality (Article 47(d) of the American Convention on Human Rights).

[12] Shany, *Competing Jurisdictions*, 142.

[13] Jonathan I. Charney, 'Is International Law Threatened by Multiple International Tribunals?', 271 *Recueil des Cours* 101 (1998); Seyed-Ali Sadat-Akhavi, *Methods of Resolving Conflicts between Treaties* (Leiden: Martinus Nijhoff, 2003).

[14] In the 1978 *Delimitation of the Continental Shelf (UK v France)* case, the arbitral tribunal declined to consider a case previously adjudicated by another arbitral tribunal.

[15] See the decisions by the Convention for the Protection of the Marine Environment of the North-East Atlantic (OSPAR) arbitration and the UN Tribunal for the Law of the Sea in the

facilitated by the differences among legal subsystems within which the bodies operate. The situation is, however, more complicated when the competition arises among courts and tribunals applying similar or identical sets of norms and when, moreover, the competition becomes more frequent. At that point the need arises for a systematic approach implying the establishment of a fixed standard of review that would be applicable in all relevant cases. The standard of equivalent protection is an example, so far probably the only one, of such a fixed standard.

Inspired by the *Solange* doctrine of the Federal Constitutional Court (FCC) of Germany, the standard of equivalent protection was introduced into the European human rights law by the European Commission on Human Rights in 1990 and embraced by the ECtHR in the 2000s. It assumes that no detailed review of a measure adopted under another legal system is needed, provided that this system ensures the material and procedural standard of human rights protection equivalent to that of the ECHR and that there is no manifest deficiency in the protection in a particular case. The standard is a complex instrument, combining elements of the fourth type of review with those of the first two types. It serves to review both the decisions of the EU courts (indirectly) and the original legal acts adopted by the EU (again indirectly), together with the implementing legislation of Member States (directly). This complex nature affects the functions that the standard serves and also helps understand its role and predict its future. The next section sketches the evolution of the standard, giving also an overview of the Strasbourg case law related to it. The following section considers the challenges that the standard faces and its prospects after the planned accession of the EU to the ECHR.

B. Standard of equivalent protection: historical evolution and case law

The standard of equivalent protection arose within the debate on the relationship between the ECHR and EU (originally EC) law. With the gradual expansion of the EU competences,[16] the law created at the European—supranational—level began to affect human rights. At the same time, the EU institutions remained shielded from the scrutiny by the ECtHR due to fact that the EU was not (and, as an international organization, was not able to become) a party to the ECHR. Thus, as De Hert and Korenica put it, 'the EU remained free from the control of the Strasbourg Court, while constantly increasing its responsibilities in the human rights area'.[17] Conscious of the delicate nature of this dilemma, the ECtHR has worked hard throughout the years to find a position which would allow it to

Mox Plant case (*Ireland v United Kingdom*) dispute (ITLOS, *The MOX Plant Case* (*Ireland v UK*), ITLOS, Case No. 10 (Interim Measures, Order of 3 December 2001).

[16] Dinah Shelton, 'The Boundaries of Human Rights Jurisdiction in Europe', 13(1) *Duke Journal of Comparative & International Law* 95 (2003).

[17] Paul De Hert and Fisnik Korenica, 'The Doctrine of Equivalent Protection: Its Life and Legitimacy Before and After the European Union's Accession to the European Convention on Human Rights', 13(7) *GLJ* 874 (2012), 877.

monitor respect for human rights standards in Europe, while at the same time not encroaching upon the autonomy of EU law. This position could be defined as follows.

First, applications directed against the EU organs had to be declared inadmissible due to the incompatibility *ratione personae* with the ECHR. In the 1978 *Confederation Française Democratique du Travail* decision, the Strasbourg Commission stated: 'the European Communities are not a Contracting Party to the European Convention on Human Rights... To this extent the consideration of the applicant's complaint lies outside the... jurisdiction *ratione personae*.'[18] Secondly, applications directed against States implementing EU law could in principle be subject to judicial review. Already in 1958, in the *X v Federal Republic of Germany* decision, the Commission declared: 'if a State contracts treaty obligations and subsequently concludes another international agreement which disables it from performing its obligations under the first treaty it will be answerable for any resulting breach of its obligations under the earlier treaty.'[19]

The latter scenario can encompass three distinct situations, which differ from each other with respect to the type of law that States implement and to the discretion that they enjoy in doing so. In the first situation, States implement EU primary law. In this case, as the Strasbourg Court concluded in the 1999 *Matthews v UK* case, 'there is no difference between European and domestic legislation'.[20] The State needs to assume responsibility independently of whether it had any discretion in implementing the EU primary law or not. The rationale behind this reasoning is that States enter the EU commitments on their free will and define the terms of these commitments; they cannot therefore be allowed to escape the consequences of their acts. The second situation pertains to cases in which States implement EU secondary law while enjoying discretion. Both the Commission, in the 1987 *Etienne Tête* case,[21] and the ECtHR, in the 1996 *Cantoni v France* case,[22] asserted that the same conclusion as in the previous situation applied here, ie State actions are open to full judicial scrutiny under the ECHR.

The third situation, when States implement EU secondary law without discretion, is the most problematic. In such a case, assessing measures carried out by States would mean engaging in a scrutiny of legislation adopted at the supranational level. Moreover, since this legislation can be challenged in the EU courts, it could also mean pronouncing indirectly on a legal opinion of the Luxembourg institutions. The third situation thus gives rise to the dilemma for the ECtHR of how to 'steer a middle ground between the necessity to confirm [the] former case law on Member States' responsibility for transferred powers so as not to give carte blanche to the EC and the difficulty of providing the EU Member States with a system of control as regards the compatibility of Community acts with the

[18] *Confederation Française Democratique du Travail v the European Communities* (app. no. 8030/77), decision of the Commission 1978, para 3.

[19] *X v Germany* (app. no. 235/56), decision of the Commission 1958.

[20] *Matthews v the United Kingdom* (app. no. 24833/94), ECtHR 1999, para 34.

[21] *Etienne Tête v France* (app. no. 11123/84), decision of the Commission 1987.

[22] *Cantoni v France* (app. no. 17862/91), ECtHR 1996.

ECHR.'[23] The standard of equivalent protection is one of the responses to this dilemma.

As mentioned above, the standard took inspiration from the *Solange* doctrine of the FCC of Germany. In its 1974 *Solange I* decision, the FCC reserved the right to review the compatibility of EC law with the German Constitution as long as the EC did not have a catalogue of fundamental rights equivalent to that included in the Constitution.[24] In the 1986 *Solange II* decision, the FCC, satisfied with the evolution of human rights under the EC law, revised its position. It claimed that:

> so long as the European Communities... generally ensured effective protection of fundamental rights... which is to be regarded as substantially similar to the protection of fundamental rights required unconditionally by the Basic Law, and in so far as they generally safeguard the essential content of fundamental rights, the... Court will no longer exercise its jurisdiction to decide on the applicability of secondary Community legislation..., and it will no longer review such legislation by the standard of the fundamental rights contained in the Basic Law.[25]

The Strasbourg institutions first used the standard of equivalent protection in the 1990 *M & Co v Germany* case.[26] In this case, a company claimed that by enforcing a fine imposed on it by the European Commission in an anti-trust proceeding, Germany had breached several provisions of the ECHR. It should be noted that Germany had no discretion and that the fine was upheld by the European Court of Justice (ECJ). In its decision, the Strasbourg Commission declared itself competent to review the measures adopted by Germany.[27] In the next step, however, acknowledging that the measures were adopted in the implementation of the EC legislation the Commission declared that 'the transfer of powers to an international organization is not incompatible with the Convention provided that within that organization fundamental rights will receive an equivalent protection'.[28] Declaring that this condition is met under EC law, since 'the legal system of the European Communities not only secures fundamental rights but also provides for control of their observance',[29] the Commission did not find it appropriate to engage in a further scrutiny of the application, which was declared inadmissible *ratione materiae* (under Article 27(2) ECHR). Later, the Commission referred to the standard of equivalent protection in several other cases, confirming its previous approach.[30]

[23] Kathrin Kuhnert, 'Bosphorus—Double Standards in European Human Rights Protection?', 2(2) *Utrecht Law Review* 177 (2006), 178.

[24] *Internationale Handelsgesellschaft GmbH v Einfuhr- und Vorratsstelle für Getreide und Futtermitte*, BVerfGE 37, 29 May 1974, 271.

[25] *WünscheHandelsgesellschaft*, BVerfGE 73, 29 October 1986, 339.

[26] *M & Co v Germany* (app. no. 13258/87), decision of the Commission 1990.

[27] 'Under Article 1 ...the Member States are responsible for all acts and omissions of their domestic organs allegedly violating the Convention regardless of whether the act or omission in question is a consequence of domestic law or regulations or of the necessity to comply with international obligations.' (*M & Co* at 6).

[28] *M & Co* at 7. [29] *M & Co* at 8.

[30] *FS and NS v France* (app. no. 15669/89), decision of the Commission 1993; *Heinz v the Contracting Parties also parties to the European Patent Convention* (app. no. 21090/92), decision of the Commission 1994; *Pafitis v Greece* (app. no. 20323/92), decision of the Commission 1998.

Following on these precedents, the ECtHR began to invoke the standard of equivalent protection in the second half of the 1990s.[31] However, the case which allowed it to elaborate upon the standard in the most detail came only in 2005. This was the *Bosphorus* case, decided by the Grand Chamber.[32] The case related to an aircraft leased by a Turkish company from a State company of the Federal Republic of Yugoslavia (FRY). After economic sanctions were imposed on the FRY by the UN Security Council, the aircraft was impounded by Ireland, enjoying no discretion, under the EC Regulation giving effect to the UN Security Council resolution. The measure was reviewed by the ECJ, which found it compatible with fundamental rights.[33] The ECtHR declared itself competent to undertake a second review of the measure, entailing an indirect review of the ECJ decision.[34] It found out that the impoundment of the aircraft constituted interference into the Turkish company's right to property granted by Article 1 of Protocol I to the ECHR. When considering whether the interference was justified, the Court, instead of engaging in a detailed scrutiny of the measure, resorted to the standard of equivalent protection.[35] Its application led it to conclude that 'the impoundment of the aircraft did not give rise to a violation of Article 1 of Protocol No. 1'.[36]

The justification of the conclusion gives an interesting account of how the Court understands the standard of equivalent protection. First, in elaborating upon the content of the standard it specifies that 'by "equivalent" [it] means "comparable",' adding that 'any requirement that the organization's protection be "identical" could run counter to the interest of international cooperation.'[37] Secondly, the Court explains the way in which the standard should be applied. It introduces a two-step procedure. In the first step, the Court verifies whether—on a general level—the protection provided by the EU is equivalent to that of the ECHR. If the outcome of this test is positive—as it is for EU law—'the presumption will be that a State has not departed from the requirements of the Convention when it does no more than implement legal obligations flowing from its membership of the organization.'[38] The presumption is not irrefutable however. It can be rebutted

[31] See *Waite & Kennedy v Germany* (app. no. 26083/94), ECtHR 1999; *Beer & Regan v Germany* (app. no. 28934/95), ECtHR 1999.

[32] *Bosphorus Hava Yollari Turizm v Ireland* (app. no. 45036/98), ECtHR 2005. See Cathryn Costello, 'The Bosphorus Ruling of the European Court of Human Rights: Fundamental Rights and Blurred Boundaries in Europe', 6(1) *Human Rights Law* 87 (2006); Frank Schorkopf, 'The European Court of Human Rights' Judgement in the Case of Bosphorus Hava Yollari Turizm v. Ireland', 6(9) *GLJ* 1255 (2005).

[33] Case C-84/95 *Bosphorus v Minister for Transport, Energy and Communications and others* [1996], ECR 3953, para 26 ('As compared with an objective of general interest so fundamental for the international community, which consisted of putting an end to the state of war in the region and to the massive violations of human rights and humanitarian international law in the Republic of Bosnia-Herzegovina, the impounding of the aircraft in question, which is owned by an undertaking based in or operating from the Federal Republic of Yugoslavia, cannot be regarded as inappropriate or disproportionate').

[34] *Bosphorus Hava Yollari Turizm v Ireland*, para 137.

[35] *Bosphorus Hava Yollari Turizm v Ireland*, para 155.

[36] *Bosphorus Hava Yollari Turizm v Ireland*, para 167.

[37] *Bosphorus Hava Yollari Turizm v Ireland*, para 167.

[38] *Bosphorus Hava Yollari Turizm v Ireland*, para 156.

'if, in the circumstances of a particular case, it is considered that the protection of Convention rights was manifestly deficient.'[39]

Third, the Court stresses that the applicability of the standard is limited to what used to be the first pillar of the EU.[40] This is logical, since only the fully communitarized areas give rise to supranational legislation which cannot be, especially if no discretion is left in its implementation, easily attributed to States. Finally, it is interesting to note that while following on the precedents set by the Commission, the Court actually makes a different use of the standard of equivalent protection. It does not resort to it in order to decide on admissibility *ratione materiae*, but in order to decide on the merits of the case.[41] This increases the potential of the standard, which can play a more efficient role in ensuring that, on one hand States will not be allowed to free themselves from human rights obligations by transferring competences to supranational bodies, while on the other hand the acts of these supranational bodies will not remain outside the scope of judicial scrutiny of the ECtHR.

Since the *Bosphorus* judgment, the Strasbourg Court has invoked the standard of equivalent protection only rarely.[42] Most recently, it revisited it in its 2011 *MSS v Belgium and Greece* judgment.[43] The case concerns an Afghan applicant, transferred from Belgium to Greece, as the latter country was competent to consider his application for asylum under the EC Dublin Regulation.[44] The applicant alleged that due to the slim chances of his application being properly examined in Greece, the transfer entailed the risk of return to Afghanistan, where he could be subject to torture and other human rights violations. In the judgment, rendered again by the Grand Chamber, the Court confirmed that 'acts falling outside... strict international legal obligations, notably where [the State] exercised discretion',[45] were subject to full judicial review, whereas State actions taken in compliance with such obligations were 'justified as long as the relevant organization is considered to protect fundamental rights in a manner which can be considered at least equivalent to that for which the Convention provides.'[46] The Court found that the

[39] *Bosphorus Hava Yollari Turizm v Ireland*, para 156.

[40] *Bosphorus Hava Yollari Turizm v Ireland*, para 72. Between 1993–2009, the EU structure encompassed three pillars—the European Communities pillar, the Common Foreign and Security Policy pillar, and the Justice and Home Affairs (later Police and Judicial Cooperation in Criminal Matters) pillar.

[41] This is also stressed in the Joint Concurring Opinion of Judges Rozakis, Tulkens, Traja, Botoucharova, Zagrebelsky, and Garlicki (*Bosphorus Hava Yollari Turizm v Ireland*, para 50).

[42] *Cooperatieve Producentenorganisatie van de Nederlandse Kokkelvisserij UA v the Netherlands* (app. no. 13645/05), ECtHR 2009. In several cases, the standard was invoked by the parties, yet the Court failed to respond to these claims. See *Al-Jedda v the United Kingdom* (app. no. 27021/08), ECtHR 2011, para 96; *Al-Saadoon and Mufdi v the United Kingdom* (app. no. 61498/08), ECtHR 2010, para 114.

[43] *MSS v Belgium and Greece* (app. no. 30696/09), ECtHR 2011.

[44] The Dublin Regulation (Council Regulation (EC) No 343/2003 of 18 February 2003 establishing the criteria and mechanisms for determining the Member State responsible for examining an asylum application lodged in one of the Member States by a third-country national OJ L 50/1) establishes the criteria and mechanisms for determining the Member State responsible for examining an asylum application lodged in one of the Member States by a third-country national.

[45] *MSS v Belgium and Greece*, para 338. [46] *MSS v Belgium and Greece*, para 338.

case at hand fell under the former category and, hence, the standard of equivalent protection was not applicable. Despite this conclusion, the case is interesting, as it confirms the definition of the standard given in the *Bosphorus* case.

II. Standard of Equivalent Protection—Challenges and Prospects

The standard of equivalent protection is now a well-established, albeit infrequently applied, standard of review used under the European system of human rights. Yet, it still gives rise to certain questions, which have been only partially addressed by scholars or the ECtHR itself. Some questions relate to the concrete parameters of the standard (Section II.A). Others pertain to the future prospects of the standard, especially in light of the planned accession of the EU to the ECHR (Section II.B).

A. Parameters of the standard of equivalent protection

Legal scholars, as well as the ECtHR itself, tend to treat the standard of equivalent protection as a settled legal institution.[47] Yet, as Section I has shown, the standard has changed considerably since the 1990s. Moreover, some of its parameters remain under-defined, in part due to the scarcity of case law. This is mainly the case of 'equivalent protection' and of 'manifest deficiency'. The concept of 'equivalent protection' constitutes the very substance of the standard of equivalent protection, as is reflected in its very designation. Despite that, the Court has not so far taken much pain to explain it in detail. It can be recalled that in the *Bosphorus* case it held that 'by "equivalent" [it] meant "comparable"', not identical.[48] This is not entirely clear. How similar does the protection need to be to be considered 'comparable'? And what is the *tertio comparationis*?

The only guidance the Court gives is that the 'equivalence' has to be considered both in the domain of material (substantive) regulation and in that of procedural guarantees offered to enforce the regulation.[49] In *Bosphorus*, the Court, rather briefly, analyses whether the EU legal system meets this test. It first looks into the substantive regulation, tracing the history of human (fundamental) rights protection at the EU level. The fact that human rights have gradually come to be recognized among the general principles of EU law and that the ECHR has been granted a special place among the sources of these rights seems to satisfy

[47] See De Hert and Korenica, 'The Doctrine of Equivalent Protection'; *MSS v Belgium and Greece* (app. no. 30696/09), ECtHR 2011.

[48] *Bosphorus v Hava Yollari Turizm Ireland*, para 156.

[49] 'In the Court's view, State action taken in compliance with such legal obligations is justified as long as the relevant organization is considered to protect fundamental rights, as regards both the substantive guarantees offered and the mechanisms controlling their observance, in a manner which can be considered at least equivalent to that for which the Convention provides.' (*Bosphorus Hava Yollari Turizm v Ireland*, para 155).

the ECtHR and to ensure their substantive equivalence. The Court then turns to procedural guarantees. Acknowledging that the 'access of individuals to the ECJ is limited',[50] it nonetheless concludes that due to the availability of national courts and the possibility of these courts and EC institutions of initiating actions before the ECJ, procedural equivalence is guaranteed within the EU as well.

This analysis reveals that when deciding on the equivalence of protection, the ECtHR focuses on the legal systems in general rather than on specific human rights (those allegedly violated in the case at hand). The legal systems are compared with respect to the existence of human rights guarantees and the availability of judicial review. 'Equivalence' then corresponds to the mere presence of these two elements, regardless of their concrete contents. At first sight, this test appears to be not only rather mechanical but also quite an easy one. Any universal or regional legal system endowed with its own judiciary could most probably meet it. Yet it is also true that currently there are no such systems in the European space apart from the EU one. This might be one of the reasons why the Strasbourg Court did not in fact find it necessary to elaborate upon the standard in more detail. Another reason might consist of the fact that, due to the close link between the two European human rights systems and the special place of the ECHR within the EU law, the equivalence of protection was more an assumption to start with than a conclusion to be reached in an analysis.

Another crucial concept under the standard of equivalent protection—'manifest deficiency'—has not been sufficiently elaborated upon by the Strasbourg Court either. In the *Bosphorus* case, in which the concept was introduced, the Court passed over it in one single paragraph declaring that 'it considers it clear that there was no dysfunction of the mechanisms of control of the observance of Convention rights'.[51] It further indicated that, when reaching this conclusion, it had taken into account the nature of the interference, the general interest pursued by the impoundment and by the sanctions regime, and the ruling of the ECJ. Yet it remains unclear what exactly would have to be deficient in any of these areas for the ECtHR to find against the EU. In his Concurring Opinion, Judge Ross sought to give some examples of what could be seen as manifest deficiency. These examples include situations in which 'the ECJ lacks competence, when the ECJ has been too restrictive in its interpretation of individual access to it; or indeed where there has been an obvious misinterpretation or misapplication by the ECJ of the guarantees of a Convention right'.[52] Interestingly, the list focuses solely on procedural shortcomings, leaving unaddressed the question as to what could constitute a manifest deficiency in the substantive area.

The lack of clarity in this regard has given rise to criticism. Judges Rozakis, Tulkens, Traja, Botoucharova, Zagrebelsky, and Garlicki, in their Joint

[50] *Bosphorus Hava Yollari Turizm v Ireland*, para 162.
[51] *Bosphorus Hava Yollari Turizm v Ireland*, para 162.
[52] *Bosphorus Hava Yollari Turizm v Ireland*, para 55.

Concurring Opinion, state that 'the criterion "manifestly deficient" appears to establish a relatively low threshold, which is in marked contrast to the supervision generally carried out under the European Convention on Human Rights.'[53] This view is largely shared in the doctrine. For De Hert and Korenica, the concept sets a 'low-bar protection'.[54] Kwiatkowska, Paulsson and Dahlin concur that 'one would be hard pressed to find an example where the ECtHR would actually go into factual detail to examine a possible deficiency.'[55] Some scholars also draw attention to a disparity between the two parts of the standard, with the general presumption of equal protection being based on an *in abstracto* comparison of legal systems, and the 'manifest deficiency' criterion requiring an *in concreto* assessment taking into account the specificities of an individual case.[56] Although this disparity could partly be overcome due to the requirement that such deficiency has to be 'manifest' and hence identifiable without any detailed analysis of the case, the criticism is, in the absence of any definition of 'deficiency', not unwarranted. This seems all the more true in that the burden of proof in rebutting the presumption of equivalent protection and proving the 'manifest deficiency' seems to lay on the applicant.[57]

The uncertainty relating to the interpretation of some of its main elements can give rise to doubts relating not only to the reliability of the standard of equivalent protection, but also to its nature. Does it truly serve as a standard of review? Or is it rather a tool to avoid review or even a legal cloak to cover up the fact that the emperor is naked, ie that no review actually takes place? This seems to be suggested by the concurring judges, who warn that:

> for the Court to leave to the Community's judicial system the task of ensuring 'equivalent protection', without retaining a means of verifying on a case-by-case basis that that protection is indeed 'equivalent', would be tantamount to consenting tacitly to substitution, in the field of Community law, of Convention standards by a Community standard which might be inspired by Convention standards but whose equivalence with the latter would no longer be subject to authorised scrutiny.[58]

This objection is made stronger by the fact that, as mentioned above, the equivalence of human rights protection in Europe seems to be presumed rather than

[53] *Bosphorus Hava Yollari Turizm v Ireland*, para 53.

[54] De Hert and Korenica, 'The Doctrine of Equivalent Protection', at 889.

[55] Agnieszka Kwiatkowska, Helena Paulsson and Gustav Dahlin, 'Will the accession of the European Union to the European Convention on Human Rights be a boost to human rights protection—A legal analysis of political argumentation', Paper at the *2010 European Integration: enhanced protection or a threat to individual freedom and liberty?*, Warsaw, 10–12 May 2010, available at <http://pl.zpc.wpia.uw.edu.pl/wp-content/uploads/2010/04/2.-EU-accession-to-the-ECHR-boosting-human-rights-protection-final2.doc> (accessed 28 March 2014).

[56] See also Costello, 'The Bosphorus Ruling'.

[57] 'In the light of these considerations, the Court cannot find that the applicant association has shown that the protection afforded to it was "manifestly deficient" because it did not have an opportunity to respond to the Opinion of the Advocate General. It has therefore failed to rebut the presumption that the procedure before the ECJ provided equivalent protection of its rights' (*Cooperatieve Producentenorganisatie van de Nederlandse Kokkelvisserij UA* at 21).

[58] *Bosphorus Hava Yollari Turizm v Ireland*, para 50.

established, and the concept of 'manifest deficiency' has not yet been used, even in controversial cases.

Still, it would be premature to conclude that the standard of equivalent protection is merely a review-avoiding technique, or even a smokescreen for a non-review. The specific nature of review which is at stake here needs to be taken into account. As discussed above, when the ECtHR addresses measures adopted in the implementation of the EU secondary law with no discretion granted to States, it reviews not only these national measures (directly) but also the EU legislation and, potentially, the ECJ decisions (indirectly). The three types of review cannot be separated, as they relate to the same acts and facts. The Strasbourg Court however only has the mandate to undertake the first type of review. It thus needs to find a standard of review which would allow it to both show a reasonable degree of deference to the EU system and also to prevent States from avoiding international scrutiny by transferring competences to the supranational level.

The standard of equivalent protection is an attempt by the ECtHR to address this dilemma. By declaring the two European systems of human rights protection generally equivalent while, simultaneously, not excluding the possibility of review in concrete cases on the 'manifest deficiency' criterion, it makes it possible for the Strasbourg Court to avoid engaging in a regular assessment of EU measures, while at the same time keeping the door open for such an assessment in cases where 'the interest of international cooperation would be outweighed by the Convention's role as a "constitutional instrument of European public order" in the field of human rights.'[59] Thus, the standard strikes a balance which, albeit not ideal, seems acceptable. It thus should be concluded that it is not merely a smokescreen for a non-review.

And it is not just a review-avoiding technique either. By imposing upon the Strasbourg Court the task of verifying the general equivalence of the protection offered by the two human rights regimes, as well as the task of assessing whether a manifest deficiency in such protection has taken place in concrete cases, the standard serves as 'the lens through which a tribunal will evaluate the determination of a prior authority'.[60] It also indicates the amount of deference given by one court in reviewing a decision of another one—fully in line with the definition of a standard of review. It however needs to be stressed that the standard of equivalent protection is highly context-specific. It is suited for indirect intra-judicial review, as it reflects its specificity consisting in the lack of formal hierarchy between the judicial body having issued a decision and the one reviewing it. It is also tailor-made for the relationship between the two European human rights systems. Since this relationship is unique, declaring the standard of equivalent protection a general standard of review under international law would be not only incorrect, but also highly risky.

[59] *Bosphorus Hava Yollari Turizm v Ireland,* para 156.

[60] *Concrete Pipe and Prod. of Cal., Inc., v Constr. Laborers Pension Trust for S. Cal.*, 508 US 602, 623 (1993).

B. Standard of equivalent protection and the EU accession to the ECHR

The standard of equivalent protection is thus tailor-made for the existing relationship between the two European human rights systems. This relationship, however, will soon undertake quite a radical change. Protocol 14 to the ECHR, adopted in 2004 and in force since 2010, made it possible for the European Union to accede to the European Convention.[61] The Lisbon Treaty, adopted in 2007 and in force since 2009, turned this option into a legal obligation.[62] The negotiations as to the concrete form of the accession have been going on for several years.[63] In April 2013, the Draft Accession Agreement was finalized.[64] Once the Accession Agreement will be ratified by all Council of Europe Member States and the EU, the European Union will become a party to the ECHR in its own capacity, with its own judge, and with the possibility of having its law, ie the full set of its secondary legislation as well as the decisions of its courts, subject to the judicial scrutiny by the Strasbourg Court.

Three main opinions exist as to the impact of the EU accession to the ECHR on the standard of equivalent protection. Some authors believe that after the accession, the standard will become obsolete.[65] Once the EU is a party to the ECHR, there are no reasons why its acts should not lend themselves to the same human rights scrutiny as acts adopted by States at the national level. There is also no reason why the decisions of the EU courts should not be subject to the same standard of review as those of domestic courts. While certainly the EU is in many respects different from States and its specificities would need to be taken into account,[66] this does not imply that its human rights performance should be measured by a different standard. The advantage of this approach would consist in the unification of the standard adopted in all types of review undertaken by the ECtHR (review of the acts of the EU and of national implementing measures adopted with or without discretion).

Other authors believe that the standard of equivalent protection could survive the accession. Van Dijk, for instance, asserts that the standard could be turned into a new admissibility criterion for cases directed against the EU institutions.[67]

[61] Article 17, inserting a new paragraph 2 to Article 59: 'The European Union may accede to this Convention.'

[62] Amended Article 6(2) TEU: 'The Union shall accede to the European Convention for the Protection of Human Rights and Fundamental Freedoms.' Further requirements for the conclusion of the Accession Agreement are set out in Protocol No. 8 to the Treaty of Lisbon.

[63] See Tobias Lock, 'End of an Epic? The Draft Agreement on the EU's Accession to the ECHR', 31(1) *Yearbook of European Law* 162 (2012).

[64] Draft revised agreement on the accession of the European Union to the Convention for the Protection of Human Rights and Fundamental Freedoms, in Final report to the CDDH, 47+1 (2013) 008rev2, 10 June 2013, 4–12.

[65] See De Hert and Korenica, 'The Doctrine of Equivalent Protection', at 890.

[66] De Hert and Korenica at 890–1.

[67] Pieter Van Dijk, *Comments on the Accession of the European Union/European Community to the European Convention on Human Rights*, 20 August 2007, available at <http://www.statewatch.org/news/2007/sep/van-dijk-eu-echr.pdf> (accessed 28 March 2014).

Such cases would, if the standard is met, be declared incompatible *ratione materie* with the ECHR (following the *M & Co* case). This opinion is shared by Bemelmans-Videc, who served as a rapporteur to the EU Committee on Legal Affairs and Human Rights in the matter of the EU accession to the ECHR. She suggests that 'if an application is brought before the ECtHR against an institution of the EU/EC [European Community], a panel will decide on whether the application will be accepted in the interest of legal protection and/or a uniform interpretation and application of the ECHR.'[68] Using the standard in this way would entail easing the workload burden placed on the ECtHR and preventing 'prestige battles'[69] between the European judicial institutions.

Finally, some scholars believe that the standard of equivalent protection could be maintained and incorporated into the new system, not solely as an admissibility criterion but as an instrument of substantive review (*meritum* standard),[70] along the lines of the *Bosphorus* case. This would mean that:

> as a rule, the decisions by the CJEC about maintaining the ECHR within the EU/EC context will be endorsed by the ECtHR, provided that the CJEC has jurisdiction over the matter, and provided that the latter does not depart from well-established Strasbourg case law and that its judgment does not concern an issue under the ECHR that has not yet been decided by the ECtHR.[71]

This option would, in addition to easing the workload of the ECtHR and preventing intra-judicial conflicts, ensure that the Strasbourg court will remain the final guardian of respect for the ECHR, able to respond to human rights excesses potentially committed in the EU framework.

It is difficult to predict which of the three scenarios *will* materialize. It is also not easy to say which of them *should* materialize, as none is without its deficiencies. The abandonment of the standard of equivalent protection could result in the ECtHR being overwhelmed with cases involving difficult issues of EU law, in which the Strasbourg judges are not necessarily trained. It could also challenge the prestige of the Luxembourg court, side-tracked in human rights issues by the ECtHR. On the other hand, preservation of the standard could put the real import of the accession by the EU to the ECHR into question. Why to undertake such a complicated process if, in the end, the EU legislation would not be subject to a standard judicial scrutiny? Would the EU gain influence (its own judges' participation in decision-making, etc) without forfeiting its legal independence? Even worse, the continued application of the standard of equivalent protection could strengthen the criticism, which has made itself heard ever since the *Bosphorus* judgment,[72] that there are double standards in human rights protection

[68] See European Parliament, *Report of the Committee on Legal Affairs and Human Rights. The accession of the European Union/European Community to the European Convention on Human Rights*, Doc. 11533, 18 March 2008, para 17.

[69] *Report of the Committee on Legal Affairs and Human Rights*, para 17.

[70] See De Hert and Korenica, 'The Doctrine of Equivalent Protection', at 891.

[71] European Parliament, *Report of the Committee on Legal Affairs and Human Rights*, para 17.

[72] See K. Kuhnert, 'Bosphorus'.

in Europe: one for EU Members, the other for non-EU States. The question would arise, as it sometimes does even now, why the standard of equivalent protection is only applied to the EU and not to other regional organizations in Europe, or even to States.

Again, some inspiration could be taken from the context in which the ECtHR resorts to the standard of equivalent protection. The context is set by a triple review involving the scrutiny of domestic acts, of international political acts, and of judicial decisions of another international court. The restraint in the approach of the Strasbourg Court has been primarily dictated by its lack of competence to scrutinize the EU acts and the decisions of the ECJ and by the impossibility of separating national implementing measures from these acts and decisions. After the accession, this lack of competence will be redressed. Consequently, the rationale for using the standard, so it seems, would collapse.

The picture however is not so simple. Besides helping the ECtHR to cope with its lack of competences, the standard of equivalent protection has also served for the Court as an instrument permitting it to walk a tightrope with respect to the delicacies implied in the relationship between the two subsystems of international law. This reason does not fully disappear with the accession, as the EU becoming party to the European Convention does not entail the EU system being placed at a par with national legal systems or the Luxembourg Court becoming just one of many supreme courts in Europe. It is thus probable that the ECtHR will not be disposed to abandon the standard lightly, nor to treat cases involving the EU in the same way as those against States. Whatever the terms of the Accession Agreement, the Strasbourg Court will certainly think twice before abandoning an instrument which has proven useful, albeit not uncontroversial, and over the years has spared some bad blood with respect to the colleagues from Luxembourg.[73]

III. Concluding Remarks

The standard of equivalent protection, inspired by the *Solange* doctrine of the FCC of Germany, has been used since the 1990s by the European Commission and the European Court of Human Rights to overcome, or prevent, normative and institutional clashes with the EU legal order. It is a rather atypical standard of review, reflecting the peculiarities of indirect intra-judicial review and tailor-made for the relationship between the European human rights systems. It assumes that no detailed review of measures adopted under the EU system is needed, provided that this system ensures the material and procedural standard of human rights protection equivalent to that of the ECHR and that there is no manifest deficiency in the protection in a particular case.

[73] See also Jana Králová, 'Comments on the Draft Agreement on the Accession of the European Union to the Convention for the Protection of Human Rights and Fundamental Freedoms', 2 *Czech Yearbook of International Law* 127 (2011).

The scarcity of cases in which the standard has been applied since the 1990s and the criticism raised against it by scholars, mainly due to the under-definition of its crucial concepts ('equivalent protection' and 'manifest deficiency'), would suggest that the standard is rather deficient. Yet, when considered in light of the function it serves, the assessment is more positive. Although not perfect, the standard strikes a rather reasonable balance between the various interests at stake. It helps ensure that the ECtHR remains the final guardian of respect for the European Convention, even in areas in which States implement EU acts without any discretion, while at the same time making it possible for the ECtHR to avoid engaging in the scrutiny of EU acts and of the decisions of the Luxembourg Court.

The accession by the EU to the ECHR is often considered as the beginning of the end of the standard of equivalent protection. Yet due to the complex reasons having led to the creation of this standard, this prediction is not uncontroversial either. It is in fact likely that the ECtHR will be reluctant to abandon an instrument which has served it rather well, helping it over the past two decades to prevent jurisdictional clashes with the EU judicial institutions. The accession by the EU to the ECHR, instead of ringing the death-knell to the standard of equivalent protection, could in fact give it a new impetus to develop inside an enlarged system of European protection of human rights.

16

Subsidiarity in the Americas

What Room Is There for Deference in the Inter-American System?

*Bernard Duhaime**

I. Introduction

Since its creation, the Inter-American Human Rights System (IAHRS) has refined its position regarding the range of Member States' human rights obligations, the extent of its jurisdiction to protect such rights in the region, and the degree of State sovereignty when it comes to these matters.

The progressive expansion of the scope of the Organization of American States (OAS) Member States' obligations flowing from the development of the applicable normative framework,[1] and liberal interpretations of the Inter-American instruments (including the OAS Charter[2] and the American Declaration of the Rights and Duties of Man[3]) are good examples of this evolution. This is also well illustrated by the very development of the Inter-American Commission on Human Rights (IACHR), which went from a body initially designed mainly to

* The author would like to thank Ms Catherine Lafontaine, Ms Myriam Cloutier and Ms Anaïs Brasier for their assistance in the preparation of this text.

[1] See eg ACHR, OAS Treaty Series No. 36, 1144 UNTS 123, 1969 (Convention); Inter-American Convention to Prevent and Punish Torture, OAS Treaty, Series No. 67, 1985; Additional Protocol to the American Convention on Human Rights in the Area of Economic, Social and Cultural Rights, OAS Treaty, Series No. 69, 1988; Inter-American Convention on Forced Disappearance of Persons, 33 ILM 1429, 1994; Inter-American Convention on the Prevention, Punishment, and Eradication of Violence Against Women, 33 ILM 1534, 1994 (Belém Do Pará Convention); Inter-American Convention on the Elimination of All Forms of Discrimination Against Persons With Disabilities, AG/RES. 1608, 7 June 1999.

[2] Charter of the Organization of American States, 119 UNTS 3, as subsequently amended.

[3] American Declaration of the Rights and Duties of Man, 2 May 1948, Res. XXX, Final Act, Ninth International Conference of American States, OAS Off. Rec. OEASer.LVII.23/Doc. 21 rev. 6, 1979. On the binding nature of the Declaration see IACHR, *Report on Terrorism and Human Rights*, OEA/Ser.L/V/ll.116 Doc. 5 rev. 1 corr., 2002, 39. See also *Interpretation of the American Declaration of the Rights and Duties of Man Within the Framework of Article 64 of the American Convention on Human Rights*, IACtHR, Advisory Opinion OC-10/89, 14 July 1989, Series A, No. 10, paras 29–47.

promote human rights, to a true authority supervising the protection of these rights, including through a complex individual petition system[4] which applies progressive admissibility criteria adapted to the region's reality.[5]

In this context, one can say that the opacity of States' sovereignty regarding human rights issues has been significantly reduced and that the Inter-American Human Rights institutions play a greater role in monitoring and verifying Member States' compliance with their obligations and in reviewing the efficiency of internal judicial mechanisms in this respect. This has naturally created tensions in the IAHRS, as evidenced by the 1984 IACHR case *Schmidt v Costa Rica*, where the State asserted that the victim's claim undermined its sovereignty and constituted an intrusion in its domestic jurisdiction, and that the Commission could not annul or reverse a judgment issued by a domestic court. In rejecting this objection, the Commission reaffirmed its capacity to verify whether a domestic law or judgment violates applicable human rights instruments.[6]

This being so, both the IACHR and Inter-American Court on Human Rights (IACtHR) exercise their jurisdiction in accordance with the principle of *subsidiarity*, as prescribed by the Preamble to the American Convention on Human Rights (ACHR or the Convention)[7] and crystallized in the rule of prior exhaustion of domestic remedies, based on the principle that a defendant State must be given the opportunity to redress wrongs on its own and within the framework of its internal legal system.[8]

This chapter will discuss, from a positive law perspective,[9] firstly the extent to which the IAHRS pays deference to States and domestic judicial institutions, beginning with the admissibility stage. It will also explore the applicability of the 'fourth instance formula'. Secondly, it will reflect on the importance of

[4] On the development of the petition system, see Bernard Duhaime, 'Protecting Human Rights in the Americas: Recent Achievements and Challenges' in Gordon Mace, Jean-Philippe Thérien and Paul Haslam (eds), *Governing the Americas: Regional Institutions at the Crossroads* (Boulder: Lynne Rienner Publishers, 2007) 216–45. See also Felipe M. González, 'La OEA y los derechos humanos despues del advenimiento de los gobiernos civiles: expectativas (in)satisfechas', 16 *Revista de Derecho (Universidad del Norte)* 1 (2003).

[5] See eg *Exceptions to the Exhaustion of Domestic Remedies (Arts. 46.1, 46.2.a and 46.2.b, American Convention on Human Rights)* (1990), Advisory Opinion OC-11/90, IACtHR, Series A, No. OC-11/90. On the Inter-American *amparo*, see generally Ariel Dulitzky, 'The Inter-American Human Rights System Fifty Years Later: Time for Changes', *Quebec Journal of International Law* (Special Edition, 2011), 127.

[6] *Schmidt v Costa Rica* (1984), IACtHR, No. 17/84, Annual Report 1984–5, para 4.

[7] Indeed, the Preamble refers to how the Convention should reinforce or complement the protection provided by the domestic law of the American States.

[8] See *Marzioni v Argentina* (1996), IACHR, No. 39/96, Annual Report 1996, paras 48 et seq. See also *Salvador Jorge Blanco v Dominican Republic* (1989), IACHR, No. 15/89, Annual Report 1988–1989, 100, para 5; *Perozo et al (Venezuela)* (1996), IACtHR, Series C, No. 195, para 64; *The Effect of Reservations on the Entry into Force of the American Convention on Human Rights (Arts. 74 and 75 of the American Convention on Human Rights)* (1982), Advisory Opinion OC-2/82, IACtHR, Series A, No. 2, para 31; *The Word 'Laws' in Article 30 of the American Convention on Human Rights* (1986), Opinion OC-6/86, IACtHR, Series A, No. 6, para 26; *Velásquez Rodríguez (Honduras)* (1988), IACtHR, Series C, No. 4, para 61.

[9] For a broader discussion regarding the concept of deference in international law see Part I of this volume, Chapters 1–4.

supervising the Member States' obligation to ensure the judicial protection of individual human rights under their respective jurisdictions, taking into consideration the spectre of impunity and the Continent's history. Finally, it will discuss the applicability of the doctrine of the margin of appreciation as well as other forms of deference in the Inter-American System.

II. Admitting Cases: Deference to National Courts and the Fourth Instance Formula

As in the European Human Rights System[10] and the United Nations Human Rights Committee,[11] the Inter-American Human Rights institutions have developed and applied the 'fourth instance formula', according to which certain decisions rendered by impartial and independent domestic courts should not be subject to scrutiny under the Convention.[12] This approach has usually been applied by the IACHR at the admissibility stage, but it has also been referred to by the IACtHR in its proceedings.

A. The concept of the fourth instance formula

While the Commission only indirectly addressed the fourth instance formula in the previously-mentioned case of *Schmidt v Costa Rica*, it later refined its doctrine in what became the leading case on the fourth instance formula in the 1997 *Marzioni v Argentina* case, dealing with the alleged inadequate application by local courts of domestic norms providing for compensation for work-related accidents. In its reasoning, the IACHR took into consideration the approach developed on this issue by the European System, including in the cases of *Alvaro Baragiola v Switzerland* and of *Gudmundur Gudmundsson v Iceland*,[13] and similarly concluded that it too could not:

> review the judgments issued by the domestic courts acting within their competence and with due judicial guarantees, unless it...portrays a claim that a domestic legal decision

[10] See eg *Anderson v the United Kingdom* (app. no. 44958/98), ECtHR 1999; *Johnson v the United Kingdom* (app. no. 42246/98), ECtHR 2001; Loukis G. Loucaides, *The European Convention on Human Rights: Collected Essays* (Leiden: MartinusNijhoff Publishers, 2007) 197.

[11] See eg *Anna Maroufidou v Sweden*, Communication No. 58/1979, UN Doc. CCPR/C/OP/1 at 80 (1985) and *G.J. v Trinidad and Tobago*, Communication No. 331/1988, UN Doc. CCPR/C/43/D/331/1988 (1991). See generally Tom Zwart, *The Admissibility of Human Rights Petitions: The Case Law of the European Commission of Human Rights and the Human Rights Committee* (Leiden: Martinus Nijhoff Publishers, 1994) 150–1.

[12] See generally Diego Rodríguez Pinzón, 'The "Victim" Requirement, the Fourth Instance Formula and the Notion of "Person" in the Individual Complaint Procedure of the Inter-American Human Rights System', 7 *ILSA Journal of International & Comparative Law* 369 (2001), 376; Monica Pinto, 'National and International Courts—Deference or Disdain', 30 *Loyola of Los Angeles International & Comparative Law Review* 247 (2008), 257 et seq. Zlata Drnas de Clément, *Corte interamericana de derechos humanos ¿CuartaInstancia?*, in *¿Se ha convertido la Corte Interamericana de Derechos Humanos en una cuarta instancia? XVIII Reunión Conjunta de Academias de Derecho de Argentina* (Buenos Aires: La Ley, 2009).

[13] See respectively application no. 17625/90, decision of the Commission 1992 and application no. 511/59, decision of the Commission 1958. See generally Frede Castberg, *The European Convention on Human Rights*, (Leiden: Sijthoff; Dobbs Ferry: Oceana Publications, 1974) 63–64.

constitutes a disregard of the right to a fair trial, or if it appears to violate any other right guaranteed by the Convention. However, if it contains nothing but the allegation that the decision was wrong or unjust in itself, the petition must be dismissed under this formula. The Commission . . . cannot serve as an appellate court to examine alleged errors of internal law or fact that may have been committed by the domestic courts acting within their jurisdiction.[14]

The IACtHR has also applied this doctrine in several cases,[15] including in *Genie Lacayo v Nicaragua*.[16] The fourth instance formula has mostly been applied in two types of situations: where the Inter-American institutions were asked to review (a) the way domestic courts appreciated the facts and the evidence of a case; or (b) how domestic courts interpreted and applied domestic law.

B. Deference regarding the appreciation of the facts

Firstly, in the 1988 death penalty case of *Wright v Jamaica*, while the IACHR declared that it could not act as a court of fourth instance and review the holdings of the domestic tribunals,[17] it concluded that it was physically impossible for the victim to have committed the murder for which he had been convicted and sentenced to death because the evidence on record clearly established that the victim was in police custody at the time of the crime. The Commission considered the factual evidence of the case only after concluding that several procedural errors had prevented the domestic judicial authorities from ensuring the victim's right to due process guarantees and to judicial protection, noting that contradictory elements of proof were not raised before the Jamaican Court of Appeal, but were rather discovered when the case was submitted to the UK Privy Council, which nevertheless refused to grant leave for appeal.[18]

Similarly, in *Andrews v United States*,[19] another death penalty case, the Commission considered that the domestic authorities had not ensured the right to judicial protection of the victim, a black man tried in front of an all-white male jury composed mainly of Mormons who believed in white supremacy. During the proceedings a note was found in the jury room stating 'Hang the Nigger'. No mistrial was ordered and the US Supreme Court confirmed the conviction because the trial judge had lectured the jury.[20] After reiterating its position on the fourth instance formula, the IACHR referred to these procedural irregularities and concluded that the victim's right to due process and to

[14] *Marzioni v Argentina*, paras 141–2.
[15] See eg *Villagrán Morales et al (Guatemala)* (2001), IACtHR, Series C, No. 77, paras 17–20.
[16] *Genie-Lacayo (Nicaragua)* (1997), IACtHR, Series C, No. 30, para 94.
[17] *Clifton Wright v Jamaica* (1988), IACHR, No. 29/88, Annual Report 1988, para 5.
[18] *Clifton Wright v Jamaica, considerando* 3 and 4.
[19] *William Andrews v United States* (1997), IACHR, No. 57/96, Annual Report 1997.
[20] See also William Schabas, *The Abolition of the Death Penalty in International Law* (Cambridge: Cambridge University Press, 2002) 322.

judicial protection had been violated, because of the hearing's lack of impartiality, based on the evidence of racial bias during his trial. It consequently ruled that the victim's right to equality had also been violated. These cases illustrate well that:

> the fourth instance doctrine is directly related to the existence of a functioning judiciary and to the level of discretion to be afforded to a domestic court in, for example, estimating the value of evidence or establishing the domestic law applicable to a case. Therefore, to override the threshold set by the Commission, a petitioner would have to prove that there is *a manifest arbitrariness that violates a right protected by the Convention in the domestic judicial proceedings*.[21]

As the Commission noted, it 'cannot assume the role of a superior court to review alleged errors of fact or law that domestic courts may have committed within their sphere of competence, *unless there is unequivocal evidence of violation of the due process guarantees of the American Convention*.'[22]

This approach was again applied in the 1990 case of *Lopez Aurelli v Argentina* dealing with the impossibility of a victim, once democracy was restored in Argentina, of accessing judicial remedies in his case alleging he had been arbitrarily convicted based on irregular evidence. In its decision, the IACHR reiterated that it could not comment on the application of domestic laws nor the determination of guilt or innocence of the applicant, matters of sole concern for the domestic judiciary. The Commission did however consider the evidence submitted (including evidence allegedly obtained illegally under coercion), the procedural irregularities at trial as well as the consequent unlawful imprisonment of the victim, and concluded that the obligations of Argentina under the Convention were not respected, notably because of the failure to review the case.[23] In its analysis of the applicability of the fourth instance formula, the IACHR again referred to the practice of the European Commission on Human Rights, which had indicated that it was 'not called upon to decide whether or not domestic courts have correctly assessed evidence before them, but whether evidence for and against the accused has been presented in such a manner and the proceedings in general have been conducted in such a way that he has had a fair trial.'[24]

In cases where it is simply requested to review evidence previously assessed by domestic authorities, and where there is no prima facie evidence of due process violations, the Commission strictly applies this doctrine. For example, it ruled in *Nelson E. Jiménez v Colombia* that the petition, which dealt with the adjudication of a family law dispute, was inadmissible on this basis because, rather than

[21] Pinzón, 'The "Victim" Requirement', 377 (emphasis added).

[22] *Wilma Rosa Posadasv Argentina* (2001), IACHR, No. 122/01, Annual Report 2001, para 10 (emphasis added). See also *Carlos Alberto López Urquía v Honduras* (2005), IACHR, No. 83/05, Annual Report 2005, at note 46.

[23] *Lopez Aurelli v Argentina* (1990), IACHR, No. 74/90, Annual Report 1990, paras 20 et seq.

[24] European Commission on Human Rights, D.6172/73 (UK) 7/7/75, 3/77. See also D.7987/77 (Aus.) 12/13/79, 18/31, where the Commission said that it could 'examine how the evidence has been obtained, but not how it has been assessed by the Court, unless there has been gross unfairness'.

demonstrating violations of the right to due process or judicial protection, the petitioners essentially asked the IACHR to re-examine the evidence presented in connection with internal disciplinary proceedings in order to evaluate a final decision pronounced by a domestic disciplinary tribunal.[25]

C. Deference regarding the legality of the application of domestic laws by national courts

As illustrated by the *Marzioni* case, the Inter-American institutions prefer to defer to national courts when it comes to interpreting domestic laws or assessing the legality of their application in the domestic sphere.[26]

In the *López Urquía v Honduras* case, where the petitioner alleged that the State had wrongly interpreted and applied the Honduran State Contracting Law in a context of public bids for service contracts, the Commission indicated that the:

> mere disagreement of the petitioners with the interpretation domestic courts have made of pertinent legal provisions does not constitute violations of the Convention. Interpretation of the law, pertinent proceedings, and weighing of evidence is, *inter alia*, the exercise of the domestic jurisdiction function, which cannot be replaced by the IACHR.[27]

However, the difference between mere errors in the interpretation or application of internal laws and those errors which result in violations of the right to judicial protection or other rights protected by the Convention is often very slim. For example, in the *Narciso Palacios v Argentina* case, the petitioner, a civil servant who had been administratively dismissed and later prevented from judicially challenging his dismissal, alleged that he could not access judicial remedies because the Argentine Supreme Court retroactively changed its interpretation on the admissibility requirements for judicial review of such administrative decisions. The Commission considered that the petitioner was denied access to effective judicial protection on the basis of the retroactive application of a legal criterion that altered the interpretation of a legal provision applicable to the petitioner's case.[28]

As this illustrates, Inter-American institutions refrain from applying the fourth instance formula where there is a prima facie case of arbitrariness in the interpretation of domestic laws by national courts. This is again exemplified by the *Carranza v Argentina* decision, dealing with the dismissal of a judge during the Argentine dictatorship, where the judicial authorities found the case non-justiciable, relying on the 'political question doctrine'. The Commission noted that:

[25] *Nelson E. Jiménez v Colombia* (1997), IACHR, No. 4/97, Annual Report 1996, para 27.

[26] *Marzioni v Argentina*, paras 50 et seq.

[27] *Carlos Alberto López Urquía*, para 72. See similarly *Juan Milla Bermúdez v Honduras* (1997), IACHR, No. 46/96, Annual Report 1996; *Carlos Alberto García Saccone v Argentina* (1998), IACHR, No. 8/98, Annual Report 1997.

[28] *Narciso Palacios v Argentina* (1999), IACHR, No. 105/99, Annual Report 1999. See also Pinzón, 'The "Victim" Requirement', 378.

[t]he removal of magistrates by order of the competent body and in accordance with established constitutional procedure is one thing, but the 'dismissal of a magistrate' by an illegitimate authority without competence, with utter disregard for the procedure prescribed by the Constitution, is quite another. The first under internal legislation, might well be non-justiciable, but the second would be unconstitutional and unlawful, and it is up to the Courts to review it and declare so.[29]

The IACHR further indicated that it could not 'pass judgment on the wisdom or efficacy of a judicial doctrine per se, unless its application results in a violation of any of the rights protected by the American Convention', and it concluded that in the case before it the effect of the political question doctrine was to preclude a decision on the merits of the petitioner's claims.[30]

In addition to the interpretation and application of domestic law, the fourth instance formula can similarly be applied to allegations regarding the compatibility of domestic norms with a State's internal legal order, or regarding the internal legality of the process used to adopt such norms.[31] Indeed, as indicated by Professor Monica Pinto, the Commission's authority to make recommendations with respect to the State's obligation to adopt progressive measures, including legislative measures, to implement the Convention,[32] does not extend to ruling 'as to how a legal norm is adopted in the internal order', a power which belongs to the competent organs of the State. In a specific case, the IACHR should only verify if a norm contradicts the Convention, not whether it contradicts the internal legal order of the State.[33]

D. Systemic preconditions for deference?

While the Commission and Court both apply the fourth instance doctrine, and accordingly defer to domestic judicial bodies, in cases where there is no prima facie evidence of *manifest arbitrariness*, or *unequivocal evidence of violations of the due process guarantees*, one can wonder to what extent they require that these judicial bodies operate in democracies which abide by the rule of law.

It should be noted that in the previously mentioned *Marzioni v Argentina* case, the IACHR indicated that:

[i]n democratic societies, where the courts function according to a system of powers established by the Constitution and domestic legislation, it is for those courts to review the matters brought before them. Where it is clear that there has been a violation of one of the rights protected by the Convention, then the Commission is competent to review. The Commission has full authority to adjudicate irregularities of domestic judicial

[29] *Gustavo Carranza v Argentina* (1997), IACHR, No. 30/97, Annual Report 1997, para 58.

[30] *Gustavo Carranza v Argentina*, paras 58 and 45.

[31] See eg *Certain Attributes of the Inter-American Commission on Human Rights (Arts. 41, 42, 44, 46, 47, 50 and 51 of the American Convention on Human Rights)* (1993), Advisory Opinion OC-13/93, IACtHR, Series A, No. 13, para 37.

[32] See Convention, Articles 1, 2 and 41.

[33] Pinto, 'National and International Courts', 262–3.

proceedings which result in manifest violations of due process or of any of the rights protected by the Convention.[34]

In fact, some of the examples presented above, illustrate well that the IACHR is unwilling to defer to domestic courts, which refuse to ensure some form of review of decisions taken under authoritarian regimes.

As indicated by Professor Diego Rodríguez Pinzón, these cases show that a greater degree of deference is given to the independent and impartial judiciaries of democracies, whereas decisions of courts lacking such qualities, including in authoritarian regimes, will be subject to closer scrutiny by the IACHR. Indeed, Professor Pinzón asserts that:

> [t]he mandate of the Commission has a dual dimension: political and judicial. In a hemisphere where States with different levels of democratic development coexist and there are certain states that still have gross and systematic violations of human rights in their jurisdiction, the Commission must use its mechanisms in a creative and effective way to induce progress in the general human rights situation.[35]

This highlights the fact that, in contexts of systemic impunity, in particular in post-armed conflict or post-dictatorship transitions towards democracy, the Commission and the Court should not and have not deferred to local institutions where domestic authorities were unable to ensure the judicial protection of rights and, consequently, permitted impunity to persist. This is further discussed below.

III. Reviewing Judicial and Legislative Processes and the Struggle against Impunity

From early on, the IAHRS has contributed significantly to the development of standards dealing with States' obligations to eliminate impunity, a problem that has marked the recent history of the Americas.[36] Both the Commission and the Court have reviewed and condemned judicial and legislative State practices that contribute to impunity.

A. Reviewing judicial processes to enforce a State's obligation to ensure effective investigations

In its emblematic 1988 *Velásquez Rodríguez v Honduras* judgment, concerning allegations of the abduction, arbitrary detention and torture of students by the Honduran security forces, the Court concluded that the State was responsible for the victims' disappearance—even though this was not necessarily directly carried out by agents of the State—because of its failure to fulfil the obligation to prevent

[34] *Marzioni v Argentina*, paras 60 et seq. See also *Abella v Argentina* (1997), IACHR, No. 5/97, Annual Report 1997, para 143.

[35] Pinzón, 'The "Victim" Requirement', 377 and 380.

[36] On this issue, see Duhaime, 'Achievements and challenges', 222 et seq.

this disappearance or to punish those responsible, thus contravening the Member States' obligation to respect and ensure human rights and guarantee the right to judicial protection, as required by the Convention.[37] While the State alleged it had carried out the adequate and relevant judicial proceedings, the IACtHR did not hesitate to review the quality of such proceedings and to conclude that the inefficiency of the judicial authorities' work triggered the State's international responsibility. More specifically, the Court indicated that the State must take reasonable steps to prevent violations and must use all means at its disposal to investigate violations, identify and punish those responsible, and compensate the victims. The State fails to comply with such an obligation if its apparatus prevents the provision of quick remedies to the victims and allows violations to go unpunished, including by allowing private persons or groups to act freely and with impunity to the detriment of the rights recognized by the Convention. Investigations must be undertaken in a serious manner, and not as a mere formality preordained to be ineffective, they must have a concrete objective and be assumed by the State as part of its legal obligations (ie not as a step taken by private interests that depends upon the initiative of the victim, without an effective search for the truth by the government).[38] The IACtHR took into consideration the systemic incapacity of the judicial authorities to resolve these types of human rights violations, namely forced disappearances, based on its finding that, at the time of the alleged violations, all *habeas corpus* motions were systematically rejected by judicial authorities and that the majority of attorneys were unable or unwilling, out of fear, to take on human rights cases.

This decision marked the inauguration of the subsequent developments of the Inter-American jurisprudence regarding the IAHRS's ability to review the quality of investigations conducted with respect to allegations of human rights violations.[39] Interestingly, when carrying out such reviews, both the Commission[40] and the Court[41] have relied on universal technical guidelines such as the *UN Manual on the Effective Prevention and Investigation of Extra-Legal, Arbitrary and Summary Executions*,[42] which provide very detailed qualitative indicators regarding criminal investigations. In addition, not only have both Inter-American bodies refused to defer to domestic investigations when there are alleged violations of the right to judicial guarantees and judicial protection leading to impunity,

[37] *Velásquez Rodríguez (Honduras)*. See also Dinah Shelton, 'Private Violence, Public Wrongs and the Responsibility of States', 13(1) *Fordham International Law Journal* 1 (1989–90).

[38] *Velásquez Rodríguez (Honduras)*, paras 174 et seq. See, more recently, *Ximenes-Lopes (Brazil)* (2006), IACtHR, Series C, No. 149, at para 148; *Goiburuet al (Paraguay)* (2006), IACtHR, Series C, No. 153, para 117. See also Shelton, 'Private Violence', 10.

[39] See eg *Manuel Stalin Bolaños Quiñones v Ecuador* (1996), IACHR, No. 10/95, Annual Report 1995, at para 76; *Abella v Argentina; Severiano Santiz Gomez and others, Ejido Morelia v Mexico* (1997), IACHR, No. 48/97, Annual Report 1997. See also *Paniagua Morales et al (Guatemala)* (1998), IACtHR, Series C, No. 37, para 173.

[40] See eg *Víctor Hernández Vásquez v El Salvador* (1999), IACHR, No. 65/99, Annual Report 1998, paras 63 et seq. See also *Manuel Stalin Bolaños v Ecuador*, paras 32–4; *Abella v Argentina*, paras 413–24 and *Ejido Morelia v Mexico*, paras 109–12.

[41] See eg *Moiwana Village (Suriname)* (2005), IACtHR, Series C, No. 124, para 124.

[42] UN Doc. E/ST/CSDHA/.12 (1991).

they have also reiterated that, at the national level, 'state authorities cannot hide behind mechanisms such as official secrets or confidentiality of the information or behind reasons of public interest or national security, to justify not providing the information required by the judicial or administrative authorities in charge of the investigation or pending proceedings.'[43]

Not surprisingly, this qualitative assessment of domestic investigations is not an easy task and may give rise to uneven results. For example, in the case of *Nogueira de Carvalhoet al v Brazil*,[44] dealing with impunity surrounding the murder of a renowned human rights defender, the judicial authorities did undertake an investigation, identify suspects, and try them. Notwithstanding the fact that the criminal trials did not lead to any conviction and that the victim's murder was left unpunished, the IACtHR did not find that the State violated the victim's right to judicial protection. Referring to language similar to that of the fourth instance formula, it stated that:

> courts of the State are expected to examine the facts and evidence submitted in particular cases. It is not the responsibility of this Court to replace the domestic jurisdiction by ordering concrete methods or forms for investigating and judging a specific case in order to obtain a better or more effective outcome; instead, its role is to find whether or not, in the steps actually taken domestically, the State's international obligations embodied in Articles 8 and 25 of the American Convention have been violated.[45]

The Court also indicated that it had taken into account 'the body of evidence and...conducted a thorough study of the entire series of police and judicial procedures conducted', before concluding that the alleged violation of the right to a fair trial had not been demonstrated.[46] Interestingly, the Court did not refer to the previously mentioned UN qualitative indicators and did not address the significant delays in the investigation, its suspension, nor the subsequent discovery of relevant evidence by the victim's relatives. One should note, however, that many of those factual elements took place before the date of the State's acceptance of the Court's mandatory jurisdiction, which could explain, in this specific instance, part of the tribunal's reserve.[47]

B. Transitional justice and the review of internal measures

Similarly, in the light of the objective of ending impunity in the region, both the Inter-American Commission and Court have not hesitated to review judicial and legislative measures adopted in contexts of post-conflict or post-dictatorship

[43] *Case Tiu Tojin (Guatemala)* (2008), IACtHR, Series C, No. 190, para 77.

[44] *Case of Nogueira de Carvalho et al (Brazil)* (2006), IACtHR, Series C, No. 161. See also *Case of Castillo Gonsález (Venezuela)* (2012), IACtHR, Series C, No. 256, paras 133-172.

[45] *Case of Nogueira de Carvalho et al (Brazil)*, para 80.

[46] *Case of Nogueira de Carvalho et al (Brazil)*, para 79.

[47] *Case of Nogueira de Carvalho et al (Brazil)*, paras 79 and 81. On this matter see also Bernard Duhaime, Ariel E. Dulitzky, 'Review of the Case Law of the Inter-American Human Rights System in 2006', 19(2) *Quebec Journal of International Law* 331 (2006), 351 et seq.

transitions, refusing to defer, ie grant appreciation, to local authorities with respect to the need to balance, in such contexts, the aims of justice, peace and reconciliation.

Accordingly, the IACHR condemned domestic laws which granted amnesty to all those who were possibly responsible for human rights violations,[48] indicating that, in such circumstances, the State cannot renounce its international obligation to investigate and punish the perpetrators, and that situations of impunity arising from de facto or de jure amnesties contravene the Convention and undermine the responsibility of the State.[49] In the 2001 *Barrios Altos v Peru* case, dealing with a massacre committed by the armed forces and the subsequent impunity resulting from the application of an amnesty law, the IACtHR reaffirmed that this type of law is incompatible with Articles 1.1, 8, and 25 of the Convention, inasmuch as '[it] precludes the identification of the individuals who are responsible for human rights violations, because it obstructs the investigation and access to justice and prevents the victims and their next of kin from knowing the truth and receiving the corresponding reparation.'[50]

In so doing, neither the Commission nor the Court ruled on the legality of the adoption process nor on the compatibility of such laws with the internal legal order itself. Rather, they verified whether these norms contradicted the Convention.[51]

Interestingly, in the similar case of *Almonacid-Arellano et al v Chile*,[52] dealing with the torture of a political dissident and subsequent impunity resulting from the self-amnesty laws adopted by the Pinochet regime, the Court not only reviewed the local legislative and judicial authorities' actions in the light of the AHCR, but it also recognized the domestic tribunals' positive obligation to conduct a similar review.[53]

Finally, in a similar manner the IAHRS has frequently reviewed the compatibility with the ACHR of institutional frameworks which allow for or encourage impunity. For example, both the Commission and the Court condemned internal laws and processes, which provided that human rights violations perpetrated by members of the armed forces be tried before military rather than civil tribunals. Both Inter-American institutions stated that military tribunals could not be considered to have the independence required to judge

[48] See eg IACHR, *Third Report on the Situation of Human Rights in Colombia*, OEA/Ser.L/V/II.102 Doc. 9 rev. 1, 26 February 1999.

[49] IACHR, *Report on the Situation of Human Rights in Peru*, OEA/Ser.L/V/II.106, Doc. 59 rev., 2 June 2000, paras 215–30.

[50] *Barrios Altos (Peru)* (2001), IACtHR, Series C, No. 75, paras 43 et seq.

[51] On this issue see Pinto, 'National and International Courts', 262.

[52] *Almonacid-Arellano et al (Chile)* (2006), IACtHR, Series C, No. 154.

[53] *Almonacid-Arellano et al (Chile)*, at para 124. On this matter see also Duhaime and Dulitzky 'Review', 353 et seq. On this complex issue see also *Gomes Lund et al (Brazil)* (2010), IACtHR, Series C, No. 219 and Andre de Carvalho Ramos, 'Crimes da ditadura militar: a ADPF 153 e a Corte Interamericana de Direitos Humanos' in Luiz Flávio Gomes, Valerio de Oliveira Mazzuoli (eds), *Crimes da ditadura militar* (São Paulo: Editora Revista dos Tribunais, 2011) 174, dealing with the challenges facing Brazil in this regard.

violations perpetrated by the armed forces, and specified that civil tribunals should hear these types of cases.[54] Similarly the IACHR and the IACtHR both denounced similar measures granting jurisdiction to ad hoc or special courts or military tribunals for judging civilians accused of security offences in times of emergency.[55]

It should however be underscored that, in cases where impunity is not a central matter, or when there is no apparent violation of the right to due process or judicial protection of rights, the IAHRS has often recognized the importance of deferring to domestic authorities and has sometimes specifically referred to and applied the doctrine of margin of appreciation, as is further examined below.

IV. The Applicability of the Doctrine of the Margin of Appreciation in the Americas

As is the case in the European and United Nations human rights systems,[56] the Inter-American institutions have also referred to the doctrine of margin of appreciation (DMA),[57] according to which:

> [b]y reason of their direct and continuous contact with the vital forces of their countries, State authorities are in principle in a better position than the international judge to give an opinion on the exact content of these requirements as well as on the 'necessity' of a 'restriction' or 'penalty' intended to meet them.... This margin is given both to the domestic legislator ('prescribed by law') and to the bodies, judicial amongst others, that are called upon to interpret and apply the laws in force.[58]

[54] On this matter see eg IACHR, *Report Colombia*. See also *Asencios Lindo et al v Peru* (2000), IACHR, No. 49/00, Annual Report 2000; *Nadege Dorzema et al (Dominican Republic)* (2012), IACtHR, Series C, No. 251.

[55] See eg IACHR, *Report on the Situation of Human Rights in Nicaragua*, OEA/Ser.L/V/II.53, doc. 25, 30 June 1981, 62 et seq; IACHR, *Report on the Situation of Human Rights in Chile*, OEA/Ser.L/V/II.66, doc. 17, 9 September 1985, 190 et seq. See also *Loayza Tamayo (Peru)* (1998), IACtHR, Series C, No. 42. See also *Castillo Petruzziet al (Peru)* (1999), IACtHR, Series C, No. 52.

[56] See eg *Hertzberg et al v Finland*, Communication No. 61/1979, UN Doc. CCPR/C/OP/1 at 124 (1985), para 10.3. See also *Handyside v United Kingdom*, 24 ECtHR, Series A at 17 (1976); *Sunday Times v the United Kingdom* (app. nos. 7151/75 and 7152/75), ECtHR 1982. See also Chapter 13, dealing with the DMA in the European system. See generally Andrew Legg, *The Margin of Appreciation in International Human Rights Law: Deference and Proportionality* (Oxford: Oxford University Press, 2012); Eyal Benvenisti, 'Margin of Appreciation, Consensus and Universal Standards', 31 *International Law and Politics* 843 (1999); Howard C. Yourow, *The Margin of Appreciation Doctrine in The Dynamics of European Human Rights Jurisprudence* (Dordrecht: Martinus Nijhoff Publishers, 1996).

[57] See generally Paola Andrea Acosta Alvarado, Manuel Núñez Poblete (eds), *El Margen de Apreciación en el Sistema Interamericano de Derechos Humanos: Proyecciones Regionales y Nacionales* (México: Instituto de Investigaciones Jurídicas, UNAM, 2012); see also Francisco R. Barbosa Delgado, 'Los límites a la doctrina del margen nacional de apreciación en el Tribunal Europeo y la Corte Interamericana de Derechos Humanos: intervención judicial en torno a ciertos derechos de las minorías étnicas y culturales', 26 *Revista Derecho del Estado* 107 (2011); Pinto, 'National and International Courts', 255 et seq.

[58] *Handyside v United Kingdom*, para 48.

Yet, the Commission and the Court have applied this doctrine with great caution and in many fewer instances than their European counterparts.[59] In addition, both bodies applied this doctrine using a great variety of names and designations, making such references sometimes difficult to recognize.[60]

This section will first present the DMA and the debates that its use has generated. It will then address its limited application in the context of state of emergency, and in the interpretation given to limitations of rights. It will finally explore the use of this approach regarding broader human rights policy issues.

A. Should the doctrine of the margin of appreciation be applied in the IAHRS?

While the Commission had referred to different variations of the DMA to interpret the scope of certain obligations imposed on States,[61] the Court mainly developed its reasoning on the use of this doctrine in its Advisory Opinion OC-4, dealing with certain proposed amendments to the naturalization provisions of the Constitution of Costa Rica. While discussing whether these provisions were discriminatory because they created different regimes of naturalization, the Court indicated that:

> Although it cannot be denied that a given factual context may make it more or less difficult to determine whether or not one has encountered the situation described in the foregoing paragraph, it is equally true that, starting with the notion of the essential oneness and dignity of the human family, *it is possible to identify circumstances in which considerations of public welfare may justify departures to a greater or lesser degree from the standards articulated above. One is here dealing with values which take on concrete dimensions in the face of those real situations in which they have to be applied and which permit in each case a certain margin of appreciation in giving expression to them.*
>
> ...as far as the granting of naturalization is concerned, it is for the granting state to determine whether and to what extent applicants for naturalization have complied with the conditions deemed to ensure an effective link between them and the value system and interests of the society to which they wish to belong. To this extent *there exists no doubt that it is within the sovereign power of Costa Rica to decide what standards should determine the granting or denial of nationality to aliens who seek it*, and to establish certain reasonable differentiations based on factual differences which, viewed objectively, recognize that some applicants have a closer affinity than others to Costa Rica's value system and interests.[62]

[59] On this issue, see Héctor Faúndez Ledesma, *El sistema interamericano de protección de los derechos humanos. Aspectos institucionales y procesales*, 3rd edn (San José: Instituto Interamericano de Derechos Humanos, 2004) 57.

[60] See eg Manuel Núñez Poblete, 'Sobre la doctrina del margennacional de apreciación. La experiencia latinoamericana confrontada y el *thelos* constitucional de una técnica de adjudicación del derecho internacional de los derechos humanos. Ensayo introductorio', in Alvarado, Poblete (eds), *El Margen de Apreciación* and Francisco R. Barbosa Delgado, 'El Margen Nacional De Apreciación En El Derecho Internacional De Los Derechos Humanos: Entre El Estado De Derecho Y La Sociedad Democrática', 58 et seq. See also Legg, *The Margin of Appreciation*.

[61] See eg *Rios Montt v Guatemala* (1993), IACHR, No. 30/93, Annual Report 1993, para 24.

[62] *Proposed Amendments to the Naturalization Provisions of the Constitution of Costa Rica* (1984), Advisory Opinion OC-4/84, IACtHR, Series A, No. 4, paras 58–9.

While it referred to the margin of appreciation enjoyed by States in their establishment of policies regarding the granting of nationality, in order to reach the conclusion that the conditions in the instant case did not amount to discrimination, the Court also provided a warning as to the limits such State discretion and as to potential discriminatory abuses, indicating that it did not approve the practice:

> which prevails in some areas to limit to an exaggerated and unjustified degree the political rights of naturalized individuals. Most of these situations... constitute clear instances of discrimination on the basis of origin or place of birth, unjustly creating two distinct hierarchies of nationals in one single country.

More precisely, the Court stated that the establishment of requirements such as demonstration of a sufficient command of the language used in the country and proof of knowledge of the country's history and values were not unreasonable nor unjustifiable conditions insofar as they are intended to establish the bonds underlying the acquisition of the new nationality. However, it noted that 'there exists the risk that these requirements will become the vehicle for subjective and arbitrary judgments as well as instruments for the effectuation of discriminatory policies which, although not directly apparent on the face of the law, could well be the consequence of its application.'[63]

There have been several views formulated in favour of or against such use of the DMA. The former Secretary General of the OAS, César Gaviria, stated in 1996 that:

> [p]articular attention needs to be paid to cases that have already undergone a thorough treatment by domestic courts. In these cases, our regional system has a real opportunity to re-connect with domestic judicial systems by articulating a specific jurisprudence of deference to domestic proceedings. What the regional court is entitled to review and what it should accept from a domestic judicial proceeding needs to be clarified. While issues of law specifically keyed to violations of the ACHR or Charter are thoroughly reviewable by the IACHR, issues of fact might receive greater deference. Note, too, that how a domestic court understands a domestic law is also presumably an issue of fact and should be granted deference.[64]

Similarly, several authors have maintained that a greater use of the doctrine could allow for a re-appropriation of local and regional particularisms that might have been pushed aside in the Americas with the ascension of human rights and the processes of democratization in the region; also arguing that it would correspond to the tendency towards greater subsidiarity of the IAHRS; and finally that it could avoid the perception of international justice as disconnected with and unrelated to local realities.[65]

[63] *Proposed Amendments to the Naturalization Provisions of the Constitution of Costa Rica* at paras 62–3.

[64] César Gaviria, 'Towards a New Vision of the Inter-American Human Rights System', 4 *Journal of Latin American Affairs* 4 (1996) 9. See also Pinto, 'National and International Courts', 256.

[65] Poblete, 'Doctrina', 40, 41, and 43. See also Delgado, 'Margen Nacional', 52 et seq.

Other experts, however, have expressed very strong reservations regarding the use of the DMA, specifically in the context of the struggle against impunity in the Americas, stating for example that 'if the Commission had deferred to the domestic courts' fact finding in the thousands of cases of "disappeared" persons that had been brought to the IACHR or those relating to persons tried by "anonymous" judges, no state would ever have been condemned.'[66] Similarly, the former President of the IACtHR, Professor Antönio Cançado Trinidade, strongly condemned the use of this doctrine. He took into consideration the limits placed on domestic judicial authorities in the region, who face problems of pressure and intimidation, and are often incapable of stopping impunity.[67]

As mentioned previously, the doctrine has been seldom used in the IAHRS and seems to have been the object of great caution, as indicated by the Commission itself, which reaffirmed 'the restrictive character that this margin of appreciation should utilize, which should always be conceived with a view to strengthening the system and its objectives.'[68]

B. The limited application of the margin of appreciation in the context of emergencies

One of the most important distinctions in the use of the DMA between the European and the Inter-American systems has been on the issue of whether or not to defer to domestic authorities in states of emergency. It has been noted that in Europe:

> [t]he margins doctrine initially responded to concerns of national governments that international policies could jeopardize their national security. This may explain the initial application of the doctrine in the context of derogations from treaty obligations due to self-proclaimed states of national emergency...This rationale later was expanded to allow each country wide discretion to select policies that would regulate potentially harmful activities, such as incitement to violence or racist speech, by means befitting each State's unique circumstances and societal constrains.[69]

In the Americas, a continent which has suffered its share of derogations in contexts of armed conflicts or of authoritarian regimes, the Commission and Court have not deferred to domestic authorities when assessing the appropriateness of declaring a state of emergency or when evaluating the types of measures adopted in such circumstances.[70] In fact, both the IACHR and the IACtHR have set very

[66] Christina Cerna, 'Clarifying a Reviewing Standard', 4 *Journal of Latin American Affairs* 54 (1996), 55. See also Pinto, 'National and International Courts', 257.

[67] Antônio Augusto Cançado Trindade, *El derecho internacional de los derechos humanos en el siglo XXI*, 2nd edn (Santiago: Editorial Jurídica de Chile, 2006), 389–91. See also Poblete, 'Doctrina', 40, 41 and 43; Delgado, 'Margen Nacional', 12 et seq.

[68] *Rios Montt v Guatemala*, para 31; Poblete, 'Doctrina', 14.

[69] Benvenisti, 'Margin of Appreciation', 845, referring to *Zana v Turkey* (app. no. 18954/91), ECtHR 1997 and to *Jersild v Denmark* (app. no. 15890/89), ECtHR 1994. On this issue, see also Chapter 14 of this volume, dealing with freedom of expression and hate speech in the European system.

[70] See generally IACHR, *Report on Terrorism*, paras 49 et seq.

strict conditions limiting the ability of States to suspend human rights in those situations and have constantly reviewed domestic decisions in this regard, applying general principles of proportionality, necessity and non-discrimination.[71]

For example, in the case of *Walter Humberto Vasquez Vejarano v Peru,* dealing with the dismissal of a judge during a state of emergency, the Commission indicated that:

> [a]lthough in general the 'margin of appreciation' is left to the states themselves to determine the need for declaring a state of emergency, inasmuch as they have direct and immediate knowledge of the factual circumstances in the country, such margin of appreciation is not unlimited. The Commission has the duty to evaluate whether the circumstances that caused the Peruvian government to declare an emergency... fit in with the conventional meaning of the terms 'war, public danger' or 'other emergency that threatens the independence or security of the State party'.

The Commission decided it had to evaluate, for instance, whether Peru exceeded 'the limited extent required by the exigencies of the situation'. Accordingly, the margin of appreciation at the internal level goes hand in hand with Inter-American supervision. The Commission must properly assess such relevant factors as the nature of the rights affected by the suspension, the circumstances behind the state of emergency and its duration.[72]

Thus, when assessing the legality of a declaration of a state of emergency, the Commission has indicated that:

> [1] There must be an extremely grave situation of such a nature that there is a real threat to law and order or the security of the state, including an armed conflict, public danger, or other emergency that imperils the public order or security of a member state; [2] Any suspension may only be for such time as is strictly required by the exigencies of the situation and may not be proclaimed for indefinite or prolonged periods; [3] Any suspension may only be effectuated to the extent strictly required by the exigencies of the situation, and thereby precludes the unnecessary suspension of rights, the imposition of restrictions more severe than necessary, or the unnecessary extension of suspension to regions or areas not affected by the emergency; [4] Any suspension of rights cannot entail discrimination of any kind on such grounds as race, color, sex, language, religion or social origin; [5] Any suspension must be compatible with all of a member state's other obligations under international law; and [6] The declaration of a state of emergency must be notified to the members states of the OAS with sufficient information that others may determine the nature of the emergency, whether the measures are strictly required by the exigencies of the situation, and whether they might be discriminatory or inconsistent with the state's other obligations under international law.[73]

[71] See eg *Neira Alegria et al (Peru)* (1995), IACtHR, Series C, No. 21. See also *Hildegard María Feldman v Colombia* (1995), IACHR, No. 15/95, Annual Report 1995, para 57.

[72] *Walter Humberto Vásquez Vejarano v Peru* (1999), IACHR, No. 48/00, Annual Report 1999. See also Poblete, 'Doctrina', 19.

[73] IACHR, *Report on Terrorism*, paras 51 et seq. See also IACHR, *Annual Report of the IACHR 1980-81*, OEA/Ser.L/V/II.54, Doc. 9 rev. 1, 16 October 1981; IACHR, *Report Peru; Asencios Lindo et al v Peru*, para 67.

In addition, the Inter-American institutions have constantly assessed the legality of measures adopted by States during states of emergency, reviewing if these actions were necessary and proportional and, when adopted in situations of armed conflict, if they respected the *lex specialis* of international humanitarian law,[74] in particular regarding the right to life, the right to physical integrity and other guarantees which cannot be suspended in time of war or similar public danger. It has done so with respect to alleged violations of due process rights in the context of the United States invasion of Grenada,[75] to evaluate allegations of torture during the Guatemalan civil war,[76] to assess the legality of the use of lethal force by the authorities during military operations in the Colombian conflict[77] and during the assault on the *La Tablada* barracks in Argentina.[78]

Finally, as mentioned above, the Commission and Court have systematically refused to defer to domestic authorities regarding extraordinary judicial processes undertaken in situations of emergency, when allegations were made that the rights to due process and judicial protection violations were violated.[79]

C. The doctrine of the margin of appreciation and the interpretation of restrictions of rights

The Inter-American institutions have referred to the DMA or some other form of recognition of deference towards States in situations where they considered measures adopted internally to limit the exercise of certain rights, when the provisions of the Convention that govern such rights allow such restrictions, as for instance is the case with the right to freedom of conscience and religion, to freedom of thought and expression, to assembly, to freedom of association, to property, to freedom of movement, to participate in government, etc. Such restrictions must generally be those 'prescribed by law that are necessary to protect public safety, order, health, or morals, or the rights or freedoms of others'. While some deference is granted to States regarding the application of such restrictions, 'they are, like derogation provisions, *governed by specific requirements that are the subject of strict and rigorous review by the supervisory bodies of the inter-American system.*'[80]

As established by the IACHR in the 1996 *X & Y v Argentina* case[81] and by the IACtHR in its Advisory Opinion OC-5/85,[82] such restrictions must be evaluated on a case-by-case basis. These measures should be previously adopted by

[74] IACHR, *Report on Terrorism*, para 61 et seq. See also Duhaime, 'Achievements and challenges'.

[75] *Coard et al v United States* (1999), IACHR, No. 109/99, Annual Report 1999.

[76] See *Bámaca Velásquez (Guatemala)* (2000), IACtHR, Series C, No. 70.

[77] See eg *Arturo Ribón Avilan v Colombia* (1997), IACHR, No. 26/97, Annual Report 1997.

[78] See eg *Abella v Argentina*.

[79] See eg IACHR, *Nicaragua Report*, 62 et seq; IACHR, *Chile Report*, 190 et seq; *Loayza Tamayo (Peru); Castillo Petruzzi et al (Peru)*.

[80] IACHR, *Report on Terrorism*, para 53.

[81] *X & Y v Argentina* (1996), IACHR, No. 38/96, Annual Report 1996, paras 54–71.

[82] *Compulsory Membership in an Association Prescribed by Law for the Practice of Journalism (Arts. 13 and 29 of the American Convention on Human Rights)* (1985), Advisory Opinion OC-5/85, IACtHR, Series A, No. 5, paras 36–7.

law (procedural requirements), be necessary for the security of all, be in accordance with the just demands of a democratic society, be applied with proportionality and be closely tailored to meeting their legitimate objective (substantive requirements).[83]

While the Inter-American institutions have reiterated their ability to review measures that restrict rights in order to assess their compatibility with the above-mentioned conditions, they have, from time to time, granted some degree of deference to States on such matters. This section does not intend to provide an exhaustive review of the jurisprudence on the topic. It will nevertheless offer a few examples to illustrate the development of the Inter-American doctrine on the matter.

Firstly, as indicated previously the Court has referred to and applied the doctrine of margin of appreciation regarding restrictions to the right to nationality (Article 20 ACHR) in the Advisory Opinion OC-4 dealing with certain proposed amendments to the naturalization provisions of the Constitution of Costa Rica.[84]

In addition, the Commission and the Court have used the DMA when addressing with the adequacy of domestic norms dealing with electoral processes and restricting the right to participate in government (Article 23 ACHR). For example, in the case of *Rios Montt v Guatemala*, regarding various acts of judicial, legislative and executive officials which resulted in the ineligibility of a former dictator to run as a candidate during a presidential election, the Commission considered that:

> the context of Guatemalan and international constitutional law in which this condition of ineligibility is placed is the appropriate dimension for analysis of the applicability of the Convention in general, and of the applicability of its Arts. 23 and 32 to the instant case, and from which the margin of appreciation allowed by international law can emerge.[85]

Nevertheless, as previously mentioned, the IACHR reaffirmed 'the restrictive character that this margin of appreciation should utilize, which should always be conceived with a view to strengthening the system and its objectives',[86] and thoroughly analysed the applicable domestic and international legislation as well as the judicial proceeding initiated by the alleged victim. While rejecting the case as inadmissible, it concluded that:

> the grounds for ineligibility emerge from an act of a Constitutional Convention elected by democratic vote in which the Guatemalan people decided through their

[83] IACHR, *Report on Terrorism*, paras 54–5. The Court has suggested that both *public order* and *general welfare* may be considered in evaluating such limitations, the former referring to the conditions that assure the normal and harmonious functioning of institutions based on a coherent system of values and principles, and the latter referring to the conditions of social life that allow members of society to reach the highest level of personal development and the optimum achievement of democratic values.

[84] Advisory Opinion OC-4/84.

[85] *Rios Montt v Guatemala*, para 24. See also Poblete, 'Doctrina', 14.

[86] *Rios Montt v Guatemala*, para 31.

representatives . . . that it was necessary to maintain such grounds, which are already founded in Guatemala's constitutional history . . . , and moreover to make them permanent. Therefore as analysed above, within those conditions any constitutional system of law possesses the right to make its operation more effective, and to defend the integrity of its citizens' rights.[87]

Similarly, in the *Statehood Solidarity Committee v United States* case, dealing with measures restricting the capacity of citizens of the District of Columbia to elect representatives to the US Congress, the IACHR indicated that:

[i]n interpreting Article 23 of the American Convention, the Commission has recognized that a degree of autonomy must be afforded to states in organizing their political institutions so as to give effect to these rights, as the right to political participation leaves room for a wide variety of forms of government. As the Commission has appreciated, its role or objective is not to create a uniform model of representative democracy for all states, but rather is to determine whether a state's laws infringe fundamental human rights.[88]

Nevertheless, the IACHR did not fully defer to domestic authorities and norms on the matter, and assessed the compatibility of the domestic restrictions with the applicable international standards, stating that:

the conduct of states in giving effect to the right to representative government, whether by way of their constitutions or otherwise, is [not] immune from review by the Commission. Rather, certain minimum standards or conditions exist respecting the manner in which this right is given effect, which must be shown to have been satisfied. These standards or conditions relate primarily to the nature of permissible limitations that may be imposed on the exercise of such rights.[89]

Ultimately, after reviewing all the information in the record, including the relevant legislation, judicial decisions and executive actions, the Commission concluded that the relevant restrictions on the right to participate in government had in fact been curtailed in such a manner as to deprive the victims of the very essence and effectiveness of that right, without adequate justification being shown by the State for this curtailment.[90]

With regard to restrictions applied to the right to freedom of expression, the Inter-American institutions have been very hesitant to grant deference to States, preferring to examine closely the scope and effect of restrictive domestic measures. Both the Commission and Court have reviewed with great scrutiny those laws and State actions which provide for prior censorship,[91] for subsequent penalties,

[87] *Rios Montt v Guatemala*, para 38.

[88] *Statehood Solidarity Committee v United States* (2003), IACHR, No. 98/03, Annual Report 2003, para 88.

[89] *Statehood Solidarity Committee v United States* at para 89.

[90] *Statehood Solidarity Committee v United States* at para101. This approach should be distinguished from the dissenting opinion of Commissioner José Zalaquett in this case, who would have favoured an approach granting more deference to the State. See similarly the dissenting opinion of Commissioner Robert Goldman in *Andrés Aylwin Azocar and Others v Chile* (1999), IACHR, No. 137/99, Annual Report 1999, paras 4 and 10.

[91] *Olmedo Bustos et al (Chile)* (2001), IACtHR, Series C, No. 73.

in particular criminal sanctions[92] and sanctions during electoral campaigns,[93] the obligation to belong to professional corporations[94] as well as other forms of indirect restrictions. In the *Herrera-Ulloa v Costa Rica* decision, more commonly known as the *La Nación* case (where a journalist was sued for reproducing someone else's web-based article alleging that a civil servant was corrupt), the Court expressly refused to apply the DMA and rather examined the effectiveness of the legal proceedings in question, indicating that States may not establish restrictions or requirements inimical to the very essence of the judicial protection of the right to freedom of expression (in the instant case, the right to appeal a judgment).[95]

D. Allowing for other forms of deference?

While it is difficult to determine whether the Inter-American institutions have developed a coherent doctrine on the margin of appreciation under other names, one could consider that both the Commission and Court sometimes defer to States, or at least contemplate doing so, in some other circumstances,[96] *inter alia* when analysing the scope of existing rights or the existence of rights not expressly provided for in human rights instruments, assessing whether distinct treatments are justified or constitute discrimination, and addressing the implementation of economic, social and cultural rights.

1. *Deference when assessing the scope of existing rights*

It has happened that the Inter-American bodies have granted some deference to States when assessing the scope of existing rights. For example, in the 1981 *Baby Boy v United States* case,[97] dealing with the issue of abortion, the Commission had to assess the scope of the right to life under the American Declaration. In doing so, the IACHR analysed the drafting history of Article I of the Declaration and concluded that the drafters had removed language, previously proposed during the negotiations over the said article, which protected the right to life *from the moment of conception*, and replaced it with its final wording ('Every human being has the right to life'), in order to avoid compatibility issues with the domestic laws of some States which allowed abortions under certain circumstances. The Commission also analysed the *travaux préparatoires* of Article 4 of the Convention and concluded that, during the drafting negotiations, the term 'in general' was inserted into the final version of the article as the result of a compromise between States that tolerated

[92] See eg IACHR, *Report on the Compatibility of 'Desacato' Laws with the American Convention on Human Rights*, OEA/Ser. L/V/II.88, Doc. 9 rev., 17 February 1995, 197–212; IACHR, *Annual Report of the IACHR, 1998* Volume III, Chapter IV A. OEA/Ser.L/V/II.102 Doc. 6 rev., 16 April 1999; and IACHR, *Annual Report of the IACHR, 2000* Volume III, Chapter III A.2. OEA/Ser.L/V/II.111 Doc. 20 rev., 16 April 2001. See also *Kimel v (Argentina)* (2008), IACtHR, Series C, No. 177.

[93] *Ricardo Canese (Paraguay)* (2004), IACtHR, Series C, No. 111.

[94] Advisory Opinion OC-5/85.

[95] *Herrera-Ulloa (Costa Rica)* (2004), IACtHR, Series C, No. 107, para 161.

[96] See Legg, *The Margin of Appreciation*; see also Delgado, 'Margen Nacional', 58 et seq.

[97] IACHR, No. 23/81, Annual Report 1980–1981.

abortion and those that were against it, and that this reflected the fact that the drafters did not intend to move away from the meaning of Article I of the Declaration. Accordingly, one could consider that the IACHR read into the text of the Declaration and of the Convention an express 'deference clause' granting some form of discretion to States on matters related to the regulation of abortion. The Commission finally concluded that the United States did not violate the American Declaration.[98]

2. *Deference when assessing the existence of rights not expressly provided for in human rights instruments*

Similarly, in cases alleging violations of rights not expressly provided for in the Convention, the Commission seems also to have deferred to States rather than expand existing rights. For example, in the case of *Cristián Daniel Sahli Vera et al v Chile*, the IACHR refused to recognize that the right to conscientious objection was contained in the right to freedom of conscience or religion or in the right to freedom from slavery. In doing so, it specifically highlighted that:

> international human rights jurisprudence recognizes the status of conscientious objectors in countries that provide for such status in their national laws. In countries that do not provide for conscientious objector status, the international human rights bodies find that there has been no violation of the right to freedom of thought, conscience or religion.[99]

3. *Deference when assessing whether different and distinct treatments are justified*

As noted in Section IV.A, the Inter-American institutions have sometimes granted some deference to States regarding measures, which treat different types of persons distinctly, when such distinctions are justified. This was precisely the issue in the Court's above-mentioned Advisory Opinion OC-4 on the proposed amendments to the naturalization provisions of the Constitution of Costa Rica, where the Court applied the DMA.[100] This is partly because, as in the case of restriction of rights (Section IV.C), both the Commission and the Court have developed tests which allow States to justify distinct treatment measures when they can be considered *necessary and proportionate*.[101] As indicated by the IACHR:

> [w]hile the doctrine of the inter-American human rights system, like that of other human rights regimes, does not prohibit all distinctions in treatment in the enjoyment

[98] See also Poblete, 'Doctrina', 19. See more generally on this issue Bernard Duhaime, 'Strengthening the Protection of Human Rights in the Americas: A Role for Canada?' in Monica Serrano (ed), *Human Rights Regimes in the Americas* (Tokyo: UN University Press, 2010).

[99] *Cristián Daniel Sahli Vera et al v Chile* (2005), IACHR, No. 43/05, Annual 2005, para 38. See also Poblete, 'Doctrina', 22.

[100] Advisory Opinion OC-5/85, paras 58–9.

[101] See generally Bernard Duhaime, 'Ver sune Amérique plus égalitaire? L'interdiction de la discrimination et le système interaméricain de protection des droits de la personne', in Ludovic Hennebel, Hélène Tigroudja (eds), *Le particularisme interaméricain des droits de l'homme* (Paris: Pedonne 2009), 151–82. See also Ariel E. Dulitzky, 'El principio de Igualdad y No discriminación. Claroscuros de la jurisprudencia interamericana', 3 *Anuario de derechos humanos* 15(2007).

of protected rights and freedoms, it requires at base that any permissible distinctions be based upon objective and reasonable justification, that they further a legitimate objective, regard being had to the principles which normally prevail in democratic societies, and that the means are reasonable and proportionate to the end sought.[102]

However, it should be noted that States enjoy very little leeway in constructing such justifications, as 'distinctions based on grounds explicitly enumerated under pertinent articles of international human rights instruments are subject to a particularly strict level of scrutiny whereby states must provide an especially weighty interest and compelling justification for the distinction'.[103] For example, in the *Ferrer-Mazorraet al v United States* case (dealing with some 3,000 Cubans said to have been detained in the United States due to their irregular entry into the country), the Commission specified that '[i]n the immigration context in particular... it is generally regarded in democratic societies as appropriate for states to afford aliens treatment that is distinct from that enjoyed by others within the State's jurisdiction to, for example, control aliens' entry into and residence in their territory'.[104] Nevertheless the IACHR added that 'any such distinctions must be shown by the State to be reasonable and proportionate to the objective sought in the circumstances.' It concluded that the distinct treatment of detention to which the victims were subjected did not meet these requirements, considering that the State had not demonstrated why and how the measures adopted—systematic administrative detention of those migrants because they were exiled by the Cuban regime—were necessary to reach the objective sought, and why other less restrictive measures could not have been implemented instead.[105]

Similarly in the *López-Álvarez v Honduras* case, the Court found that prohibiting a detainee from using his native Afro-descendent language in prison constituted a violation of the victim's right to freedom of expression and to equality. The IACtHR did not accept the State's justification—ensuring security within the detention centre—because the treatment was deemed obviously unnecessary and disproportionate. While reviewing the adequacy of the measure, the Court applied a particularly strict test, noting that:

the observance of rules in the collective treatment of the detainees within a criminal center, does not give the State, in the exercise of its power to punish, the legal authority to limit, in an unjustified manner, the freedom of the people to express themselves through any means and in the language chosen by them. [Here] the prohibition was issued regarding the native language of [the victim], which is the form of expression of the minority to which [he] belongs. Therefore the prohibition acquires a special seriousness, since the mother tongue represents an element of identity of [the victim and] affected his

[102] IACHR, *Report on Terrorism*, para 338. See also Advisory Opinion OC-5/85, para 56. See eg*Juridical Condition and Rights of the Undocumented Migrants* (2003), Advisory Opinion OC-18, IACtHR, Series A, No. 18; *Rafael Ferrer-Mazorra et al v United States* (2000), IACHR, No. 51/01, Annual Report 2000, para 238.

[103] See IACHR, *Report on Terrorism*, para 338.

[104] See *Rafael Ferrer-Mazorra et al v United States*, para 239.

[105] *Rafael Ferrer-Mazorra et al v United States* at paras 241–2.

personal dignity as a member of that community…States must take into consideration the information that differentiates the members of the Indian populations from that of the population in general, and that make up their cultural identity. Language [is] one of the most important elements of identity of any people, precisely because it guarantees the expression, diffusion, and transmission of their culture.[106]

Finally, one should note on this issue that, contrary to the European System where the lack of Member State consensus on specific complex social issues[107] has prompted the European Court to have recourse to the doctrine of the margin of appreciation—including when dealing with equality-related cases[108]—the Inter-American Court has been very reluctant to adopt such an approach in similar cases. For example, in the case of *Atala Riffo and Daughters v Chile,* dealing with the right of a lesbian woman to have guardianship of her children, the IACtHR expressly rejected the State's argument on the matter, pointing out that:

the alleged lack of consensus in some countries regarding full respect for the rights of sexual minorities cannot be considered a valid argument to deny or restrict their human rights or to perpetuate and reproduce the historical and structural discrimination that these minorities have suffered. The fact that this is a controversial issue in some sectors and countries, and that it is not necessarily a matter of consensus, cannot lead this Court to abstain from issuing a decision, since in doing so it must refer solely and exclusively to the stipulations of the international obligations arising from a sovereign decision by the States to adhere to the American Convention.[109]

4. *Deference regarding the implementation of economic, social and cultural rights*

Lastly, one could also conclude that the IAHRS has granted States significant deference when dealing with the general implementation of economic, social and cultural rights (ESCR). It should be noted however that recent developments related to supervision of the implementation of the *Additional Protocol to the American Convention on Human Rights in the Area of Economic, Social and Cultural Rights* (also called the Protocol of San Salvador) through a periodic reporting system have provided the IACHR with some form of authority to assess the adequacy of State policies and actions regarding such rights and to formulate recommendations on the matter. In fact, this new reporting procedure has also led to the establishment of detailed quantitative and qualitative indicators used by the Commission and other competent OAS bodies

[106] *López-Álvarez (Honduras)* (2006), IACtHR, Series C, No. 141, paras 168 et seq.

[107] See eg *Schalk and Kopf v Austria* (app. no. 30141/04), ECtHR 2010, para 58. See also *H. v Finland* (app. no. 37359/09), ECtHR 2012.

[108] See generally Benvenisti, 'Margin of Appreciation'. See also Legg, *The Margin of Appreciation*, 116.

[109] *Atala Riffo and Daughters (Chile)* (2012), IACtHR, Series C, No. 239, para 92. Cf with *Schalk and Kopf v Austria* and *H. v Finland.*

to review the State measures.[110] However, this new procedure only allows the Commission and other competent OAS bodies to make a general assessment of the situation of ESCR in a specific country during a determined period of time. Accordingly, it does not provide for a review per se of individualized decisions of the domestic authorities on specific issues or cases.[111]

In addition, the Commission has pronounced itself on the scope of the States' discretion while adopting and implementing policies and programmes regarding ESCR. In its 2007 *Report on Access to Justice as a Guarantee of Economic, Social, and Cultural Rights*,[112] the IACHR indicated that States had to respect several specific procedural obligations when implementing such policies, that these measures could not be arbitrary, and that they needed to satisfy some level of transparency and foreseeability. Accordingly, States must ensure access to justice and eliminate obstacles to the exercise of such rights, including undue delays and costs.[113] In addition the IACHR has specified that States also have the obligation to ensure all guarantees in judicial and administrative proceedings dealing with economic, social and cultural rights,[114] including the right to be heard and represented,[115] the right to be informed of administrative proceedings potentially limiting the exercise of such rights,[116] the right to obtain a motivated decision,[117] the right to publicity of certain administrative proceedings,[118] the right to a recourse within a reasonable time,[119] and the right to judicial review.[120] In fact, both the Commission and the Court have established that administrative entities mandated to implement ESCR policies need to apply clear, objective and

[110] See on this issue IACHR, *Guidelines for preparation of progress indicators in the area of economic, social and cultural rights*, Doc. off. OEASer.L/V/II.132 Doc. 14 rev. 1 (19 July 2008). See also OAS GA resol. AG/RES. 2713 (XLII-O/12) and AG/RES. 2798 (XLIII-O/13).

[111] On the limits of this new periodic reporting procedure see Bernard Duhaime, 'L'OEA et le Protocole de San Salvador' in Lucie Lamarche, Pierre Bosset (eds), *Donner droit de cité aux droits économiques, sociaux et culturels—La Charte des droits et libertés du Québec en chantier* (Cowansville: Yvon Blais, 2011), 363–405. See also Bernard Duhaime, 'Le système interaméricain et la protection des droits économiques, sociaux et culturels des personnes et des groupes vivant dans des conditions particulières de vulnérabilité', 44 *Canadian Yearbook of International Law* 95 (2006).

[112] IACHR, *Access to Justice as a Guarantee of Economic, Social, and Cultural Rights. A Review of the Standards Adopted by the Inter-American System of Human Rights*, Doc. off. OEA/Ser.L/V/II.129 (2007).

[113] IACHR, *Access to Justice*, at para 48 et seq. See also *Exceptions to the Exhaustion of Domestic Remedies (Arts. 46.1, 46.2.a and 46.2.b, American Convention on Human Rights)* (1990), Advisory Opinion OC-11/90, IACtHR, Series A, No. OC-11/90, para 22.

[114] IACHR, *Access to Justice*, paras 95 et seq. See also *Baena Ricardo et al (Panama)* (2001), IACtHR, Series C, No. 72, paras 95–105; *Sawhoyamaxa Indigenous Community (Paraguay)* (2006), IACtHR, Series C, No. 146, paras 81, 82, and 11.

[115] See *Loren Laroye Riebe Star, Jorge Barón Guttlein and Rodolfo Izal Elorz v Mexico* (1999), IACHR, No. 49/99, Annual Report 1998.

[116] See *Ivcher Bronstein (Peru)* (2001), IACtHR, Series C, No. 74; *Elías Gattass Sahih v Ecuador* (2005), IACHR, No. 9/05, Annual Report 2005.

[117] See *Claude Reyes et al (Chile)* (2006), IACtHR, Series C, No. 151.

[118] See IACHR, *Report on Terrorism*, para 287.

[119] *Indigenous Community Yakye Axa (Paraguay)* (2005), IACtHR, Series C, No. 125, paras 66–88, 158, and 207.

[120] *Yean and Bosico (Dominican Republic)* (2005), IACtHR, Series C, No. 130, paras 132–9.

pre-established criteria that limit the authorities' discretion, which could lead to the violation of such rights.[121]

Notwithstanding these positions, which obviously dictate limitations on State discretion in the implementation of ESCR, the Inter-American institutions have on the whole been very reluctant to review specific legislative, administrative and judicial decisions adopted by domestic authorities in individual cases. While the Commission did adopt certain decisions in this regard, declaring States' measures which appeared to limit the progressive development of such rights to be in violation of the Convention, the Court, in its 2003 decision in the *'Five Pensioners' v Peru*, seemed to prefer to defer to domestic authorities when dealing with such matters. Rejecting allegations of violations of Article 26 of the Convention, the Court indicated that ESCR:

> have both an individual and a collective dimension. [Their] progressive development...should be measured in function of the growing coverage of economic, social and cultural rights in general, and of the right to social security and to a pension in particular, of the entire population, bearing in mind the imperatives of social equity, and not in function of the circumstances of a very limited group of pensioners, who do not necessarily represent the prevailing situation. It is evident that this is what is occurring in the instant case; therefore, the Court considers that it is in order to reject the request to rule on the progressive development of economic, social and cultural rights in Peru, in the context of this case.[122]

It can be observed that the Court's position further highlights the challenges facing the efforts to 'judicialize' the supervision of States' implementation of ESCR generally, and debates continue as to whether international tribunals should have the authority to review local decisions dealing with such rights, or whether democratically elected governments and legislatures alone should adopt and implement such programmes and policies.[123]

[121] See eg *Baena Ricardo et al (Panama)*, para 126; *'Five Pensioners' (Peru)* (2003), IACtHR, Series C, No. 98, para 117; *Eduardo Perales Martínez v Chile* (2005), IACHR, No. 57/05, Annual Report 2005, paras 13–36.

[122] *'Five Pensioners' (Peru)*, para 147. But see *Community of San Mateo De Huanchor and its Members v Peru* (2004), IACHR, No. 504/03, Annual Report 2004; *Jesús Manuel Naranjo Cárdenas et al [Pensioners of the Venezuelan Aviation Company—Viasa] v Venezuela* (2004), IACHR, No. 70/04, Annual Report 2004, OEA/Ser.L/V/II.122 Doc. 5 rev. 1 at 569; *Luis Rolando Cuscul Pivaral et al (Persons Living With HIV/Aids) v Guatemala* (2005), IACHR, No. 32/05, Annual Report 2005; *Jorge Odir Miranda Cortez et al v El Savador* (2009), IACHR, No. 27/29, Annual Report 2009, paras 107 et seq. See also *National Association of Ex-Employees of the Peruvian Social Security Institute v Peru* (2009), IACHR, No. 38/09, Annual Report 2009. For a discussion on this issue see Duhaime, 'Protocole de San Salvador', 363–405. See also Duhaime, 'Le système interaméricain'.

[123] On this broader debate, see generally Duhaime, 'Protocole de San Salvador', 363–405. See also Duhaime, 'Le système interaméricain'; Tara Melish, *Protecting Economic, Social and Cultural Rights in the Inter-American Human Rights System: A Manual on Presenting Claims* (New Haven: Yale Law School and Centro de Derechos Económicos y Sociales, 2002); James L. Cavallaro and Emily J. Schaffer, 'Less as More: Rethinking Supranational Litigation of Economic and Social Rights in the Americas', 56 *Hastings Law Journal* 217 (2004). See also the dissenting opinion of Judge Antônio Augusto Cançado Trinidade in *Dismissed Congressional Employees (Aguado—Alfaro et al) (Peru)* (2007), IACtHR, Series C, No. 174, para 17.

V. Conclusions

As this chapter has illustrated, the Inter-American institutions have been very hesitant to defer to domestic legislative, administrative and judicial institutions when assessing cases of human rights violations.

However, as the famous *Marzioni* precedent seems to indicate, the IAHRS is ready to apply the fourth instance formula in situations where domestic courts adequately function in accordance with a system of powers established by a Constitution and domestic legislation in a democratic State governed by the rule of law. In very limited circumstances this formula has been applied and the Commission has refrained from second-guessing how domestic authorities have dealt with certain proceedings or how local legislatures have adopted internal norms.

Part of the IAHRS's hesitation to defer seems to stem from the limited capacity on the part of national agencies to effectively protect human rights in the region. Accordingly, when faced with allegations of systemic impunity and violations of the right to judicial protection, both the IACHR and the IACtHR have refused to defer to judicial authorities with the mandate to resolve such matters. Similarly, in contexts of democratic transitions both institutions have similarly refused to defer to laws of amnesty or reconciliation, because they did not ensure the victims' right to justice.

This certainly explains the reservations expressed by some critics of the application of doctrine of the margin of appreciation in the Inter-American System.[124] Nevertheless, as the region progresses towards democracy and consolidates its institutions and practices towards States governed by the rule of law—with more effective judicial authorities—one could expect a greater use of this doctrine by the Commission and Court,[125] as has been observed also with the fourth instance formula.[126]

In a context where the IAHRS is facing an important crisis regarding the quantity of petitions submitted and the resulting formidable delays in the processing of such cases—owing to, *inter alia*, the institutions' lack of proper funding, amongst others[127]—it has been suggested that part of the solution lies in strengthening, through greater technical cooperation and institutional collaboration, the capacity of domestic judicial and administrative authorities in order to enable them to provide effective solutions to human rights problems.[128] Indeed, the Inter-American

[124] Cerna, 'Clarifying a Reviewing Standard', 55. See also Pinto, 'National and International Courts', 257; Cançado Trindade, 'El derechointernacional', 389–391; Poblete, 'Doctrina', 40, 41, and 43.

[125] Legg, *The Margin of Appreciation*, 75.

[126] Pinzón, 'The "Victim" Requirement', 377 and 380.

[127] See eg Dulitzky, 'Time for Changes'; Brian D. Tittemore, 'The Mandatory Death Penalty in the Commonwealth Caribbean and the Inter-American Human Rights System: An Evolution in the Development and Implementation of International Human Rights Protections', 13(2) *William & Mary Bill of Rights Journal* 445 (2004–2005).

[128] See Duhaime, 'Achievements and Challenges'.

human rights petition system cannot continue to act as a substitute for deficient domestic authorities by admitting cases that, in the majority, meet the conditions to qualify as exceptions to the rule requiring prior exhaustion of domestic remedies. Ultimately, for the Inter-American human rights regime to function effectively, reforms need to be made at the national level, so that the Commission and the Court can actually process cases that have been *fully and effectively* dealt with by local authorities, as provided by the Convention, in accordance with the general principle of subsidiarity.

In addition, efforts to ensure effective respect by local administrative and legal authorities of the rights to due process and to judicial protection will certainly allow both the Commission and the Court to make greater use of the doctrine of the margin of appreciation. Of course caution will remain key, since the application of this doctrine can still raise important problems, even when such authorities function adequately and effectively, in particular with respect to persons or groups placed in situations of vulnerability. As rightly posited by Professor Benvenisti, the application of this doctrine in the absence of regional normative consensus can leave human rights victims, in particular those belonging to minorities, without proper justice.[129] In this sense, the doctrine that the IACtHR seems to have adopted on this issue, as shown in the above-mentioned *Atala Riffo and Daughters v Chile* decision (at Section IV.D.3),[130] is certainly promising.

[129] Benvenisti, 'Margin of Appreciation'.
[130] *Atala Riffo and Daughters (Chile)*, para 92.

PART V

OTHER INTERNATIONAL COURTS

17

Standard of Review and the Margin of Appreciation before the International Court of Justice

*Chiara Ragni**

I. Introduction

The concept of standard of review, which originates in domestic administrative legal systems, generally refers to the degree of deference that a court grants to institutional decisions taken by other authorities. In the context of international law it can be seen, broadly speaking, as the lens through which international courts or tribunals evaluate actions and decisions of States or of other international bodies in light of international law. More precisely, it can indicate whether, and to what extent, an international court may assess factual or legal findings made by a State (or by another international body) as regards the adoption of domestic measures, when their compliance with international law is at issue.

Unlike national legislation, the applicable standards of review are almost never explicitly articulated in statutes of international adjudicating bodies or in other relevant treaties. In the absence of any provisions in this regard, each tribunal may in principle set its own standard. In other words, it is for the international court itself to determine whether deference to national authorities' determinations should be warranted and to what extent; or if, on the contrary, judges may substitute their own assessment for that of the State concerned and arrive at a different conclusion (this latter case is generally referred to as *de novo* review).

While some international tribunals, such as the European Court of Human Rights (ECtHR), have articulated their own principles in this regard,[1] the International Court of Justice (ICJ or the Court) has hardly ever made express reference to concepts like standard of review or margin of appreciation. The question of whether a doctrine of judicial deference to other bodies' actions or to

* The information included in this chapter is accurate as of January 2014. The author is grateful to Professor Tullio Treves for his valuable comments.

[1] On the practice of the ECtHR see Chapter 13 by Mónika Ambrus in this volume.

national decision-making exists, and if so, what the applicable standard is, therefore remains controversial. Not only are both the ICJ Statute and the United Nations (UN) Charter silent in this respect, but, more generally, they do not expressly provide for a separate power of judicial review.[2]

The lack of any provisions regulating the matter does not, however, in itself preclude the Court from exercising such a power, when it is required to pronounce on questions whose solution implies assessment of the decisions or actions of States or of other bodies. The analysis of the jurisprudence of the Court seems in principle to confirm this assumption, at least with regard to States, while it is still uncertain whether the Court is, for example, competent to pronounce on acts of other UN bodies in the absence of any relevant provisions expressly so providing.[3] It can be inferred from the Court's practice in this last regard that it has adopted a quite cautious approach. In the *Advisory Opinion on Certain expenses of the United Nations*,[4] the Court, while clearly stating that according to its Statute it lacks judicial power over the acts of other UN bodies,[5] seemed to acknowledge a limited competence to pronounce on the matter in cases where the proper exercise by the Security Council or by the General Assembly of their powers was the subject of contention in light of the competences given to the UN by the Charter, to the extent that this evaluation was necessary to pronounce on the case.[6] The same approach was confirmed

[2] It is worth noting in this regard, that in the absence of any explicit provisions, such a competence cannot be inferred through the interpretation of Article 92 UN Charter. The norm, while identifying the Court as the main judicial organ of the UN, does not say anything about a power of appraisal over the institutional acts of other international bodies or States. As regards actions and decisions of other international bodies, the question whether the Court can pronounce on their lawfulness is still far from clear, except of course in those instances where the statutes of some international organizations provide for such a competence. See on this point Kaiyan Homi Kaikobad, *The International Court of Justice and Judicial Review: A Study of the Court's Powers with Respect to Judgments of the ILO and UN Administrative Tribunals* (The Hague: Brill, 2000). With regard to State institutional acts, a power of judicial review cannot be derived from either the Charter or from the Statute of the ICJ, which more generally entrusts the Court with contentious jurisdiction over inter-State legal disputes regarding questions of application or interpretation of international law (Statute of the ICJ, Article 36), and with the competence to give advisory opinions when requested by an authorized body (Article 65). In this regard see Andreas Zimmermann et al (eds), *The Statute of the International Court of Justice: A Commentary* (Oxford: Oxford University Press, 2006) 97 ff.

[3] This issue was widely debated by scholars, especially with regard to the existence of such a power of judicial review over UN Security Council resolutions. See eg Mohammed Bedjaoui, 'Un contrôle de légalité des actes du Conseil de Sécurité est-il possible?' in *Société française pour le droit international, Colloque de Rennes, Le chapitre VII de la Charte des Nations Unies, 50e anniversaire des Nations Unies* (Paris: Pedone, 1995); Bernd Martenczuk, 'The Security Council, the International Court and Judicial Review: What Lessons from Lockerbie?', 10(3) *EJIL* 517 (1999). For a comprehensive study of the relationship between the ICJ and the UN Security Council, see also Maria I. Papa, *I rapporti tra la Corte internazionale di giustizia e il Consiglio di sicurezza* (Padova: Cedam, 2006) 295 ff.

[4] ICJ, *Certain expenses of the United Nations (Article 17.2, of the Charter)*, Advisory Opinion, ICJ Rep 1962.

[5] The Court quite clearly stated: 'In the legal systems of States, there is often some procedure for determining the validity of even a legislative or governmental act, but no analogous procedure is to be found in the structure of the United Nations', meaning that, in principle, a power of judicial review should be excluded (ICJ, *Certain expenses*, 168).

[6] See in this regard Papa, *I rapporti*, 310. On the question whether the ICJ can also pronounce on the validity of other UN bodies' acts, see the Separate Opinions of Judges Morelli and Fitzmaurice

in the *Namibia* opinion,[7] and it was, to some extent, reiterated some years later in the *Lockerbie* and in the *Genocide* cases, where the Court avoided taking any position on the issue, implicitly suggesting that this was not necessary for ruling on the dispute.[8]

(respectively, paras 223 and 204–5) in the *Certain expenses* case, where they make reference to *ultra vires* acts as being one of the cases which should justify the exercise of a power of judicial review.

[7] ICJ, *Legal Consequences for States of the Continued Presence of South Africa in Namibia (South West Africa) notwithstanding Security Council Resolution 276 (1970)*, Advisory Opinion, ICJ Rep 1971, para 89. On the specific question at issue see E. Gordon, 'Old Orthodoxies Amid New Experiences: The South West Africa (Namibia) Litigation and the Uncertain Jurisprudence of the International Court of Justice', 1 *Denver Journal of International Law and Policy* 65 (1971), 83 ff. The approach taken by the ICJ with regard to its power of judicial review was criticized by some of the judges in their separate opinions. It was contended that the '[t]he Court's powers are clearly defined by the Statute, and do not include powers to review decisions of other organs of the United Nations; but when, as in the present proceedings, such decisions bear upon a case properly before the Court, and a correct judgment or opinion could not be rendered without determining the validity of such decisions, the Court could not possibly avoid such a determination without abdicating its role of a judicial organ' (Separate Opinion of Judge Onyeama, 131 ff). For stronger criticism with regard to the attitude of the Court, cf Dissenting Opinion of Judge Gros, 331 ff. See also Separate Opinion of Judge Padilla Nervo, 105.

[8] ICJ, *Questions of Interpretation and Application of the 1971 Montreal Convention arising from the Aerial Incident at Lockerbie* (*Libyan Arab Jamahiriya v United States of America*), Provisional Measures, ICJ Rep 1992 (Order of 14 April 1992). Here the Court was requested by the Libyan government to grant provisional measures that would have clashed with the sanctions imposed by Security Council's Resolution 748 (1992), the validity of which was contested by the State. The Court refused to grant the measures and demurred on the issue of judicial review of other bodies' acts, stating: 'The right of the Parties to contest such issues at the stage of the merits must remain unaffected by the Court's decision' (16). On this point see Geoffrey R. Watson, 'Constitutionalism Judicial Review and the World Court', 34 *Harvard International Law Journal* 1 (1993), 27; Gaetano Arangio-Ruiz, 'The ICJ Statute, the Charter and Forms of Legality Review of Security Council Decisions' in Lal C. Vohrah et al (eds), *Man's Inhumanity to Man: Essays on International Law in Honour of Antonio Cassese* (The Hague: Kluwer Law International, 2003) 41 ff, 59. Cf ICJ, *Questions of Interpretation and Application of the 1971 Montreal Convention arising from the Aerial Incident at Lockerbie* (*Libyan Arab Jamahiriya v United States of America*), Preliminary Objections, ICJ Rep 1998, paras 49–50. See also on this point, Joint Declaration of Judges Bedjaoui, Ranjeva, and Koroma. See the Dissenting Opinions of Judges Schwebel (7–13) and Jennings (10). The case was then discontinued and removed from the list, with the result that the Court has never pronounced on the matter (Order of 10 September 2013). In *Case Concerning the Application of the Genocide Convention*, the decision on the provisional measures requested by Bosnia once again required the Court to pronounce on Security Council Resolutions, the appropriateness of which was contested in light of a change of the circumstances that accompanied their adoption. The Court refused the measures by denying its jurisdiction in the case, without therefore pronouncing on the question raised by the applicant. ICJ, *Application of the Convention on the Prevention and Punishment of the Crime of Genocide*, Provisional Measures, ICJ Rep 1993, para 41 (Order of 13 September 1993). The issue was however addressed by Judge Lauterpacht in his Separate Opinion. While stating that the Court possesses a power of judicial review over the acts of other UN bodies, he acknowledged that in any case this competence can never be exercised where, as in the *specie*, a discretional power of a political organ is under discussion, unless the validity of a Security Council's resolution is contended as being in conflict with a *jus cogens* norm. In this hypothetical situation, the Court should refer the matter to the Security Council for its reconsideration. See *contra* Lucius Caflisch, 'Is the International Court Entitled to Review Security Council Resolutions Adopted under Chapter VII of the United Nations Charter?' in Najeen M. Al-Nauimi and R. Meese (eds), *International Legal Issues Arising under the United Nations Decade of International Law* (The Hague, London, Boston: Martinus Nijhoff, 1995), where the authors argue: 'It is impossible to find in the Order anything resembling a "window of opportunity" for judicial review of binding Security Council resolutions' (649–650).

According to this reasoning, it can been argued that, as regards UN bodies' actions, the Court is not entrusted with competences comparable to those exercised by constitutional or administrative judicial bodies in a domestic system. Rather, it seems that it can only proceed to the interlocutory examination of the lawfulness of an act when such is strictly necessary for pronouncing on a case that falls under its jurisdiction.[9] However, it is unclear (or at least it does not emerge from the jurisprudence) what should be the applicable standard for such a review.

As regards States, the jurisdiction of the Court is adversarial in nature and this extends to disputes regarding questions concerning the application or interpretation of international law. Judicial review may therefore, in principle, be exercised when the appraisal of a domestic measure or of the national decision-making process that led to its adoption is relevant to decide whether a specific conduct amounts to a breach of an international obligation, or whether it represents the proper exercise of a discretionary power by the State. Standard of review problems may therefore come up in such cases, to the extent that the Court has to determine the degree of deference (if any) to be granted to legal or factual determinations made by the State when applying international law norms. This issue is likely to arise mostly in cases where the interpretation or the application of an international rule includes some elements that need to be clarified, and where the question of the State's degree of flexibility in its implementation is at stake. Standard-type norms, which resort to concepts like proportionality, necessity, security, public policy or public concerns, may for example give rise to these kinds of questions. In international law, they are largely included in exceptions clauses, which in principle allow the State a certain level of discretion as to the enforcement of its obligations when an essential national interest, regarded as worthy of protection, is at stake.

Flexible provisions, which raise standard of review issues, can also be found in international law norms that provide a limited conduct-guidance and preserve a significant 'zone of legality' within which States are free to operate. These kinds of rules, which might, at least in principle, facilitate the exercise of judicial deference are included, for example, in end-oriented norms that bind the State to obtain a certain result, leaving free the choice of means by which this can be achieved.[10]

[9] On the incidental nature of the competence of the ICJ to pronounce on the lawfulness of an action of the UN, see Enrico Milano, 'Security Council Action in the Balkans: Reviewing the Legality of Kosovo's Territorial Status', 14 *EJIL* 999 (2003), 1016. In this regard, see also Susan Lamb, 'Legal Limits to United Nations Security Council Powers' in Guy S. Goodwin-Gill and Stefan Talmon (eds), *The Reality of International Law: Essays in Honour of Ian Brownlie* (Oxford: Oxford University Press, 1999) 361 ff. According to Lamb: 'The unique character of the UN system may ensure that judicial review of Security Council resolutions occurs incidentally, indirectly, and infrequently, but it does occur.' In the same vein, Papa, *I rapporti*, 366 ff.

[10] See Jean-Pierre Cot, 'Margin of Appreciation' in Rüdiger Wolfrum (ed), *Max Planck Encyclopedia of Public International Law* (Oxford: Oxford University Press, 2012), 1012, para 13 ('Among the criteria allowing for application of margin of appreciation, the nature of the applicable norms is paramount. Obligations of conduct, as opposed to obligations of results, are particularly amenable to such a standard').

This analysis will be conducted taking first into consideration the jurisprudence of the ICJ with regard to exceptions clauses, and making a distinction according to both the characteristics of the relevant norms and the nature of the obligation to which they consent to derogate. The study will then focus on the problem of whether, as regards norms which by themselves leave a wide margin of discretion as to their implementation, the ICJ retains a power of review and, if so, what is the appropriate standard. In this regard, this chapter will also attempt to provide an answer to the question whether good faith can be regarded as a standard of review, as the jurisprudence of the Court seems to suggest, and if so, how it has been applied (or should have been applied) according to the relevant practice.

II. Derogation Clauses and the Standard of Review: The Restrictive Approach Taken by the ICJ as Regards the Proportionality and Necessity Test

When analysing the jurisprudence of the ICJ, the issue of standard of review first comes into play in the application of derogation clauses, which are designed to preserve the exercise of a State's sovereignty in areas which are traditionally considered as unsuitable for judicial assessment, such as in the case where security concerns are at issue.[11] The application of this kind of norm therefore requires a balance between the international obligation required by international law and the interest of the State concerned by its implementation.

With regard to the first element, a distinction may be traced in the practice of the ICJ between the standards for assessing so-called self-judging clauses—that expressly provide for a discretional power of the State as regards their application (by generally using expressions such as 'if the State considers')—and other provisions which do not include any similar wording.

This distinction was first articulated in the *Nicaragua* case, where the Court had to assess the relevance of the security exception in Article XXI(d) of the Treaty of Friendship, Commerce and Navigation (TFCN) concluded between the United States and Nicaragua. The norm, which was invoked by the United States in order to justify its conduct (which, according to Nicaragua, amounted to a violation of international law) was aimed at excluding the illegality of a national measure which was contrary to the TFCN if its application was 'necessary to protect... essential security interests'. In the judgment of 27 June 1986, the ICJ held that the exception raised by the United States could not be regarded as self-judging and that the arguments put forward by the respondent in this regard must therefore be rejected. According to the Court, the derogation clause provided for in the TFCN could not be equated to other security exceptions, such as

[11] Clauses of this kind are, for example, included in security exceptions. In this regard it has been argued that 'national security is a matter of which the government is sole trustee. It is eminently a matter on which an international court can have no useful opinion.' See Robert Jennings, 'Recent Cases on "Automatic" Reservations to the Optional Clause', 7 *ICLQ* 349 (1958), 362.

for example that included in Article XXI General Agreement on Tariffs and Trade (GATT), which expressly grants to the State a wide margin of discretion as to the assessment of the existence of a national security interest to be defended and of the action it 'considers necessary' to ensure its protection.[12] In the light of the different language used by the norm which was invoked by the United States, the Court concluded that in the case at issue the question 'whether a measure is necessary to protect the essential security interests of a party is not... purely a question for the subjective judgment of the party; the text [of the Treaty] does not refer to what the party "considers necessary" for that purpose.'[13] Notwithstanding that the word 'purely' seems to imply some degree of deference to the State in the assessment of the circumstances for invoking the security exception, the Court remained silent as to the extent of such discretion and to the adequate standard of review to be eventually applied in evaluating the lawfulness of its exercise. Once it established that the measure taken by the United States amounted to the use of armed force, it clarified that in this case any evaluation of its legality can only be made in the light of international customary rules on self-defence. Given the importance of the interests involved and the customary nature of the norms providing for such an exception, the Court further concluded that the assessment on the necessity and proportionality of the national measure concerned cannot be left to the State, but must be subjected to strict judicial control in accordance with international law.

This conclusion was confirmed in *Oil Platforms*, where the ICJ assumed an even more restrictive approach regarding the discretion of a State on the matter of the application of security exceptions. The dispute arose out of the attack on and destruction of three offshore oil production complexes (owned and operated for commercial purposes by the National Iranian Oil Company) by several warships of the United States Navy. One of the questions brought before the Court, which is broadly reminiscent of the *Nicaragua* case, was whether this action amounted to a violation of the 1955 Treaty of Amity, Economic Relations and Consular Rights between the United States and Iran, or whether, on the contrary, it could be justified under the security exception included in its Article XX.1(d) and regarded, as it was claimed by the United States, as a legitimate response to actions taken by Iran which involved, *inter alia*, mining and other attacks on United States vessels. Since once again the measure taken by the United States amounted to the use of armed force, the ICJ reiterated its view that any evaluation on its necessity inevitably overlaps with that of its validity as an act of self-defence.[14] In this regard, the

[12] ICJ, *Military and Paramilitary Activities in and against Nicaragua* (*Nicaragua v United States of America*), Merits, Judgment, ICJ Rep 1986, para 222.

[13] ICJ, *Nicaragua v United States of America*, para 282.

[14] The Court argued: 'the measures taken must not merely be such as tend to protect the essential security interests of the party taking them, but must be necessary for that purpose; and whether a given measure is "necessary" is not purely a question for the subjective judgment of the party..., and may thus be assessed by the Court. In the present case, the question whether the measures taken were "necessary" overlaps with the question of their validity as acts of self-defense. As the Court observed in its [*Nicaragua*] decision of 1986, the criteria of necessity and proportionality must be observed if a measure is to be qualified as self-defence'; ICJ, *Oil Platforms* (*Islamic Republic of Iran v United States of America*), Judgment, ICJ Rep 2003, para 43. According to the United States, on the

Court once again rejected the argument put forward by the United States that the evaluation of whether the necessity and proportionality test was *in specie* satisfied is for the State to make. It stated that:

> measures taken avowedly in self-defence must have been necessary for that purpose is strict and objective, leaving no room for any 'measure of discretion'. The Court will therefore turn to the criteria of necessity and proportionality in the context of international law on self-defence.[15]

In the light of these cases, it can be contended, by way of implication, that the margin of appreciation granted to the State in assessing whether a national interest requires safeguarding, and in deciding on the protective measure to be adopted, is mostly linked to the nature, the effects and the importance of the norm which is alleged to have been violated.[16] As regards this matter the Court, in both the *Nicaragua* and *Oil Platforms* cases, seems first to endorse the view that no margin of discretion should be left to the State in relation to an imperative norm (such as prohibition of aggression). It then argues that judicial review of legal determinations made by national authorities is always admissible when the provision which is invoked by the State to validate its conduct requires, for its application, resort to standards governed and defined by customary international law. The restrictive perspective adopted by the ICJ in this case may also be grounded in the need to ensure the legal certainty of international law and to prevent divergent interpretations of the same rule, which may lead to its fragmentation.[17]

This reasoning is confirmed in *Gabčíkovo-Nagymaros Project*; a dispute which arose out of a treaty signed in 1977 between Hungary and Czechoslovakia concerning the construction of a 'System of Locks' on the Danube River, to be operated jointly by the parties. In the face of growing domestic ecological concerns, the Hungarian government suspended works on its part of the project and terminated the treaty, arguing that the 'state of ecological necessity' justified its conduct. Hungary argued before the Court that the question of whether necessity and its elements applied, as specified in Article 25 of the International Law Commission's Articles on State Responsibility, was to be determined by the State invoking the exception. This argument was rejected by the ICJ. It first considered that:

contrary, a measure of discretion should be afforded to a party's good faith application of measures to protect its essential security interests.

[15] On the matter of proportionality in international law see Enzo Cannizzaro, *Il principio della proporzionalità nell'ordinamento internazionale* (Milan: Giuffè, 2000). On the application of the proportionality principle in the practice of other international dispute settlement bodies (ie Court of Justice of the European Union, WTO panels and the Appellate Body) see Chapter 12 by Alexia Herwig and Asja Serdarevic in this volume.

[16] Yuval Shany, 'Toward a General Margin of Appreciation Doctrine in International Law', 16 *EJIL* 907 (2005), 925. According to the author: 'strict scrutiny by international courts is more responsive to the gravity of the interests at stake.'

[17] Shany, 'Toward a General Margin of Appreciation', 934, where the author argues that: 'since international courts are typically better situated than national actors to identify and interpret the relevant norms of international law, they play a crucial part in ensuring the legal appropriateness of national decisions.'

the state of necessity is a ground recognized by customary international law for precluding the wrongfulness of an act not in conformity with an international obligation. It observes moreover that such ground for precluding wrongfulness can only be accepted on an exceptional basis... the state of necessity can only be invoked under certain strictly defined conditions which must be cumulatively satisfied; and the State concerned is not the sole judge of whether those conditions have been met.[18]

The ICJ concluded that necessity, being an exception to an international legal obligation, provided for by customary rules, does not allow for the unilateral determination by national authorities, but it can be invoked under the strict conditions established by international law. The ICJ then determined, without paying deference to the decision-making process of the State concerned, whether the substantive elements of necessity (namely, the existence of a serious impairment of an essential interest) were met, and whether Hungary's reaction was objectively necessary to protect the interests concerned.

The above analysis seems to suggest that the margin of appreciation left to a State, when dealing with derogation rules which resort, for their enforcement, to a standard governed by general international law, is restrained to the appraisal of the factual circumstances surrounding the adoption of the measure concerned. Deference to national authorities' determination in this respect is justified firstly on the basis that they are better placed than an international judge to decide on the matter. Second, the evaluation as to the existence of a public concern worthy of protection and to the appropriate measure to be undertaken, given its prominent political implications, is primarily for the State. It may, however, be subjected to ICJ review if its consistency with international law is contested in the light of imperative rules protecting fundamental international interests.

III. In Search of a Balance between International Interests and Unilateral State Concerns in the Self-judging Clauses Regime: Is Good Faith an Appropriate Standard of Review?

The reasoning of the ICJ in *Nicaragua* appears *a contrario* to suggest that a more flexible standard of review should be used when dealing with treaty provisions which, by their wording, expressly grant a margin of discretion to the State as regards the assessment of the circumstances giving rise to their invocation.

The restrictive perspective assumed by the ICJ when dealing with security or necessity exceptions has not, in fact, been adopted when the norm invoked by the State to justify its conduct has been included in self-judging treaty clauses,[19]

[18] ICJ, *Gabčíkovo-Nagymaros Project* (*Hungary v Slovakia*), Judgment, ICJ Rep 1997. The Court confirmed this assumption some years later in its Advisory Opinion of 9 July 2004 on the *Legal Consequences of the Construction of a Wall in the Occupied Palestinian Territory*, para 140.

[19] 'By means of these clauses, states reserve to themselves the right to unilaterally declare such obligations to be non-binding if the state in question determines that its essential interests are at stake and, according to its determination, should take precedence over international law.' Robyn Briese and Stephan Schill, '"If the State Considers": Self-Judging Clauses in International Dispute

namely provisions which authorize the State not to comply, in particular circumstances, with certain obligations *if it considers* that essential public interests could be jeopardized. Such circumstances may encompass, for example, preservation of security interests, public policy or, more generally, essential public concerns. With regard to these clauses it has been observed that a 'sufficiently robust standard of review' should be applied to prevent their abuse, while at the same time preserving the discretion granted to the State that invokes the exception.[20]

Even if the practice of the ICJ is rather constrained in this regard, it reveals a slightly deferential approach towards national decision-making when the application of these kinds of rules is at issue. This approach is reflected in the *Djibouti v France* case,[21] which is the only one to date where the ICJ has expressly recognized the self-judging character of the international norm whose violation was alleged by the applicant State. In this case the Court was required to determine whether France's refusal to execute a rogatory letter notified by Djibouti constituted a breach of the Mutual Assistance Convention concluded in 1986 between the two States, or whether it rather represented the correct exercise of a discretionary power justified under the public concerns exception provided for by Article 2(c) of the treaty.[22] The ICJ first remarked that in such cases, where treaty norms *expressly* provide for a wide discretion in terms of their application,[23] the State potentially enjoys a broad margin of appreciation in assessing the institutional measure to be taken to protect its essential interests, with this power only being subjected to the obligation of good faith as codified in the Vienna Convention on the Law of the Treaties (VCLT),[24] and reflected in the customary law principle *pacta sunt servanda*.

In the *Djibouti* case, the ICJ held it to be sufficient for the State, in order to comply with its good faith obligation, to show that the reasons for its refusal to execute the rogatory letter fell within those provided for in Article 2, and concluded that

Settlement', 13 *Max Planck Yearbook of United Nations Law* 61 (2009); Robyn Briese and Stephan Schill, 'Djibouti v France: Self-Judging Clauses before the International Court of Justice', 10 *Melbourne Journal of International Law* 308 (2009).

[20] Briese and Schill, 'Djibouti v. France' 63.

[21] ICJ, *Certain Questions of Mutual Assistance in Criminal Matters* (*Djibouti v France*), Judgment, ICJ Rep 2008.

[22] Article 2(c) of the Convention provides that assistance in proceedings relating to criminal offences 'may be refused...if the requested State considers that the execution of the request is likely to prejudice its sovereignty, its security, its ordre public or other of its essential interests.' As is clear by the wording of this clause, the Contracting Parties thereby established a subjective test of whether the exception is applicable in any given circumstances and assigned the power of assessment to the State refusing cooperation.

[23] The self-judging character of a provision cannot be presumed, but it must clearly result from the wording of the treaty; on this point, emphasized by the ICJ in the *Nicaragua* and *Oil Platforms* cases, para 4, see Tarcisio Gazzini, 'Interpretation of (Allegedly) Self-judging Clauses in Bilateral Investment Treaties' in Malgosia Fitzmaurice et al (eds), *Treaty Interpretation and the Vienna Convention on the Law of the Treaties: 30 Years On* (Leiden-Boston: Martinus Nijhoff, 2010) 239 ff.

[24] 1969 Vienna Convention on the Law of Treaties, Article 26: 'every treaty in force is binding upon the parties to it and must be performed by them in good faith.' The principle of bona fides is also included in Article 31(1) as regards the rules governing the interpretation of international treaties.

France's refusal to comply with Djibouti's request was not in breach of the Mutual Assistance Convention. This argument was criticized by Judge Keith in his Separate Opinion, in which he argued that the Court should have first interpreted the exception clause in the light of the objective pursued by the Convention and then it should have assessed whether France's refusal to cooperate was consistent with Article 2, rather than limiting itself to the mere ascertainment that the exception invoked by the State was among those provided for by the treaty.[25]

In other words, in *Djibouti* the ICJ seems to have applied good faith as a standard of review, by implicitly arguing that, in the absence of more restrictive rules it is the principle itself that defines the boundaries within which the discretion of a State should be exercised. This argument is consistent with the past jurisprudence of the Court, which has often made reference to good faith as an obligation incumbent on the State, therefore constraining its discretion, in the implemention of treaty norms.[26]

As regards the scope and the content of this standard however, the ICJ made no reference to its previous practice, which taken together with the deferential approach applied in the case, provides little clarification with respect to the requirements for an act to be consistent with the principle of good faith. The *Djibouti* judgment has been rightly criticized in this respect. It has, for example, been suggested that the Court should at least have made reference to its precedent in the *Gabčíkovo* case,[27] where it stated that the principle of bona fides, as enshrined in the VCLT, implies that a State party to a treaty should apply it 'in a reasonable way and in such a manner that its purpose can be realized'.[28] This would imply that, when dealing with self-judging treaty clauses, which by their nature grant a State the possibility to depart from its international obligations when bound by the need to safeguard its public concerns, unilateral considerations should be balanced against the need for international cooperation.

In the light of these considerations, good faith may be regarded as an appropriate standard of review for self-judging clauses,[29] provided that the assessment of a

[25] 'The Court begins its examination of Article 2 of the 1986 Convention by observing that, while it is correct, as France claims, that the terms of Article 2 provide a State to which a request for assistance has been made with a very considerable discretion, this exercise of discretion is still subject to the obligation of good faith codified in Article 26 of the 1969 Vienna Convention on the Law of Treaties... This requires it to be shown that the reasons for refusal to execute the letter rogatory fell within those allowed for in Article 2' (*Djibouti* Judgment, para 145).

[26] On the practice of the ICJ in this regard, see John F. O'Connor, *Good Faith in International Law* (Aldershot: Dartmouth Publishing, 1991) 81 ff; Markus Kotzur, 'Good Faith (Bona fide)' in Rüdiger Wolfrum (ed), *Max Planck Encyclopedia of Public International Law* (Oxford: Oxford University Press, 2012) 508.

[27] *Djibouti v France*, Judgment, Separate Opinion of Judge Keith.

[28] *Gabčíkovo-Nagymaros Project*, para 142.

[29] For a consistent view, see ICJ, *Case concerning the Application of the Convention of 1902 governing the Guardianship of Infants* (*Netherlands v Sweden*), Judgment, Separate Opinion of Judge Sir Hersch Lauterpacht, para 99. For a comment, see Sir Gerald Fitzmaurice, *The Law and Procedure of the International Court of Justice* (Grotius Publications Ltd, 1986), Vol. 2, 668–9. More recently, good faith has been consistently described as a general principle of international law that has as its aim 'to blunt the excessively sharp consequences sovereignty and its surrogates (eg the principle of consent, no obligation without consent) may have in the international society, in ever-increasing

State's conduct in the light of this principle would not be limited, as it was in the *Djibouti* case, to the mere ascertainment that the national action was aimed at realizing one of the national purposes considered by the invoked norm. Otherwise the result would be that the pursuit of a national interest, regarded as worthy of protection, could in principle justify any conduct contrary to applicable international rules.

For that reason, treaties containing exception clauses, especially if they are self-judging in nature, often include mechanisms aimed at limiting instances of abuse by providing for a means for monitoring the exercise of State discretion. In the Mutual Assistance Convention, for example, this mechanism amounts to the obligation on the part of a State invoking the exception clause to give the reasons for its refusal to cooperate. It is not enough to say that a security, or another public interest among those included in Article 2, is at stake. According to Article 17 of the Convention, a State shall also notify the reasons why it considers that the execution of the request of judicial cooperation would amount to putting such an interest at risk.

The aim of this procedural obligation is to allow another Contracting Party to verify whether the limits of the self-judging clause were respected in a case where the assessment made by the State invoking the exception is questioned. In the *Djibouti* case, however, the Court, while recognizing the importance of the obligation in Article 17 in preventing the abuse of self-judging clauses, concluded that 'in spite of the non-respect by France of Article 17, the latter was entitled to rely upon Article 2(c) and that, consequently, Article 1 of the Convention [which obliges the parties to afford each other the wider measure of mutual assistance in criminal matters] has not been breached.'[30] In this regard it has been contended that the Court should have applied procedural grounds of review in order to assess whether France's decision to refuse cooperation was properly taken and whether the good faith principle was respected.[31] State discretion, granted by the exception clause, would have thereby been preserved against any judicial hindrance, but at the same time the Court could have verified that it had not been exercised arbitrarily, but in a reasonable way given the particular circumstances.

need of cooperation': Robert Kolb, 'Principles as Sources of International Law (with Special Reference to Good Faith)', 53(1) *Netherlands International Law Review* 1 (2006), 18. On this point see also Chapter 5 by Andrei Mamolea in this volume.

[30] ICJ, *Djibouti v France*, Judgment, para 156.

[31] In particular it has been argued: 'a finding that [in the light of procedural grounds of review] a State has exercised its power improperly and has yet to make a decision according to law does not prevent the State from making the same substantive decision on review... It is possible that in Djibouti v France, this would have been the outcome if the Court had ordered France to remake its decision given the further reasons for its refusal... such a standard of review upholds a State's sovereign discretion to determine its own essential interests and the circumstances in which they may be prejudiced or require protection, as envisaged by a self-judging clause. At the same time, such a standard of review ensures that State discretion is not misused by imposing concrete procedural controls through an independent international dispute settlement body' (Briese and Schill, 'Djibouti v France', 26).

IV. The Need to Clarify What Is Required by the Good-faith Standard: Possible Recourse to a Reasonableness Test and to Procedural Safeguards as Grounds for Review

The suggested approach—according to which good faith cannot be presumed (when it is contested by another State) but should be verified through an assessment of whether the State has properly exercised its powers when entrusted with a margin of discretion in implementing international law—is also consistent with ICJ jurisprudence. The Court has, in fact, on several occasions clarified that in order to comply with the bona fide principle, international rules should always be applied in a reasonable manner.[32]

For example, in the *Case concerning the Application of the Convention of 1902 governing the Guardianship of Infants*, individual judges, in their separate opinions, considered the relevance of good faith in the invocation by the State of a public policy exception to its obligation under the Convention.[33] In particular Judge Lauterpacht observed: 'The Court is competent to decide not only whether the [national] law…falls within the notion of *ordre public*, but also whether it has been applied *reasonably* and so as not to defeat the true objects of the Convention.'[34] That principle was confirmed by subsequent decisions—for example, in *Barcelona Traction, Gabčíkovo*,[35] and more recently in *Navigational and Related Rights*, where the Court required that State powers must be exercised *properly*, that is, for the purpose for which they have been given.[36] Similarly, the Court has also stressed that State discretion should not be exercised in a manner that would undermine the object and purpose of the provisions of the treaty granting such a power (the principle of *effectiveness*).[37]

Furthermore, the jurisprudence of the Court in this regard seems to suggest that the reasonableness test, in its formal meaning, implies an assessment on the application of appropriate procedural safeguards, especially if they are provided for by the norm whose violation is alleged. An example of this approach can be

[32] On the concept of reasonableness in international law and its function as a limit to the discretion of a State, see Olivier Corten, *L'utilisation du 'raisonnable' par le juge international: discours juridique, raison et contradictions* (Bruxelles: Bruylant, 1997), paras 112–19; Olivier Corten, 'Reasonableness in International Law' in Rüdiger Wolfrum (ed), *Max Planck Encyclopedia of International Law* (Oxford: Oxford University Press, 2012), 645.

[33] On the use of public policy exception in the practice of international courts and tribunals (ie Court of Justice of the European Union, WTO panels and the Appellate Body, international investment tribunals) see Chapter 3 by Ilona Cheyne in this volume.

[34] ICJ, *Case concerning the Application of the Convention of 1902 governing the Guardianship of Infants* (*Netherlands v Sweden*), Judgment, ICJ Rep 1958. Separate Opinion of Judge Sir Hersch Lauterpacht, para 99.

[35] In the *Barcelona Traction* judgment, the ICJ stated: 'in all [the] fields of international law, it is necessary that the law be applied reasonably.' ICJ, *Case concerning the Barcelona Traction, Light and Power Company, Limited (New Application: 1962)* (*Belgium v Spain*), Second Phase, Judgment, ICJ Rep 1970, para 9; in the same way, *Gabčíkovo-Nagymaros Project*, para 142.

[36] ICJ, *Dispute regarding Navigational and Related Rights* (*Costa Rica v Nicaragua*), Judgment, ICJ Rep 2009, para 61.

[37] ICJ, *Case Concerning Territorial Dispute* (*Libyan Arab Jamahiriya/Chad*), Judgment, ICJ Rep 1994, para 51.

found in the *Pulp Mills* judgment,[38] where Argentina claimed that Uruguay had breached its treaty obligations under the 1975 Statute of the River Uruguay when it authorized the construction of two specific pulp mills and failed to provide for the environmental impact of these activities on the surrounding area. According to Article 27 of the Statute, the violation of which was alleged by the applicant:

the right of each Party to use the waters of the river, within its jurisdiction, for domestic, sanitary, industrial and agricultural purposes shall be exercised without prejudice to the application of the procedure laid down in [the Statute] when the use is liable to affect the regime of the river or the quality of its waters.

The norm, according to the ICJ:

embodies... interconnectedness between equitable and reasonable utilization of a shared resource and the balance between economic development and environmental protection that is the essence of sustainable development.[39]

In other words, notwithstanding the fact that State enjoys a margin of discretion in evaluating the existence of a national interest, represented in the Treaty, which justifies the adoption of measures encompassing the use of shared waters, this power should be reasonably exercised, including by taking into account environmental concerns. To that end, according to the Court, a reasonable—and well-balanced—application of the right descending from the Treaty entails the obligation not to grant any permission to use the river's water without having previously conducted an environmental impact assessment of the activity concerned. As regards the authority entitled with the competence to make such an assessment, the ICJ argued:

it is for each State to determine in its domestic legislation or in the authorization process for the project, the specific content of the environmental impact assessment required in each case, having regard to the nature and magnitude of the proposed development and its likely adverse impact on the environment as well as to the need to exercise due diligence in conducting such an assessment.[40]

The conclusion which seems to arise from this reasoning is that, once the State proves it has conducted an evaluation of the possible environmental impact of the project to be authorized, and such evaluation is well-reasoned and supported by substantial evidence taking into account all the possible circumstances, its good faith can be considered as established and any further review of its decision to grant the permission should, in principle, be excluded.[41]

A somewhat similar approach could be eventually taken by the Court in a pending case concerning *Whaling in the Antarctic*, where Australia has claimed a violation by Japan of the International Convention for the Regulation of Whaling,

[38] ICJ, *Pulp Mills on the River Uruguay* (*Argentina v Uruguay*), Judgment, ICJ Rep 2010.

[39] ICJ, *Pulp Mills*, Judgment, para 177.

[40] ICJ, *Pulp Mills*, Judgment, para 205.

[41] In this regard, Alan Boyle, 'Developments in the International Law of Environmental Impact Assessments and their Relation to the Espoo Convention', 20(3) *Review of European Community & International Environmental Law* 227 (2011), 231.

which entrusts each Party with the right to grant to its nationals special whaling permits:

> for purposes of scientific research subject to such restrictions as to number and subject to such other conditions as the Contracting Government thinks fit... Each Contracting Government shall report at once to the Commission all such authorizations which it has granted.[42]

Australia first denies the self-judging character of the norm, which was on the contrary maintained by Japan, by arguing that the assessment of the scientific purpose is not only for the State to make, it being also subject to the review of the Scientific Committee, to which, under the consistent practice of the Whaling Commission, all the proposed permits should be submitted. It then refers to fundamental principles of interpretation relied upon by the Court, in order to conclude that the exception to whaling included in Article VIII of the Convention must be applied for its stated purpose, ie 'scientific research', 'in a reasonable way', and in such a manner that the main objective of the treaty can be realized.[43] It finally argues that the evaluation whether an activity under Article VIII has been performed in good faith for the purpose of scientific research must be assessed on the basis of objective criteria established by experts and not in the light of the State decision-making process.[44] Respect for the procedural safeguard provided for by the Convention should help to prevent the arbitrary employment of State discretion and ensure that the powers granted to a State will be exercised properly and in a reasonable way.

To sum up, in the case where an international norm by itself grants a State a margin of appreciation with respect to its application or enforcement of the reasonableness principle—the respect of which may be ensured *inter alia* through the provision of procedural safeguards—could be regarded as an effective means both to assess that a particular conduct was exercised in good faith and to balance the latitude of discretion left to public authorities against the need to preserve international obligations and interests.

It is worth noting however that in the Whaling affair the appropriateness of this argument was challenged by Japan in its Counter-Memorial of 9 March 2012.[45] According to the respondent, the evaluation as to what the term 'research purposes' refers to is exclusively for the national authorities to make, and the standard of review to be adopted in assessing the exercise of this discretion is that of margin of appreciation, which the State assumes to have been consistently applied even in the past practice of the Court. Notwithstanding that the question

[42] International Convention for the Regulation of Whaling (Washington, 2 December 1946), Article VIII, para 1.

[43] It is worth mentioning, even if this is not the place to go deeper into the issue, that the exact determination of the objective of the Whaling Convention is one of the most controversial issues between the parties to the dispute.

[44] ICJ, *Whaling in the Antarctic* (*Australia v Japan*), Memorial of Australia, vol. 1, chapter 4, paras 4.24 and 4.33 ff.

[45] ICJ, *Whaling in the Antarctic* (*Australia v Japan*), Counter-Memorial of Japan, vol. 1, Section B.

will be probably addressed in the judgment of the ICJ, it is still worthwhile to make a few final remarks on the issue at this point in time.

V. Is There a Place and a Rationale for the Margin of Appreciation Doctrine in the Jurisprudence of the ICJ?

In light of the analysis in Section IV, a question that needs to be clarified is whether, in situations where the ICJ has recognized, or should recognize, any margin of discretion to a State with respect to the assessment of international law norms, such a recognition can be regarded as amounting to judicial deference towards national decision-making, and if so, whether the margin of appreciation doctrine may be applied.

This problem has already been addressed in the literature in the context of disputes regarding the appropriateness of national measures taken to comply with an obligation of result. Reference is made to the *LaGrand* and *Avena* judgments, both concerning violations by the United States of its obligation under the 1963 Vienna Convention on Consular Relations, by failing to give notice of the arrest and the sentencing of foreign citizens to the competent national authorities. In both cases the Court endorsed the view that the review(s) and reconsideration(s) of the convictions pronounced against individuals whose right to notification under the Treaty had been violated should be carried out by means of choice of the State to which the obligation is addressed.[46] The same flexible perspective has been more recently taken in the *Jurisdictional Immunities* case where the Court recognized the respondent as having:

> the right to choose the means it considers best suited to achieve the required result [namely, it refers to the obligation of restitution, ie to take all steps to ensure that all the decisions of Italian courts and other judicial authorities infringing Germany's sovereign immunity become unenforceable]. Thus, the Respondent is under an obligation to achieve this result by enacting appropriate legislation or by resorting to other methods of its choosing having the same effect.[47]

In all these cases the Court limited itself to binding the State to the achievement of a specific result, leaving it free as to the choice of means to perform its obligation.

Even if it is quite clear that the ICJ has adopted a deferential approach towards legal and factual determinations made by States, the question whether this attitude

[46] ICJ, *LaGrand* (*Germany v United States of America*), Judgment, ICJ Rep 2001, paras 125–6; ICJ, *Avena and Other Mexican Nationals* (*Mexico v United States of America*), Judgment, ICJ Rep 2004, para 127. On this aspect, see Bernardo Sepúlveda-Amor, 'Diplomatic and Consular Protection: the Right of the State and the Rights of Individual in the LaGrand and Avena Cases' in Ulrich Fastenrath et al (eds), *From Bilateralism to Community Interest: Essays in Honour of Judge Bruno Simma* (Oxford: Oxford University Press, 2011) 1099.

[47] ICJ, *Jurisdictional Immunities of the State* (*Germany v Italy: Greece intervening*), Judgment, ICJ Rep 2012, para 137.

may be regarded as an application of a 'margin of appreciation-type' decision-making methodology or rather is the result of a different reasoning is still to be answered.[48] In this regard it should be noted that margin of appreciation is a concept which has essentially been developed by the ECtHR; it has been described as 'the measure of discretion allowed to the Member States in the manner in which they implement the [ECHR's] standards, taking into account their own particular circumstances and conditions.'[49] It is inversely proportional to the level of consensus reached by States on the interpretation and the application of a norm, and it is conditioned on the respect of the proportionality test. The doctrine was initially elaborated by the ECtHR in response to the concerns of national governments that international policies could jeopardize their national security interests. It has been further extended to non-security issues, and is aimed at 'enabling the [ECtHR] to balance the sovereignty of Contracting Parties with their obligation under the Convention.'[50] In other words, the doctrine is aimed at preserving a zone of legality where the State is free to act in order to safeguard its fundamental interests without violating international obligations. It does not extend to the entire Convention, but only to provisions that could give rise to cultural, moral, environmental or security concerns. It never applies to norms protecting fundamental rights (such as the right to life). The objective is to put the State in the position to regulate, according to its own fundamental values, matters that traditionally fall within its domestic jurisdiction, yet at the same time without violating the Convention.

The question which is at issue here, and which has also been raised before the ICJ by Japan in the *Whaling* case, is whether the margin of appreciation approach is applied by the Court. According to literature: 'A conspicuous recent example of resort by the ICJ to a decision-making methodology compatible with the margin of appreciation doctrine may be found in the discussion of appropriate remedies in the two consular assistance cases.'[51] While it is therefore undeniable that in this regard the ICJ recognized a wide power of discretion to the State, it is however questionable whether this can be interpreted as amounting to application of the margin of appreciation approach by the ICJ.[52] In the context of the ECtHR, the margin of appreciation doctrine is grounded on the need to balance the supervisory powers of the European Court over domestic conduct while respecting the primary responsibility of the State for the protection of human rights and freedoms of individuals within its jurisdiction in situations where the safeguard of fundamental national values is concerned.[53] The idea is that, owing to their

[48] Shany, 'Toward a General Margin of Appreciation'.

[49] Yutaka Arai-Takahashi, *The Margin of Appreciation Doctrine and the Principle of Proportionality in the Jurisprudence of the ECHR* (Oxford: Intersentia, 2002) 2.

[50] R. St. John Macdonald, 'The Margin of Appreciation in the Jurisprudence of the European Court of Human Rights', Collected Courses of the Academy of European Law (1992), 95 ff.

[51] Shany, 'Toward a General Margin of Appreciation', 935. In the same vein Jean-Pierre Cot, 'The Law of the Sea and the Margin of Appreciation' in Tafsir M. Ndiaye and Rüdiger Wolfrum (eds), *Law of the Sea, Environmental Law and Settlement of Disputes: Liber Amicorum Judge Thomas A. Mensah* (Leiden: Martinus Nijhoff, 2007) 391.

[52] On this and on its practical implications, see Cot, 'Margin of Appreciation', para 34.

[53] On this point see Arai-Tajharashi, *The Margin of Appreciation*, 236 ff.

direct knowledge of the society and its needs, national authorities are in principle better placed than the international judge to appreciate the existence of a public interest to be safeguarded and to decide how to implement the rights enshrined in the ECHR without putting such an interest at risk. The perspective is different however with respect to the ICJ, whose jurisdiction is of a general character and it extends to inter-State disputes concerning the violation or interpretation of international law. In this context the interests to be balanced by the Court are primarily those of the competing States, and the development or application of a uniform standard of review (and *a fortiori* of a doctrine in this regard) is difficult to conceive. The conclusion that can be drawn therefore is that the margin of appreciation doctrine, as it has been developed by the ECtHR, has never been applied as such in the context of the ICJ. The Court has rather made recourse to a similar reasoning—that national authorities may be better positioned than international judges to determine the domestic measures to be taken in order to achieve a given result—only with regard to the application of open-ended norms in *LaGrand, Avena* and the *Jurisdictional Immunities* cases, where it adopted a flexible standard of judicial review which is similar to that applied by the ECtHR in its jurisprudence.[54]

VI. Concluding Remarks

In the light of the reasoning carried out so far, one may question the rationale for the standard of review issue concerning the ICJ. As the analysis of its jurisprudence has shown, the existence and the grounds of judicial deference accorded to State decision-making may in fact be heterogeneous and depend on different circumstances—such as the character of the norm which is alleged to have been violated and the purpose for which it is intended, the importance of the value that it aims to protect, and the degree of legal certainty the judges aim to achieve in order to avoid divergent means of enacting an international norm; with the consequence that uniform standards may be difficult to identify and establish.

It should be further noted that the question of applicable standard of review has hardly ever been considered directly by the Court, so that the criteria that it applies in this respect may be only drawn by way of inference from the analysis of its jurisprudence.

In this context, standard of review, margin of appreciation or deference problems may be traced in cases where a question of interpretation of an international rule is at issue and the State to which the violation of the norm is ascribed claims to have acted within the proper exercise of its discretion, in accordance with international law. This situation occurs, for example, when the conduct performed

[54] On the application of the margin of appreciation as a standard of review see Cot, 'Margin of Appreciation', para 34.

by the national authorities has been justified under norms (including derogating clauses) which resort, for their application, to elements that need to be clarified or that provide only for an obligation to obtain a required result. In these cases the Court has to first establish whether the State enjoys a certain degree of discretion as concerns the interpretation of the rule or the choice of the means of implementation, and then what are the grounds for the deference granted to its legal and factual determinations.[55]

The jurisprudence of the Court in this last regard seems to suggest that the standard of review to be applied depends on the nature, aim and characteristics of the norm concerned, being quite restrictive when fundamental concerns of the international community as a whole are at stake, while granting a greater degree of deference to national decision-making process in situations where self-judging clauses or result-oriented norms are at issue. Even in these latter cases however, the margin of discretion allowed to the State is not unlimited, its exercise being subject to the obligation of good faith,[56] respect of which should strike a reasonable balance between domestic interests and international cooperation.

[55] As it has been rightly suggested by literature, 'the margin of appreciation implies a degree of review. It runs against the principle of absolute sovereignty and calls for some form of challenges and monitoring' (Cot, 'Margin of Appreciation', para 34).

[56] Cot, 'Margin of Appreciation', para 34.

18

Standard of Review in the International Tribunal for the Law of the Sea

Rosemary Rayfuse

I. Introduction

The concept of the 'standard of review' is well known in international law. Related to the concept of the 'margin of appreciation' applied in human rights tribunals,[1] it refers to the degree of deference shown by an international tribunal to the decisions and actions of national authorities.[2] As Caroline Henckels notes in Chapter 7 of this volume, the aim of the standard of review in the international context is to 'strike an appropriate balance between the need for compliance with international obligations and national autonomy'.[3] Key to its invocation is the exercise of a regulatory or judicial discretion on the part of a State.[4] Most often discussed in the context of World Trade Organization,[5] European,[6] or human rights[7] law, the concept has received little attention in the context of the law of the sea. Many of the rules laid down in the 1982 Law of the Sea Convention (LOSC)[8] do not involve or relate to the exercise of regulatory or judicial discretion by a State. For those that do, the complex dispute settlement provisions in Part XV of the LOSC ensure that few disputes arising from their interpretation or application will be resolved by an international tribunal.[9] Nevertheless, the concept of the standard of review has been identified as relevant to the International Tribunal for the Law of the Sea

[1] For a discussion of the margin of appreciation in the ECtHR see Chapter 13 by Mónika Ambrus and Chapter 14 by Uladzislau Belavusau in this volume.

[2] Jan Bohannes and Nicholas Lockhart, 'Standard of Review in WTO Law' in Daniel Bethlehem et al (eds), *The Oxford Handbook of International Trade Law* (Oxford: Oxford University Press, 2009) 379.

[3] Caroline Henckels, Chapter 7 in this volume (Section II).

[4] Caroline Henckels, Chapter 7 in this volume (Section II).

[5] See eg Chapter 9 by Lukasz Gruszczynski and Valentina Vadi and Chapter 12 by Alexia Herwig and Asja Serdarevic, both in this volume.

[6] See eg Chapter 12 by Alexia Herwig and Asja Serdarevic in this volume.

[7] See eg Mónika Ambrus, Chapter 13 in this volume.

[8] 1982 United Nations Convention on the Law of the Sea, 1833 UNTS 31363.

[9] Rosemary Rayfuse, 'The Future of Compulsory Dispute Settlement under the Law of the Sea Convention', 36 *Victoria University of Wellington Law Review* 1 (2005).

(ITLOS), most notably in the context of its prompt release jurisdiction where the issue to be determined relates to the reasonableness of the bond set by a coastal State for release of a vessel and its crew alleged to have infringed certain coastal State laws, and the maintenance of the appropriate balance between coastal and flag State rights.[10]

This chapter examines the concept of standard of review as developed and applied in the prompt release jurisprudence of ITLOS. The chapter begins with a brief discussion of the jurisdiction of ITLOS and the history of its prompt release jurisdiction, an understanding of which is essential to an appreciation of the Tribunal's approach to the concept of the standard of review in prompt release proceedings. It then discusses the Tribunal's general approach to the standard of review and the content of that standard. The chapter then examines the manner in which the standard has been applied by the Tribunal. In doing so the chapter seeks to illuminate the extent to which ITLOS either implicitly or explicitly relies on the concept of the standard of review in prompt release cases, the content of that standard, and the extent to which the Tribunal succeeds in meeting that standard in adjudicating and reviewing State conduct.

II. The Jurisdiction of the International Tribunal for the Law of the Sea: A Brief Primer

The ITLOS was established in 1996 pursuant to Annex VI of the LOSC which sets out its structure, composition and basic rules of procedure. The Tribunal's jurisdiction is determined by the dispute settlement provisions contained in Part XV of the LOSC which provide, in default of other agreement between States, for compulsory recourse to a range of procedures including various arbitral tribunals, the International Court of Justice (ICJ) and ITLOS.[11] The terminology of 'compulsory dispute settlement' is, in truth, something of a misnomer given that the limitations and exclusions set out in Part XV effectively exclude a broad range of ocean disputes from the compulsory procedures. Moreover, in the absence of any exclusivity of jurisdiction or hierarchical superiority over other courts or tribunals disputes can only be submitted to ITLOS where both parties have made a declaration formally accepting its jurisdiction.[12] With few States having chosen ITLOS as their forum of preference, fears of the Tribunal's underutilization that were expressed during the negotiation of the LOSC may have been well-founded.[13]

[10] Seline Trevisanut, 'The Exercise of Administrative Functions by ITLOS: A Comment on Prompt Release Cases' in Nerina Boschiero et al (eds), *International Courts and the Development of International Law: Essays in Honour of Tullio Treves* (The Hague: Asser Press, 2013).

[11] LOSC, Article 287.

[12] LOSC, Article 287.

[13] As of December 2013 there are 166 States parties to the LOSC. Of those, only 45 States have made declarations under Article 287, only 36 of whom have indicated ITLOS as their first preference. See <http://www.un.org/Depts/los/settlement_of_disputes/choice_procedure.htm> (accessed 28 March 2014).

Nevertheless, ITLOS does have residual compulsory jurisdiction in two particular types of cases: those relating to the prompt release of vessels and crews, and requests for the prescription of provisional measures pending the constitution of an Annex VII or Annex VIII arbitral tribunal.[14] Needless to say, it is these two types of applications that have formed the bulk of the Tribunal's work to date. Of the twenty-two cases that have reached ITLOS, nine have involved prompt release applications while five have involved requests for provisional measures. It is the Tribunal's prompt release jurisdiction, in particular, in which the concept of standard of review is enlivened. The following discussion therefore focuses on the prompt release cases. Before turning to the jurisprudence, however, a brief explanation of the concept and nature of prompt release proceedings is warranted.

III. The History of ITLOS Prompt Release Jurisdiction

The origins of the prompt release jurisdiction of ITLOS lie in the extension of coastal state jurisdiction effected by the LOSC. With the adoption of the exclusive economic zone (EEZ) concept, the LOSC conferred significant jurisdictional capacity on coastal States, affording them sovereign rights for the purpose of exploring, exploiting, conserving and managing the natural resources found with their EEZs as well as the power to enforce laws and regulations adopted pursuant to the exercise of these rights. In particular, Article 73 allows coastal States to board, inspect, arrest and take judicial proceedings against foreign flagged vessels and crews for breaches of their fisheries regulations. Article 220 similarly allows the coastal state to detain foreign vessels that have violated laws and regulations with respect to the prevention, reduction and control of pollution in the coastal State's EEZ or territorial sea where the violation has resulted in a discharge causing major damage or threat of major damage to the coastline or marine environment of the coastal State while Article 226 allows detention for the purpose of investigations provided for in Article 220.

In recognition of the potential for abuse by coastal States of their enforcement powers, and in order to reconcile the interests of coastal States with the competing interests of flag States in the freedom of navigation, certain substantive safeguards were included in these provisions. Article 73(2) requires the prompt release of arrested vessels and their crews upon the posting of a reasonable bond or other security and prohibits the imprisonment of crew members unless an agreement to the contrary exists between the States concerned. For its part, Article 220 similarly requires compliance with release, bonding and other financial security arrangements to which the States may be party.[15] Article 226 is more explicit and requires delay of a vessel to be for no longer than essential for the purposes of conducting the relevant investigations. Where a violation of coastal State regulations

[14] LOSC, Article 292.

[15] Such arrangements are found, for example, in the 1969 International Convention on Civil Liability for Oil Pollution Damage, Articles V and VI, 9 ILM 45 (1970).

is confirmed, detained vessels are to be promptly released subject to reasonable procedures such as bonding or other appropriate financial security.

Not content with these substantive protections, during the negotiation of the LOSC a number of delegations pushed for the inclusion of further procedural safeguards to ensure the prompt release of arrested or detained vessels.[16] These safeguards were incorporated into Article 292, which provides that, unless the parties otherwise agree, the jurisdiction of the Tribunal is mandatory in cases relating to the prompt release of vessels and crews. The Tribunal must deal with the application for release without delay and must deal only with the question of release, without prejudice to the merits of any case before the appropriate domestic forum against the vessel, its owner or its crew. By virtue of the reference to compliance with the Convention provisions on prompt release this jurisdiction is, however, limited to cases involving claims relating to illegal fishing or to claims in respect of pollution caused by unauthorized dumping or discharge as those are the only matters where prompt release is specifically addressed within the LOSC provisions. While ITLOS has considered requests for the prompt release of vessels in other cases alleging violations of other coastal State laws and regulations,[17] these requests have been made in the context of provisional measures proceedings where the decisions of the Tribunal have been based on considerations of international legality, imminent risk of irreparable harm and humanitarian concerns arising as a result of the time lag involved in establishing an Annex VII tribunal, and not on any concept of a standard of review.

IV. The Nature and Scope of Prompt Release Proceedings

Prompt release proceedings are a special procedure having a character somewhat analogous to but different from dispute settlement.[18] In this respect they differ from trade, human rights or other proceedings in which the concept of the standard of review is relevant. This difference is manifest in the exhortation in Article 292(3) that prompt release proceedings shall deal only with the question of release and that they shall do so without prejudice to the merits of any case in a domestic forum against the vessel, its owner or crew. This special nature of prompt release proceedings is reflected in the Tribunal's judgments which make clear that these procedures are not to be considered as equivalent to judicial review.[19]

[16] Myron H. Nordquist et al (eds), *United Nations Convention on the Law of the Sea 1982: A Commentary, vol. V* (The Hague: Kluwer Law International, 1989) Article 292, 66–71 at 67.

[17] See the *ARA Libertad* case (*Argentina v Ghana*), ITLOS, Case No. 20, 15 December 2012; The *M/V Lousia* case (*Saint Vincent and the Grenadines v Kingdom of Spain*), ITLOS, Case No. 18, 23 December 2010; and the *Arctic Sunrise* case (*Kingdom of the Netherlands v Russian Federation*), ITLOS, Case No. 22, 22 November 2013.

[18] David H. Anderson, 'Investigation, Detention and Release of Foreign Fishing Vessels under the United Nations Convention on the Law of the Sea 1982 and Other International Agreements', 11 *International Journal of Marine and Coastal Law* 177 (1996).

[19] The *Camouco* case (*Panama v France*), ITLOS, Case No. 5, 7 February 2000, Dissenting Opinion of Judge Anderson.

They are neither preliminary nor incidental, but rather separate, independent proceedings based on the interpretation and application of the LOSC.[20] Unlike provisional measures proceedings which are incidental to the proceedings on the merits, prompt release proceedings form a discrete case which results in a definitive final determination.[21] They are 'not a first phase in a case which proceeds on to the merits'.[22] Rather, they are 'definitive proceedings in which a court or tribunal is required to decide whether a case has been made that the allegation of non-compliance (with prompt release obligations under Article 73, 220 or 226) is well founded'.[23] Thus, they are 'an independent remedy and not an appeal against a decision of a national court'.[24]

The sole purpose of prompt release proceedings, and thus the sole determinant of the standard of review, is to balance 'the interest of the coastal state to take appropriate measures as may be necessary to ensure compliance with the laws and regulations adopted by it on the one hand and the interest of the flag state in securing prompt release of its vessels and crews from detention on the other'.[25] A more detailed rationale for such proceedings involves 'the interests of shipping companies in minimizing economic loss, of crews in avoiding physical suffering due to vessel detention, and of detaining states in avoiding a serious safety and environmental hazard'.[26] Essentially, their purpose is a balance between the right to prompt release on the one hand and the right to try and punish on the other.[27]

As independent proceedings, the scope of prompt release jurisdiction is circumscribed by the requirement in Article 292(3) that the determination regarding prompt release be made without prejudice to the merits of the case in the domestic forum. The determination should also not prejudice the merits of any case 'that may be brought before an international court or tribunal concerning the compatibility with international law of any national laws or of measures taken by national authorities on the basis of such laws against a ship, its cargo or fishing gear, including arrest, detention or judicial proceedings'.[28] However, the independence of the proceedings works both ways. As noted by the Tribunal in the *Saiga* case,[29] while the States involved in prompt release proceedings will be bound by the Tribunal's judgment as far as release of the vessel and payment of the bond or other security are concerned, 'their domestic courts in considering the merits of the case, are not

[20] The *M/V Saiga* case (*Saint Vincent and the Grenadines v Guinea*), ITLOS, Case No. 1, 4 December 1997 (*Saiga No. 1*), para 50.

[21] *Saiga No. 1,* Dissenting Opinion of Judge Mensah, para 5.

[22] *Saiga No. 1,* Dissenting Opinion of Judge Anderson, para 5.

[23] *Saiga No. 1,* Dissenting Opinion of Judge Mensah, para 5.

[24] The *Monte Confurco* case (*Seychelles v France*), ITLOS, Case No. 6, 18 December 2000, para 58.

[25] *Monte Confurco*, para 70.

[26] *Camouco*, paras 57–58.

[27] Bernard H. Oxman and Vincent P. Bantz, 'The "Camouco" (Panama v. France) (Judgment). ITLOS, Case No. 5', 94(4) *AJIL* 713 (2000), 720.

[28] The *Juno Trader* case (*Saint Vincent and the Grenadines v Guinea-Bissau*), ITLOS, Case No. 13, 18 December 2004, Joint Separate Opinion of Judges Wolfrum and Mensah, para 4.

[29] *Saiga No. 1* (*Saint Vincent and the Grenadines v Guinea*), ITLOS, Case No. 1, 4 December 1997.

bound by any findings of fact or law that the Tribunal may have made in order to reach its conclusions.'[30]

Two important consequences relating to the admissibility of claims flow from the nature of prompt release proceedings. The first relates to the application of the domestic remedies rule. In the *Camouco* case,[31] France argued that the application for prompt release was premature given that domestic legal proceedings, the purpose of which were to achieve precisely the same result as the prompt release proceedings brought before the Tribunal, were currently pending. According to France, this created a situation of *lis pendens*, rendering the ITLOS application inadmissible. In truth, no situation of *lis pendens* arises, given that separate and distinct issues are at stake in the two proceedings, one of which is governed by national law and the other by international law.[32] Moreover, Article 292 allows for proceedings to be brought within ten days of the date of detention and requires the Tribunal to proceed 'without delay'. The Tribunal thus rejected France's argument on the basis that to read a requirement of exhaustion of domestic remedies into Article 292 would defeat its very object and purpose.[33]

The second and related consequence arises from the requirement to consider only the question of release without prejudice to the merits of proceedings in the domestic courts. The Tribunal has repeatedly noted that questions relating to the legality or illegality of the actions taken by the coastal State against a vessel found or suspected to have engaged in illegal fishing or polluting activities are irrelevant.[34] The only issue to be considered in prompt release proceedings is compliance or non-compliance by the detaining State with a provision of the LOSC for the prompt release of a vessel upon posting of a reasonable bond.[35] Thus, the laws of the detaining State and the decisions of its courts are to be treated only as relevant facts and only to the extent necessary for a proper appreciation of the reasonableness of the bond.[36] While, as discussed in Section VI below, this has implications for the standard of review, it also has implications for the admissibility of an application for prompt release in that the rendering of a final judgment by the national courts of a detaining State may effectively preclude an order for prompt release.[37]

This possibility was first raised in the *Grand Prince* case[38] where France argued that an application brought by Belize had been rendered moot by reason of an

[30] *Saiga No. 1*, para 49.

[31] The *Camouco* case (*Panama v France*), ITLOS, Case No. 5, 7 February 2000.

[32] Oxman and Bantz, 'The "Camouco"', 719.

[33] *Camouco*, paras 55–8.

[34] *Camouco*, Dissenting Opinion of Judge Anderson.

[35] *Grand Prince* case (*Belize v France*), ITLOS, Case No. 8, 20 April 2001, Separate Opinion of Judge Treves.

[36] *Camouco*, Dissenting Opinion of Judge Anderson; *Monte Confurco*, para 74; *Grand Prince*, para 72; and *Hoshinmaru case* (*Japan v Russian Federation*), ITLOS, Case No. 14, 6 August 2007, para 89.

[37] Yoshifumi Tanaka, 'Prompt Release in the United Nations Convention on the Law of the Sea: Some Reflections on the ITLOS Jurisprudence', 51(2) *Netherlands International Law Review* 237 (2004), at 257–8.

[38] *Grand Prince*, paras 57–61.

order of a French criminal court confiscating the vessel, its equipment and the fishing gear, fish products and catch on board. The issue was not decided because the Tribunal held that Belize lacked standing to bring the application. The issue was raised again in the *Juno Trader* case, where Guinea-Bissau argued the case was moot because the vessel had been confiscated and both its ownership and flag had reverted to the State pursuant to administrative procedures as a result of non-payment of a fine.[39] However, the evidence revealed that the confiscation order had been suspended upon judicial review by a national court pending settlement of the case, thereby rendering 'inapplicable any sanction for non-payment, including confiscation'.[40] As the vessel could not be considered confiscated, the argument was rejected.

In the *Tomimaru* case, the Tribunal resolved the issue holding that the effect of final confiscation was, indeed, to render an application for prompt release without object. The *Tomimaru* had been arrested by Russia for illegal fishing within the Russian EEZ and, after rather complex domestic legal processes, had been seized by the State. Domestic appeal and judicial review processes had ended many months later in the confirmation of the confiscation and reversion of the vessel to the Russian State. All of this had transpired before the application for prompt release was submitted to ITLOS. In the circumstances, the Tribunal held that while a decision to confiscate would not prevent it from considering an application for prompt release while domestic proceedings were ongoing, once those proceedings had reached their final conclusion an application for prompt release was without object. To order the release of the vessel 'would contradict the decision which concluded the proceedings before the appropriate domestic fora and encroach upon national competencies, thus contravening Article 292, paragraph 3, of the Convention'.[41] Thus while non-exhaustion of domestic remedies will not be a bar to an application for prompt release, subject to issues of timeliness and due process discussed below, their exhaustion will be.

V. The General Approach to the 'Standard of Review'

Given the nature of prompt release proceedings it can come as no surprise that the Tribunal has interpreted the standard of review in which it engages in a very circumscribed manner. As noted in Section IV above, the only issue to be considered in prompt release proceedings is compliance or non-compliance by the detaining State with a provision of the LOSC for the prompt release of a vessel upon posting of a reasonable bond. Issues relating to the legality or illegality of actions taken are irrelevant.[42] The most significant aspect of the Tribunal's prompt release jurisprudence has therefore involved establishing and applying the criteria for determining the 'reasonableness' of the bond. The concept of reasonableness is

[39] The *Juno Trader* case (*Saint Vincent and the Grenadines v Guinea-Bissau*), ITLOS, Case No. 13, 18 December 2004, Joint Separate Opinion of Judges Wolfrum and Mensah, para 58 (*Juno Trader*).

[40] *Juno Trader*, para 62.

[41] The *Tomimaru* case (*Japan v Russian Federation*), ITLOS, Case No. 15, 6 August 2007.

[42] *Saiga No. 1*, para 62.

related to the standard of review to be applied by the Tribunal by virtue of the fact that 'provided that the bond is not "unreasonable", the Tribunal does not have to substitute its discretion for that of the coastal state.'[43]

Two approaches to determining the standard of reasonableness, or the 'margin of appreciation', have emerged in the Tribunal's jurisprudence; one of strong deference to the regulations and decisions of the coastal State and another that seeks to assess reasonableness by reference to some sort of international standard. Essentially these approaches mirror those taken in the trade and human rights situations.[44]

Early articulation of these approaches was on display in the *Camouco* case. Taking a restrictive approach, Judge Anderson considered that national courts should be accorded a broad 'margin of appreciation' as they were 'best placed to appreciate the relevant considerations of fact and law in the States concerned'.[45] Judge Wolfrum, too, favoured a restrictive approach, noting 'it is not for the Tribunal to establish a system of its own which does not take into account the enforcement policy by the coastal state in question,' or 'to substitute its own decision for the discretionary power of the coastal state' which enjoyed a 'considerable margin of appreciation'. Referring to the standards adopted in human rights courts, Judge Wolfrum considered that the Tribunal should only interfere where the national decisions or measures were unlawful under international law, arbitrary, an abuse of authority, made in bad faith or disproportionate.[46] Judge Treves, on the other hand, was of the opinion that the notion of 'reasonable bond' 'must be an international notion, based on the Convention' and that it did not 'have to coincide with what can be considered as reasonable from a domestic point of view.'[47] Judge Laing similarly considered the appropriate standard to be an international one as determined by the Tribunal, the content of which could certainly differ from that in domestic law. The role of the Tribunal was neither to enforce the domestic laws of the detaining State nor the substantive provisions of the LOSC but to apply an internationally determined objective standard of reasonableness.[48]

Certainly, if the bond requirements in the LOSC are separate and distinct from national law, then arguably the standards used to review the reasonableness of the application of those requirements should also be autonomous and not dependent on national law.[49] Thus, it is hardly surprising that the notion of an international standard of reasonableness of bond appears to be that which has won favour in the Tribunal. As confirmed in the *Monte Confurco* case, the Tribunal's determination

[43] The *Volga* case (*Russian Federation v Australia*), ITLOS, Case No. 11, 23 December 2002, Separate Opinion of Judge Cot, para 22.

[44] See Chapter 13 by Mónika Ambrus, Chapter 12 by Alexia Herwig and Asja Serdarevic, and Chapter 9 by Lukasz Gruszczynski and Valentina Vadi, all in this volume.

[45] *Camouco*, Dissenting Opinion of Judge Anderson.

[46] *Camouco*, Dissenting Opinion of Judge Wolfrum, paras 11–14.

[47] *Camouco*, Dissenting Opinion of Judge Treves, para 4.

[48] *Camouco*, Declaration of Judge Laing.

[49] Oxman and Bantz, 'The "Camouco"', 720.

of reasonableness 'must be based on the Convention and other rules of international law not incompatible with the Convention'.[50] This does not, however, mean that national law is irrelevant. On the contrary, the Tribunal has made it clear that in assessing the reasonableness of the bond the laws of the detaining State and the decisions of its courts are relevant. However, as discussed below, they are to be treated only as relevant facts[51] to be considered in the context of all the information provided by the parties in arriving at an objective assessment of the reasonableness of the bond.[52]

VI. The Content of the 'Standard of Review': Determining the Reasonableness Criteria

'Reasonableness' has been described as 'both an instrument for preserving the margin of appreciation of States and an instrument for courts to control the exercising of the discretionary power of the State'.[53] The LOSC provides no guidance as to the substantive content of the reasonableness criteria other than it is to be assessed in light of the object and purpose of Article 292, to wit the balance of interests between detaining and flag States. Thus, ITLOS has had to work out for itself what its international standard of reasonableness entails. To that end the Tribunal has held that reasonableness encompasses the amount, nature and form of the bond or financial security.[54] Factors relevant to the assessment of reasonableness include the gravity of the alleged offences, the penalties imposed or imposable under the laws of the detaining State, the value of the detained vessel and of the cargo seized, the amount of the bond imposed by the detaining State and its form,[55] although the list is not exhaustive and no strict rules exist as to the weight to be accorded to each factor.[56] As a general matter 'due account must be taken of the bond or other security set by the detaining state, having regard to all the circumstances of the particular case',[57] and 'the assessment of the relevant factors must be an objective one, taking into account all information provided' by the parties.[58] The guiding criterion for the Tribunal in the assessment of the reasonableness of the bond must, however, at all times be the balance of interests between the flag State's right to prompt release and the coastal State's right to try.[59]

Also identified as relevant to a reasonableness review have been the concepts of proportionality, humanity and due process relied on by other tribunals such as the European Court of Human Rights and the Court of Justice of the European Union.[60] The concept of proportionality is relevant both to assessing the reasonableness of the detaining State's bond and of that eventually set by the Tribunal.

[50] *Monte Confurco*, para 75. [51] *Monte Confurco*, para 74.
[52] *Juno Trader*, para 85. [53] *Volga*, Separate Opinion of Judge Cot, para 18.
[54] *Saiga No. 1*, para 82. [55] [56] *Monte Confurco*, para 76.
[57] *Volga*, para 65. [58] *Juno Trader*, para 85. [59] *Monte Confurco*, para 72.
[60] See Chapter 13 by Mónika Ambrus, Chapter 14 by Uladzislau Belavusau, and Chapter 12 by Alexia Herwig and Asja Serdarevic, all in this volume.

The concept was first mentioned by Judge Laing in the *Camouco* case, where he called for the careful development of the Tribunal's jurisprudence in light of the concepts of consistency and proportionality.[61] Of concern to Judge Laing was the Tribunal's failure to explain the significant difference between the amount of bond set in the *Saiga* and *Camouco* cases. The issue of proportionality of aggregate potential liability under national law to the bond set was again raised in the *Monte Confurco* case, although there is nothing in the judgment to suggest that the Tribunal accepted the argument. Indeed, given the broad differences in national laws and potential penalties imposable it seems difficult to argue that a fixed ratio of bond to potential liability or bond to vessel value could provide an objective criterion applicable in all cases.[62] Nevertheless, proportionality has not been irrelevant. Implicit in the Tribunal's judgments has been the notion that the amount of bond set in individual cases should be proportionate to the gravity of the alleged offences. This was made explicit in the *Hoshinmaru* case.[63] Thus it is clear that the State behaviour should be proportional to the aim legally pursued.[64]

The concepts of humanity and due process have also been considered by the Tribunal as relevant to the assessment of the reasonableness of coastal State actions. In the *Juno Trader* case, Guinea-Bissau had ignored representations from the vessel owners, who had posted a bond to secure the release of the vessel and the crew, and had simply carried on with its domestic administrative processes, detaining the crew, assessing fines and, upon their non-payment, ordering confiscation of the vessel. In considering whether Guinea-Bissau had violated its obligations under Article 73, the Tribunal noted that 'the obligation of prompt release of vessels and crews includes elementary considerations of humanity and due process of law'.[65] The Tribunal went on to say that the criteria of reasonableness 'indicates that a concern for fairness is one of the purposes of' Article 73.[66] For his part, Judge Treves considered the articulation of a requirement for due process a 'very relevant and welcome new development in the jurisprudence of the Tribunal'.[67]

The issue of due process was again discussed in the *Tomimaru* case and again in the context of a confiscation order. Starting from the premise that confiscation must not be used in such a manner as to upset the balance of interests between the flag and coastal State, the Tribunal stated:

> A decision to confiscate eliminates the provisional character of the detention of the vessel rendering the procedure for its prompt release without object. Such a decision should not be taken in such a way as to prevent the shipowner from having recourse to available domestic judicial remedies, or as to prevent the flag state from resorting to the prompt release procedure set forth in the Convention; nor should it be taken through proceedings inconsistent with international standards of due process of international

[61] *Camouco*, Declaration of Judge Laing. [62] Tanaka, 'Prompt Release', at 267.

[63] *Hoshinmaru*, para 88.

[64] *Case Concerning Filleting within the Gulf of St Lawrence* (*Canada v France*), Arbitral Award 17 July 1986, 82 ILR, 631, para 54, cited in *Volga*, Separate Opinion of Judge Cot, para 21.

[65] *Juno Trader*, para 77. [66] *Juno Trader*, para 77.

[67] *Juno Trader*, Separate Opinion of Judge Treves.

law. In particular, a confiscation decided in unjustified haste would jeopardize the operation of article 292 of the Convention.[68]

However, in that case there had been no allegation of undue haste or of inconsistency of domestic law with international standards and no allegation that the confiscation procedures had been followed to thwart the possibility of recourse to international or national remedies. Moreover, the applicant, Japan, had not contested that the domestic proceedings had been completed and that there was no further avenue of appeal. Since a decision for prompt release would contradict the decision of the national court and encroach on national competencies the application was considered without object and moot. It is important to note, however, that the result in this case was made possible because of excessive delay by Japan in bringing the application more than eight months after the detention of the vessel. As Judge Lucky noted, there is a presumption in favour of States adhering to due process. Nevertheless, that presumption may be overcome.[69] The question thus remains whether, and if so under what conditions, a 'too swift' confiscation might yet be considered an abuse of process sufficient for the Tribunal to effectively overturn an order of confiscation and order release.[70]

VII. Applying the Reasonableness Criteria

Articulating standards of review is one thing; applying them in such a way as to ensure the appropriate balance between coastal State and flag State rights is quite another. Indeed, it is not entirely clear that the Tribunal always succeeds in doing so. On several issues the application by the Tribunal of its standard of review has led to controversial outcomes seen as unduly interfering with the rights and interests of coastal States.

In its first case, the *Saiga* case, an oil tanker engaged in bunkering fishing vessels had been charged with customs offences for which no obligation of prompt release is found in the LOSC. In finding the application admissible the Tribunal recharacterized the alleged offences to ones related to fishing, considering itself not bound by the classification given by the detaining State.[71] In hindsight this result is somewhat surprising given that when the case was eventually heard on the merits, the Tribunal found that bunkering was not an activity related to fishing.[72] While the Tribunal's recharacterization of the offence can certainly be explained by reference to the independent nature of the prompt release proceedings and the desire to ensure that coastal States do not emasculate Article 73 by

[68] *Tomimaru*, para 76. [69] *Tomimaru*, Separate Opinion of Judge Lucky.

[70] Vincent P. Cogliati-Bantz, 'International Tribunal for the Law of the Sea, *Hoshinmaru* and *Tomimaru (Japan v Russian Federation)*, Prompt Release Judgments of 6 August 2007', 58 *ICLQ* 241 (2009), 257.

[71] *Saiga No. 1*, paras 62–72.

[72] *Saiga No. 2* (*Saint Vincent and the Grenadines v Guinea*), ITLOS, Case No. 2, 1 July 1999 (Merits).

unilaterally characterizing fishing activities as non-fisheries related offences,[73] it is perhaps better explained by the fact that this was the first case heard by a tribunal that may simply have been anxious not to turn applicants away and render itself redundant from the start. Nevertheless, in ordering prompt release in that case, the Tribunal effectively undermined the potential penalties and legal remedies ultimately available to the coastal State.

The problem of potentially undermining national penalties has also arisen in the context of the Tribunal's attempts to achieve objectivity through a balancing of the aggregate potential liability (potential penalties imposable) with the bond set. It will be recalled that the power to order prompt release upon payment of a reasonable bond 'constitutes, to a certain extent "an interference" with the coastal state's judicial authorities' which allows the Tribunal to 'put a brake on the discretionary power of the coastal state with respect to the fixing of bonds in certain circumstances.'[74] Of concern to the Tribunal is the possibility that States might deliberately seek to impose unduly harsh and disproportionate penalties which may either be unreasonable or may otherwise be contrary to the LOSC or other rules of international law.[75] Thus, in several cases the Tribunal has refused to accept the aggregate potential liability, or the maximum penalties imposable, as the appropriate measure, reducing by significant amounts the bond requested by the detaining State.

In the *Saiga* and *Camouco* cases the bonds were set at 9 and 26 per cent of what had been sought by the detaining State, respectively. In the former case the detaining State appears to have been penalized for its refusal to engage with the flag State by failing to set a bond in the first place. In the latter the Tribunal accepted that the gravity of the alleged offences and the range of penalties that could be imposed under French law for those offences was relevant. However, charges had not yet been laid against the vessel owners and it appears the Tribunal considered that since maximum penalties had not yet been sought, they should play no role in the Tribunal's assessment of what was reasonable. In the *Monte Confurco* case the Tribunal adjusted downwards the bond that had been set by the detaining State which had taken into account the value of the allegedly illegal catch on the basis that the evidence appeared to indicate the possibility that not all of the fish had been taken in the French EEZ. In doing so the Tribunal openly criticized the assumptions that had been made by the domestic court in setting the bond. This earned a stern rebuke from Judge Mensah who suggested that this came 'perilously close to an attempt by the Tribunal to enter into the merits of the case pending before the domestic forum in France'.[76]

Although more careful with its language in subsequent cases the effect has been the same. In the *Hoshinmaru* case the vessel had a valid licence to fish in in

[73] Bernard H. Oxman, 'The M/V "Saiga" (Saint Vincent and the Grenadines v Guinea) ITLOS, Case No 1', 92(2) *AJIL* 278 (1998).

[74] *Monte Confurco*, Separate Opinion of Judge Nelson.

[75] Thomas A. Mensah, 'The Tribunal and the Prompt Release of Vessels', 22(3) *International Journal of Marine and Coastal Law* 425 (2007), 441.

[76] *Monte Confurco*, Declaration of Judge Mensah.

the Russian EEZ but was accused of having exceeded its quota of certain species and falsely recording its catch to conceal the overage. The bond eventually set by Russia was based on the maximum imposable fines and penalties. However, the Tribunal considered this approach unreasonable. While at pains to note that 'the offence committed by the Master of the *Hoshinmaru* should not be considered as a minor offence or an offence of a purely technical nature', the Tribunal considered that it was not realistic to expect that the Russian courts would impose the maximum penalties.[77] The bond was therefore reduced by some 50 per cent.

While this critique may seem like unduly pedantic 'number crunching', the gap between the Tribunal's reasoning and the amount of bond ultimately set by it cannot go unnoticed. By refusing to provide guidance on the weight to be attached to the factors relevant to the setting of a reasonable bond the objectivity, or at any rate transparency, of the Tribunal's assessments is open to criticism for failing to provide clear rules on which domestic courts can rely in performing their functions in compliance with international law.[78] Moreover, in each case in which prompt release has been ordered, the coastal State's ultimate ability to impose its penalties—which have not otherwise been found to be disproportionate or unreasonable—may have been compromised. Given the unlikely ability to recover amounts in excess of the bond upon completion of the domestic proceedings, the penalty recovered will be limited to the amount of bond set by the Tribunal and may thus fall short of securing enforcement of the domestic judgments.[79]

Moreover, the deference (or lack thereof) paid by the Tribunal to coastal State laws and regulations has had serious implications not only for the sovereign rights of coastal States but also for the implementation of other LOSC provisions and the more than thirty years of post-LOSC developments relating to the conservation and management of marine living resources both within and beyond areas under national jurisdiction. The Tribunal has made clear that reference to penalties imposed or imposable under national law is relevant to the determination of the gravity of the offence.[80] However, by substituting its own appreciation of the penalties imposable, the Tribunal has, on occasion, been criticized for substituting its own, too limited, appreciation of the gravity of the offence and, in particular, of undermining global efforts to reduce, prevent, and eliminate illegal, unregulated and unreported (IUU) fishing. In the *Volga* case, although noting the concerns of the international community about IUU fishing in the Southern Ocean, the Tribunal rejected Australia's argument that these concerns, and its obligations as a party to the Convention on the Conservation of Antarctic Marine Living Resources, were relevant to an assessment of the gravity of the offence and the reasonableness of the bond it had set.[81] Although concurring in the result,

[77] *Hoshinmaru*, para 93.

[78] Gao Jianjun, 'Reasonableness of the Bond under Article 292 of the LOS Convention: Practice of ITLOS', 7(1) *Chinese Journal of International Law* 115 (2008) at 129 and 136.

[79] Gao, 'Reasonableness of the Bond under Article 292', at 136.

[80] *Camouco*, para 67.

[81] *Volga*, para 69.

Judge Cot considered that the Tribunal had failed in its duty to respect Australia's measures, particularly as they were taken in the context of concerted international efforts to control IUU fishing.[82] This opinion was shared by Judge Anderson and Judge ad hoc Shearer in dissent, both of whom considered that the Tribunal had failed to consider all the relevant factors relating to the IUU activities of the vessel.

The *Volga* decision was criticized by commentators as having shifted the balance of interests too far in favour of the flag State by failing to recognize the legitimate rights and duties of coastal States in seeking to protect their marine living resources from IUU fishing and the established obligation on all States to cooperate in their conservation.[83] Admittedly, like beauty, the gravity of an offence may be in the eye of the beholder and not easily admit of objective determination. However, it has been suggested that the Tribunal should not be the one to ignore the implications of its decisions on other rights and duties of States under the LOSC, even in prompt release cases.[84] Perhaps mindful of this criticism, in the *Juno Trader* case the Tribunal 'took note' of the concern of Guinea-Bissau that IUU fishing in its EEZ had resulted in a serious depletion of its fisheries resources and indicated that this was one of the considerations to be taken into account in determining the amount of the reasonable bond, although no explanation was given of the manner in which this was done.[85]

Other aspects of the Tribunal's application of its reasonableness criteria might also be construed as potentially skewing the balance in favour of either the flag State or the coastal State. On the one hand, in considering the value of the detained vessel the Tribunal appears consistently to have favoured the lower vessel valuations presented by the applicant flag State over higher valuations presented by the respondent detaining State. On the other hand, detaining States have prevailed when it comes to excluding the value of the catch seized from the amount of the bond ordered, at least when seizure and confiscation of illegally obtained catch is provided for in the domestic legislation.[86] More significantly, it will be recalled that the LOSC provides no guidance as to the nature, form or amount of the bond and it provides no guidance as to the penalties that might be imposed by States other than prohibiting imprisonment (unless otherwise agreed to by the States concerned) and corporal punishment. Two issues of particular interest to

[82] *Volga*, Separate Opinion of Judge Cot, paras 11–12.

[83] See eg Donald R. Rothwell and Tim Stephens, 'Illegal Southern Ocean Fishing and Prompt Release: Balancing Coastal and Flag State Rights and Interests', 53(1) *ICLQ* 171 (2004) 184; Chester Brown, '"Reasonableness" in the Law of the Sea: The Prompt Release of the Volga', 16(3) *Leiden Journal of International Law* 621 (2003), 629; Warwick Gullet, 'Prompt Release Procedures and the Challenge for Fisheries Law Enforcement: The Judgment of the International Tribunal for the Law of the Sea in the "Volga" Case (Russian Federation v Australia)', 31 *Federal Law Review* 395 (2003), 406; Taisaku Ikeshima, 'The "Reasonableness" of Unreasonable Arguments in Prompt Release Cases in the ITLOS', 6 *Waseda Global Forum* 107–28 (2009), 121.

[84] Vaughan Lowe, 'The International Tribunal for the Law of the Sea: Survey for 2000', 16 *International Journal of Marine and Coastal Law* 549 (2001), 570. In his Declaration in the *Volga* case, Judge Marsit also suggested that the Tribunal's interpretation of a reasonable bond should take into account the interests not only of the parties but also of developing States.

[85] *Juno Trader*, paras 87 and 94–5.

[86] *Volga*, para 86.

the current discussion have been the Tribunal's interpretation of the nature (as opposed to amount) of the bond and the meaning of detention.

With respect to the bond, the obvious expectation is of a financial bond. However, non-financial conditions may actually be more effective in preventing a vessel from returning to IUU fishing or other illegal activities once it is released.[87] Indeed, non-financial aspects are specifically provided for in the context of protection of the marine environment in Article 226(1)(c) which provides for the release of a vessel to be refused or made conditional upon proceeding to the nearest repair yard where its release would present an unreasonable threat of damage to the marine environment. In the *Volga* case Australia sought to make release of a fishing vessel conditional upon both the posting of a bond and on the fulfilment of two other, non-financial, conditions: carriage by the vessel of a vessel monitoring system (VMS); and submission of details of the ownership and beneficial ownership of the vessel to the Australian authorities. In interpreting the phrase 'bond or other security' in Article 73(2), the Tribunal took a restrictive approach, confining the interpretation to a bond or other security of 'a financial nature' on the basis that, had it been intended otherwise, the LOSC would have provided for non-financial components in Article 73 as it had in Article 226. Even though Australia had quantified the VMS requirement in financial terms the Tribunal considered this was in essence a 'good behaviour bond' aimed at preventing future violations.[88] Since the only function of a bond or other financial security for the purposes of Article 292 was to ensure full protection of the coastal State's potential right in the vessel and possible fines against the crew members,[89] the measures sought by Australia were, in effect, an impermissible non-financial security. Analogizing to the 'minimum control' criteria applied by courts dealing with human rights cases, Judge Cot considered that Australia had committed an error of law with regard to the lawful nature of the reasonable bond. 'Attaching conditions to the bond would transform the very nature of' the prompt release procedure from prompt and final to delayed and conditional.[90] Thus it was appropriate for the Tribunal to reject Australia's claim.

This narrow interpretation was heavily criticized by Judges Anderson and ad hoc Shearer in dissent who pointed out that it was commonplace in national legal systems for bonds to include non-financial conditions and who criticized the Tribunal's decision as representing an unwarranted diminution in the ability of coastal States to control IUU fishing. However, as the Tribunal itself noted, it was taking no position on the legality of Australia imposing such obligations under its domestic legislation in the exercise of its sovereign rights over its EEZ. The issue under consideration related purely to the interpretation of the phrase in the context of prompt release proceedings.

The final issue of interest relates to the Tribunal's interpretation of the concept of 'detention'. The issue has arisen in the context of confiscation of vessels where

[87] Tanaka, 'Prompt Release', 268. [88] *Volga*, paras 77 and 79–80.
[89] *Volga*, para 85. See also Tanaka, 'Prompt Release', at 269–70.
[90] *Volga*, Separate Opinion of Judge Cot, para 27.

coastal States have argued that confiscation of the vessel effectively terminates any detention thereby rendering the issue moot. As revealed by the *Grand Prince, Juno Trader* and *Tomimaru* cases discussed in Section IV above, the balance between coastal and flag State interests in respect of vessels will depend on the circumstances and finality of the confiscation.

The more interesting discussion relates, however, to the Tribunal's interpretation of 'detention' in the context of crew members. In the *Camouco* and *Monte Confurco* cases, the Masters had been charged with fisheries offences, placed under court supervision, and their passports confiscated in an effort to ensure their presence at trial. According to the Tribunal this constituted detention and their release was ordered along with that of the vessels.[91] In the *Juno Trader* case disagreement existed as to whether the crew, a number of whose passports had been seized, were being 'detained'. Although the passports were returned during the Tribunal's deliberations, the crew members were still in Guinea-Bissau and under its jurisdiction. In the circumstances, the Tribunal considered it necessary to place on record an undertaking given by Guinea-Bissau that all crew members were free to leave the country and to declare that they should be free to leave with no conditions attached.[92] In the *Hoshinmaru* case, despite requests from the flag State for their release, no bond had been set for the release of the vessel and crew until one week after the application for prompt release had been filed which was more than five weeks after the vessel had been arrested. The detaining State, Russia, then advised the flag State, Japan, that the crew would be free to leave Russia upon payment of the bond. Before the Tribunal, Japan argued that the crew were 'in detention' while Russia argued that they had never been detained in respect of the alleged offences and that their ability to enter and leave Russia was merely subject to formal immigration permission that the vessel owner was obliged to apply for. In the event, while making no specific finding that the Master and crew were detained, the Tribunal noted that 'they still remain in the Russian Federation'[93] and included in its order a requirement that the Master and crew be free to leave Russia without any conditions.[94]

The Tribunal has clearly given a functional rather than a formal interpretation to the meaning of 'detention',[95] considering it to encompass 'all cases in which the movement of a vessel or its persons is prevented by authority'.[96] As Judge Treves suggested in the *Hoshinmaru* case, the requirement to release without conditions attached should not be read as suggesting that the crew members are 'detained', but rather 'as a compliment to the provision for the release of the vessel' the function of which is to 'prevent resort to conditions of any kind, bureaucratic or otherwise,

[91] *Monte Confurco*, para 90. [92] *Juno Trader*, para 79. [93] *Hoshinmaru*, para 77.

[94] *Hoshinmaru*, para 120(4).

[95] Vincent P. Bantz, 'Views from Hamburg; The Juno Trader Case or How to Make Sense of the Coastal State's Rights in the Light of its Duty of Prompt Release', 24 *The University of Queensland Law Journal* 415 (2005), 434.

[96] Tullio Treves, 'The Proceedings Concerning Prompt Release of Vessels and Crews before the International Tribunal for the Law of the Sea', 11 *International Journal of Marine and Coastal Law* 179 (1996), 182.

concerning the departure of Master and crew, that might delay the departure of the vessel'.[97] Terminological issues aside, however, an order declaring that all members of the crew should be free to leave without any condition can thus be expected in any case where the crew are unable, for either legal or practical reasons, to leave the detaining State, or have not yet done so.[98] Moreover, as with the Tribunal's refusal to countenance non-financial conditions attached to the release of a vessel, inclusion of the words 'without any conditions' appears to indicate that non-financial conditions will also be refused in the case of the release of crew members. When combined with the limitations on the inclusion of maximum imposable penalties in setting the bond, and the reality that, once freed, crew members are unlikely to return to the coastal State to stand trial, the effect of these orders arguably compromises the interests of the coastal State in favour of those of the flag State.[99]

VIII. Conclusion

While the question of the standard of deference to be applied to national measures may not be relevant in all cases that come before ITLOS, it is most certainly relevant in the context of the prompt release procedures. ITLOS has explicitly referred to the analogous concept of 'margin of appreciation' articulated in human rights cases in establishing the parameters of the standard of review in which it will engage and the criteria to be applied in assessing whether and, if so, under what conditions to order prompt release. Coastal States are given a wide discretion or 'regulatory autonomy'[100] under the LOSC to adopt laws and regulations relating to the exercise of their sovereign rights in the EEZ. However, these rights are subject to the interests of flag States. The Tribunal has made clear that the balance between these interests is to be found in the application not of total deference to coastal State measures but rather of an international standard of reasonableness as determined by the Tribunal. That standard requires the rejection of excessive or disproportionate domestic penalties and the objective application of relevant criteria embodying the internationally recognized concepts of fairness, humanity and due process.

Whether ITLOS has, in fact, achieved the requisite balance between coastal and flag State interests remains something of an open question. In all cases where a bond was set by the national authorities the Tribunal has reduced that bond by significant amounts, arguably undermining the ability of the coastal State to secure enforcement of its laws. In doing so the Tribunal has run the risk of determining not only the reasonableness of the bond but also that of the entire domestic enforcement mechanism permitted to coastal States under Article 73 of the LOSC.[101] In addition, in refusing to provide for the inclusion in the bond of

[97] *Hoshinmaru*, Declaration of Judge Treves.

[98] Bantz, 'Views from Hamburg', 435.

[99] Gao, 'Reasonableness of the Bond', 137.

[100] See Caroline Henckels, Chapter 7 in this volume.

[101] Cogliati-Bantz, 'International Tribunal', 257.

non-economic values relating to the conservation of marine living resources the Tribunal has arguably undermined the fight against IUU fishing and the relevant provisions of the LOSC.[102] Commentators have thus suggested that the effect of the Tribunal's decisions has been an overly intrusive approach to the regulatory autonomy of coastal States.[103] Be that as it may, prompt release proceedings are clearly not the forum in which to right all the wrongs of the law of the sea. In the final analysis the careful circumscription by the Tribunal of its review function in prompt release cases has resulted in a degree of clarity with respect to the content of the international standard of reasonableness of bond on which States can rely. Given the ingenuity of both flag and coastal States, its evolution will no doubt continue in future cases where, while its application may, at times, be open to contestation, the appropriateness and legitimacy of the approach cannot be.

[102] Rothwell and Stephens, 'Illegal Southern Ocean Fishing', 184.
[103] Rothwell and Stephens, 'Illegal Southern Ocean Fishing', 184.

19

Deference in the ICC Practice Concerning Admissibility Challenges Lodged by States

*Karolina Wierczynska**

I. Introduction

The International Criminal Court (ICC or the Court) is a permanent judicial body, complementary to national jurisdictions. This means that it is primarily the 'duty of every State to exercise its own criminal jurisdiction' while the ICC may exercise it only in certain situations. According to Article 17 of its Statute (Rome Statute or Statute), which regulates issues of admissibility of a case, the ICC can, in the case of a grave crime, exercise its jurisdiction only when the relevant State 'is unwilling or unable genuinely to carry out the investigation or prosecution'[1] of the case. This formulation provides, therefore, 'the built-in deference of the ICC to national prosecutions [that] respects state sovereignty and places significant control within national jurisdictions'.[2] On the other hand, the Court has a right to activate its jurisdiction *ex officio*, and in doing so it additionally decides whether the national authorities are acting properly.[3]

Despite the authority given to the Court, the Statute does not specify how to evaluate the actions taken by a State. In principle, this is not a problem when a

* The author wishes to acknowledge that her research was financed by the Polish National Science Center pursuant to grant number DEC-2011/01/M/HS5/03846. The author also wishes to thank the Editors of this volume for their comments and help, and Sarah Nouwen for her insightful remarks on an earlier draft.

[1] See Article 17 of the Rome Statute of the International Criminal Court, 2187 UNTS 90, entered into force 1 July 2002; *Prosecutor v Lubanga, Decision on the Prosecutor's Application for a Warrant of Arrest*, ICC-01/04-01/06-8, 10 February 2006, para 40, and PTC II, Decision Pursuant to Article 15 of the Rome Statute on the Authorization of an Investigation into the Situation in the Republic of Kenya, ICC-01/09, 31 March 2010, paras 52–54; cf also Mohamed El Zeidy, *The Principle of Complementarity in International Criminal Law: Origin, Development and Practice* (Leiden: Martinus Nijhoff, 2008).

[2] Linda E. Carter, 'The Future of the International Criminal Court: Complementarity as a Strength or a Weakness', 12 *Washington University Global Studies Law Review* 451 (2013), 451.

[3] Hector Olásolo, The triggering procedure of the International Criminal Court, procedural treatment of the principle of complementarity, and the role of Office of the Prosecutor, Guest Lecture Series of the Office of the Prosecutor, 24 March 2004, available at <http://www.icc-cpi.int/iccdocs/asp_docs/library/organs/otp/040326_Olasolo.pdf> (accessed 28 March 2014).

State is not conducting any proceedings; in such instances a case is practically 'automatically' admissible before the ICC.[4] It becomes more problematic when the State is actually acting but its actions may be deemed insufficient. The ICC's Office of the Prosecutor is authorized to assess the activities taken by the State and ultimately can take over a case if it decides that the conduct of a State does not meet the required threshold. The State, in turn, can oppose such an intervention by contesting admissibility.[5] However, the assessment of State actions by the ICC presents a serious challenge, as the criteria and intensity of such scrutiny are not specified in the Statute and have never been addressed systematically. In this context, Hansen notes: '[t]he Rome Statute itself offers little guidance concerning the criteria that should be used to determine whether national proceedings exist—or, in the words of the Statute, whether a "case is being investigated or prosecuted"'.[6]

The enigmatic language of the Statute therefore calls for formulation of a clear set of admissibility criteria, and as a corollary the need to apply an appropriate standard of review by the ICC. Formulation of such a standard should be consistent with the principle of complementarity, which implies that at some level the Court needs to respect national jurisdiction (thus granting a certain degree of deference to a State). If the Court interprets the statutory provisions too broadly, it would grant itself powers which could undermine the purpose of the Statute and intervene in situations when the jurisdiction should be left to the State. This in turn can discourage countries from cooperation with the ICC and/or undermine the legitimacy of the Court decisions. Hence it follows that the credibility of the Court requires clear, not arbitral standards that respect State autonomy.

This brings us to the core issue of this chapter, which aims at analysing the criteria developed by the Court in assessing domestic conduct (including various determinations made at the municipal level) in the admissibility challenges and enquiring into the level of intrusiveness expressed in the Court's approach. In this context, the chapter will pay special attention to two related (but also distinct) mechanisms that may control the extent of the Court's scrutiny: standard of review and standard of proof. The chapter will also offer some normative conclusions on the desirable level of deference.

The chapter proceeds in five sections. The next section (Section II) briefly addresses the notions of standard of review and standard of proof. Section III critically analyses the four cases (one by the Democratic Republic of Congo, one by Kenya, and two by Libya) in order to reconstruct the nature of the Court's review, concentrating in this context on the same person and same conduct tests, and criteria used in the assessment of the quality of national proceedings. It should

[4] When a State triggers ICC jurisdiction by making a self-referral, the ICC can accept its competence on the grounds of inactivity of a State, and therefore the ICC does not have to decide whether the State is willing or able to prosecute. See for example: PTC II, Office of the Prosecutor, Request for authorization of an investigation pursuant to Article 15, ICC-01/09, 26 November 2009, para 52.

[5] Article 19(2)(b) of the Statute.

[6] Thomas O. Hansen, 'A Critical Review of the ICC's Recent Practice Concerning Admissibility Challenges and Complementarity', 13 *Melbourne Journal of International Law* 217 (2012), 223.

be noted that the selection of cases is not accidental. Except for the case of the Democratic Republic of Congo (DRC), which must be perceived as a point of reference in the context of discussed issues, all of them are admissibility challenges lodged by States where the issue of deference granted by the Court to States is of prime importance. Section IV looks at the problem of deference afforded to States by the ICC in admissibility proceedings through the lens of two mechanisms: standard of review and standard of proof. Section V offers some (normative) conclusions.

II. Standard of Review and Standard of Proof

Standard of review, in the international context, is conventionally understood as 'the nature and intensity of review by a court or tribunal of decisions taken by another governmental authority or, sometimes, by a lower court or tribunal'.[7] The standard may vary, ranging from a deferential approach to strict scrutiny. The notion of standard of review is hardly ever, however, associated with the activities of the ICC.[8] While many scholars have noted that the ICC must provide guidance as to what would constitute sufficient domestic proceedings in the context of Article 17 of the Statute,[9] rarely has the notion of standard of review been explicitly used.[10] The Court itself only connects the notion of standard of review with the decisions of the Appeal Chamber (AC) vis-à-vis the decisions of a Pre-Trial Chamber (PTC).[11]

Among the few scholars who have mentioned the standard of review in the context of the ICC's assessment of a State's activities, Shany noted:

[7] Jan Bohanes and Nicolas Lockhart, 'Standard of Review in WTO Law' in Daniel Bethlehem et al (eds), *The Oxford Handbook of International Trade Law* (Oxford: Oxford University Press, 2009) 379.

[8] Cf Chapter 20 by Diane Bernard in this volume (Section II).

[9] William Burke-White and Scott Kaplan, 'Shaping the Contours of Domestic Justice: The International Criminal Court and an Admissibility Challenge in the Uganda Situation' in Carsten Stahn and Göran Sluiter (eds), *The Emerging Practice of the International Criminal Court*, (Leiden: Martinus Nijhoff, 2009) 114.

[10] The notion of 'standard of review' in international criminal law is also used with respect to the relation between the Security Council (SC) and criminal courts in order to discuss the judicial scrutiny over actions of the SC, eg Dagmar Richter, 'Judicial Review of Security Council Decisions—A Modern Vision of the Administration of Justice?', 32 *Polish Yearbook of International Law* 271 (2012).

[11] See Corrigendum to Prosecution Response to the 'Document in Support of the Government of Libya's Appeal against the Decision on the admissibility of the case against Saif Al-Islam Gaddafi', Situation in Libya, ICC-01/11-01/11, 23 July 2013, paras 29–32; Judgment on the appeal of the Prosecutor against the decision of PTC I of 16 December 2011 entitled 'Decision on the confirmation of charges, Situation in the Democratic Republic of the Congo', ICC-01/04-01/10 OA 4, 30 May 2012, para 15; Hector Olásolo, 'International Criminal Court and International Tribunals: Substantive and Procedural Aspects' in Carlos Jiménez Piernas (ed), *The Legal Practice in International Law and European Community Law* (The Hague: Brill, 2007) 159–204; José Doria, 'Standards of Appeals and Standards of Revision' in José Doria et al (eds), *The Legal Regime of the International Criminal Court, Essays in Honour of Professor Igor Blishchenko* (The Hague: Brill, 2009) 945–74.

So far there has been little discussion before international criminal courts of the standards of review... In fact, it may be argued that the special nature of criminal proceedings puts into question the applicability of any general international law margin of appreciation doctrine: since courts sitting in criminal cases exercise judicial supervision over individual conduct, considerations of deference which might be appropriate vis-à-vis state conduct might be irrelevant. At the same time, principles of criminal justice introduce independent reasons for judicial restraint: for instance, they militate in favour of a cautious approach towards statutory construction (especially interpretation in favour of the accused) and toward a high evidentiary threshold for conviction. Hence, interpretation of criminal norms might raise analogous considerations to the margin of appreciation methodology.[12]

It should be noted that Shany's observation on the standard of review (or margin of appreciation, which denotes the deferential form of the review) contains an important omission. He refers only to the competence of the ICC concerning the responsibility of an individual, omitting the fact that the ICC, when deciding on admissibility challenges made by States, must assess the actions of States, hence his dismissal of 'considerations of deference which might be appropriate vis-à-vis State conduct' seems ill-founded in the context of admissibility challenges. In that concrete situation the ICC establishes a methodology for its scrutiny over actions of national authorities. In this context, it is also worth recalling Olásolo, who called for the formulation of the applicable standard of review relating to admissibility questions, stating that 'Art. 19 ... does not specify the applicable standard of review for admissibility of cases and, thus, the PTC and the AC will also have to give some guidance on whether they embrace a balance of probabilities standard, an "intimate conviction" standard or any other conceivable standard.'[13] Consequently, it is legitimate to talk about standard of review applicable to admissibility challenges (ie nature and intensity of review by a court over a State's determinations). One of the advantages of such an approach is that the concept of standard of review can operate as a formal tool to be used by the Court for establishing the extent of deference granted to States.

Before going further, it is also worth noting that the standard of review can be directly linked to the standard of proof—the lower the standard of proof for a State challenging admissibility, the more lenient will be the standard of review. Standard of proof as such refers to evidentiary considerations[14]—it is the level of proof required in a given case. According to the Informal Expert Paper, 'the appropriate burden is a simple balance of probabilities, rather than any higher standard such as "proof beyond reasonable doubt"'.[15] Different

[12] Yuval Shany, 'Toward a General Margin of Appreciation Doctrine in International Law?', 16(5) *EJIL* 907 (2005), 930.

[13] Hector Olásolo, *The Triggering Procedure of the International Criminal Court* (Leiden: Martinus Nijhoff, 2005) 168 (note certain confusion in this statement, the terms used by Olásolo are conventionally connected with standard of proof, not review).

[14] Marc Klamberg, *Evidence in International Criminal Law. Confronting Legal Gaps and the Reconstruction of Disputed Events* (Leiden: Martinus Nijhoff, 2013) 129–32. See also Chapter 13 by Mónika Ambrus and Chapter 14 by Uladzislau Belavusau, both in this volume, discussing the relationship between standard of review and standard of proof in the context of the ECtHR.

[15] Informal Expert Paper, *The principle of complementarity in practice*, ICC-OTP 2003, 16.

standards can be applied depending on the type and phase of proceedings such as the 'full certainty' standard and the 'reasonable grounds to believe' standard.[16] For example, the Rome Statute provides that '[i]n order to convict the accused, the Court must be convinced of the guilt of the accused beyond reasonable doubt' (Article 66(3)). The Statute, however, does not set any standard of proof for determination of the admissibility of a case. Having reference to the lack of a precise standard, Kleffner noted that '[t]he resulting lack of transparency would likely have a detrimental effect on the Court's legitimacy and make it liable to the accusation by the Parties to admissibility proceedings that it acts arbitrarily.'[17] Instead he claims that such standard 'should be flexible enough to take account of possible context-specific situations in which States fail to cooperate.'[18]

Consequently, there are compelling reasons to determine both standard of proof and standard of review; their establishment can not only contribute to transparency and predictability of Court's operations but also respond to the need for operationalization of deference, which is embedded in the idea of complementarity.

III. Admissibility Criteria in the Practice of the ICC

A. Same person and same conduct test

Any discussion on admissibility criteria needs to start from the *Lubanga* case where the standard of the same person and same conduct was used for the first time. The situation in the DRC was referred (via self-referral) to the ICC by the President of the DRC, who claimed that national authorities were not able to prosecute the alleged crimes committed in the territory of the DRC since the entry into force of the Rome Statute. In 2006 the ICC decided to issue an arrest warrant for Thomas Lubanga relating to the war crimes of enlistment of children under the age of fifteen; of conscription of children under the age of fifteen; and of using children under the age of fifteen to participate actively in hostilities children.[19]

The Court, while analysing the admissibility test, stated that 'the case would be admissible only if States remained inactive... or unwilling or unable'[20] to proceed with a case.[21] According to the Court the '*condition sine qua non* for a case arising from investigation of a situation to be inadmissible is that national proceedings encompass both the person and the conduct which is the subject of a case before

[16] Klamberg, *Evidence*, 136.

[17] Jann K. Kleffner, *Complementarity in the Rome Statute and National Criminal Jurisdictions* (Oxford: Oxford University Press, 2008), 207.

[18] Kleffner, *Complementarity in the Rome Statute*, 214.

[19] *Prosecutor v Lubanga*, 'Decision on the Prosecutor's Application for a Warrant of Arrest', ICC-01/04-01/06-8, 10 February 2006, paras 31 and 37–9.

[20] *Lubanga*, Arrest Warrant Decision, para 29.

[21] The second part of the test of admissibility refers to the gravity threshold and will not be discussed in the chapter, as not being a part of the evolving standard of review.

the Court.'[22] The concept of a case[23] has been defined as the 'specific incidents during which one or more crimes within the jurisdiction of the Court seem to have been committed by one or more identified suspects.'[24] The ICC found that the DRC proceedings against Lubanga, although they concerned the same person, did not refer to the same conduct as the arrest warrant issued by the Prosecutor of the ICC as the national authorities did not encompass such crimes as practice of enlistment/conscripting/or using children under the age of fifteen to participate in hostilities. On that basis, the Court found the DRC inactive in the given case.[25]

Three cases that followed (one Kenyan and two Libyan cases—Saif Gaddafi and Abdullah Al-Senussi) provided some additional insight into the same person and same conduct test. With respect to Kenya, the situation that gave rise to the ICC actions centred around the post-election violence in the country between 2007 and 2008. On 31 March 2010 the PTC issued a decision authorizing an investigation into the situation in the Republic of Kenya.[26] On 8 March 2011 the PTC decided to issue Summonses to Appear for three persons, specifically Francis Muthaura, Uhuru Kenyatta and Mohammed Hussein Ali.[27] On 31 March 2011 the Kenyan government contested this decision by filing an application pursuant to Article 19 of the ICC Statute, challenging the admissibility of the case before the Court.[28] The decision of the PTC was presented on 30 May 2011, while the decision of the AC on 30 August 2011.

With regard to the same person test, the Kenyan government argued that the word 'case' meant that the national investigation had to 'cover the same conduct in respect of persons at the same level in the hierarchy being investigated by the ICC',[29] and added that its proceedings did relate to the 'highest levels for all possible crimes.'[30] In other words the Kenyan government preferred a test which applied to the broader situation and not to the specific case. The Pre-Trial Chamber II (PTC II) disagreed however and explained that national proceedings

[22] *Lubanga*, Arrest Warrant Decision, para 31; 'Same person, same conduct' test was also elaborated in further decisions of the ICC which are not developed here, see eg PTC I, *The Prosecutor v Thomas Lubanga Dyilo*, 'Decision concerning Pre-Trial Chamber I's Decision of 10 February 2006 and the Incorporation of Documents into the Record of the Case against Mr Thomas Lubanga Dyilo', ICC-01/04-01/06-8-Corr, 24 February 2006, para 31, PTC I, *The Prosecutor v Ahmad Muhammad Harun and Ali Muhammad Ali Abd-Al-Rahman*, 'Decision on the Prosecution Application under Article 58(7) of the Statute', ICC-02/05-01/07-l-Corr, 27 April 2007, para 24.

[23] It must be noted that States are not obliged to incorporate the crimes as defined in the Rome Statute into their penal codes. As a consequence, it is possible that national conduct may be focused on murder and persecution while the conduct before the ICC will refer to crimes against humanity or genocide.

[24] *Lubanga*, Arrest Warrant Decision, para 31.

[25] *Lubanga*, Arrest Warrant Decision, paras 37–40.

[26] PTC II, 'Decision Pursuant to Article 15 of the Rome Statute on the Authorization of an Investigation into the Situation in the Republic of Kenya', ICC-01/09, 31 March 2010.

[27] PTC II, 'Decision on the Prosecutor's Application for Summonses to Appear for Francis Kirimi Muthaura, Uhuru Muigai Kenyatta and Mohammed Hussein Ali', ICC-01/09-02/11-01, 8 March 2011.

[28] PTC II, Application on behalf of the Government of the Republic of Kenya pursuant to Article 19 of the ICC Statute, ICC-01/09-02/11-26, 31 March 2011.

[29] PTC II, Application on behalf of the Government of the Republic of Kenya, para 32.

[30] PTC II, Application on behalf of the Government of the Republic of Kenya, para 32.

must concern exactly the same persons that are subject to the Court's proceeding.[31] The AC confirmed, holding that the same person test refers to the same individual.[32] As a consequence, both chambers dismissed the arguments of Kenya.[33] At the same time, the AC added a new element to the same conduct test, as it observed, without however providing any further explanation, that conduct only needs to be substantially the same.[34] This was clarified only in the Libyan cases, to which we now turn.

The situation in Libya was referred to the Court by the Security Council (SC) in reliance on Article 13(b) of the Statute. In its resolution no. 1970 of 16 February 2011[35] the SC decided to refer the situation in Libya (Muammar Gaddafi was accused of using lethal force against protestors) to the Prosecutor of the ICC, and also declared that Libya should fully cooperate with the Court and provide all necessary assistance. In June 2011 the ICC issued arrest warrants against Muammar Gaddafi, Saif Al-Islam Gaddafi and Abdullah Al-Senussi for alleged criminal responsibility for crimes against humanity, consisting of murder and persecution. Following Gaddafi's overthrow and death, the Libyan Prosecutor-General commenced its own investigative procedures against S. Gaddafi. On 1 May 2012 Libya submitted to the ICC its application pursuant to Article 19 ICC Statute,[36] challenging the admissibility of the case before the ICC relating to Gaddafi (the decision of the PTC was issued on 31 May 2013). The admissibility challenge in the context of Al-Senussi was filed on 2 April 2013 while the PTC presented its decision on 11 October 2013.

Libya referred in its application both to the question of conduct and incidents.[37] Describing the actions of its Prosecutor-General, Libya underlined that his investigation covered factual incidents charged as murder and persecution before the ICC; and the same allegations of individual conduct by Mr Gaddafi which formed the basis for his alleged participation in crimes mentioned in the ICC's decision.[38] Libya's argument was that a conduct in order to be qualified as substantially the same, did not have to 'mirror' the case before the ICC. In other

[31] PTC II, 'Decision on the Application by the Government of Kenya Challenging the Admissibility of the Case Pursuant to Article 19(2)(b) of the Statute, 30 May 2011', para 50.

[32] AC, *The Prosecutor v Francis Kirimi Muthaura, Uhuru Muigai Kenyatta and Mohammed Hussein Ali*, Judgment on the appeal of the Republic of Kenya against the decision of PTC II of 30 May 2011 entitled 'Decision on the Application by the Government of Kenya Challenging the Admissibility of the Case Pursuant to Article 19(2)(b) of the Statute', ICC-01/09-02/11 O A, 30 August 2011, paras 39–40.

[33] The PTC I confirmed that approach in the Libyan case, but found on the basis of presented evidence that this condition was met (see PTC I, 'Decision on the admissibility of the case against Saif Al-Islam Gaddafi', ICC-01/11-01/11-344-Red, 31 May 2013, paras 76–7).

[34] AC, Judgment on the appeal of the Republic of Kenya, para 39.

[35] Resolution of the Security Council no. 1970, 16 February 2011, S/Res 1970 (2012).

[36] Application on behalf of the Government of Libya pursuant to Article 19 of the ICC Statute, ICC-01/11-01/11, 1 May 2012.

[37] PTC I, 'Decision on the admissibility of the case against Saif Al-Islam Gaddafi', ICC-01/11-01/11-344-Red, 31 May 2013, para 47.

[38] PTC I, 'Decision on Prosecutor's Application Pursuant to Article 58 as to Muammar Mohammed Abu Minyar Gaddafi, Saif Al-Islam Gaddafi and Abdullah Al-Senussi', ICC-01/11-12, 27 June 2011, paras 15–65, 72–90.

words, the argument was that Libya did not need to charge Gaddafi under the same legal qualification as the acts alleged before the Court if those acts are substantially the same.[39] In Libya's opinion a strict same conduct standard would be 'inconsistent with the presumption in favour of the primacy of national proceedings' (ie the complementarity principle).[40]

The Prosecutor of the ICC joined this debate by stating that the substantially same conduct test is satisfied when:

> at a minimum, the national authorities are focused on the same course of conduct and series of events as the ICC, meaning that they are examining the person's criminal responsibility in the context of substantially the same incidents and underlying facts and allegations of criminal responsibility.[41]

The Prosecutor added that if the national authorities refer to all the incidents, facts and allegations of criminal responsibility investigated or prosecuted by the ICC exactly, this part of the test will automatically be satisfied.[42] At the same time the Libyan attempt to weaken the test in the context of a 'limited' number of incidents was opposed by the Prosecutor, who believed that substantially same conduct has to refer to the same incidents, facts and allegation as before the ICC.

The position of the Prosecutor was not, however, endorsed by the Court. The PTC found that rather than referring to the issue of incidents, the AC referred to conduct 'as alleged in the proceedings before the Court', and added that 'the investigation or prosecution must cover substantially the same conduct'.[43] In this context, two sets of conduct must be compared—the one attributed to Gaddafi in the Warrant of Arrest (WA), and its Libyan equivalent.[44] The PTC noted that the WA did not relate to specific instances of killing and persecution, but referred to acts of such nature being the result of Gaddafi's actions. Those events did not represent unique manifestations of the form of criminality, but rather samples of a course of conduct. The Libyan proceedings, in the opinion of the ICC, did not have to cover exactly the same acts.[45]

In the proceedings concerning the admissibility challenge in the case of Al-Senussi, the Prosecutor focused on the incident-specific characterization and criticized this position of the PTC, adding that the notion of 'incidents' refers to 'criminal acts that occur in a particular location and at a specific time and in the framework of a course of conduct and series of events'[46] and that those

[39] Decision on the admissibility of the case against Saif Al-Islam Gaddafi, paras 62–3.

[40] Decision on the admissibility of the case against Saif Al-Islam Gaddafi, para 62.

[41] Prosecution's Response to 'Libyan Government's further submissions on issues related to the admissibility of the case against Saif Al-Islam Gaddafi', ICC-01/11-01/11, 12 February 2013, para 31.

[42] Prosecution's Response to 'Libyan Government's further submissions on issues related to the admissibility of the case against Saif Al-Islam Gaddafi', para 32.

[43] Decision on the admissibility of the case against Saif Al-Islam Gaddafi, para 76.

[44] Decision on the admissibility of the case against Saif Al-Islam Gaddafi, para 78.

[45] Decision on the admissibility of the case against Saif Al-Islam Gaddafi, para 82; this was also confirmed in the decision concerning Al-Senussi, para 76.

[46] Decision on the admissibility of the case against Abdullah Al-Senussi, para 47.

circumstances may change, which is why each case should be assessed on a case-by-case basis.[47] The Prosecutor also found that analysis of the term 'substantially' in the context of the same conduct 'serves to explain, in relation to what "sameness" attaches, namely to the substance of the criminal behavior'. In that context, the same conduct can be substantially the same only if differences between the two conducts are minor. In the opinion of the Prosecutor, if Libya in its proceedings did not cover all the incidents enumerated in the Article 58 decision, the difference cannot be substantial for the proceedings to be described as essentially the same.[48] Libya, on the contrary, found the notion of 'incident' not relevant to the conduct.

The ICC confirmed, as the Prosecutor suggested, that every case has to be described with reference to precise temporal, geographic and material parameters, however such a conduct does not have to necessarily be composed of specific incidents of a 'pre-determined breadth'.[49] Contrary to the Prosecutor, the Court found that the reference to incidents (as mentioned in Article 58 of the Decision) is not necessary in order to define or narrow down the proceedings against Al-Senussi.[50] However the Court underlined that the reference to incidents or facts can be an indicator 'that the case subject to said proceedings is indeed the same as the one before the Court.'[51]

Additionally the question of ordinary crimes had been also raised in the cases of both Gaddafi and Al-Senussi. In particular it was contested whether charges of ordinary crimes, instead of using 'international crimes labels', are sufficient in domestic proceedings. The PTC found that a domestic investigation or prosecution for 'ordinary crimes', to the extent that the case covers the same conduct (substance rather than form), could be considered sufficient.[52]

B. Assessment of the genuineness of a national proceeding

A State that wishes to challenge the admissibility of a case before the Court has to focus not only on the same person/same conduct test but also on the quality of its procedure. In particular it needs to pay attention to the question of genuineness of the investigation or prosecution[53] (as provided in Article 17 of the Statute), and the evidentiary issues that come out under the standard of proof (which is

[47] Decision on the admissibility of the case against Abdullah Al-Senussi, para 48.

[48] Decision on the admissibility of the case against Abdullah Al-Senussi, paras 49–50.

[49] Decision on the admissibility of the case against Abdullah Al-Senussi, para 75 (in other words, the ICC seems to depart from the understanding that the case needs to be composed of concrete predefined incidents; this obviously gives States some margin of appreciation).

[50] Decision on the admissibility of the case against Abdullah Al-Senussi, para 77.

[51] Decision on the admissibility of the case against Abdullah Al-Senussi, para 79.

[52] Decision on the admissibility of the case against Abdullah Al-Senussi, para 66; Decision on the admissibility of the case against Saif Al-Islam Gaddafi, para 88. This might look like an odd conclusion as one of the ideas behind the ICC was to carve out certain crimes that affect the world community. On the other hand, such an approach provides an additional margin of appreciation to States.

[53] For more extensive discussion of this criterion, see Diane Bernard, Chapter 20 in this volume.

discussed in the next section). The term 'genuinely' is not elaborated in the Statute and it is left to the Court's determination. Nevertheless, it should be added that the term was included to the Statute as being the 'least subjective concept considered' among the other alternatives, such as 'ineffective' or 'good faith'.[54] As noted in the Informal Expert Paper:

> [t]he term 'genuinely' restricts the class of national proceedings that require deference from the ICC. Without such a qualifier, any national proceeding would preclude ICC action, even if the national proceeding were fraudulent or hopelessly inadequate. This balance was one of the key compromises of the Rome Statute, giving the ICC a certain scope to assess the objective quality of a national proceeding, but setting a standard no higher (but no lower) than that the proceedings be carried out 'genuinely'.[55]

Of course, the question of genuine proceedings does not arise in the situation of a State's inaction, as in the Kenyan cases where the Court was not convinced that there was any ongoing investigation with respect to the three suspects summoned by the ICC, and qualified this as a situation of inactivity. Consequently, it was not necessary for the Court to determine whether Kenya was unwilling or unable to genuinely prosecute the case.[56]

Genuineness of the proceedings was assessed in the two Libyan cases, as Libya was challenging admissibility on the grounds that it was actively investigating the case. In the Gaddafi case, the Court found Libya unable to genuinely conduct the investigation or prosecution (the unavailability of a national system) for three reasons.[57] First, Libya could not secure the transfer of Gaddafi from the place of his detention under the custody of Zintan militia into State authority (and the trial could not take place in his absence); second, it was not able to ensure a lawyer for the suspect; and third, it did not demonstrate any progress in this area, nor did it indicate when it would overcome these difficulties.[58] But in the Al-Senussi case, the PTC found that Libya is not unable and unwilling to genuinely carry out its proceedings (despite the fact that Al-Senussi could not meet with his lawyer) and held the case inadmissible before the Court.[59] These two decisions, as relating to the same State, may be seen as demonstrating a certain inconsistency in the approach of the Court to the question of genuineness of domestic proceedings, as the only difference between two cases is that, unlike Al-Senussi, Gaddafi was under the control of forces not directly connected with the government. Rightly or not, such an approach also reflects the ICC's policy dilemmas relating to the degree of deference that can be given to a State.

[54] John Holmes, 'Complementarity: National Courts versus the ICC' in Antonio Cassese et al (eds), *The Rome Statute of the International Criminal Court: A Commentary*, vol. 1 (Oxford: Oxford University Press, 2002), 674.

[55] Informal Expert Paper, *The principle of complementarity*, 8.

[56] PTC II, 'Decision on the Application by the Government of Kenya Challenging the Admissibility of the Case Pursuant to Article 19(2)(b) of the Statute', 30 May 2011, para 66.

[57] Decision on the admissibility of the case against Saif Al-Islam Gaddafi, paras 208–14.

[58] Decision on the admissibility of the case against Saif Al-Islam Gaddafi, para 214.

[59] Decision on the admissibility of the case against Abdullah Al-Senussi, para 311.

IV. Deference in the Practice of the ICC: Standard of Review and Standard of Proof

The analysis of the ICC jurisprudence, as discussed above in Section III, shows that the Court is aware of its complementary role in the international administration of justice in criminal matters. At the same time, the level of deference that is expressed by the ICC varies between the different criteria used. When it comes to the same person test, the Court is reluctant to afford any deference to a State and applies strict scrutiny. As a consequence, the State's prosecutorial or investigative activities have to specifically involve the same individual, not a person from the same hierarchical level. This is true 'even if national prosecutions encompassed persons with greater responsibility, different and arguably more serious crimes and different incidents'.[60] This is not a surprising result as criminal responsibility is of an individual rather than collective character.

Having said this, it also needs to be added that the same person test can raise concerns when the same person is prosecuted by national and international courts. First, the problem can appear in a situation when the same person is prosecuted for crimes against humanity before a national court and for genocide before the ICC. As both charges are extremely grave crimes, the question arises whether in such a case the ICC should defer to national prosecution? The issue could be, as suggested by Robinson[61] and subsequently by Nouwen,[62] addressed by the cooperation regime (not the admissibility regime), but will the ICC with its hunger for cases tend to accept such a solution? Secondly, how should the charges (of the national court and the ICC) against the same person be compared? Should the character of the alleged crime be compared (whether international or ordinary crime), or the penalties provided for the commission of the crime, or maybe, as suggested by Schabas,[63] the 'assessment of relative gravity of offences' would be a better approach? This problem also raises another concern, ie how to compare genocide with crimes against humanity if it is generally accepted that these are crimes of comparable gravity? Such situations call for the Court's deference to the national proceedings and domestic law (in context of penalties for instance), if the domestic conduct is genuine, meaning that the State is actively investigating a given case and its conduct covers the acts of the same nature as before the ICC, or if 'such proceedings advance the goals of international criminal justice'.[64]

[60] Sarah Nouwen, 'Fine-tuning Complementarity' in Bartram Brown (ed), *Research Handbook on International Criminal Law* (Cheltenham: Edward Elgar Publishing, 2011), 211.

[61] Daryl Robinson, 'Three Theories of Complementarity: Charge, Sentence, or Process?', 53 *Harvard International Law Journal* 85 (2012), 179.

[62] Sarah Nouwen, *Complementarity in the Line of Fire: The Catalysing Effect of the International Criminal Court in Uganda and Sudan* (Cambridge: Cambridge University Press, 2013) 56.

[63] William A. Schabas, *An Introduction to the International Criminal Court* (Cambridge: Cambridge University Press, 2007) 182.

[64] Linda M. Keller, 'The Practice of the International Criminal Court: Comments on the Complementarity Conundrum', 8(1) *Santa Clara Journal of International Law* 199 (2010), 228.

As far as the same conduct test is concerned, the approach of the ICC has evolved over the years. While the early jurisprudence suggested a similar level of strictness as demanded under the same person test, the subsequent case law has loosened these requirements. As noted by Jelloh in the context of the Kenyan case, 'by essentially retaining the strict same-person, same-conduct test, which on its face granted no margin of appreciation for States to make different investigative or charging decisions from those of the ICC prosecutor, the Appeals Chamber places stringent demands on States.'[65] Under the more recent case law, the applicable test calls only for 'substantially the same conduct', which means that the national conduct does not have to refer to exactly the same acts and the same incidents but rather acts of the same nature. Moreover, national proceedings referring to ordinary crimes, as opposed to international crimes, may be considered as sufficient to the extent that the case covers '*substantially* the same conduct'. In other words, the State does not have to investigate exactly the same facts and incidents or crimes 'under the international crime label' to prove that it is actively investigating the case. Such formulation of the test definitively leaves a certain margin of flexibility to a domestic prosecutor concerning the selection of specific conduct. At the same time, it must be stressed that the test remains very casuistic and context-dependent, without clear guidance as to the extent of existing deference.

Application of the test also raises concerns relating to the meaning of the word 'conduct'[66] (it is definitely not a synonym of the word 'crime') and the standard to be used in order to compare crimes regulated in national penal codes with crimes under the jurisdiction of the Court (which is subsequently related to the scope of the ICC's deference in context of the same conduct criterion). For example, the question arises whether the Court will be deferential if a State is actively investigating, but the domestic proceedings cover, let's say, only three crimes against humanity rather than four (compared with the proceedings before the ICC), or if national conduct refers only to genocide, instead of genocide and crimes against humanity? Under the *Lubanga* approach, the answer would be negative, while under more recent case law, it is unclear at best. Even without focusing on the same incidents, the same conduct test can still be very narrow and strict if it refers to the same charges. In such situation the case could be considered as admissible before the ICC, although the application of the cooperative approach, in the form of deference to States and consequently accepting national jurisdiction, would better fit the overall idea of complementarity.

The extent of deference that is granted by the ICC to States is also affected by the allocation of burden of proof and applicable standard of proof. It is worth noting that the Statute determines none of these issues and it was (and still is) the task of the Court to provide relevant standards. The ICC, rather uncontroversially and in line with the regular practice of international courts (ie it is the party that

[65] Charles C. Jalloh, 'International Decision: Situation in the Republic of Kenya. No. ICC-01/09-02/11-274. Judgment on Kenya's Appeal of Decision Denying Admissibility', 106 *AJIL* 119 (2012), 122.

[66] See the elaboration of Nouwen, *Complementarity*, 213.

claims something which needs to substantiate its claim), found that the burden of proof is placed on the State challenging admissibility. As to the standard of proof in admissibility challenges, the practice of the Court seems to be both underdeveloped and unprincipled. Instead of focusing on a specific type of standard, the ICC has preferred to determine it in a more descriptive way, by mentioning features such as a 'sufficient degree of specificity and probative value', 'progressive steps', etc.[67] Such a policy not only creates additional, new standards, but leaves a State with very limited guidance as it does not refer to any known and accepted standard of proof which could be easily applied by States. What remains clear is that a State needs to submit concrete, exhaustive information in a detailed manner about the activities taken, about suspects, about their names, about witnesses interviewed, etc. A State has to prove that it is conducting proceedings directed at collecting evidence that specific suspects are responsible for substantially the same conduct alleged. The evidence should also demonstrate that the State is taking concrete and progressive steps.[68]

This unprincipled approach was criticized by Judge Ušacka who, in a dissenting opinion, noted that the Court had failed to explain such fundamental matters as standard of proof or the type of evidence necessary to meet the burden.[69] Overall she characterized the Court's approach as requiring a relatively high standard of proof[70] (and as a consequence limiting the extent of deference that is granted to States). At the same time the standard of proof applied was arguably not the strictest 'beyond a reasonable doubt' standard, which is an appropriate standard for the criminal conviction of a person, but not for the review of a State's actions when determining the admissibility of a case. The subsequent case law has not clarified this picture. While the Court directly referred to the standard of proof in the Gaddafi case, it did not explain the nature of such a standard (eg whether the admissibility determination should be based on a 'beyond reasonable doubt' standard, or 'substantial grounds to believe' standard, or eventually 'reasonable grounds to believe' standard).

Finally, it also needs to be stressed that the ICC practice has not yet addressed many issues where the question of applicable standard of review could be of prime importance. For example, it is not clear to what extent the Court should express deference to a State which challenges the admissibility 'on the grounds that non-prosecution and the upholding of amnesties are necessary to prevent the resumption of violence and bring about lasting political reconciliation.'[71] Or to what extent, if at all, the Court needs to be deferential to 'non-prosecutorial

[67] Judgment on the appeal of the Republic of Kenya, para 61, similarly, the Gaddafi decision, para 135 and Al-Senussi decision, para 66.

[68] Gaddafi decision, paras 54–5 and Al-Senussi decision, para 66.

[69] Dissenting Opinion of Judge Anita Ušacka, ICC-01/09-01/11OA, 20 September 2011, paras 20–28.

[70] Dissenting Opinion of Judge Anita Ušacka, para 25. A similar observation is made by Stahn, who notes that the AC set a very high threshold (Carsten Stahn, 'A Test for "Shared Responsibility"', 19(2) *Journal of International Criminal Justice* 325 (2012)).

[71] Cedric Ryngaert, 'State Responsibility, Necessity and Human Rights', 41 *Netherlands Yearbook of International Law* 79 (2010), 91.

alternatives such as a truth commission or a traditional justice mechanism like Uganda's *Acholi mato oput* ceremony'.[72] Due to the lack of space and also because this issue does not fall within the scope of this chapter, I will not attempt to answer these questions. Nevertheless, it is worth adding that while to date the ICC has not shown much respect for those 'non-prosecutorial alternatives',[73] its jurisprudence will have to face such mechanisms (as pardons, amnesties, truth commissions, etc) in the future and assess the degree of deference that should be granted in this context as the State practice referring to them is widespread.[74]

V. Some (Normative) Conclusions

In the context of the present discussion one may ask whether the Court has, in its admissibility jurisprudence, expressed a sufficient level of deference. The answer is not an easy one as both standards (that of review and that of proof) used by the ICC are still *in statu nascendi*, with their nature determined on a case-by-case basis while the methodology is not yet settled. Moreover, the answer also depends on the normative stance that is taken. On the one hand, one may argue that the principle of complementarity, being at the heart of the Statute, mandates the Court to grant States a broad margin of appreciation in the way they investigate, qualify and prosecute crimes. For example, Newton claims that 'the ICC should [always] defer to the good faith reasoning of domestic officials applying the law of the sovereign.'[75] Although the standard of good faith is in itself very ambiguous,[76] it definitely can be read as calling for a large degree of deference. Going beyond the argument on the centrality of the complementarity principle in the Rome Statute, it may be also argued that deference is justified by pragmatic reasons, such as superiority of a State, as compared to the ICC, to access and decide on evidence, witnesses and suspects. The ICC as such is not equipped with any enforcement mechanisms and must cooperate with States in every single case, beginning with interviews of witnesses, to collecting evidence and to the enforcement of sentences.

On the other hand, if one subscribes to the position that the Court's jurisdiction should be reconstructed with a due regard to the other objectives of the Rome Statute, as provided in its preamble,[77] such as the need to put an

[72] Keller, 'The Practice', 227. See also Diane Bernard, Chapter 20 in this volume (Section V).

[73] For a more in-depth discussion, see Sarah Nouwen and Wouter Werner, 'Monopolising Global Justice: International Criminal Law as Challenge to Human Diversity' (unpublished manuscript, on file with the author).

[74] Similarly, Nidal N. Jurdi, *The International Criminal Court and National Courts: A Contentious Relationship* (Farnham: Ashgate Publishing, 2011), 73–100.

[75] Michael A. Newton, 'The Complementarity Conundrum: Are We Watching Evolution or Evisceration?', 8(1) *Santa Clara Journal of International Law* 115 (2010), 145.

[76] For criticism of such an approach, see Keller, 'The Practice', 226. See also Andrei Mamolea, Chapter 5 in this volume.

[77] The Preamble to the Rome Statute recognizes various objectives of the treaty ('[d]etermined to put an end to impunity for the perpetrators of these crimes and thus to contribute to the prevention of such crimes'; '[e]mphasizing that the International Criminal Court established under this Statute

end to impunity or to guarantee lasting respect for international justice, some limitations on the deference are warranted. This more nuanced approach is arguably to be preferred as it ensures the effectiveness of the international system of criminal justice without compromising the complementarity principle. At the same time, such an interpretation is compatible with the customary rules of interpretation provided in the Vienna Convention on the Law of Treaties, which mandate consideration of the purpose(s) and the objective(s) of a treaty. Of course, such a general statement does not provide a clear demarcation line that would allow for precisely determining the extent of the required deference. What it does, however, it excludes two extremes of judicial review—*de novo* and full deference (an analogous conclusion can be reached with respect to standard of proof and its extremes).[78] Any assessment of the Court's practice that goes beyond this conclusion therefore needs to be subjective. Bearing in mind this limitation I would like, nevertheless, to offer a couple of observations.

Probably the most compelling task for the Court is to clarify the applicable standards of review and proof, thus providing States with a clear set of criteria about what makes a case admissible. In doing so, the Court should bear in mind that the complementarity principle requires that a certain margin of appreciation (deference) be granted to States. However it cannot be unlimited, as the Rome Statute provides for multiple objectives and these must be taken into account in determining the requisite standard. At the same time, defining the deference which is warranted under the complementarity principle in terms of applicable standard of review will provide States with clear and familiar standards with respect to the jurisdiction of the Court.

Complementarity as such should operate, on one hand, as a mechanism of a dialogue with States, while on the other it is a mechanism of control over States' actions. At the moment the complementarity principle, as interpreted by the ICC, seems mainly focused on the mechanism of control.

While the Court has granted States a certain degree of deference, some standards have been construed in a way which may unnecessarily limit the discretion of States. For instance, the same conduct test in its original interpretation offered only a small chance to positively challenge the admissibility of a case before the Court (this objection relates specifically to those States with limited resources to conduct proceedings covering the same acts/incidents/facts). This aggressive approach could lead to a situation when the State's admissibility challenge referring to serious crimes (more serious that those before the ICC) could be rejected because the prong of the same conduct test with respect to incidents was not satisfied. Such a situation may discourage States from cooperation with the Court,

shall be complementary to national criminal jurisdictions'; [r]esolved to guarantee lasting respect for and the enforcement of international justice').

[78] Cf Michael Ioannidis, Chapter 6 in this volume, who discusses a similar approach of the Appellate Body in the context of the WTO.

specifically if the standard of review applied is perceived as too strict.[79] The same observation applies to an overly high standard of proof.

Although the eagerness of the Court to consider cases, which is implied in the moderate level of deference expressed in the admissibility cases so far, is understandable (the Court is still a relatively young institution that seeks to establish its presence in the international community); in the long term such an approach 'could undermine reasonable national efforts to prosecute by going against the logic of the burden-sharing goals of complementarity.'[80]

[79] Charles C. Jalloh, 'Kenya vs. The ICC Prosecutor', 53 *Harvard International Law Journal Online* 238 (2012).
[80] Jalloh, 'International Decision', 122.

20

Beyond Hierarchy

Standard of Review and the Complementarity of the International Criminal Court

Diane Bernard

I. Introduction

The International Criminal Court (ICC) exercises a 'complementary' jurisdiction in the repression of genocide, war crimes, crimes against humanity and aggression.[1] According to this original allocation of jurisdictional powers, States have *priority* in the prosecution and punishment of mass atrocities; the Court may only intervene if States do not genuinely combat impunity. Indeed, according to the Preamble of the Statute, States are determined to 'put an end to impunity' for the perpetrators of these crimes, which 'must not go unpunished'—and the ICC completes their actions only if needed.[2] The principle of complementarity therefore implies an assessment of national processes: the Court must appraise the actions of national authorities in order to decide whether or not to exercise its jurisdiction.

This assessment constitutes a complex operation, involving political tensions and technical challenges. The exercise of *ius puniendi* is traditionally a sovereign right of a State, which makes the complementarity mechanism an important innovation,[3] as well as a source of tensions between international and national

[1] Rome Statute of the International Criminal Court, 2187 UNTS 90, came into force 1 July 2002 (see particularly Articles 1 and 17). For an extensive analysis, see eg Jann K. Kleffner, *Complementarity in the Rome Statute and National Criminal Jurisdictions* (Oxford: Oxford University Press, 2008); Jo Stigen, *The Relationship between the International Criminal Court and National Jurisdictions* (Leiden/Boston: Martinus Nijhoff, 2008); Mohamed El Zeidy, 'The Principle of Complementarity: A New Machinery to Implement International Criminal Law', 23 *Michigan Journal of International Law* 869 (2002); for a contextualized and critical approach, see Sarah Nouwen, *Complementarity in the Line of Fire. The Catalysing Effect of the International Criminal Court in Uganda and Sudan* (Cambridge: Cambridge University Press, 2014).

[2] Rome Statute, Preamble, clauses 4, 5, and 10.

[3] See eg Robert Cryer, 'International Criminal Law vs State Sovereignty: Another Round', 16(5) *EJIL* 979 (2006); Morten Bergsmo and Yan Ling (eds), *State Sovereignty and International Criminal Law* (Beijing: Torkhel Opsahl, 2012).

authorities.[4] Both the drafters of the Statute and the judges of the ICC have consequently formulated various criteria of assessment in order to maximize the 'objectivity' of international intervention in national (failing) judicial orders. These criteria act as markers of the *deference* shown by the Court to national reactions to mass atrocities, albeit always in the light of the general target of fighting impunity. While the ICC may well have an international jurisdiction in criminal matters, it still shows respect towards the exercise of *ius puniendi* by individual States. This chapter focuses on such 'respect' in procedural matters, ie it focuses on the degree of deference towards national actions, and the requirements expressed by the ICC regarding the type and quality of national processes which should take place following mass atrocities.

The key ideas of 'deference' and 'assessment' are common to both the concept of 'complementarity' as well as 'standard of review', which justifies a joint analysis despite all existing differences (Section II). The hermeneutical potential of various aspects connected with 'standard of review' will then be scrutinized through a brief presentation of complementarity (Section III), followed by a specific analysis of the norms of due process (Section IV) and judicial processes which are potentially required from States by the Rome Statute (Section V). Along with this technical presentation, the chapter also addresses certain aspects of 'standard of review' as applicable to complementarity, ie its inherent criminal teleology. In international criminal law, everything seems to converge towards punishment (even though many other reactions to mass atrocities might be implemented). This penal bias illustrates the fact that no mechanism can pretend to be entirely neutral or purely objective. In conclusion, the chapter suggests that, 'standard of review' might contribute to conceptualizing the general structure of international criminal law (Section VI).[5]

II. Intersection of Complementarity and Standard of Review

As a new and complex mechanism, complementarity requires theoretical and practical refinement. In this light one can suggest that the notion of 'standard of review' could, despite contextual and material differences between it and 'complementarity', help to conceptualize the relationship between a 'complementary'—but not superior—international court, and an 'assessed'—but still sovereign—national authority. Indeed, the concept of standard of review allows the

[4] For more on the political debates surrounding the exercise of international criminal jurisdiction within States' orders, see John T. Holmes, 'The Principle of Complementarity', in Roy S. Lee (ed), *The International Criminal Court: The Making of the Rome Statute* (Den Haag: Kluwer, 1999) 41–78 (about the negotiation) or Nouwen, *Complementarity in the Line of Fire* (in Uganda and Sudan specifically).

[5] In this chapter, I will use 'international criminal law' as a synonym for 'the law applied to and by the ICC', which offers a very narrow definition of this branch of law; for a definition of international criminal law in general, not restricted to the ICC, see eg Antonio Cassese and Paola Gaeta, *Cassese's International Criminal Law* (Oxford: Oxford University Press, 2008) 3–9.

combination of political respect for national sovereignty (ie deference) with the quest for effectiveness in the struggle against impunity.

The concept of 'standard of review' comes from the Common Law tradition, where it is used in several legal contexts (such as judicial review of jury decisions, of legislation or actions of administrative agencies, and as appellate review of trial court decisions). It may be defined as the degree of deference given by a reviewing court to the actions and decisions under review, eg 'a statement of the power not only of the appellate court but also of the tribunal below, measured by the hesitation of the appellate court to overturn the lower court's decision'[6] (with respect to intra-judicial review). At the international level the concept has been extensively used, for example, in the area of trade law.[7] Standards may vary from strict scrutiny to deferential ones, in the latter case with a court showing respect for the first decision-maker, either due to its inherent authority (eg with respect to a jury's finding of fact) or because of its expertise in a given matter. This variation also depends on the type of issue under review: a *de novo* standard often applies to determinations of law, while more deference is usually shown to factual findings. The same ambiguity characterizes complementarity. States maintain their priority in fighting impunity, but this power is inherently limited by the potential intervention of the Court.

Based on this conceptual similarity, the key concepts underlying 'standard of review' will be woven into the analysis of complementarity in procedural matters. My hypothesis is that, on the one hand, the concept of 'standard of review' might play an interesting role in the theorization of the relationship of the ICC with domestic orders, while on the other hand an analysis of the complicated relationship between an (international) reviewer and (national) first decision-maker could reciprocally give the concept of 'standard of review' a new dimension.

Such an experimental application of the concept of 'standard of review' requires two clarifications. First, the concept is hardly ever applied to the relationship between international criminal courts and national authorities,[8] but is frequently used in its classical sense in the jurisprudence concerning appeals lodged with the ICC and the International Criminal Tribunals for the former Yugoslavia (ICTY) and for Rwanda.[9] Despite the silence of the Statutes and Rules in this

[6] Martha S. Davis, 'Standards of Review: Judicial Review of Discretionary Decisionmaking', 2 *Journal of Appellate Practice and Process* 47 (2000).

[7] See for example Chapter 6 by Michael Ioannidis and Chapter 9 by Lukasz Gruszczynski and Valentina Vadi, both in this volume.

[8] For a similar observation see Chapter 19 by Karolina Wierczynska in this volume (Section II).

[9] ICTY, Appeals Chamber, *Dusko Tadic*, IT-94-1-A, 15 July 1999, Judgment, paras 64, 115, and 149; Appeals Chamber, *Anto Furundzija*, IT-95-17/1-A, 21 July 2000, Judgment, paras 34–40; *Dragoljub Kunarac et al*, IT-96-23-A, 12 June 2002, paras 35–48; *Mitar Vasiljevic*, IT-98-32-A, 25 February 2004, Judgment, 4–12. For a summary of the standards of review of use before the ICTs, see *Tihomir Blaskic*, IT-95-14-A, 29 July 2004, Judgment, paras 8–24. About the ICC, see eg Appeals Chamber, *Callixte Mbarushimana*, ICC-01/04-01/10 OA4, 30 May 2012, Judgment on the appeal of the Prosecutor against the decision of Pre-Trial Chamber I of 16 December 2011 entitled 'Decision on the confirmation of charges', para 15. In the literature, see eg Robert Cryer et al, *An Introduction to International Criminal Law and Procedure* (Cambridge: Cambridge University Press, 2010) 471–73.

regard, the judges have implemented standards of review which date from the very first appeals. Already in the *Tadic* case, the Appeals Chamber determined that only unreasonable *factual* determinations of the Pre-Trial Chamber may be overturned, while *legal* determinations are subject to *de novo* review.[10] In the same sense, the ICC Appeals Chamber promptly distinguished *legal* errors (no deference) from errors of *fact* (standard of reasonableness in reviewing the findings), and *procedural* errors (some deference).[11] However, application of the concept of standard of review to the assessment implied by complementarity constitutes an innovation, if not a wager. The concept has not been used as such by the drafters of the Rome Statute, and if the term 'standard of review' has incidentally come up in this regard in the international criminal law literature, it has been through an American or Canadian scholar perspective.[12] These lexical occurrences, arising out of their authors' legal education, do not justify this chapter (even if they might reinforce its relevance). My interest in the concept lies much more in its paradoxical combination of *deference* and *assessment* than in its textual usage. As aforementioned, these two key ideas may help to define complementarity.

A second clarification relates to the respective 'objects' of standard of review and complementarity. While 'complementarity' is used to determine the *admissibility* of a case before the ICC, standard of review serves to assess the *legality* of national measures or previous decisions.[13] Nevertheless, this difference does not reduce their similar articulations of deference and assessment, which justifies the approach of this chapter.

In Sections III, IV and V, I address some aspects of complementarity, with a focus on its application in procedural matters. The use of 'standard of review' as a grid, or as a conceptual tool, should help conceptualize the assessment of national reactions to mass atrocities.

[10] ICTY, Appeals Chamber, *Dusko Tadic*, paras 64, 115, and 149. Article 83-2 of the Rome Statute specifies a kind of standard of review, but without any great detail or clarity.

[11] See the clear summary in ICC, Office of the Prosecutor, *Mathieu Ngudjolo Chui*, ICC-01/04-02/12 A, 3 April 2013, Prosecution's Document in Support of Appeal against the 'Jugement rendu en application de l'article 74 du Statut', paras 33–6.

[12] See eg Benjamin R. Dolin, 'International Criminal Court: American Concerns about an International Prosecutor' (Parliamentary Research Branch, 14 May 2002), available at <http://publications.gc.ca/Collection-R/LoPBdP/BP/prb0211-e.htm> (accessed 28 March 2014); Michael A. Newton, 'The Complementarity Conundrum: Are We Watching Evolution or Evisceration?', 8 *Santa Clara Journal of International Law* 136 (2010); Jimmy Gurule, 'United States Opposition to the 1998 Rome Statute Establishing an International Criminal Court: Is the Court's Jurisdiction Truly Complementary to National Criminal Jurisdictions?', 35 *Cornell International Law Journal* 9 (2001–2002).

[13] Similarly to the concept of 'margin of appreciation' developed by the European Court of Human Rights (ECtHR), which provides 'the space for manoeuvre that the Strasbourg organs are willing to grant national authorities, in fulfilling their obligations under the European Convention on Human Rights' (Steven Greer, *The Margin of Appreciation: Interpretation and Discretion under the European Convention on Human Rights* (Council of Europe, 2000) 5). The 'margin of appreciation' is of less interest in this chapter, since it relates to the reviewed actor's autonomy in itself more than to the *relationship* between the reviewer and reviewed, or the articulation of deference in reviewing. For more detailed discussion of the 'margin of appreciation', see Chapter 13 by Mónika Ambrus (in the ECtHR context) and Chapter 16 by Bernard Duhaime (in the context of the Inter-American Human Rights System).

III. Criteria of Complementarity

The principle of complementarity 'means that the Court will *complement but not supersede* national jurisdiction.'[14] It was initially intended to protect national sovereignty, with the States remaining masters of their own judicial systems and national courts keeping their priority in the investigation and prosecution of crimes committed within their jurisdiction. But as States and the ICC share concurrent jurisdiction, the Court is entitled to intervene—if and only if—no concerned State is *genuinely* reacting to mass atrocities. The ICC thus holds a residual power, to be exercised in case of inactivity or inappropriate and ineffective activity by the State. This regime is the result of 'politically sensitive and legally complex' negotiations about the articulation of national sovereignties with respect to the first international and permanent criminal court. It constitutes a delicate balance between the desire to prevent grave crimes from going unpunished on the one hand, and the desire to preserve the autonomous sovereignty of national judicial systems on the other.[15]

In order to determine its own jurisdiction over a case, the ICC must assess the struggle against impunity pursued by States *in specie*. According to Article 17 of the Rome Statute, a case is inadmissible when '[it] is being investigated or prosecuted by a State which has jurisdiction over it, *unless* the State is unwilling or unable genuinely to carry out the investigation or prosecution' (emphasis added). So *unwillingness* and *inability*, together with the requirement of gravity, constitute the criteria of assessment.[16]

Gravity, as an implicit criterion, is indeed included in the material jurisdiction of the ICC: the crimes within its jurisdiction are 'the most serious crimes of concern to the international community.'[17] The Pre-Trial Chamber nonetheless clarified that 'the fact that a case addresses one of the most serious crimes for the international community as a whole is not sufficient to be admissible before the Court.'[18] Rules 145-1-C and 2-B-iv of Procedure and Evidence provide some

[14] Roy S. Lee, 'The Rome Conference and its contribution to International Criminal Law: Introduction' in Roy S. Lee (ed), *The International Criminal Court: The Making of the Rome Statute* (Den Haag: Kluwer, 1999) 27.

[15] El Zeidy, 'The Principle of Complementarity' 970; Stigen, *The Relationship* 17; Michael A. Newton, 'Comparative Complementarity; Domestic Jurisdiction Consistent with the Rome Statute of the International Criminal Court', 167 *Military Law Review* 20 (2001) 23.

[16] For an extensive analysis of this criterion, see Margaret deGuzman, 'Gravity and the Legitimacy of International Criminal Court', 32 *Fordham International Law Journal* 1400 (2008).

[17] As formulated, *inter alia*, in the Preamble to the Statute, clause 4. Gravity as a criterion of admissibility was already discussed in the first projects of the Statute, see Report of the International Law Commission to the General Assembly on the work of its 46th session, A/CN.4/SER.A/1994/Add.l (Part 2), 52.

[18] ICC, *Situation of the Democratic Republic of the Congo in the case of Thomas Lubanga*, ICC-01/04-01/06, 24 February 2006, Decision concerning Pre-trial Chamber I's decision of 10 February 2006 and the incorporation of documents into the record of the case against M. Thomas Lubanga Dyilo, para 41 or, as confirmation, ICC, *Situation in Darfur in the Case of Bahar Idriss Abu Garda*, ICC-02/05-02/09, 8 February 2010, Public redacted version of the Decision on the confirmation of charges, para 30; see also ICC (Pre-Trial Chamber), Decision pursuant to Article 15 of the Rome Statute on the authorization of an investigation into the situation of the Republic of Kenya, ICC-01/09, 31 March 2010, para 56.

indicators of gravity, without defining the criterion itself. These indicators include the extent of damage caused to victims and their families, the nature of the unlawful behaviour, and the means used to execute the crime.[19]

Regarding *unwillingness*, three scenarios are described in Article 17(2) of the Rome Statute: the 'purpose of shielding the person concerned from criminal responsibility', an 'unjustified delay in the proceedings', and a lack of independence or impartiality. The *unwillingness* criterion was initially focused on situations where a State was conducting a *sham trial/investigation*, but it has found new significance already, for example with respect to self-referrals (ie in situations where States declare their will to see the ICC intervene for them).[20] The criterion of *inability*, established by Article 17(3), covers the 'total or substantial collapse or unavailability of [State's] national judicial system'. It would appear to be more concrete than unwillingness, and consequently easier to allege, as it refers to factual capacity instead of subjective alacrity (how could the national *will* be anything else than subjective?).[21] Nevertheless, both remain hard to evaluate, *a fortiori* in post-conflict periods.[22] The recent analysis of the ICC on the 'unavailability of the national Libyan system' properly illustrates this complexity, on both the legal and political levels.[23]

Gravity, unwillingness and/or inability determine the admissibility of a case before the ICC, ie these elements condition the complementarity of the Court. But the 'genuineness' of national actions is the 'key qualification of ability or willingness to conduct proceedings'.[24] It might take on various senses: 'good faith'[25] or 'not in a sham manner' when applied to (un)willingness; not lacking legal certainty when applied to (in)ability. Despite the intention of the drafters 'to reduce

[19] These elements are not exhaustive, see ICC (Pre-Trial Chamber), (Public) Decision pursuant to Article 15 of the Rome Statute on the Authorisation of an investigation into the situation in the Republic of Côte d'Ivoire, ICC-02/11, 3 October 2011, paras 202–3. For a complete reference in the matter, see Kevin J. Heller, 'Situational Gravity under the Rome Statute', in Carsten Stahn and Larrisa van den Herik (eds), *Future Directions in International Criminal Justice* (Cambridge: TMC Asser/Cambridge University Press, 2009).

[20] The three first situations before the ICC came to the Court in this way (Democratic Republic of Congo, Uganda, and Central African Republic).

[21] Some drafters were against the inclusion of this criterion in the Statute, arguing that it excessively impinged on States' sovereignty, see eg Mohamed El Zeidy, *The Principle of Complementarity in International Criminal Law: Origin, Development and Practice* (Leiden: Brill, 2008) 163.

[22] See eg ICC, *Situation of the Democratic Republic of the Congo in the case of Thomas Lubanga Dyilo*, ICC-01/04-01/06, 10 February 2006, Decision on the Prosecutor's application for a warrant of arrest, para 36.

[23] ICC, *Situation in Libya in the case of the Prosecutor v Saif al-Islam Gaddafi and Abdullah Al-Senussi*, ICC-01/11-01/11, 31 May 2013, Decision on the admissibility of the case against Saif al-Islam Gaddafi, paras 199–218.

[24] Bartram Brown, *Research Handbook on International Criminal Law* (Cheltenham: Edward Elgar Publishing, 2011) 216–20. For instance, the Court concluded very recently that Libya was unable to *genuinely* try Saif Gaddafi thus avoiding an assessment of its willingness), see ICC, *Situation in Libya in the case of Saif al-Islam Gaddafi and Abdullah Al-Senussi*, ICC-01/11-01/11, 31 May 2013, Decision on the admissibility of the case against Saif al-Islam Gaddafi, paras 138 and 218.

[25] For an analysis of good faith review across different international courts, see Chapter 5 by Andrei Mamolea in this volume.

the number of terms that included subjective elements,'[26] in a classical but vain quest for objectivity, genuineness presents a subjective aspect as well.[27] The Court did specify that national investigations and prosecutions must be assessed in the context of the relevant national system,[28] which opens the possibility of a flexible implementation of the complementarity criteria, depending on the situation. This also enables the Court to balance the political and contextual aspects of its intervention.

Translated into 'standard of review' language, these constitutive elements of complementarity would certainly imply a 'deference' to national decisions/actions. As mentioned, 'complementarity substantially safeguards States' sovereignty'.[29] Due to this political intricacy, and to its negotiated origin, the ICC certainly could not review *de novo* national intentions, good faith or ability: it must show a certain degree of deference.[30] Moreover, the negotiators of the Rome Statute repeatedly emphasized the difference between the complementary ICC and a court of appeal:[31] in order to limit international interferences into national orders, the action of the Court was limited by allegedly objective criteria in order to restrict too wide a review. The issue is highly debatable of course. No criterion can be completely objective, interpretation cannot be avoided, and law has always to be contextualized.

Moreover, complementarity to some extent lacks determinacy (see Section V). But at the same time, stricter requirements for States might be deduced from a closer look at the Rome Statute with regard to due process (Section IV) and judicial process (Section V). These lacunae and extensions of complementarity might be enlightened once again by the concept of 'standard of review', while at the same time the latter might find some refinement in such an application.

IV. Reviewing Fairness and/or Punishing at Any Price

Within the general requirement of the genuineness of judicial proceedings, Articles 17 and 20(3) of the Rome Statute make specific reference to the 'norms of due process recognized by international law'. If Articles 17 and 20 are deemed to incorporate the due process guarantees within the general fairness required from States, they do not specify whether this constitutes a stand-alone criterion of admissibility, or only is an element, among others, of *unwillingness* or *inability*. By referring in the Statute to the 'norms of due process recognized by international law', the drafters apparently wanted to provide the ICC with an *objective* criterion of assessment, without raising these guarantees to a positive obligation.[32] Still, the

[26] Holmes, 'The Principle of Complementarity', 49. [27] Stigen, *The Relationship*, 215.

[28] Decision on the admissibility of the case against Saif al-Islam Gaddafi, ICC-01/11-01/11, 31 May 2013, 138.

[29] Kleffner, *Complementarity*, 314.

[30] Cf also Chapter 19 by Karolina Wierczynska for a similar observation.

[31] See the summary of drafting and negotiation process by Holmes, 'The Principle of Complementarity', 49–50.

[32] See Holmes, 'The Principle of Complementarity', 53–4; Enrique Carnero-Rojo, 'The Role of Fair Trial Considerations in the Complementarity Regime of the International Criminal

wording of the Statute does not rule out such an interpretation. Consequently, these terms have provoked active debates among experts.[33] Can the Court assess the general fairness of domestic actions, therefore exceeding its initial mandate (limited to ensuring that States fight impunity, regardless of their methods)? This issue directly refers to questions of deference to be shown to national processes.

Scholars have been considering this issue for years now. In this context, the 'due process thesis' has been developed, according to which[34] a national failure to offer a defendant (all or basic) guarantees of due process makes a case admissible before the ICC because it shows an 'unwillingness' or 'inability' to genuinely react to mass atrocities (therefore meeting the admissibility criteria), even if the whole trial is not thereby vitiated. In their very specific contexts (of the Tribunals for former Yugoslavia and Rwanda), Rules 11*bis* of Procedure and Evidence before the International Criminal Tribunals could constitute a precedent reinforcing this position.[35] They have indeed blocked deferrals to national jurisdictions for reasons linked to the (unfair) trial that would have been reserved to the transferred defendant at the national level. However, one should note that this requirement was part of a global collaboration between international and national authorities that does not occur in all situations.[36] This 'due process thesis' is nevertheless seductive, given the current trend to fairer trials and the universal implementation of human rights.

On the other hand, one could argue that violating a party's due process rights does not denote *inability*, as the trial is effectively taking place. Nor does it comply with the initial interpretation of *unwillingness*; in fact it reflects the exact opposite (there is no *sham trial* protecting the defendant from effective prosecution). More generally, important issues arise on the legitimacy of an international *criminal* court to assess fairness of trials within national systems, and on the links of this praetorian extension with national sovereignty. Apart from the explicit mention of the 'norms of due process', there is little in the Statute that suggests that the respect of procedural human rights in court could be imposed on the States as a *required* way to react to mass atrocities. The ICC is a *criminal court*, and its Statute

Court: From "No Peace without Justice" to "No Peace without Victors' Justice"?', 18(4) *Leiden Journal of International Law* 829 (2005), 851; Markus Benzing, 'The Complementarity Regime of the International Criminal Court: International Criminal Justice between State Sovereignty and the Fight against Impunity', 7 *Max Planck Yearbook of UN Law* 591 (2003), 606; Kleffner, *Complementarity*, 127.

[33] Eg recently through specialized blogs, as *EJIL:Talk!*

[34] Kevin J. Heller, 'The Shadow Side of Complementarity: The Effect of Article 17 of the Rome Statute on National Due Process', 17 *Criminal Law Forum* 255 (2005), 255–6. For an excellent summary of positions on this matter, see Elinor Fry, 'Between Show Trials and Sham Prosecutions: The Rome Statute's Potential Effect on Domestic Due Process Protections', 23 *Criminal Law Forum* 35 (2012).

[35] These rules have been developed within the Completion Strategies of the International Criminal Trials for the former Yugoslavia and for Rwanda.

[36] See the Libyan case before the ICC. Libya's admissibility challenge has been rejected on other grounds despite several due process violations in the case of Saif Gaddafi, who has been detained by a special militia for months in complete isolation and very questionable conditions, his ICC counsel having been detained for a few weeks during a visit to Libya in June 2012, etc. The Defence vainly relied on the due process thesis in its Urgent request for measures to remedy ongoing violations of Mr Saif al-Islam Gaddafi's right before the ICC, ICC-01/11-323-Conf-Exp, 16 April 2013.

does not include an equivalent to Article 6 of the European Convention of Human Rights (ECHR). While the ICC must respect the norms of due process in its own proceedings, this does not translate into a mandate to assess the national ways of conducting trials. Its mission is to verify that trials actually take place and that States effectively fight impunity. Of course, international criminal law springs from, and makes constant reference to, human rights.[37] There is a substantial and institutional relationship between human rights and international criminal law, variously referred to as 'faux-frères':[38] 'Siamese twins with a single head',[39] or 'tangled' disciplines.[40] Human rights humanize criminal trials, and criminal law is increasingly used to punish breaches of human rights guarantees.[41] But if Article 21(3) of the Statute refers to internationally recognized human rights, it applies to the activities of the Court itself.[42] The ICC is not competent to deal with human rights matters: it is a *criminal* court, granted with an exceptional power of intervention in failing domestic orders because of the gravity of the crimes concerned. As a consequence, any extension of this aspect of complementarity goes beyond the Statute.[43] The ICC is not competent to evaluate the way in which States apply human rights, but only their struggle against impunity for the 'worst crimes'. Both theoretically and textually, it cannot force States to implement fair trials.[44] Only a very wide interpretation of the Statute would give the Court such an extensive dimension.[45]

In conclusion, the due process thesis is thrilling for those who maintain faith in the highest aims of justice, equity and universality. But it is legally uncertain

[37] See the references to these texts eg in ICC, *Thomas Lubanga Dyilo*, ICC-01/04-01/06, 31 March 2006, Décision relative à la requête du Procureur sollicitant l'autorisation d'interjeter appel de la décision de la Chambre du 17 janvier 2006 sur les demandes de participation à la procédure de VPRS 1, VPRS 2, VPRS 3, VPRS 4, VPRS 5 et VPRS 6, para 34.

[38] William A. Schabas, 'Droit pénal international et droit international des droits de l'homme: faux frères?', in Marc Henzelin and Rober Roth (eds), *Le droit pénal à l'épreuve de l'internationalisation* (Paris, etc: LGDJ/Georg/Bruylant, 2002) 165–81.

[39] Paul Tavernier, 'Les tribunaux pénaux internationaux et le droit international des droits de l'homme' in Mireille Delmas-Marty et al (eds), *Les sources du droit international pénal—l'expérience des Tribunaux Pénaux Internationaux et le Statut de la Cour Pénale Internationale* (Paris: Société de Législation comparée, 2004) 395–402.

[40] See eg Yves Cartuyvels et al (eds), *Les droits de l'homme: bouclier ou épée du droit pénal?* (Brussels: FUSL-Bruylant, 2007).

[41] Alvaro P. Pires, 'Quelques obstacles à une mutation du droit pénal', 26 *Revue Générale de Droit* 133 (1995), 136.

[42] Frederic Mégret and Marika G. Samson, 'Holding the Line in Complementarity in Libya: The Case for Tolerating Flawed Domestic Trials', 11 *Journal of International Criminal Justice* 573 (2013).

[43] Report of the International Law Commission to the General Assembly on the work of its 46th session, A/49/10, *Yearbook of the ILC*, vol. II (part 2), 2 May–22 July 1994, para 72; Topical summary of the discussion held in the 6th Committee of the General Assembly during its 49th session, A/CN.4/464/Add.1, para 159; Holmes, 'The Principle of Complementarity', 50 ('many delegations believed that procedural fairness should not be a ground for the purpose of defining complementarity'); Heller, 'The Shadow Side of Complementarity', 264.

[44] See eg Rolf E. Fife, 'The International Criminal Court. Whence It Came, Where It Goes', 69 *Nordic Journal of International Law* 63 (2000), 66–7.

[45] Christine van den Wyngaert and Tom Ongena, 'Ne bis in idem Principle, Including the Issue of Amnesty' in Antonio Cassese, Paola Gaeta and John R. Jones (eds), *The Rome Statute of the International Criminal Court* (Oxford: Oxford University Press, 2002) 725.

whether violations of party's right to a fair trial before domestic courts suffice to make a case admissible before the ICC. Pragmatically, the Court will probably require some basic guarantees of fairness from States,[46] which might appease (without solving) the contradictions inherent to this predilection for punishment at all costs.[47]

This controversy is relevant for our discussion as it provides a better understanding of complementarity and highlights issues where analysis of the concept of 'standard of review' may be helpful. While the ICC holds one of the fundamental sovereign rights, ie the *ius puniendi*, it cannot interfere (for now) into the qualitative aspects of the national exercise of this same right. In other words, the degree of deference shown here appears to be very high. Objective criteria of a fair trial however exist: the ECtHR, in particular, offers a comprehensive jurisprudence based on Article 6 ECHR (ie the right to a fair trial). We concluded Section III by observing that despite a prevailing subjectivity in the assessment of national decisions, a limited deference to States had to be shown (under the condition of maximizing objectivity of the review). In other words, fair trial standards could help better guarantee such objectivity, but nevertheless a deference to national decisions must be kept (while the 'more objective' criteria of fairness could open a window to greater intervention by the ICC). Consequently, the translation of issues relating to complementarity into the language of 'standard of review' reveals that objectivity is not the key point in the assessment of national actions. Another aspect of the complex relationship between international and national decision-makers is at stake. My hypothesis is that *punishment* is the central issue—penal repression may sweep away issues of sovereignty and deference, as well as fairness and objectivity. The next section tries to clarify this point.

V. Reviewing Choices of Processes and/or Requiring Criminal Trials

The ICC aims at combating impunity (especially when it is organized by the State), and does so by requiring efficient actions from States. Pushing this assertion to the extreme, one could conclude that the end might justify the means: even if they lacked quality, national trials would still be trials, and therefore able to block the ICC's complementary intervention. As mentioned previously, I believe that the

[46] Pragmatically, Fry has recently pleaded for a 'moderate' interpretation of the 'due process thesis', as including only basic norms of due process; see Fry, 'Between Show Trials and Sham Prosecutions'. As an extreme example, the possibility that Said El Gaddafi may be sentenced to death in Libya has been raised as a strong argument in favour of the admissibility of his case before the ICC, but as previously mentioned, the ICC did not take a position in this regard; see Fry, 'Between Show Trials and Sham Prosecutions'.

[47] See Section V on the possible moderation of this tendency through an emphasis on 'interests of justice'.

Court will preferably opt for a middle ground, still requiring some basic guarantees from States.

Nevertheless, an analysis of the assessment of national trials, as set up by the Rome Statute, does confirm the general emphasis on punishment or, at least, on penal proceedings. According to Article 20(3) of the Statute, judicial processes within domestic orders will be assessed as follows:

No person who has been tried by another court for conduct also proscribed under article 6, 7, 8 or 8*bis* shall be tried by the Court with respect to the same conduct unless the proceedings in the other court:

(a) were for the purpose of shielding the person concerned from criminal responsibility for crimes within the jurisdiction of the Court; or

(b) otherwise were not conducted independently or impartially in accordance with the norms of due process recognized by international law and were conducted in a manner which, in the circumstances, was inconsistent with an intent to bring the person concerned to justice.

A conviction or an acquittal by a national judge will consequently be determined to be valid before the ICC on the basis that: (a) it took the shape of a trial; (b) judgment was given by a jurisdiction *stricto sensu*; in the case of a conviction, (c) this conviction is enforceable; and (d) the sentence was sufficiently severe. The trial should moreover (e) be genuine, independent and impartial, and consistent with the norms of due process, which refers to general criteria of complementarity already analysed in Sections III and IV.[48] Below I analyse each of these points.

(a) First, the term 'tried' instead of 'convicted or acquitted' indicates that any *final* and *judicial* decision would block the complementarity of the Court (in other words, it would activate the principle of *ne bis in idem*). A decision on the merits is not required from national courts;[49] the decision of a national judge to end the process for formal reasons (eg because a reasonable time had been exceeded, or to have the accused committed for medical reasons), could be considered as valid and sufficient by the ICC. This high degree of deference shown to national judges reflects the core idea of complementarity: States are primarily competent in their judicial affairs.[50] At the same time, it illustrates the political weight of the issue of reviews by the ICC: the Statute could not go too far in establishing international intervention within national judicial affairs.

[48] The qualification used by national judges could also be commented on, as a trial for an ordinary crime could be considered as insufficient. *A contrario*, see Kevin J. Heller, 'A Sentence-based Theory of Complementarity', 53 *Melbourne Journal of International Law* 86 (2012). This chapter nevertheless only covers purely procedural issues, as indicated in the introduction. For an analysis of the 'same conduct same person' criterion, see Chapter 19 by Karolina Wierczynska, Section III.A.

[49] Benzing, 'The Complementarity Regime', 618.

[50] Gerard Conway, 'Ne bis in idem and the International Criminal Tribunals', 25 *Criminal Law Forum* 361 (2003).

(b) In addition, the terms 'tried by another *court*' in Article 20(3) imply that national decisions should be taken by an (ordinary or military) judicial organ, *stricto sensu*.[51] This textually excludes administrative sanctions,[52] transactions, mediations,[53] and alternative reactions to mass atrocities, such as Truth and Reconciliation Commissions or other extra-judicial processes. This issue was inconclusively addressed by the drafters of the Statute and still appears as confusing.[54] Genuine extra-judicial efforts (eg Truth and Reconciliation Commissions), even if they lead to a final decision, would not be considered judgments (although they could be recognized as inquiries followed by a decision not to prosecute, according to Article 17(1)).[55]

(c) Enforcement constitutes one of the classical criteria of recognition of a foreign judgment by a national jurisdiction.[56] Authors agree that the enforcement of the sentence is an indispensable corollary to the struggle against impunity.[57] The ICC could consider pardon, parole or commutation of sentence as reliable,[58] but these declarations must follow the pronouncement of an *enforceable* sentence: they could not apply to a sentence of a symbolic nature, for instance. This requirement implies that the absence of enforcement could reveal a failure in the national trial.[59] A sentence without full enforcement would also show too much mercy to the accused, and only an enforced conviction *stricto sensu* mobilizes the complementarity mechanism and the *ne bis in idem* rule (thereby preventing

[51] Bruce Broomhall, 'La Cour pénale internationale: directives pour l'adoption des lois nationales et d'adaptation', in Association International de Droit Pénal (ed), *ICC ratifications and national implementing legislation* (Toulouse: Erès, 1999) 155; Stigen, *The Relationship*, 206.

[52] Stigen, *The Relationship*, 211.

[53] John Dugard, 'Possible Conflicts of Jurisdiction with Truth Commissions' in Antonio Cassesse, Paola Gaeta and John R. Jones (eds), *The Rome Statute of the International Criminal Court* (Oxford: Oxford University Press, 2002) 702.

[54] Cf Holmes, 'The Principle of Complementarity', 59; Report of the Preparatory Committee on the Establishment of an International Criminal Court, vol. 2, A/51/22, *GAOR*, 51st sess., Suppl. 22, para 174; A/CONF.183/2/Add.1, 14 April 1998, fn 42; J. Stigen, *The Relationship*, 211; Dugard, 'Possible Conflicts', 693 and 702; William W. Burke-White, 'Complementarity in Practice: The International Criminal Court as Part of a System of Multi-level Global Governance in the Democratic Republic of Congo', 18(3) *Leiden Journal of International Law* 582 (2005); El Zeidy, 'The Principle of Complementarity', 947.

[55] See also discussion in Section IV of Chapter 19, by Karolina Wierczynska, in this volume.

[56] Van den Wyngaert and Ongena, 'Ne bis in idem', 712.

[57] El Zeidy, 'The Principle of Complementarity' 947, about genocide, torture and serious violations of the Geneva Conventions (as implemented according to the Convention against Torture and other Inhuman or Degrading Treatment or Punishment, adopted by GAUN Res. 39/86, 10 December 1984, entered into force on 26 June 1987, Article 7; Convention on the Prevention and Punishment of the Crime of Genocide, adopted by GAUN Res. 260 (III), 9 December 1948 and entered into force on 11 January 1951, Article 4; Convention (I) for the Amelioration of the Condition of the Wounded and Sick in Armed Forces in the Field, Article 49; Convention (II) for the Amelioration of the Condition of Wounded, Sick and Shipwrecked Members of Armed Forces at Sea, Article 50; Convention (III) relative to the Treatment of Prisoners of War, Article 129; Convention (IV) relative to the Protection of Civilian Persons in Time of War, Article 146, all four were adopted on 12 August 1949 in Geneva and entered into force on 21 October 1950).

[58] Broomhall, 'La Cour pénale', 153.

[59] See eg Report of the Preparatory Committee on the Establishment of an International Criminal Court, A/CONF.183/2/Add.1, 14 April 1998, at 46.

the ICC from 'completing' a national action).[60] Without such enforcement, the force of *res judicata* is questionable, and the national effort to combat impunity could be considered as insufficient, hence the Court could admit the case. This is consistent with the *penal* project promoted by the Rome Statute.

(d) Article 20(3) of the Rome Statute also seems to require national jurisdictions to have pronounced a *sufficiently severe* sentence in case of a conviction.[61] A lenient sentence could be regarded as showing undue mercy towards the accused, concluding a partial or sham trial—therefore in contradiction with points (a) and (b) of the article, ie with the requested 'intent to bring the person to justice' (in a penal sense).[62]

(e) As an exception to the primacy of the national jurisdiction, decisions that are not genuinely made cannot be recognized. This expresses the core idea of complementarity;[63] that the ICC 'needs to step in when national justice fails'.[64] As aforementioned, the criteria to assess such a failure are (at least partially) subjective, in particular when they refer to (un)willingness (logically speaking, when a trial has been conducted 'inability' does not apply).[65] Again, the criteria of complementarity (as *unwillingness* and/or *inability*) do not appear as neutral technical tools, but as expressions of the larger aim pursued by international criminal law. They primarily cover situations where national proceedings make an accused more difficult to convict,[66] rather than offering a general protection to any citizen against abuse by their sovereign. These criteria contribute to assuring that States effectively punish perpetrators of the so-called 'worst crimes'.

Collectively, these five criteria of the assessment of judicial proceedings show a limited deference to national processes, ie the standard of review is rather strict. Here again, objectivity does not appear as essential as the struggle against impunity. The desire to effectively punish 'the worst crimes' limits the deference to be shown towards States' exercise of their *ius puniendi*. This re-formulation of the

[60] Rober Kolb and Damien Scalia, *Droit international pénal* (Basel: Helbing, 2012) 105.

[61] Similarly, see Adan Nieto Martin, 'Introduccion: El principio de ne bis in idem en el Derecho penal europeo en internacional' in Luis Arroyo Sapatero and Adan Nieto Martin (eds), *El principio de ne bis in idem en el Derecho penal europeo en internacional* (Cuenca: Ed. de la Universidad de Castilla—La Mancha, 2007) 15.

[62] Broomhall, 'La Cour pénale', 163.

[63] See eg El Zeidy, 'The Principle of Complementarity', 931; van den Wyngaert and Ongena, 'Ne bis in idem', 721; Holmes, 'The Principle of Complementarity', 42; Kai Ambos, 'The International Criminal Court and the Traditional Principles of International Cooperation in Criminal Matters', 9 *Finnish Yearbook of International Law* 419 (2000).

[64] Immi Tallgren, 'Article 20: *Ne bis in idem*', in Otto Triffterer (ed), *Commentary on the Rome Statute of the International Court. Observers' Notes, Article by Article* (Oxford: Hart Publishing, 2008) 688.

[65] Heller, 'The Shadow Side of Complementarity', 257. It has been asserted that the criterion of 'independence' is more *institutional*, as it applies to the relationship between judges and government, whilst 'impartiality' refers more subjectively to the *attitude* required of the judge during the exercise of his or her duty; Stefan Trechsel, *Human Rights in Criminal Proceedings* (Oxford: Oxford University Press, 2005) 53–61 and generally 45–80.

[66] Heller, 'The Shadow Side of Complementarity', 257.

criteria into the vocabulary of 'standard of review' underlines some fundamental (but not always explicit) features of complementarity.

This strictly *penal* conception, as identified within complementarity, could nevertheless find an extended and opportune interpretation through Article 53 of the Statute. This provision declares that, on the basis of 'the interests of justice', the Prosecutor of the ICC may decide not to prosecute, considering that current traditional or local processes, ie amnesty, compensation or the public discovery of the truth, would be more appropriate in the rebuilding of public peace.[67] Tacitly at least,[68] it is acknowledged that Truth and Reconciliation Commissions, as an alternative to criminal trials, could therefore have an impact on the international reaction to mass atrocities. And the 'interests of justice' would then constitute a new benchmark for determining the applicable standard of review, hopefully supplanting the actual emphasis on punishment through criminal law.

V. Beyond Hierarchy

The previous sections have demonstrated the hermeneutical potential of 'standard of review' with respect to 'complementarity'. Despite all the existing differences, the similarities between the two have probably increased their mutual relevancy and their joint analysis is at least partially justified by their common key ideas of 'deference' and 'assessment'. While the concept of 'standards of review' has broadened the analysis of complementarity, the very same exercise has also demonstrated the non-neutrality of the (variable) deference mechanism (as any procedural or analytical tool actually). The degrees of deference shown to national decisions and actions also rely on the general target of combating impunity. This conclusion could dampen propositions for very deferential standards of review to be applied by international courts, as a greater and more objective way to empower national and international actors.[69] No mechanism can pretend to complete neutrality or objectivity; in the current state of international criminal law everything seems to converge towards *punishment*, including procedural mechanisms, despite the fact that many other reactions to mass atrocities could be (and are) implemented. Standards of review serve this *ratio puniendi* more than any sovereign ideal or national order.

Despite this position, 'standard of review' might contribute to the structural conceptualization of international criminal law. Indeed, the degrees of deference towards States' penal sovereignty, as expressed in the variable 'standards of review', reveals a subtle structure, far from the basic hierarchy.[70] First, these variations in deference show that the ICC does not exercise a primacy upon States, which

[67] See Darryl Robinson, 'Serving the Interests of Justice: Amnesties, Truth Commissions and the International Criminal Court', 14 *EJIL* 481 (2003).

[68] Unfortunately, the Prosecutor may but does not have to justify her decisions not to prosecute.

[69] See eg Gurule, 'United States Opposition', 9.

[70] Yuval Shany, *The Competing Jurisdictions of International Courts and Tribunals* (Oxford: Oxford University Press, 2003) 127.

remain the first masters of penal reactions to mass atrocities. Secondly, standards frame a flexible but equitable system of criminal law: without requiring homogeneous reactions from States, they contribute to enforcing a side effect of the ICC, ie that States, in their struggle against impunity, are called upon to implement judicial actions based on *common criteria*,[71] each and every one being subject to the same requirements. In this sense, standards of review contribute to a seductive implementation of pluralism: they tend to facilitate the struggle against impunity without (completely) imposing a strict and single way to react to mass atrocities. That would fruitfully exceed the utopia of universal objectivity and univocality.

[71] Stefano Manacorda and Gerhard Werle, 'L'adaptation des systèmes pénaux nationaux au Statut de Rome. Le paradigme du "Volkërstrafgesetzbuch" allemand', 3 *Revue de science criminelle et de droit pénal* 501 (2003).

Bibliography

Abbott Kenneth W., Robert O. Keohane, Andrew Moravcsik, Anne-Marie Slaughter and Duncan Snidal, 'The Concept of Legalization', 54 *International Organization* 401 (2000).

Accetto Matej and Stefan Zleptnig, 'The Principle of Effectiveness: Rethinking its Role in Community Law', 11 *European Public Law* 375 (2003).

Acosta Alvarado Paola A. and Manuel Núñez Poblete (eds), *El Margen de Apreciación en el Sistema Interamericano de Derechos Humanos: Proyecciones Regionales y Nacionales* (México: Instituto de Investigaciones Jurídicas, UNAM 2012).

Alemanno Alberto, *Trade in Food—Regulatory and Judicial Approaches in the EC and the WTO* (Colwick: Cameron May, 2007).

Alemanno Alberto, 'EU Risk Regulation and Science: The Role of Experts in Decision-making and Judicial Review' in Ellen Vos (ed), *European Risk Governance—Its Science, its Inclusiveness and its Effectiveness* (Mannheim: Connex Report Series No. 6, 2008).

Alemanno Alberto, 'The Shaping of European Risk Regulation by Community Courts', *Jean Monnet Working Papers No. 18/2008.*

Alemanno Alberto, 'Case C-77/09, Gowan Comercio Internacional e Servicos Lda v Ministero della Salute, Judgment of the Court of Justice (Second Chamber) of 22 December 2010, nyr', 48(4) *CMLR* 1329 (2011).

Allan T.R.S., 'Human Rights and Judicial Review: A Critique of "Due Deference"', 65 *CLJ* 671 (2006).

Allan T.R.S., 'Judicial Deference and Judicial Review: Legal Doctrine and Legal Theory', 127(1) *Law Quarterly Review* 96 (2011).

Alexy Robert, *A Theory of Constitutional Rights* (Oxford: Oxford University Press, 2002).

Alvarez José E., 'The Return of the State', 20(2) *Minnesota Journal of International Law* 223 (2009).

Ambos Kai, 'The International Criminal Court and the Traditional Principles of International Cooperation in Criminal Matters', 9 *Finnish Yearbook of International Law* 419 (2000).

Ambrus Mónika, 'Comparative Law Method in the Jurisprudence of the European Court of Human Rights in the Light of the Rule of Law', 3 *Erasmus Law Review* 353 (2009).

Ambrus Mónika, *Enforcement Mechanisms of the Racial Equality Directive and Minority Protection* (The Hague: Eleven International Publishing, 2011).

Andenas Mads and Stefan Zleptnig, 'Proportionality: WTO Law in Comparative Perspective', 42 *Texas International Law Journal* 371 (2006).

Anderson David H., 'Investigation, Detention and Release of Foreign Fishing Vessels under the United Nations Convention on the Law of the Sea 1982 and Other International Agreements', 11 *International Journal of Marine and Coastal Law* 177 (1996).

Arai-Takahashi Yutaka, *The Margin of Appreciation Doctrine and the Principle of Proportionality in the Jurisprudence of the ECHR* (Oxford: Intersentia, 2002).

Arangio-Ruiz Gaetano, 'State Fault and the Forms and Degrees of International Responsibility: Questions of Attribution and Relevance' in Michael Virally (ed),

Le Droit International au Service de la Paix, de la Justice et du Développement (Paris: A. Pedone, 1991).

Arangio-Ruiz Gaetano, 'The ICJ Statute, the Charter and Forms of Legality Review of Security Council Decisions' in Lal C. Vohrah, Fausto Pocar, Yvonne Featherstone, Olivier Fourmy, Christine Graham, John Hocking and Nicholas Robson (eds), *Man's Inhumanity to Man. Essays on International Law in Honour of Antonio Cassese* (The Hague: Kluwer Law International, 2003).

Arendt Hannah (edited by Jerome Kohn), *The Promise of Politics* (New York: Schocken Books, 2005).

Aristotle, *Nicomachean Ethics* (Indianapolis, IN: Hackett Publishing, 1999).

Arnull Anthony, 'The Principle of Effective Judicial Protection: An Unruly Horse?', 36 *ELR* 51 (2011).

Avbelj Matej, 'Supremacy or Primacy of EU Law—(Why) Does it Matter?', 17 *ELJ* 744 (2011).

Bantz Vincent P., 'Views from Hamburg; The Juno Trader Case or How to Make Sense of the Coastal State's Rights in the Light of Its Duty of Prompt Release, 24 *The University of Queensland Law Journal* 415 (2005).

Barak Aharon, *Proportionality: Constitutional Rights and Their Limitations* (Cambridge: Cambridge University Press, 2012).

Barbier Eric de la Serre and Anne-Lise Sibony, 'Expert Evidence before the EC Courts', 45 *CMLR* 948 (2008).

Barcelo III John J., 'Burden of Proof, Prima Facie Case and Presumption in WTO Dispute Settlement', 42(1) *Cornell International Law Journal* 23 (2009).

Barnard Catharine, 'Derogations, Justifications and the Four Freedoms: Is State Interest Really Protected?' in Catherine Barnard and Okeoghene Odudu (eds), *The Outer Limits of European Union Law* (Oxford: Hart Publishing, 2009).

Bates Ed, *The Evolution of the European Convention on Human Rights—From Its Inception to the Creation of a Permanent Court of Human Rights* (Oxford: Oxford University Press, 2010).

Beck Ulrich, *Risk Society: Towards a New Modernity* (London: Sage, 1986).

Becroft Ross, *The Standard of Review in WTO Dispute Settlement: Critique and Development* (Cheltenham: Edward Elgar Publishing, 2012).

Bedjaoui Mohammed, 'Un contrôle de légalité des actes du Conseil de Sécurité est-il possible?' in Société française pour le droit international, *Colloque de Rennes, Le chapitre VII de la Charte des Nations Unies, 50e anniversaire des Nations Unies* (Paris: Pedone, 1995).

Belavusau Uladzislau, 'A Dernier Cri From Strasbourg: An Ever Formidable Challenge of Hate Speech', 16(3) *European Public Law* 373 (2010).

Belavusau Uladzislau, 'Judicial Epistemology of Free Speech through Ancient Lenses', 23 *International Journal for the Semiotics of Law* 165 (2010).

Belavusau Uladzislau, 'Fighting Hate Speech through EU Law', 4(1) *Amsterdam Law Forum* 20 (2012).

Belavusau Uladzislau, 'Historical Revisionism in Comparative Perspective: Law, Politics, and Surrogate Mourning', *EUI Law Research Paper No. 12/2013.*

Belavusau Uladzislau, 'A Penalty Card for Homophobia from EU Non-Discrimination Law: Comment on Asociaţia ACCEPT', *Columbia Journal of European Law* (2014) (forthcoming).

Beloff Michael, 'The Concept of Deference in Public Law', 11 *Judicial Review* 213 (2006).

Benvenisti Eyal, 'Margin of Appreciation, Consensus and Universal Standards', 31 *International Law and Politics* 843 (1999).

Benvenisti Eyal, 'Sovereigns as Trustees of Humanity: On the Accountability of States to Foreign Stakeholders', 107 *AJIL* 295 (2013).

Benzing Markus, 'The Complementarity Regime of the International Criminal Court: International Criminal Justice between State Sovereignty and the Fight against Impunity', 7 *Max Planck Yearbook of United Nations Law* 591 (2003).

Bergsmo Morten and Ling Yan (eds), *State Sovereignty and International Criminal Law* (Beijing: Torkhel Opsahl, 2012).

Bernard Nicolas, 'On the Art of Not Mixing One's Drinks: *Dassonville* and *Cassis de Dijon* Revisited' in Miguel P. Maduro and Loic Azoulai (eds), *The Past and Future of EU Law—The Classics of EU Law Revisited on the 50th Anniversary of the Rome Treaty* (Oxford: Hart Publishing, 2010).

Bickel Alexander, *The Least Dangerous Branch: The Supreme Court at the Bar of Politics*, 2nd edn (New Haven, CT: Yale University Press, 1986).

Bohanes Jan and Nicolas Lockhart, 'Standard of Review in WTO Law' in Daniel Bethlehem, Donald McRea, Rodney Neufeld and Isabelle van Damme (eds), *The Oxford Handbook of International Trade Law* (Oxford: Oxford University Press, 2009).

Bourgeois Jacques H.J., 'GATT/WTO Dispute Settlement Practice in the Field of Anti-Dumping Law' in Ernst-Ulrich Petersmann (ed), *International Trade Law and the GATT/WTO Dispute Settlement System* (London: Kluwer Law International, 1997).

Bown Chad P. and Joel P. Trachtman, 'Brazil—Measures Affecting Imports of Retreaded Tyres: A Balancing Act', 8(1) *WTR* 85 (2009).

Boyle Alan, 'Developments in the International Law of Environmental Impact Assessments and their Relation to the Espoo Convention', 20(3) *Review of European Community & International Environmental Law* 227 (2011).

Brady Alan D.P., *Proportionality and Deference under the UK Human Rights Act: An Institutionally Sensitive Approach* (Cambridge: Cambridge University Press, 2012).

Brauch Jeffrey A., 'The Margin of Appreciation and the Jurisprudence of the European Court of Human Rights: Threat to the Rule of Law', 11 *Columbia Journal of European Law* 113 (2004–2005).

Brems Eva, 'The Margin of Appreciation Doctrine in the Case-Law of the European Court of Human Rights', 56 *Zeitschrift für Auslandisches Öffentliches Recht und Volkrecht* 240 (1996).

Briese Robyn and Stephan Schill, 'Djibouti v France: Self-Judging Clauses before the International Court of Justice', 10 *Melbourne Journal of International Law* 308 (2009).

Briese Robyn and Stephan Schill, '"If the State Considers": Self-Judging Clauses in International Dispute Settlement', 13 *Max Planck Yearbook of United Nations Law* 61 (2009).

Broomhall Bruce, 'La Cour Pénale Internationale: directives pour l'adoption des lois nationales et d'adaptation' in Association International de Droit Pénal (ed), *ICC ratifications and national implementing legislation* (Paris: Erès, 1999).

Brown Bartram S., 'Primacy of Complementarity: Reconciling the Jurisdiction of National Courts and International Criminal Tribunals', 23 *Yale Journal of International Law* 383 (1998).

Brown Bartram S., *Research Handbook on International Criminal Law* (Cheltenham: Edward Elgar Publishing, 2011).

Brown Chester, '"Reasonableness" in the Law of the Sea: The Prompt Release of the Volga', 16(3) *Leiden Journal of International Law* 621 (2003).

Brown Chester, 'The Inherent Powers of International Courts and Tribunals', 76 *BYIL* 195 (2005).

Burke-White William W., 'Complementarity in Practice: The International Criminal Court as Part of a System of Multi-level Global Governance in the Democratic Republic of Congo', 18(3) *Leiden Journal of International Law* 582 (2005).

Burke-White William W. and Andreas von Staden, 'Investment Protection in Extraordinary Times: The Interpretation and Application of Non-Precluded Measures Provisions in Bilateral Investment Treaties', 48 *Virginia Journal of International Law* 307 (2008).

Burke-White William W. and Scott Kaplan, 'Shaping The Contours of Domestic Justice: The International Criminal Court and an Admissibility Challenge in the Uganda Situation' in Carsten Stahn and Göran Sluiter (eds), *The Emerging Practice of the International Criminal Court* (Leiden: Martinus Nijhoff, 2009).

Burke-White William W. and Andreas von Staden, 'Private Litigation in a Public Law Sphere: The Standard of Review in Investor-State Arbitrations', 35 *Yale Journal of International Law* 283 (2010).

Butler Judith, *Excitable Speech: A Politics of the Performative* (London: Routledge, 1997).

Button Catherine, *The Power to Protect: Trade, Health and Uncertainty in the WTO* (Oxford: Hart Publishing, 2004).

Buyse Antoine, 'Dangerous Expressions: The ECHR, Violence and Free Speech', 63(2) *ICLQ* 491 (2014).

Caflisch Lucius, 'Is the International Court Entitled to Review Security Council Resolutions Adopted under Chapter VII of the United Nations Charter?' in Najeen M. Al-Nauimi and Richard Meese (eds), *International Legal Issues Arising under the United Nations Decade of International Law* (The Hague: Martinus Nijhoff, 1995).

Cançado Trindade Antônio A., *El derecho internacional de los derechos humanos en el siglo XXI*, 2nd edn (Santiago: Editorial Jurídica de Chile, 2006).

Cannizzaro Enzo, *Il principio della proporzionalità nell'ordinamento internazionale* (Milan: Giuffè, 2000).

Caoimh Aindrias Ó., 'Standard of Proof, Burden of Proof, Standards of Review and Evaluation of Evidence in Antitrust and Merger Cases: Perspective of Court of Justice of the European Union' in Mel Marquis and Claus-Dieter Ehlermann (eds), *European Competition Law Annual 2009* (Portland, OR: Hart Publishing, 2011).

Carnero-Rojo Enrique, 'The Role of Fair Trial Considerations in the Complementarity Regime of the International Criminal Court: From "No Peace without Justice" to "No Peace without Victors' Justice"?', 18(4) *Leiden Journal of Int. Law* 829 (2005) 851.

Carozza Paolo G., 'Subsidiarity as a Structural Principle of International Human Rights Law', 97 *AJIL* 38 (2003).

Carter Linda E., 'The Future of the International Criminal Court: Complementarity as a Strength or a Weakness', 12 *Washington University Global Studies Law Review* 451 (2013).

Cartuyvels Yves, Hugues Dumont, François Ost, Michel van de Kerchove and Sébastien Van Drooghenbroeck (eds), *Les droits de l'homme: bouclier ou épée du droit pénal?* (Brussels: FUSL-Bruylant, 2007).

Cass Deborah Z., 'The "Constitutionalization" of International Trade Law: Judicial Norm-Generation as the Engine of Constitutional Development in International Trade', 12 *EJIL* 39 (2001).

Cass Deborah Z., *The Constitutionalization of the World Trade Organization* (Oxford: Oxford University Press, 2005).

Cassese Antonio and Paola Gaeta, *Cassese's International Criminal Law* (Oxford: Oxford University Press, 2008).

Castberg Frede, *The European Convention on Human Rights* (Leiden: Sijthoff; Dobbs Ferry: Oceana Publications, 1974).

Cavallaro James L. and Emily J. Schaffer, 'Less as More: Rethinking Supranational Litigation of Economic and Social Rights in the Americas', 56 *Hastings Law Journal* 217 (2004).

Chalmers Damian, Gareth Davies and Giorgio Monti, *European Union Law*, 2nd edn, (Cambridge: Cambridge University Press, 2010).

Chalmers Damian, Christos Hadjiemmanuil and Giorgio Monti, *European Union Law: Texts and Materials* (Cambridge: Cambridge University Press, 2006).

Charney Jonathan I., 'Is International Law Threatened by Multiple International Tribunals?', 271 *Recueil des Cours* 101 (1998).

Chen Tsai-fang, 'The Standard of Review and the Roles of ICSID Arbitral Tribunals in Investor-State Dispute Settlement', 5(1) *Contemporary Asia Arbitration Journal* 23 (2012).

Chen Tsai-fang, 'What Exactly is the Panel Reviewing: The First Step in the Standard of Review Analysis in the WTO Dispute Resolutions', 4 *Asian Journal of WTO, Health Law and Policy* 467 (2009).

Cho Sungjoon, 'Global Constitutional Lawmaking', 31 *University of Pennsylvania Journal of International Law* 621 (2010).

Çoban Ali Riza, *Protection of Property Rights within the European Convention on Human Rights* (London: Ashgate Publishing, 2004).

Cogliati-Bantz Vincent P., 'International Tribunal for the Law of the Sea, *Hoshinmaru (Japan v Russian Federation)* and *Tomimaru (Japan v Russian Federation)*, Prompt Release Judgments of 6 August 2007', 58 *ICLQ* 241 (2009).

Conway Gerard, 'Ne bis in idem and the International Criminal Tribunals', 25 *Criminal Law Forum* 361 (2003).

Corkin Joseph, 'Science, Legitimacy and the Law: Regulating Risk Regulation Judiciously in the European Community', 33(2) *ELR* 359 (2008).

Corten Olivier, *L'utilisation du 'raisonnable' par le juge international: discours juridique, raison et contradictions* (Bruxelles: Bruylant, 1997).

Corten Olivier, 'Reasonableness in International Law' in Rüdiger Wolfrum (ed), *Max Planck Encyclopedia of International Law* (Oxford: Oxford University Press, 2012).

Costello Cathryn, 'The Bosphorus Ruling of the European Court of Human Rights: Fundamental Rights and Blurred Boundaries in Europe', 6(1) *Human Rights Law* 87 (2006).

Cot Jean-Pierre, 'Margin of Appreciation' in Rüdiger Wolfrum (ed), *Max Planck Encyclopedia of Public International Law* (Oxford: Oxford University Press, 2012), also as online version (<http://opil.ouplaw.com/home/epil>).

Cot Jean-Pierre, 'The Law of the Sea and the Margin of Appreciation' in Tafsir M. Ndiaye and Rüdiger Wolfrum (eds), *Law of the Sea, Environmental Law and Settlement of Disputes: Liber Amicorum Judge Thomas A. Mensah* (Leiden: Martinus Nijhoff, 2007).

Cottier Thomas and Satoko Takenoshita, 'The Balance of Power in WTO Decision-Making: Towards Weighted Voting in Legislative Response', 58 *Aussenwirtschaft* 171 (2003).

Cottier Thomas, 'Risk Managment Experience in WTO Dispute Settlement' in Thomas Cottier (ed), *The Challenge of WTO Law: Collected Essays* (London: Cameron May, 2007).

Craig Paul, *Administrative Law*, 7th edn (London, Sweet & Maxwell, 2008).

Craig Paul and Gráinne de Búrca, *EU Law Text Cases Materials*, 5th edn (Oxford: Oxford University Press, 2011).

Craig Paul, 'Judicial Review, Intensity and Deference in EU Law' in David Dyzenhaus (ed), *The Unity of Public Law* (Oxford: Hart Publishing, 2004).

Craig Paul, 'Proportionality, Rationality and Review', *New Zealand Law Review* 265 (2010).

Craig Paul, *EU Administrative Law*, 2nd edn (Oxford: Oxford University Press, 2012).

Cram Ian, 'Coercing Communities or Promoting Civilised Discourse? Funeral Protests and Comparative Hate Speech Jurisprudence', 12(3) *Human Rights Law Review* 455 (2012).

Craufurd Smith Rachael, 'Remedies for Breaches of EU Law in National Courts: Legal Variation and Selection' in Paul Craig and Gráinne De Búrca (eds), *The Evolution of EU Law* (Oxford: Oxford University Press, 1999).

Crawford James, *The ILC's Articles on State Responsibility. Introduction, Text and Commentaries* (Cambridge: Cambridge University Press, 2002).

Crema Luigi, 'Disappearance and New Sightings of Restrictive Interpretation(s)', 21(3) *EJIL* 681 (2010).

Croley Steven P. and John H. Jackson, 'WTO Dispute Procedures, Standard of Review, and Deference to National Governments', 90 *AJIL* 193 (1996).

Cryer Robert, 'International Criminal Law vs State Sovereignty: Another Round', 16(5) *EJIL* 979 (2006).

Cryer Robert, Hakan Friman, Darryl Robinson and Elizabeth Wilmshurt, *An Introduction to International Criminal Law and Procedure* (Cambridge: Cambridge University Press, 2010).

Dąbrowska Patrycja, 'GM Foods, Risk, Precaution and the Internal Market: Did Both Sides Win the Day in the Recent Judgment of the European Court of Justice?, 5(2) *GLJ* 151 (2004).

Dąbrowska-Kłosińska Patrycja, 'EU Courts, Global Risks, and the Health and Environmental Safety Revisited: On Nuances of a Less Deferential Standard of Review', *RSCAS EUI Working Papers Series 63* (2013).

Dąbrowska Patrycja and Patricia Quillacq, 'Science Goes to Court. Some Considerations on the Precautionary Principle in the Community Jurisprudence' in Francesco Francioni (ed), *The Future of Environmental Law: International and European Perspective*, 5 *EUI Law Working Paper 59* (2006).

Damaska Mirjan R., *Evidence Law Adrift* (New Haven, CT: Yale University Press, 1997).

Damaska Mirjan, 'Propensity Evidence in Continental Legal Systems', 70 *Chicago-Kent Law Review* 55 (1994).

Davies Arwel, 'Interpreting the Chapeau of GATT Article XX in Light of the "New" Approach in *Brazil-Tyres*', 3 *JWT* 507 (2009).

Davies Gareth, 'Understanding Market Access: Exploring the Economic Rationality of Different Conceptions of Free Movement Law', 11 *GLJ* 671 (2010).

Davis Martha S., 'Basic Guide to Standards of Judicial Review', 33 *South Dakota Law Review* 469 (1988).

de Búrca Gráinne, 'The Principle of Proportionality and its Application in EC Law', 13 *Yearbook of European Law* 105 (1993).

deGuzman Margaret, 'Gravity and the Legitimacy of International Criminal Court', 32 *Fordham International Law Journal* 1400 (2008).

de Hert Paul and Fisnik Korenica, 'The Doctrine of Equivalent Protection: Its Life and Legitimacy Before and After the European Union's Accession to the European Convention on Human Rights', 13(7) *GLJ* 874 (2012).

de la Rasilla del Moral Ignacio, 'The Increasingly Marginal Appreciation of the Margin-of-Appreciation Doctrine', 7 *GLJ* 611 (2006).

Delgado Francisco R. Barbosa, 'El Margen Nacional De Apreciación En El Derecho Internacional De Los Derechos Humanos: Entre El Estado De Derecho Y La Sociedad Democrática' in Paola A. Acosta Alvarado and Manuel Núñez Poblete (eds), *El Margen de Apreciación en el Sistema Interamericano de Derechos Humanos: Proyecciones Regionales y Nacionales* (México: Instituto de Investigaciones Jurídicas, UNAM 2012).

Delgado Francisco R. Barbosa, 'Los límites a la doctrina del margen nacional de apreciación en el Tribunal Europeo y la Corte Interamericana de Derechos Humanos: intervención judicial en torno a ciertos derechos de las minorías étnicas y culturales', 26 *Revista Derecho del Estado* 107 (2011).

Del Mar Katherin, 'The International Court of Justice and Standards of Proof' in Karine Bannelier, Theodore Chistakis and Sarah Heathcote (eds), *The ICJ and the Development of International Law. The Lasting Impact of the Corfu Channel Case* (New York: Routledge, 2011).

Delmas-Marty Mirellie and Izroche Marie-Laure, 'Marge Nationale d'Appréciation et Internationalisation du Droit: Réflexions sur la Validité Formelle d'un Droit Commun Pluraliste', 52 *Revue internationale de droit comparé* 753 (2000).

de Sadeleer Nicolas, 'Procedures for Derogations from the Principle of Approximation of Laws under Article 95 EC', 40 *CMLR* 911 (2003).

de Sadeleer Nicolas, 'The Precautionary Principle in European Community Health and Environmental Law: Sword or Shield for the Nordic Countries?' in Nicolas de Sadeleer (ed), *Implementing the Precautionary Principle: Approaches from the Nordic Countries, EU and USA* (London: Earthscan, 2007).

Desierto Diane A., 'Development as an International Right: Investment in the New Trade-Based IIAs', 3 *Trade, Law and Development* 296 (2011).

Desmedt G. Axel, 'Hormones: "Objective Assessment" and (or as) Standard of Review', 1 *JIEL* 695 (1998).

Desmedt G. Axel, 'Proportionality in WTO Law', 4(3) *JIEL* 441 (2001).

Diggelmann Oliver and Tilmann Altwicker, 'Is There Something Like a Constitution of International Law? A Critical Analysis of the Debate on World Constitutionalism', 68 *Zeitschrift für ausländisches öffentliches Recht und Völkerrecht* 623 (2008).

Diebold Nicolas, *Non-Discrimination in International Trade in Services* (Cambridge: Cambridge University Press, 2010).

Dolin Benjamin R., 'International Criminal Court: American Concerns about an International Prosecutor', Law and Government Division, 14 May 2002, available at <http://publications.gc.ca/Collection-R/LoPBdP/BP/prb0211-e.htm>.

Dolzer Rudolf and Christoph Schreuer, *Principles of International Investment Law* (Oxford: Oxford University Press, 2008).

Doria Jose, 'Standards of Appeals and Standards of Revision' in José Doria, Hans-Peter Gasser and M. Cherif Bassiouni (eds), *The Legal Regime of the International Criminal Court, Essays in Honour of Professor Igor Blishchenko* (The Hague: Brill, 2009).

Dougan Michael, *National Remedies before the Court of Justice. Issues of Harmonisation and Differentation* (Portland, OR: Hart Publishing, 2004).

Dougan Michael, 'The Vicissitudes of Life at the Coalface: Remedies and Procedures for Enforcing Union Law before the National Courts' in Paul Craig and Gráinne de Búrca (eds), *The Evolution of EU Law* (Oxford: Oxford University Press, 2011).

Drnas de Clément Zlata, 'Corte interamericana de derechos humanos ¿Cuarta Instancia?' in *¿Se ha convertido la Corte Interamericana de Derechos Humanos en una cuarta* *instancia? XVIII Reunión Conjunta de Academias de Derecho de Argentina* (Buenos Aires: La Ley, 2009).

Dugard John, 'Possible Conflicts of Jurisdiction with Truth Commissions' in Antonio Cassesse, Paola Gaeta and John R. Jones (eds), *The Rome Statute of the International Criminal Court* (Oxford: Oxford University Press, 2002).

Duhaime Bernard and Ariel E. Dulitzky, 'Review of the Case Law of the Inter-American Human Rights System in 2006', 19(2) *Quebec Journal of International Law* 331 (2006).

Duhaime Bernard, 'Le système interaméricain et la protection des droits économiques, sociaux et culturels des personnes et des groupes vivant dans des conditions particulières de vulnérabilité', 44 *Canadian Yearbook of International Law* 95 (2006).

Duhaime Bernard, 'Protecting Human Rights in the Americas: Recent Achievements and Challenges' in Gordon Mace, Jean-Philippe Thérien and Paul Haslam (eds), *Governing the Americas: Regional Institutions at the Crossroads* (Boulder: Lynne Rienner Publishers, 2007).

Duhaime Bernard, 'Vers une Amérique plus égalitaire? L'interdiction de la discrimination et le système interaméricain de protection des droits de la personne' in Ludovic Hennebel and Hélène Tigroudja (eds), *Le particularisme interaméricain des droits de l'homme* (Paris: Pedonne, 2009).

Duhaime Bernard, 'Strengthening the Protection of Human Rights in the Americas: A Role for Canada?' in Monica Serrano (ed), *Human Rights Regimes in the Americas* (Tokyo: UN University Press, 2010).

Duhaime Bernard, 'L'OEA et le Protocole de San Salvador' in Lucie Lamarche, Pierre Bosset (eds), *Donner droit de cité aux droits économiques, sociaux et culturels—La Charte des droits et libertés du Québec en chantier* (Cowansville: Yvon Blais, 2011).

Dulitzky Ariel E., 'El principio de igualdad y no discriminación. Claroscuros de la jurisprudencia interamericana', 3 *Anuario de derechos humanos* 15 (2007).

Dulitzky Ariel E., 'The Inter-American Human Rights System Fifty Years Later: Time for Changes', *Quebec Journal of International Law* (Special Edition, 2011), 127.

Dunoff Jeffrey L., 'Constitutional Conceits: The WTO's "Constitution" and the Discipline of International Law', 17 *EJIL* 647 (2006).

Dunoff Jeffrey L. and Joel P. Trachtman (eds), *Ruling the World?: Constitutionalism, International Law, and Global Governance* (Cambridge: Cambridge University Press, 2009).

Dupuy Pierre-Marie, Francesco Francioni and Ernst-Ulrich Petersmann (eds), *Human Rights in International Investment Law and Arbitration* (Oxford: Oxford University Press, 2009).

Dworkin Roland, *Law's Empire* (Cambridge, MA: Harvard University Press, 1986).

Eeckhout Piet, 'The EU Charter of Fundamental Rights and the Federal Question', 39 *CMLR* 945 (2002).

Eeckhout Piet, 'The Scales of Trade—Reflections on the Growth and Functions of the WTO Adjudicative Branch', 13(1) *JIEL* 3 (2010).

Ehlermann Claus-Dieter, 'Six Years on the Bench of the "World Trade Court": Some Personal Experiences as Member of the Appellate Body of the World Trade Organization', 36 *JWT* 605 (2002).

Ehlermann Claus-Dieter and Nicolas Lockhart, 'Standard of Review in WTO Law', 7(3) *JIEL* 491 (2004).

Ehring Lothar, 'De Facto Discrimination in WTO Law: National and Most-Favored-Nation Treatment—Or Equal Treatment?', *Jean Monnet Working Paper No. 12/2001.*

Eliantonio Mariolina, *Europeanisation of Administrative Justice? The Influence of the ECJ's Case Law in Italy, Germany and England* (Groningen: Europa Law Publishing, 2008).

Elliott Mark, 'Proportionality and Deference: The Importance of a Structured Approach' in Christopher Forsyth, Mark Elliott, Swati Jhaveri, Michael Ramsden, and Anne Scully Hill (eds), *Effective Judicial Review: A Cornerstone of Good Governance* (Oxford: Oxford University Press, 2010).

Ely John H., *Democracy and Distrust—A Theory of Judicial Review* (Cambridge, MA: Harvard University Press, 1980).

El Zeidy Mohamed, 'The Principle of Complementarity: A New Machinery to Implement International Criminal Law', 23 *Michigan Journal of International Law* 869 (2002).

El Zeidy Mohamed, *The Principle of Complementarity in International Criminal Law: Origin, Development and Practice* (Leiden: Martinus Nijhoff, 2008).

Emilio Nicholas, *The Principles of Proportionality in European Law: A Comparative Study* (London: Kluwer Law International, 1996).

Engström Johanna, 'The Principle of Effective Judicial Protection after the Lisbon Treaty. Reflection in the Light of Case C-279/09 DEB Deutsche Energiehandels- und Beratungsgesellschaft mbH', 4 *Review of European Administrative Law* 53 (2011).

Eskridge William N. Jr and Lauren E. Baer, 'The Continuum of Deference: Supreme Court Treatment of Agency Statutory Interpretations from Chevron to Hamdan', 96 *The Georgetown Law Journal* 1083 (2007–2008).

Esty Daniel C., 'Good Governance at the Supranational Scale: Globalizing Administrative Law', 115 *Yale Law Journal* 1490 (2006).

European Union Agency for Fundamental Rights, *Access to Justice in Europe: An Overview of Challenges and Opportunities* (Luxembourg: Publication Office of the European Union, 2011).

European Food Safety Authority, 'Review of the Séralini et al Publication on a 2-year Rodent Feeding Study with Glyphosate Formulations and GM Maize NK603 as Published Online on 19 September 2012 in Food and Chemical Toxicology', 10(10) *EFSA Journal* 2910 (2012).

Faber Michael J., *Our Federalist Constitution—The Founder's Expectations and Contemporary American Government* (El Paso, TX: LFB Scholarly Publishing, 2011).

Fauchald Ole Kristian, 'The Legal Reasoning of ICSID Tribunals—An Empirical Analysis', 19 *EJIL* 301 (2008).

Faúndez Ledesma Héctor, *El sistema interamericano de protección de los derechos humanos. Aspectos institucionales y procesales*, 3rd edn (San José, CA: Instituto Interamericano de Derechos Humanos, 2004).

Fawcett James E.S., *The Application of the European Convention on Human Rights* (Oxford: Oxford University Press, 1968).

Fife Rolf E., 'The International Criminal Court—Whence It Came, Where It Goes', 69 *Nordic Journal of International Law* 63 (2000).

Fisher Elizabeth, *Risk Regulation and Administrative Constitutionalism* (Oxford: Hart Publishing, 2007).

Fitzmaurice Gerald, 'The Law and Procedure of the International Court of Justice, 1951–54: General Principles and Sources of International Law', 35 *BYIL* 183 (1959).

Fitzmaurice Gerald, *The Law and Procedure of the International Court of Justice*, vol. 2 (Grotius Publications Ltd, 1986).

Fortier L. Yves, 'Indirect Expropriation in the Law of International Investment: I Know It When I See It, or Caveat Investor', 19 *ICSID Review* 293 (2005).

Foster Caroline E., *Science and the Precautionary Principle in International Courts and Tribunals: Expert Evidence, Burden of Proof and Finality* (Cambridge: Cambridge University Press, 2011).

Franck Susan D., 'The Legitimacy Crisis in Investment Treaty Arbitration: Privatizing Public International Law Through Inconsistent Decisions', 73 *Fordham Law Review* 1521 (2005).

Franck Thomas M., *Fairness in International Law and Institutions* (Oxford: Clarendon Press, 1995).

Fry Elinor, 'Between Show Trials and Sham Prosecutions: The Rome Statute's Potential Effect on Domestic Due Process Protections', 23 *Criminal Law Forum* 35 (2012).

Fukunaga Yuka, 'Standard of Review and "Scientific Truths" in the WTO Dispute Settlement System and Investment Arbitration', 3(3) *JIDS* 559 (2012).

Gazzini Tarcisio, 'Interpretation of (Allegedly) Self-judging Clauses in Bilateral Investment Treaties' in Malgosia Fitzmaurice, Olufemi Elias and Panos Merkouris (eds), *Treaty Interpretation and the Vienna Convention on the Law of the Treaties: 30 Years On* (Leiden: Martinus Nijhoff, 2010).

Gerards Janneke H., *Judicial Review in Equal Treatment Cases* (Leiden: Martinus Nijhoff, 2005).

Gerards Janneke, 'Pluralism, Deference and the Margin of Appreciation Doctrine', 17(1) *ELJ* 80 (2011).

Gaviria César, 'Towards a New Vision of the Inter-American Human Rights System', 4 *Journal of Latin American Affairs* 4 (1996).

Gilmour D.R., 'The Sovereignty of Parliament and the European Commission of Human Rights', *Public Law* 62 (1968).

Ginsburg Tom, 'International Substitutes for Domestic Institutions: Bilateral Investment Treaties and Governance', 25 *International Review of Law and Economics* 107 (2005).

Goldman Alvin, 'Epistemic Paternalism: Communication Control in Law and Society', 88(3) *Journal of Philosophy* 113 (1991).

González Felipe M., 'La OEA y los derechos humanos despues del advenimiento de los gobiernos civiles: expectativas (in)satisfechas', 16 *Revista de Derecho (Universidad del Norte)* 1 (2003).

Gordon Kathryn and Joachim Pohl, 'Environmental Concerns in International Investment Agreements: A Survey', *OECD Working Papers on International Investment, No. 2011/1.*

Grando Michelle, *Evidence, Proof, and Fact-Finding in WTO Dispute Settlement* (Oxford: Oxford University Press, 2010).

Greer Steven, *The Margin of Appreciation: Interpretation and Discretion under the European Convention on Human Rights* (Strasbourg: Council of Europe, 2000).

Gruszczynski Lukasz, 'SPS Measures Adopted in Case of Insufficiency of Scientific Evidence: Where Do We Stand after EC-Biotech Products Case' in Julien Chaisse and Tiziano Balmelli (eds), *Essays on the Future of the World Trade Organization* (Geneva: Edis, 2008).

Gruszczynski Lukasz, *Regulating Health and Environmental Risks under WTO Law: Critical Analysis of the SPS Agreement* (Oxford: Oxford University Press, 2010).

Gruszczynski Lukasz, 'Standard of Review of Health/Environmental Regulation by WTO Panels' in Gert Van Calster and Denise Prévost (eds), *Research Handbook on Environment, Health and the WTO* (Cheltenham: Edward Elgar Publishing, 2013).

Gruszczynski Lukasz, 'The Role of Experts in Environmental and Health Related Trade Disputes in the WTO: Deconstructing Decision-Making Processes' in

Monika Ambrus, Karin Arts, Ellen Hey and Helena Raulus (eds), *Irrelevant, Advisors or Decision-Makers? The Role of 'Experts' in International Decision-Making* (Cambridge: Cambridge University Press, 2014, forthcoming).

Guglya Leonila, 'The Interplay of International Dispute Resolution Mechanisms: The Softwood Lumber Controversy', 2(1) *JIDS* 175 (2011).

Gullet Warwick, 'Prompt Release Procedures and the Challenge for Fisheries Law Enforcement: The Judgment of the International Tribunal for the Law of the Sea in the "Volga" Case (Russian Federation v Australia)', 31 *Federal Law Review* 395 (2003).

Gurule Jimmy, 'United States Opposition to the 1998 Rome Statute Establishing an International Criminal Court: Is the Court's Jurisdiction Truly Complementary to National Criminal Jurisdictions?', 35 *Cornell International Law Journal* 9 (2001–2002).

Guzman Andrew T., 'Why LDCs Sign Treaties that Hurt Them: Explaining the Popularity of Bilateral Investment Treaties', 38 *Virginia Journal of International Law* 639 (1998).

Guzman Andrew T., 'Dispute Resolution in SPS Cases' in Dan Horowitz, Daniel Moulis and Debra Steger (eds), *Ten Years of WTO Dispute Settlement* (London: International Bar Association, 2007).

Guzman Andrew T., 'International Tribunals: A Rational Choice Analysis', 157 *University of Pennsylvania Law Review* 171 (2008).

Guzman Andrew T., 'Determining the Appropriate Standard of Review in WTO Disputes', 42 *Cornell International Law Journal* 45 (2009).

Habermas Jurgen, *Between Facts and Norms: Contributions to a Discourse Theory of Law and Democracy* (translated by William Rehg, Cambridge: Polity Press, 1996).

Hamburger Philip, *Law and Judicial Duty* (Cambridge, MA: Harvard University Press, 2008).

Hansen Patricia I., 'Transparency, Standards of Review, and the Use of Trade Measures to Protect the Global Environment', 39 *Virginia Journal of International Law* 1017 (1999).

Hansen Thomas O., 'A Critical Review of the ICC's Recent Practice Concerning Admissibility Challenges and Complementarity', 13 *Melbourne Journal of International Law* 217 (2012).

Harbo Tor-Inge, 'The Function of the Proportionality Principle in EU Law', 16 *European Law Journal* 158 (2010).

Hart Herbert L.A., *The Concept of Law* (Oxford: Oxford University Press, 1994).

Hay Bruce, 'Allocating the Burden of Proof', 72 *Indiana Law Journal* 651 (1997).

Helfer Laurence R. and Anne-Marie Slaughter, 'Toward a Theory of Effective Supranational Adjudication', 107 *Yale International Law Journal* 273 (1997).

Heller Kevin J., 'A Sentence-based Theory of Complementarity', 53 *Melbourne Journal of International Law* 86 (2012).

Heller Kevin J., 'Situational Gravity under the Rome Statute' in Carsten Stahn and Larrisa van den Herik (eds), *Future Directions in International Criminal Justice* (Cambridge: TMC Asser/Cambridge University Press, 2009).

Heller Kevin J., 'The Shadow Side of Complementarity: The Effect of Article 17 of the Rome Statute on National Due Process', 17 *Criminal Law Forum* 255 (2005).

Henckels Caroline, 'Indirect Expropriation and the Right to Regulate: Revisiting Proportionality Analysis and the Standard of Review in Investor-State Arbitration', 15(1) *JIEL* 223 (2012).

Henckels Caroline, 'Balancing Investment Protection and the Public Interest: The Role of the Standard of Review and the Importance of Deference in Investor-State Arbitration', 4(1) *JIDS* 197 (2013).

Hennette-Vauchez Stephanie, 'Constitutional v International? When Unified Reformatory Rationales Mismatch the Plural Paths of Legitimacy of ECHR Law' in Jonas Christoffersen and Mikael R. Madsen (eds), *The European Court of Human Rights between Law and Politics* (Oxford: Oxford University Press, 2011).

Henry Laura, 'Investment Agreement Claims under the 2004 Model U.S. Bit: A Challenge for State Police Powers?', 31 *University of Pennsylvania Journal of International Law* 935 (2010).

Herwig Alexia, 'Lost in Complexity? The WTO's Panel Report in the EU Seals Case', 5 *European Journal of Risk Regulation* 97 (2014).

Heyvaert Verlee, 'Facing the Consequences of the Precautionary Principle in European Community Law', 31 *ELR* 185 (2006).

Higgins Rosalyn, 'The Taking of Property by the State: Recent Developments in International Law', 176 *Recueil des Cours* 259 (1982).

Higgins Rosalyn, 'Accountability and Liability: The Law of State Responsibility' in Rosalyn Higgins, *Problems and Process: International Law and How We Use It* (Oxford: Oxford University Press, 1995).

Hilf Meinhard, 'The Power, Rules and Principles—Which Orientation for WTO/GATT Law?', 4(1) *JIEL* 111 (2001).

Holmes John T., 'The Principle of Complementarity' in Roy S. Lee (ed), *The International Criminal Court: The Making of the Rome Statute* (Den Haag: Kluwer Law International, 1999).

Holmes John, 'Complementarity: National Courts versus the ICC' in Antonio Cassese, Paola Gaeta and John R.W.D. Jones (eds), *The Rome Statute of the International Criminal Court: A Commentary*, vol. 1 (Oxford: Oxford University Press, 2002).

Horlick Garry N. and Peggy A. Clarke, 'Standards for Panels Reviewing Anti-dumping Determinations under the GATT and WTO' in Ernst-Ulrich Petersmann (ed), *International Trade Law and the GATT/WTO Dispute Settlement System* (London: Kluwer Law International, 1997).

Horn Henrik and Petros Mavroidis, 'Still Hazy after All These Years: The Interpretation of National Treatment in the GATT/WTO Case-law on Tax Discrimination', 15 *EJIL* 39 (2004).

Howse Robert, 'Democracy, Science, and Free Trade: Risk Regulation on Trial at the World Trade Organization', 98 *Michigan Law Review* 2329 (2000).

Howse Robert and Donald H. Regan, 'The Product/Process Distinction—An Illusory Basis for Disciplining "Unilateralism" in Trade Policy', 11 *EJIL* 249 (2000).

Howse Robert, 'The Legitimacy of the World Trade Organization' in Jean-Marc Coicaud and Veijo Heiskanen (eds), *The Legitimacy of International Organizations* (Tokyo: UN University Press, 2001).

Robert Howse and Nicolaidis Kalypso, 'Legitimacy and Global Governance: Why Constitutionalizing the WTO Is a Step Too Far' in Roger B. Porter, Pierre Sauvé, Arvind Subramanian and Americo Beviglia Zampetti (eds), *Efficiency, Equity, and Legitimacy: The Multilateral Trading System at the Millennium* (Washington: Brookings Institution, 2001).

Howse Robert and Nicolaidis Kalypso, 'Democracy without Sovereignty: The Global Vocation of Political Ethics' in Tomer Broude and Yuval Shany (eds), *The Shifting*

Allocation of Authority in International Law. Considering Sovereignty, Supremacy and Subsidiarity (Oxford: Hart Publishing, 2008).

Howse Robert and Joanna Langille, 'Permitting Pluralism: The Seal Products Dispute and Why the WTO Should Accept Trade Restrictions Justified by Noninstrumental Moral Values', 37 *Yale Journal of International Law* 367 (2012).

Huerta-Goldman Jorge A., 'Trade Remedies Disputes—Reciprocal Relationships between WTO and NAFTA Tribunals' in Filippo Fontanelli, Giuseppe Martinico and Paolo Carrozza (eds), *Shaping Rule of Law through Dialogue* (Groningen: Europa Law Publishing, 2010).

Huls Nick, Maurice Adams and Jacco Bomhoff (eds), *The Legitimacy of Highest Courts' Rulings. Judicial Deliberations and Beyond* (Cambridge: Cambridge University Press, 2009).

Ikeshima Taisaku, 'The "Reasonableness" of Unreasonable Arguments in Prompt Release Cases in the ITLOS', 6 *Waseda Global Forum* 107 (2009).

Ioannidis Michael, 'A Procedural Approach to the Legitimacy of International Adjudication: Developing Standards of Participation in WTO Law', 12 *GLJ* 1175 (2011).

Jackson John H., 'Remarks, Panel on Trading in a Post-Uruguay World: The New Law of the GATT/World Trade Organization', 88 *Proceedings of the Annual Meeting (American Society of International Law)* 136 (1994).

Jalloh Charles C., 'Kenya vs. The ICC Prosecutor', 53 *Harvard International Law Journal Online* 238 (2012).

Jans Jan H., 'Proportionality Revisited', 27(3) *Legal Issues of Economic Integration* 239 (2000).

Janssen Anne-Marie and Marjolein B.A. van Asselt, 'The Precautionary Principle In Court: An Analysis of Post-Pfizer Case Law' in Marjolein B.A. van Asselt, Esther Versluis and Ellen Vos (eds), *Balancing between Trade and Risk Integrating Legal and Social Science Perspectives* (Oxford and New York: Routledge, 2013).

Jennings Robert, 'Recent Cases on "Automatic" Reservations to the Optional Clause', 7 *ICLQ* 349 (1958).

Jianjun Gao, 'Reasonableness of the Bond under Article 292 of the LOS Convention: Practice of ITLOS', 7(1) *Chinese Journal of International Law* 115 (2008).

Joerges Christian and Jürgen Neyer, 'Politics, Risk Management, World Trade Organization Governance and the Limits of Legalisation', 30 *Science and Public Policy* 219 (2003).

Joerges Christian, 'Free Trade in Hazardous Products. The Emergence of Transnational Governance with Eroding State Government', 10(4) *European Public Affairs Review* 553 (2005).

Joerges Christian, '"Deliberative Political Processes" Revisited: What Have We Learnt About the Legitimacy of Supranational Decision-Making', 44 *Journal of Common Market Studies* 779 (2006).

Jurdi Nidal N., *The International Criminal Court and National Courts, A Contentious Relationship* (Farnham: Ashgate Publishing, 2011).

Kaikobad Kaiyan Homi, *The International Court of Justice and Judicial Review: A Study of the Court's Powers with Respect to Judgments of the ILO and UN Administrative Tribunals* (The Hague: Brill, 2000).

Kakouris Constantinos, 'Do the Member States Possess Judicial Procedural Autonomy?' 34 *CMLR* 1389 (1997).

Kascian Kiryl, 'Die Litauische Verfassung und die Auslegung des Begriffes "Volk" in historischer Perspektive', 5 *Osteuropa-Recht* 290 (2008).

Kazazi Mojtaba, *Burden of Proof and Related Issues: A Study on Evidence Before International Tribunals* (The Hague: Kluwer Law International, 1996).

Kavanagh Aileen, 'Deference or Defiance? The Limits of the Judicial Role in Constitutional Adjudication' in Grant Huscroft (ed), *Expounding the Constitution: Essays in Constitutional Theory* (Cambridge: Cambridge University Press, 2008).

Kavanagh Aileen, *Constitutional Review under the UK Human Rights Act* (Cambridge: Cambridge University Press, 2009).

Kavanagh Aileen, 'Defending Deference in Public Law and Constitutional Theory', 126 *Law Quarterly Review* 222 (2010).

Keane David, 'Attacking Hate Speech under Article 17 of the European Convention of Human Rights', 25(4) *Netherlands Quarterly of Human Rights* (2007).

Keohane Robert, 'Global Governance and Democratic Accountability' in David Held and Mathias Koenig-Archibugi (eds), *Taming Globalization: Frontiers of Governance* (Cambridge: Polity Press, 2003).

Keohane Robert O. and David G. Victor, 'The Regime Complex for Climate Change', 9(1) *Perspectives on Politics* 7 (2011).

Kilinç Umit, *La liberté d'expression en Turquie à l'épreuve de la Convention Européenne des Droits de l'Homme* (Paris: L'Harmattan, 2010).

King Jeff, '*Institutional Approaches to Judicial Restraint*', 28 *OJLS* 409 (2008).

Kingsbury Benedict, Nico Krisch and Richard B. Stewart, 'The Emergence of Global Administrative Law', 68 *Law and Contemporary Problems* 15 (2005).

Kingsbury Benedict and Stephan W. Schill, 'Public Law Concepts to Balance Investors' Rights with State Regulatory Actions in the Public Interest—The Concept of Proportionality' in Stephan W. Schill (ed), *International Investment Law and Comparative Public Law* (Oxford: Oxford University Press, 2010).

Kingsbury Benedict, 'International Courts: Uneven Judicialisation in Global Order' in James Crawford and Martti Koskenniemi (eds), *The Cambridge Companion to International Law* (Cambridge: Cambridge University Press, 2012).

Kinsch Patrick, 'On the Uncertainties Surrounding the Standard of Proof in Proceedings before International Courts and Tribunals' in Gabriella Venturini and Stefania Bariatti (eds), *Diritti Individuali E Giustizia Internationazionale. Liber Fausto Pocar* (Milan: Giuffre, 2009).

Klabbers Jan, 'Constitutionalism Lite', 1 *International Organizations Law Review* 31 (2004).

Klabbers Jan, Anne Peters and Geir Ulfstein, *The Constitutionalization of International Law* (Oxford: Oxford University Press, 2009).

Kläger Roland, *'Fair and Equitable Treatment' in International Investment Law* (Cambridge: Cambridge University Press, 2011).

Kleffner Jann K., *Complementarity in the Rome Statute and National Criminal Jurisdictions* (Oxford: Oxford University Press, 2008).

Kolb Rober and Scalia Damien, *Droit international pénal* (Basel: Helbing, 2012).

Kolers Avery H., 'Dynamics of Solidarity', 20 *Journal of Political Philosophy* 365 (2012).

Koskenniemi Martti, 'The Politics of International Law—20 Years Later', 20 *EJIL* 7 (2009).

Koskenniemi Martti, 'Law, Teleology and International Relations: An Essay in Counterdisciplinarity', 26 *International Relations* 1 (2012).

Kotzur Markus, 'Good Faith (Bona fide)' in Rüdiger Wolfrum (ed), *Max Planck Encyclopedia of Public International Law* (Oxford: Oxford University Press, 2012).

Králová Jana, 'Comments on the Draft Agreement on the Accession of the European Union to the Convention for the Protection of Human Rights and Fundamental Freedoms', 2 *Czech Yearbook of International Law* 127 (2011).

Kratochvíl Jan, 'The Inflation of the Margin of Appreciation by the European Court of Human Rights', 29 *Netherlands Quarterly of Human Rights* 324 (2011).

Kriebaum Ursula, 'Regulatory Takings: Balancing the Interests of the Investor and the State', 8 *Journal of World Investment and Trade* 717 (2007).

Krisch Nico and Benedict Kingsbury, 'Introduction: Global Governance and Global Administrative Law in the International Legal Order', 17(1) *EJIL* 1 (2006).

Krueger Anne, 'The Political Economy of the Rent-Seeking Society', 64 *The American Economic Review* 291 (1974).

Kuhnert Kathrin, 'Bosphorus—Double Standards in European Human Rights Protection?', 2(2) *Utrecht Law Review* 177 (2006).

Kulick Andreas, 'Book review, Stephan W. Schill (ed). International Investment Law and Comparative Public Law. Oxford: Oxford University Press, 2010', 22 *EJIL* 917 (2011).

Kumm Mattias, 'The Legitimacy of International Law: A Constitutionalist Framework of Analysis', 15 *EJIL* 907 (2004).

Kumm Mattias, 'The Cosmopolitan Turn in Constitutionalism: On the Relationship between Constitutionalism in and beyond the State' in Jeffrey L. Dunoff and Joel P. Trachtman (eds), *Ruling the World? Constitutionalism, International Law, and Global Governance* (Cambridge: Cambridge University Press, 2009).

Kunsch Kelly, 'Standard of Review (State and Federal): A Primer', 18 *Seattle University Law Review* 11 (1994–1995).

Kurtz Jürgen, 'Access to Justice, Denial and Justice and International Investment Law: A Reply to Francesco Francioni', 20 *EJIL* 1077 (2009).

Kurtz Jürgen, 'Adjudging the Exceptional at International Investment Law: Security, Public Order and Financial Crisis', 59 *ICLQ* 325 (2010).

Kurtz Jürgen, 'The Australian Trade Policy Statement on Investor-State Dispute Settlement', 15(22) *ASIL Insights* (2011).

Kurtz Jürgen, 'Australia's Rejection of Investor–State Arbitration: Causation, Omission and Implication', 27(1) *ICSID Review* 65 (2012).

Kwiatkowska Agnieszka, Helena Paulsson and Gustav Dahlin, 'Will the accession of the European Union to the European Convention on Human Rights be a boost to human rights protection—A legal analysis of political argumentation', paper at the *2010 European Integration: enhanced protection or a threat to individual freedom and liberty?, Warsaw, 10–12 May 2010*, available at <http://pl.zpc.wpia.uw.edu.pl/wp-content/uploads/2010/04/2.-EU-accession-to-the-ECHR-boosting-human-rights-protection-final2.doc>.

Lash Kurt T., 'Three Myths of the Ninth Amendment', 56 *Drake Law Review* 875 (2007–2008).

Lauterpacht Hersch, *Oppenheim's International Law*, 8th edn (London: Longmans, Green & Co, 1955).

Leach Philip, Costas Paraskeva and Gordana Uzelac, *An Analysis of the Fact-Finding Missions Conducted by the European Commission & the Court of Human Rights*, Report by the Human Rights & Social Justice Research Institute at London Metropolitan University (February 2009).

Lee Roy S., 'The Rome Conference and Its Contribution to International Criminal Law. Introduction' in Roy S. Lee (ed), *The International Criminal Court: the Making of the Rome Statute* (The Hague: Kluwer Law International, 1999).

Legg Andrew, *The Margin of Appreciation in International Human Rights Law: Deference and Proportionality* (Oxford: Oxford University Press, 2012).

Lenaerts Koen, '"In the Union We Trust": Trust-enhancing Principles of Community Law', 41 *CMLR* 317 (2004).

Lenaerts Koen, Dirk Arts, Ignace Maselis and Robert Bray, *Procedural Law of the European Union* (London: Sweet & Maxwell, 2006).

Lenaerts Koen, 'Consumer Protection, Free Movement and Harmonisation' in Evelyne Terryn, Gert Straetmans and Veerle Colaert (eds), *Landmark Cases of EU Consumer Law* (Antwerp: Intersentia, 2013).

Leonhardsen Erlend M., 'Looking for Legitimacy: Exploring Proportionality Analysis in Investment Treaty Arbitration', 3 *JIDS* 95 (2012).

Lester Lord, 'Freedom of Expression', 19 *Commonwealth Law Bulletin* 1722 (1993).

Lester Simon, 'The Development of Standards of Appellate Review for Factual, Legal and Law Application Questions in WTO Dispute Settlement', 4 *Trade, Law and Development* 125 (2012).

Letsas George, *Theory of Interpretation of the European Convention* (Oxford: Oxford University Press, 2007).

Letsas George, 'Two Concepts of the Margin of Appreciation', 26 *OJLS* 705 (2006).

Lock Tobias, 'End of an Epic? The Draft Agreement on the EU's Accession to the ECHR', 31(1) *Yearbook of European Law* 162 (2012).

Loucaides Loukis G., *The European Convention on Human Rights: Collected Essays* (Leiden: Martinus Nijhoff, 2007).

Lovric Daniel, *Deference to the Legislature in WTO: Challenges to Legislation* (Alphen aan den Rijn: Wolters Kluwer, 2010).

Lowe Vaughan, 'The International Tribunal for the Law of the Sea: Survey for 2000', 16 *International Journal of Marine and Coastal Law* 549 (2001).

Lubbers Jeffrey S., *A Guide to Federal Agency Rulemaking*, 4th edn (Chicago, IL: ABA Publishing, 2006).

Macdonald Ronald St. J., 'The Margin of Appreciation' in Ronald St. J. Macdonald, Franz Matscher and Herbert Petzold (eds), *The European System for the Protection of Human Rights* (Dondrecht: Martinus Nijhoff, 1993).

Macdonald R. St. John, 'The Margin of Appreciation in the Jurisprudence of the European Court of Human Rights', 1 *Collected Courses of the Academy of European Law* 95 (1992).

Maduro Miguel P., *We, the Court: the European Court of Justice & the European Economic Constitution* (Oxford: Hart Publishing, 1998).

Majone Giandomenico, *Europe as the Would-be World Power. The EU at Fifty* (Cambridge: Cambridge University Press, 2008).

Maletic Isidora, *The Law and Policy of Harmonisation in Europe's Internal Market* (Cheltenham: Edward Elgar Publishing, 2013).

Manacorda Stefano and Werle Gerhard, 'L'adaptation des systèmes pénaux nationaux au Statut de Rome. Le paradigme du "Volkërstrafgesetzbuch" allemand', 3 *Revue de science criminelle et de droit pénal* 501 (2003).

Marks Susan, 'The European Convention on Human Rights and its "Democratic Society"', 66 *BYIL* 209 (1995).

Marlles Justin R., 'Public Purpose, Private Losses: Regulatory Expropriation and Environmental Regulation in International Investment Law', 16 *Journal of Transnational Law and Policy* 275 (2007).

Martenczuk Bernd, 'The Security Council, the International Court and Judicial Review: What Lessons from Lockerbie?', 10(3) *EJIL* 517 (1999).

Mathisen Gjermund, 'Consistency and Coherence as Conditions for Justification of Member State Measures Restricting Free Movement', 47 *CMLR* 1021 (2010).

Matthews Jud and Alec Stone Sweet, 'All Things in Proportion? American Rights Review and the Problem of Balancing', 60(4) *Emory Law Journal* 799 (2011).

Matsui Yoshiro, 'Transformation of the Law of State Responsibility', 20 *Thesaurus Acroasium* 5 (1993).

Marceau Gabrielle and Joel P. Trachtman, 'A Map of the World Trade Organization Law of Domestic Regulation of Goods' in George Bermann and Petros Mavroidis (eds), *Trade and Human Health and Safety* (New York: Cambridge University Press, 2006).

Mavroidis Petros, *Trade in Goods—The GATT and the Other Agreements Regulating Trade in Goods* (Oxford: Oxford University Press, 2007).

McGinnis John O. and Mark L. Movsesian, 'The World Trade Constitution', 114 *Harvard Law Review* 511 (2000).

McGrady Benn, *Trade and Public Health: The WTO, Tobacco, Alcohol and Diet* (Cambridge: Cambridge University Press, 2010).

McKendrick John, 'Modifying Procedural Autonomy: Better Protection for Community Rights', 8 *European Review of Private Law* 565 (2000).

McNelis Natalie, 'The Role of the Judge in the EU and WTO. Lessons from the BSE and Hormones Cases', 4(1) *JIEL* 698 (2001).

Mégret Frederic and Marika G. Samson, 'Holding the Line in Complementarity in Libya. The Case for Tolerating Flawed Domestic Trials', 11 *Journal of International Criminal Justice* 573 (2013).

Melish Tara, *Protecting Economic, Social and Cultural Rights in the Inter-American Human Rights System: A Manual on Presenting Claims* (New Haven, CT: Yale Law School and Centro de Derechos Económicos y Sociales, 2002).

Mensah Thomas A., 'The Tribunal and the Prompt Release of Vessels', 22(3) *International Journal of Marine and Coastal Law* 425 (2007).

Merrill Thomas W., 'Judicial Deference to Executive Precedent', 101 *Yale Law Journal* 969 (1992).

Michaels Ralf and Joost Pauwelyn, 'Conflict of Norms or Conflict of Laws? Different Techniques in the Fragmentation of International Law' in Tomer Broude and Yuval Shany (eds), *Multi-Sourced Equivalent Norms in International Law* (Oxford: Hart Publishing, 2011).

Milano Enrico, 'Security Council Action in the Balkans: Reviewing the Legality of Kosovo's Territorial Status', 14 *EJIL* 999 (2003).

Milanović Marko, 'State Responsibility for Genocide: A Follow Up', 18 *EJIL* 669 (2007).

Milewicz Karolina, 'Emerging Patterns of Global Constitutionalization: Toward a Conceptual Framework', 16 *Indiana Journal of Global Legal Studies* 413 (2009).

Mills Alex, 'Antinomies of Public and Private at the Foundations of International Investment Law and Arbitration', 14(2) *JIEL* 469 (2011).

Ming Du Michael, 'Standard of Review under the SPS Agreement after EC–Hormones II', 59 *ICLQ* 441 (2010).

Mitchell Andrew D. and Caroline Henckels, 'Variations on a Theme: Comparing the Concept of "Necessity" in International Investment Law and WTO Law' 14 *Chicago Journal of International Law* 93 (2013).

Mitchell Andrew D., *Legal Principles in WTO Disputes* (Cambridge: Cambridge University Press, 2008).

Moloo Rahim and Justin Jacinto, 'Standards of Review and Reviewing Standards: Public Interest Regulation in International Investment Law' in Karl P. Sauvant, *Yearbook of International Investment Law and Policy 2011-2012* (New York: Oxford University Press, 2013).

Montt Santiago, *State Liability in Investment Treaty Arbitration: Global Constitutional and Administrative Law and the BIT Generation* (Oxford: Hart Publishing, 2009).

Morrisson Clovis Jr, 'The Margin of Appreciation in European Human Rights Law', 6 *Revue des Droit de l'Homme* 263 (1973).

Mortenson Julian D, 'The Meaning of "Investment": ICSID's Travaux and the Domain of International Investment Law', 51 *Harvard International Law Journal* 257 (2010).

Nebbia Paolise, 'Do the Rules on State Aids Have a Life of Their Own? National Procedural Autonomy and Effectiveness in the Lucchini Case', 33 *ELR* 427 (2008).

Newcombe Andrew and Lluís Paradell, *Law and Practice of Investment Treaties: Standards of Treatment* (Alphen aan den Rijn: Kluwer Law International, 2009).

Newton Michael A., 'Comparative Complementarity; Domestic Jurisdiction Consistent with the Rome Statute of the International Criminal Court', 167 *Military Law Review* 20 (2001).

Newton Michael A., 'The Complementarity Conundrum: Are We Watching Evolution or Evisceration?', 8(1) *Santa Clara Journal of International Law* 115 (2010).

Ní Aoláin Fionnuala, 'From Discretion to Scrutiny: Revisiting the Application of the Margin of Appreciation Doctrine in the Context of Article 15 of the European Convention on Human Rights', 23 *Human Rights Quarterly* 625 (2001).

Nieto Martin Adan, 'Introduccion: El principio de ne bis in idem en el Derecho penal europeo en internacional' in Luis Arroyo Sapatero and Adan Nieto Martin (eds), *El principio de ne bis in idem en el Derecho penal europeo en internacional* (Cuenca: Ed. de la Universidad de Castilla—La Mancha, 2007).

Nielsen Laura, *The WTO, Animals and PPMs* (Leiden: Martinus Nijhoff, Publishers 2007).

Nollkaemper Andre, *National Courts and the International Rule of Law* (Oxford: Oxford University Press, 2011).

Nordquist Myron H., Satya Nandan and Shabtai Rosenne (eds), *United Nations Convention on the Law of the Sea 1982: A Commentary*, vol. V (The Hague: Kluwer Law International, 1989).

Nouwen Sarah, *Complementarity in the Line of Fire: The Catalysing Effect of the International Criminal Court in Uganda and Sudan* (Cambridge: Cambridge University Press, 2013).

Nouwen Sarah, 'Fine-tuning Complementarity' in Bartram Brown (ed), *Research Handbook on International Criminal Law* (Cheltenham: Edward Elgar Publishing, 2011).

O'Connor John F., *Good Faith in International Law* (Aldershot: Darmouth Publishing, 1991).

Oesch Matthias, *Standards of Review in WTO Dispute Resolution* (Oxford: Oxford University Press, 2003).

Olásolo Hector, 'International Criminal Court and International Tribunals: Substantive and Procedural Aspects' in Carlos Jiménez Piernas (ed), *The Legal Practice in International Law and European Community Law* (The Hague: Brill, 2007).

Olásolo Hector, *The Triggering Procedure of the International Criminal Court* (Leiden: Martinus Nijhoff, 2005).

Olásolo Hector, *The triggering procedure of the International Criminal Court, procedural treatment of the principle of complementarity, and the role of Office of the Prosecutor*, Guest Lecture Series of the Office of the Prosecutor, 24 March 2004, available at: <http://www.icc-cpi.int/iccdocs/asp_docs/library/organs/otp/040326_Olasolo.pdf>.

Orellana Marcos, 'The Role of Science in Investment Arbitrations Concerning Public Health and the Environment', 17(1) *Yearbook of International Environmental Law* 48 (2006).

Ortino Federico, *Basic Legal Instruments for the Liberalisation of Trade: A Comparative Analysis of EC and WTO Law* (Oxford and Portland: Hart Publishing, 2004).

Ortino Federico, 'The Investment Treaty System as Judicial Review: Some Remarks on its Nature, Scope and Standards' (2012), available at <http://papers.ssrn.com/sol3/papers.cfm?abstract_id=2181103>.

Oxman Bernard H. and Vincent P Bantz, 'The "Camouco" (Panama v. France) (Judgment). ITLOS Case No 5', 94(4) *AJIL* 713 (2000).

Oxman Bernard H., 'The M/V "Saiga" (Saint Vincent and the Grenadines v Guinea) ITLOS Case No 1', 92(2) *AJIL* 278 (1998).

Papa Maria I., *I rapporti tra la Corte internazionale di giustizia e il Consiglio di sicurezza* (Padova: Cedam, 2006).

Paulus Andreas, 'International Adjudication' in Samantha Besson and John Tasioulas (eds), *The Philosophy of International Law* (New York: Oxford University Press, 2010).

Pauwelyn Joost, *Optimal Protection of International Law: Navigating between European Absolutism and American Voluntarism* (Cambridge: Cambridge University Press, 2008).

Peel Jacqueline, *Science and Risk Regulation in International Law* (Cambridge: Cambridge University Press, 2010).

Peel Jacqueline, 'Of Apples and Oranges (and Hormones in Beef): Science and the Standard of Review in WTO Disputes under the SPS Agreement', 61 *ICLQ* 427 (2012).

Perez Oren and Reut Snir, 'Global Environmental Risk Governance under Conditions of Scientific Uncertainty: Legal, Political and Social Transformations', 2(1) *Transnational Environmental Law* 7 (2013).

Perkams Markus, 'The Concept of Indirect Expropriation in Comparative Public Law—Searching for Light in the Dark' in Stephan Schill (ed), *International Investment Law and Comparative Public Law* (Oxford: Oxford University Press, 2010).

Peters Anne and Klaus Armingeon, 'Introduction—Global Constitutionalism from an Interdisciplinary Perspective', 16 *Indiana Journal of Global Legal Studies* 385 (2009).

Petersmann Ernst-Ulrich, 'Administration of Justice in the WTO: Did the WTO Appellate Body Commit "Grave Injustice"?', 8 *The Law and Practice of International Courts and Tribunals* 329 (2009).

Petersmann Ernst-Ulrich, 'Can the EU's Disregard for 'Strict Observance of International Law' (Article 3 TEU) Be Constitutionally Justified?' in Marco Bronckers, Inge Govaere and Reinhard Quick (eds), *Trade and Competition Law in the EU and Beyond* (Cheltenham: Edward Elgar Publishing, 2011).

Petersmann Ernst-Ulrich, *International Economic Law in the 21st Century. Constitutional Pluralism and Multilevel Governance of Interdependent Public Goods* (Oxford: Hart Publishing, 2012).

Petersmann Ernst-Ulrich, *The GATT/WTO Dispute Settlement System* (London: Kluwer Law International, 1997).

Pinto Monica, 'National and International Courts—Deference or Disdain', 30 *Loyola of Los Angeles International & Comparative Law Review* 247 (2008).

Pires Alvaro P., 'Quelques obstacles à une mutation du droit pénal', 26 *Revue Générale de Droit* 133 (1995).

Pirker Benedikt, *Proportionality Analysis and Models of Judicial Review—A Theoretical and Comparative Study* (Groeningen: Europa Law Publishing, 2013).

Pirker Benedikt, 'Seeing the Forest without the Trees—The Doubtful Case for Proportionality Analysis in International Investment Arbitration' in Alexia Herwig, Christian Joerges and George Pavlakos (eds), *Proportionality in a Post-National Context* (forthcoming 2014).

Poblete Manuel Núñez, 'Sobre la doctrina del margen nacional de apreciación. La experiencia latinoamericana confrontada y el *thelos* constitucional de una técnica de adjudicación del derecho internacional de los derechos humanos. Ensayo introductorio' in Paola A. Acosta Alvarado and Manuel Núñez Poblete (eds), *El Margen de Apreciación en el Sistema Interamericano de Derechos Humanos: Proyecciones Regionales y Nacionales* (México: Instituto de Investigaciones Jurídicas, UNAM 2012).

Porges Amelia and Joel P. Trachtman, 'Robert Hudec and Domestic Regulation: The Resurrection of Aim and Effects', 37 *JWT* 783 (2003).

Post Robert C., *Democracy, Expertise, Academic Freedom. A First Amendment Jurisprudence for the Modern State* (New Haven, CT: Yale University Press, 2012).

Prechal Sacha and Rob Widdershoven, 'Redefining the Relationship between "Rewe-effectiveness" and Effective Judicial Protection', 4 *Review of European Administrative Law* 31 (2011).

Rawls John, *A Theory of Justice* (Oxford: Oxford University Press, 1999).

Rayfuse Rosemary, 'The Future of Compulsory Dispute Settlement under the Law of the Sea Convention', 36 *Victoria University of Wellington Law Review* 1 (2005).

Raz Joseph, *Practical Reasons and Norms* (Oxford: Oxford University Press, 1999).

Regan Donald H., 'The Supreme Court and State Protectionism: Making Sense of the Dormant Commerce Clause', 84 *Michigan Law Review* 1091 (1986).

Regan Donald H., 'Judicial Review of Member-State Regulation of Trade within a Federal or Quasi-Federal System: Protectionism and Balancing, "Da Capo"', 99 *Michigan Law Review* 1853 (2001).

Regan Donald H., 'The Meaning of "Necessary" in GATT Article XX and GATS Article XIV: The Myth of Cost-Benefit Balancing', 6 *WTR* 347 (2007).

Reisman W. Michael and Robert D. Sloane, 'Indirect Expropriation and its Valuation in the BIT Generation', 74 *BYIL* 115 (2003).

Richter Dagmar, 'Judicial Review of Security Council Decisions—A Modern Vision of the Administration of Justice?', 32 *Polish Yearbook of International Law* 271 (2012).

Rivers Julian, 'Proportionality and Variable Intensity of Review', 65 *CLJ* 174 (2006).

Roberts Anthea, 'Clash of Paradigms: Actors and Analogies Shaping the Investment Treaty System', 107 *AJIL* 45 (2013).

Roberts Anthea, 'Power and Persuasion in Investment Treaty Arbitration', 104 *AJIL* 176 (2010).

Roberts Anthea, 'The Next Battleground: Standards of Review in Investor-State Arbitration' in Albert Jan Van Den Berg (ed), *Arbitration—The Next Fifty Years* (Alphen aan den Rijn: Kluwer Law International, 2012).

Robinson Daryl, 'Three Theories of Complementarity: Charge, Sentence, or Process?', 53 *Harvard International Law Journal* 85 (2012).

Rodríguez-Pinzón Diego, 'The "Victim" Requirement, the Fourth Instance Formula and the Notion of "Person" in the Individual Complaint Procedure of the Inter-American Human Rights System', 7 *ILSA Journal of International & Comparative Law* 369 (2001).

Rothwell Donald R. and Tim Stephens, 'Illegal Southern Ocean Fishing and Prompt Release: Balancing Coastal and Flag State Rights and Interests', 53(1) *ICLQ* 171 (2004).

Russell Gillian and Graff Fara Delia (eds), *The Routledge Companion to Philosophy of Language* (London: Routledge, 2012).

Ryngaert Cedric, 'State Responsibility, Necessity and Human Rights', 41 *Netherlands Yearbook of International Law* 79 (2010).

Sabel Charles F. and Oliver Gerstenberg, 'Constitutionalising an Overlapping Consensus: The ECJ and the Emergence of a Coordinate Constitutional Order', 16 *ELJ* 511 (2010).

Sadat-Akhavi Seyed-Ali, *Methods of Resolving Conflicts between Treaties* (Leiden: Martinus Nijhoff, 2003).

Salacuse Jeswald W., *The Law of Investment Treaties* (Oxford: Oxford University Press, 2010).

Sandifer Durward V., *Evidence Before International Tribunals* (Chicago: Foundation Press, 1975).

Sauter Wolf, 'Proportionality in EU Law: A Balancing Act?', *TILEC Discussion Paper No. 2013-003*, available at <http://ssrn.com/abstract=2208467>.

Sauter Wolf and Harm Schepel, *State and Market in European Union Law: The Private and Public Spheres of the Internal Market before the EU Courts* (Cambridge: Cambridge University Press, 2009).

Schabas William, 'Droit pénal international et droit international des droits de l'homme: faux frères?' in Marc Henzelin and Rober Roth (eds), *Le droit pénal à l'épreuve de l'internationalisation* (Paris etc: LGDJ/Georg/Bruylant, 2002).

Schabas William, *The Abolition of the Death Penalty in International Law* (Cambridge: Cambridge University Press, 2002).

Schauer Frederic, 'Freedom of Expression Adjudication in Europe and America: A Case Study in Comparative Constitutional Architecture', *Faculty Research Working Paper Series, Harvard University, RWP05-019.*

Shelton Dinah, 'Private Violence, Public Wrongs and the Responsibility of States', 13(1) *Fordham International Law Journal* 1 (1989–90).

Schill Stephan and Robyn Briese, '"If the State Considers": Self-Judging Clauses in International Dispute Settlement', 13 *Max Planck Yearbook of United Nations Law* 61 (2009).

Schill Stephan W., *International Investment Law and Comparative Public Law* (Oxford: Oxford University Press, 2010).

Schill Stephan, 'W(h)ither Fragmentation? On the Literature and Sociology of International Investment Law', 22 *EJIL* 875 (2011).

Schill Stephan, 'Deference in Investor-State Arbitration: Re-Conceptualizing the Standard of Review', 3 *JIDS* (2012).

Schneiderman David, 'Judicial Politics and International Investment Arbitration: Seeking an Explanation for Conflicting Outcomes', 30 *Northwestern Journal of International Law & Business* 383 (2010).

Schorkopf Frank, 'The European Court of Human Rights' Judgement in the Case of Bosphorus Hava Yollari Turizm v. Ireland', 6(9) *GLJ* 1255 (2005).

Schreuer Christoph, 'Denunciation of the ICSID Convention and Consent to Arbitration' in Michael Waibel, Asha Kaushal, Kyo-Hwa Liz Chung and Claire Balchin (eds), *The Backlash against Investment Arbitration: Perceptions and Reality* (Alphen aan den Rijn: Kluwer Law International, 2010).

Schwöbel Christine E. J., *Global Constitutionalism in International Legal Perspective* (Leiden: Martinus Nijhoff, 2011).

Scott Joanne, Ellen Vos, 'The Juridification of Uncertainty: Observations on the Ambivalence of the Precautionary Principle within the EU and the WTO' in Christian Joerges and Renaud Dehousse (eds), *Good Governance in Europe's Integrated Market* (Oxford: Oxford University Press, 2002).

Scott Joanne, 'The Precautionary Principle before the European Courts' in Richard Macrory (ed), *Principles of European Environmental Law* (Groningen: Europa Law Publishing, 2004).

Scott Joanne, 'Comment in the Panel "Dispute Settlement: Jurisprudential and Procedural Features"' in Mads Andenas and Federico Ortino (eds), *WTO Law and Process* (London: BIICL, 2005).

Scott Joanne and Susan Sturm, 'Courts as Catalysts: Rethinking the Judicial Role in New Governance', 13(3) *Columbia Journal of European Law* 565 (2007).

Scott Joanne, 'European Regulation of GMOs: Thinking about "Judicial Review" in the WTO' in Ellen Vos and Michelle Everson (eds), *Uncertain Risks Regulated* (London: Routledge, 2009).

Segnana Oliver, 'The Precautionary Principle: New Developments in the Case Law of the Court of First Instance', 3(10) *GLJ* 5 (2002).

Sepúlveda-Amor Bernardo, 'Diplomatic and Consular Protection: the Right of the State and the Rights of Individual in the LaGrand and Avena Cases' in Ulrich Fastenrath, Rudolf Geiger, Daniel-Erasmus Khan, Andreas Paulus, Sabine von Schorlemer and Christoph Vedder (eds), *From Bilateralism to Community Interest: Essays in Honour of Judge Bruno Simma* (Oxford: Oxford University Press, 2011).

Seralini Gilles-Eric, Emilie Claira, Robin Mesnagea, Steeve Gressa, Nicolas Defargea, Manuela Malatestab, Didier Hennequinc and Joël Spiroux de Vendômoisa, 'Long Term Toxicity of a Roundup Herbicide and a Roundup-tolerant Genetically Modified Maize', 50(11) *Food and Chemical Technology* 4221 (2012).

Shaffer Gregory, 'Power, Governance, and the WTO: A Comparative Institutional Approach' in Michael Barnett and Raymond Duvall (eds), *Power in Global Governance* (Cambridge: Cambridge University Press, 2005).

Shaffer Gregory, Trachtman Joel, 'Interpretation and Institutional Choice the WTO', 52 *Virginia Journal of International Law* 103 (2011).

Shany Yuval, *The Competing Jurisdictions of International Courts and Tribunals* (Oxford: Oxford University Press, 2003).

Shany Yuval, 'Toward a General Margin of Appreciation Doctrine in International Law?', 16(5) *EJIL* 907 (2005).

Shany Yuval, *Regulating Jurisdictional Relations between National and International Courts* (Oxford: Oxford University Press, 2007).

Shany Yuval, 'No Longer a Weak Department of Power? Reflections on the Emergence of a New International Judiciary', 20(1) *EJIL* 73 (2009).

Shapiro Martin, 'The Institutionalization of European Administrative Space' in Alec Stone Sweet, Wayne Sandholtz and Neil Fligstein (eds), *The Institutionalization of Europe* (Oxford: Oxford University Press, 2001).

Shapiro Martin, Alec Stone Sweet, *On Law, Politics, and Judicialization* (Oxford: Oxford University Press, 2002).

Shelton Dinah, 'The Boundaries of Human Rights Jurisdiction in Europe', 13(1) *Duke Journal of Comparative & International Law* 95 (2003).

Snell Juka, *Goods and Services in EC Law: A Study of the Relationship Between the Freedoms* (Oxford: Oxford University Press, 2002).

Snyder Timothy, *The Reconstruction of Nations: Poland, Ukraine, Lithuania, Belarus, 1569–1999* (New Haven, CT: Yale University Press, 2004).

Sornarajah Muthucumaraswamy, 'Evolution or Revolution in International Investment Arbitration? The Descent into Normlessness' in Chester Brown and Kate Miles (eds), *Evolution in Investment Treaty Law and Arbitration* (Cambridge: Cambridge University Press, 2011).

Spamann Holger, 'Standard of Review for World Trade Organization Panels in Trade Remedy Cases: A Critical Analysis', 38 *JWT* 509 (2004).

Spielmann Dean, 'Allowing the Right Margin: The European Court of Human Rights and the National Margin of Appreciation Doctrine: Waiver or Subsidiarity of European Review?', 14 *Cambridge Yearbook of European Legal Studies* 381 (2011–2012).

Stahn Carsten, Sluiter Goran, *The Emerging Practice of the International Criminal Court* (Leiden: Brill, 2009).

Steele Jenny, *Risks and Legal Theory* (Oxford: Hart Publishing, 2004).

Steger Debra P., 'Comment in the Panel "Dispute Settlement: Jurisprudential and Procedural Features"' in Mads Andenas and Federico Ortino (eds), *WTO Law and Process* (London: BIICL, 2005).

Stewart Richard B., Michelle Ratton Sanchez Badin, 'The World Trade Organization: Multiple Dimensions of Global Administrative Law', 9 *International Journal of Constitutional Law* 556 (2011).

Stigen Jo, *The Relationship between the International Criminal Court and National Jurisdictions* (Leiden/Boston: Martinus Nijhoff, 2008).

Stone Sweet Alec, 'Sur la constitutionnalisation de la Convention européenne des droits de l'homme', 80 *Revue trimestrielle des droits de l'homme* 923 (2009).

Sunstein Cass R., *Risk and Reason: Safety, Law, and the Environment* (Cambridge: Cambridge University Press, 2002).

Taggart Michael, 'Proportionality, Deference, *Wednesbury*', 1 *New Zealand Law Review* (2008).

Taillant Jorge D. and Jonathan Bonnitcha, 'International Investment Law and Human Rights' in Marie-Claire Cordonier Segger, Markus W. Gehring and Andrew Newcombe (eds), *Sustainable Development in World Investment Law* (Alphen aan den Rijn: Wolters Kluwer, 2011).

Tallgren Immi, 'Article 20: *Ne bis in idem*' in Otto Triffterer (ed), *Commentary on the Rome Statute of the International Court. Observers' Notes, Article by Article* (Munich etc: Beck/Hart/Nomos, 2008).

Tanaka Yoshifumi, 'Prompt Release in the United Nations Convention on the Law of the Sea: Some Reflections on the ITLOS Jurisprudence', 51(2) *Netherlands International Law Review* 237 (2004).

Tavernier Paul, 'Les tribunaux pénaux internationaux et le droit international des droits de l'homme' in Mireille Delmas-Marty, Emanuela Fronza and Elisabeth Lambert Abdelgawad (eds), *Les sources du droit international pénal—l'expérience des Tribunaux Pénaux Internationaux et le Statut de la Cour Pénale Internationale* (Paris: Société de Législation Comparée, 2004).

Thompson-Flores Thomas L., 'Brazil Begins to Investigate Its Dark Past, But Is It Too Little Too Late?' *ExpressO*, 2012, available at <http://works.bepress.com/thomas_thompson_flores/2>.

Teitelbaum Ruth, 'Recent Fact-Finding Developments at the International Court of Justice', 6 *Law & Practice of International Courts & Tribunals* 119 (2007).

Tittemore Brian D., 'The Mandatory Death Penalty in the Commonwealth Caribbean and the Inter-American Human Rights System: An Evolution in the Development and Implementation of International Human Rights Protections', 13(2) *William & Mary Bill of Rights Journal* 445 (2004–2005).

Trachtman Joel P., 'The Constitutions of the WTO', 17 *EJIL* 623 (2006).

Trechsel Stefan, *Human Rights in Criminal Proceedings* (Oxford: Oxford University Press, 2005).

Treves Tullio, 'The Proceedings Concerning Prompt Release of Vessels and Crews before the International Tribunal for the Law of the Sea', 11 *International Journal of Marine and Coastal Law* 179 (1996).

Trevisanut Seline, 'The Exercise of Administrative Functions by ITLOS: A Comment on Prompt Release Cases' in Nerina Boschiero, Tullio Scovazzi, Chiara Ragni and Cesare Pitea (eds), *International Courts and the Development of International Law: Essays in Hinour of Tullio Treves* (The Hague: Asser Press, 2013).

Tridimas Takis, 'Proportionality in Community Law: Searching for the Appropriate Standard of Scrutiny' in Ellis, Evelyn (ed), *Principle of Proportionality in the Laws of Europe* (Oxford: Hart Publishing, 1999).

Tridimas Takis, *The General Principles of EU Law* (Oxford: Oxford University Press, 2006).

UNCTAD, 'Denunciation of the ICSID Convention and BITS: Impact on Investor-State Claims', *IIA*, December 2010: No. 2.

Vadi Valentina, 'Overlapping Regulatory Spaces: The Architecture of NAFTA Chapter 11 and the Regulation of Toxic Chemicals', 4 *European Journal of Risk Regulation* 586 (2011).

Vadi Valentina, 'Global Health Governance at a Crossroads: Trademark Protection v. Tobacco Control in International Investment Law', 48 *Stanford Journal of International Law* 93 (2012).

Vadi Valentina, *Public Health in International Investment Law and Arbitration* (London: Routledge, 2012).

Vadi Valentina, 'The Beauty of Unity? Intellectual Property Rights v. Public Health in International Investment Arbitration' in Christian J. Tams and Rainer Hoffmann (eds), *Investment Law and Its Others* (Berlin: Nomos, 2012).

Vadi Valentina and Lukasz Gruszczynski, 'Standards of Review in International Investment Law and Arbitration: Multilevel Governance and the Commonweal', 16(3) *JIEL* 613 (2013).

Van Cleynenbreugel Pieter, 'Judge-Made Standards of National Procedure in the Post-Lisbon Constitutional Framework', 37 *ELR* 92 (2012).

Van Cleynenbreugel Pieter, 'The Confusing Constitutional Status of Positive Procedural Obligations in EU Law', 5 *Review of European Administrative Law* 98 (2012).

Van Cleynenbreugel Pieter, 'Transforming Shields into Swords. The Vebic Judgment, Adequate Judicial Protection Standards and the Emergence of Procedural Heteronomy in EU Law', 18 *Maastricht Journal of European and Comparative Law* 511 (2011).

Van den Wyngaert Christine, Ongena Tom, 'Ne bis in idem Principle, Including the Issue of Amnesty' in Antonio Cassese, Paola Gaeta and John R. Jones (eds), *The Rome Statute of the International Criminal Court* (Oxford: Oxford University Press, 2002).

Van Dijk Pieter, *Comments on the Accession of the European Union/European Community to the European Convention On Human Rights*, 20 August 2007, available at <http://www.statewatch.org/news/2007/sep/van-dijk-eu-echr.pdf>.

Van Gerven Walter, 'Of Rights, Remedies and Procedures', 37 *CMLR* 500 (2000).

Van Harten Gus, *Investor-State Arbitration and Public Law* (Oxford: Oxford University Press, 2007).

Van Harten Gus, 'Reforming the NAFTA Investment Regime', 1 November 2009, unpublished paper available at SSRN: <http://ssrn.com/abstract=1687263>.

Verdier Pierre-Hugues, 'Cooperative States: International Relations, State Responsibility and the Problem of Custom', 42 *Virginia Journal of International Law* 839 (2002).

Viñuales Jorge E., 'Foreign Investment and the Environment in International Law: An Ambiguous Relationship', 80 *BYIL* 244 (2009).

von Bogdandy Armin, 'Law and Politics in the WTO—Strategies to Cope with a Deficient Relationship', 5 *Max Planck Yearbook of United Nations Law* 609 (2001).

von Bogdandy Armin, 'Rechtsnatur und Finalität der WTO—eine Analyse der Präambel' in Hartmut Bauer, Detlef Czybulka, Wolfgang Kahl and Andreas Voßkuhle (eds), *Wirtschaft im offenen Verfassungstaat: Festschrift für Reiner Schmidt zum 70 Geburtstag* (Munchen: Beck, 2006).

von Bogdandy Armin and Ingo Venzke, 'Beyond Dispute: International Judicial Institutions as Lawmakers', 12 *GLJ* 979 (2011).

von Staden Andreas, 'Deference or No Deference, That Is the Question: Legitimacy and Standards of Review in Investor-State Arbitration', 2 *Investment Treaty News* 3 (2012).

von Staden Andreas, 'The Democratic Legitimacy of Judicial Review Beyond the State: Normative Subsidiarity and Judicial Standards of Review', 19 *International Journal of Constitutional Law* 1023 (2012).

Vos Ellen, 'The European Court of Justice in the Face of Scientific Uncertainty and Complexity' in Mark Dawson, Bruno de Witte and Elise Muir (eds), *Judicial Activism at the European Court of Justice* (Cheltenham: Edward Elgar Publishing, 2013).

Vranes Erich, *Trade and the Environment—Fundamental Issues in International Law, WTO Law, and Legal Theory* (Oxford: Oxford University Press, 2009).

Waibel Michael, Asha Kaushal, Liz Kyo-Hwa Chung and Claire Balchin, *The Backlash against the Investment Arbitration* (Alphen aan den Rijn: Kluwer Law International, 2010).

Wälde Thomas, Abba Kolo, 'Environmental Regulation, Investment Protection and "Regulatory Taking" in International Law', 50 *ICLQ* 811 (2001).

Walzer Michael, 'Philosophy and Democracy', 9(3) *Political Theory* 379 (1981).

Watson Geoffrey R., 'Constitutionalism Judicial Review and the World Court', 34 *Harvard International Law Journal* 1 (1993).

Weiler Todd, 'Methanex Corp. v. USA. Turning the Page on NAFTA Chapter Eleven?', 6 *Journal of World Investment & Trade* 903 (2005).

Weiler Joseph H.H., 'Epilogue: Towards a Common Law of International Trade' in Joseph Weiler (ed), *The EU, the WTO, and the NAFTA: Towards a Common Law of International Trade* (Oxford: Oxford University Press, 2000).

Weiler Joseph H.H. and Marlene Wind (eds), *European Constitutionalism Beyond the State* (Cambridge: Cambridge University Press, 2003).

Wigmore John Henry, *The Principles of Judicial Proof as Given by Logic, Psychology, and General Experience* (Boston: Little, Brown and Company, 1913).

Winickoff David, Sheila Jasanoff, Lawrence Busch, Robin Grove-White and Brian Wynne, 'Adjudicating the GM Food Wars: Science, Risk, and Democracy in World Trade Law', 30 *Yale Journal of International Law* 81 (2005).

Wolfrum Rüdiger, 'International Courts and Tribunals, Evidence' in Rüdiger Wolfrum (ed), *Max Planck Encyclopedia of Public International Law* (online version available at <http://opil.ouplaw.com/home/epil>).

Wouters Jan and Nicolas Hachez, 'The Institutionalization of Investment Arbitration and Sustainable Development' in Marie-Claire Cordonier Segger, Markus W. Gehring and Andrew Newcombe (eds), *Sustainable Development in World Investment Law* (Alphen aan den Rijn: Wolters Kluwer, 2011).

Yourow Howard C., *The Margin of Appreciation Doctrine in the Dynamics of European Human Rights Jurisprudence* (Dordrecht: Martinus Nijhoff, 1996).

Ziccardi Capaldo Giuliana (ed), *Repertory of Decisions of the International Court of Justice 1947–1992,* vol. II (Dordrecht: Martinus Nijhoff, 1995).

Zimmermann Andreas, Christian Tams, Karin Oellers-Frahm and Christian Tomuschat (eds), *The Statute of the International Court of Justice: A Commentary* (Oxford: Oxford University Press, 2006).

Zingales Nicolo, 'Member State Liability vs. National Procedural Autonomy: What Rules for Judicial Breach of EU Law?', 11 *GLJ* 419 (2010).

Zleptnig Stefan, 'The Standard of Review in WTO Law: An Analysis of Law, Legitimacy and the Distribution of Legal and Political Authority', *European Integration Online Papers*, vol. 6, no. 17 (2002).

Zurn Christopher F., *Deliberative Democracy and the Institutions of Judicial Review* (New York: Cambridge University Press, 2007).

Zwart Tom, *The Admissibility of Human Rights Petitions: The Case Law of the European Commission of Human Rights and the Human Rights Committee* (Leiden: Martinus Nijhoff, 1994).

Index